Isabel Allende

McFarland Literary Companions

by Mary Ellen Snodgrass

1. *August Wilson* (2004)

2. *Barbara Kingsolver* (2004)

3. *Amy Tan* (2004)

4. *Walter Dean Myers* (2006)

5. *Kaye Gibbons* (2007)

6. *Jamaica Kincaid* (2008)

8. *Peter Carey* (2010)

10. *Leslie Marmon Silko* (2011)

13. *Isabel Allende* (2012)

by Phyllis T. Dircks

7. *Edward Albee* (2010)

by Erik Hage

9. *Cormac McCarthy* (2010)

by Rocky Wood

11. *Stephen King* (2011)

by Tom Henthorne

12. *William Gibson* (2011)

Isabel Allende

A Literary Companion

Mary Ellen Snodgrass

McFarland Literary Companions, 13

McFarland & Company, Inc., Publishers
Jefferson, North Carolina, and London

ISBN 978-0-7864-7127-0
softcover : acid free paper ∞

Library of Congress cataloguing data are available

British Library cataloguing data are available

On the cover: Isabel Allende, 2010
(AP Photo/Peter Morgan); background image (Hemera/Thinkstock)

Manufactured in the United States of America

McFarland & Company, Inc., Publishers
Box 611, Jefferson, North Carolina 28640
www.mcfarlandpub.com

For Miguel Gonzalez,
my friend and source

Acknowledgments

Anne Benham, reference librarian,
University of Virginia,
Charlottesville, Virginia

Commerce Public Library,
Commerce, Georgia

Joyner Library,
East Carolina University,
Greenville, North Carolina

McConnell Library,
Radford University,
Radford, Virginia

Martin Otts,
reference librarian,
Patrick Beaver Library,
Hickory, North Carolina

Hannah Owen,
children's librarian,
Patrick Beaver Library,
Hickory, North Carolina

Mark Schumacher,
reference librarian,
Walter Jackson Library,
University of North Carolina,
Greensboro, North Carolina

Smith Library,
High Point University,
High Point, North Carolina

Walter R. Davis Library,
University of North Carolina,
Chapel Hill, North Carolina

Special thanks go to Eileen Lawrence, vice president of Alexander Street Press for access to online databases and to reference librarians Beth Bradshaw and Martin Otts of the Patrick Beaver Library in Hickory, North Carolina.

Table of Contents

Acknowledgments vi

Preface 1

Introduction 3

Chronology of Allende's Life and Works 5

Allende Genealogy 27

Isabel Allende: A Literary Companion 29

Glossary 305

Appendix A: Historical Timeline from the Allende Canon 310

Appendix B: Writing and Research Topics 315

Bibliography 321

Index 339

"Each person has his own truth, and ... all are valid."
— *Forest of the Pygmies*

Preface

For a wide readership of Isabel Allende's vivid canon of young adult, feminist, Latina, and American literature, *Isabel Allende: A Literary Companion* outlines the themes and styles that govern her works. Essays inform the reader, feminist, historian, linguist, student, researcher, teacher, reviewer, and librarian of respected commentaries on characters, plots, humor, symbols, wisdom, and pervasive gender concepts in Allende's range of texts. Opening with a chronology of Allende's life and Chilean heritage, the companion introduces her early works, self-exile to Venezuela, and award-winning titles. A family lineage of the Allende-Gordon families clarifies kinship of people who fill her memoirs and interviews.

The 84 A-to-Z entries summarize twenty-first century commentary from scholars, literary historians, biographers, and reviewers with generous citations from primary and secondary sources and comparisons to classic and popular literature. Entries feature references to the works from which each event derives. Analysis from Australia, Canada, Chile, England, India, Ireland, New Zealand, Scotland, Spain, Tasmania, Tobago, and Trinidad and from American and Hispanic consortia illustrates the range of scholarly and popular response to Allende's titles. Each entry concludes with selected source material on such subjects as adaptation, music, order, reading, food, feminism, male persona, writing, and achievement. Annotated charts substantiate dates and events and identify interrelated casts of characters, notably, both fictional and historical characters in the *House of the Spirits* trilogy and *Inés of My Soul*. Generous cross references point to divergent strands of thought and direct the user toward related ideas, from violence to war and from adaptation to wisdom.

Back matter aids the student, reviewer, and researcher in locating and elucidating details. A glossary of 212 terms enlightens readers to the significance of the *mestizo*, *picaro*, scapular, *zhong-yi*, *loa*, *qi*, and Alta California. "Appendix A: Historical Timeline from the Allende Canon" orders background data on the Inquisition, student activism at Berkeley, singsong girls, 9/11, Diego de Almagro's exploration of Chile, and the original version of the Zorro myth. A second appendix provides 43 topics for group or individual projects, composition, analysis, background material, and comparative literature, notably, themes of social issues and conflict, the impact of settings, contrasts of mothering instincts, shifts in family power, evidence of the supernatural, focal terms, and gendered rules for behavior or career advancement as revealed in works by Paolo Coelho, Hannah Pakula, Douglass G. Brinkley, Rita Dove, Jessamyn West, Bernard Malamud, and Eve Ensler.

Back matter concludes with an exhaustive alphabetic listing of primary sources followed by a general, biographical, and interview bibliography and a literary booklist organized by each of the 18 Allende titles that the sources discuss. Many entries derive from journal and periodical articles, interviews, and critiques of Allende's public appearances, memoirs, novels, and short fiction in major newspapers from the Americas, Great Britain, and the Pacific. Secondary sources, particularly those by experienced reviewers, justify the inclusion of Allende's publications in feminist, Latina, and postcolonial literature and on high school and college reading lists. A comprehensive index directs users of the literary companion to major and minor characters and peoples, divinities, events and historic eras, significant figures, place names, published titles, literary motifs, period terms, genres, and issues, e.g., Maurice Mbembelé and Yanacona, Erzulie and *loas*, earthquake and Treaty of Guadalupe Hidalgo, Napoleon and Jean Lafitte, *cordillera* and San Francisco, "Tosca" and "The Proper Respect," autodidacticism and pseudonym, Bal de Cordon Bleu and concentration camp, beast fable and magical realism, racism and war.

Introduction

A feminist powerhouse, Latina author Isabel Allende contributes to the world canon a rich variety of stories, historical fiction, and autobiographical reflection. A native of Lima, Peru, she invigorates her works with a South American perspective tinged with the worldly wisdom of a global traveler. Her characters dramatize the myriad stories of the conquest and miscegenation of peoples of the Western Hemisphere, from the war of Francisco Pizarro against the Inca in *Inés of My Soul* to the mongrelized settlement of San Francisco by foreigners and Americanos in *Daughter of Fortune*, from the emancipation of Haitian slaves by Toussaint L'Ouverture at Le Cap in *Island Beneath the Sea* to the return of soldiers and war orphans from Vietnam, a troubling era in *The Infinite Plan*. Her stories capture the dark corners of repression and the human retreats into food lore, fashion, crafts, child rearing, and storytelling, all incorporated in *The House of the Spirits*, the first of a post-colonial trilogy on the del Valle clan. Her blend of realism with supernatural elements energizes everyday scenes—the prescience of White Owl in *Zorro*, the welcome and camaraderie of village gatherings in Agua Santa in *Eva Luna*, prayers for the sick in a Madrid hospital in *Paula*, the curse of Férula's spirit on her self-ennobling brother in *The House of the Spirits*, and revelations from photos of a disloyal bridegroom, Diego Dominguez, the bittersweet triumph of *Portrait in Sepia*. By enlarging normal life with intuition and foresight, Allende welcomes the deceased to guide and hearten the living, as with visitations from the spirit of Tao Chi'en's Cantonese wife Lin in *Portrait in Sepia*, a tender leave-taking of husband from wife in the story "Walimai," and a blessing from Allende's dying daughter in the thanatography *Paula*.

From a career in playwriting and journalism for *Paula* magazine in Santiago, Chile, in the 1960s and early 1970s, Allende became a respecter of detail that depicts the sorrows of amputees following the War of the Pacific, the freedom of camp followers in Sacramento's mining country, and the upbringing of Los Angeles barrio children amid family meals, workplace prejudice, parental disintegration, and gang violence. The author turns naturally to the ambitions and accomplishments of females—Inmaculada Morales's welcome to *gringo* strangers, Blanca del Valle's crêches, Alba del Valle's assistance to arms smugglers, Eliza "Chile Boy" Sommers's empanadas made from wilderness game, Tamar's gypsy garments and accessories, Aurora del Valle's photos, Irene Beltrán's fashion interviews, and Digna Ranquileo's rearing of an infant switched at birth with her own daughter. In *The House of the Spirits* trilogy, Allende's most honored works, female casts exhibit fortitude and compensation through cooking, herbalism, photography, music, murals, sewing, and sisterhood, skills that lighten the burdens of the underclass and ready the young, such as Alba, Lynn, and Aurora del Valle, for their own turn at adult endeavors. Allende's inclusion of healthy matings— Severo del Valle's siring of fifteen children with Nivea, Aurora del Valle's passionate relationship with Iván Radovic, Paulina del Valle's marriage to her butler, Frederick Williams— accords to male characters the contentment of a fulfilling love life and the partnership of supportive and imaginative mates.

Unlike the first generation of the Latino literary "boom," Allende frees herself to try a variety of perspectives and genres, as with her travelogue "The Amazon Queen" and the collection of recipes in *Aphrodite* that ponder the atmosphere of a sultan's seraglio and the male fantasy of owning a harem. Her venture into young adult quest fiction reveals a sensitivity toward youthful idealism and the formation of an inclusive world view, as demonstrated by Nadia Santos's concern for indigenous Brazilian culture and ecology in *City of the Beasts*, King Dil Bahadur's replacement of a Himalayan icon in *Kingdom of the Golden Dragon*, and Alex Cold's training in medicine in *Forest of the Pygmies*. Allende incorporates the Zeitgeist in historic losses following revolutions in France, Haiti, and the United States as well as the defeat of Napoleon, the rise of Augsto Pinochet's corrupt regime, and involvement of the CIA in destabilizing Latin American governments. The author substantiates her forays into alarming events with research focusing on the lives of women and families, such as the women who sew records of *desaparecidos* and the female inmates in concentration camps who survive the political intimidation and torture following the death in 1973 of Chilean president Salvador Allende. Through solidarity and concerted protest, Allende's female characters fight the uncertainties of socioeconomic change and the exigencies forced on their children and neighbors by bondage, rationing, insurgency, imprisonment, and war.

Readers and reviewers admire Allende for her gift of engaging storytelling heightened by memorable character decisions, as with Angel Sánchez's nativist treatment of illness in "Ester Lucero," the collection of sensual recipes in *Aphrodite*, and the on-the-spot courtship of strangers in "The Guggenheim Lovers." Her pictorial skills enhance the terrors of corpses suspended from meat hooks in *Of Love and Shadows*, a pirate slave auction in *Zorro*, and the author's formation of a blended family with second husband Willie Gordon and his dysfunctional children in *The Sum of Our Days*. Her gift for poetry and humor inject self-reclamation into Tété's African dance in *Island Beneath the Sea* and La Señora's witty comments on a corrupt vice squad in *Eva Luna*. Sure-footed in varied genres, Allende seems at home with psychological fiction in "Wicked Girl," religious satire in "A Discreet Miracle," mythology in *Kingdom of the Golden Dragon*, and personal sorrow in *Paula*. The magnetic pull of Allende's writings keeps readers coming back for more, embracing her heroic pastiche in *Zorro*, the confessional of a nineteen-year-old addict in *Maya's Notebook*, and the first-person account of Inés Suarez, an historic nation builder in *Inés of My Soul*.

Chronology of Allende's Life and Works

The rise of Isabel Allende to Chile's first mass-marketed writer and the world's most widely read Spanish-language author of all time coincides with the emergence of multiculturalism and global feminism. NPR critic Michael Schaub called her "that rarest of people: a foreign-language author whose books sell well in the United States" (Schaub, 2010). Her artistry has added to the male-dominant Western literary canon powerfully honest, revelatory works by female and non–European authors who touch the pulse points of humankind. Her bravura study of the interwoven roles of women in family history opens the minds of outsiders to the sufferings of females and their children during years of social and political nightmare. Chileans reverence her as "la Famosa."

Throughout the Americas and Europe, readers lionize Allende as Latin America's foremost female proponent of socialism and women's rights. Critic Shannin Schroeder credits the author with dispelling "distrust of the powerful, magical mother figure," an archetype begun with Clara del Valle, protagonist of *The House of the Spirits* and extended with Iyomi and Nana-Asante in the *City of the Beasts* trilogy and White Owl in *Zorro* (Schroeder, 2004, 139). By valorizing women's literary conventions, Allende claims to have liberated the roles of females, emigrants, blacks, Chicanos, and Indians from formulaic and deprecatory fiction. Critics remark favorably on her creation of an enigmatic demarcation between fantasy and reality and praise her acknowledgment of the female spiritual quest.

August 2, 1942 Isabel Allende Llona was born in Lima, Peru, to a Basque-Chilean heritage. She is the first of three children and only daughter of bank clerk Francisca "Doña Panchita" Llona Barros, a sheltered romantic, and Tomás Allende Pesce de Bilbaire, an egotistical wastrel and secretary of the Chilean embassy in Peru fifteen years older than his wife. The author also claims kinship with the Araucan or Mapuche Indians: "If I am not Mestisa by blood — because my family would deny any Indian blood, although I would be very proud to have it — I am Mestisa by culture," an unusual claim for a woman of the privileged caste (Norris, 2006).

The author's homecoming set a pattern of nonconformity to cultural mores, especially for the ambassadorial class. Her maternal grandmother, Isabel Barros Moreira, attended the birth at an American clinic and helped Francisca steal Isabel from the nursery. The family lived in grand style in the historic district of Miraflores on the Pacific coast, where Tomás developed a raffish persona as a literary wit, apostate, and ladies' man.

Narrative soaked in from gossipy servants and from operatic *telanovelas* (soap operas) on the radio that held listeners rapt for the next episodes. Tomás introduced his firstborn to art books, history, classical music, and mythology. To his discredit, the dramatic marital scenes between him and his wife impressed Isabel with the effects of rumors, social climbing, sporadic separations, and emotional outbursts behind closed doors. From the domestic division, she developed ease with lunar reality, nighttime shadows and secrets growing out of ungovernable passion. Her comfort level with the occult enabled her to endure domestic discomfort by retreating into memory, a crucible a-swirl with enigmatic feelings.

1945 Dogged by debt and scandals involving gambling and women, Tomás Allende left the foreign service and abandoned his wife, daughter, and sons Francisco and the infant Juan. To Isabel, the betrayal felt like an amputation. She retreated into disturbing images and lost her trust of males, whom her works tend to depict as tyrants, lotharios, and villains. Because of Chile's rejection of divorce, Francisca remained legally shackled to Tomás. She retaliated by obtaining an annulment and cutting his face from family photos. Ramón Huidobro, a Chilean consul in Peru with regal manners, arranged the family's sea passage from Callao to Valparaíso aboard the *Aconcagua,* a 25-passenger vessel built by the South American Steamship Company in 1922 as a hedge against U.S. prohibitionism.

In the patriarchal household of her grandparents—dwarf-size Isabel "Memé" Barros Moreira and Basque sheep rancher Agustín "Tata" Llona Cuevas—at 081 Calle Suecia near Avenida Providencia in northeastern Santiago, Isabel lived an upbringing she summarized as "conservative, Catholic, Basque" (Miller, 2006). She accepted the sovereignty of Tata, whom she described as "like God: infallible, omniscient, and omnipotent" and "a severe although always just Zeus" (Allende, 2003, 29; 1998, 35). The sharing of a room with her mother and brothers magnified family closeness. Despite two jobs—bank clerk and hat maker—Francisca entertained the trio with Gothic stories such as Robert Browning's "The Pied Piper of Hamelin" (1842) and utopian fantasies about a place where the family could be happy again. From "her whole soul," Memé told bizarre tales so casually that the children believed them (Allende, Summer 1996, 24).

The author came of age among strong female models. She later recalled transformation into a feminist: "I just wanted to own my own rights. I didn't want to obey the church, the police, or a bunch of males," a veiled reference to the *machismo* that monopolized Chilean society (Timpane, 2010). Of women's struggles into the twenty-first century, she identified with the females whom society "sold into menial labor, prostitution, and marriages they don't want," an image of bondage that resonates in her stories and novels (*Ibid.*). Sympathy with gendered obstacles resounded in subsequent works, including her short stories and the memoir *The Sum of Our Days* (2008).

Nonetheless, Allende identified with her maternal grandfather, who was born with a crippled hip and one short leg. Tata possessed a peasant background in adages, folk tales, and narrative verse. In a turbulent era, her aristocratic paternal grandfather died from an unexplained shotgun blast. In addition to family catastrophes, Allende discovered a skull in the family basement and added it to her collection of exotica before using it as a prop in her first novel, *The House of the Spirits* (1985). From her father's trunk, she retrieved pirate novels and Jules Verne's *20,000 Leagues Under the Sea* (1870).

From domestic disorder, Allende's mother sank into fits of weeping, fever, and headaches, a retreat for the fictional Eugenia García del Solar of Madrid in *Island Beneath the Sea* (2010). A solace for the author, Tío Pablo's library contained books he stole from friends' shelves and bookstores. Pablo described the mingling of characters as "maidens and courtesans, warriors and pirates, angels and demons, all busy with their adventures and overwhelming passions" (Allende, April 1996, 43).

1947 By age five, Allende stoked rage at Latino patriarchy and Catholic conservatism, which enforced *marianismo*, the Virgin Mary's chaste model of womanly passivity. Allende's mother compared her daughter to Genghis Khan, a conqueror of women in serial sexual assaults. Some 15 years later, Allende acquired the proper term for her attitudes and principles from first wave feminism.

1948 German Ursuline nuns expelled Allende from elementary school, ostensibly for organizing a show of underpants. In reality, the staff ejected the six-year-old because Francisca took up with Huidobro, a married man and a stunning intellect educated by Jesuits. On the northeastern rim of Santiago, Isabel enrolled at Dunalastair, a bilingual English academy that required uniforms.

Through painting, reading in the cellar, and verbal invention, Allende worked her way toward adult truths. A copy of Hans Christian Andersen's fairy tales improved her reading and her grasp of narration. She entertained her brothers with storytelling and affirmed that oral skills set her apart from other narrators less observant, less creative than she. To her chauvinist stepfather, she insisted that he not denigrate her as a helpless female. She insisted, "Please respect what I say and my right to say it. That is how to show me you care for me" (Flores, 2002).

December 25, 1950 Molestation by a fisherman terrorized Isabel, who accompanied him to the woods out of curiosity. She retreated from physical violation into solitude and reading.

December 26, 1950 Allende witnessed the fisherman's corpse, felled by a blow to the head. Ironically, her narration of the pedophile's advances angered parents in Fayetteville, Arkansas, who petitioned in 2003 to have the school board ban Allende's *Paula* from the high school library.

1951 Swift changes of the guard in Allende's life followed Memé's death from leukemia. Tata lived on in stoic sorrow for his beloved wife, whom Isabel welcomed into her reveries as a guardian angel. Tata shepherded his grandchildren to the zoo and on vacations to La Playa Grande and Patagonia.

1952 After Francisca's quasi-marriage to Tío Ramón Huidobro, he never gained an annulment from his legal wife María. The Allende family and Ramón traveled northeast by train from Antofagasta and settled in La Paz, Bolivia, far from Isabel's Tata. The night before her departure to La Paz, Allende bade farewell to her bedroom mural, a montage of events in her life. She recorded thoughts in a journal and defended her Chilean heritage from unfavorable histories of war with Bolivia and Peru.

1953 After Tío Ramón Huidobro transferred to Buenos Aires to become secretary of the Chilean embassy, he and Panchita quarreled frequently. Allende entered a private school and began reading Shakespeare's plays, a gift from Tata along with a world map.

1955 During her teens, for three years, Isabel lived in Beirut in a third-floor apartment with her mother and stepfather, who enabled Francisca to travel for two months through Genoa and Rome to reach Lebanon. In a cloistered British private school, the author learned French and, under instructor St. John, read from the Bible. At the academy, the diminutive five-footer became shy and withdrawn because of isolation and homesickness for Chile. Consumed by adolescent stoicism, she contemplated entering a convent.

Equal rights appealed to Allende. A feminist in early womanhood, she described herself as a short bulldozer. She rebelled against traditional Catholic mores and the rigid Chilean class structure. Among Lebanese peers, she learned French and Arabic to add to the Spanish she spoke at home and English in class.

1956 Illuminating pages by flashlight, Allende became an under-the-covers reader and the prototype for Irene Beltrán, the rebel journalist in *Of Love and Shadows* (1987). Allende sank into perusal of *One Thousand and One Nights*, which she purloined from her stepfather's locked armoire. The compendium introduced her to eroticism and fantasy. She later described how the story collection furthered a love of storytelling and "lascivious visions" (Allende, 1998, 78).

1957 In a lively household, Allende's stepfather taught her to samba. An epiphany awakened the budding feminist to the one oppressor she had overlooked, conservative Catholicism. She concluded that, in a league with chauvinism and male authority, the power of popery held women like her mother and aunts in unrelenting bondage.

July 15, 1958 After the Suez Canal crisis, when U.S. Marines occupied Beirut to quell a Lebanese Muslim demand for Arab nationalism, Isabel encountered a soldier at an ice rink who kissed her. As the crisis worsened, she and her brothers returned to Chile on the last commercial flight. In *My Invented Country* (2003), she repined, "I didn't fit in there either, because I'd been away too long" (Allende, 2003, 78). She received tutoring in math and began home schooling in geography, handwriting, grammar, and history under Tata's instruction before entering Colegio La Maisonette, a secondary academy at 6076 Louis Pasteur Avenue in northeastern Santiago.

Because Allende's mother and stepfather moved to a new post in Turkey, mother and daughter began a ritual of daily letters. Isabel promised to destroy the missives after Francisca's death. They grew so close that they shared the same dreams. The author valued the exercise of replying to her mother as an extension of journaling—a record of her life from two perspectives. She valued the letters, bundled and labeled by year, "to keep pulsing the cord that has joined us since the instant of my conception" (Flores, 2008, PA-20).

January 1, 1959 Allende began treasuring passion over security and yearning for independence and connection with other free-spirited women. Her daily debates with Tata sharpened her distaste for Latino *machismo.*

Fall 1959 After graduating from high school, Allende lived in the La Reina hills while managing the data of a forestry census and working as press officer for the U.N. Food and Agricultural Organization in Santiago and Brussels. Her refinement of vision coincided with "el Boom," the world acclamation of upbeat Latino fiction that followed the victory of Fidel Castro during the Cuban Revolution. Fans adored Gabriel García Márquez's *One Hundred Years of Solitude* (1967), a witty saga of a Colombian family, and lionized Peruvian Nobelist Vargas Llosa, Argentine surrealist Julio Cortázar, and Mexican historical novelist Carlos Fuentes. Allende concurred with her fellow writers on the inclusion of the invisible sphere of passion and emotion, a literary revolt against the tyranny of fact over impression. She noted that she belonged to the first generation schooled in "the long list of remarkable fabulists from Latin America" (Austerlitz, 2006).

September 8, 1962 At age 19, Allende married an English-speaking Anglican, Miguel "Michael" Frías, an engineering student at the University of Chile. Panchita sold a rug to pay for the nuptials. In place of the bride's father, Salvador Allende Gossens, Tomás's idealistic cousin and Isabel's godfather, gave Isabel away at the altar. Panchita and Tío Ramón, who were moving to the United Nations office in Geneva, Switzerland, offered the newlyweds a home rent free until March 1963.

During the first months, thieves robbed Isabel and Miguel of clothing, pantry goods, three cars, and wedding gifts. Under her maiden name, Allende worked in media journalism and as a dramatist and translator of the romance novels of Barbara Cartland from English to Spanish. The latter job ended after Allende injected realistic dialogue and altered endings to reflect women's independence. In an interview, Allende explained, "The female protagonists were all retarded. I improved them, and of course I was fired" (Mabe, 2012). Meanwhile Tata retired from sheep raising and settled at the beach, leaving his Santiago manse to the newlyweds until they could build their first home.

October 22, 1963 After Allende gave birth to Paula by caesarean section, she and Miguel received fellowships to study radio and television journalism and engineering in Brussels, Belgium. She made their home in a garret apartment and attended class with Congolese males, who demeaned her as a mere woman. The author absorbed American and European feminism by reading anti-patriarchal authors. Without tactile connection to her Chilean roots, she developed alternate handholds on memory.

1964 Following tours of Norway, Italy, and Spain in a Volkswagen and living among hippies in Geneva, Switzerland, the author returned to Santiago. She became a correspondent for Channel 13, a job that Tata considered too proletarian for his elite granddaughter. She later admitted her flair for snooping: "I'm a story junkie. I hunt stories everywhere" (Hawley, 2008). She narrated the weekly show *Listen Up!* for the United Nations Department of Information and disclosed the lives of felons, hookers, abortionists, and drug dealers. Her bent for muckraking remained strong in the writing of "The Road North," an adoption story about the illicit sale of human organs harvested from orphaned children.

1966 Upon return to Chile, while Miguel worked on an engineering project, Allende lived a block from her in-laws' home. She produced son Nicolás and began composing stories to entertain the children. She later observed, "Kids say wonderful things and they keep you alive. There's something so vital about them" (Locke, 2008).

August 1967 At an auspicious time in the development of a writing persona, Isabel joined the editorial staff of *Paula,* a pace-setting feminist magazine that she co-founded with journalist Delia Vergara, an intellectual rebel. For working-class and middle-class female readers, Allende produced a horoscope, advice to the lovelorn in the column "Love Mail," and radical satire in the column "The Impertinents." Under the pen name Francisca Román, her critiques surveyed stage and television productions. While covering one exposé of women's lives, she appeared in a G-string as a chorus girl in the follies. Serious criticism of her later works denigrated what analyst Veronica Cortínez termed Allende's "professionally embarrassing" past as "frivolous" (Lindsay, 2003, 116).

1969 Allende dreamed of scripting a *telanova* for television, a career later filled by the title character in *Eva Luna* (1987). For *Mampato,* a children's magazine, Allende served as editor in chief and issued the children's stories "Grandmother Panchita" and "Mouselets and Mice, Ratlets and Rats." For satire, she targeted political graft, aging roués, and women's obsessions with cosmetics and *The Cat,* a popular *telenovela.*

October 24, 1970 The founder of Chile's socialist party, Salvador Allende became Chile's first Marxist-Leninist president and an ally of Fidel Castro. The author referred to Salvador Allende as *tío* (uncle) and, in fiction, depicted him as a nearsighted physician. By charismatic speeches, he won the vote of the urban working class and appointed Ramón Huidobro ambassador to Argentina. The auspicious presidency invited undermining by U.S. president Richard Nixon. The president's self-assured leadership spawned insecurity and jealousy in his commander in chief, General Augusto Pinochet Ugarte.

Pinochet trained for the role of minister of defense with courses from Panama's School of the Americas. Analysts Herman Gray and Macarena Gómez-Barris affirm that "Allende renders the story of Chile in ways that make the U.S. state accountable to the historical record" (Gray and Gómez-Barris, 2010, 239). In retrospect, in 1999, Allende proclaimed, "A man who had the gall to pose as his nation's saviour will take his place alongside Caligula and Idi Amin" (Allende, 1999, 24). For the author's role in demanding acknowledgment of U.S. culpability, she has become what Gray and Gómez-Barris call a "public intellectual."

After the author began interviewing on television for Canal 7, a humor and opinion site, she answered a police request to identify the remains of her father, who died on the street in Santiago from heart failure. Her stepfather recognized the corpse as that of Tomás Allende.

The author learned that Tomás had sired four children by two mistresses. The disengagement between father and daughter returns to Allende's *The House of the Spirits* in the relationship between Alba and Blanca's husband, Count Jean de Satigny, whom Clara del Valle erases from family memory by destroying his photos and fabricating his demise in the desert.

December 13, 1971 Pablo Neruda, Allende's favorite poet, received the Nobel Prize for Literature, which he dedicated to the Chilean people.

1972 The author read the popular feminist texts of the era — the works of Simone de Beauvoir, an existential philosopher and activist and Germaine Greer's *The Female Eunuch* (1970). Of Greer's feminism, Allende declared, "Suddenly I felt someone understood me and I could finally cope with my emotions" (Levine, 2002, 6).

Winter 1972 At lunch on Isla Negra with Pablo Neruda, Allende accepted the poet's mockery of her attempts at objective journalism and began to think of herself as a storyteller and fiction writer. To Margaret Munro-Clark, an interviewer for *Antípodas*, Allende considered the shift to fiction as a compromise: "Literature is a very limited tool when you want to change the world. If you could be a very effective journalist that would be much better" (Lindsay, 2003, 116). Nonetheless, she found uses for her skills at community interaction, research, interviewing, and reporting.

Summer 1973 Allende's play *The Ambassador,* which opened in Santiago, earned little remuneration for its nightmarish story of a diplomat's kidnapping. On commission, she followed with *The Ballad of a Nobody* and, the following year, *The Seven Mirrors.* She later credited her love of the stage to its immediacy, a quality she observed in dramatic version of her fiction. Because acting companies interpreted the playwright's dialogue, Allende decided to give up stage plays for storytelling, over which she had complete control.

September 11, 1973 Bombs and a military coup backed by President Richard Nixon, Secretary of State Henry Kissinger, and the American CIA ousted Chile's Marxist government from the Palacio de la Moneda, the presidential residence. Rebels placed Pinochet in control of what the author describes as "the most solid and the longest democracy in the continent" (Norris, 2006). Within five hours, Tomás's cousin, Salvador Allende, died during the coup by an allegedly self-inflicted pistol wound.

Allende mourned, "One day it was a beautiful country, and in 24 hours they had erected torture centers and concentration camps," an outrage she compared to Guantanamo and Abu Ghraib (May, 2010). The regime stayed in power for sixteen years because of complicity of fascists with the press and with the "gente decente" (decent people), who chose consumerism and faux patriotism over human rights (McKale, 2002, 127). Isabel's brother Francisco found himself marooned in Moscow. Tío Ramon resigned his post. In musings about those calamitous events, in 2006 Allende exonerated most Americans of "the evil that their government has done ... the atrocities that have been committed in their name and with their tax money" (Allende, 2006, 7). She charged United States citizens with being apathetic toward world tyranny, which Congress aided by passing the "Torture Bill," her term for the Patriot Act, enacted on October 26, 2001.

September 12, 1973 Immediately, the *junta* dissolved the legislature, abolished unions, banned political parties, rescinded agrarian reform, and outlawed collective bargaining and strikes. The author and journalistic friends began collecting sources of information about the regime's terrorism and its perpetrators, facts suppressed by regime censorship and persecution of reporters. She realized "There were no rules, just brutality" (Miller, 2006). Pinochet, like a sociopathic batterer isolating his mate, began reducing sources of support for Allende. The dictator made fraudulent claims that the coup prevented the former president from violating Chilean democracy and touching off civil war. Pinochet's censors padlocked the door of *Paula* magazine for its audacious feminism, an anti-woman event that Allende turned to comedy in

Of Love and Shadows. The author experienced silencing as insomnia, hives, and a metallic taste in the mouth. No longer a spoiled aristocrat, she grew up rapidly into a savvy survivor of political isolation and daily menace.

The fascist trouncing of human rights by Pinochet's jack-booted military introduced Allende to the alienation that had limited lower class and Indian females since the arrival of Spain's conquistadors in 1536. To the detriment of workers, greed became the national religion. For the first time, she identified with the invisible "other," a citizenry set apart by gender prejudice. She later proclaimed her liberalism a benefit: "I never asked myself if it was worthwhile. Of course it was worthwhile" (Moran, 2000).

Allende's work with the underground introduced her to the era's heroes. She reflected on survivors: "I saw many such stories in Chile during the military coup—people who within a horrible life experience solidarity, integrity, compassion.... For every person tortured, there were a thousand willing to risk their lives to help others" (Timpane, 2010). In all, 3,000 died and another 1,200 were *desaparecidos* (disappeared).

September 23, 1973 After Chile's beloved poet, Pablo Neruda, died, Allende walked in his funeral cortege. Chilean liberties sank under the regime's capricious curfews, censorship, terrorism, corruption, food insecurity, and tyranny. At high risk, Allende pressed her Citroen into service. She hid dissidents at home and an infant in a carload of vegetables. She worked to arrange asylum for some of the thousands locked out of factories, kidnapped, jailed, tortured, and slain. Journalist Maria-Belen Moran noted, "Allende risked her life over and over again, maneuvering in the shadows of foreign embassies, becoming so familiar with the getaway routes that she knew exactly when and where to slow down so her passengers could jump out" (Moran, 2000). The author kept lists of death squad members and *desaparecidos* and addresses of torture centers and petitioned Amnesty International to trace the missing.

1974 Allende published a sheaf of comic columns called *The Impertinents*, including the sarcastic "Civilize Your Troglodyte," which spawned angry letters to the editor. In July, the response influenced Allende to publish 10,000 copies of the anti-male satire.

Summer 1974 The author visited Easter Island, "the Navel of the World," a Chilean possession that sparked her interest in mystery and religion (Allende 1998, 85). In *Aphrodite,* the author describes the birth of the island from volcanic lava and the production of a magnetic point that confuses compasses and watches.

September 30, 1974 After the secret police car bombing of General Carlos Prats González, former vice president under Salvador Allende and commander of the Chilean military, Allende's mother and stepfather eluded possible execution by considering immigration to New Zealand, then by fleeing to Caracas, Venezuela. In *Paula,* Allende described antipathy of Venezuelans toward the intellectual refugees arriving from Argentina, Chile, and Uruguay who competed for top-level positions. The author developed respect for the voyeur, the *hors de combat* observer who must view without taking action, a characteristic reflected in the fictional snooping of Clara del Valle, who witnesses the autopsy that Dr. Cuevas performs on Clara's sister Rosa, and of Férula Trueba and Esteban García in *House of the Spirits,* Aurora del Valle in *Portrait in Sepia* (1995), and Gregory Reeves in *The Infinite Plan* (1993).

1975 The Chilean women's movement gained global prestige from the United Nations, which declared 1975 the International Women's Year. The backing of world feminists bolstered solidarity during the long years under Pinochet until re-democratization in 1989. Like her peers, Allende backed the underdog: "My position is always to defend the least favored," in this case, members of the Chilean Socialist Party (Gough, 2004, 103).

June 1975 Twenty-four hours after Allende received two telephoned death threats and saw her name on an execution list, she realized the danger of Pinochet's spite. Traveling on a passport, she journeyed to Venezuela and lived alone for five weeks. She carried with her "some clothes, family pictures, a small bag with dirt from my garden, and two books," one of the them the poems of Neruda (Allende, 1997, 6). The keepsakes embody what analyst Roberta Rubenstein calls "cultural mourning," a sorrow at the loss of motherland, lifestyle, and ethnic history (Rubenstein, 2001, 79).

July 1975 Miguel and the children joined Allende in Caracas. The home they left unoccupied suffered theft and vandalism. The two displaced families—Isabel's and her mother's—reunited on the second and third floors of an apartment complex. Because of the trauma of the next 13 years, the author cultivated themes of separation, displacement, homesickness, and nostalgia and generated details and minutia drawn from her identity with Chile and Chileans. The experience altered her life and perspective on world slavery, torture chambers, and starvation. She acknowledged the change: "In exile, literature gave me a voice; it rescued my memories from the curse of oblivion; it enabled me to create a universe of my own" (Allende, 2008).

The move stressed the family, who found Venezuela rife with burglary and car theft. Without a job in journalism, she felt overwhelmed by narrative: "The stories just kept piling up within me, and they were suffocating me" (Savio, 2002). Because the refugees found little work, Miguel joined a dam project at Puerto Ordaz and commuted home after separations of weeks and months. The marriage foundered. Rootless and silenced from journalism, Isabel abandoned raffish costumes, the garments she later assigned to Irene Beltrán in *Of Love and Shadows.*

Returning to work, the author wrote television scripts. To escape despair, she returned to journalism with a nine-year column for *El Nacional,* Venezuela's largest newspaper. She explained in an interview, "I needed to lose my country to start writing" (Edemariam). Among her subjects, she featured Chilean survivors of Pinochet's concentration camps.

1978 Retreating into sensuality, Isabel initiated short-lived love affairs. For two months, she separated from her husband and lived in Madrid with an Argentine flute player before returning home to Las Colinas de Bello Monte.

1979 For four years, in lieu of journalistic jobs, Allende served as administrator to the Colegio Marroco, a school with 400 students. She worked two shifts, from 7 A.M. to 1 P.M. among elementary students and in the high school from 1 P.M. to 7 P.M. She later recalled from an American perspective a student body of "nasty brats; here you call them children with disabilities" (Allende, Summer 1996, 21).

January 8, 1981 Because the author remained exiled from Chile, she began typing a letter on her portable Underwood to her 99-year-old grandfather Tata. In decline, he welcomed death by refusing nourishment. The narrative, "an attempt to recreate the country I had lost, the family I had lost," cured the author's homesickness (Edemariam, 2007). As she explains in "Interminable Life," "To exorcise the demons of memory, it is sometimes necessary to tell them as a story" (Allende, 1991, 237). In "great outpourings," the unstructured epistle took shape on the table that her grandmother Memé once used for conducting séances (Correas de Zapata, 2002, 45).

Within 12 months, the letter had grown to a 500-page saga incorporating a half millennium of colonial exploitation. She later confessed, "I was totally innocent: I didn't know anything about writing, the literary critics and professors, the publishing world, or the press. I didn't even know if my manuscript was ever going to be published!" (Cruz-Lugo, 2008, 55). The focus on love and revolt in the lives of three generations of del Valle-Trueba women won readers, while the exposé of injustice, misery, and violence enraged Pinochet.

1982 Influenced by the verse of Neruda and the fiction of Gabriel García Marquez, Allende began designing a fictional character, Clara del Valle, based on Isabel's beloved grandmother, Isabel Barros Moreira. Allende became enamored of storytelling, which she described as "unwinding a ball of yarn" (DeSalvo, 2000, 36). The outlet for rage and sorrow made living more tolerable and saved her grandparents' spirits from oblivion.

Hesitant to call herself a writer, a profession that Latino cultures denied to women, Allende hunkered down at the kitchen table to refine her 500-page text, which she secured in a canvas bag. She stretched the missive into journalistic fiction, *The House of the Spirits*, a gynocentric pseudo-memoir and the first of a bestselling trilogy that exposed the terrorism under Chile's dictator. An example of the dictator novel pioneered by Miguel Angel Asturias, *The House of the Spirits* belongs in a Latin American genre furthered by Mario Vargas Llosa, Augusto Roa Bastos, Manuel Puig, and Roberto Bolano.

The work became the second-largest seller written in Spanish. Enthusiasts embraced the baroque saga as "the major literary event in Spanish America during the early eighties" (Buedel, 2006). Critic Sophie Ratcliffe described Allende's style as "ardent breathlessness" and "giddy freedom," two descriptors of the author's vigor and drive (Ratcliffe, 2001). To accusations that she framed her novel on originals by García Márquez, she lashed out at critics who expect every successful female author to have a male mentor.

Rather than particularize the historical setting, which mimics the grand home of her maternal grandparents, Allende freed herself from fact. The liberation established a technique she later explained: "I prefer the ambiguity of an unnamed place and an undetermined time. It gives me a sort of mythical or legendary tone" (Allende, Summer 1996, 24). Academics lambasted her for playful scenarios and the lack of the political and psychological complexity more readily acceptable to pundits and university specialists. Nonetheless, the world took Allende's three-dimensional reportage for fact and extended empathy to exiled Chileans.

The text, which Magda Bogin translated into English, succeeded works by the big four of the boom years—Cortázar, Fuentes, Llosa, and Márquez. Critic Ilan Stavans elevated Allende's novel as a womanly triumph in the spirit of Nobelist Gabriela Mistral. Reviewer Helen Falconer described the reprise of hellish Chilean history as the author's "exercise in understanding" (Falconer, 2001). *The House of the Spirits* symbolized "the end of the old-boys club in Latin American letters" and a resurgence of world fiction devoid of European dominance (Edemariam, 2007). The author remained oblivious to her global fame until she received royalties and press clippings.

1983 Excerpted in a *Vogue* magazine serial, *The House of the Spirits* won a Chilean novel of the year citation and a *Panorama Literario* selection of the best in Latino literature. In this same period, Miguel's construction company went bankrupt. He developed porphyria, an enzyme disorder.

January 8, 1983 Under the influence of voices of murdered Chileans of the Maurella family, Allende began her second novel, *Of Love and Shadows,* a political exposé of human rights violations committed by the Pinochet regime. While driving, she recalled, "I would start sweating, just like when you put on the brakes and you have this adrenalin coming all over your body" (Hague, 2003, 121). She developed a ritual of locking herself away from distractions and surrounding herself with photos of departed loved ones to summon their spirits. Her son insisted she give up the typewriter and buy a computer.

For text, according to analyst Margaret McKale, Allende drew on "journal articles and recordings, ... letters that her mother had written her over the years, and her grandmother's old diaries and notebooks" (McKale, 2002, 75). She researched press clippings and details at abandoned lime kilns at Lonquén outside Santiago, where the military massacred and buried 15 *campesinos* in 1973. The text honored the persecuted, tortured, repressed, disappeared, and summarily slain at the Los Riscos mine, a source of Bentonite, an aluminum silicate found in volcanic ash. She later discovered that fictional events actually occurred. She credited data "[flowing] in a very mysterious way" that made her the conduit for historical testimony (Hague, 2003, 122).

1984 Germany declared Allende and *The House of the Spirits* the writer and book of the year. Literary historian Raymond L. Williams described the year as a watershed for the revelation of "the Latin American writer as public intellectual on the international stage" (Williams, 2010, 162). From France, she received the *Grand Prix d'Evasion.* Literary historian Donald Leslie Shaw justified Allende's duty "to embrace political commitment," the source of tone and motif in the second half of *The House of the Spirits* (Shaw, 2002, 182). Her ease with notoriety gave her the courage to predict the fall of Pinochet and his fascist hit squads.

January 8, 1984 As a form of discipline, Allende began another project on her chosen date of beginnings. She initiated each new work by lighting candles and meditating. In Madrid, she composed *The Porcelain Fat Lady,* a children's allegory that never pleased her.

1985 Allende received the *Grand Prix de la Radio Télévision Belge;* Mexico declared *Of Love and Shadows* a best novel for reclaiming the humanity of Pinochet's victims. Book dealers recognized Allende as a bankable author; fellow novelist Amy Tan dubbed her contemporary a story giver.

Spring 1985 In New Jersey, Allende taught Latin American literature at Montclair State College.

1986 A global celebrity, Allende received an "author of the year" title from Germany and Mexico's Colima Literary Prize as well as a nomination for the Quality Paperback Book Club New Voice. While visiting Paula, who studied community psychology at the University of Virginia in Charlottesville, Allende led seminars for Spanish majors.

June 1987 In Venezuela, where divorce was legal, the author parted from Miguel Frías. After the couple split their belongings in front of their college-age children, Allende began a lecture tour from Iceland to Puerto Rico and lectured at San Jose State University.

September 1987 Following issuance in Spain of *Eva Luna,* a picaresque narrative about a writer of soap operas, critics applauded the work as "a dialectic between art and life" (Buedel, 2006). More international acclaim derived from Portugal's *Premio Mulheres a la Mejor Novela Extranjera* (first woman author of a major foreign novel), the Swiss book of the year, and the Italian *XV Premio Internazionale I Migliore dell'Anno* (international prize for the year's best). The *Los Angeles Times* nominated her for its book prize. Media broadcasts boosted her from spokeswoman for Latinas to the voice of all Latin America.

October 1987 On a book tour to California to publicize *Of Love and Shadows,* the author met Sausalito attorney and noir crime novelist William "Willie" C. Gordon, a graduate of the University of California at Berkeley and Hastings College of Law. A tattooed Spanish-speaking gringo dressed like an aristocrat, he adored her liberal spirit and called her "my woman, my soul" (Allende, 1995, 110). On return to Venezuela, she drew up a marital contract and sent it to Willie, who accepted the formal proposal. Of her bold actions, she once claimed, "I don't think I would go anywhere for gold or fame, but I would go to the end of the world following a man that I'm in love with" (Norris, 2006).

December 1987 While writing about Eva Luna, a character who seduces by means of storytelling, Isabel directed her own love to a man who listened. In an emotional whirlwind, she settled with Willie and a "tribe" of 17 people at 5 Marina Way in San Rafael overlooking San Francisco Bay. She confided to National Public Radio interviewer Lynn Neary, "We share food, we share clothes, we share children, we help each other. Very much the way I grew up" (Neary, 2008).

1988 The year Allende became a U.S. resident, she accepted a *Library Journal* best book award. She lived for eight months with Willie, then demanded marriage to provide her with a visa.

July 17, 1988 Wed in San Francisco, Isabel and Willie Gordon cultivated harmony in their mixed families, who lived within minutes of each other. She joked that "not even marriage has made me stop liking him" (Correas de Zapata, 2002, 79). Two decades later, she admitted, "It's very difficult to be married to me! I am a bossy, jealous, and demanding Latin American wife" (Cruz-Lugo, 2008, 55).

The author slipped away during heavy writing time and, from 9 A.M. to 7 P.M., barricaded herself in a *cuchitril* (study), a former pool house. In a trance, she allowed a fictional voice to speak: "That first sentence usually determines the whole book. It's a door that opens into an unknown territory that I have to explore with my characters" (McNally, 2010). Willie's inventive Spanglish influenced the author's language, forcing her to hire Spanish grammarian Jorge Manzanilla to correct her manuscripts.

August 1988 An amnesty for 500 exiles allowed Allende a visit to her homeland. On her return to Santiago to vote, the expatriate made peace with Miguel, who had remarried. She found fans thronging the airport and waving pirated copies of *The House of the Spirits,* a contraband book in Chile.

Fall 1988 While traveling cross country for brief reunions with Willie, Allende worked as guest teacher at the University of Virginia and received appointment as Gildersleeve Lecturer at Barnard College.

1989 A Before Columbus Foundation Award acknowledged Allende's recognition of aboriginal contributions to history. During the writing of *The Stories of Eva Luna* (1991), the author described a vulnerability: "I felt naked the whole time I was writing ... very sensitive to everything that was going on" (Gregory, 2003, 91). A compelling story of Omaira Sánchez, a girl killed in a mud slide from the Nevado del Ruiz volcano on November 16, 1985, nagged at the author for narration in "And of Clay Are We Created." After Allende published the anthology, she left her post at a school for the handicapped. Her collection received film options in Canada and the U.S. and appeared as opera, stage adaptation, and radio and television versions.

Spring 1989 The author taught creative writing and long narrative at the University of California at Berkeley.

December 14, 1989 The return of political stability to Chile allowed the author to visit home. She renewed family relationships and celebrated Pinochet's loss of supreme power to Christian Democrat Patricio Aylwin.

January 1991 *Mother Jones* published "Two Words," the first entry in *The Stories of Eva Luna.* With details drawn from the life of Willie Gordon, Allende completed her third novel, *The Infinite Plan,* her first fiction set in America. She justified the focus: "The U.S. is the center of the world. Whatever happens here is reflected in the rest of the world" (Mabe, 2012). Perhaps because she chose a male protagonist, the novel received a lukewarm reception.

December 6, 1991 Shortly after Paula's marriage to Ernesto Díaz in Venezuela, she worked in a Catholic school as a volunteer psychologist and teacher. Allende interrupted the celebration of *The Infinite Plan,* and the writing of *Daughter of Fortune* (1999) in Barcelona to drive to Madrid and rush up six flights of hospital stairs to comfort Paula during treatment for unexplained convulsions. The author's broad world view shrank to a twelve-bed ward and a tangle of monitors and lab tests. Her body shut down, throwing her into menopause. To assuage her terror, Allende indulged in five helpings of rice pudding, a dessert that took her back to childhood comforts to enable her to "bear the anguish of seeing my daughter so ill" (Allende, 1998, 24).

January 28, 1992 Allende's mother observed the stress that hospital stays inflicted and ordered Isabel to seize life by writing. *Time* magazine reported Allende's comment on loss: "It was destiny—and it was bad luck. After they told me, I went on writing because I could not stop. I could not let anger destroy me." Carmen Balcells, Allende's Spanish agent, presented her a ream of yellow foolscap along with nougats, sausage, and armloads of red roses. The author opted to fill the sheets with nonfiction that structured her pain. Allende wrote a memoir of her mother-daughter relationship with Paula, a mythic blend of dark and light paralleling the Greek myth of Persephone and Demeter, the earth mother who literally harrowed the underworld to retrieve her child. A family history defying death, Allende's text relived Paula's life and released the sorrow that temporarily silenced the novelist, leaving what reviewer Sarah Vine called an "aching, gaping void" (Vine, 2008, 10). A reviewer for *USA Today,* Deirdre Donahue, called the memoir one of the most poignant ever written about sorrow.

March 16, 1992 After weeks of tending Paula, Francisca flew back to Chile.

May 1992 In the year-long coma, like Sleeping Beauty under glass, Paula remained in intensive care. After neurologists diagnosed irreversible brain damage, Allende transferred Paula to San Rafael via a 20-hour pilgrimage. The patient languished in a rehabilitation center for one month.

June 1992 At home once more, Allende held Paula with the tenderness of a new mother while hospice nurses, an acupuncturist, astrologer, Apache shaman, and hypnotist continued treatment regimens. Diagnosis targeted porphyria, an enzyme deficiency inherited from Miguel Frías, and the Madrid hospital staff for overdosing sedatives.

November 15, 1992 When Paula's death seemed ineluctable, Allende seesawed between wanting to sue the hospital and wanting to kill herself. She needed to savor moments, to read stories slowly to extract the pleasure of the telling and the motivations of the characters. An apparition of Paula readied Allende for letting go and accepting an inevitable death. Allende prepared to ingest Paula's spirit, love, gestures, and voice.

November 30, 1992 Allende and Ernesto gave Paula permission to die. For six days, she sank deeper into a moribund state.

December 6, 1992 Without regaining consciousness, Paula died of cerebral hemorrhage at 3 A.M. by candlelight at her mother's home. Allende observed a gathering of family spirits, including her clairvoyant Grandmother Isabel and Basque patriarch Agustin.

December 7, 1992 At Paula's direction from her last letter, the family scattered her ashes in a stream running through a redwood forest.

1993 Paula's death left the author angry, confused, and despondent, a complex of emotions that critic Anita Savio called "an emotional fugue" (Savio, 2002). Allende tried "to exorcise ... sadness with futile rituals" (Allende, 1998, 24). More honoraria — the XLI Bancarella Literary Prize from Italy and the Brandeis University Major Book Collection Award from the U.S.— extended the author's fame.

June 1993 Allende received the Independent Foreign Fiction Award from England. To publicize *The Infinite Plan,* she conducted an 18-city tour.

August 1993 Director Michael Batz and Yorick theatre company's seven-hour stage version of *The House of the Spirits* opened in London.

October 22, 1993 To mixed reviews, the screen version of Allende's first novel debuted in Munich, starring Antonio Banderas, Glenn Close, Jeremy Irons, Vanessa Redgrave, Winona Ryder, and Meryl Streep.

1994 The Feminist Majority Foundation declared Allende Feminist of the Year. The French presented her the *Chevalier des Artes and des Lettres* (knight of arts and letters). Allende joined Gloria Steinem in presenting views on international transpersonal experience at the conference entitled *Spirit in Action: Awakening to the Sacred in Everyday Life.*

January 1994 Antonio Banderas co-starred with Jennifer Connelly in the Spanish-Argentine film version of *Of Love and Shadows.*

March 1994 Analyst John Rodden, a fellow teacher with Allende at the University of Virginia, noted that the author experienced a spiritual transformation that made her "more reflective, less goal-directed, more self-revealing, less guarded" (Rodden, 2010, 184). She received more joy from composition and less concern for critical acclaim.

The author flew to Santiago to become the first female recipient of the Gabriela Mistral Order of Merit. She attended the birth of granddaughter Andrea and cut the umbilical cord. The experience, which left the author with a sense of identity with life and spirit, enacted the poet David's reminder of the essence of deity: "Be still and know that I am God" (Psalm 46:10).

1995 Well received by Allende fans and boosted to #8 on *The New York Times* bestseller chart, *Paula* blended misfortune with a celebration of life. The memoir drew on the love letters between Paula and Ernesto, who shared the sexual, pornographic side of Allende's daughter. The brutal honesty of a mother's ruminations shocked Allende's mother, who edited the work.

April 11, 1995 To promote *Paula,* her most popular work, the author began a 12-city book tour in Austin at the University of Texas. Of personal sorrow, she remarked, "I think very few people pass through life without suffering. And my suffering is no different from that of others and it's not great" (Ratner-Arias, 2010). Allende began to see "strokes of color" and to experience "a tremendous desire to eat and cuddle once again" (Allende, 1998, 25). On a trip to New Delhi, a bizarre incident determined how she would invest the royalties from *Paula.* A woman handed her a female newborn. Allende's driver explained, "Who wants a girl?"

The BBC Channel 1 screened *Listen, Paula,* a documentary on Allende's reduction of a miserable year into a vivid catastrophe narrative. Renewed interest in the family's loss generated competition for the Paula Scholarships, awarded to the Canal Community Alliance and at the University of San Jose.

January 16, 1996 Los Angeles celebrated "Isabel Allende Day" funded by Miller Brewing Company and led by public librarians. The author promoted ethnic inclusion by touring with the "Read about Me" program, a public library initiative promoting literacy and literature. For her activism, she received the designation of "Author of the Year." At the East Los Angeles Public Library, she stressed that "a world without books without reading would be a cold, impersonal place.... My dream is to see a world agenda where race, nationality or class will not define or determine a nation's destiny" (Lamolinara, 1996).

May 16, 1996 In a speech for the Institute of Noetic Sciences, Allende described how despair preceded the opening of her mind to composition, an escape from feelings of failure. In the wake of Paula's death, Isabel underwent a period of being rather than doing. Lacking any way to intervene in her daughter's suffering, the author recognized a need for unconditional love and patience. At the moment when Paula slipped away, Isabel felt a sacred aura, the same that accompanied the birth of granddaughter Andrea. In retrospect, Allende described the life force that yanked her out of the underworld and equipped her with compassion and strength.

Summer 1996 Allende accepted a Critics' Choice award and honorary doctorate from Columbia College and, at the Chicago Public Library, became the first Hispanic to receive the Harold Washington Literary Award. More honors from the U.S. Hispanic Heritage Award in Literature and the American Library Association Books to Remember boosted her name recognition.

December 9, 1996 To honor Paula, the author launched the Isabel Allende Foundation to champion the rights of women and children. With the royalties from *Paula,* Isabel and her husband hosted an outreach to the poor in a Victorian house, a former Sausalito brothel. Daughter-in-law Lori Barra directed the charity and supported Mujeres Unidas y Activas (women united and active), which promoted empowerment for Latina immigrants, reproductive rights, health care, and protection of girls and women.

1997 Allende collected condolence letters in *Cartas a Paula* (Letters to Paula). Three years of silence ended with Allende's choice of food, love, and sex as her next subject. Abetted by her mother, at porn shops in Castro, a seedy section of San Francisco, Allende collected love charms and recipes to test on Willie. The publication of humorous erotica in *Aphrodite: A Memoir of the Senses* swelled her mail with pleadings from men to enliven their sex lives. She began a series of creative writing workshops at Book Passage Cafe and Book Store in Madera, California.

March 25, 1997 Publication of a travelogue, "The Amazon Queen," in *Salon* prefaced a repeat of the details for Allende's 2002 YA novel *City of the Beasts.* Her depiction of Manaos as a has-been center of the rubber trade precedes a ten-day perusal of the Brazilian jungle. Upon return, she felt unburdened of a three-year case of writer's block.

January 8, 1998 After an eight-year hiatus in fiction writing, Allende picked up the del Valle saga to begin *Daughter of Fortune.* Critic Efraín Kristal noted the post–1980 rise of women's history studies and gender criticism, a feminist triumph that Allende reflects with the bold travels and exotic experiences of Eliza Sommers with Chinese comfort girls immured in San Francisco. The feminist quest novel, woven into the history of the California gold rush, spent eleven weeks on the *New York Times* list of bestsellers, boosting the author to the world's most-read writer of translated fiction.

October 13, 1998 At a presentation by International PEN, the novelist received the Dorothy and Lillian Gish Prize—a silver medallion and $200,000—for contributions to beauty and enjoyment of life. Allende also accepted Italy's Donna Citta di Roma (female citizen of Rome), a Malaparte Amici di Capri, and the Sara Lee Foundation citation, a $200,000 stipend, and a $50,000 donation to the charity of her choice.

December 1998 To advertise *Daughter of Fortune,* until November 1999, Allende traveled in Europe and the Americas.

1999 The author's son married Lori Barra, Allende's second daughter-in-law.

2000 The PBS broadcast of "Woman's Place: Voices of Contemporary Hispanic American Women" featured Allende alongside Bianca Jagger and Puerto Rican novelist Esmeralda Santiago.

February 17, 2000 After Oprah Winfrey chose *Daughter of Fortune* as her thirtieth novel selection, Allende became the first Hispanic author so honored. To meet demand, the publisher printed 600,000 additional copies.

October 2000 Allende issued *Portrait in Sepia*, a baroque delight that critic Kris Dinnison called "another luxurious read" (Dinnison, 2002). A reviewer for *Hispanic Outlook in Higher Education* compared the novel's epic sweep to "I-Max, Cinerama, Three-D, or Cinemascope" ("Review," February 2005). The plot continued the saga of Eliza Sommers with the life of her daughter Lynn and granddaughter Aurora del Valle. The author described the three sagas of the del Valle family—*The House of the Spirits, Daughter of Fortune*, and *Portrait in Sepia*—as a trilogy. She observed that the 1800s created Latino interest because Chile underwent one revolution and five wars. She added, "I think a big part of the national character was forged there" (Moran, 2000). Ironically, between 1990 and 2000, Allende's *The House of the Spirits* earned a position of 67 on the American Library Association list of the 100 most banned books.

September 2000 Disclosures by the CIA admitted underhanded media and propaganda tactics in the elevation of Pinochet to power in 1973. After the election of George W. Bush to the U.S. presidency, she regretted the Republican politics that exacerbated poverty and terrorism.

January 2001 A school board in Newport-Mesa, California, debated the advisability of teaching Allende's *Of Love and Shadows* and David Guterson's *Snow Falling on Cedar,* both frankly sexual in content. In mid-February, the school board overrode parental objections and restored both novels to the high school curriculum.

February 12–March 3, 2001 At the Deckchair Theatre in Perth, Australia, Angela Chaplin and Kavisha Mazzella's *Luna* saluted Allende's *The Stories of Eva Luna.* A dreamscape allegory punctuated by 15 original songs, the action melded political oppression with passion.

March 28, 2001 Allende appeared on Oprah Winfrey's show and described the loss of Paula.

September 11, 2001 Terrorist attacks jolted Allende into reliving the coup that killed Salvador Allende. She realized that she shared with Americans a sense of helplessness in the face of political evil. Of the motivation for 9/11, she declared, "Every form of imperialism is the same—a mission to impose your values on those who do not want them. Every great power has done it" (Pamela Miller, 2006).

October 2001 A writer for the *Rocky Mountain News* balked at the idea of a feminist producing a romance as lush and languorous as *Portrait in Sepia.* From a positive perspective, Jonathan Yardley, reviewer for the *Washington Post,* declared the novel Allende's finest. The *Weekend Australian* dubbed the writer a "hussy of a storyteller" (Rodden, 2005, 65).

2002 To rid herself of writer's block, the author consumed ayahuasca, an hallucinogenic alkaloid brewed from *Banisteriopsis* or "spirit vine." The two-day experience purges the body of tropical parasites and produces a shamanic experience. Allende also aided her husband to write *The Chinese Jars,* a noir mystery set in San Francisco's Chinatown and starring detective Samuel Hamilton.

Fulfilling her promise to write works for each of Nicolás's children, the novelist published the eco-thriller *City of the Beasts,* the first of the Jaguar and Eagle YA trilogy brought out in annual installments. Critic Santa L. Beckett described the trio as "a kind of Latin American *Harry Potter*" (Beckett, 2009, 165). Brian Stableford termed the quest novel series "an elaborate Odyssean fantasy" (Stableford 2005, 7). The ambiguous tone and themes enabled German and British booksellers to profit from two editions, one young adult and one adult. The grown-ups' edition cost more and featured Allende's name in larger type, an appeal to author recognition.

American hero Alexander Cold and his sidekick, Brazilian-Canadian teenager Nadia Santos, join Stone Age Amerindians in a magical venture into Amazonia, an escape into non-Western reality. Contributing an air of the supernatural are episodes of shapeshifting, magical spaces, animal speech, and ESP set on the Upper Orinoco. Allende objected to jacket blurbs and promotions for *City of the Beast,* which showcase protagonist Alexander Cold to the exclusion of the co-protagonist, Nadia Santos. The author regretted that "at even this age there are prejudices against the feminine presence in important roles" (Flores, 2002). In a vision of "the last stand of the old male order," the author pictured healthy older women seizing power and engineering a new gender balance (Flores, 2002). She omitted younger women from the vision because they tend to identify with the artifice of beauty and allure advertised in the media rather than the raw need of third world women.

April 2002 The author visited 30 students at Northern New Mexico Community College in Española. Each received a $1,000 scholarship from Allende.

October 25, 2002 A performance of *Two Words,* Denise Blinn and Gabrielle Kemeny's adaptation of two Allende stories, opened in Toronto at the Tarragon Extra Space. Of the power of drama, she exulted, "Live theatre has magic different from any other art" ("Allende Is All," 2002).

November 17, 2002 The *San Francisco Chronicle* chose *City of the Beasts* among the year's best sci-fi novels for young readers, an honorarium echoed by *Book* magazine.

May 2003 The author acquired dual citizenship by becoming an American and issued a meandering memoir, *My Invented Country: A Nostalgic Journey Through Chile.* The text clarifies her sense of "American-ness" on September 11, 2001, when she watched the World Trade Center collapse and burn. Still a South American nostalgic for customs and rituals, she pictured herself as the autocratic Godfather controlling family lives. She received the Premio Iberoamericano de Letras (Iberian-American literature award) from the University of Talca, Chile.

June 13, 2003 In a PBS interview with Bill Moyers, Allende explained how writing untangled the author's confusion about events and their meaning.

August 2003 John Gertz and Sandra Curtis, representatives of Zorro Productions, arrived at Allende's home with books and videos and a proposal: that she write *The Origins of the Legend of Zorro,* a literary prequel to the mestizo swordsman's adventures, another crossover from her established literary modes. The 85-year-old legend grew from the pulp serial *The Curse of Capistrano,* which Johnston McCulley issued in 1919. The plot draws on episodes in the life of the California *bandito* Joaquin Murieta, the avenger of Mexican losses to the United States under the 1848 Treaty of Guadalupe Hidalgo.

Allende admitted, "I couldn't talk about anything else for three months or more" (Keenan, 2005). She envisioned an Arthurian epic incorporating a secret Spanish brotherhood with denizens of the Old West and a Mexican child of disparate circumstances. Her Dickensian image focused on Antonio Banderas, the star of the film *The Mask of Zorro* (1998), as well as the historical figures Marie Laveau, a voodoo priestess, privateers Jean and Pierre Lafitte, and Jean's quadroon wife, Catherine Villars.

2004 Allende received membership in the American Academy of Arts and Letters, a life association with leading American artists, and traveled to Copenhagen as ambassador to the Hans Christian Andersen Bicentenary. She completed *Kingdom of the Golden Dragon,* part two of her young adult trilogy. The Seattle Public Library chose Allende as the year's featured author and named her the "Author That Everyone Should Read." Staff gathered 600 fans in a community center gym to welcome her to a poor neighborhood.

Summer 2004 Willie, Isabel, Nico, Lori, and the three grandchildren swam with turtles and sea lions off the Galapagos Islands.

2005 Composer Michael Djupstrom, a 25-year-old native of St. Paul, Minnesota, wrote "Walimai," a fourteen-minute solo piece for piano and alto saxophone or viola expressing the animism and anti-colonialism of Allende's short story.

January 8, 2005 Setting out to write *Inés of My Soul,* Allende expressed her antipathy toward the Bush administration for using terrorism as "an excuse for a culture of fear" (Pamela Miller, 2006). Because of the high romantic flourishes, reviewer Antonella Gambotto-Burke accused the author of "[working] a hypnagogic literary realm" (Gambotto-Burke, 2006). Celia McGee, in a review for *USA Today,* credited Allende for writing "her surest work since *The House of the Spirits*" (McGee, 2006).

Spring 2005 Allende's *Zorro,* which reset the legends of a hero, allowed her to fantasize about a handsome masked intruder on her balcony and in her bed. Her version, unlike comic strips and adventure movies, characterized Zorro's childhood and young manhood as the mestizo son of an Indian mother and Spanish father. The plot served as a series on U.S. Telemundo and a musical performed in Brazil, England, and France.

That same year, Allende published *Forest of the Pygmies,* the last of the trilogy that began with *City of the Beasts.* The opening text expresses Allende's commitment to ecofeminism through the *Defenders of the Chilean Forests.* Critic Donnarae MacCann and reviewer Reyhann Harmanci of the *San Francisco Chronicle* charged Allende with Eurocentric cliché by retreating to a virulent face mask on the cover and to disturbing images of helpless African Bantus and Pygmies—a demeaning term for the Aka, Mbuti, and Twa—in need of direction by Brother Fernando and Catholic missionaries from Spain. The character of Má Bangesé, an African priestess, recedes into caricature from protruding eyes and guttural voice, elements of the Hollywood stereotype of the witch doctor.

Summer 2005 On safari in Kenya, Willie, Isabel, Nico, Lori, and the three grandchildren observed the Masai and Samburu.

August 12, 2005 At the Armory for the Arts in Santa Fe, New Mexico, director John Flax and the Theater Grottesco opened *A Dream Inside Another,* an adaptation of three of Eva Luna's stories—"The Little Heidelberg," "Tosca," and "Wicked Girl."

2006 By the year's beginning, Allende had sold 50 million books in 30 languages. Actor Blair Brown's reading of *Inés of My Soul* on CD revived Allende's readership.

January 8, 2006 A call from Allende's agent in Spain rechanneled plans for her next novel into suggestions for a second memoir, *The Sum of Our Days.* Like the autobiographical elements of works by Tim O'Brien, Tennessee Williams, and Leslie Marmon Silko, the second memoir enabled Allende to reappraise her life. By reviewing changes and aging, like Alice Walker and Virginia Woolf, Allende became a witness to impermanence and enabled herself to accept the worst along with the best. Therapy assisted her in accepting the unalterable and preparing for the unpredictable.

January 15, 2006 Walden Media purchased rights to Allende's young adult *City of the Beasts* trilogy. The company CEO chose the trio because it bases action on the intergenerational relationship between a 15-year-old boy and his writer grandmother, Kate Cold. The company CEO, Cary Granat, praised the series for placing a male teen under the care and influence of a grandparent. Granat explained, "Kids today have lost that ability to connect with the older generation" (Lia Miller, 2006). Another plus for the trio, it exhibits the value of spirituality without subjecting readers to religious orthodoxy or proselytizing.

mid–February 2006 At the opening ceremony of the Winter Olympics in Turin, Italy, Allende joined actors Sophia Loren and Susan Sarandon, Kenyan activist Wangari Maathai, and Cambodian anti-slavery crusader Somaly Mam in carrying the Olympic flag.

August 2006 Allende dramatized the life of an historic female, Inés Suárez, as the heroine of 16th-century Chile in *Inés of My Soul,* a Chilean bestseller.

November 4–11, 2006 The author read from *Inés of My Soul* at the Miami Book Fair, which featured Hispanic works.

2007 *Latino Leaders Magazine* acclaimed Allende as a Latina who influences the world. The Bancroft Library of the University of California at Berkeley presented the author the Hubert Howe Bancroft Award.

January 8, 2007 Allende began composing her second memoir, *The Sum of Our Days,* including the growth of the Allende-Gordon clan after the death of Paula Allende and Jennifer Gordon.

April 2007 Enraged at the shackling of a seven-year-old to his father in a raid led by the Immigration and Customs Enforcement, Allende joined San Francisco Latinos on a march to the mayor's office. The protesters chanted their trust in the people to unite against tyranny. That night, she suffered a panic attack from a flashback to the Pinochet military coup in Chile that had forced her out of her motherland for a 13-year exile.

May 2007 At Trento, Italy, the novelist accepted the Premio Honoris Causa (cause of honor award) for language and literature of a modern Euro-American.

June 8–24, 2007 In celebration of the 25th anniversary of *The House of the Spirits,* adapter Myra Platt's stage version opened in Seattle, Washington, at the Book-It Repertory Theatre. The production reduced the saga into 75 roles played by 18 actors, nearly half of them Latino.

September 26, 2007 Allende and William Gordon received honorary doctorates from Whittier College for their humanitarian outreach to the San Francisco Bay area through the Isabel Allende Foundation.

2008 Critic Nick Rennison, who writes for the London *Sunday Times* and edits *The Bloomsbury Good Reading Guide*, chose *The House of the Spirits* for inclusion in *100 Must-Read Life-Changing Books.*

Spring 2008 At commencement, San Francisco State University awarded the author an honorary doctorate for her humanitarianism and contributions to literature. She issued *The Sum of Our Days,* an autobiographical sequel to *Paula.* Completion of the manuscript required long conversations with family members and recasting of events to voice individual memories. Of the exercise, the author declared, "It enriched us all" (Richards, 2008).

April 21–28, 2008 The author promoted her memoir in Great Britain and Ireland.

July 15–25, 2008 Stephen Clark's musical adaptation of *Zorro,* directed by Christopher Renshaw, opened in London at the Garrick Theatre. Set in 1805, it featured the villain Ramón, ingenue Luisa, and Inez, queen of a troop of Gypsies in episodes from Diego de la Vega's adventures in Barcelona and California. As preparation for staging, Allende choreographed dueling scenes before a mirror.

2009 The London *Times* named *The House of the Spirits* one of the top 60 books in the past six decades. Allende addressed attendees at the Göteborg Book Fair in Sweden. Matt Wagner and Francesco Francavilla issued a young adult graphic novel based on Allende's backstory of the Zorro legends. The comic book version features White Owl, a powerful female spiritualist reminiscent of Clara del Valle and Queen Nana-Asante in *Forest of the Pygmies.* The episodes picture young Diego developing a liberator's virtues—endurance, loyalty, and strength—and an affinity for communicating with nature.

March 9, 2009 Caridad Svich's four-act adaptation of Allende's "La Casa de Los Espíritus" premiered in Spanish at the Repertorio Español at New York City's Gramercy Arts Theater. The production featured puppetry, video, and original songs performed by eleven actors. Critics applauded Svich's version for its lyric subtleties and nimble language.

October 2009 Allende fostered the work of Jamaican composer Eleanor Alberga, adapter of "Letters of Love Betrayed" from *The Stories of Eva Luna* for Music Theatre Wales.

October 13, 2009 Isabel presented the Frederick Douglass Freedom Award before the Free the Slaves organization. She used her notoriety to protest pockets of slavery around the globe, primarily in southeast Asia, where slaves are "as disposable as paper cups" (May, 2010). She pinpointed bondage among the indebted, Cambodian concubines, Haitian and Nepalese domestics, African diamond miners and child soldiers, Pakistani field drudges, and slaves to fishing, logging, and sweatshops. For blame, she accused all forms of "power with impunity" (May, 2010).

October 23, 2009 The Spanish cabinet appointed Allende to the Council of the Cervantes Institute, which champions Spanish language and culture.

2010 After the retirement of 83-year-old English translator Margaret Sayers Peden, Allende hired Anne McLean.

March 2010 Allende responded to an earthquake in Chile by appearing on the telethon "Chile Helps Chile" and donating $500,000 to the cause. Of the nation's response to need, she observed that catastrophe "brings out the best in us—courage, solidarity, generosity, and I hope too, joy" (Beaubien, 2010).

April 29, 2010 Four years in the making and dedicated to son Nicolás and his wife Lori, Allende's novel *The Island Beneath the Sea* drew on her research for *Zorro.* Research into racial atrocities made her physically ill, but clarified why New Orleans changed completely with the influx of refugees from the Haitian Revolution of 1791. She stalled to wait for the "moment when it's ready," a coalescing of character with historical milieu (Gumbrecht, 2010). Harper debuted the novel at the National Cathedral to 1,000 fans.

The text pictures the milieu of Haiti during a slave revolt and the 10,000 refugees who flee to Cuba, France, and New Orleans. Critic Michael Schaub credits her handling of "a difficult issue with, for the most part, considerable restraint and grace," notably, an era of grand arson and beheadings in Le Cap (Schaub, 2010). The novel, filled with loss and sorrow, reached print in the same year as the earthquake that devastated Haiti (Bahadur, 2010, 26). The author's book tour included Philadelphia and Union Square in New York City. Of the hurricane-like protagonist, Zarité "Tété" Sedella, sex slave at age 11 to 20-year-old planter Toulouse Valmorain, Allende described her as made from the author's own rib.

August 5, 2010 After the Chilean earthquake, Allende flew home to a damaged airport and no electricity or telephones. She participated in a television fundraiser to aid victims. Of the conjunction of the disaster with the publication of *Island Beneath the Sea,* she regretted any suggestion of exploitation, but applauded the return of Haiti to public interest: "It's on the map again.... People are talking about Haiti, a marvelous country in need of help" (Ratner-Arias, 2010).

September 2, 2010 Allende received Chile's National Literature Prize, a $30,000 purse and a lifetime stipend of $17,000 per year.

September 19, 2010 Isabel spoke by video to 33 Chilean miners trapped underground. The rescue coincided with preparations for director Marcela Lorca's October presentation of *The House of the Spirits,* an adaptation staged and choreographed by the Minneapolis Mixed Blood Theatre. Lorca admired Allende's fictional cast: "These women are very spirited, peculiar, artistic, political. Some are off the wall, some not so good. I call myriad people like that family" (Preston, 2010). To assist actors in understanding the characters, Allende visited them during rehearsal to display photos of her grandparents.

September 25, 2010 An introduction to Allende's address to the National Book Fair in Washington, D.C., pictured her as an "unbelievable workhorse." In her account of the basis of *Island Beneath the Sea,* she described the "experience of the divine" that strengthened Haitian blacks to overthrow Napoleon's troops (Allende, 2010). In an overview of her career, she rejected the workings of the white suburban middle class, Wall Street, and Washington to focus on marginal non-white people who are vulnerable to bastions of power.

Winter 2010 Caridad Svich published his 150-minute stage adaptation of *The House of the Spirits* in TheatreForum featuring photos of the premiere in September 2009 at Houston's Main Street Theater. Svich chose the work for stage because he found it "fascinating, turbulent, beautiful, sensual, and compelling ... grand narrative tradition" (Aparicio, 2011, 1). His notes designate Alba the "witness and archivist of her history" (Svich, 76). For the part of Barrabás, the director, José Zayas, employed a puppet.

2011 With the contemporary suspense novel *Maya's Notebook,* the author contrasted Chiloé, Chile, with Berkeley, California. In Spain, Allende accepted the City of Alcalá Arts and Letters Award.

January 1, 2011 The novelist began a year's sabbatical.

June 9, 2011 *Forbes* named Allende one of the ten most powerful female authors.

July 8, 2011 Emerging female playwright Caridad Svich won the 2011 American Theatre Critics Association Francesca Primus Prize of $10,000 for adapting for stage Allende's *The House of the Spirits.* Critics rewarded Svich for a concise version of the novel spiked with realism, verse, and song. Allende admired the adaptation for its originality and fluidity.

September 2011 The debut of the documentary film *Santiago Files* featured Isabel Allende's overview of the collapse of the Salvador Allende government as told through interviews and archival news clips.

October 10, 2011 Sony Pictures began developing a film about the legendary Zorro based on Isabel Allende's novel, adapted for the screen by television writers Matthew Federman and Stephen Scaia. The prequel carried the working title *Zorro: The Legend Begins.*

March 5, 2012 Florida International University in Miami honored Allende with the Lawrence A. Sanders Award for Fiction, an acknowledgment of her 19 books carrying a monetary prize of $5,000 and trophy sculpted by Ignacio Castaneda. Combining popular appeal with literary excellence, her works have sold 57 million copies in 35 languages.

March 7, 2012 In Mexico City, the author delivered a speech, "Stories of Passion," on behalf of Mexico's Council for Culture and Art detailing the inequalities and violence suffered by women globally. At the crux of the oration, she asserted, "It's not about changing the women so that they fit in the world, but changing the world so that it fits women," a reference to the "gendercide" that kills girl babies and to the rape that is a "weapon of war" (Arvide, 2012, 1, 2).

June 24, 2012 At a time when immigration centered political discussion on both left and right, Allende joined the 500 marchers at San Rafael, California, honoring immigrants with dance, food, games, and music.

September 30, 2012 For her nineteen works, Allende became the third writer to receive the Hans Christian Andersen Literature Award, a storyteller's prize of $90,000 presented by Crown Princess Mary at Odense, the Danish raconteur's boyhood home.

May 19, 2013 The L.A. Opera Off Grand premiered *Dulce Rosa,* composer Lee Holdridge and Richard Sparks's adaptation of Allende's story "An Act of Vengeance," conducted by Placido Domingo. A fable of forgiveness set in the early 1950s, the story depicts a father, Senator Orellano, trying to save his daughter Rosa from torture by the bandit Tadeo Cespedes.

• *References and Further Reading*

Allende, Isabel. *Aphrodite: A Memoir of the Senses.* New York: HarperCollins, 1998.
_____. "Breath of Hope: On the Writings of Eduardo Galeano," *Monthly Review* 48:11 (April 1997): 1–6.
_____. *Inés of My Soul.* New York: HarperCollins, 2006.
_____. "My House Is Full of People," American Libraries 27:4 (April 1996): 42–43.
_____. *My Invented Country.* New York: HarperCollins, 2003.
_____. *Paula.* New York: HarperCollins, 1995.
_____. "Pinochet Without Hatred," *New York Times* (17 January 1999): 24–27.
_____. "The Short Story," *Journal of Modern Literature* 20:1 (Summer 1996): 21–28.
_____. *The Stories of Eva Luna.* New York: Atheneum, 1991.
_____. "2010 National Book Festival," www.youtube.com/watch?v=61RL2aiuLi4, accessed May 29, 2012.
_____. "Zorro—My Ultimate Hero," (London) *Times* (3 March 2008).
"Allende Is All about Storytelling," *Toronto Star* (23 October 2002).
Aparicio, Alfredo. "'The House of the Spirits": A Multi-Layered Saga," *Florida International University Student Media* (31 October 2011).
Arvide, Cynthia. "Author Isabel Allende Proves Strategic Funding Changes Lives for the Better," *Women News Network* (16 April 2012): 1–2.
Austerlitz, Saul. "Chile's Colonial History Given Life," *San Francisco Chronicle* (7 November 2006).
Axelrod-Contrada, Joan. *Isabel Allende.* New York: Marshall Cavendish Benchmark, 2011.

Bahadur, Gaiutra. "All Souls Rising," *New York Times Book Review* (2 May 2010): 26.
Barbas-Rhoden, Laura. *Writing Women in Central America: Gender and the Fictionalization of History.* Athens: Ohio University Press, 2003.
Beaubien, Jason. "Chile's Edge over Haiti When It Comes to Quakes," (NPR) *Morning Edition* (8 March 2010).
Beckett, Sandra L. *Crossover Fiction: Global and Historical Perspectives.* New York: Routledge, 2009.
Buedel, Barbara Foley. "Magical Places in Isabel Allende's Eva Luna and Cuentos de Eva Luna," *West Virginia University Philological Papers* (22 September 2006).
Correas de Zapata, Celia. *Isabel Allende: Life and Spirits.* Houston, TX: Arte Público, 2002.
Cruz-Lugo, Victor. "The Love That Binds," *Hispanic* 21:4 (April 2008): 54–56.
DeSalvo, Louise A. *Writing as a Way of Healing: How Telling Our Stories Transforms Our Lives.* Boston: Beacon Press, 2000.
Dinnison, Kris. "Review: *Portrait in Sepia,*" (Spokane) *Pacific Northwest Inlander* (21 February 2002).
Edemariam, Aida. "The Undefeated," (Manchester) *Guardian* (27 April 2007).
Elsworth, Catherine. "Isabel Allende: Kith and Tell," (London) *Telegraph* (21 March 2008).
Falconer, Helen. "Colouring the Family Album," (Manchester) *Guardian* (17 November 2001).
Flores, Camille. "The Power to Transform," (Santa Fe) *New Mexican* (12 April 2002).
_____. "Review: *The Sum of Our Days,*" (Santa Fe) *New Mexican* (8 August 2008): PA-20.
Gambotto-Burke, Antonella. "Putting the Romantic before the Authentic," *The Australian* (23 December 2006).
Gough, Elizabeth. "Vision and Division: Voyeurism in the Works of Isabel Allende," *Journal of Modern Literature* 27:4 (Summer 2004): 93–120.
Gray, Herman, and Macarena Gómez-Barris. *Toward a Sociology of the Trace.* Minneapolis: University of Minnesota Press, 2010.
Gregory, Stephen. "Scheherazade and Eva Luna: Problems in Isabel Allende's Storytelling," *Bulletin of Spanish Studies* 80:1 (January 2003): 81–101.
Gumbrecht, Jamie. "Isabel Allende to Discuss New Novel, 'Island Beneath the Sea,'" *Atlanta Journal-Constitution* (4 May 2010).
Hague, Angela. *Fiction, Intuition, & Creativity: Studies in Brontë, Woolf, and Lessing.* Washington, DC: Catholic University of America Press, 2003.
Hawley, Janet. "A Woman of Spirit," *The* (Melbourne) *Age* (15 March 2008).
Keenan, John. "Novelist Allende Playful with Book for Young Adults," *Omaha World-Herald* (24 November 2002): 8.
Kristal, Efraín, ed. *The Cambridge Companion to the Latin American Novel.* New York: Cambridge University Press, 2005.
Lamolinara, Guy. "San Antonio ALA," *ALA Bulletin* (19 February 1996).
Levine, Linda Gould. *Isabel Allende.* New York: Twayne, 2002.
Lindsay, Claire. *Locating Latin American Women Writers: Cristina Peri Rossi, Rosario Ferré, Albalucía Angel, and Isabel Allende.* New York: Peter Lang, 2003.
Locke, Michelle. "Author Isabel Allende Chronicles Her Own Real-Life Drama in New Book," *Canadian Press* (28 March 2008).
Mabe, Chauncey. "A Few Words with FIU Honoree Isabel Allende," (South Florida) *SunSentinel* (29 February 2012).
MacCann, Donnarae. "White Supremacy in Isabel Allende's Forest of the Pygmies," *Journal of African Children's and Youth Literature* 17–18 (2007): 60–75.
Martin, Karen Wooley. *Isabel Allende's House of the Spirits Trilogy: Narrative Geographies.* Rochester, NY: Tamesis, 2010.
May, Meredith. "Allende Takes on Slavery," *San Francisco Chronicle* (28 April 2010).
McGee, Celia. "'Ines' Captures Chile's Soul in 1500s," *USA Today* (9 November 2006).
McKale, Margaret A. Morales. *Literary Nonfiction in Works by Isabel Allende and Guadalupe Loaeza.* Columbus: Ohio State University, 2002.
McNally, Frank. "An Irishman's Diary," *Irish Times* (8 January 2010).
McNeese, Tim. *Isabel Allende.* New York: Chelsea House, 2006.
Miller, Lia. "Walden Acquires Film Rights to a Trilogy by Isabel Allende," *The New York Times* (16 January 2006).
Miller, Pamela. "Isabel Allende's New Novel Is Set in the 1500s, But the Parallels to Contemporary Issues Are Unmistakable," (Minneapolis) *Star Tribune* (31 October 2006).
Moran, Maria-Belen. "Isabel Allende," *AP Online* (27 September 2000).
Neary, Lynn. "In Memoir, Allende Reveals Life to Late Daughter," *Weekend Edition (NPR)* (13 April 2008).
Norris, Michele. "Allende Reimagines Life of Conquistador 'Ines,'" *All Things Considered* (NPR) (6 November 2006).

Preston, Rohan. "Tapping a Vein of Grace and Pain," (Minneapolis) *Star Tribune* (21 October 2010).
Ratcliffe, Sophie. "Branching Off," (London) *Times* (1 December 2001).
Ratner-Arias, Sigal. "Isabel Allende Sets New Book in Haiti with Theme of Slavery and Regrets Timing," *Canadian Press* (18 May 2010).
"Review: *Portrait in Sepia," Hispanic Outlook in Higher Education* (14 February 2005).
Richards, Jonathan. "Summing Our Mysterious Days," (Santa Fe) *New Mexican* (19 September 2008): PA-22.
Rodden, John. "Isabel Allende, Fortune's Daughter," *Critical Insights* (October 2010): 184–194.
_____. "Technicolored Life," *Society* 42:3 (March/April 2005): 62–65.
Rubenstein, Roberta. *Home Matters: Longing and Belonging, Nostalgia and Mourning in Women's Fiction.* New York: Palgrave, 2001.
Savio, Anita. "A Teller of Tales: Isabel Allende," *Latino Leaders* (1 October 2002).
Schaub, Michael. "Dreams of Freedom in Allende's 'Island,'" www.npr.org/templates/story/story.php?storyId=126892427, accessed on April 4, 2010.
Schroeder, Shannin. *Rediscovering Magical Realism in the Americas.* Westport, CT: Praeger, 2004.
Shaw, Donald Leslie. *A Companion to Modern Spanish-American Fiction.* Rochester, NY: Tamesis, 2002.
Stableford, Brian. *The A to Z of Fantasy Literature.* Lanham, MD: Scarecrow, 2005.
Svich, Caridad. "The House of the Spirits, a New Play," *TheatreForum* 36 (Winter/ Spring 2010): 76–104.
Taylor, Tracey. "Nurturing Her Family and Her Tribe," *The New York Times* (11 April 2010: 25A.
Timpane, John. "Isabel Allende's Heroines Are, Like Their Feminist Creator, Strong and Independent," *Philadelphia Inquirer* (5 May 2010).
Vine, Sarah. "Humanity Laid Bare," (London) *Times* (12 April 2008): 10.
Wilkinson, Marta L. *Antigone's Daughters: Gender, Family, and Expression in the Modern Novel.* New York: Peter Lang, 2008.
Williams, Raymond L. *A Companion to Gabriel García Márquez.* Rochester, NY: Tamesis, 2010.

Allende Genealogy

```
Luis Barros Mendez=Teresa Moreira Urrejola     Ester Cuevas Ovalle=Agustin Santiago Llona Alvizú
Minister of Justice   |                        pianist              | suicide by shotgun
1861-1906             |                                             |
                      |                                             |
________________________                  _______________________________________________
|       |       |     |                         |                   |          |        |
Teresa  ten     Rosa  Isabel Barros Moreira=Agustín José=second   Tío Nicolas  Tío Pablo  Tío Jorge=wife
winged  more          "Memé," clairvoyant |Llona Cuevas  wife     flier        book thief
d.1951                d. of leukemia 1951 | "Tata"                             d. 1962
                                          | 1882-1981
Tomás Allende Castro=Laura Pesse Guerra   |                       ______________________
                      |                   |                       |                 |
_____cousins______________                |                       father            bishop
|                         |               |                       |
Salvador="Tencha"     Tomás Allende Pesse=Francisca Llona Barros=Tió Ramón Dominguez Huidobro=María
Allende     |         ambassador          | b. 12/18/1920         ambassador            |
1908-1973 |           left 1945           | m. 1941               ca. 1916-1987     four children
            |         d. 1970             | bank clerk            m. 1953
_________________                         |
|              |                          |
Carmen Paz     two other daughters        |
                                          |
```

```
Granny=German                 _____________________________________________________
Paulita |                     |                                 |                  |
1978    |                     |       knife sharpener           |                  |
__________                    |       convict in Australia      |                  |
|        |                    |               |                 |                  |
|        |                    |       William Lindsay Gordon    |                  |
|        |                    |       d. 1943 of cirrhosis      |        Hilda     |
|        |                    |               |                 |          |       |
sister   Miguel Frías=Isabel Allende Llona=William C. Gordon  Francisco "Pancho"=Hildita   Juan A.
Uruguay  m. 9/8/1962   | 8/2/1942    b. 1937     |  b. 1944          |=Blanca     professor
         div. 1987     |             m. 7/7/1988 |                   |            b. 1945
______________________________                   |  ______________________
|   grandfather                  |               |  |               |     |
|   executed in Spain            |               |  Francisco Javier   Adriana  Jimena
|        |                       |               |
|   father          Lucille=Tom  |               ______________________________
|        |             |         |               |       |        |           |
Paula=Ernesto Díaz=Giulia   Lori=Nicolás=Celia=/=Sally=/=Jason   Jennifer   Lindsay   Harleigh
10/22/1963-    |     Barra b. 1966 |        stepson   heroin addict   ex-con   former
12/6/1992      |     m. 1999       |        writer    vanished                 addict
m. 1991        |     ______________________              | Fu=/=Grace
_______twins______   |       |        |                  | foster mothers
|                |   Alejandro   Nicole   Andrea         |    |
Cristina      Eiisa  b. 5/1990            b. 9/1993      Sabrina Gordon
b. 6/2004                                 suffers from   b. 5/25/1993
                                          porphyria      HIV positive
```

Isabel Allende: A Literary Companion

achievement

Achievement takes unpredictable forms in Allende's writings as diverse as the bride Dulce Rosa Orellano's suicide that accomplishes retribution in "Revenge," the flight from a bad marriage in "The Guggenheim Lovers," and the conquering of personal nightmares by the photojournalist in "And of Clay Are We Created." From the beginning of her career, for *The House of the Spirits* trilogy, the author foresaw the humbling of grand plans by orchestrating diabolical situations that placed a nation in peril. To survive under insurgency, bondage, and war required perseverance and cunning, two qualities that sustained Chileans during atrocities perpetrated by Augusto Pinochet's sixteen-year regime from 1974 to 1990. To Allende's credit as a global writing success, she chose the romance of storytelling about peasant uprisings as a fictional relief of the paralysis thrust upon her in young womanhood by class distinction and socioeconomic upheaval. The selection of narration—"stories of poverty and accumulated injustice, of every form of violence, of children dead before term and lovers who had run away"—countered both exile and the fragmentation of family and country (Allende, 1991, 151).

In the maturation of fictional achiever Pedro Tercero García, a folk singer in *The House of the Spirits*, Allende reveals the evolution of the Chilean revolt from idealistic beginnings to a pragmatic victory. Unlike his old-fashioned grandfather, healer and storyteller Pedro García, and hot-tempered father, farm manager Pedro Segundo, the third in the male lineage possesses the clarity of vision to best Senator Esteban Trueba and his entrenched autocracy. Pedro Tercero internalizes his grandfather's beast fable of the fox and hens, a prophetic parable that calls for solidarity within the working class to defeat a common enemy. By yoking variant levels of laborers into a strong comradeship, followers enthralled by Pedro Tercero's songs on the radio arouse a "giddy popularity" that subverts a tyrant and overthrows a dictatorship (Allende, 1985, 260).

As literary historian Amanda Hopkinson notes in the author's own experience, the "way of assimilating and conquering her many experiences is to write stories about them" (Hopkinson, 2003). In Allende's second novel, *Of Love and Shadows*, testimony empowers the fictional journalist Irene Beltrán to control the trajectory of her career by overcoming public apathy and ignorance. With her colleague, photojournalist Francisco Leal, she investigates a national atrocity, the murder and mass burial of fifteen citizens by the Political Police. The crafting of narrative from life serves Allende as a vindication of the *desaparecidos* and later during the loss and mourning of daughter Paula, a personal blow that forced the author to take up pen and paper to assuage sorrow and re-situate her career. Faith in successful writing made Allende the first Latin American woman writer to merit global success and keeps her at the top of the list of writers with a worldwide following.

Achievement Through Self-Expression

In a description of her style and thrust, Isabel Allende stated a feminist creed: "My writing is always about freedom, about owning your own life. What always draws me is the story of the survivor," such as the street waif Eva Luna, Eva's prostitute friend La Señora, and the transdressing singer Mimí in the confessional saga *Eva Luna* (Timpane, 2010). The title character in Allende's third novel, Eva yearns for belonging, which she achieves in Agua Santa when she redefines the extended household: "My *patrones* were my family" (Allende, 1987, 157). Striving to put composition to good use, Eva manages to write a *telenovela* that morphs into a reprise of a prison break that she helps to engineer. Critic Karen Castellucci Cox notes that "Eva Luna understands her limited position and depends only on herself and her writing abilities to gain financial and emotional independence" (Cox, 2003, 91). At the crux of Eva's literary success, she realizes that reality, when transposed on the screen by costumed actors, bears little resemblance to the immediacy and terror of the original actions. The source of the story's appeal lies in her rephrasing of history with touches of imagination, a skill she shares with Allende.

In *My Invented Country*, Allende develops the notion of reclamation through creativity, a method adaptable to the repressed and the inarticulate. She lionizes women for their commitment to husbands and domesticity. The text explains wifely liberation in terms of resolve: "Free and well organized, they keep their maiden names when they marry, they compete head to head in the workforce and not only manage their families but frequently support them" (Allende, 2003, 29). As an adjunct to heading a household, she demonstrates the worth of art to Blanca, the sculptor of folk crêches in *The House of the Spirits*, photography to the abandoned wife Aurora del Valle in *Portrait in Sepia*, and jewelry to the merchant designer Carmen Morales in *The Infinite Plan*. Like the wood carver trapped in an industrial ghetto in Harriette Arnow's *The Dollmaker*, Allende's women refuse to be defeated by the repetition and ennui of household tasks.

The spirit of attainment in *Daughter of Fortune*, a sequel to *The House of the Spirits*, invigorates the least likely heroine, Eliza Sommers, a sixteen-year-old pregnant runaway who appears at a dead end of her dreams to marry Joaquín Andieta. To fund a scouring of mining camps for her wayward lover, she relies on piano playing, cooking tarts and empanadas, and reading and writing letters for the illiterate while alternately posing as Chilean, Mexican, or Chinese male or female, depending on the situation. Her companion, herbalist Tao Chi'en, admires Eliza for surviving a stillbirth during a trans–Pacific voyage and resettling in a brash California setting during the 1849 gold rush. Archly, he observes, "It was not for nothing that the most celebrated heroines of Chinese literature always died at the precise moment of their greatest charm," a salient comment on the grandeur of martyrdom in the formulation of such legends as Joan of Ark and numerous Christian saints (Allende, 1999, 171).

Unlike stereotypical achievers, both Tao and Eliza outlive challenges and deterrents to their pilgrimage and enjoy a mutually satisfying family life, which the author extends in the third volume, *Portrait in Sepia*. The successes of Tao, Eliza, their daughter Lin/Lynn, and Lynn's daughter Aurora derive from innate competencies—Tao with healing, Eliza with operating a pastry shop and tea room, Lynn with modeling for a sculptor, and Aurora with taking unposed photos of simple, but fulfilling human activities. For Aurora, glimpses of domestic truths in candid photos strengthen her to abandon a sham marriage and to set the parameters of a gratifying live relationship. To her credit, she chooses free love with physician Iván Radovic over marriage as an expression of self "to define my identity, to create my own legend," a personal story written in word and picture (Allende, 1999, 304).

VICTORY AS ACHIEVEMENT

Triumph over violence and war is a benchmark of characters in Allende's historical fiction in *House of the Spirits* trilogy as well as *Inés of My Soul* and *Island Beneath the Sea*, significant contributions to historical fiction of the Western Hemisphere. For Inés Suarez, the *conquistadora* of Chile, the author depicts historic skirmishes won at great personal cost and regret in the passing of two mates. Analyst Hendrik Marthinus Viljoen focuses on Allende's recreation of "history in which women have played a crucial though underestimated role" (Viljoen, 2004, 71). Through imagination and the composition of a new narrative built on fragments of identity and action, Allende valorizes lovers Inés Suarez and Pedro de Valdivia, who intend not only to survive but prevail on their march south to Chile. After Pedro's ignoble death at the hands of Indians, the protagonist reflects on the prophecy of a long life for her and savors the social position as "widow of the Most Excellent Gobernador don Rodrigo de Quiroga, conquistador and founder of the kingdom of Chile," which he wrested from the Mapuche (Allende, 2006, 3). Of the price of Spanish triumph over Indians, Inés admits, "This conquest cost enormous suffering," a residue of guilt that clings to her final memories as the invader's price of claiming a country from its aborigines (*ibid.*, 313). In the review "A Conquistadora Comes to Life," Ashley Simpson Shires exulted, "It's a joy to see Inés triumph," a tribute to Allende's creation of a sympathetic character crafted from historical strands (Shires, 2006).

Similar in hearthside values to those of Clara del Valle, the success of nation builder Inés Suarez and her community demonstrates the implementation of family in constructing a complex aim. The communal effort advances from individual exploits to the glory of Santiago, a city built on martyrdom and sacrifice in what critic Jonathan Yardley terms "one of the bloodiest periods in human history" (Yardley, 2006). The arrival of two relief ships from Peru before Christmas 1543 enables Spanish villagers and new arrivals to employ technical marvels in the layout and erection of a permanent colony. With the addition of herding, quarrying, milling, lumbering, tanning, pottery, furniture making, and chandlery, the Spaniards raise their level of subsistence at least to the sophistication of the late medieval era. The addition of a physician, veterinarian, scribes, and tailors provides professional knowledge to a raw village in need of sophisticated know-how. Allende's ordering of a Renaissance hierarchy of workmanship and professionalism epitomizes the period concept of the good life displayed by the city-states of Genoa, Lübeck, and Venice and the trading centers in Beijing, Istanbul, Kyoto, London, and Paris, the municipalities that dominated commerce long before competition from New York and San Francisco.

At the core of *Island Beneath the Sea*, Allende dramatizes the opposite of Inés in the underdog's triumph from the perspective of Tété, an enslaved concubine. The author soaks a revealing scene in the running, wading, and climbing of Gambo, the sixteen-year-old West African abductee who vows to end his year of kitchen vassalage to Haitian sugar planter Toulouse Valmorain. Like the doughty African father before him, Gambo sees himself seated at his father's side at mealtime to "hear familiar tongues and known stories," the impetus to excellence (Allende, 2010). Gambo reminds himself that duty to Guinea's male code of honor requires him to continue running, however painful or terrifying. A touch of magical realism summons the father's spirit to rout a hovering vulture, a reminder of mortality to a boy who has only limbs and muscles to carry him away from Antillean bondage.

Island Beneath the Sea evokes epic struggle, recalling the vanquishing of natural obstacles by Greek strongman Hercules, Sumerian wanderer Gilgamesh, Hebrew savior Moses, Danish defender Beowulf, and the early nineteenth-century African hero Shaka Zulu. At the nadir of the lad Gambo's strength, he sinks toward death, then awakens at a Maroon outpost, the endpoint of his flight to freedom. The author crowns his feat with a gulp of water, a guerrilla campfire, and a dish of fufu, an African staple that his mother once made from pounded starchy tubers. Both water and fufu represent women's gifts to Gambo, the leader who grows into La Liberté, the lieutenant of Toussaint L'Ouverture, Haiti's savior. Self-naming symbolizes Gambo's self-actualization, the drive to apply the philosophies of the French Revolution of 1789 to despairing field hands in Haiti.

Triumph Over Self

The author's regard for Haiti's freedom fighters—Gambo, the martyred Macandal, Boukman, Toussaint L'Ouverture, and General François Dessalines—echoes in her admiration for more mundane scrappers. She lionizes the partnership of two rivals, wife Antonia Sierra and mistress Concha Díaz, in "The Gold of Tómas Vargas" and pals Gregory Reeves and Carmen Morales in *The Infinite Plan*. In the second instance, the author depicts the blossoming of Greg's innate faculties through contrasting experiences that include defeating addiction during the Vietnam War. A sound student and bilingual orator, Greg applies his gifts to law school and a legal career dedicated to assisting urban Chicanos. Allende comments, "No one could censure his ambition, because an impending era of unbridled greed was already gestating," her description of the Reagan years (Allende, 1993, 379). Greg escapes the greed-centered law firm climate and opens a string of offices that rate achievement on aiding rather than fleecing clients. The author's respect for Greg parallels her bent for lauding the unusual self-starter, from bandit Joaquín Murieta, a former hourly laborer, and herbalist Tao Chi'en, an unwanted son, in *Daughter of Fortune*, to Zorro, the self-appointed rescuer of the afflicted.

From an expansive perspective of women's roles, Allende's canon envisions the efforts of the female doer, developing the successful gender adaptation of Mimí in *Eva Luna*, the native acumen of Nadia Santos and Iyomi in *City of the Beasts*, and the charitable thrust of her own daughter, educator Paula Frías, protagonist of *Paula*. In *The Infinite Plan*, the author juxtaposes Greg's mounting notoriety at law with the parallel achievements of Carmen Morales, his blood sister and boon companion. Lacking success at formal education, she excels at learning from a string of faulty love relationships and from literally turning scraps into art, an aptitude traditionally allotted to female quilters and crafters that Allende champions in the foreword to *Tapestries of Hope*. Under the career name of Tamar, Carmen uses her experiences with Gypsies and Asians as sources of ethnic costume, a peak seller among hippies and young urbanites. From shards of wood, bone, shell, and stone, she shapes jewelry suited to the multicultural movement and arrives at the crest of a global demand for individualized apparel. Thus, both luck and pluck contribute to her fame. Nonetheless, she never overvalues monetary returns above personal satisfaction. Her weighting of emotional satisfaction amid fiscal attainments illustrates a major feat that Greg fails to accomplish.

As models of maturation and responsibility, Allende's trio of YA quest novels depicts achievement in Alex Cold, the protagonist of the *City of the Beasts* trilogy. He pairs with Nadia Santos, three years his junior, to aid animals and people in distress. In unfamiliar climes amid variant dialects, the duo manages to preserve the closed society of the People of the Mist by halting a genocidal plot to kill indigenous Brazilians with a smallpox epidemic. A similar respect for natives and cultures in *Kingdom of the Golden Dragon* furthers the cooperation of Yetis, soldiers, and three teenagers of different nationalities to foil a plot to steal a precious statue and kidnap King Dorji.

In the second novel's resolution, the king's death from a bullet to the lungs and the destruction of the statue in a helicopter crash introduce the individual achievement of Prince Dil Bahadur, whom conflict energizes from a nine-year period of instruction to action as the succeeding monarch. By the opening of the third novel, *Forest of the Pygmies*, King Dil and Queen Pema have reshaped national symbolism with a replacement statue and secured the dynasty with the birth of their first son. Allende rounds out the trio of adventures with the restoration of the Pygmies of Ngoubé to sovereignty. Rather than applaud the daring of Alex and Nadia, the author focuses on the courage of native Africans to rid themselves of fear of a tyrant and return their relationship with the Bantus to its former symbiotic arrangement.

• *References and Further Reading*

Cox, Karen Castellucci. *Isabel Allende, a Critical Companion*. Westport, CT: Greenwood, 2003.

Hopkinson, Amanda. "Isabel Allende" in *Contemporary Literary Criticism*. Farmington Hills, MI: Gale Cengage, 2003.

Shires, Ashley Simpson. "A Conquistadora Comes to Life," *Rocky Mountain News*(10 November 2006).

Timpane, John. "Isabel Allende's Heroines Are, Like Their Feminist Creator, Strong and Independent," *Philadelphia Inquirer* (5 May 2010).

Viljoen, Hendrik Marthinus. *Storyscapes: South African Perspectives on Literature, Space, and Identity*. New York: Lang, 2004.

Yardley, Jonathan. "Review: *Inés of My Soul*," *Washington Post* (12 November 2006).

adaptation

Much of the dramatic intensity of Allende's fiction derives from the acclimation of characters to fearful threats or deprivations, for example, the adaptation of Marcia Lieberman to kidnap and immurement in the jungle in "Phantom Palace," Tao Chi'en's acceptance of Western cultural codes in *Daughter of Fortune* and *Portrait in Sepia*, and Clara del Valle's life with a fractious bully and her granddaughter Alba's mental retreat from torture and solitary confinement in a prison "doghouse" in *The House of the Spirits*. The onslaught of national chaos forces characters to turn talents and material assets into strengths, as with the composition of narratives that brings success to the title figure in *Eva Luna* and the partnership of a wife and concubine in destabilizing a tyrant in "The Gold of Tomás Vargas."

In Allende's initial novel, Jaime and Nicolás, Alba's twin uncles, weather an era of violence, curfews, and food rationing — Jaime by offering his medical skills to aid the poor and Nicolás by retreating into imagination to seek universal truth in outlandish religions, rituals, and stunts. At an upturn in the lengthy saga, Senator Esteban Trueba, previously the villain, sheds greed and arrogance to shelter his daughter Blanca and her outlaw lover, Pedro Tercero. Complicity with Tránsito Soto, a prostitute known to liberal guerrilla forces, enables Trueba to bargain for Alba's life and to live out old age in a modicum of contentment. The episodic examples of adjustment confer longevity on the del Valle-Trueba clan, allowing Alba an opportunity to write a hopeful family history free of hatred, "terrors of my own," and vengeance (Allende, 1985, 491).

From a negative perspective, the adaptation of Beatriz Alcántara to a right-wing junta in *Of Love and Shadows* requires daily self-deception. By turning the ground floor of her mansion into The Will of God rest home for the elderly, she maintains the aura of wealth and privilege on the second floor. Surrounded by material comforts and artistic bibelots, Beatriz assesses changes in the authoritarian government as necessary adjustments to ensure "democracy." Acclimation to age and weathered skin demands anti-wrinkle creams and lotions plus seasonal trysts with young men who assure her that she is still desirable. The jolt that follows the lethal assault on her daughter, journalist Irene Beltrán, fails to purge Beatriz's make-believe utopia or to impart the horrors that Irene and her photographer uncover among the peasantry. Clinging to the myth of patriarchal patriotism, Beatriz commiserates with a mass killer, Lieutenant Juan de Dios Ramírez, and murmurs, "No one stops to remember that he helped liberate us from Communism," a ridiculous claim that inflates previous dangers to elevate a phony military icon (Allende, 1987, 247).

Allende's works picture physical as well as social adaptations. The adjustment of Guinean domestics and field hands and Spanish brides to fierce heat and mosquitoes of the "sordid parallel universe" discloses the "malicious menace" of tropical Haiti that critic Olga Ries defines in *Island Beneath the Sea* (Ries, 2011, 4). In the novel's second half, Allende presents modification of a different type, the making of homes for French refugees in the disapproving Creole society of New Orleans. After escaping the rejection of the Spanish in Havana, Tété, the heroine, allies with fellow immigrant Violette Boisier at Rampart Street, a haven to "many free women of color" bearing a name suggesting reinforcement for battle (Allende, 2010, 313). Similar in strength to the pact of marginalized women in Dolen Perkins-Valdez's *Wench*, daily collaboration with seamstress Adèle and the slave Loula gradually rids the newcomers of their Haitian idiosyncrasies and refugee insecurities. Simultaneously, says critic Ries, ecstatic rhythms at place Congo revitalize spirituality with "dancing scenes, medicinal and religious rituals occupying a central place in the narrative and in the characters' psyche as elements of strength" (Ries, 2011, 4).

Allende's feminism favors women of color for their versatile solutions to problems. The female enclave, a given in feminist literature, encourages pragmatic settling in through shared proficiencies—makeup, nursing, herbal treatments, Creole cookery, couturier, corsetry, perfume—and the plotting of the first Bal de Cordon Bleu. A credit to biracial female intrigue, the presentation of attractive quadroon girls to likely white bachelors encourages more stable love relationships than more casual alliances. To make a success of the first invitation-only cotillion, the mulattas display fashion sense and social savoir faire gained from observations of pretentious white Creoles. As a result, the philosophy of "give them what they most want" serves the refugees and initiates Rosette and the rest of the upcoming generation of biracial females into more promising connubial circumstances.

The Determined Survivor

On a par with Tété's Rosette, a resilient character in *Daughter of Fortune*, the foundling Eliza Sommers, escapes the invisibility of the illegitimate waif in Chile and wrests a vigorous, interethnic future from California's mining camps and Tao Chi'en's medical practice. Editor Michael D. Sollars describes the feat of adaptation as a struggle with "emotional attachments and social restrictions in a journey of self-discovery and self-realization" (Sollars, 2008, 199). During San Francisco's early years, Eliza's nonconformist activities belie Miss Rose's vision of British ladyhood and the appropriate attire and behavior of genteel Anglo-Chilean women in Valparaíso. To facilitate a search for Joaquín Andieta, Eliza's lost love, she mimics the demeanor and gestures of a young male. Residual training from girlhood betrays her as a sissy and potential homosexual, a diagnosis of Babalú the Bad, who attempts to erase any femininity in "Chile Boy." Allende extends the invisibility of a girl in men's clothing by depicting males as uninterested in examining Chile Boy more closely or discovering why he seems clumsy at typically male behaviors.

In the sequel, *Portrait in Sepia*, Eliza excels at three languages—the Spanish of her Chilean childhood, the Chinese of husband Tao Chi'en, and the English of the American frontier. To refresh her first language, she visits Spanish-speaking groups in San Francisco and retrains her ear to a dialect no longer prominent in her life as a pastry chef. Similarly adept at fitting in, her granddaughter, Aurora del Valle, a perceptive photographer, slips behind the camera to ease herself into family scenarios among her in-laws. Not only adapting, but analyzing the subtleties of relationships, Aurora recognizes that her husband, Diego Domínguez, has gulled her into counterfeit wedlock. The exposure of his matrimonial hoax requires courage and truth to self for Aurora, who abandons her in-laws' home in the country and returns to the city to thrive on taking honest cameos of people and enjoying a sincere relationship with Iván Radovic, the man she loves. A gesture at realistic romance, Allende's pairing of Aurora with her lover reveals the author's faith in instinct as a guide to intimate pleasures and personal contentment.

For the three works in the *City of the Beasts* trilogy, Allende depicts the acclimation of Alexander Cold to climates and atmospheres much different from his native California. While navigating the Upper Orinoco river on the Brazil-Venezuela border, he overcomes pickiness about food and expands on traits of the Jaguar, his totemic identity. Adaptation requires willingness to suffer fear of enclosed spaces and of the unknown, two terrors that threaten his mission to find curative water to heal his mother's cancer. Learning to overcome self-imposed limitations, Alex discovers that his capabilities lie under the surface awaiting his summons, a mature perception common to coming-of-age scenarios. Allende creates subtle humor in Alex's need to appear strong and unwavering in the midst of challenges that hold no terrors for Nadia Santos, a girl three years his junior.

Alex's adaptability serves him in the sequel, *Kingdom of the Golden Dragon*, in which he applies skill at rappelling to a dangerous rescue mission in the Himalayas of the Forbidden Kingdom. His ability to survive without complaint on yak butter tea and Tibetan mountain rations displays an older, more self-confident sixteen-year-old on his way to manhood. Potentially lethal challenges amplify Alex's need to reach inside for poise and willingness to endanger himself to help others. In the role of mentor, Alex introduces Prince Dil Bahadur to modern technology, a mini-cam and GPS that lead the way over treacherous passages. In the third novel, *Forest of the Pygmies*, Alex acclimates to riding a testy bull elephant and to organizing a revolution of Aka and Bantus against a tyrant. By age twenty, Alex applies his self-assurance to a career in medicine, a profession he intends to practice "in the poorest corners of the earth" (Allende 2005, 292). The choice implies that Alex's adaptability in teen adventures prepares him for tests of courage and devotion to duty in situations where rappelling and riding an elephant play no part.

Reprogramming Self

In the more realistic *The Infinite Plan*, protagonist Gregory Reeves, like the adult Alex Cold, chooses a future based on a reasonable evaluation of personal strengths and needs. Greg exits a nomadic existence with his father, the peripatetic philosopher Charles Reeves, to settle in a Los Angeles barrio among Latinos. Central to adaptation, a knowledge of Spanish language and culture enables the boy to elude gang-style torment and to nest in a gendered Mexican home governed by obdurate patriarchy and maternal acceptance and affection. By accepting the gendered principles of the Morales family, Gregory spans the gap between his failing caucasian parents and the loving haven maintained by Inmaculada and Pedro Morales for their rambunctious brood and their newly received "blond son" (Allende, 1993, 71). Allende indicates that Greg's extensive changes in himself and his behavior as an interracial trailblazer derive from a deep-seated longing for stability and affection, which win out over racial and ethnic identity.

Into manhood, Gregory's challenges continue to range toward fight-or-flight situations, a fictional version of Allende's experience with self-exile and retrenchment in Venezuela after her blacklisting by the Pinochet regime in Chile. In Vietnam, acclimating to combat with a wily Asian foe forces Gregory to shed his cinema-bred misperception of heroism and to rely on a brotherhood of fellow infantrymen locked into a no-win war where he "felt the darkness closing in" (Allende, 1993, 197). Reliance on marijuana and drugs presses Gregory to his psychic limit; reclamation of his sanity demands rehabilitation and a revamping of values and aims. Because he over-corrects and swerves toward greed and sexual sybaritism, he thrusts himself into a more treacherous jungle of 15-hour workdays and drinking bouts in San Francisco that debilitate rather than relax. A second major adaptation requires the protagonist to examine himself in middle age and "gradually [impose] some order" (*ibid.*, 380). To actualize his role as parent, he redirects his energies and experience toward more realistic attainments that allow him to harmonize client obligations with time left over to reclaim and socialize his children, Margaret and David.

Allende impresses on both the reader and protagonist the roots of wisdom that grow from faulty choices and errors in judgment. As Gregory draws on the combined female strengths of Dr. Ming O'Brien and old friend Carmen Morales, he shapes a workable late-in-life philosophy: adaptation emerges from a day-by-day plan of action, a recognition that postponing financial debt and paternal responsibilities results in an all-at-once crisis beyond one person's ability to cope. From his acceptance of mundane decisions and actions, Gregory creates for himself a realistic outlook that gradually restores organization and direction to his office and home life. By advancing the fictional Reeves family toward a potential personal and financial catastrophe, Allende builds a literary theme that outlines the steps toward resolving problems via incremental adaptation.

See also wisdom

- *References and Further Reading*

Ries, Olga. "Latino Identity in Allende's Novels," *Comparative Literature and Culture* 13:4 (2011): 1–8.
Seaman, Donna. "Review: *Island Beneath the Sea*," *Booklist* 106:13 (1 March 2010): 5.

Sollars, Michael D. *The Facts on File Companion to the World Novel, 1900 to the Present*. New York: Facts on File, 2008.

Allende, Isabel

Isabel Allende, whom newspaper reviewer Laura Wides-Munoz calls "the grande dame of Latina lit," clings easily to prominence outside the dictates of literary convention and academic strictures (Wides-Munoz, 2006). Allende chose the hybridity of new journalism by symbolically placing opposing forces in fiction, beginning with colonizer Esteban Trueba and his plantation peons in a matrilineal saga, *The House of the Spirits*, and expanding to a documentary romance, *Of Love and Shadows*, and a cohesive series of short fiction in *The Stories of Eva Luna*. The author immersed herself in testimonials to national subversion under the Pinochet regime and determined how and why "a country with such a large middle class and history of democracy could put up with a sixteen-year dictatorship" (McKale, 2002, 127). Her distaste for tyranny buoyed her story collection with further perusals of the Jiménez regime in Venezuela, which she recreated in the building of a grandiose summer residence in "Phantom Palace."

Allende's splash in world publishing launched the "post-boom" or "boom feminino," a Latina venture into the global literary spotlight. Literary historian Efraín Kristal defended her inclusion in listings of major works by validating her relationship to "el Boom" and her avoidance of elitism in favor of readability, optimism, and sociopolitical analysis (Kristal, 2005, 94). Unlike Gabriel García Márquez's choice of ambiguity and fantasy over realistic representation of Chilean history, Allende rearticulated magical realism through shamanism, telepathy, spiritualism, healing, and channeling of energy through her choice of a clairvoyant protagonist named Clara (clear). The narrative gradually homed in on transparent scenarios of the Pinochet coup and the institutional injustices and atrocities committed by unrestrained political police.

The author's fictional accounts of human rights violations as stark as the hoisting of cadavers on meat hooks and the entombment of victims in a mine shaft transcend limitations on emotion and subjective response. Critic Shannin Schroeder declares that Allende's modes of magical realism liberate a history of imperialism and dispel the fragmentation in Latin America's chronicles. For the sake of continuity, Allende produces a fictive borderland in scenes unavailable in textbooks and academic history by saying "what the press can't say" about individual families and their survival of arbitrary arrests and mass killings, as with the arbitrary arrest and torture of a fifteen-year-old oracle in *Of Love and Shadows* and the barbarous sweep of bandits through a hacienda in "Revenge" (Schroeder, 2004, 128). Allende's insider's knowledge placed in these humanistic scenarios the details that censorship distorted and that covert military trials concealed under lies and obfuscation.

For facts that extend outside her grasp during exile in Caracas, Venezuela, Allende relies on interviews and her mother's notebook of places, sense impressions, and moral judgments. Where Allende interprets events beyond her range of experience, she sometimes discovers that her fiction contains unforeseen truths because events "happened that way, and I didn't have any way of knowing that it was that way" (*ibid.*, 129). Thus, according to Schroeder, Allende's magical realism influences the North American novelists Toni Morrison and Maxine Hong Kingston and reconciles "the history of the Americas with the reality of the present" (*ibid.*). The academic obstruction to the postmodern magical realists lies in the xenophobia and ignorance of "Anglophonic Departments of Literature" that continue to anchor curricula to nineteenth-century European, North American, and Russian classics that rule out the Latino experience (*ibid.*).

Allende's success with the first four titles raised questions about her place in the Latin American canon. Analyst Ana Patricia Rodríguez noted, "Because of her mass-market cachet, some critics have harshly and hastily critiqued the literary merit of Allende's work," dismissing her as a spinner of romantic fluff (Farr and Harker, 2008, 195). The subsequent popularity and academic kudos for *Daughter of Fortune*, *Portrait in Sepia*, *Inés of My Soul*, *Island Beneath the Sea*, and *Zorro*, especially as choices for community reading projects, refute critical derogation of a writer who follows her own notions of narrative integrity. Most difficult of her beliefs for hard-edged critics, the place of human affection in a ranking of redeeming traits derives from the "vital brew of diversity," a survey of humankind from which Allende draws unlikely pairings and loyalties, as with the stable commitment of herbalist Tao Chi'en and Eliza Sommers in *Daughter of Fortune* and the father-daughter love between Riad Halabí and the title figure in *Eva Luna* (*ibid.*, 202).

Rather than comply with outworn archetypes and academic criteria, Allende obeys the inner voice that demands an honest, intuitive narration about diverse characters and situations drawn from her experiences and glimpses from the media, such as threats to Amazonian denizens from exploiters in *City of the Beasts* and the death of a girl in a mud avalanche in "And of Clay Are We Created." Rodríguez notes the use in *Daughter of Fortune* of eroticism and romantic sex "to represent larger issues of national history, politics, and social and racial engineering" (*ibid.*, 200). Intimacy between narrator and audience allows the author to fine tune the lives of marginal and secondary characters, notably, a wife and mistress in "The Gold of Tomás Vargas" and the guests in "The Little Heidelberg," and to convince readers that there are no throw-away people, from the dignified Indian beggars at Agua Santa in *Eva Luna* and the Bantu guards in *Kingdom of the Pygmies* to the moribund singsong girls dying in subterranean cells in *Daughter of Fortune*. David Walton, a book critic for the Minneapolis *StarTribune*, credits the author with popularizing "multigenerational, multiracial, multicultural, multinational perspectives," an inclusion that radiates a generous inclusivity (Walton, 2005). Stephen Hart praises her authorship for its "trend towards readability, structural clarity, sociopolitical commentary, and relative optimism," even to the down-and-out who populate such stories as "Walimai" and "The Road North" (Kristal, 2005, 94).

Nuala Finnegan, on staff at the National University of Ireland, described Allende's rebel nature in "effortlessly crossing boundaries between high and low culture, First and Third Worlds, and questioning the very concepts and limits of literature and fiction," accomplishments suited to the demands of the *City of the Beasts* trilogy (Ramblado-Minero, 2003, xiii). The analyst focused on Allende's blurring of the division between fiction and autobiography, a source of the novelist's elusive identity as woman, observer/interviewer, Latina, and refugee. Ironically, critics denigrate Allende's works for being bankable and "dismiss her as popular, too open, too facile, too feminist, or not feminist enough" (Timpane, 2010). The mishmash of charges suggests a complexity in her writing not easily categorized on a continuum from intellectualism to fluff. C.R. Perricone sheds light on Allende's appeal by noting that she "embodies, contradicts, or transcends the patriarchal system," thus producing "a greater understanding of a culture in transition" (Perricone, 2002, 84). Perricone's insight suggests that Allende is adept at perceiving and depicting increments of change as they impact individual lives, as with the rehabilitation of Greg

Reeves in *The Infinite Plan* and the maturation of protagonist Alex Cold over the sequential adventures of three YA quest novels.

Of the source of characters and quirky situations, Allende noted, "With a family like mine, you don't need to have an imagination" (Ojito, 2003). The author revels in the human condition and credits it with generating stories "like a candy store," a term suggesting her delight in creating the title figure in "Clarisa" and the shared sufferings of lovers in "Our Secret" (Miller, 2006). Reviewer Jane Dickson, who described Allende as "a writer with the wind at her back," admired her buoyance, a boundless faith in people that transcends extremes of anguish, disempowerment, and bereavement (Dickson, 2001, 13). Through identifiable sovereignties and social situations, Allende chooses to remain apolitical, yet fiercely involved in freeing nations from tyranny and immigrants from degradation. In tribute to their courage and hardihood, she ennobles the humiliation and brutality endured by Jaime and Alba in *The House of the Spirits* and female enslavement in brothels in "Walimai," *Daughter of Fortune*, and *Portrait in Sepia*. Her novels remain attuned to artistic independence rather than message, which she describes as a poor basis for fiction.

Accolades present the author a mixed bag of rewards. Of the resultant notoriety, she acknowledged, "Celebrity is intangible, fleeting, capricious, uncontrollable, and, to tell you the truth, not always desirable," an oblique reference to her loss of privacy (Richards, 2008, PA-22). Although she enjoys the perks of fame, the publicity infringes on her family compound and intimate retreats with family and friends. With a ready repartee, she added that she possesses only a small draw, much less significant than "the real celebrities like Madonna or any serial killer" (*ibid.*). The quip epitomizes her skill at self-deprecation, a satiric turn that endows her deft turns of phrase in oratory and printed word.

• *References and Further Reading*

Dickson, E. Jane. "Word of Mouth," (London) *Times* (3 February 2001): 13.

Farr, Cecilia Konchar, and Jaime Harker, eds. *The Oprah Effect: Critical Essays on Oprah's Book Club*. Albany: State University of New York Press, 2008.

Kristal, Efraín, ed. *The Cambridge Companion to the Latin American Novel*. New York: Cambridge University Press, 2005.

McKale, Margaret A. Morales. *Literary Nonfiction in Works by Isabel Allende and Guadalupe Loaeza*. Columbus: Ohio State University, 2002.

Miller, Pamela. "Isabel Allende's New Novel Is Set in the 1500s, but the Parallels to Contemporary Issues Are Unmistakable," (Minneapolis) *Star Tribune* (31 October 2006).

Ojito, Mirta. "A Writer's Heartbeats Answer Two Calls," *The New York Times* (28 July 2003).

Perricone, C.R. "Allende and Valenzuela: Dissecting the Patriarchy," *South Atlantic Review* 67:4 (Fall, 2002): 80–105.

Ramblado-Minero, María de la Cinta. *Isabel Allende's Writing of the Self: Trespassing the Boundaries of Fiction and Autobiography*. Lewiston, NY: E. Mellen Press, 2003.

Richards, Jonathan. "Summing Our Mysterious Days," (Santa Fe) *New Mexican* (19 September 2008): PA-22.

Schroeder, Shannin. *Rediscovering Magical Realism in the Americas*. Westport, CT: Praeger, 2004.

Timpane, John. "Isabel Allende's Heroines Are, Like Their Feminist Creator, Strong and Independent," *Philadelphia Inquirer* (5 May 2010).

Walton, David. "Review: *Portrait in Sepia*," (Minneapolis) *Star Tribune* (18 December 2005).

Wides-Munoz, Laura. "Concubines and Queens Inspire Scribes Isabel Allende, Gioconda Belli," *Canadian Press* (11 November 2006).

ambition

Allende's choice of fiction as a conduit for character ambition endows the reader with subliminal instruction, as with the hardships and losses that color the life of Inés Suarez, the mother of Chile in *Inés of My Soul*, and the selfless heroism of photographer Rolf Carlé in "And of Clay Are We Created" and of Haitian Maroons in *Island Beneath the Sea*. E.L. Doctorow explains that such vicarious readings create a bond between writer and audience: "A novel is a printed circuit through which flows the force of a reader's own life" (McKale, 2002, 93). By dramatizing the desire of Aurora del Valle to capture reality in photos in *Portrait in Sepia*, the curiosity of Irene Beltrán and Francisco Leal to publicize covert operations of the Political Police in *Of Love and Shadows*, and the need of Gregory Reeves to champion the Latino underdog in *The Infinite Plan*, Allende confers an indirect opportunity on the reader to profit from the drive and resolve of fictional characters. To contrast personal strivings with outcomes, she outlines Greg's upbringing by an egomaniac father, Charles Reeves, and the boy's selfish motive to become an authority figure in his own right, even at the expense of his family and soul. Greg's fantasy pictures lesser beings kowtowing to professional prominence and gaudy materialism because "no one could censure his ambition" (Allende, 1987, 279). Underneath the "bacchanal of conspicuous consumption," Greg conceals "exorbitant bank loans ... the bold juggling of credit cards," the true sources of his ready money and the venality of his spirit (*ibid.*, 320, 280).

In a characterization of males over time, Allende risked a stern generalization: "Greed has been the great motivation in history — greed and power and sex are the great driving forces of men" (Wides-Munoz, 2006). In *The Sum of Our Days*, she differentiates female motivations: "They throw themselves into adventure without measuring the risks or looking back, because to remain paralyzed in the place society holds for them is much worse" (Allende, 2003, 267). As proof, Allende notes in the foreword to *Tapestries of Hope* that women "record the truths of history — not the struggles for power or the vanity of emperors, but the pains and hopes of everyday life" (Allende, 2007, ix). Without these strands of truth, the people have no voice.

Ambition and Success

Allende employs the fatal three — greed, power, and sex — in the characterization of the fearsome miner and planter Esteban Trueba in *The House of the Spirits*. In a reflection over his goals, he chortles to prostitute Tránsito Soto, "I had stared at ambition so many times in the mirror when I was shaving in the mornings that I was able to recognize whenever I encountered it in others" (Allende, 1985, 137). Unlike the prostitute, who sees the wisdom in cooperatives, Esteban clings to tunnel vision of himself as senator and shaper of the nation's destiny. Allende mocks his efforts by envisioning Trueba's fiancée Rosa sitting home imagining him "piling up boulders in the hope that by subjecting them to God only knew what wicked incinerating processes, they would eventually spit out a gram of gold," a fantasy that links Trueba's dreams of wealth to medieval alchemy (*ibid.*, 12).

As a gender contrast, the author juxtaposes the gentle seer Clara del Valle as wife of Esteban. By being loyal to self, family, and other women, Clara finds contentment and fulfillment in a balance of family responsibilities with obligations to society and plantation and with fulfillment of self. To Clara, assistance to the underclass of Las Trés Marias requires constant attention and compassion to peons. The pattern holds in the career contentment of storyteller Belisa Crepusculario, aide to the vainglorious Colonel in "Two Words," and in *The Infinite Plan* in the depiction of Carmen Morales, who rears her adopted son Dai and supports the family with costume designs, which mesh into Carmen's compensation for childlessness and a satisfying life for new mother and son. In each case, investment in giving proves valuable to women like Clara, who invest themselves without counting the cost or predicting returns.

Characters from the colonial era display ruthless self-betterment at the cost of others' lives, the story of Général Pedro de Valdivia's establishment of Santiago in *Inés of My Soul*, El Benefactor's grandstanding in "Phantom Palace," and the slave manager Prosper Cambray's success at Habitation Saint-Lazare in *Island Beneath the Sea*. During Cambray's three years in Haiti's mounted militia, he parades the "balls and red blood" of a plantation manager and evolves a "brutal character and killer's physique," a physiognomy that serves him well as overseer for his master, Toulouse Valmorain (Allende, 2010, 46). Allende overturns Cambray's supervisory strutting by replacing him with Owen Murphy, a decent Irish family man who needs neither lash nor threats to operate a profitable sugar plantation. The contrast in superintendents reveals in Murphy a strain of self-respect that draws more cooperation from workers than the swaggering and lashings of Cambray, an archetype that influences the creation of Captain Ariosto and entrepreneur Mauro Carías in *City of the Beasts* and Commandant Maurice Mbembelé in *Forest of the Pygmies*.

In contrast to commercial mentorship for the sake of profit, the philosophical teachings and demonstrations of the guru Tensing to apprentice Dil Bahadur in *Kingdom of the Golden Dragon* nurture a specific ambition meant to secure the throne of the Forbidden Kingdom after the death of Dil's father, King Dorji, a "generous man with no personal ambition, dedicated wholly to the well-being of his kingdom" (Allende, 2005, 267). Prince Dil's suitability for the role takes dramatic proportions as he leads attackers to the palace, threads his way over obstacles to the oracular room, and learns his destiny following Dorji's death and the end of the apprenticeship with Tensing. Suddenly and violently thrust into manhood and kingship, Dil opts for the wise choices of a king in the making by marrying the brave Pema and siring a son, thus ensuring another link in the royal dynasty. More crucial to his rule, Dil overcomes the loss of traditions by replacing the former gold statue and instituting new customs to unify his people.

At a turning point in her career, Allende achieved international regard for *Daughter of Fortune*, a treatise on ambition and greed, which surveys the checkered history of the 1849 California gold rush. A window of opportunity on the American frontier, the discovery of gold introduces seekers to a disorderly milieu, where nonconformists and divergent thinkers fit goods and services to the needs of a motley populace. Allende pictures "Hundreds of men [passing] through, aflame with hope and ambition, headed for the placers" (Allende 1999, 243). For personal reasons, Eliza Sommers joins the rush and applies her gift for cooking and keyboard skills to a need for funds. Allende turns into humor the playing of rowdy songs for a brothel caravan and builds Eliza's character with occasions where frying empanadas wins the thanks and admiration of peers in Joe Bonecrusher's caravan. To her benefit, Eliza's aid to Tao Chi'en in rescuing singsong girls from peril results in a firm basis for life partnership, even though Eliza wonders how a Chilean woman and Chinese man can survive in a racist, anti-woman atmosphere.

For the sequel, *Portrait in Sepia*, the author depicts the sons of Paulina and mine owner Feliciano Rodríguez de Santa Cruz as disaffected family members who strive for self alone. Matías, the sybarite, pleasures himself by despoiling San Francisco's desirable exotic model, Lynn Sommers, the heretofore "inaccessible prey" (Allende, 2001, 57). His purpose, winning a bet with his pals that he can deflower the pristine virgin, results in the conception of daughter Aurora, whose paternity he denies. Self-satisfying to the point of casual cruelties toward others, Matías departs for Europe, leaving his kinsman Severo del

Valle to assume the role of Lynn's husband and Aurora's surviving parent. The author saves up poetic justice until Aurora's adulthood, when Matías lies crippled and dying from syphilis, a fitting nemesis for a womanizer.

In the denouement of *Inés of My Soul*, Allende applies historical foils to account for the failure of the Pizarro brothers and Diego de Almagro in subduing southern Chile, the region that accords glory to the ambitious Pedro de Valdivia. The author dismisses Pizarro as an overreaching "marqués gobernador of Peru [who] was crushed by his ambition and multiple betrayals" (Allende, 2006, 2). More driven than his predecessor, Valdivia accepts a clear destiny for himself and an expansionist era: "Spain was the past. Chile was the future" (*ibid.*, 91). Allende admits the sway of the zeitgeist—a time when "everything had a price, including honor" (*ibid.*, 103). The text pictures the conqueror "with the brio of a stallion," yet dramatizes the comeuppance of the faithless colonizer (*ibid.*, 12). Like King Midas in Herodotus's *Histories*, Valdivia suffers the poetic justice of the avaricious, a gulp of melted gold poured down his throat. Despite his ignoble end, his venture south of Peru to found a new colony contributes to Chile the vision of an ambitious nation builder.

See also achievement

• *References and Further Reading*

Cox, Karen Castellucci. *Isabel Allende, a Critical Companion*. Westport, CT: Greenwood, 2003.

McKale, Margaret A. Morales. *Literary Nonfiction in Works by Isabel Allende and Guadalupe Loaeza*. Columbus: Ohio State University, 2002.

Wides-Munoz, Laura. "Concubines and Queens Inspire Scribes Isabel Allende, Gioconda Belli," *Canadian Press* (11 November 2006).

Aphrodite

A bolder, more playful departure than previous works from her early period, Allende's *Aphrodite: A Memoir of the Senses* offers an encyclopedic mix of cookery, folklore, and erotic whimsy. On a par with the carnal celebration of *Inés of My Soul*, "Simple María," "The Little Heidelberg," and "Toad's Mouth," the text investigates creativity as an expression of a unique self, dramatized by Aunt Burgel's adaptation of Central European apple strudel with guava and mango, common local ingredients in the Caribbean. In reflections on the first century C.E., Allende dismisses asceticism as "the first teachings of the new fanatics" that, by the Middle Ages, transformed the body into an incarnation of Satan, the soul's adversary (Allende 1998, 79). With humor and gusto, the author claims that gluttony and lust are "the only cardinal sins worth paying a penance for" (Allende, 2003, 195). She backs up her belief with Eggplant to a Sheik's Taste, Harem Turkey, lovers' soup, Novices Nipples, and Odalisques' Salad, evocative dish names to implant naughty thoughts about otherwise ordinary combinations.

Realistically, like the cook Rosa in *Of Love and Shadows*, the wife and concubine in "The Gold of Tomás Vargas," and Nana in *Eva Luna*, Allende uses both sins—gluttony and lust—to escape the paralyzing crisis and sorrow over her daughter Paula's death. In the embrace of life, the author's health recovered from a numbing of the senses and a ritualized exorcism of grief. For precision, she outlines carnal pleasures that breach the division "between love and appetite" (Allende, 1998, 11). Analyst Lisa Bach notes that "women's connection to food is both personal and communal," one reason she finds commonalities between *Aphrodite* and the "food porn" in feminist films *Babette's Feast*, *Chocolat*, and

Like Water for Chocolate, with their delight in cooking, serving, arranging, and devouring meals as introits to bedding lovers (Bach, 2001, xv).

Allende accentuates methods of rejuvenating a damaged outlook. Her purpose, in the view of analyst Vincent Kling, involves "exciting and prolonging sexual desire" to yield a "higher plane of awareness, acceptance, and integration of self" (Kling, 2010, 250–251). The outcome celebrates the five senses through camaraderie, savor, and physical pleasure, the complete opposite of the months of sadness when "universal grayness had spread inexorably over every surface (Allende, 1995, 25). Kling stresses that the "deepest core conviction" places compassion and reconciliation along the path to wisdom and enlightenment, a coming to knowledge that Allende welcomes about a full year of watching Paula succumb to porphyria (Kling, 2010, 252).

From the beginning of her recovery of vivacity and appetite, the author dreams of food. On the mend at last, she experiences a resurgence of hunger for imagination and cuddling, which Rodden terms "the primal drives that create and perpetuate life and make it pleasurable" (Rodden, 2010, 188). The reconnection with inborn pleasures fulfill a second need, the author's dearth of kitchen and bedroom experiences to refresh her narrative source. From a new embrace of love, Allende recoups "a keen taste for life's sweetness—and bittersweetness," a reflection of the sexual and realistic awakening of Irene Beltrán in *Of Love and Shadows* and Aurora del Valle, the unloved wife in *Portrait in Sepia* (*ibid.*).

Allende's text touts variety, a pattern that influences Joan and Susan's restaurant meals in *The Infinite Plan* and the adaptable empanadas that feed the poor in *Inés of My Soul*. The author asserts that indulgence in eroticism varies with the individual. She refers to a litany of frolicsome character situations, as with the exhilarating sexual shenanigans of Hortense Guizot with husband Toulouse Valmorain in *Island Beneath the Sea* and the annual trysts that Beatriz Alcántara arranges with a bullfighter in *Of Love and Shadows*. The totality of sexual pleasure from the French dishes, "daring games, massages, shows, erotic literature, and art" enliven the ploys of *Aphrodite*, all catalysts to passion and satiety (Allende, 1998, 26).

Satire resonates through *Aphrodite* with a joyful mockery of people too tight-laced for fun, a grim social malaise that possesses islanders in Isak Dinesen's food fable *Babette's Feast*. For an orgy, the author excludes melancholics, hypochondriacs, and those "overly married," a wry jab at couples too uptight to indulge in a bedroom frolic (Allende, 1998, 86). Allende ridicules bureaucrats, fundamentalists, and soldiers, who avoid good food and lusty lovemaking and expend their energies on "more disciplined methods of killing one another," a grim reminder of the sexual foundations of torture and murder displayed by Colonel Esteban García, the warped police commandant in *The House of the Spirits* and of the necrophilia that exacerbates the crimes of Lieutenant Juan de Dios Ramírez in *Of Love and Shadows* (Allende, 1998, 27).

The book earned from critic Abigail Dennis the term "gastroporn," a polite term for lascivious recipes and coital advice (Dennis, 2008, 1). Written while Allende's "mind and heart were still in a giant blur of grief" from the slow demise and death of daughter Paula in December 1992, the text explodes with bawdy merriment as though the writer has no other refuge but frivolity (Hawley, 2008). In the introduction, Allende makes light of chastity by referring to virgin's urine as an endangered species and tweaks Catholicism for the concept of cyclical sin interrupted at intervals by confession. She credits "the Pill, hippies, and women's lib" for relieving women of the burden of "obsessive monogamy," a hint that Allende values an occasional carnal side trail (Allende, 1998, 14).

• *References and Further Reading*

Bach, Lisa. *Her Fork in the Road: Women Celebrate Food and Travel.* San Francisco: Travelers' Tales, 2001.
Dennis, Abigail. "From Apicius to Gastroporn: Form, Function, and Ideology in the History of Cookery Books," *Studies in Popular Culture* 31:1 (Fall 2008): 1–18.
Hawley, Janet. "A Woman of Spirit," *The* (Melbourne) *Age* (15 March 2008).
Kling, Vincent. "Archetype, Not Ideology: Isabel Allende's Balance of Opposites," *Critical Insights* (October 2010): 239–257.
Rodden, John. "Isabel Allende, Fortune's Daughter," *Critical Insights* (October 2010): 184–194.

belonging

Allende exposes from personal history the longings of the outsider to achieve affiliation or, at the least, tolerance from the majority, a focal theme among laborers in "Toad's Mouth" and Haitian refugees in *Island Beneath the Sea* and for the storygiver Belisa Crepusculario in "Two Words." In her first novel, *The House of the Spirits*, the del Valle-Trueba household lives in peace until Esteban assaults his wife Clara, knocking out teeth because Clara exonerates their daughter Blanca's affair with a peasant, Pedro Tercero. The event severs the del Valle-Trueba marriage, sending Clara into withdrawal and Esteban into physical and emotional alienation. Husband and wife follow divergent paths toward belonging—Clara toward the city to nurture and feed the poor and live among friends, artists, and the Mora sisters, with whom she practices clairvoyance. While refusing reconciliation, Clara forms a stronger bond with granddaughter Alba. In contrast to female intimacy at the residence, Esteban relies on the political old guard of males for acceptance. After election to the senate, he discovers that political alliances offer an arid substitute for blood relations. Upon Clara's death, Esteban views the deep love of people for a woman devoted to the needy, whether family or strangers.

For *Of Love and Shadows*, Allende confers belonging on Francisco Leal, the beloved son of Spanish emigrés Hilda and Professor Leal. Far from their homeland, they create a haven of affection, good food, and cultural activities to compensate for their refugee status. Francisco, a consulting psychologist, teams with his brother, the priest José Leal, for subversive work among the poor and suffering. In contrast to the loving foursome, the older son Javier loses the warmth of family, both with his parents and his wife and three children. He departs from them with wordless violence: "He had never spoken of suicide; he had told no one goodbye; he left no notes of farewell" (Allende, 1987, 122). After the Leals witness Javier's suicide by hanging, their unity increases with the inclusion of Francisco's lover, Irene Beltrán, a duo that forms a lasting romance on a par with that of the Leals.

For the working-class Ranquileos, belonging takes a twisted path that generates the conflict in *Of Love and Shadows*. The hospital error that awards Digna the wrong daughter introduces a faulty belonging for Evangelina, a blonde fifteen-year-old conceived by the Flores. Allende turns the inclusion of the outsider into a source of incestuous love by Digna's son Pradelio. During Evangelina Ranquileo's noontime seizures, she mimics a fierce physical passion, the cause of her arrest and murder by the Political Police. The misalliance within the Ranquileo household forces the self-exile of Pradelio to the mountains, but advances a search and mitigation of sufferings for other families of the *desaparecidos*. On a national scale, the resolution of Evangelina's disappearance confers a universal belonging on victims of a corrupt regime, who unify to unseat a tyrant.

Allende recognizes the racial disjunction in the life of her husband, William C. Gordon, source of the plot of *The Infinite Plan*. Protagonist Gregory Reeves speaks the despair of the caucasian at standing out from the dark-skinned majority in a barrio on the eastern edge of Los Angeles: "I experienced the unpleasantness of being different, I did not fit in; I wanted to be like everyone else" (Allende, 1993, 54). The separation of white from brown carries greater cultural overtones in a neighborhood where "no one understood or cared about the law of the gringos" (*ibid.*, 60). Lacking structure and supervision during free time, boys like Gregory cling to gang membership, a belonging tinged with ritual colors, dope, homemade weapons, hand signals, and codes of brotherhood. Shut out by his blond coloring, "all he wanted was to survive" the years preceding manhood (*ibid.*, 71). Following hellish derangement during the Vietnam War, he finds contentment and acceptance in a mountain community. Because of his skill at the Vietnamese language, he surprises himself by developing oneness with Asians that includes card playing and storytelling. Allende extends the irony of Greg's adaptation to disparate ethnic groups by returning him to the military and rehabilitation among disabled soldiers.

Acceptance eludes other newcomers to the California frontier in *Daughter of Fortune* and outsiders to the Amazon in the *City of the Beasts*. More insidious, according to Allende's foreword to *Tapestries of Hope*, the plight of the underprivileged reduces them to "the disposable sector of the population" (Allende, 2007, ix). Editors Herman Gray and Macarena Gómez-Barris note that Allende herself, like Spanish immigrant Inés Suarez, a Spanish colonist of Chile in *Inés of My Soul*, maneuvers away from the margins toward full membership in her adopted land, a sense of oneness with North Americans that she fosters in the memoir *My Invented Country*. The author identifies her platform as that of a low social caste, the Latina, a status she brandishes as "a position of responsibility and privilege that I plan to use and abuse" (Rodden, 2004, 143). In comic mode, she jokes about her liminal position as an American: "In California I'm a misfit; I wear silk while the rest of the population wears sneakers, and I order beef when everyone else in on a kick for tofu and green tea" (Boss, 2006, 126).

While Allende's books contribute to the "multicultural debates in public intellectual spheres," she simultaneously establishes a need to be truly American following her move from South America, marriage to a U.S. attorney, and citizenship (Gray and Gómez-Burris, 2010, 246). Analysts Herman Gray and Macarena Gómez-Barris note that "Her work depends on the post-civil rights era, where claims for recognition are rearticulated in the dominant media and political-racial landscape into multiculturalism" (Gray and Gómez-Barris, 2010, 246). The duo's assessment places Allende in the arenas "that put questions of race ... at the center of political discourses and practices" (*ibid.*, 247). Of particular distress to the author lies the post–9/11 foreignness that the George W. Bush administration foisted on residents who lacked the "sense of racial purity and ethnic homogeneity that even naturalization and citizenship cannot erase" (*ibid.*, 251). In *City of the Beasts*, Allende stresses the presumption of the birthright American, "those arrogant gringos [who] thought the world belonged to them" (Allende, 2002, 366). The YA trilogy further undermines white American egotism by picturing ineffectual Catholic missionaries in Central Africa in *Forest of the Pygmies*, where Aka and Bantu natives throw off tyranny through their own efforts rather than a rescue operation arranged by white outsiders.

Analysts affirm that "Allende benefited from the widening terrain" that accepted discourse on race and culture, particularly international concern for the community of relatives protesting loss of the *desaparecidos* (Gray and Gómez-Barris, 2010, 247). As critics Ana Nogales and Laura Golden Bellotti explain, through the bilingual community of *comadres*, Allende promotes a "redefinition of belonging" and states, "You need the company of women in order to survive" (Nogales and Bellotti, 2003, 76, 78). She proclaims community and individual witness as bases of democracy: "Just by being together you can create a spiritual energy, very humane" (*ibid.*, 78).

See also marginalism

• *References and Further Reading*

Boss, Pauline. *Loss, Trauma, and Resilience: Therapeutic Work with Ambiguous Loss.* New York: W.W. Norton, 2006.

Gómez-Barris, Macarena, and Herman Gray, eds. *Toward a Sociology of the Trace.* Minneapolis: University of Minnesota Press, 2010.

Gray, Herman, and Macarena Gómez-Barris. *Toward a Sociology of the Trace.* Minneapolis: University of Minnesota Press, 2010.

Nogales, Ana, and Laura Golden Bellotti. *Latina Power!* New York: Simon & Schuster, 2003.

Rodden, John, ed. *Conversations with Isabel Allende.* 2nd ed. Austin: University of Texas Press, 2004.

Beltran-Leal genealogy

The alliance of an elite Latin American family with a refugee clan from Franco's Spain in *Of Love and Shadows* connects from opposite sides of the globe the plight of the innocent under ruthless tyrants. Allende rounds out the marriage of Irene Beltrán to Francisco Leal by sending them from their troubled country to the abandoned Leal home in Teruel, Spain. The creation of a loving couple and new sept of the family tree mitigates in part the desertion of Eusebio Beltrán from his family and the unforeseen suicide of Javier. The possibility of children from Irene and Francisco also makes up for the celibacy of Father José Leal and the dead end of the Beltrán line.

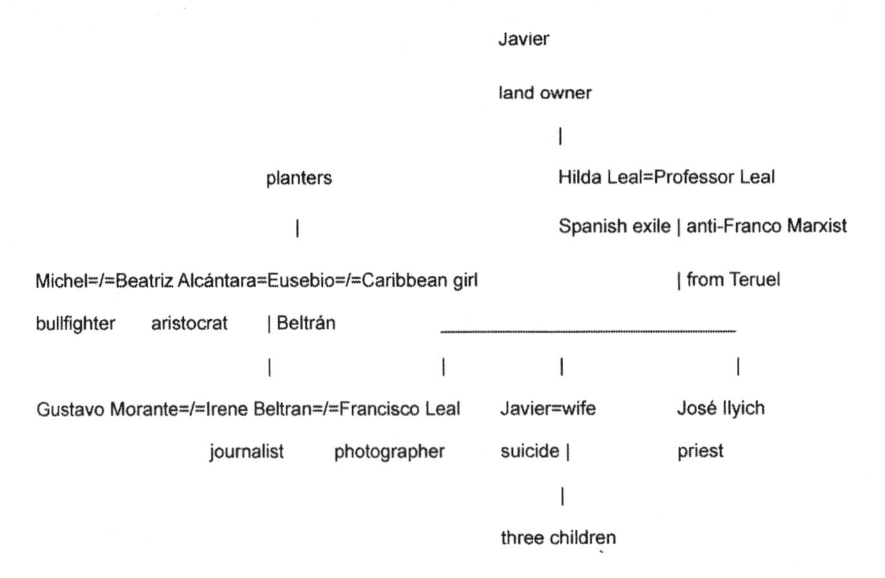

See also belonging

• *References and Further Reading*

Kristal, Efraín. *The Cambridge Companion to the Latin American Novel.* New York: Cambridge University Press, 2005.

Toomey, Mike. "Love and Chaos," (Melbourne) *Herald Sun* (7 August 2007).

betrayal

The duplicity of humankind resonates in Allende's fiction as a grievous sin, a violation of trust dramatized in fraudulent police raids on prostitutes in *Eva Luna* and by elected officials against peasants in *The House of the Spirits*. In her own life, she considered betrayals "serious ... they leave indelible scars" (Correas de Zapata, 2002, 820). For Clara del Valle, the devolution of husband Esteban Trueba into physical violence destroys marital intimacy while foreshadowing a national political disjuncture, the breakdown of the patriarchal junta that embroils the Latin American nation in arbitrary arrests, abductions, torture, and execution. The suffering of Alba, Trueba's beloved granddaughter, slaps him with a painful truth, that political betrayal can escalate to harm the most vulnerable citizens.

In like fashion, Lieutenant Juan de Dios Ramírez's flouting of due process in *Of Love and Shadows* escalates mounting oppression into death squads and mass graves, the hiding places where the guilty inter their sins. Allende indicates a futile attempt by Captain Gustavo Morante to forestall the mass treachery, but affirms his martyrdom by a corrupt system that media exposure can only disclose and censure. As an antidote to hidden treachery, Allende creates a fictional conduit in the travels of Evangelina Flores to "the United Nations, in press conferences, on television, at congresses, universities—everywhere—speaking about the *desaparecidos*, to insure that the men, women, and children swallowed up by that violence would never be forgotten" (Allende, 1987, 272). Historically, these infractions of codes of humane governance resonated through families, clans, communities, and nations, notably, the global outcry against the flesh trade and the denunciation of Augusto Pinochet for concealing crimes against humanity in Chile.

Allende's summation of depravity incorporates personal relationships, especially the disingenuous marriage of Diego Domínguez to Eliza Sommers in *Portrait in Sepia*, the flight of false lover Joaquín Andieta from Eliza Sommers in *Daughter of Fortune*, and the womanizing of Rafael Moncada in *Zorro* and Matías Rodríguez de Santa Cruz in *Portrait in Sepia*. A case in point, the infidelities of wives Samantha and Shannon against lawyer Gregory Reeves in *The Infinite Plan*, illustrate the failings of dishonest parents toward their children. From the beginning of her relationship with Greg, Samantha Ernst "never showed him her true face," a cloaking of intent unworthy of a wife and mother (Allende, 1993, 171). Allende vilifies the second wife, Shannon, for being unsuitable mother material because she "loved trips, buying sprees, and parties," all the result of her "restless and adventurous" spirit, which son David pictures as "a gentle mirage" (*ibid.*, 305, 376). The resultant family chaos scuttles the attorney's attempts to stabilize his two children, whom divorce sets adrift.

With a look toward Latin America's colonial era, in *Inés of My Soul*, Allende features the downfall of the infamous conqueror Francisco Pizarro and the trickery of Pedro de Valdivia in swindling Santiagans of their gold. The motif of double-dealing parallels the trickery of Felipe/Lautaro, the docile paddock boy who conceals under servility the bold spirit of a rebel Indian leader. Swift and invisible, he "flees Santiago on the darkest night of summer, unseen by the sentinels, and unbetrayed by the dogs" (Allende 2006, 271). A puzzle to the protagonist, the dissimulation of Felipe/Lautaro prompts Allende's review of the boy's subsequent role in a Mapuche ambush of Spanish forces. By posing as a sweet-natured lad, Felipe lures the Spaniards into trusting him and allowing his observation of their fortifications and military strength. From months of insider observation, Lautaro easily outflanks Général Valdivia in one of Allende's most blatant models of military deception. The author closes the one-on-one confrontation with Lautaro's spitting in Valdivia's face, the moment of payback that the turncoat awaits "for twenty-two years" (*ibid.*, 312).

Heinous perfidy characterizes Allende's more recent works. To serve the conventions of the *City of the Beasts* quest novels, betrayal heightens suspense and enhances the satisfaction of resolution. The combined evil of entrepreneur Mauro Crías, the murderous Captain Ariosto, and Dr. Omayra Torres, the innoculator of Amazonian natives with the smallpox virus, demands on-the-spot retribution by Alex Cold and his cohort, Nadia Santos, as well as by Alex's grandmother Kate and the invisible People of the Mist. The abrupt action and operatic tone recur in the sequel, *Kingdom of the Golden Dragon*, in which, once more, a devious female, Judit Kinski, threatens the expedition as well as the life of King Dorji and the national treasure of the Forbidden Kingdom. As an antidote to duplicity, Allende resets the monarchy under King Dil Bahadur and Queen Pema, who establish an orderly family and produce a prince, a contribution to a stable dynasty.

Allende depicts bondage as a vile extreme of the genteel life of the Caribbean investor. In a discussion of the roots of slavery in *Forest of the Pygmies* and *Island Beneath the Sea*, she surveys what critic Margo Hammond identifies as "themes of national identity (and racial confusion) set against a background of family loyalties (and class betrayals)," elements that "find echoes in today's headlines" (Hammond, 2010). The texts stress the source of moral insufficiency: "If you give power to human beings, and they are unaccountable, they can do whatever they want with another human being, they become capable of unspeakable horrors," a description of the wretched lives of Central African domestics and press gangs and the cane field workers in colonial Haiti (May, 2010).

In *Forest of the Pygmies*, the diminutive size of slaves increases the pathos of their suppression by Commandant Maurice Mbembelé. Allende compounds the grotesque situation by frequent referrals to his muscles, his Bantu security guards, and a crocodile pond, the execution site for his enemies. The poignance of enslaved women attempting to prevent the sale of their children accounts for the uprising of females in the resolution. At a dramatic overturn of Mbembelé's tyranny, Queen Nana-Asante liberates the mothers "so they could fight along with their men" (Allende, 2005, 246). By providing the conclusion with a touch of magic from Alex's shapeshifting, Allende restores balance and trust to the Pygmies and the Bantu, who realize a mutual need to collaborate.

On an historical level in *Island Beneath the Sea*, the Haitian emancipation struggle from 1791 to 1804 incurs a series of shifts in loyalty as black Maroons determine whether to ally with the French or Spanish or continue to fight alone for freedom. Although parted from her lover, Gambo La Liberté, Tété trusts his intent to free all slaves, even after the French trick and deport emancipator Toussaint L'Ouverture. The author dramatizes the era's duplicity with General Dessalines's covert sale of the very Haitian blacks he pledges to liberate. At a slave auction, Tété struggles with disgust at the sight of a woman on the auction block pleading to remain with her child.

The profitability of the flesh trade reaches untenable proportions: "Thousands of slaves arrive in Saint-Domingue, but never enough to fill the insatiable demands of the planters," the offenders of the social order (Allende, 2010, 113). Revolt against the phony gentility of French islanders unveils a social rot that the wealthy cloak with a pretense of civilizing and Christianizing African abductees. The source of generations of resentment, cane field labor destroys the health of black workers, "but when they began to emerge from the thick vegetation it could be seen that they were hundreds," the nightmare of retribution to exploiters of the black race (Allende, 2010, 186).

Allende's skill at portraying tricksters and sharpers has earned a devoted audience. In 2009, director Donald Sturrock partnered with Jamaican composer Eleanor Alberga to turn one of *The Stories of Eva Luna* into an opera. Both artists chose "Letters of a Love Betrayed," the story of Analía Torres, an orphan deluded into marrying her cousin Luis. The melodrama suited the purpose and style of vocal drama with a standard motif from fairy tale and vengeance parables—the elevation of a poor, innocent young girl and her triumph in adulthood over a cozening uncle. Because Allende set the story in a convent and a Colombian hacienda, the contrast provided the adapters with an engaging social platform for libretto and music for guitar and harp. Alberga admired "the mystery, the slight undercurrent of darkness and a sense of Analía's spirituality," both of which elucidate the suspenseful double-cross (Devine, 2009, 15).

See also evil

• *References and Further Reading*

Correas de Zapata, Celia. *Isabel Allende: Life and Spirits.* Houston, TX: Arte Público, 2002.
Devine, Rachel. "Passion, Betrayal and Love in a Hot Climate," (London) *Sunday Times* (15 November 2009): 15.
Hammond, Margo. "A Slave Makes History in Allende's New Novel," *Pittsburgh Post-Gazette* (6 June 2010).
May, Meredith. "Allende Takes on Slavery," *San Francisco Chronicle* (28 April 2010).
Santiago, Sylvia. "Portrait in Sepia," *Herizons* 16:2 (22 September 2002): 44.

Carlé-Luna genealogy

The Carlé-Luna family pictures the loosely connected cast of characters that forms Eva Luna's family. As Mimí constructs a female life for her male body, Eva Luna searches for photos of the Dutch grandfather and ambassadorial ancestor to pair with an idealized portrait of Consuelo with a parasol and lace dress. The revelation of family traits and actions continues in the story "The Little Heidelberg."

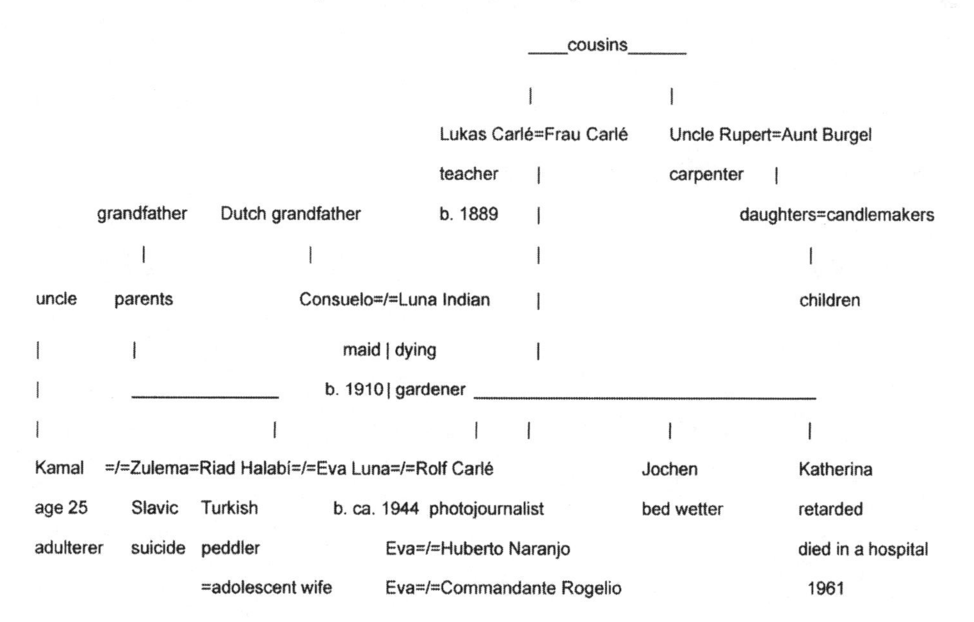

• *References and Further Reading*

Axelrod-Contrada, Joan. *Isabel Allende*. New York: Marshall Cavendish Benchmark, 2011.

Chi'en–del Valle–Sommers genealogy

The Chi'en–del Valle–Sommers alliance distinguishes the ethnicities of three continents—Chinese, Latino, Mapuche, and British—united in one family tree. Eliza, an Anglo-Mapuche foundling, acquires education in Mapuche and Spanish languages and rituals as well as the graces of an English aristocrat. From experience, she adds an introduction to Chinese ancestor worship. Jacob Todd, a visitor from England to Valparaíso, Chile, views the Spanish reverence for family in the lives of the del Valles, "a large family united by intricate bloodlines and an inflexible code of honor" (Allende, 1999, 41). The intractability of characters underscores the collision of nationalities at Eliza's unforeseen conception and her successful union of English, Chilean, Spanish, and Chinese traits and loyalties in her story.

```
        ____________
        |            |
        Eliza=father       aunt in Scotland
        widow | bibliophile

____________________________________________________________
|        |          Bastille jailer                      |
|        |             |                                 |
Jeremy   Dame Rose Sommers=/=Karl=/=Frenchwoman=/=Marquis   John Sommers=/=Mapuche
merchant pornographer       Bretzner=wife      de Sade    sea captain  |woman
b. 1802  b. 1812            Viennese |                    suicide      |
                            tenor    |                                 |
                              two children                             |
merchant class      _____________________________________________
grandfather          |    grandfather in Kwangtung
|                    |       |
seamstress=/=ravisher |      ______________                conquistadors
|                    |       |              |                   |
Joaquín Andieta=/=Eliza Sommers=Tao Chi'en=Lin     sister      Emilia=Agustín del Valle
radical       | 3/15/1832   | healer     |        b. 1828        | agriculturist
1827-1853     | pastry chef | murdered   girl     Sephardic Jewish  | in Valparaíso
                            | by tongs   stillborn widow      ___________________
                            1824-1885    1848      |          |      |          |
                            |            _________            |      bastards   |
```

```
                          |          |          |          |                      |
                          |      attorney       |          |                      |
                          |                     |          |                      |
_________________________    Amanda Lowell =/=Feliciano=Paulina del Valle=Frederick   Severo del Valle
|                        |   Irish actor     Rodríguez  | entrepreneur  Williams          |
Ebanizer Sommers=mail order |  courtesan    de Santa Cruz  | 1824-1890   convict      Severo=Nívea
| "Lucky"        | bride  |              gold mine owner |              butler     del Valle | b. 1861
b. 1854          |        |                             |                           b. 1857 |
        children   Severo=Lynn Sommers=/=Matías Rodríguez de=/=Amanda              ______________
                   del Valle | 1860-1880    | Santa Cruz          Lowell            |            |
                   lawyer  | artist's model | dies of syphilis, 1893               Clara        Rosa
                           |                                                      del Valle    la Bella
                           |            Sebastián=Doña Elvira                                  poisoned
                           |            Domínguez |
                           |                      |
                           |           _________________________________
                           |           |                  |           |
Iván Radovic=/=Aurora del Valle (Lai-Ming)=Diego Domínguez=/=Susana=Eduardo    Adela
physician    | b. 10/12/1880         b. 1874          b. 1873  | b. 1873
             | photographer                                 m. 1893
                                                            three children
```

See also del Valle–García–Trueba genealogy

• *References and Further Reading*

Carvalho, Susan E. *Contemporary Spanish American Novels by Women: Mapping the Narrative.* Rochester, NY: Tamesis, 2007.

Macpherson, Heidi Slettedahl. *Women's Movement: Escape as Transgression in North American Feminist Fiction.* Amsterdam: Rodopi, 2000.

Chile

The mythic homeland of Isabel Allende's nostalgic fiction, Chile "lies at the end of all roads," a lance flung south of Peru and the Atacama Desert along the southwestern coast of South America to the island of Chiloé (Allende, 2003, 1). Her characters range over disparate terrain as brutally rugged as the *cordillera* in *Inés of My Soul*, as remote as the Domínguez cattle ranch in *Portrait in Sepia*, and as sophisticated as Santiago's city center in *Paula*. Analyst Shannin Schroeder notes the recurrence of Chilean themes and attitudes in the writer's canon: "Chilean author Isabel Allende now lives in San Francisco; however, in spite of her increasingly North American settings and interests, her fiction is still synonymous with Latin America (and specifically Chile)" (Schroeder, 2004, 4). For the expatriate author, her homeland fleshes out the edenic other world of longing and fantasy, a place that reviewer Helen Falconer calls the "tragic land of (Allende's) upbringing" (Falconer, 2001). In *The Sum of Our Days*, Allende admits, "my memories of Chile are covered with a golden patina, like the altarpieces of colonial churches" (Allende, 2008, 414–415).

In *Inés of My Soul*, the author debates the racism of colonization, which pitted Araucan and Mapuche Indians against savage Spanish military armed with swords and the Christian cross to conquer "the Spanish burying ground" (Allende, 2006, 108). The Europeans who found Santiago walk one thousand kilometers "weighed down in heavy iron armor; they crossed mountains, rivers, and the world's most arid desert" (Allende, 1999, 41). Wandering the wilderness, Spaniards under Général Pedro de Valdivia search for precious metals, "bearing off everything they found" from an unclaimed province that they consider "the backside of the world" (*ibid.*, 52). In the nation's rape, Chile takes on new parameters from the conquistadors and their culture. Valdivia, after defeating Diego de Almagro, visits his foe in prison and elicits details of the first European expedition south from Peru over the *cordillera* in a milieu of "rock, wind, ice, and solitude" (Allende, 2006, 71). Valdivia profits from descriptions of the Yanacona who freeze each night or die of thirst and of soldiers who remove boots and gloves along with frozen fingers and toes. As contrast, the author revels in Almagro's description of Chile's wonders—"gentle hills, fragrant forests, fertile valleys, bounteous rivers" and a pleasing climate (*ibid.*, 72).

According to reviewer Susannah Goddard, the meeting of Europeans with Amerindians presages an end to primitivism and the rise of a world capital at Santiago: "The Conquistadors changed a culture, a race, a religion. They changed a whole continent" (Goddard, 2006). Among the curious tribes, Valdivia hopes "to found a just, and strong, society" based on Iberian principles and virtues Allende, 2006, 110). Inés Suarez adds her own perspective in describing the blends of arrogant hidalgos with doughty Mapuche, producing "a people of demented pride" (Allende, 2006, 149). Only after concerted efforts do characters discover sources of wealth in steamships and the sale of guano from caves, ice from the islands bordering Antarctica, and red wine from outlying vineyards.

In the contrasting worlds brought together in *Daughter of Fortune*, the author spars with characters over the true nature of colonial Chile. Allende romanticizes the terrain as "a wild geography of imposing mountains, cliff-lined coasts, fertile valleys, ancient forests, and eternal ice ... bathed top to tail by the Pacific Ocean ... [and] the impossible fragrance of sirens" (Allende, 1999, 14, 15). British immigrants complain that "the exigencies of landscape, climate and life in Chile had forced substantial changes" in the genteel existence they had known in the British Isles (Allende, 1999, 6). For Jeremy Sommers, a Valparaíso import-export manager, the truth lies closer to the misery of icy gales and whirlwinds, heat, downpours, and earthquakes and the squalor of shacks and slums, which prevent him from fantasizing that the city resembles London. His brother John, a sea captain, adds the terror of tidal waves. Jeremy disdains Chilean women, whom he deems "fatal ... short, broad through the posterior, and they have most unpleasant voices" (*ibid.*, 19). Bible salesman Jacob Todd learns too late that "all newcomers fell ill when first they visited Chile," ostensibly from tainted water (*ibid.*, 29).

Enlarging on the sober note, the author acknowledges the parade of disasters that mark Chilean history, including cholera and smallpox epidemics among Indians, the War of the Pacific, and mud slides resulting from winter snowmelt. In *Paula*, the author catalogues the country's seasonal calamities— droughts and wildfire, volcanic eruptions, insects, and earth tremors, much of which assaults her characters and impacts their outlooks and destinies. Socially, she compares the layered Chilean society to a "mille-feuille pastry. It had more castes than India, and there was a pejorative term to set every person in his or her rightful place," from commoners, refugees, and the *nouveau riche* to socialists and Marxists (Allende 1995, 6). For *Portrait in Sepia*, Allende orchestrates entrepreneur Paulina del Valle's homecoming from San Francisco to the aristocratic address on Ejército Libertador in the center of Santiago. Although Paulina profits by establishing steamer lines for shipping ice, fruits, and vegetables from Chile to frontier California, she varies her estimations of the region from a "sleepy city filled with the odors of flowering gardens and horse manure" to "an ass-backward corner of the world" (Allende, 2001, 141, 211).

As a control of chauvinism, in *My Invented Country*, the author restrains the urge to rhapsodize on snowy mountains and summer air scented with peaches with reminders of a closed society steeped in snobbery, arrogance, and Catholic close-mindedness and surrounded by vendors' cries, ragged child beggars, and the barking of stray dogs. The arrival of so eccentric a couple as Paulina and former butler Frederick Williams sparks exaggerated rumors of his past as a ruined oligarch who scrupulously avoids the underclass. To Amanda Lowell, the former top courtesan of San Francisco, Santiago lacks the sparkle of Paris and flounders in meaningless luxury and "brazen ostentation" (Allende, 2001, 220). In 1898, conditions worsen with high infant mortality, slums, unemployment, and bureaucracy. For Aurora del Valle, immured at Cleufú in May 1899 by a rainy winter, moaning winds and muddy roads turn the dark months into a seasonal imprisonment. Allende sums up the country's destiny as a bureaucratic nightmare with "one foot in the poorhouse," a reference to the lack of easy sources of wealth from gold, silver, or copper mines or coffee, cotton, or tobacco plantations (Allende, 2003, 82).

Imbued with sense impressions from the author's childhood and young womanhood, in *The House of the Spirits*, the unnamed nation—obviously modeled on Chile—crumbles under violence, a parallel to the September 11, 1973, bombing of Chile's presidential palace and the alleged suicide of Salvador Allende, Isabel's godfather. In his place, Augusto Pinochet set up an adamantine dictatorship. Analyst Marta L. Wilkinson explains the late ripening of Chilean democracy, "Due to the timing and effects of colonization in the New World, the demands for reform of government and oligarchic practices do not surface ... until the mid- and late twentieth century" (Wilkinson, 2008, 151). In *The Sum of Our Days*, the expatriate author recalls "images of the military coup in Chile, the dead in the streets, the blood, the sudden violence, the sensation that at any moment something fatal could happen, that no one was safe anywhere" (Allende 2008, 278). Conservatives bolted before 1973, political refugees fled from 1973 to 1978, and economic exiles dribbled across the borders after 1978 to more promising climes. Those who remained "learned to keep their opinions to themselves" of brigades of young Communist thugs, drive-by shootings, gun running, and rivers clogged with rotting carcasses of swine and dairy herds (Allende, 2003, 47).

Sorrow for her afflicted homeland returns in *Of Love and Shadows*, when the fictional Journalist Irene Beltrán mourns "My country, oh, my country" (Allende, 1987, 289). Irene and Francisco Leal feel "dwarfed, alone, vulnerable, two desolate sailors adrift on a sea of mountain peaks and clouds amid a lunar silence" (*ibid.*). The "shadows" that engulf survivors cloak corrupt politicians and military who spread propaganda and pervert truth for the sake of upper caste empowerment. In contrast, the Roman Catholic cardinal examines the incriminating photos of cadavers sequestered in a mine tunnel and thinks of a treasured home, where his large family shared "succulent vegetable soups, corn cakes, chicken stews, highly spiced seafood chowder, and, above all, homemade desserts," the food of the past (Allende, 1987, 207). Memories of the family table sustain the cardinal in hard times while rumors spread fear for *desaparecidos* and their unknown fate.

Food continues to particularize the good life that Chileans enjoy. While Irene digs for details of crime from Sergeant Faustino Rivera, the two receive servings of soup, fried potatoes, and a roast pig, a symbol of Chile's victimization of vulnerable peasants during the dictatorship. The next phase of the investigation takes Irene to the Los Riscos market, heaped with corn and potatoes, vegetables, and caged rabbits and chickens alongside chilled seafood, cheese, and meat. While admiring clams, grapes, and strawberries, Irene ponders the illusion that "nothing terrible could befall a world where such abundance flowered," a momentary denial of reality (Allende, 1987, 231).

Allende admires the investigative journalists for refusing protection by the establishment. Rather than sink into apathy, Irene and Francisco grapple for internal fortitude to face an anonymous enemy. The text represents peasant resistance in the miraculous overpowering of Lieutenant Juan de Dios Ramirez by a wonder worker, Evangelina Ranquileo. The author remarked on "this incredible source of energy inside ... it's there when we reach for it" (Ford, 2007). By identifying with victims of dictatorship and mass murder, Allende assuages her personal nostalgia for Chile in what novelist Antonella Gambotto-Burke calls "her true home ... her writing, a dimension inaccessible to matter" (Gambotto-Burke, 2006, 15).

After years of self-exile in Venezuela, Allende's relationship to her motherland underwent cycles of revisitation and change. Following the publication of *The House of the Spirits*, shrill criticisms vilified what critic Karen Wooley Martin called a subversion of "patriarchal norms that have governed politics, sexuality, and ethnicity" (Martin, 2010, back cover). In deflating chauvinistic notions of where and how Chile came to be and how it survived revolution, Allende both revitalized South American history and reclaimed female activism in guiding the nation out of nineteenth-century *machismo* and racism into postmodern multiethnic egalitarianism.

The recreation of home in *My Invented Country* pictures a land of nitrate exports, copper mining, the mystic energy of Elqui Valley, and lip service to Roman Catholicism and its anti-choice views on contraception. Striking at the heart of the people, the stereotypical Catholic conservatism, a guilt-ridden androcentrism, forbids abortion and divorce but does not prevent employers from exploiting workers. Amid false modesty and Puritanism, Chileans live pessimistic days and secretive nights. In reflective passages, Allende blames the double sexual standard in part on Chilean women. The servile nature of mothers and daughters toward the males of the household nurtures expectations of servile treatment from all females. Kept out of sight, the creation of womanizers produces more males who "went to bed with anyone and at any time he pleased" (Allende, 2003, 54–55).

In a less humorous vein, the author charged the American CIA with unseating a duly elected socialist government under Salvador Allende, thus engendering a military fascism in Chile. Macarena Gómez-Barris points out the nose-to-nose confrontation: "Allende renders the story of Chile in ways that make the U.S. state accountable to the historical record" (Gómez-Barris, 2010, 239). Beyond issues of sovereignty, U.S. meddling in Chilean politics in the 1970s rested on overt racism, a denial of the rights of peons to land that they had worked from prehistory. Once settled in California, Allende viewed her homeland with renewed vigor and wisdom. In California, she saw Latino ghettoes as the residence of thousands who lived in poverty and distrust, but who imparted to their adopted homeland "music, highly spiced food, and exuberant sense of color" (Allende, 1993, 35).

Holding them back from assimilation, elements of superstition, patriotism, and *machismo* reduced Hispanics to low-end jobs and a life of penury and pride.

See also food

• *References and Further Reading*

Falconer, Helen. "Colouring the Family Album," (Manchester) *Guardian* (17 November 2001).
Ford, Karen. "Triumph of Truth and Love," *The* (Melbourne) *Age* (23 September 2007).
Gambotto-Burke, Antonella. "Novelist's Purest Symphony of Being," *The* (Sydney) *Australian* (5 April 2008): 15.
Goddard, Susannah. "The Woman Who Built a City," (Melbourne) *Herald Sun* (25 November 2006): W26.
Gómez-Barris, Macarena, and Herman Gray, eds. *Toward a Sociology of the Trace*. Minneapolis: University of Minnesota Press, 2010.
Martin, Karen Wooley. *Isabel Allende's House of the Spirits Trilogy: Narrative Geographies*. Rochester, NY: Tamesis, 2010.
Schroeder, Shannin. *Rediscovering Magical Realism in the Americas*. Westport, CT: Praeger, 2004.
Wilkinson, Marta L. *Antigone's Daughters: Gender, Family, and Expression in the Modern Novel*. New York: Peter Lang, 2008.

City of the Beasts

A trilogy of problem novels beginning with *The City of the Beasts* and moving chronologically to *Kingdom of the Golden Dragon* and *Forest of the Pygmies* illustrates the universal reach of Allende's twenty-first century canon to young adults. For facts about the first setting, Manaos, Brazil, she draws on "The Amazon Queen," a travelogue she published in *Salon* on March 25, 1997. The adventure genre, according to critic Philip Swanson, "seeks to invert the traditional message" of the "*conquista* or conquest and colonizing of the Americas" through the actions of idealistic youth, fifteen-year-old Alexander "Jaguar" Cold and twelve-year-old sidekick Nadia "Eagle" Santos, an archetype of the wise, intuitive child (Swanson, 2006, 173). For the adventure along the Amazon, Allende emphasizes language barriers with Indians. Two characters— Nadia and Padre Valdomero— master the indigenous language and communicate well in native dialects. Nadia also speaks English, Portuguese, and Spanish. Like the Indians' clothing and food, language derives from nature with sounds "gentle as the breeze, as water, as birds" (Allende, 2002, 85).

British reviewer Carol Birch notes Nadia's value as "a brave and loyal child who tutors her more educated and linear-thinking male sidekick in the art of living intuitively," a motif that continues in the two sequels through clairvoyance and telepathy (Birch, 2002, 33). Through a mutually beneficial partnership, the plucky, physically fit protagonists from North and South America contrast the menacing entrepreneur Mauro Carías, genocidal Dr. Omayra Torres, murderous Captain Ariosto, and greedy *garimpeiros* (prospectors) who die in the jungle from desperate scrabbles for gold and jewels.

As an introduction, Allende juxtaposes disparate generations. Grandmother Kate Cold tests her grandson's adaptability and logic by listing hazards of the Amazon. Her description of a nine-foot humanoid piques Alex's curiosity and gives evidence that the boy has inherited some of Kate's insouciant courage and inquisitiveness. For setting, the story extends the contrast of the north and south of the Western Hemisphere, a theme that Allende peruses in *Daughter of Fortune* and *Portrait in Sepia*. More exotic than urban California, Indian territory on the Brazil-Venezuela border reveals the influx of foreigners who threaten native survival while exploiting gold, cattle, diamonds, lumber, and rubber or trafficking in contraband birds, drugs, and arms along the Upper Orinoco. Unlike other of Allende's migration scenarios, the tone demeans usurpers who harm the fragile Amazon environment for the sake of profit.

Thematically, the *City of the Beasts* trilogy stresses the potential of the individual, a quality that Eliza Sommers, Tao Chi'en, and Aurora del Valle share with Eagle and Jaguar. In the estimation of critic Mel Boland, the assimilation and quest motifs foreground the author's "broaching contemporary issues relevant to the conservation of the environment and the efforts to protect indigenous lands, people, and traditions" that date back twenty thousand years (Boland, 2003, 453). By picturing the danger of microbes, animal extinction, and deforestation, the text imparts the paradoxical perils and fragility of a land that threatens to eradicate the strongest, wiliest, and most technologically advanced white insurgent — Mauro Carías, who survives the expedition on life support.

Begun with a nightmare, the action of *City of the Beasts* unites the youthful duo of Cold and Santos in varied genres — adventure, mystery, history, and ecological heroism — as part of their maturation. Critic Philip Swanson admires the picaresque young adult trilogy for "[mobilizing] the sense of magical freedom and innocence implicit in children's fiction to convey ... the postcolonial experience to a wide and often implicitly 'First-World' public" (Swanson, 2006, 267). As models of institutional obstacles to native survival, Allende sets up Captain Ariosto (military), Mauro Carías (capitalism), and Dr. Omayra Torres (medicine), an array of villains defeated by the optimism and teamwork of youth aided by the People of the Mist, New World Yetis, and Grandmother Cold.

A shadow plot resonates with the terrors of the Amazonian jungle, which amplify the endangerment of Alex's mother Lisa from cancer and chemotherapy in a Texas hospital. In frustration, Alex "Jaguar" Cold destroys the model planes and toys of childhood, a symbolic abandonment of childish frivolity to free him for adult responsibilities. Significant to standard adventure motifs, he battles the terrifying reality of his mother's disease, a reason for his grasping at magical remedies to cure larger-than-life menace. His encounter with the totemic black jaguar satisfies a boy's need to find mystic power in natural healing, the last resort when technology fails to relieve Lisa of the miseries of chemotherapy. By drawing on identification with a great jungle cat, at a crucial time, Alex feels "powerful, feared, solitary, invincible," a mental armament that prepares him for the worst (Allende, 2002, 225).

As the teen duo advances into Alex's first foray into the Upper Orinoco, the text builds tension through short statements and succinct dialogue, especially the pithy remarks of Walimai, a shaman in the tradition of the biblical Eli, Merlin of Arthurian lore, Gandalf of J.R.R. Tolkien's epic *Lord of the Rings*, and Obi-Wan Kenobi from *Star Wars*. Allende illustrates the supernatural concept of the "People of the Mist," an airy race so enfolded in nature that individual members elude national boundaries and merge into a mystic environment. As in the real world, defenders of the wild contend with greed, an abstract evil encompassing abusers of the outdoors as models of self-enriching capitalism, a theme that dominates the story "Toad's Mouth" and the premise of the historical novel *Inés of My Soul*. On a personal level, native modeling of climbing a slick waterfall draws Alex into a life-or-death feat that earns him respect and election to a chiefdom. To prepare him for jungle survival, control of out-of-body shapeshifting enables indigenous people to initiate Jaguar into a transformative encounter with psychic death, an introit into manhood.

Allende aims the text toward the exposure of an Amazonian Bigfoot, a prehistoric sloth based on a fossil found in Amazonia an dating to 7300 B.C.E. The author's fanciful suppositions about the hiding of local beings from conquistadors and airplanes in the "last refuge of prehistoric times" poses the antithesis of Darwin's theories of evolution and natural selection (Allende, 2002, 318). Sustaining the small clutch of eleven Beasts, three males and eight females, the oral epics that Walimai recites educate them on tribal history. The animals preserve their past with an eagerness parallel to that of Grr-ympr, the chief of the Yetis in *Kingdom of the Golden Dragon*.

The testing of Alex and Nadia involves them in displays of physical strength, judgment, inner control, adaptability, and daring. Their individual challenges require the recovery of what they most want—the water of life and three crystal eggs—and impose artificial strictures in separate missions to be completed in one day without turning back, limitations common to fairy tales and quest lore. The text depicts Nadia shapeshifting into "eagle-girl" by relying on a talisman and on skill "from a hidden and mysterious place" in her heart, a metaphor for intuition and instinct (Allende, 2002, 291–292). The feat concludes with reciprocity, the giving of a gift to replace the precious eggs. The parallel test for Alex takes on an Indiana Jones intensity as he plays his grandfather Cold's flute to subdue a huge albino bat and abandons his instrument in exchange for curative waters.

As the dynamic teens face down the corrupt Captain Ariosto, money-grubbing Mauro Carías, lethal Dr. Omayra Torres, and fatuous Professor Ludovic Leblanc, the blend of eco-justice and youthful idealism proves mutually beneficial to Eagle and Jaguar and to the People of the Mist, represented by Chief Iyomi, an archetype of the prehistoric queen/matriarch. As critic Don Latham explains, teenagers like Eagle and Jaguar share characteristics of "the politically and culturally disempowered," a category that exposes them to the inconsistencies and conflicts that threaten endangered species and native cultures (Latham, 2007, 61). Jaguar sheds the certainties of the social order and reaches beyond civilization for truths older than rational intellectualism, a self-empowerment slated to serve him in his grandmother's next two adventures.

See also Forest of the Pygmies; *Kingdom of the Golden Dragon*; nativism

• *References and Further Reading*

Birch, Carol. "Review: *City of the Beasts*," (Manchester) *Guardian* (30 November 2002): 33.
Boland, Mel. "'Orienting' the Text: Eastern Influences in the Fiction of Isabel Allende" in *Cross-Cultural Travel*, ed. Jane Conroy. New York: Peter Lang, 2003.
Latham, Don. "The Cultural Work of Magical Realism in Three Young Adult Novels," *Children's Literature in Education* 38 (2007): 59–70.
Swanson, Philip. "Z/Z: Isabel Allende and the Mark of Zorro," *Romance Studies* 24:3 (November 2006): 265–277.

Cold genealogy

A blend of disparate talents, the Cold family tree reveals sources of musicality from Alex's paternal grandfather and endurance and rationality from his mother and father, Lisa and John Cold. By allying with Nadia Santos, Alex acquires communication skills that are both lingual and telepathic. His extensive of native abilities enables him to engage with the prehistoric People of the Mist, Yetis, gorillas, mandrills, and Kobi, a curmudgeon bull elephant.

See genealogy chart on page 58.

• *References and Further Reading*

Birch, Carol. "Review: *City of the Beasts*," (Manchester) *Guardian* (30 November 2002): 33.
Boland, Mel. "'Orienting' the Text: Eastern Influences in the Fiction of Isabel Allende" in *Cross-Cultural Travel*, ed. Jane Conroy. New York: Peter Lang, 2003.
Latham, Don. "The Cultural Work of Magical Realism in Three Young Adult Novels," *Children's Literature in Education* 38 (2007): 59–70.

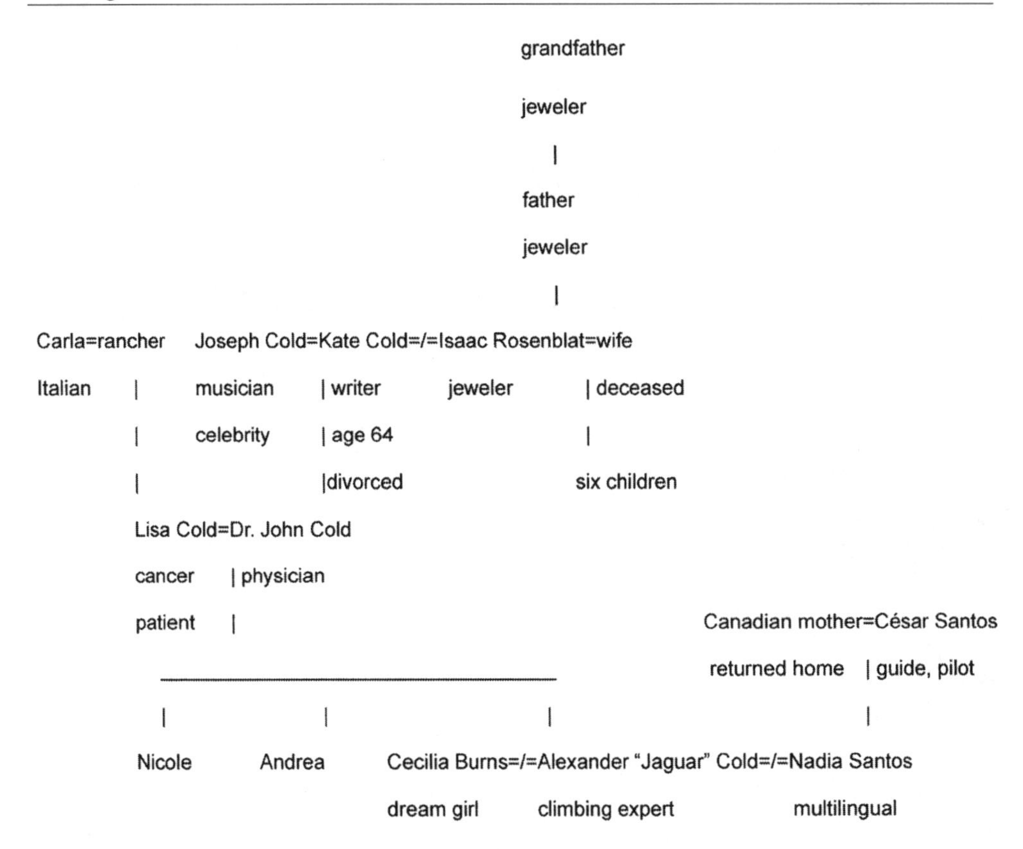

coming of age

In Allende's writings, rites of passage bear opportunities and choices that influence both present and future. At the foundation of character growth in her major novels, the author sets the parent/child relationship as the basis for identity, a pairing paralleled by the psychic tethering of Allende to her mother in *Paula*. The author explains how she learned female roles: "My mother and I were the only females, along with the maidservants who were females and who were serving everybody else. That was the model I had" (Rodden, 2011, 190). She accounts for the familial yoking: Francisca Llona Barros "is the longest love affair of my life. We have never cut the umbilical cord" (O'Reilly, 2010, 48).

The long-lived relationship influences the author's fictional families, including Téte's devotion to daughter Rosette in *Island Beneath the Sea* and the daughter-in-law/mother-in-law camaraderie in *Portrait in Sepia*. In the latter, Aurora del Valle experiences a "volcanic transformation" from childhood (Allende 20021, 179). In her apprenticeship as a newlywed, she observes in her mother-in-law, Doña Elvira Domínguez, the traits that sustain a family: "as ethereal as an angel ... a simple woman, pure goodness and will to serve, [a] transparent soul" (*ibid.*, 239, 242). The model materfamilias has a calming effect on Aurora, who must make serious evaluations of marriage and correct her romantic view of intimacy and domesticity. To rid herself of a loveless marriage doomed by her husband Diego's concealment of adultery with his sister-in-law Susana and complete her maturation, Aurora seeks self-expression through photography, a learning experience that looks beyond social posturing to genuine feelings and loyalties more important than the fakery of a happy union with Diego.

As in Rudolfo Anaya's *Bless Me, Ultima*, Piri Thomas's *Down These Mean Streets*, and Sylvia Lopez-Medina's *Cantora*, adolescence perplexes Allende's characters with temptations and decisions beyond the experience and wisdom of youth, as dramatized in *Zorro* by White Owl's initiation of Diego and Bernardo into the meaning of sacred power symbols. By approaching a numinous presence with good intentions, White Owl explains that the "body opens to receive blessing; that is the only way to prepare yourself for *okahué* ... the five basic virtues: honor, justice, respect, dignity, and courage" (Allende, 2005, 37, 38). Critic Karen R. Tolchin notes that Allende presents young characters like Bernardo and Diego with "substantive concerns" that can be "political, social, moral, or ethical in nature," for example, attitudes toward patriotism and the powers of the church, two entwined themes in *The House of the Spirits* and *Of Love and Shadows* and contributing factors to dilemmas in *Portrait in Sepia* (Tolchin, 2007, 15).

Among the memorable coming-of-age narratives, the story "Wicked Girl," a fable of domestic realism in the same mode as Gish Jen's "Fish Cheeks" and Jamaica Kincaid's "Girl," dramatizes recognizable phases of puberty, particularly what Joyce Carol Oates calls "a revelation of the 'insupportable longing' of sexual infatuation — and its eventual denouement" (Berliner and Oates, 2000, x). In Allende's own growing up, as she describes in *Paula*, Chilean women lived under a culture of silence and had limited knowledge of sex education and contraception, although "the age of The Pill arrives in time for me" (Allende, 1995, 15). She recalls, "I was paralyzed by fear of the consequences of sex; nothing cools one off like the threat of an unwanted pregnancy" (*ibid.*, 103).

Maturity and Social Conventions

As models of normal maturation, Allende grasps, outlines, and contextualizes the metaphors and traditional codes of puberty. Her *House of the Spirits* trilogy makes sense of the embodiments of feminism and gendered thinking for young Latinas of the late nineteenth through early twentieth centuries. Critic Janet McCain notes that the trio of novels "shares the theme of women's special gifts and abilities within a violent society run by men" (McCann, 2010). As proof of the empathies incubating in teenage females, Allende catalogs the sexual awakening and fornication of Blanca with Pedro Tercero and Alba with Miguel in *The House of the Spirits* and of Eliza Sommers with Joaquín Andrieta in *Daughter of Fortune*. In each case, the girls conceive and weigh the options for an unwed mother and illegitimate child in an era when traditional wedlock remains the norm, especially for the upper class. Throughout Eliza's lengthy search for Joaquín, she clings to love letters, a conventional affirmation to the forsaken partner, as "irrefutable proof that their delirious love was not an invention of her adolescent imagination" (Allende, 1999, 108). As evidence that Eliza outgrows infatuation during a fruitless quest to restore youthful love, she declares herself free of her illusions about Joaquín.

Beyond the usual rites of passage, Allende's the enlightenment of innocence in Irene Beltrán in *Of Love and Shadows* characterizes the late blooming of a professional woman. An untried journalist from the privileged class reared under patriarchal values, Irene tackles moral shifts brought about by modern socialist thought amid urban conflicts between peons and the ruling class. For Irene, the post-puberty education gained in her career on a slick magazine forces her to look subsurface for the reality of peasant life in a tyrannized country, a fictional version of Chile under the Pinochet dictatorship. In her final view of the motherland as she retreats into exile, she expresses a mature political consciousness and grieves wholeheartedly for all classes of citizens, not just the elite. With renewed perceptions, she recognizes the status of "the tortured, the dead, the wretched, poor, the rich who were profiting from the nation as if it were just another business" (Allende, 1987, 254).

The normal stages of growth and emotional blossoming make a fuller appearance in *Eva Luna*, in which the main character progresses from conception and birth to a complex adulthood reflecting the whole range of maturation. Coinciding with the issues of mother loss and child labor, the text pictures the coming of age of filmmaker Rolf Carlé, a teenager growing up under domestic duress under the Nazi regime of World War II. At crucial points in his grasp of adult reality, Rolf witnesses the humiliation of his mother by her fiendish husband Lukas and the father's eventual hanging by defiant students. The pall of dysfunction clings to Rolf throughout his career in photojournalism until he leads an attempt to rescue Azucena, a dying child in "And of Clay Are We Created," which concludes Rolf's character analysis with a test of compassion and acceptance of death. With adult comprehension, he recognizes the purpose of his risky job, "an exercise of courage, training by day to conquer the monsters that tormented him by night" (Allende, 1991, 328).

Attaining Resilience

More specific to the quests and concerns of youth at the edge of adulthood, like Esmeralda Santiago's immigration conventions in *When I Was Puerto Rican*, Carmen Deedy's *Growing Up Cuban*, and Andrés Wood's film *Machuca*, Allende's literary novel *The Infinite Plan* and a trio of El Dorado–style adventures stories—*City of the Beasts*, *Forest of the Pygmies*, and *Kingdom of the Golden Dragon*—interweave realism and contemporary politics with survival lore. For Judy Reeves in *The Infinite Plan*, an experimental novel, the onset of womanhood changes her from a lovely, docile girl into a "sea lion" clothed in menswear, "her hair cut like a jailbird" (Allende, 1993, 68). For most of young womanhood, Judy internalizes the rage and despair generated by the pedophiliac gropings of her father, Charles Reeves. Simultaneously, her brother Greg flounders in a welter of strutting gangbangers and alluring Chicanas, his contemporaries in a Los Angeles barrio. His daily skirmishes thrust him into new routes to avoid the ambush of the Martínez gang and introduce him to methods of seducing girls.

Allende texturizes the narrative with quasi-comic dodgings and grapplings, the ongoing saga of a boy shoving his way into manhood, much as Alex forces his way in the Amazonian tunnel. In both cases, the siblings, Judy and Greg Reeves, reach maturity only partially equipped for adult decisions. The absence of nurturing parents leaves Judy longing for maternal outlets and Greg vulnerable to false notions of how husband and wife establish a family. Because of inadequate parenting, Greg Reeves nests in an adopted family, a transition that requires acquisition of Latino culture and language. Allende illustrates how faulty socialization sloshes over into the lives of Greg's addicted daughter Margaret and hyperactive son David, both of whom fight their own coming-of-age battles without adequate family guidance. Like the origin stories in Genesis about family miscalculations by Isaac and Jacob, Greg must learn through frustration and loss how to compensate for substandard preparation for fatherhood. His friend Carmen offers worthy advice: "I suggest that you enter therapy yourself.... If you don't correct your own problems, you won't be able to help your son" (Allende, 1993, 325).

For her young adult trilogy, Allende dramatizes the joys and foibles of the immature, especially those under the influence of hormones. For mountain climber Alexander Cold, tests of courage and problem solving provide the hands-on necessities of a full education much as they did for Judy and Greg Reeves. For Alex Cold, "adolescence was the pits ... a hurricane inside" (Allende, 2002, 132). After destroying the tokens of childhood, he pays for his lack of self-control by accepting the quasi-parentage of Grandmother Kate, a dour eccentric. On the bus from the New York airport, he credits himself with skill at the flute and mountain climbing and with the sense to refuse alcohol, drugs, and marijuana. On the long boat ride through Amazon territory, he observes the bodies of Nadya, Omayra Torres, and Grandmother Kate and realizes that females appeal to the eye at different stages "each in her own way" (*ibid.*, 133). The conclusion suggests maturity in Alex as he completes a jungle journey among strangers and re-evaluates the character of the three women who impact his first adventure away from home and country.

To introduce the supernatural, Allende falls back on a Gothic convention, the intuitive power over evil of children at the threshold of adulthood. For Nadia, proof of womanhood begins with the passive acceptance of menarche. First blood evidences her arrival into womanhood and her magical powers to "make people," a reproductive capability that fosters the divine in the eternal female (Allende, 2002, 232). For Alex, coming of age requires passing tests of manhood. As the author explains, "the body has to experience certain things that are important for the soul" (Rodden, 2011, 185). The summoning of inner reserves enables him to prove to male villagers that he controls inborn potencies and that he can draw on manly strengths to withstand the pain of ant stings on his left arm. Surprisingly, Alex also finds himself clairvoyant, a quality that enables him to visit his mother in Texas through spiritual telepathy, a connection with maternity that sustains him in a foreign land.

Multiple tasks require of Alex the maturation of boys from the People from the Mist and demand that he search for a cure for Lisa's illness. By contrasting esoteric challenges with real confrontations, Allende retains command of the framework narrative and the conflict within Alex concerning the possible death of a parent. Alex quickly surmises that, because of destruction in the Amazon forest and threats to the survival of aborigines of the First World, he has to improvise, since "the rules he was used to didn't count ... in the hazy territory of dreams, intuition, and magic" (Allende, 2002, 279). Part of his efficacy as a leader involves the formal acceptance of manhood, which requires a primitive ritual—the metaphoric death of boyhood followed by birth into adulthood. Allende deepens the challenge to Alex's world view in the tunnel to the fountain, a tight, hot encasement symbolizing emergence from the birth canal into individuality.

Alex's rapid acceptance of adult responsibilities begins with his efforts to atone for a childish misstep. As his home life returns to normal, he works in a pizzeria and gives music lessons to fund a restoration of the room decor that he smashes in a fit of frustration. Wisely, his grandmother maneuvers him into accompanying her to the Himalayas, which he has researched. Only six months after his first adventure, in *Kingdom of the Golden Dragon*, he recognizes growth in himself in the form of self-confidence and emotional control. The change in Alex parallels the demands on Dil Bahadur, the prince who studies under the guru Tensing before assuming the throne of Dil's father, King Dorji. At the pivotal moment when monarchy requires a change of command, Tensing realizes that character must emerge from a worthy pupil: "All the training in the world" was wasted unless Dil "proved to have superior intelligence and a spotless heart" (Allende, 2004, 72). The teamwork of Alex and Dil concludes the novel with a satisfying symbiosis that introduces Dil to the technological wizardry of a Global Positioning System and to the sobering challenge of bidding farewell to his father and accepting the rule of the Forbidden Kingdom.

The maturation motif intensifies in *Forest of the Pygmies* as Nadia reaches age fifteen and Alexander, eighteen. In emails, the pair ponders the "torment of growing up," a shared anxiety that they discuss via coded messages (Allende, 2005, 6). In a single paragraph, Allende accounts for Alex's teen angst as "hormonal explosions of adolescence" that bedevil him, causing restlessness, boredom, depression, and a lack of concentration, the normal symptoms of late puberty that make "his body ... his enemy" (*ibid.*, 197). His retreat into vigorous surfing and to dreams of majoring in holistic medicine precedes the possibility of marrying Nadia, a more practical choice of wife than the trivial-minded Cecilia Burns, Alex's first fantasy girlfriend. Thoughts of intimacy with his best friend loom more dangerously in Alex's mind than fear of overcoming King Kosongo, Commandant Maurice Mbembelé, and the sorcerer Sombe. Qualms at the transition from friend to lover predict that Alex will follow a natural arc toward loving mate and future father.

- *References and Further Reading*

Berliner, Janet, and Joyce Carol Oates. *Snapshots: 20th Century Mother-Daughter Fiction*. Boston: David R. Godine, 2000.
McCann, Janet. *Critical Survey of Long Fiction*. 4th ed. New York: Salem, 2010.
O'Reilly, Andrea. *Encyclopedia of Motherhood*. Thousand Oaks, CA: Sage, 2010.
Rodden, John. *Critical Insights: Isabel Allende*. Pasadena, CA: Salem, 2011.
Tolchin, Karen R. *Part Blood, Part Ketchup: Coming of Age in American Literature and Film*. Lanham, MD: Lexington, 2007.

confinement

Episodes of confinement afflict Allende's characters, offering them periods of safety and contemplation as well as obstacles to personal liberty and intellectual curiosity. Restraint takes the form of the rainforest canopy that restricts a view of the Brazilian sun in *City of the Beasts*, the corridors of the Red Fort and the social immurement of castes in India in *Kingdom of the Golden Dragon*, and the "visceral terror" that engulfs photojournalist Rolf Carlé on viewing Avucena's submergence in mud in "And of Clay Are We Created" (Allende, 1991, 327). While Rolf guards and distracts the dying thirteen-year-old with stories and Austrian folk songs, the lethal muck reveals to Rolf his own conflicted memories of his retarded sister, Katherina Carlé, hiding under a table from their father's rages. Rolf views himself "trapped in a pit without escape, buried in life, his head barely above ground," still fighting the darkness of the armoire in which his father once locked him (*ibid.*). Through the assignment to report the news of Azucena's burial by a volcanic mudslide, Rolf achieves catharsis and a coming to knowledge of his subconscious burdens. The ironic twist — the serendipity of a rescuer gaining self-knowledge from a doomed child — unleashes an unnamable "sweet, sad emotion" generated by pity and frustration at an unfeeling bureaucracy. With a compassion born of shared ordeal, he accepts death that receives Azucena like "a flower in the mud" (*ibid.*, 330, 331).

Allende fuses compound confinements in *The House of the Spirits*. An architectural hodgepodge as rampant as the title edifice in "Phantom Palace," the iconic del Valle-Trueba residence morphs into a maze of "extra little rooms, staircases, turrets and terraces" that conceals from the public the doghouses, stable, chicken coops, and staff quarters out back (Allende, 1985, 224). Built in the capital's High District, the circuitous halls and additions symbolize the ins and outs of history and the dark corners of political intrigue that foreground the coming revolt. Analyst Susan R. Frick notes that Esteban Trueba's breach with his wife Clara by slapping her for revealing his sexual sins results in his social, connubial, and spatial confinement in a small portion of the mansion. Just as Tránsito Soto predicts, Esteban enters a period of isolation and loneliness that shrivels his soul while the del Valle women "invent a place and time alternative to male history and use that female creation in order to survive" (Frick, 2001, 40). As Esteban shrinks, Clara and Amanda superintend the birth of Alba, a mestizo tier to the family tree sired by an indigenous father, Pedro Tercero García, the beginning of a blended aristocratic and peon heritage in the del Valle-Trueba line.

The author depicts Esteban's misperception of space allotment as a foretokening of his personal and political downfall. The demarcation of male from female space parallels the demographics of "the conservatives he represents [who] oversee only a tiny percentage of the population politically" (Frick, 2001, 33). Esteban retreats to the library, where he plots with the conservative party and releases rage, frustrations, and sorrow at unpredictable election outcomes. In contrast, Clara, "and not Esteban, fills the niches and crevices of the house, haunting his space with spirits," beneficent presences summoned by empathetic females (*ibid.*). As Clara and her specters enjoy free range over a trove of "the magic books from Uncle Marcos's enchanted trunks and other treasures" in the basement and living area, they welcome truths from the past as well as the living refugees and political activists who engineer revolt (*ibid.*, 115). By making the most of her realm, Clara defeats patriarchy while freeing herself to drift unmolested in the phantom realm, the existence that awaits her in death.

Outwardly, the heroic style of Esteban's dwelling appears as formidable and stable as the Sommers mansion in *Daughter of Fortune* and Paulina del Valle's San Francisco home in *Portrait in Sepia*. Invisible to the public, the architecture of the Trueba compound lapses into gradual disrepair and erosion, a symbol of the stodgy status quo that the female del Valles, like a colony of termites, undermine from within. Because of domestic decline after Clara's death, Esteban further contracts his living quarters to the library and bedroom, a shrinking residency commensurate with his diminishing self-image. He admits that his sister's "curse came true and I began to shrink" (Allende, 1985, 45). After the "infamous military pyre" that devours the house and its rambling trove of exotica, in a triumph of the spiritual over the material, only the truths of Clara's ribbon-bound notebooks survive their years of confinement to a male realm (*ibid.*, 36).

Analyst Margaret McKale describes how Allende's recreation of terror allows the reader to absorb complex, intuitive, and nonverbal understandings of the Pinochet regime and to profit from "instructive emotion ... from the illusion of suffering an experience not his own" (McKale, 2002, 93). For Alba, jailing under a tyrannical police regime forces her to determine whether life is worth living under extreme internment by a madman. In the doghouse, she cowers in a "small, sealed cell like a dark, frozen, airless tomb," a Gothic chamber suggesting premature burial (Allende, 1985, 466). By communing with the wraith of her deceased grandmother Clara, Alba taps into the wealth of spiritual wisdom accruing in a strong matriarchy. In retreat from the vengeance of Colonel Esteban García, Alba finds in Clara's spiritual visitation the bulwark and "sure refuge" she had known all her life (*ibid.*, 321).

The immurement of Alba in authoritarian detention generates a phobia that destroys her visits to the zoo. In sympathy with the animals, she weeps at the "horror of enclosures, walls, cages, and isolation," a hint at the torture she survives in adulthood under Esteban García's torments (Allende, 1985, 317). The author inserts a witty mirroring of Alba's fear in her mother's courtship by the "King of the Pressure Cookers," a Jewish survivor of a concentration camp who drives a tiny car (*ibid.*). Less entertaining looms Alba's knowledge that the cook drowns unwanted kittens in pails of water. In the novel's resolution, the confinement to quarters that saddens Trueba provides shelter for his old enemy, Pedro Tercero, who hides in an empty room, a suggestion of the solitary existence in ungratifying fame as a radio star that keeps Pedro from a full life with Blanca.

Extending Allende's condemnation of the Pinochet regime, the grisly events in *Of Love and Shadows* move beyond Alba's experience in Esteban's fetid lockup to the entombment of victims of the Political Police. Allende creates Irene Beltrán, a character much like herself during her journalistic career, to search out and accuse the death squads that murder the *desaparecidos*. Depiction of the defunct Los Riscos mine introduces shredded garments on skeletons and the reek of decaying flesh from "the Vesuvius of piled-up bones, hair, and tattered cloth" (Allende, 1987, 225). The discovery carries to completion the viewing of corpses "contained in the refrigerated units" in the morgue to the ignoble dumping of remains in a tunnel, a confinement intended to conceal the regime's secret executions (*ibid.*, 116). Metaphorically, the opening of the tunnel opens Irene's mind and career to more than fashion models and hair styles by revealing the sufferings of people who have no sanctuary.

Controls and Concealment

For the title figure in *Eva Luna*, jobs equate with boundaries and containment of her natural exuberance. As helper to a maid, Eva ranges no farther than the garden, where sounds from the street cause her mind to wander from work. Living in La Señora's apartment proves as restrictive as Eva's labor for the *patrona*. As a companion to Zulema Halabí, Eva enjoys welcome in the rural community of Agua Santa, a metaphorical free zone in which she can blossom in a house with "many doors" where "doors were always open" (Allende, 1987, 144, 151). The Tableaux Vivants of Christmas and events in the public square for St. John's Day, Annunciation, and the crowning of the village queen delight Eva, revealing a "happy, defiant, mingling with the others, rejoicing" in a belonging devoid of curbs on her imagination (Allende, 1987, 151). In addition to free association, Eva learns the everyday mathematics of shopkeeping and the euphoria of literacy, a true freeing of the mind and spirit.

Unlike the elation of Eva's birth and childhood, the confinements in *Daughter of Fortune* begin with the recovery of an infant from a soap crate and reach dramatic irony in the deflowering of Eliza Sommers in a stash of "mirrors, furniture, and draperies" in a storage room, a complex image of reflection, accommodation, and concealment (Allende, 1999, 87). Choosing the lot of the stowaway to follow her lover, she elects to sail north to San Francisco on the brigantine *Emilia* hidden among the ship's stores, which resonate with the secrecy and illusions wrought by teenage coitus amid "flowered cretonne draperies" (*ibid.*, 111). Her narrow world parallels that of Tao Chi'en, an herbalist who initiates the healer's trade while living in a garret measuring one by three meters and who survives in airless ship's quarters allotted to Chinese and Africans, a metaphor for the social smothering of nonwhites. While Tao treats Eliza for nausea and blood loss, the limited space robs her of modesty and any other choice of medical care. The space dims Eliza's visions of motherhood while providing a suitable birthing chamber for her stillborn child.

During the 1891 Civil War in *Portrait in Sepia*, the third novel in the *House of the Spirits* triad, Allende returns to the trope of the cooped-up female. Paulina's mansion in Santiago, ostensibly protected by a British ensign on the roof, shelters liberals from the predations of state torturer Joaquín Godoy. The extent of house-to-house searches for dissidents discloses the secret printing press that Don Pedro Tey, Señorita Matilde Pineda, and Nívea del Valle operate to spread anti-government "lampoons and revolutionary pamphlets" satirizing the fraudulent President José Manuel Balmaceda, who crushes the congress (Allende, 2001, 158). In one of the numerous enclosed scenarios in Allende's works, the characters realize that printing operations and propaganda dissemination from under Señorita Pineda's cape must end and the family disperse to protect the household from mass arrest. The decision elucidates critic Clarence Major's discussion of ambiguity and irony in Allende's presentation of secrets that "sometimes link people or generations" and sometimes "break such human ties" (Major, 2001, 178).

Significantly, emergence from sequestering introduces a clearer view of government corruption. The dispersal of the subversive cell forces the family to evaluate loyalties to clan and nation and the burden of what critic María Inés Lagos calls "gender-based repression" (Lagos, 2002). In a country villa, characters retreat from the urban maelstrom and reflect on the causes and outcomes of civil unrest. Aurora, at age 11, uses rural confinement as an opportunity to study adult females and the rigors of Nívea's pregnancy and birthing, a necessary freeing of Aurora's curiosity to observe womanhood at close range. For the occasion, Aurora "was crouched in a corner of the hall, trembling with terror" at the initiation rite (Allende, 2001, 167). Upon return to Santiago, Nívea rejects the notion of confinement during pregnancy and exhibits "her bulging womb like a shameless country woman" (*ibid.*, 172). The bold maternal gesture illustrates Nívea's rebellion against traditional coercion and the concealment of the facts of parturition from young girls as tender and uninformed as Aurora.

Historical Confinements

Allende applies to *The Infinite Plan* a similar study of male chafing at social and institutional confines, beginning with the coming of age of Greg Reeves in a Latino barrio, where he contends with "differences of race and custom" (Allende, 1993, 23). As an army reserve officer during the Vietnam War, he affirms "my friends, my brothers, all united in the same desperate fraternity," but regrets the merger of "blacks and poor whites, country boys, boys from small towns, from the worst barrios" in doomed combat (*ibid.*, 183, 191). During the "national nightmare," he frets at his body's betrayal (*ibid.*, 252). The period of rehabilitation in Hawaii enables him to reevaluate the daily retreat into marijuana and drugs for stamina during hazardous patrols and firefights. At home, he celebrates liberation from the military with a bonfire of photos, letters, tapes, uniforms, and a medal for bravery. Unfortunately, he requires a second confinement from near nervous collapse and alcoholic bingeing and a lengthy psychiatric treatment to retrain himself to enjoy freedom of choice.

In her later works, Allende focuses on the confinement of slavery, a controlling theme in *Island Beneath the Sea* and *Forest of the Pygmies.* Colonial confinement on Caribbean sugar plantations in *Island Beneath the Sea* immures slaves out of the public eye under the whip of men like overseer Prosper Cambray. In solitude at the island retreat, Tété, the female protagonist, superintends housekeeping, the nursing of Eugenia, and child care of Maurice, the presumptive heir to Habitation Saint-Lazare. Tété endures isolation from the cane fields in concubinage to the master, Toulouse Valmorain. He makes an effort to conceal sexual depravity from his wife Eugenia, the crazed plantation mistress—to "hide from her what was happening in her own house," where Tété went "every time he wished"

(Allende, 2010, 96, 131). Outside the house, Cambray earns his keep as a slave catcher, "the thankless task of capturing Negroes in that wild geography of hostile jungles and steep mountains" with the aid of dog packs (*ibid.*, 46). The women he immures in his hammock, where "he could fornicate at will," a sexual enslavement that double compromises African females (*ibid.*, 115).

A public exposé of the secrets of bondage and the Code Noir ignite Haiti and much of France and the Caribbean in a frenzy of conflict over colonial greed and inhumanity perpetrated under the cloak of European refinement and gentility. During the Haitian Revolution of 1791, at the fall of the last compound, liberation for Tété begins with "glass breaking in the windows of the first floor," a symbolic opening of eyes to the hidden depravity of whites (Allende, 2010, 222). The torching of the Lacroix and Valmorain estates frees slaves from restraint and leaves the manager Cambray no choice. Immured behind debris in the storage room at the height of Maroon rebellion, he shoots himself through the mouth, creating a paradox of his given name and the hellish immurement he superintends for black field laborers.

Some critics express dismay that the vivid action of *Island Beneath the Sea* shifts in the second half to drawing room concerns. Socio-economic taboos extend the immurement of slavery into a period of partial freedom in New Orleans, where slavery remains legal until the Emancipation Proclamation on January 1, 1863. In the interim preceding the Louisiana Purchase of 1803, mulattas amid the self-absorbed Creole society build a lifestyle based on the bedroom freedoms of sexuality. To ensure the liberation of daughters from the shame of slave-time concubinage, biracial mothers support Violette Boisier in the foundation of the *Bal de Cordon Bleu*, a form of social insurance that pits the lust of white youths against the allure of quadroon girls trained in good grooming and seduction. Nonetheless, the illicit bargain again frames female lives in a confinement fenced by white wealth, racial convention, and sexual compromise.

• *References and Further Reading*

Frick, Susan R. "Memory and Retelling: The Role of Women in *La casa de los espíritus*," *Journal of Iberian and Latin American Studies* 7:1 (June 2001): 27–41.

Lagos, María Inés. "Female Voices from the Borderlands: Isabel Allende's *Paula* and *Retrato en Sepia*," *Latin American Literary Review* 30:60 (2002): 112–127.

Major, Clarence. *Necessary Distance: Essays and Criticism*. Minneapolis: Coffee House Press, 2001.

Vidimos, Robin. "Slave Uprising in Colonial Haiti at Heart of Isabel Allende's Latest," *Denver Post* (2 May 2010).

costume

Allende's knowledge of wrappings of the human form add intrigue and enticement to narratives, as with the masked holiday outfits and the henna that decorates Nadia's hand in *Kingdom of the Golden Dragon*, the pilot's cornrows and the herbalist's dusty dreadlocks in *Forest of the Pygmies*, and the kohl-darkened eyes of Indian women, the lust of Solomon for the brilliantly arrayed Sheba, and the swish of hippies' long skirts in *Aphrodite*. For the sake of multicultural contrasts within aristocratic New Orleans, in *Island Beneath the Sea*, the author depicts the slaves' sweaty wigs and the wrist and ankle shells that Tété wears to dance to the drums. Coordination of outfits with the times requires the investigative research Allende learned from journalism and from interviewing people. From authentic data she creates the tattooed Domingo Toro and the ostentatious outfits of social climber Abigail McGovern in "The Proper Respect" and the sedate European dress of an immigrant couple, Ana and Roberto Blaum, in the poignant story "Interminable Life." In both narratives, costume cloaks an unrest that belies the prestige of fashionable dress and surroundings.

In her first novel, *The House of the Spirits*, Allende chooses chaste nightdresses for female garments indicating purity and integrity, the traits that protagonist Clara del Valle maintains even as a spirit. In childhood, Clara observes the investiture of her sister Rosa's autopsied body in a maidenly gown appropriate to her virginal state. The use of simple undyed garments for Clara's attire and for Férula's departure from Las Tres Marías dramatizes the women's roles as unaffected instruments of truth and beneficence in a hacienda tricked out in refined European furnishings, the trappings of Esteban's bid for social approval. From his pretentious perspective, his sister's simple raiment represents both an emotional disjuncture and a shroud, evidence of the banishment of Férula from his life as though she had died. To seduce Clara, Esteban dons a "plush ecclesiastic dressing gown" which "she never seemed to notice," a disregard in keeping with Clara's rejection of the pomposity of the elite (Allende, 1985, 207).

In subsequent scenes, Allende stresses outfits as evidence of states of mind. Upon reunion with her sister-in-law, Clara observes a Gothic hoard of "inexplicable admirals' jackets and bishops' chasubles" hanging amid outdated dresses and hats, rhinestoned finery, makeup, purses, and wigs, "all thrown together in grotesque fraternity" (Allende, 1985, 175). Within the abysmal slum apartment, Férula lies in make-do splendor like "an Austrian queen," her face at peace with a sweetness lacking during her miserable residence with Esteban's family (*ibid.*, 178). As Clara prepares the body for interment, she discloses a nearly bald head and honors the pathetic body with powder and cologne before choosing "eccentric and elegant rags" for the laying out of a beloved friend (*ibid.*, 179). The bag lady attire attests to the garbage that Férula combs for additions to her wardrobe and a life of self-denial among the poor.

Disguise takes on a beneficence in later episodes during the love affair of Pedro Tercero and Blanca, the daughter of Esteban, Pedro's *patrón*. Under pain of death, Pedro dons countrified garb that conceals his presence at Las Trés Marías. From a tinsman selling pots and pans to a postman's uniform, preacher's attire, a Jesuit priest's cassock, and the guise of a gypsy, Pedro bobs up in Blanca's presence, his piercing black eyes unconcealed by shaggy eyebrows, hair, and beard. For political symbolism, he wears canvas pants, wool poncho, and homemade sandals, an appropriate garb to pair with Blanca's "whorish underwear" for their unconventional courtship (Allende, 1985, 356). Peasants so rely on Pedro's messages of hope that women make him ponchos and socks. Pedro Segundo, torn between love and fear for his son, admires the spunk that frees Pedro Tercero of the peasant's unending cycle of subservience.

The loss of luster to the del Valle-Trueba clan worsens after the death of Clara, the controller of domestic affairs. To prevent taking money from Esteban, Blanca whittles at the family budget and fights the signs of aging with applications of Harem Cream, a subtextual dig at her celibate lifestyle. In a chill house, she sleeps in a hand-knitted gloves and a "novitiate's nightgown," an echo of her aunt Rosa's burial clothes (Allende, 1985, 347). For day wear, she allots herself "an apron and cloth sandals," the attire of servants on a par with Pedro's social status (*ibid.*, 346). Their daughter Alba, as unimpressed with aristocratic dress as her mother and grandmother, presents a motley appearance in her cousins' hand-me-downs. In a prophetic scene, the intrusion of police at a university sit-in reminds Alba of the repulsive Colonel Esteban García, who appears in a green uniform, a costume she relates to a green beast, an outgrowth of the jungly countryside that houses his family.

Unlike his liberal daughter and granddaughter, Esteban shuffles about in ecclesiastical bathrobe and slippers by night while dressing for public appearances in an uncompromising black that echoes his unyielding conservatism. On his visit to the Christopher Columbus "cooperative of prostitutes and homosexuals," the clownish majordomo dressed in Turkish slippers and turban presents a catalog of prostitutes decked in the costumes of amazons, madams, nuns, and nymphs, a handy advertising gimmick and a sop to clients who require fantasy to quicken withered loins (Allende, 1985, 357). After Tránsito arranges Alba's freedom, Alba departs a world of grimly uniformed guards, leaving behind a woolen sweater for female prisoners to "unravel it and knit something warm," a subtle expression of women's ability to transform and renew (*ibid.*, 485). Reunited with her beloved grandfather, Alba, wrapped in a blanket by a female rescuer, observes that Esteban retains the appearance of a grandee with "his leonine white mane and his heavy silver cane," a dignified pose that he maintains into his ninetieth year (*ibid.*, 480). Although he grooms himself in the semblance of the landed gentry, his change of heart enables him to aid the flight of his granddaughter and Miguel to freedom.

The contrast in costume continues in *Of Love and Shadows*. Allende outfits her peasant families in cast-offs and sweaters knitted from raveled and recycled yarn with the same pragmatism as the female prisoners in *House of the Spirits*. In peasant style, Hipólito Ranquileo makes espadrilles for his children. A more revealing role of costume occurs in the shift of journalist Irene Beltrán from romantic peasant skirts, loose hairstyle, and tingling brass and copper bangles to a single braid and khaki pants, evidence of her loss of innocence and somber mind-set as she shifts from outfitting fashion models to researching the story of a *desaparecida*, Evangelina Ranquileo. The austere dress becomes a necessity for Irene's climb to Pradelio's mountain hideout and forays into the burial tunnels of the Los Riscos mine. A series of disguises during her flight with Francisco from the Political Police contributes to the aura of spying and intrigue and to the change of residence from Latin America to the couple's new home and conjugal contentment in Spain.

The effect of theatrical costuming in *Daughter of Fortune* guides the destiny of Rose Sommers, who gains her first backstage experience at the London opera. In the clutches of tenor Karl Bretzner, she allows the unbuttoning of her bodice and removal of white stockings, embroidered garters, and kid-skin boots, the dainties of a virgin. Amid worldly "brocades, feathers, velvets, and faded laces," Rose enjoys the fantasy of love for its brief duration, then immures herself in reality during her family's retreat from scandal to Valparaíso, Chile (Allende, 1999, 93). The hasty migration, however, serves only surface needs until family disorder over Eliza's pregnancy and flight destroys the illusion of British refinement and social conformity. The result, in the words of critic Ana Patricia Rodríguez, immerses the Sommers clan in "the melting pot, social uplifting, individual remaking, and cultural hybridization" (Farr and Harker, 2008, 206).

During the realignment of the Sommers clan with reality, Allende turns costume into the elements of self-invention. Rose, tainted by the perils of sexuality, protects her daughter from the raffish life. Elegance conferred by "blue velvet, white high-button shoes, and a bonnet embroidered with flowers" propels Eliza from orphanhood to the bosom of English aristocrats (Allende, 1999, 29). Even the myth of her abandonment insists that the babe came to the Sommers residence in a basket topped by batiste sheets "edged with brussels lace" and a mink coverlet (*ibid.*, 4). Rose, Eliza's adoptive mother, maintains the English mania for porcelain skin and avoids the Spanish black mantle in favor of bonnets and capes. Trained in piano, French, ballroom dance, and embroidery, Eliza grows up in princess attire — a dress that covers batiste camisoles, whalebone corset, and starched petticoats, an extended image that creates the illusion of a slim waistline, which an unplanned pregnancy threatens. Rose loses her battle for Eliza's innocence, which the teen-ager surrenders in a storage room for hats, clothing, and "flowered cretonne draperies" as florid as Eliza's romantic ideal (*ibid.*, 111).

In impressionistic glimpses, clothing identifies the provenance and degree of prosperity in the characters who flock to San Francisco, as with the conical *maulino* hats of Chileans. Allende chooses for herbalist Tao Chi'en a muslin smock over short trousers, a cloth sash and slippers, and straw hat above a trailing queue, a hairstyle emblematic of the Han Chinese during the Qing dynasty. Mama Fresia, endowed with foresight, packs for Eliza stout boots and a wool mantle, items geared to hardships that materialize in Sacramento. The prostitutes aboard the brigantine *Emilia* shuck their "whoring clothes" and retreat into plain shirts and blouses to remind sailors that the women abjure their trade for the passage to California (Allende, 1999, 209). The dream of Azucena Placeres to earn a fortune and return with a queen's wardrobe and "one gold tooth" epitomizes the stir of gold fever, especially among marginalized women (*ibid.*, 215). Upon arrival at her destination, she chooses a feathered blue V-necked gown, turquoise brooch, and hat to display her wares. Because of tightened accountability at dockside, Eliza emerges at the same time virtually invisible in smock, pants, and straw hat, her gender concealed and her security ensured by suppressing femininity and abandoning womanly garb.

Ironically, the costume of a poor Asian swabby posing as a deaf mute gives Eliza a freedom common to lowly males and a chance to savor coastal breezes without the bulwark of petticoats and corset, the epitome of Victorian womanhood. A subsequent shift of attire to miner's pants, shirt, and gloves introduces a new identity, Elías "Chile Boy" Andieta, a lad safe from the advances of lusty males in clothing suited to such camp dwellers as Joaquín Murieta and Three-Finger Jack. Analysts Reginald Dyck and Cheli Reutter characterize the Western gear as part of the "role and stature traditionally held by the cowboys of western fiction," the knockabout laborers who frequent ranch paddocks and cattle trails (Dyck and Reutter, 2009, 15). Around Eliza swarm a variety of costumes identifiable by nationality — Indians in military jackets, Chinese in quilted tops, Mexicans under sombreros, and the bouncer Babalú the Bad in scruffy wolf furs, pirate earrings, and Russian boots. Other cultural outfits link ponchos with South Americans, silk sashes with Hawaiians, and Jacob Todd with the stereotype of the garish Yankee in checkered suit, planter's hat, and snakeskin boots, the vulgar attire of the upstart.

Episodes call for frequent changes of costume, as with the myth of *bandito* Joaquín Murieta's black velvet and leather outfit and the gifts of housewifely dresses from Quakers after a fire destroys the gaudy frippery of Joe Bonecrusher's prostitute caravan. As the prostitutes attempt a recovery from penury and Joe's flagging interest in commerce, Eliza reunites with Tao Chi'en, an Americanized "celestial" who presents himself in short hair, severely tailored overcoat and top hat, glasses, and umbrella, the elements of British respectability that cloak his ethnicity (Allende, 1999, 334). The author states the loss of Tao's sacred queue as evidence he no longer wants to return to Hong Kong. The adoption of American costume also gives him "access to the world of the Americans" and a conservative air that Eliza connects with gravediggers (*ibid.*). The vast change in Tao Chi'en imparts the sacrifices of custom and dignity that Asians make to blend in with California's frontier society.

Adjustments to clothing mark the novel's denouement with character choices and coming to knowledge. For Rose Sommers, the loss of a daughter saps her usual interest in finery during times when she was "caught up in her own frivolities" (Allende, 1999, 378). Rose ceases to trim hats and neglects her brother, whose "shirts were badly ironed and his suits not brushed" (*ibid.*, 380). Her drab appearance in outmoded outfits befits the sorrow and regret of four years without Eliza. Simultaneous with Rose's search for Eliza, her daughter abandons male attire, which transforms her "into a strange, asexual creature" (*ibid.*, 387). She smartens up her suitcase of dresses by sending them to the laundry and, for a photo, resumes a female identity. After months of trickery and disguise, Eliza stands naked and explores the female treasure within, "confirming her desire to be a woman again," a realistic transformation that ends her unwieldy gender disguise (Allende, 1999, 393).

Allende gives costume a staged air in the extreme situations of *Eva Luna* in the generalized glamour of La Señora, one of the "women who moved like toreadors" and who outfits the bedraggled title character in full skirts, tight belts, and ballet slippers (Allende, 1987, 119). Huberto Naranjo, Eva's pseudo-sibling, returns her to innocence by buying little-girl frills, "baby-doll shoes, and little-girl pocketbooks" (*ibid.*, 111). The return of the Austrian deserter Lukas Carlé to his family creates immediate recognition of hardship in his dirty kerchief, worn jacket, and rags tied to his shoeless feet, a parallel to Eva's hardships as a storyteller on the streets. After Uncle Rupert establishes a Caribbean Eden, his two daughters dress German style in felt skirts and vests topped with aprons and stockings and ribbons in their hair, a visible recreation of Alpine frauleins for the entertainment of tourists. The least satisfying costumes, those that Melesio wears for cabaret performances as Mimí, make no progress in changing his gender by decking him in ostrich plumes, platform shoes, a blond wig, and glitter, the female getup that he identifies as "the best of himself" (*ibid.*, 128).

A source of humor and character delineation, the clothing of Paulina del Valle, the investment maven of *Portrait in Sepia*, fuses into a symbol of vanity and profusion. *Kirkus Reviews* finds the grandmother figure, "bejeweled and bedecked in fussy Victorian finery," all fascinatingly grotesque on an oversized matron ("Review," 2001). Central to the image, her "throne," a carved Florentine bed edged in mythic scenarios, recedes from her bedroom to the basement as Paulina herself loses steam in widowhood. The gradual wasting of flesh and fortune accompanies the inevitable decline of Paulina to old age and a stomach tumor and her gulling by a rapacious Catholic priest. As evidence of her disinterest in vanity, she "dressed any which way" and admits "I'm getting on," a hint at her acceptance of the compromises of advanced age (Allende 2001, 207, 216).

Allende's commentary on outfits segues from humor and whimsy into thematic indicators, as with the similarity of suits worn by a Cabinet Minister and his chauffeur in *Eva Luna* and the nudity and breechclouts of Indians in *City of the Beasts*, an indication of immodesty by the standards of insurgent whites. Allende's young adult trilogy continues the use of costume as a gauge of character and theme. The demands of clothing in the latter title contrasts citified needs with the Amazonian environment, with its sudden downpours and humidity and the attacks of mosquitoes and leeches. Wise jungle travelers choose cottons and tend to their feet, which suffer chafing from damp, shrinking leather boots. On a peaceful day, Alex and Nadia enjoy a swim following by body decoration with vegetal paint and the playing of children with beetles and butterflies on tethers. The adornment of women with fireflies, feathers, orchids, and picks through the lips seems normal in an Upper Orinoco setting, where singers and dancers imitate bestial mating rituals as an everyday part of village activity. The danger posed by Captain Ariosto grows in part from the "confidence bestowed by his uniform," an arrogance and privilege that reprises the menace of guards in *The House of the Spirits* and *Of Love and Shadows* and anticipates the palace security guard in *Kingdom of the Golden Dragon* (Allende, 2002, 359). By offsetting harmless adornments with authoritative posturing, Allende builds to a tense confrontation that ends with Ariosto's death and the freeing of natives from potential harm.

Similar to the old lady dignity of Paulina del Valle, the delineation of change in the title figure in *Inés of My Soul* begins with the mourning and heavy veil she chooses as a "widow of the Americas" (Allende, 2006, 15). In a New World setting, she finds that heavy underskirts, shawl, and dress shoes encumber her riding "a thousand leagues sidesaddle," a miserable posture inflicted on proper European women whom social dictates refuse to allow to ride astride (*ibid.*, 141). In old age, Inés Suarez pines most for her sword and coat of mail, the conquistador's outfit that enabled her to seize and dominate Chile. Upon her reunion with her former lover, General Pedro de Valdivia, she manipulates an uncomfortable social situation by ironing an elegant Spanish fashion of "iridescent coppery silk," a subtle gesture toward the skin tones of Chilean Indians (*ibid.*, 289). The dress fails to outclass the array of Cecilia in sky blue with a gold sash and Inca jewelry dramatized by a feather fan, the author's gesture toward the magnificence of an antique South American civilization.

In scenarios in *The Infinite Plan*, a shift in costume indicates deception, as with the change from Olga's workman's pants, undershirt, and cap for driving to Gypsy skirt, revealing blouse, jingly necklaces, and yellow boots for fortune telling. In the seer's garb, she advances to fake healing with herbs, amulets, and sugar pills and to pulling teeth, stitching wounds, and aborting fetuses, the multitasking expected of the *curandera*. Likewise out of place, Gregory Reeves abandons southern California wear to ingratiate himself with hippies and protesters at Berkeley. For Carmen Morales, the return to the flashy Chicana skirts of her girlhood in the Los Angeles barrio enhances her profession as jewelry maker among Spanish Gypsies. The shift in persona requires a new name, Tamar, which suits both her business and an emerging adult self, which balances business travel and commerce with her devotion to Dai, an adopted son.

In *Island Beneath the Sea*, the mulatta servant displays dignity and a sense of place in the washing and starching of her *tignon*, the emblem of black servitude that black females develop into a socio-economic diadem. Unlike Tété, the mulatta courtesan Violette Boisier earns her living by conjuring images of personal luxury and allure. Reviewer Gaiutra Bahadur noted that Allende "revels in period detail: ostrich-feathered hats, high-waisted gowns," the details that draw attention to Violette and away from her humble beginnings (Bahadur, 2010, 26). After soothing her skin and body with caramel depilatory, coconut milk, bath oil, and herbal tea, she slips on colorful silk and taffeta tunics, slippers, jewels, beaded turbans, plumes, scarves, and furs, the froufrou of the demimonde. Reviewer Marcela Valdes refers to the treatments, interior decor, and personal baubles as "Cosmo elements" that set Violette apart from black slaves and elite whites (Valdes, 2010). Violette's competition, Eugenia García del Solar, wife of Toulouse Valmorain, degenerates rapidly in Haiti's heat and humidity. Eugenia's personal maid, Tété, divests the plantation mistress of corset, petticoats, and hose, leaving her in a shift for all obligations except dinner. Stripped of the accoutrements of wealth and social class, Eugenia seems more vulnerable to the dangers of life among rebellious island slaves.

The symbolism of class-based costume takes on significance at the fast-paced climax of *Island Beneath the Sea*. In the rush over rocks and roots into the Haitian hills, Tété suffers from cuts to her feet. Gambo La Liberté unwinds Tété's *tignon* and turns the head cloth into bindings for her bleeding feet. A parallel image pictures Valmorain removing boots from raw flesh that reminds Gambo of "skinned rabbits" (Allende, 2010, 188). A subsequent encounter with Maroons reveals a necklace of human ears, a detail that marks the savagery of American soldiers during the Vietnam War in Tim O'Brien's *The Things They Carried*. From the torture of cuts, exhaustion, and thirst, Valmorain grasps safety in the decorum of a mounted French militia, seeing only their uniforms, not the mulatto soldiers within and rushing to thank official rescuers.

Betrayal coalesces in characters with the dressing of the French in their former finery, including the "opera-admiral's uniform" worn by Zacharie, the 38-year-old republican majordomo of the Intendance. An avowed monarchist following the French Revolution of 1789, the chevalier Valmorain, his dignity restored, equips himself regally at Le Cap and hires servants liveried in blue and gold to serve a 15-course dinner "with the discipline of a battalion" (Allende, 2010, 201). The master himself appears regal in a vest brocaded with gold and silver embroidery. Completing the outfit of lace cuffs and neck, pink hose, and dancing shoes, Valmorain dons a lavender wig that a wig maker convinces him to wear for the occasion. Allende's snide humor wrings satire out of an artisan advising a grandee on the choice of accessories.

The decline of French dignity returns during the civil war at Le Cap, where even Général Galbaud abandons the self-importance of his "medal-festooned red uniform" for a dark traveling suit, his disguise for blending in with the fleeing citizenry (Allende, 2010, 212). As he rushes to the defense of his beloved wife, she struggles barefoot through the phalanx of guards wearing only her night attire—a negligee and shawl—while Galbaud leads forces without concern for his bloody, soot-stained clothes and singed hair and beard. Because the unnamed wife becomes a hostage during white flight from Le Cap on June 24, 1793, her dishabille seems all the more pathetic, but effective in securing a boat for Valmorain and his family.

The novel depicts clothing as an essential illusion for the retreating Valmorain household, which escapes a conflagration at Le Cap to a luxury hotel in Cuba. Upon the family's move to property among the elite in Louisiana, Tété must dress herself and the children in finery to blend in. Her one concession to European tastes, high-top shoes, torment her feet, which she prefers unshod. Upon gaining freedom and acquiring panache from Violette's makeup and lessons in deportment, Tété attends a pirates' auction, at which Jean Lafitte poses among bidders in black suit with white lace collar and cuffs, the modish habiliment of a gentleman. These references to appropriate attire illustrate the shallow state of New Orleans society, where even a Haitian slave and a well-dressed pirate can achieve stature.

For *Zorro*, Allende showcases clothing for histrionic effect, such as Rafael Moncada's silks for his fake serenade to Juliana, the circus cape and tights that Bernardo and Diego don for performing with the Gypsies, and the trappings of livery that disguise Diego while he delivers drugged wine to the barracks. Diego's mother, Toypurnia/Regina, manipulates her dual presence at the hacienda in Alta California by letting her hair go wild and her feet bare and by donning a papoose carrier while she takes intrepid horseback rides and visits Indians. When she campaigns among Spaniards for justice, she "dressed in Spanish style, combed her hair into a severe bun, wore an amethyst cross upon her breast," the conventional pose of the sedate Catholic colonial matron (Allende, 2005, 34). Bernardo, a deceptively simply 13-year-old, wears the convert's linen outfits topped with sash, serape, and headband. His braid proclaims his Indian pride and his disinterest in posing as anything other than his original self. For the sake of the Zorro legend, Bernardo adds to Diego's black cape and gloves with a kerchief pierced with eye holes, the vizard mask that enables Diego to engage in daring escapades.

Challenging frontier hierarchies, the two brothers perpetuate disguises during the freeing of hostages, Diego's first act of justice in Barcelona, which begins with Bernardo seizing a French army uniform and Diego/Zorro adding a mustache to his appearance. Contributing to the role of garments during the feat, Agnès Duchamp's handkerchief convinces Chevalier Roland Duchamp to comply with extortion; even the horse wears rags on his feet to silence his hooves. For normalcy, Zorro enhances the everyday life of Diego with unheroic touches. To cloak Diego thoroughly in the guise of a lesser man, Allende adds hypochondria in the form of asthma, coughing, heart palpitations, migraines, and myopia.

See also duality; migration literature; nativism

• *References and Further Reading*

Bahadur, Gaiutra. "All Souls Rising," *New York Times Book Review* (2 May 2010): 26.

Dyck, Reginald, and Cheli Reutter. *Crisscrossing Borders in Literature of the American West.* New York: Palgrave Macmillan, 2009.

Farr, Cecilia Konchar, and Jaime Harker, eds. *The Oprah Effect: Critical Essays on Oprah's Book Club.* Albany: State University of New York Press, 2008.

González, Aníbal. *Love and Politics in the Contemporary Spanish American Novel.* Austin: University of Texas Press, 2010.

McKale, Margaret A. Morales. *Literary Nonfiction in Works by Isabel Allende and Guadalupe Loaeza.* Columbus: Ohio State University, 2002.

"Review: *Portrait in Sepia,*" *Kirkus Reviews* (15 August 2001).

Valdes, Marcela. "Isabel Allende on Haiti's Slave Rebellion: A Lost Cause," *Washington Post* (8 June 2010).

Daughter of Fortune

For a picaresque novel about duality, transnationalism, and the female quest, Allende calls on her own upbringing and young womanhood for a story to counter the sorrow of losing daughter Paula. The perspective opens on a red-haired Englishman, Jacob Todd, a "false missionary" whose liberal notions elucidate his views on social and religious hypocrisy in the "English royal family, the military and the police, the system of class privilege ... and Christianity in particular" (Allende, 1999, 65, 66). From the novel's beginning, secrecy, mendacity, and ambiguity conceal a variety of actions—Jacob's waste of mission funds, Rose Sommers's pornographic writings, and the provenance and racial background of the foundling Eliza, fathered on a Mapuche girl by Captain John Sommers and abandoned in a soap crate. Coincidences—Paulina's residence in San Francisco, Tao Chi'en's service to Captain John Sommers, and Azucena Placeres's turquoise brooch—link people and quests with a boldness drawn from Greek stage drama and the intricacies of Dickensian fiction.

For structure, Allende develops the nineteenth-century parameters of the babe left on a doorstep and the transdressing female swashbuckler into urban history and the birth of a multicultural city, San Francisco. Central to the defeat of Victorian socio-economic standards, the plot requires a setting rich in caste subversion and deceits that enable the ambitious to attain wealth and prominence on the American frontier. For contrast, the life of Fourth Son, Tao Chi'en, echoes the biblical sale of Joseph into slavery and his advance in the Egyptian court of Pharaoh in Genesis in the rise of a Cantonese herbalist through intellect and agency. Parallel to the Victorian orphan of Joseph Fielding's novel *Tom Jones* and George Bernard Shaw's play *Major Barbara,* the plot carries protagonist Eliza Sommers from a foundling and pampered adoptee in Valparaíso, Chile, to pregnant stowaway in "the belly of the *Emilia,*" which holds "assorted luggage" as well as a parturient teen approaching death during childbirth (Allende, 1999, 149).

Eliza and Tao Chi'en share the outlook of the adventurer willing to sample the culture and lore of unknown settings. Eliza's luck in encountering Tao Chi'en, who "knows how to cure almost any ailment," rescues her from an ignoble death in a "two-by-two-meter hole" (Allende, 1999, 132, 149). Fortunately, he carried a gold acupuncture kit and essential curatives for healing, some from *zhong yi* (Chinese herbalism) and some adapted from the Western medicine of colleague Ebanizer Hobbs. In fractious situations among racist whites, he knows how to "play a part, act stupid, not provoke them" (*ibid.*, 229). Allied with Tao Chi'en, Eliza adapts transcultural dress, food, healing, and language to create a new identity superior in character and pluck to the privileged girl schooled for Anglo-Chilean society and marriage. On a landscape still taking shape in frontier California, with Tao Chi'en's help, she self-styles herself the heroine in an individualized cosmos.

The Disguise Motif

Like the Greek seer Teiresias, Eliza views the gendered sides of society from both perspectives, female and male. As a girl, she acquires the social polish of the British immigrant in South America, a setting that builds on the lives of the Boultons in a British colony in "A Discreet Miracle." After posing as a deaf-mute Chinese ship's boy, Eliza concludes, "It is tedious to be a man, but being a woman is worse still," the author's comment on costume and social strictures on females as opposed to the obstacles faced by a handicapped Asian (Allende, 1999, 227). For a living, Eliza puts to daily use piano playing for Joe Bonecrusher's troupe of entertainers and, as Elías "Chile Boy" Andieta, cooks beans, beef, and bacon into savory entrees while pretending to search for her "brother," Joaquín. The lengthy pilgrimage from Sacramento back to San Francisco enables Eliza to mother an orphan, Tom No-Tribe, and to accept her worth as a vigorous, self-assertive female of English-Mapuche Indian origin capable of fending for herself. Tao Chi'en, her faithful companion, explains her failure to reunite with her lover as evidence that Joaquín "doesn't deserve" a woman as fine as Eliza (*ibid.*, 335).

With feminist zeal, Allende pictures the down side of the womanly arts, a confining code of behaviors and expectations that socially prominent females enforce as controls on scandalous extremes. According to analyst Ana Patricia Rodríguez, gender subjugation, like colonialism, "challenges the notion of the democratizing forces of education and literacy," which equip Eliza with relative freedom of choice on the frontier (Farr and Harker, 2008, 193). In the rarefied Sommers household at Cerro Alegre, a snooty British enclave in Valparaíso, Chile, the child undergoes grooming intended to rid her of mestizo coarseness to prepare her for the self-valorized Anglo-Chilean microcosm. Through British club activities and items that Jeremy Sommers purchases by catalog, the family lives the illusion of British aristocratic refinement. Victorian ladyhood requires corseting and embroidery and piano lessons for posture. As a contrast, the text retraces the marriage of Lin to Tao Chi'en, a traditional Cantonese male dazzled by his wife's "golden lilies," the Asian euphemism for bound feet (*ibid.*, 170). By minimizing the couple's interest in their stillborn daughter, the text imparts the Chinese prejudice favoring male infants.

Allende applauds her protagonist's innate wisdom. To Eliza's credit, she rejects the pretense modeled by Miss Rose Sommers and chooses as maternal comfort the love of Mama Fresia, the Mapuche housekeeper and cook who shares ethnicity with Eliza's anonymous birth mother. Ironically, the 16-year-old's sexual awakening in the arms of Joaquín Andieta, an employee of the British Import and Export Company, begins the process of self-discovery as a stowaway dressed like a Chinese male in the hold of a ship bound for California. As critic Karen Martin explains, the journey begins "the process of integrating the contradictory elements of her ethnic identity," ironically, by altering her gender, social class, and race (Martin, 2007, 4). A change of clothing strips Eliza of lady's garments as she enters a "new story in which she was both protagonist and narrator," a scenario consistent with American feminism (Allende, 1999, 152). While gold fever inflames Joaquín and other prospectors arriving from Chile, Eliza searches for an ideal love, a pipe dream as ephemeral as El Dorado.

Coming to Knowledge

The exuberant style of *Daughter of Fortune* reviewer Jane Dickson calls hyperfiction, "a highly coloured, turbo-charged version of possible truths" about Eliza's coming-to-knowledge during a vibrant decade from 1843–1853 and the revelation of family secrets in the Sommers household (Dickson, 2001, 13). At first, according to the author, Eliza "closes down" over the emotional and physical trauma of the abandonment of her Chilean home and family and the stillbirth of the child sired by Joaquín (Rodden, 2010, 190). By choosing which elements of her bicultural background to emphasize, she navigates the Asian, Caucasian, Indian, and Latino regions of a fluid New World microcosm. A grim theme in the economic prosperity of Hong Kong and California, the rise of racial animosity targets coolie laborers, comfort girls, blacks, and Mexicans who maintain Latino claim to territory lost in 1848 at the end of the Mexican War. By 1853, urban unity depends on unprecedented cultural alliances, as symbolized by the assistance of Quaker James Morton to Joe Bonecrusher's brothel and the romance and medical practice of Eliza Sommers and Tao Chi'en.

Allende overleaps questions of sovereignty by dramatizing a witty, ironic challenge to Manifest Destiny. The backdrop of strong-arming and lynching offsets evidence of opportunity for immigrant whites and women of color, a motif that *Daughter of Fortune* shares with Margaret Walker's *Jubilee*, Leslie Marmon Silko's *Garden in the Dunes*, and Toni Morrison's *Paradise*. Potential savagery incises Allende's coming of age story with a reminder that those who transgress borders and shortcut society's rituals accept the risks, an axiom imbedded in Allende's life story as expatriate and new U.S. citizen (Meacham, 2007, 29–45). Themes of home and foreignness ricochet across Eliza's biography, leaving open to interpretation where she belongs and to what culture she owes allegiance.

Eliza's betrayal by a confining romantic ideal underscores the universality of Allende's tropes as they apply to female coming of age, whether that of Clara del Valle in *The House of the Spirits* or of Judy Reeves and Carmen Morales in *The Infinite Plan*. Heightening Eliza's marginality in an emerging California port, her affection for a Chinaman sets her further apart from other Americans as she "clung to Tao Chi'en's fingers but moved forward with determination" toward the end of her illusory romance with Joaquín Andieta (Allende, 1999, 299). Rodríguez notes the value of Allende's interracial and interethnic conundrum to discussions of "the cultural anxieties of living in the United States, then and now" (Farr and Harker, 2008, 206).

See also costume

• *References and Further Reading*

Dickson, E. Jane. "Word of Mouth," (London) *Times* (3 February 2001): 13.
Dyck, Reginald, and Cheli Reutter. *Crisscrossing Borders in Literature of the American West.* New York: Palgrave Macmillan, 2009.
Farr, Cecilia Konchar, and Jaime Harker. *The Oprah Effect: Critical Essays on Oprah's Book Club.* Albany: State University of New York Press, 2008.
Martin, Karen. "Mapping Ethnicity in Isabel Allende's *Daughter of Fortune* and *Portrait in Sepia,*" *Grafemas* (December 2007): 1–8. McClennen, Sophia A. Meacham, Cherie. "Resisting Romance: Isabel Allende's Transformation of the Popular Romance Formula in *Hija de la Fortuna,*" *Latin American Literary Review* 35:69 (January–June 2007): 29–45.
Rodden, John. "Isabel Allende, Fortune's Daughter," *Critical Insights* (October 2010): 184–194.

death

With existential calm and surrender to the inevitable, Allende applies paradox to the great mystery of physical decline and death. Her writings forge inward into thoughts and yearnings, embracing the scars resulting from her own struggle and loss and venturing on toward serenity and joy. Mother-daughter separation angst heightens the falling action in *Daughter of Fortune.* The motif of decline pictures the flagging of female vanity in Rose Sommers, whose spirit withers after the disappearance of her adopted daughter. In mourning, Rose wears black in the style of sorrowing Chilean widows, a self-immurement she had previously rejected as too severe. As a result of the mother's dejection, Allende describes as morose the mausoleum air of the Sommers home, where Rose "ached with pure loneliness" and infects the rest of the family with grief (Allende, 2001, 379).

In a memoir, *The Sum of Our Days,* Allende acknowledges the fear of death, but rejects the paralysis inflicted by the unknown. The author's courage explains her stance in the valiant embrace of mortality in *Inés of My Soul.* Rather than obsess over interment and the grave, the text energizes mortality with the image of flight: "To die is to fly like an arrow through dark reaches toward the firmament, toward infinite space, where I must look for my loved ones, one by one" (Allende, 2006, 260). Unlike the plodding aspects of earthly life, the arrow's arc symbolizes a freedom from impermanence that is unimaginable to the living. In her last months, Inés gazes over her house in Santiago and recognizes death as a comforting mother scented like fresh laundry, a "large, roly-poly woman with an opulent bosom and welcoming arms: a maternal angel" (*ibid.,* 83). Allende accords her protagonist a writer's concern, that she not fade away leaving too many memories "in the inkwell" (*ibid.,* 209). The metaphor pictures the author's belief that memory is the true antidote to death.

For the author, senescence is another matter. A moribund characterization of Inés reveals old age as a betrayal more grievous for the title character than her experiences with perfidy or war, where "death is a constant companion" (Allende, 2006, 21). Already bereft of a husband and a lover, Inés regrets the betrayal of her unreliable body from aching joints and diminished eyesight. The physical decline of her beloved second husband, Rodrigo de Quiroga, weights her seventh decade with sadness from yet another parting. She recalls the last kiss to "receive my husband's last breath," a romantic farewell common to drama and opera (*ibid.,* 5). Returning to thoughts of her prime, Inés pines for the loss of strength to ride once more into battle. At Pedro's gruesome execution, she dispatches her soul to accompany him and weeps "for him and for all the other victims of those years" that saw the birth of Santiago (*ibid.,* 313). In a verbal lament, Inés retreats into memory to assuage absences that can only worsen in her final days.

For Allende, death may gradually overtake mortal life, as revealed by the unsound physical condition of the Yeti wise woman Grr-ympr and the sickness of village babies in *Kingdom of the Golden Dragon* and the preserved beauty of Rosa the Beautiful during an autopsy in *The House of the Spirits*. A lapse of appetite and visible signs of aging in Grr-ympr imply that the "bundle of rickety bones covered with a greasy hide" has little time left to protect the Yetis from extinction (Allende, 2004, 324). The text contrasts the robust health of her people with the foul secretions and "smell of filth and decay she emitted," a sure sign of waning life in her body (*ibid.*). Yet, for Grr-ympr, the decease of her body lacks the greater tragedy of the demise of the Yeti.

Through foreshadowing, Allende permeates the opening chapter of her first novel with a cataclysmic family demise. Isabel Dulfano explains that "deaths that alter the course of a generational line are extremely disruptive, particularly when the unexpected death is of a child who had already reached adulthood" (Dulfano, 2006, 504). Allende pictures on Maundy Thursday, the beginning of Easter, the iconic suffering of Saint Sebastián, riddled with arrows ordered by the Roman emperor Diocletian, symbols of earthly strife. After the unanticipated arrival of Uncle Marcos's remains from Africa, the text discloses a more immediate, shocking loss of Rosa the Beautiful from drinking brandy spiked with rat poison, a toxin intended to kill her father. In the ensuing autopsy scene, Allende enlarges on the juxtaposition of rosy youth with rigor mortis. Interpreter Anne J. Cruz refers to the presentation of Rosa as "beautiful and distant, asexual, perfect, or goddess-like ... a necrophilic esthetic" that leaves the undertaker's assistant panting (Cruz, 2003, 239). Overwhelmed by the delicacy of the corpse, he kisses it "on the lips, the neck, the breasts, and between the legs," a further acknowledgement of Rosa's unplucked ripeness (Allende, 1985, 54).

The theme of unrequited love enhances the poignance of a brutal murder of one so young and maidenly. Alongside the coffin with its silver rivets, miner Esteban Trueba regrets never knowing the corporal wonders of his fiancée's body. Instead, he views her "outlined against the satin pleats in her virginal coffin," lying in the standard pious pose with rosary in hand and a bride's blossoms in her hair, a visual statement of her purity (Allende, 1985, 51). Rather than comfort the mourner, the all-night vigil sets Esteban to cursing his ill luck, a suggestion of the anger and possessiveness that marks his downfall. A second evil omen, the stabbing death of the dog Barrabás, marks Clara and Esteban's ring ceremony with portents of a difficult marriage, which ends with another ineffectual outburst from the possessive husband.

Inevitable Change

At significant points of the action in *The House of the Spirits*, death precedes a plot change — the demise of Doña Ester Trueba before her son Esteban's marriage to Clara del Valle, the sudden death of Nana the morning of the earthquake that levels Las Tres Marías, and the passing of Pedro García before the presidential elections of 1948. Allende implies that change requires the expiration of antique traditions and beliefs to make way for untried philosophies that challenge outmoded principles with modernity. With the loss of Old Pedro goes "his memory of the past and the immediate present," a storehouse of knowledge that parallels Clara's journal entries on memorable events (Allende, 1985, 220). Esteban takes stock of Pedro's many contributions to the welfare of Las Tres Marías and "wanted everyone to remember this funeral as a major event" (*ibid.*). At Pedro's wake, Clara overrules Esteban's ostentation by welcoming Father José Dulce María, who brings "a little order to matters of the spirit," a necessary restoration of mourners' hopes (*ibid.*, 219).

Upon Clara's preparation for death, characters again display their attitudes toward change and loss. The gentle leave-taking occurs with "detaching herself from the world, growing ever lighter, more transparent, more winged," a suggestion of upward thrust (*ibid.*, 331). The end comes with a "contented sigh," a waft from Earth suited to a woman who had occupied a liminal existence between the living and dead (*ibid.*, 333). Jaime, who calls on a medical specialist to corroborate the diagnosis, admits that Clara's departure causes an ineluctable change of place for the spirit, for which "science has no cure" (*ibid.*, 332). Unlike the *patrón's* noble acceptance of Pedro's death, Esteban, the generator of chaos, smashes china and lamps in frustration at losing his estranged wife. Allende creates irony from Esteban's agitation at loss as opposed to seven-year-old Alba's wise observation that Clara's spirit will remain close by. The statement presages a time when Alba profits from her grandmother's comforting words.

Portrait in Sepia, the sequel of *Daughter of Fortune*, reprises the sadness of a family grieving the loss of a young woman. Allende returns to the Chi'en household at the family's unforeseen leave-taking with daughter Lin/Lynn, who dies after "a dry, difficult birth" attended by her father, Tao Chi'en, an herbalist (Allende, 2001, 80). Motionless in "absolute silence," the Chi'en family meditates on the mysterious departure of the spirit, a scene replicated at the passing of Grandmother Paulina (*ibid.*, 84). Tao's Asian upbringing enables him to comfort his son-in-law, Severo del Valle, with a murmured "It's all right, it's all right" (*ibid.*, 85). The verbal reassurance discloses Tao's Buddhist upbringing in beliefs in reincarnation and ultimate Nirvana, the cessation of human suffering.

In a subsequent mortal challenge, Allende contrasts Severo's brush with a soldier's death on January 16, 1881, in a Lima field hospital during the War of the Pacific. Crazed with pain and fear, he imagines death in the form of a female buzzard "awaiting her chance for the last slash of her claws" and perceives hope in the vision of Nívea, his fiancée, who charges him "with an instinct to life" (*ibid.*, 114). The female's healing power in Nívea, like Clara's abiding spirit, dispels the death bird and fills Severo with resolve to join the ten percent of amputees to survive blood loss and gangrene. Allende credits Nívea with the knowledge and initiative to continue retrieving Severo's spirit from despair, a common recurrence in one-legged veterans. From newfound courage and anticipation of reward, Nívea exults that touching the hearts of others imprints their life forces with understanding and acceptance.

In "Interminable Life," Allende takes the opposite stance by admitting that death can relieve unbearable suffering. Through the perspective of Dr. Roberto Blaum, she justifies euthanasia, an ethically taboo topic clarified via Blaum's image of the reunion of the spirit with the oversoul. Blaum maintains that "death, with its ancestral weight of terrors, is merely the abandonment of an unserviceable shell," a release of a struggling spirit from its temporary housing to reintegrate into the universe (Allende, 1991, 242). Blaum's transcendental philosophy echoes the acquiescence of Clara and Alba del Valle and Tao Chi'en. The pro-life tumult that arises over Blaum's bold statement reveals two extremes of professional and public opinion—those who accuse Blaum of Naziism and admirers who deck him with sainthood. The end of life for Blaum and his wife Ana tests the theory close to home. Editor Daniela Carpi describes the urgent conclusion as experience "not limited to theoretical considerations, but clashes with a real choice ... the true Gordian knot" (Carpi, 2011, 109).

A Living Will

Allende views wisdom as an ongoing gift to those who cherish the advice and example of the departed. As summarized by critic Vincent Kling, the author's resolutions of paradox place "contradictory terms in harmonious, creative tension ... into a yet more encompassing reality," a perception revealed in the parting of a loving couple in the mystic fable "Walimai," the struggle to save the title figure from a gut wound in "Ester Lucero," and King Dorji's brave acceptance of death in *Kingdom of the Golden Dragon* (Kling, 2010, 243). From an autobiographical view, the author stated that she wanted to leave a living legacy to her family: "I hope that when I die I will have been able to, during my life, plant little seeds in the souls of my children and my grandchildren so that when they need something from me I will always be available" (Kennedy, 2001, 25). Kling explains that the contrast between absence and availability "fosters profusion and inclusion ... into the peace that passes all understanding, and an assertion of life in all its fecundity" (Kling, 2010, 243).

The author's pact with Tata in *Paula* to help him die when he becomes too feeble to end his life foretokens Allende's negotiation with death during her daughter Paula's year-long coma. Allende recoils from the obvious arc toward death as an end to the fundamental tasks of mothering, a part of the author's identity similar to the self-definition that poet Adrienne Rich posits in *Of Woman Born*. In Allende's approach-avoidance of Paula's death, Carpi summarizes the quandary as "the legitimacy of actions or omissions that are consistent with the patient's will and suitable to produce or accelerate his or her death" (Carpi, 2011, 110). While pondering a wish to end Paula's suffering, the author consoles the wife of Don Manuel, the elderly farmer slowing expiring from gastric disease in the same ward. Allende's charity toward a fellow sufferer predicts kindness toward herself when her turn to grieve wounds her heart. She observed the random nature of such losses: "You don't plan it, it happens" (Moline, 2003. 92). Of the turn of fate, she added, "We don't have to understand it. It is enough to be aware that it exists" (*ibid.*).

At Paula's death on December 6, 1992, "everything stopped" for Allende (Moline, 2003, 92). Former colleague John Rodden noted that the author's life "lost its goal-directed focus yet not its spirit and drive" (Rodden, 2005, 64). The defeat that consumed Allende transformed the mother/author into the matriarch of her tribe and a more compassionate, intuitive survivor/writer. Isabel Dulfano accounts for the change in Allende as the result of an I-thou perspective: "Isabel cannot accept the separation between herself and daughter and therefore appropriates the I/You model in order to integrate with Paula," an immersion that resuscitates the dying 28-year-old (Dulfano, 2006, 499).

Boldness in reclaiming Paula through confessional memoir replaces terrors of loving too much, too deeply. *Paula* and *The Sum of Our Days* reinstate the daughter through what reviewer Karen Moline calls "an exorcism of death and a celebration of life" (Moline, 2003, 88). Reviewer Michelle Locke observes that the author "always seems to find strength and healing and even joy in writing her way through sorrow and through the obstacles that life throws up" (Locke, 2008). As Allende explains in the latter memoir, she gathers her tribe, an assortment that reviewer Sarah Vine dubs a "sprawling, peculiar, imperfect, and yet ultimately loving group of friends and relations" (Vine, 2008, 10). Vine adds that, "if only books were people, her beloved daughter Paula would once again be alive and well" (*ibid.*). Lest Allende lose her gift for narrative, she determines to inscribe amorphous impressions that should be remembered, notably, the fictional loved ones who pass to the spirit world, such as Eugenia García del Solar in *Island Beneath the Sea*, Tao Chi'en in *Portrait in Sepia*, and King Dorji in *Kingdom of the Golden Dragon*.

From an opposite perspective on survival, Gregory Reeves's combat experience in *The Infinite Plan* forbids him to muse on death or trust, a risky abandonment of the army's gung-ho *esprit de corps*. Lacking control of the conscious mind, he regrets that his "head is filled with visions of death, words of death" (Allende, 1993, 196). A brutal nighttime assault leaves him so deranged that, like the Incredible Hulk, he morphs into an invincible rescuer of eight comrades. As dislodged from self as the protagonist of Stephen Crane's *The Red Badge of Courage* and Tim O'Brien's *The Things They Carried*, Gregory solidifies into a rigid humanity shaken by terrors and uncertainty, which he stores in his subconscious. In the next military assignment gathering information under the guise of a village English teacher, he takes on surreal elements that he later dismisses with a too-slick cliché, "Kill or be killed," an either-or philosophy that overlooks the terrors of the living death of post-traumatic stress syndrome (*ibid.*, 219).

On return to civilian California, the protagonist faces another wartime onus, the report to Inmaculada and Pedro Morales of Juan José's combat death. Disabused of childhood fantasy drawn from Hollywood film, Greg recalls his blood brother chopped into half a man and fearful of the dark chasm that awaited his remains. Greg spews his rage at war's Gothic savagery: "We don't die cleanly, we die stricken with terror in a pool of blood and shit" (Allende, 1993, 221). More damning for the survivor, he admits missing the blood-rush of firefights and describes the adrenaline flow as "an atrocious pleasure ... a divine revelation," an admission that introduces him to an unknown sector of his own psyche (*ibid.*, 223). In a nightmare, he launches a scream that disintegrates into "shards of ice," a metaphor that characterizes the fragility of the inner man (*ibid.*, 224).

Allende restructures the novel's meditation on death by picturing the gentle departure of Thui Morales. After securing for her toddler son Dai a workable relationship with Dai's aunt Carmen, Thui retreats into terminal cancer with the reminder, "We do what we can," a sad but true commentary on the lives of the Vietnamese during two decades of civil war (Allende, 1993, 270). Her stoicism supports one life's end, but leaves the blunt truncation of mother-son love for Dai to heal with Carmen's help. Olga, Carmen's mentor, diagnoses the remnants of the past that rob Dai of appetite. She describes Thui's influence as a living weight on the boy: "The dead go hand in hand with the living" (*ibid.*, 272). Once Dai accepts the image of his mother shadowing him like an invisible angel, he begins to eat again.

The Deaths of Others

The mother-son relationship recurs in Allende's YA trilogy, creating a hovering anxiety that deeds cannot lessen. During the venture of Alex Cold along the upper Amazon in *City of the Beasts*, the concern for his mother back in Texas becomes an invisible burden. He allows himself to ponder the chemotherapy and the advance of cancer in Lisa Cold, but he stops short of considering her death, "something disagreeable that happened to other people" (Allende, 2002, 249). At a precipice, he re-channels the grievous possibilities toward positive thoughts and directs the energy toward allaying her pain. As with prayers for healing, the act of hope does more for the son than for the mother.

A similar refocus of emotion occurs at Tapirawa-teri, where villagers adorn themselves in ash, charcoal, and mud to mourn the passing of Chief Mokarita and symbolically battle the enemy responsible for the death. Although pagan, the animistic ceremony provides physical outlets for bereavement and loyalty, just as Alex's expedition to the Upper Orinoco provides him with challenges to mind and body to absorb the passive hurt for his ailing mother. Dulfano acknowledges that "death can help develop a deeper appreciation of oneself and the importance of human relations," a bond that Alex develops with Nadia Santos and the People of the Mist, who face possible extinction (Dulfano, 2006, 504–505).

In *Kingdom of the Golden Dragon*, Allende groups in the mind of Nadia mortal inklings from the story "Walimai" and *City of the Beasts.* As the temperature drops and she nears freezing to death in the Himalayas, she ponders the in-between state occupied by Walimai's wife, who accompanies her mate as a disembodied spirit. By emitting a telepathic message in the form of a white eagle, "the essence of her character," Nadia signals distress that takes the form of a "knot in her throat" (Allende, 2004, 295). Rather than bemoan the quandary of dying from hypothermia, she considers opportunities to assuage sorrow in her father and Alex. Allende pictures Nadia in a moribund state that releases earthly bonds and benignly drifts away from pain toward the moon. In a similar lost-cause episode, when an avalanche threatens Alex as he crosses a bridge, he shapeshifts into the totemic jaguar and leaps from the precipice at the same time that Nadia flies overhead in the form of an eagle. The grandeur of telepathic avoidance of harm illustrates the trilogy's commendation of the supernatural as a boost to the courage of young readers.

For historical fiction, Allende acknowledges periods of unfathomable amounts of suffering. Deaths heap *Island Beneath the Sea* with the emaciation and demise of Eugenia García del Solar and the grisly torture and slaughter of slaves and white planters who, before the Haitian Revolution of 1791, accepted attrition among blacks as "a calculated loss" (Allende, 2010, 45). Allende appears to sweep murder and execution from *Island Beneath the Sea* after Toulouse Valmorain makes a new start in Cuba and New Orleans. Once he sails from Haiti, he leaves behind the unburied remains of his wife Eugenia, which burn in the conflagration that sweeps Le Cap, and Prosper Cambray, who commits suicide rather than submit to murderous black rampagers. Allende's preference for paradox marks the scene that destroys Eugenia and Prosper's corpses at the same time that it rids the island of bondage and Valmorain's role in enslaving Africans for the sake of profit.

In the view of Toulouse's servant/concubine Tété, life seems amicable to the Valmorain household, which flourishes after the horrendous mass killings, burnings, and public hangings in Le Cap. Following an annual hurricane and flood, the author makes light sport of the problem of floating coffins in New Orleans, a perennial problem in a city built below sea level. Allende satirizes the differentiation of social strata in the harborage of "the wealthy dead in their mausoleums" (Allende, 2010, 280). In contrast to the moneyed class, the New Orleans poor lose bones to stray dogs, an indignity consistent with the destiny of the lower class and subtly reminiscent of the outré deaths caused by the Haitian Revolution.

Death becomes more personal to Valmorain after symptoms of obesity, high blood pressure, and cardiovascular problems predict a premature end from overeating and debauchery that precipitate a stroke. In a flurry of self-absorption, Valmorain not only adopts Dr. Parmentier's diet, but also consults with herbalists, *gris-gris* merchants, and Sanité Dédé to extend his life through supernatural intervention. Like Ebenezer Scrooge beset by visions of Jacob Marley's ghost in Dickens's *A Christmas Carol*, Valmorain reveals residual guilt for purloining the bank account of Lacroix and declares, "I hope to live long enough for me to correct some of my errors" (Allende, 2010, 454). Details of suffering and regret suggest that, for all Valmorain's good intentions, he has little time left to make amends. Allende depicts Valmorain's too-little-too-late change of heart in the fear of "the abysmal silence and inconsolable solitude of the tomb" (*ibid.*, 438). In a mockery of confession to Père Antoine and extreme unction, the former planter glosses over his crimes against blacks but admits to thievery lest death "catch him unprepared" (*ibid.*).

• *References and Further Reading*

Carpi, Daniela, ed. *Bioethics and Biolaw Through Literature*. Berlin: William de Gruyter, 2011.
Cruz, Anne J., Rosilie Hernández-Pecoraro, and Joyce Tolliver, eds. *Disciplines on the Line: Feminist Research on Spanish, Latin American, and U.S. Latina Women*. Newark, DE: Juan de la Cuesta, 2003.
Dulfano, Isabel. "The Mother/Daughter Romance—Our Life: Isabel Allende in/and *Paula*," *Women's Studies* 35:5 (2006): 493–506.
Kennedy, Alexandra. *The Infinite Thread: Healing Relationships Beyond Loss*. Hillsboro, OR: Beyond Words, 2001.
Kling, Vincent. "Archetype, Not Ideology: Isabel Allende's Balance of Opposites," *Critical Insights* (October 2010): 239–257.
Locke, Michelle. "Author Isabel Allende Chronicles Her Own Real-Life Drama in New Book," *Canadian Press* (28 March 2008).
Moline, Karen. "The Spirit of Love," *Australian Woman's Weekly* 73:8 (August 2003): 88–92.
Vine, Sarah. "Humanity Laid Bare," (London) *Times* (12 April 2008): 10.

Del Valle–García–Trueba genealogy

For the del Valle–García–Trueba clan, whom Allende calls "a family of passionate barbarians," vigor and direction determine a series of iconoclastic behaviors, from Nívea del Valle's appearance in maternity clothes in public to Blanca del Valle's sexual alliance with the folksinger Pedro Tercero, a plantation peon (Allende, 2001, 142). Ironically, the sin that plunges the family into turmoil, Esteban Trueba's adulteries with plantation laborers, raises no eyebrows and draws no complaints from his aristocratic peers, who deem colonial males unaccountable for fornication and bastardy.

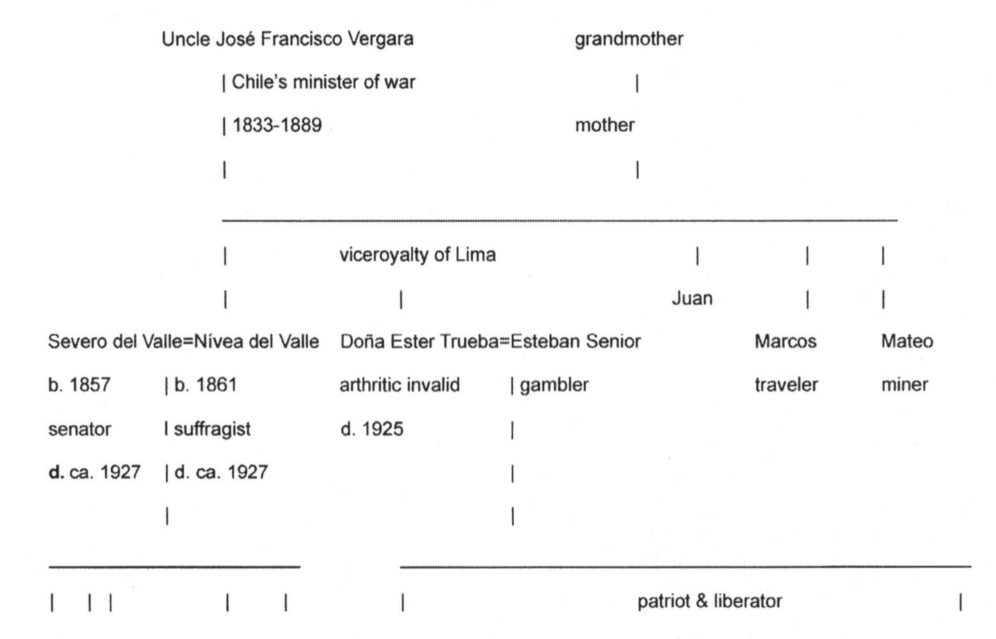

| | tutor | nun | Pedro García, patriarch and fablist |

| | | | | |

| Teresa | | ____________ |

| | | | | |

Rosa Clara del Valle=Esteban Trueba=/=Pancha García Pedro Segundo Férula Trueba

eldest ca. 1905-1958 | b. ca. 1890 | dies of diarrhea farm manager reclusive seamstress

1895-1915 m. ca. 12/1925 | Esteban García | ca. 1880-1940

| | |

| Colonel Esteban García |

| b. ca. 1938 |

| snitch, torturer |

____twins____________________________________ |

| | | |

| | Jean de Satigny=Blanca Trueba=/=Pedro Tercero=/=groupies

| | pervert ceramicist | folksinger

| | b. ca. 11/1926 |

| ______________________ |

| | | |

Jaime del Valle=/=Amanda=/=Nicolás Miguel =/=Alba Trueba=/=Colonel Esteban García

liberal journalist debater rebel | muralist rapist

physician b. ca. 1923 lawyer | b. ca. 1951

1927-9/13/1973 |

the "little *patrón*" unborn daughter

See also Chi'en–del Valle–Sommers genealogy

• *References and Further Reading*

Rodden, John, ed. *Isabel Allende.* New York: Salem Press, 2011.

duality

The merger of characters in Allende's canon derives from both magical and realistic circumstances, as with the human and bestial forms of Eagle and Jaguar in the *City of the Beasts* trilogy and the human and spiritual incarnations of Clara del Valle in *The House of the Spirits.* For Eliza Sommers, the headstrong protagonist of *Daughter of Fortune* and grandmother of Aurora in *Portrait in Sepia,* a drastic flight from the confines of Anglo-Chilean society in Valparaíso to the gold fields of California requires gender masking. Dressed as a man, she embraces the freedom accorded males, even the lowly Elias "Chile Boy" Andieta, pianist, letter writer, and cook for a caravan of prostitutes. The two-sided persona functions profitably on the frontier, yet Eliza maintains a suitcase of female attire by which to retrieve her femininity. From bold decision making, Eliza shapes her own destiny apart from that of her lover, Joaquín Andieta/Murieta, the Pan-American myth. In the estimation of editor Michael Sollars, Eliza thrives under outré situations because she accepts "that she must answer to no one except herself," including the man she once identified as her life's love (Sollars, 2008, 200). Her metamorphosis into a compatible friend and aide to herbalist Tao Chi'en rewards her with a workable, Americanized individuality suited to time and place. Nonetheless, she continues wearing men's attire "because it contributed to the invisibility so necessary in the quixotic mission" (*ibid.*, 360).

In a more physical form of duality, the title figure in *Eva Luna* dramatizes the control of the storykeeper over circumstance by allowing the narrator to shapeshift into fantastic forms. Eva, upon learning about snow, becomes the "abominable snow woman" in her own stories (Allende, 1987, 73). Her dream states prefigure camaraderie with the tormented transsexual singer Melesio, who regrets having a "woman inside him and she could not get used to the male body in which she was trapped" (*ibid.*, 121). In a household where members work by night and sleep away the day, "Melesio was without sex or age" (*ibid.*, 126). After applause for his cabaret performance of French songs as Mimí, Melesio retreats to El Negro's bar and relives the joy of cross-dressing for the stage before retiring to the dreary lifestyle that society accords him. Like Gregory Reeves, the faux Latino in *The Infinite Plan*, Melesio/Mimí feels marginal in both extremes until he allows Mimí to erase Melesio.

A witty irony sustains the last one-third of *Eva Luna* in the duality of Mimí, who, like Teiresias from Greek myth, knows human life from both male and female perspectives. As a woman, she manages hair, wardrobe, and makeup with panache and decorates her apartment according to fashion from the proceeds of a singing career. As a male, Mimí recognizes the deception of Eva Luna by Huberto Naranjo, a peripatetic lover who strings his paramour along on an erratic schedule to suit the life of a terrorist. Integral to Eva's fantasy, the disguises the guerrilla warrior adopts make him seem like "several lovers at the same time" (Allende, 1987, 229). Whereas wishful thinking forces Mimí to accept realistic compromise, Eva's phantom lover encourages lies about the past and the possibility of a normal life with Huberto.

Allende challenge Huberto's duality by inserting moral questions after the assassination of two factory guards, whose deaths Huberto rationalizes as executions. In the jungle, he transforms himself into Comandante Rogelio, the mentor to naive recruits to the revolution. However, Mimí's assumptions proves correct: during forays to the city, Huberto must admit that his pose as a normal citizen is unrealistic: "he was not like everyone else, he was a guerrilla fighter" (Allende, 1987, 236). By accepting his militant side, Huberto opts to return to the "affectionate and slightly incestuous brother" in Eva's life, a relationship more easily sustained during his unpredictable comings and goings (*ibid.*, 286).

For Dil Bahadur, heir apparent to the throne of the Forbidden Kingdom in *Kingdom of the Golden Dragon*, a nine-year apprenticeship to the guru Tensing introduces the prince to the physical, emotional, and psychic skills required of a monarch. Out of humility and a need to protect himself, Dil conceals his future role from outsiders. Allende presents him as a normal teen-aged boy until a cataclysm rips away his concealment in the mountains and thrusts him into the tasks of replacing his father, King Dorji, and supplying the Forbidden Kingdom with a new symbolic statues. The sudden emergence of the young king parallels similar royal advancement of eighteen-year-old Queen Victoria of England and fifteen-year-old King Chulalongkorn of Siam upon the death of previous monarchs.

With no opportunity to assuage the dying king or mourn his passing, Dil sits quietly for an hour a secret chamber while receiving the charge to rule his people with the aid of a treasured oracle. By the opening of *Forest of the Pygmies*, Dil has married, sired the next heir apparent, and begun modernizing his nation, an accomplishment also achieved by Victoria and Chulalongkorn.

Allende implements the dual nature of characters as a means of heightening drama. A surprising character in *Inés of My Soul*, Felipe, a young Mapuche paddock boy, involves himself so thoroughly in the lives of the title character and her lover, Général Pedro de Valdivia, that he easily acquires an education in Spanish military tactics and horsemanship. In young manhood, he retreats from Santiago to reclaim the name Lautaro and the title of chief as "the most famous *toqui* in the land of the Araucans, a feared demon to the Spaniards, a hero to the Mapuche, a prince of the epic war" (Allende 2006, 269). With the outrageous act of beheading Valdivia's horse Sultán, Felipe/Lautaro obliterates the image of faithful stablehand and moves sure-footedly by night to his redoubt in the forest. While leading his people to victory against the colonizers of Chile, Lautaro dramatically lifts his mask to his enemy, Valdivia, achieving the satisfaction of surprise and vengeance through the unveiling.

So successful is the turncoat that Allende accords him honor and admiration for his amalgamation of native pride and stealth with centuries of European infantry and cavalry stratagems. So thoroughly did the act impact Chilean history that "the spirit of Lautaro continues to lead his armies and his name will resound through the centuries" (*ibid.*, 270). As a symbol of the shift from docile servant to grim avenger, the text, composed in historical present tense, pictures him baptized in the river and reborn in spirit and hope for his people's reclamation of Chile, a mission fraught with the tragic theme of an honorable martyrdom to freedom. Allende grooms the legend with Lautaro's delight in Guacolda, the native foil of the Spaniard Inés. Both women who groom their mates for greatness, Inés and Guacolda retain iconic stature, especially the devotion of Guacolda to her beloved in Canto XIII of the epic verse of Alonso de Ercilla y Zuñiga, a treasured document of Spain's golden age. However, unlike Inés, whom literate Europeans lionize, Guacolda disappears from history in a primitive society not yet introduced to reading and writing.

After the issuance of the adventure novel *Zorro*, critics accounted for dual nature in Allende's Diego de la Vega as an innate gift rather than a burden or ultimate persona. His birth in May 1795 to a Spanish hidalgo and Shoshone mother and his breastfeeding by Ana, an Indian wet nurse, presage ambivalence toward class and racial superiority that only a European grandee can claim. Enlarging the concept of duality, Diego shares feedings with Bernardo, a milk brother born to Ana on the day of Diego's birth. Reviewer Shaun Charles characterized the pairing as "the Old World colliding with the New, driven by a power higher than the everyday, yet rooted firmly in the tangible ... a fusion of strict European traditions and indigenous mysticism" (Charles, 2005, M8). While fighting an implacable enemy, at the novel's climax, Diego summarizes his two-part persona—"one part Diego de la Vega, elegant, affected, hypochondriac, and the other part El Zorro, audacious, daring, playful" (Allende, 2006, 232). By straddling the contentions of his era, Diego/Zorro plots methods of securing justice for the underclass.

A corresponding duality fills the thoughts and colors the actions of Tété, housekeeper and nanny for Toulouse Valmorain in *Island Beneath the Sea*. The moiling emotions of newly captured Guineans stoke the flames lit by Macandal, the mythic martyr to black freedom in Haiti. Tété speaks nightly with her master, cloaking hints of insurrection to conceal the coming liberation prophesied by Tante Rose, a voodoo high priestess. Overt signs of defiance force planters to import French soldiers, but the murmur persists, predicting vengeance on the whites who perpetrate daily forced labor and nightly sexual thralldom, a French duality that generates a growing mulatto subclass.

By 1791, blacks, who "didn't count because they were property," realize their dreams of a conflagration of plantations and a return to full humanity (Allende, 2010, 212). The mulatto overseer, Prosper Cambray, deludes himself that an armed militia and whip-swinging stewards can easily suppress ignorant drones like the African field hands. Belying his confidence, he sleeps with two pistols, "always on guard" (*ibid.*, 114). In the "cruel anarchy reigning in the colony" that forces Cambray to shoot himself, Guineans divorce themselves from press gangs (*ibid.*, 230). Through what analyst Philip Swanson calls "dynamic transformation," the hero, Toussaint, abandons the identity of both slave and rebel to create a new life story by naming himself L'Ouverture and leading a state of self-governing blacks.

See also clothing

• *References and Further Reading*

Charles, Shaun. "Marking Zorro's Place in History," *The* (Brisbane) *Courier Mail* (23 April 2005): M8.

Sollars, Michael D. *The Facts on File Companion to the World Novel, 1900 to the Present.* New York: Facts on File, 2008.

Swanson, Philip. "Z/Z: Isabel Allende and the Mark of Zorro," *Romance Studies* 24:3 (November 2006): 265–277.

Eva Luna

Based on thirteen years as an expatriate in Caracas, Venezuela, Allende expresses populism and feminism in *Eva Luna* and its sequel, *The Stories of Eva Luna*, a story collection that extends character information and themes. According to analyst Alice Nelson, the author's method of communing with readers revives *la fábula*, a transgenerational vehicle for messages of hope and love based on "universalized archetypes acting against a fairy tale backdrop" (Nelson, 2002, 196, 198). Eva exults in "the slightest effort of imagination to pass through the door and enter the extraordinary stories unfolding on the other side of the walls" (Allende, 1987, 111). For characters, except for Riad Halabí, Allende emulates real life by drawing on actual people, notably, Mimí the cross-dresser and the prostitute La Señora, who recurs in the story "Clarisa."

The author sets picaresque conventions through episodic glimpses of camaraderie, collaboration, and sensuality. Beginning with the childhood of Consuelo, the red-haired orphaned mother of raconteur Eva Luna, storytelling serves "to add a little color to life and to allow [the teller] to escape to other worlds when reality became too difficult to bear" (Allende, 1987, 212). Critic Hendrik Marthinus Viljoen states that Eva's life resembles that of Scheherazade, "one long concatenation of improbable characters and stories" intended to spare her execution (Viljoen 2004, 80). Her listeners declare, "You're stories are better than the movies, there's more suffering" (Allende, 1987, 127). These narratives equip Eva with the power to navigate through imagined scenarios in the *telenovela* series *Bolero*, which, according to Viljoen, "might be preferable to life" for offering listeners a level of identification and sympathy with female suffering (Viljoen 2004, 82).

According to critic Beth E. Jorgensen's survey of the author's early works, the plot-driven text thrives as Allende's "most celebratory and upbeat" (Jorgensen, 2002, 137). As with most of Allende's canon, Gothic elements rub elbows with lyricism and realism, particularly the hardships of the poor villagers of Agua Santa, Huberto Naranjo's doomed rebel army, and the lives of abandoned children like Consuelo and Eva Luna. At the death of Professor Jones, a dismemberment motif seizes the action with the dissemination of his personal effects and with the hacking up of his mummies into "unsavory mincemeat" to disclose the secrets of embalming, a ghoulish reality in the home where Eva comes of age (Allende, 1987, 53).

Life in the Margins

Viljoen acknowledges Eva's flight to a "contradictory world where the whores and thieves who populate the red light district are more honest and better organized than the police force" (Viljoen, 2004, 80). Within the demimonde, Eva finds beauty and generosity among society's outcasts, the marginal people who dominate Allende's fiction. By shaping and reshaping the dreams and passions of these pariahs, Eva seizes "the opportunity for self-representation through tactics that reveal and reverse relationships of power" (*ibid.*, 81). By succeeding at a writing career, she gains a measure of control: "Little by little, the past was transformed into the present, and the future was also mine" (Allende, 1987, 224).

The intercalary chapters on Rolf Carlé's childhood exhibit the narrative horror of a Grimm's fairy tale, especially the discovery of Rolf's evil father, Lukas Carlé, found hanging from a noose. He follows Eva's escapism with the request, "Tell me a story, to get our minds off things" (Allende, 1987, 280). The qualities of farmers' daughters jokes and fool tales persist, including the bedding of voluptuous Germanic sisters, the birth of a two-headed baby, and a voodoo exorcism of "The Little Monster Murderess" (Allende, 1987, 105). Central to the political subtext, the boyish idealism of university students and young recruits singing by the campfire shifts to a Gothic tale of modern invention—"a conflict without mercy or restraint" plotted by Comandante Rogelio and his henchmen according to a "revolution code of ethics" (*ibid.*, 237, 238).

For Eva Luna, writing becomes a means of raising consciousness in herself and others to social and political injustice, such as the shooting death of the son of Inés the schoolteacher for stealing a mango, a tragedy repeated in "The Schoolteacher's Guest." To ensure the storyteller's survival through vivid composition, scenes of self-reliance and invention reset the freedom of Scheherazade in Harun al-Rashid's story compendium *A Thousand and One Nights.* The creation of a storytelling voice suited Allende as an alter ego. The author felt Eva "inside me, as if I were a glove and she were the hand inside the glove," an image paralleling puppetry (Gregory, 2003, 82). Through imaginary collaboration, the pairing gave Allende a fictional "dreamself" (*ibid.*). Literary historian Donald Leslie Shaw links Eva Luna's "self-affirmation ... through the medium of writing" to that of Alba del Valle in *The House of the Spirits* (Shaw, 2002, 182). Later characters, including Alexander Cold and his writer grandmother Kate in *City of Beasts,* frame stories as a means of capturing historical events worth remembering and disseminating.

The Extrovert's Creation

A brash, optimistic mestiza, Eva reinvents Eve, the Old Testament mother of humankind, as a moon-driven female creator blessed with street smarts. A literary sister of Jane Eyre, the protagonist milks from Riad Halabí the elements of personhood that she lacks.

Their daily fun consists of gab fests, cooking Arab recipes, and silly attempts at belly dancing. With a birth certificate and literacy, Eva advances to teacher of Riad's wife and to seducer, thus elevating Riad's importance from *patrón*/parent to playful lover of a pseudo-daughter. Simultaneously, Rolf Carlé becomes the sole journalist to follow the overthrow of a German dictatorship and the rise of guerrilla warfare; however, the novel's action directs violence away from the Germany mountains to Zulema, who shoots herself in the mouth to elude guilt. Eva's description, a stream of consciousness outpouring after a day of torture by police, connects Kamal's disappearance with the unsatisfied wife's seduction and depression. As self-assuagement, Eva spills the details, an "uncontainable outpouring, one after the other ... I didn't do it, didn't do it, didn't do it" (Allende, 1987, 198).

A reflection of Catherine Earnshaw's spiritual presence in *Wuthering Heights*, Eva's metamorphosis into a libido-crazed enamorata of guerrilla chief Huberto Naranjo unleashes a daring self, a female persona drawn to secret assignations with a self-styled terrorist. At a climax of self-awareness, Eva realizes a feminist truth: "As long as I lived I would still have to make my own way," an epiphany she shares with Eliza Sommers in *Daughter of Fortune* (Allende, 1987, 233). With Eva's new typewriter, she unfurls a clean sheet as though making a bed for welcoming a lover. Unfettered imagination provides materials as "characters stepped from the shadows where they had been hidden for years" (*ibid.*, 251). She interprets the natural flow of narrative as innate: "I could see an order to the stories stored in my genetic memory since before my birth" (*ibid.*, 251).

Critic Francis Abao refers to Eva's epiphany as a metatext—a romantic heroine summarizing the flaws of romantic idealism. As Eva views the sanitized pairings of romance novels, she pictures metaphoric passion between the deserving fictional virgin and her muscular, steely-eyed seducer. The epitome of the stereotypical union resides in ritual wedlock, the closed curtains that shield the tender reader from wild carnality on the lawn or an elemental coupling to the sweep of the tide. Eva shortcuts the romantic finis by celebrating love with Rolf Carlé, the photojournalist whose uninhibited fling with a professional writer foretells a shared sexuality alive with joy. Their union, a parallel to that of Irene Beltrán and Francisco Leal in *Of Love and Shadows*, recurs in the story "And of Clay Are We Created," a tale of the disorder wrought by calamity and the job of the photojournalist to report the news. The storyteller projects a godlike power in tales where "every birth, death, and happening depended on me" (Allende, 1987, 188). Even death fails to sober Eva, who anticipates creating a fateful end for herself in the story of her choice.

• *References and Further Reading*

Abao, Frances Jane P. "The Power of Love: Rewriting the Romance in Isabel Allende's *The House of the Spirits* and *Eva Luna*," *Humanities Diliman* 1:2 (July–January 2000): 87–99.

Gregory, Stephen. "Scheherazade and Eva Luna: Problems in Isabel Allende's Storytelling," *Bulletin of Spanish Studies* 80:1 (January 2003): 81–101.

Jorgensen, Beth E. "'Un Punado de Criticos': Navigating the Critical Readings of Isabel Allende's Work," *Latin American Literary Review* 30:60 (July–December, 2002): 128–146.

Nelson, Alice A. *Political Bodies: Gender, History, and the Struggle for Narrative Power in Recent Chilean Literature*. Danvers, MA: Bucknell University Press, 2002.

Shaw, Donald Leslie. *A Companion to Modern Spanish-American Fiction*. Rochester, NY: Tamesis, 2002.

Viljoen, Hendrik Marthinus. *Storyscapes: South African Perspectives on Literature, Space, and Identity*. New York: Lang, 2004.

evil

Allende contemplates the dual nature of evil as both a tangible and abstruse enemy of good. Critic Alice Nelson applauds the author for "narratively [countering] evil in society with a promise of redemption, of restored innocence," such as the apology of Valmorain for theft in *Island Beneath the Sea*, Captain John Sommers's acknowledgement of his illegitimate child in *Daughter of Fortune*, and the repentant robber in the story "Clarisa" (Nelson, 2002, 197). Of the erratic nature of punishment, Allende once observed that there are too many villains in the world to requite them all for their crimes. In stories, like Eva Luna, the author is free to avenge offenses, as with the coma she inflicts on the plotter Mauro Carías in *City of the Beasts* and the fiery helicopter crash that incinerates Tex Armadillo in *Kingdom of the Golden Dragon*.

Allende chose raw evil as a text for her first novel, *The House of the Spirits*, a reenactment of her country's suffering under colonial masters and dictator Augusto Pinochet. In a hierarchy of criminality, miner and planter Esteban Trueba, proud and willful, misdirects his energies toward sexual debauchery, cruelty toward peons, and free-floating rage. As a senator, he uses power and prestige for pernicious purposes. Age and diminished wealth prevent him from fulfilling his goal of restoring Las Tres Marías to colonial splendor of the grandee lifestyle. Analyst Marta L. Wilkinson comments that Esteban "is horrified to find out that the family is aware of some of his sinful crimes, and never thinks that those acts will have repercussions within his 'legitimate' family, or upon later generations" (Wilkinson, 2008, 156). As his sister Férula predicts, he grows more frustrated and isolated, confined by a maleficent heart and unwillingness to love. He equates human achievement with control at any cost, even the subversion of a democratic government under tyranny. The fruit of his malignancy, the mestizo grandson, Colonel Esteban García, appears as a dark little boy who "would one day be the instrument of a tragedy that would befall [the] family" (Allende, 1985, 218). Critic Vincent Kling describes the irredeemable child as "unregenerate brutality, never to emerge into a new form" (Kling, 2010, 245).

Secrecy and collusion worsen after the election of a leftist president in 1970. Esteban departs his urban refuge and attends a secret lunch of military men, politicians, and white CIA agents to plot the downfall of the Marxist regime by sabotaging the economy. Symbolically, the cabal gathers at a "colonial-style house," a refuge for conservative ideas dating to the Spanish colonization in the Americas (Allende, 1985, 390). The scenario resonates with hints at conniving, from "cold fish" to "roast suckling pig," an image projecting the heartlessness of the coterie and their victimization of the hapless working class (*ibid.*, 391). Trueba vows, "We won't give him any peace," a strategy of ongoing vexation similar to that formulated by U.S. Republicans during the presidencies of Democrats Bill Clinton and Barack Obama (*ibid.*).

After choosing to "stockpile hatred," (Allende, 1985, 392), the reactionaries generate shortages, which fuel a black market, strikes, factionalism, and rationing of necessities—gasoline, soap, and sugar. Allende describes the left's retort to economic sabotage as a call to organize "as if for war" (*ibid.*, 397). Trueba's next move is to demand a military coup and to amass "pistols, submachine guns, rifles, and hand grenades" (*ibid.*, 401). The coming-to-knowledge that fascism curtails citizen rights overwhelms Trueba and his family with the horrendous execution of Jaime under a tank, a symbolic bludgeoning of an altruistic physician. The grip of dictatorship compounds opportunism through blacklisting, citizen disappearances, curfews, torture, and spying, a motif that Allende extends in her two subsequent novels. The depiction of Trueba recognizing the "hour of truth" and pouring out his sins to Tránsito Soto begins the healing of past wrongs for the family, symbolized by the arrival of three amputated fingers in the mail (*ibid.*, 457).

In Allende's third novel, *Of Love and Shadows*, the incubation of evil in the career of the narcissistic Lieutenant Juan de Dios Ramírez echoes the malice of Esteban García, the perverted military torturer in *The House of the Spirits*, and anticipates the unbridled savagery of Tadeo Céspedes in "Revenge." Allende moves from a four-generation saga to one event, the abduction and live burial of fifteen citizens at Lonquén, Chile, on October 7, 1973, who turned up as corpses five years later. The plot accounts for the "shadows"—the lieutenant's decline into bullying, sadism, murder, and necrophilia. She speaks the details of an individual slide into mayhem through the eyewitness account of Corporal Faustino Rivera, a soldier under Ramírez's command who accounts for the growth of authoritarian malevolence in a leader who once "had all the virtues of a good military man" (Allende, 1987, 131).

Critic Karen Ford identifies the shadow figures—the military police—as liars who propagate "the evil that lurks around every corner ... a star reminder of the ugliness of class and the perversion of power and truth," the downward trajectory that destroys Ramírez (Ford, 2007). In retrospect, the vainglory that fifteen-year-old Evangelina belittles by tossing the lieutenant onto the patio results in her torture, rape, and slaughter and the lieutenant's need to conceal a loss of status among his men. Additional torment of her brother Pradelio dramatizes the lieutenant's effort to recoup stature by obliterating evidence and memory "to repay to some degree the humiliation he had suffered at her hands" (Allende, 1987, 198). The nonspecific nature of place, time, and actors represents a broad swath of Latin American history while placing peripheral blame on American-trained economists and the CIA backing of tyrants, which critic Laurie Clancy terms "the macho element so common in Latin American culture" (Clancy, 2008).

As in Allende's first novel, the suppression of investigative reporting miscarries, further disclosing the see-no-evil mask of authoritarianism, which cloaks censorship, curfews, random murders, the blacklisting of radicals and union members, and the ban on public meetings and the media. Gradually, muted news of atrocities becomes more evident in the demand of families to learn the fate of the *desaparecidos* and "to insure that the men, women, and children swallowed up by that violence would never be forgotten" (Allende, 1987, 272). Change comes slowly through Irene's rejection of passivity and submission and her bravery in allying with the Catholic bishop to report depravity in an army official. The author describes Irene as one of the political heroes "who stand on the edge and therefore are not sheltered" (Ford, 2007). The passion and courage that energize Irene, her sidekick Francisco, and Mario the disguise artist to combat evil, even at the risk to their own lives, derive from "inner strength, a strength that is not based on social codes or expectations" (*ibid.*).

Military Evil

In fiction set in the late 1900s, Allende's masterful internal dialogue in *The Infinite Plan* words the mental dissolution of Gregory Reeves, a reserve officer in the Vietnam War whose grasp of morality crumbles under a barrage of inexplicable stimuli. Reared in a Los Angeles barrio under the implacable grasp of the Catholic church, he lives the daily chaos of kill or be killed. Ringed by the dead after a mountaintop firefight, he and the rest of the nine platoon members who survive all-night combat anticipate the overhead chop-chop of helicopters. In the light of one more survival of the impossible, Gregory perceives the damage that a fight to the death inflicts on his values, a mental lambasting that pits patriotism against moral rectitude. He fears "I've completely crossed over the line, lost any sense of good and bad, of what's decent" (Allende, 1993, 194).

The text flows hither and yon with wartime musings, the ineluctable torment of the contemplative man. Contributing to the gray gloom that enshrouds him, his wife Samantha's betrayal in casual couplings with other men inhibits a comforting fantasy of wife and home. On his own time, Gregory tries to offer courtesy to hospitable Vietnamese. In his head rings an existential truism: "We can't go through life without owing something to somebody" (Allende, 1993, 196). From the teachings of Cyrus, the elevator operator, Gregory repeats to himself, "The only power that counts is the power of morality," a truism that proves hard to live by (*ibid.*, 205). Because Greg returns to civilian life bearing the onus of post-traumatic stress disorder, he blunders at attempts to achieve Cyrus's ideal.

An antiphonal refutation strikes Greg's brain, reminding him of patient, generous Pedro Morales, "another victim of this shithole society" who works hard to provide his urban family with the rudiments of success (*ibid.*). Greg contrasts Pedro's grit with the inadequacies of eighteen-year-old recruits. Instead of clarity of endeavor, Gregory views the emptiness in the eyes of young soldiers. Uncertain of the unit's aims and beliefs, he quibbles, "We're the good guys, aren't we? (*ibid.*, 210). He lapses into cynicism and pictures himself profiting from power and prestige, his version of the success enjoyed by black marketer Leo Galupi. Although the soul wrestling leaves Greg in amoral limbo, the struggle at least saves him from becoming "an alcoholic-drug-addict-dregs-of-the-world veteran" (*ibid.*, 206). His reason remains ignobly pragmatic: "There's enough of them already" (*ibid.*). Rather than accept the vision of himself as a combat-crazed derelict, he thinks of his daughter Margaret and looks to the color-burst of sunrise for hope.

Civil Struggles

In her more recent fiction, Allende sets characters in national and global conflicts too pervasive, too complicated for one person to combat. For Le Cap, Haiti, in *Island Beneath the Sea*, vice and opportunism dominate human relationships, especially between high and low caste and between whites and people of color. In the pervasive opinion in a place where "vice was the norm, honor for sale, and laws made to be broken, ... he who did not abuse power did not deserve to have it" (Allende, 2010, 15). Planter Toulouse Valmorain, a wine smuggler, discerns a similar pattern of dissipation in Cuba by men like Sancho García del Solar, a "rowdy bachelor" with a brazen imagination given to gambling and posturing to cover his indebtedness (*ibid.*, 25). Valmorain's literary foil, Dr. Parmentier, asserts that his observations in Africa lead him to agree only that whites are greedier and more violent that blacks: "That explains our power and the extent of our empires" (*ibid.*, 84). Valmorain, reared in inherited wealth and privilege, bases his riposte on the exigencies of a slave economy—without bondage, the plantation system would collapse.

Allende contrasts the lackadaisical Valmorain with his sinister overseer, Prosper Cambray, a hireling who "lacked fortune or patrons" (Allende, 2010, 46). A cruel driver of blacks to extremes of exhaustion, he makes up for penury with a "brutal character and killer's physique" (*ibid.*). Cambray enjoys sexual debauchery with women and raises black gladiators for the ring and snarling mastiffs to devour fugitives on the run. With whip and pistol, he subdues field hands and replaces the dead as easily as buying livestock to replace slaughtered beasts. Valmorain's less barbarous methods of discipline clash with Cambray's personal preference roasting incorrigibles "over a slow fire," a torment dramatized in Toni Morrison's *Beloved* (*ibid.*, 163). Within Cambray's gaze, slaves can only hope for invisibility and a lengthy span between applications of the lash.

For greed-based plots in *City of the Beasts*, Allende stresses the concealment of evil under an appealing appearance and technology, a method, according to veteran reviewer Hazel Rochman, that "shakes up all the usual definitions of savagery and civilization" (Rochman, 2002, 590). Through what Nora Krug characterizes as "bickering and double-crossing," characters reveal their dominant traits (Krug, 2003, 21). Mauro Carías, an industrialist who milks the Amazon for its riches, poses behind white teeth, clean hands, and impressive sports wear. Although rumors of criminal behavior circulate, accusers hesitate to breach the exterior pose of propriety and politesse. Additional evidence of hospitality from a lunch of meat and cheese, shellfish, fruit, and ice cream imply graciousness. The entrepreneur demonstrates his acquisitive, overbearing nature by caging a jaguar, a status pet he intends to display in his private zoo in Rio de Janeiro. As comic relief to the machinations of a killer, Allende poses anthropologist Ludovic Leblanc, an egotistical fool whom reviewer Carol Birch identifies as "a complete caricature of a colonial twit," the foil of the wise shaman Walimai and the odious Carías (Birch, 2002).

The cast of characters aroused conflicting critical opinions about intent and harm. Birch accused Allende of reducing Amazonian Indians to a new version of the noble savage "as if they simply do not have the same human qualities as the rest of us" (*ibid.*). In the council session in the land of the gods, Alex tries to mediate native decisions involving saving the fragile People of the Mist from extinction by outsiders. He admits the evil of greedy whites, yet maintains "not all *nahab* were evil demons" (*ibid.*, 223). He nurtures a rosy belief that good whites can halt the destruction wrought by malicious ones and that his grandmother's articles for the *International Geographic* can stop exploiters from "committing crimes in this part of the world with the same impunity as always" (*ibid.*, 391). Allende implies that Alex, like idealistic world leaders, confronts immediate perils, but has no plan for controlling the plunder of Brazil or for preserving the natural wonders of the Eye of the World.

In the sequel, *Kingdom of the Golden Dragon*, the identification of evil in the collusion and secrecy of Tex Armadillo and a man tattooed with a scorpion suggests a poisonous presence within the tourist celebration of a Tibetan holiday, when the Blue Horsemen kidnap six girls. Reviewer Susan Carlile describes the scorpion sect as "an ancient fighting troupe that today functions as a mercenary band," a fair assessment of dacoity recycled from the Indian thuggee traditions in Kipling's short stories in *Actions and Reactions* and Mark Twain's travelogue *Following the Equator* (Carlile, 2005, 170). Allende identifies pernicious elements in the abductors, particularly filth and oral faults— garlic breath, the smells of liquor and tobacco, missing teeth, and teeth blackened from chewing betel nut, all emblematic of deception and lies. The action implies a phallic threat from Pema's admirer, a Blue Horseman who fondles his dagger's handle. Worsening the menace, a statue to Kali "the black one" discloses the worship of the death goddess with skulls and poisonous vermin.

Allende reveals the Blue Horsemen's intent to hobble and silence six girls by branding feet and cutting out tongues, standard ploys of female disempowerment of action and words. Contrasting the kidnappers' gang mentality, the monomaniacal Collector prefers abduction of a prince or bribery as the means of obtaining the dragon statue and its interpretive code. An impatient, behind-the-scenes villain, the Collector operates under the First World assumption that "little kings of second-rate countries are all corrupt" and therefore susceptible to pain, greed, lust, and the will to control nuclear power (Allende, 2004, 209). Lacking understanding of mysticism, the Collector compares the spiritual detachment of "the king of some dinky country" to the trickery of circus fakirs, a devaluation common to ethnocentrists (*ibid.*, 211). The overthrow of an evil regicide and female insurgent requires a *tour de force* cooperation of soldiers, Yetis, American adults, a Buddhist guru, a royal prince, and teenagers, who employ what reviewer Hazel Rochman summarizes as "a mix of telepathy, technology, guns, and Tao-shu," an Asian form of martial arts (Rochman, 2004, 1050).

The collaborative overthrow of villainy recurs in *Forest of the Pygmies*, in which the hunter Beyé-Dokou and native women, led by Alex Cold, Nadia Santos, and Kenyan pilot Angie Ninderera, ramp up combined powers to bring down a poacher and enslaver. In place of torture and murder, Allende substitutes a pond of crocodiles, thus according ultimate blame to an African carnivore. Reviewer Janet hunt characterizes "sinister undertones: the cruel dictator; a fetishistic, mask-wearing mad king; a witch doctor," elements of Joseph Conrad's *Heart of Darkness* as well as "bitter realities of modern Africa" under Idi Amin, Joseph Mugabe, and Moammar Qaddafi (Hunt, 2005). The falling action deflates evil in Central Africa with a cooperative model by which "Bantus needed the meat the hunters provided, and the little people couldn't live without the products they obtain in Ngoubé" (Allende, 2005, 288). With a gesture of faith in women, Queen Nana-Asante trusts African females to establish peace by disseminating goodness.

See also violence; war

• *References and Further Reading*

Birch, Carol. "Review: *City of the Beasts*," (Manchester) *Guardian* (30 November 2002): 33.

Carlile, Susan. "Review: *Kingdom of the Golden Dragon*," *Journal of Adolescent & Adult Literacy* 49:2 (1 October 2005): 170.

Clancy, Laurie. "Isabel Allende's 1988 Novel Looks Again at Love and Dictators," *The* (Melbourne) *Age* (11 February 2008).

Ford, Karen. "Triumph of Truth and Love," *The* (Melbourne) *Age* (23 September 2007).

Hunt, Janet. "Review: *Forest of the Pygmies*," *New Zealand Herald* (7 May 2005).

Kling, Vincent. "Archetype, Not Ideology: Isabel Allende's Balance of Opposites," *Critical Insights* (October 2010): 239–257.

Krug, Nora. "Review: *City of the Beasts*," *The New York Times* (9 February 2003): 21.

Nelson, Alice A. *Political Bodies: Gender, History, and the Struggle for Narrative Power in Recent Chilean Literature*. Danvers, MA: Bucknell University Press, 2002.

Rochman, Hazel. "Review: City of the Beasts," *Booklist* 99:6 (15 November 2002): 590.

_____. "Review: *Kingdom of the Golden Dragon*," *Booklist* 100:12 (15 February 2004): 1050.

Wilkinson, Marta L. *Antigone's Daughters: Gender, Family, and Expression in the Modern Novel*. New York: Peter Lang, 2008.

female persona

Allende regards women as the fulcrums by which society moves mountains: "Around them revolve their own children and others they have taken in; they care for the aged, the ill, the unfortunate—they are the axis of the community" (Allende, 1994, 140). The comment encompasses a cast of whores, shamans, consolers, nanas, cooks, and volunteers. The list encompasses Azucena Placeres, the Indian prostitute who tends Eliza in *Daughter of Fortune*, the oracle Má Bangesé in *Forest of the Pygmies*, the nameless woman who retrieves Alba from the dump in *The House of the Spirits*, and Doña Elvira Domínguez, the teacher of sewing classes for wives of tenant farmers in *Portrait in Sepia*. In the style of other Latin American writers of the feminist renaissance—Argentinian Luis Valenzuela, Mexican Elena Poniatowska, Puerto Rican Rosario Ferré, and Uruguayan Cristina Peri Rossi—Allende allies female characters with the themes of labor, sacrifice, optimism, and joy in womanhood. In the estimation of critic Marta L. Wilkinson, the alliance of women "fuses the domestic and public spheres in the feminine experience" (Wilkinson, 2008, 151). The descriptors apply to Isabel and Francisca in *Paula*, to Toypurna and White Owl, the mother and grandmother of Diego de la Vega in *Zorro*, and, in *Portrait in Sepia*, to Eliza and Nívea del Valle, whom reviewer Falconer calls "the sex-obsessed revolutionary wife with fifteen children" who teaches Eliza by example how to produce and nurture a family (Falconer, 2001).

Horror marks the author's perusals of history, which critic Yvonne Zipp admires for avoiding "politically correct revisionism" (Zipp, 2006, 17). The title figure in *Inés of My Soul* recognizes the hypocrisy of church tradition, which places the burden of fidelity on wives while freeing males to indulge their carnal and military fantasies. After her husband departs for the New World, Inés prays for the opportunity to escape female bondage and join adventurers in the Western Hemisphere. Reviewer Celia McGee lauds the move that turns the grass widow into a "smart, ambitious, self-made colonista" with a "utopian streak" (McGee, 2006).

According to Adriana Herrera, a critic writing for *Americas*, by the choice of female space for her fiction, the author opens her work to denigration by academics who disdain love stories and women's domain, particularly kitchen work and child care. In retort to carping by academics, Allende embraces gynocentric literature featuring rebel females who are "always passionate in their lives and loyal to other women ... not moved by ambition but by love" (Pabst, 2008). The designations characterize the work of liberal anti-government, anti–Catholic subversives in *Portrait in Sepia*, notably, Sor María Escapulario, the "nun with the heart of a lioness," and Señorita Matilde Pineda, the tutor endowed with socialistic fervor during the 1891 Chilean Civil War (Allende, 2001, 25).

In a foreword to *Imagining Ourselves: Global Voices from a New Generation of Women* (2007), Allende stated, "I am startled by the assured attitude of these young women, their creative force, and their capacity for leadership. Nothing can stop them" (Allende, 2007). Her choice of qualities begins with self-assurance and moves in two directions—creativity and self-empowerment. Like the tetrad of Nívea, Clara, Blanca, and Alba in *The House of the Spirit*, Allende's celebration of sisterhood allots to each woman new opportunities to express individual strengths and perspectives, particularly suffrage and social reform. As Marta Wilkinson explains, Alba becomes "not just the last generation, but an intricate, valid, and significant part of her family's history" (Wilkinson, 2008, 156).

The author recognizes in females a skill for weaving narrative "while stirring soup, sowing fields, or mending fishing nets," a commentary on the humble endeavors of the peasant (Allende, 2008, ix). She notes, moreover, that women's perspective lies in mundane activities rather than macho power struggles or "the vanity of emperors," such as the everyday telepathy of the Mora sisters in *My Invented Country* (*ibid.*). Because shantytown females in Chile resided in the domestic sphere and provided meager incomes to replace missing sons and husbands, Pinochet labeled women expendable. Like the repressed women in Barbara Kingsolver's *Animal Dreams*, Chilean women made *arpilleras*, scraps of cloth stitched with yarn in narrative patterns and raised as humble banners of resistance. An emblem of frugal recycling elevated to folk art, each story cloth increased female solidarity against repression. Like the AIDS quilt's witness to official disinterest in a gay sickness and children born with HIV, female labor demanded in vivid shape and color the return of justice to Chile.

Networking

Allende creates networks of female characters who share trials and sisterhood like siblings, a loving bond such as that of La Señora and the title figure in *Eva Luna*, among the enslaved Aka maidservants in *Forest of the Pygmies*, and between Antonia Sierra and Concha Díaz in "The Gold of Tomás Vargas." The friendship between Pema and Nadia in *Kingdom of the Golden Dragon* illustrates the strength of gender over cultural and racial differences. Reviewer Susan Carlile remarks on the presence of Nadia as a "precious asset ... a steady reminder that the young and the small in stature have an essential role to play in the most stressful and dangerous situations," particularly scaling and rappelling in the Himalayas and leading victims out of danger (Carlile, 2005, 170). More crucial to Allende's style, according to critic Shannin Schroeder, women provide magical realism with children, home, and revolt, elements evident in oppositional feminist works by Maxine Hong Kingston, Leslie Marmon Silko, Amy Tan, and Toni Morrison.

Females express curiosity about the privileges and strictures affecting the lives of other women, such as the domestic discipline governing the life of the Tibetan girl Pema in *Kingdom of the Golden Dragon*. Her father Wandgi insists that "No respectable girl went out alone at night and without her parents' permission" (Allende, 2004, 170). Tibetan peasants enhance drama after Scorpions dressed like devils kidnap Pema, her friend Nadia, and four local girls, ostensibly to enslave them until the "young slave girls died of illness or mistreatment, or were simply murdered" (*ibid.*, 173). Allende allows freelance writer Kate Cold, whom analysts Yulisa Maddy and Donnarae MacCann call a self-conscious nonconformist, to surge to prominence as persuader of General Myar Kunglung to organize a regional search for the girls (Maddy and MacCann, 2009, 56). The scenario falls back on time-honored humor featuring a pompous male hounded by a relentless female.

Critics Gary Bridge and Sophie Watson note the inevitability of survival in women who overcome indifference and alienation through female bonding. In a parallel of the ambitious prostitute Tránsito Soto in *The House of the Spirits*, the warmth of Joan, a restaurant owner in *The Infinite Plan*, allies with the friendship of Susan. Devoted to "the feminist struggle and the culinary chemistry" of vegetarianism, the duo thrives in business (Allende, 1993, 172). After overcoming the clumsy lie that Carmen utters to get a job, Joan sweeps over the deception and embraces Carmen as a friend in need. To seal the womanly collaboration, Carmen adds brio to the menu and shapes earrings as a thank-you gift. Partners Joan and Susan welcome the baubles and declare themselves "feminists but still feminine," a version of the Three Musketeers' declaration "All for one and one for all" (*ibid.*, 232).

Variety in Activism

As Joan's faith in women illustrates, the gendered activism of Allende's female casts develops individuality through blended character traits and beliefs:

woman	*title*	*role*
Adèle	*Island Beneath the Sea*	seamstress, concubine
Alba del Valle	*House of the Spirits*	freedom fighter, collator of family history

woman	*title*	*role*
Amanda	*House of the Spirits*	sexual adventurer, victim of abortion and drugs
Amanda Lowell	*Portrait in Sepia*	entertainer, courtesan
Ana	*Zorro*	wet nurse, mother
Angie Ninderera	*Forest of the Pygmies*	pilot, adviser
Aurora del Valle	*Portrait in Sepia*	photographer, scandalous wife
Beatriz Beltrán	*Of Love and Shadows*	mother, supporter of fascism
Blanca del Valle	*House of the Spirits*	rebel, wife of a revolutionary
Carmen Morales	*The Infinite Plan*	friend, jewelry maker
Clara del Valle	*House of the Spirits*	peacemaker and redeemer, spiritualist, recorder of events
Consuelo	*Eva Luna*	comforter, mother
Digna Ranquileo	*Of Love and Shadows*	devout Catholic, responsible farm wife
Elena Mejías	*Stories of Eva Luna*	schoolgirl, seductress
Eliza Sommers	*Daughter of Fortune* *Portrait in Sepia*	risk taker, idealist, pastry chef
Elvira	*Eva Luna*	cook, surrogate grandparent
Eva Luna	*Eva Luna* *Stories of Eva Luna*	feminist storyteller, shopkeeper
Evangelina	*Of Love and Shadows*	teen rape victim
Férula	*House of the Spirits*	repressed lesbian, handmaiden
Granny	*Paula*	mother, protester
Hilda Leal	*Of Love and Shadows*	refugee, mother
Inés Suarez	*Inés of My Soul*	widow, conquistadora
Inmaculada	*The Infinite Plan*	mother figure, worker
Irene Beltrán	*Of Love and Shadows*	witness to corruption, investigator
Isabel	*Zorro*	observer, storyteller
Joe Bonecrusher	*Daughter of Fortune*	brothel owner, rescuer
Juliana	*Zorro*	heiress, rehabilitator
Kate Cold	*City of the Beasts* *Kingdom of the Golden Dragon* *Forest of the Pygmies*	writer, adventurer
Light-in-the-Night	*Zorro*	companion, mother
Loula	*Island Beneath the Sea*	slave, usurer
Madrina	*Eva Luna*	cook, godmother
Mama Fresia	*Daughter of Fortune*	cook, healer, mother
Mora sisters	*House of the Spirits*	spiritualists
Nadia Santos	*City of the Beasts* *Kingdom of the Golden Dragon* *Forest of the Pygmies*	adventurer, shapeshifter, rescuer
Nana-Asante	*Forest of the Pygmies*	queen, hermit, peacemaker
Nívea	*House of the Spirits*	feminist, suffragist
Nora Reeves	*The Infinite Plan*	ineffectual parent, idealist
Olga	*The Infinite Plan*	healer, fortune teller
Paulina del Valle	*Daughter of Fortune* *Portrait in Sepia*	investor, grandmother
Pema	*Kingdom of the Golden Dragon*	friend, leader, risk taker
Regina	*Zorro*	warrior, visionary
Rose Sommers	*Daughter of Fortune*	secretive erotic novelist, foster mother
Tante Rose	*Island Beneath the Sea*	healer, high priestess
Tránsito Soto	*House of the Spirits*	courtesan, self-actualizer
Violette Boisier	*Island Beneath the Sea*	courtesan, usurer
White Owl	*Zorro*	healer, educator
Zarité	*Island Beneath the Sea*	sex slave, survivor
Zulema	*Eva Luna*	wife, adulterer, suicide

The uniqueness of womanhood sets apart woman's work in terms of its contribution to culture, as with the funeral arrangements that Nana makes for Rosa in *The House of the Spirits* and the tasks of Madame Odilia and Marie Laveau in *Zorro* to superintend Pierre's birth and the burial of his mother, Catherine Villars, a victim of puerperal fever. While Odilia possesses the magic potions to ensure the success of Juliana de Romeu as Pierre's stepmother and the second wife of Jean Lafitte, Juliana's earthly talents and willing heart to promote the formation of the new family and the perpetuation of life. Their teamwork dramatizes a pervasive strange in Allende's feminism, which maintains faith in women's cooperatives, a motif the recurs in the mining camps in *Daughter of Fortune* and in the unseating of a dictator in *Forest of the Pygmies*.

For *Of Love and Shadows*, Allende crafts a three-fold view of Latinas suffering a magnitude of governmental crimes. At the top, Beatriz Alcántara and daughter Irene Beltrán represent the diminishment of the upper class. At the middle, Hilda Leal, a refugee from Franco's Spain, applies intellectualism and prayer vigils to the hardships of émigrés under the junta. After breakdowns into tears, she "dried her tears, gathered strength from the reserves in her innermost being, and prepared to fight once again for her own" (Allende, 1987, 126). Allende validates the friendship of Hilda with Irene as a preface to a stable relationship as mother-in-law and daughter-in-law, a pairing that recurs in *Portrait in Sepia* between Aurora and Doña Ester Domínguez.

At bottom of the socio-economic hierarchy, the laboring-class difficulties of Digna Ranquileo illustrate the vulnerability of peasants. The poorest, least educated are the least likely to relieve poverty and ward off the atrocities of an egotistical military, which captures, rapes, and murders Digna's daughter Evangelina. Alike in their rebellion through silence and unvoiced ritual, the five women—Beatriz, Hilda, Irene, Digna, and Evangelina—clash with a patriarchal army that oppresses the citizenry. Eventually, popular anger foments riots so vigorous that "not even the police shock troops and Army heavy equipment could control the people" (Allende, 1987, 274).

Domestic Sisterhood

Each of Allende's texts sets action in domestic interiors, as demonstrated by the storyteller's tent in "Two Words" and the compact barrio homes in *The Infinite Plan*. Within the positive aura of home, such as the Domínguez ranch in *Portrait in Sepia*, Joe Bonecrusher's caravan in *Daughter of Fortune*, Paulina's mansion during the looting of Santiago in *Portrait in Sepia*, and Violette's town house and Eugenia's quarters in the Habitation of Saint-Lazare in *Island Beneath the Sea*, women find ways to survive chaos and threat. Critic Susan Carvalho admires the female quest for self and sexual liberation, qualities in Eliza Sommers that the author mirrors in her granddaughter Aurora, a survivor of a sham marriage. Even in the contrast between the private quarters that immure the del Valle women in *The House of the Spirits* to their urban mansion and their hacienda at Las Tres Marías, female characters manage to work together, educating peasant children and undermining the caching of weapons by suppressors of the citizenry.

To survey feminists, Allende chooses Carmen Morales, the jewelry artist in *The Infinite Plan*, the belligerent prostitute in "Simple María," and Eliza Sommers, the tempestuous wanderer in *Daughter of Fortune* and pastry shop owner in *Portrait in Sepia*. In the estimation of reviewer Kris Dinnison, Eliza, her daughter Lin/Lynn, Lynn's daughter Aurora, and Aurora's paternal grandmother Paulina "pick their way around society's expectations" and set unique courses (Dinnison, 2002). They rebel against the previous generation's gendered obstacles and free their spirits from patriarchal constraints demanding chastity and sexual abstinence. Eliza, who "fell in love with freedom," invests her future with the energy and promise of the California gold rush of 1849 (Allende, 1999, 275). She eludes the claustrophobic childhood home and frilly outfits that infantilized her, keeping her timid, ignorant, and dependent. Through Eliza, other women gain support, a source of spirituality that becomes the gateway to wisdom. Female passages mark high points in ritual detail, such as the parallel arrival of Aurora at adolescence, Nívea into labor and birthing, and Grandmother Paulina into menopause in *Portrait in Sepia*. In *Zorro*, Light-in-the-Night uses the blood of menarche to paint a ritual rune of her devotion, which she shapes into two flying birds. For Aurora, whom a reviewer for *Irish Times* views as a "child of passion and tragedy," intellectual curiosity empowers her to elude the pitfalls of sentimental Catholicism and the customary straitjacketing by church and male family moguls ("Review," August 2002). Education under Sor María Escapulario and Señorita Matilde Pineda replaces the ritual upbringing of Catholic youth in androcentric church dogma with a free-thinking study of research and logical debate, a liberal departure from readying young women for the marriage market.

The Historical Heroine

On a more stirring plane of action, in *Inés of My Soul*, adventurer Inés Suárez becomes what reviewer Amber Haq terms "the visionary architect of the nation of Chile" (Haq, 2006). The protagonist internalizes the mission of her lover, Général Pedro de Valdivia, who epitomizes the glory hounds who conquered Latin America. Critic Celia McGee pictures the Spanish heroine as she "sits astride her own epic," a defiant posture in an era when women rode side saddle (McGee, 2006). According to reviewer Pamela Miller, Inés is "wholly a woman of her day," a blend of warrior and nurturer (Miller, 2006). Among phalanxes of soldiers, she "walked with the long strides of a Gypsy ... pure energy, like a contained cyclone" (Allende, 2006, 91, 92). Her innate qualities parallel the vigor of the New World, where lowered social mores encourage newcomers— male and female — to set their own values. Relying on dreams and the divination of her servant Catalina, Inés recognizes in Valdivia the man destined to be her lover. Her chutzpah in seducing and overpowering him presages the role that Inés plays in Valdivia's career and in the founding of Santiago.

Late in the colonial era, the unique powers of Tante Rose as a *mambo* or priestess in *Island Beneath the Sea* derive from her skill at birthing and curing and from her prominence among blacks as a high priestess of voodoo. For Tété, advice from Tante Rose convinces the girl to spare her fetus, whose mixed blood will not dismay a master inured to mulattos and quadroons. The emergence of Tété's regard for voodoo *loa*, especially her patron goddess Erzulie, arouses what critic William Kowalski terms "a talent for manipulation and a mystical connection to the divine feminine," a quality that Tété passes to daughter Rosette (Kowalski, 2010). At a critical moment in the preparation of Gambo for his mission of freedom, Tante Rose tutors him in trail lore, naming deadly plants and snakes and describing how to greet Ghede, the spirit of the dead, and choose a path from the crossroads between the living and the underworld.

Because of women's diminished roles in the Haitian revolt, Allende is slow to reveal Tante Rose's centrality to the slave grapevine and to her night passages to the Maroon villages in the impenetrable mountains. At a public revelation, she levitates "straight up to double her size, with neither lameness nor years on her back, ... made an astounding leap and landed nearly ten feet away" (Allende, 2010, 160). The old woman knows how to poison mastiffs with chili powder and how to recognize zombies by looks and odor.

Significant to the historicity of the text, Tante Rose's value to the Haitian Revolution involves her background role as an adviser. With an elder's wisdom, she distracts Gambo from his phobias by warning "you need to fear some of the living" (Allende, 2010, 143). Central to his physical exertions, the magic leaves of "nature's fresh greenery" from Rose's pharmacopoeia energize the sixteen-year-old with a natural substance similar to the coca that revives Mapuche warriors in *Inés of My Soul*, highland Indians in *Portrait in Sepia*, the table steward in *The House of the Spirit*, patients in *Daughter of Fortune*, and travelers in *Paula* and receives mention as a satisfier of hunger in Allende's *Aphrodite* (*ibid.*, 73). Through Rose's immersion with island powers and her dissemination of curatives, she abets the slave insurrection that spreads the cry of liberty from Haiti across the Caribbean and the Americas.

See also feminism; male persona; marriage

• *References and Further Reading*

Abao, Frances Jane P. "The Power of Love: Rewriting the Romance in Isabel Allende's *The House of the Spirits* and *Eva Luna*," *Humanities Diliman* 1:2 (July–January 2000): 87–99.
Carlile, Susan. "Review: *Kingdom of the Golden Dragon*," *Journal of Adolescent & Adult Literacy* 49:2 (1 October 2005): 170.
Dinnison, Kris. "Review: *Portrait in Sepia*," (Spokane) *Pacific Northwest Inlander* (21 February 2002).
Falconer, Helen. "Colouring the Family Album," (Manchester) *Guardian* (17 November 2001).
Haq, Amber. "The Mother of Chile: Isabel Allende's New Novel Celebrates the Spanish Conquistadora Who Helped Create a New Nation," *Newsweek* (13 November 2006).
Herrera, Adriana. "And God Made Me a Woman," *Americas* 61:6 (November/ December 2009): 48–51.
Kowalski, William. "A Mixed Outcome," (Toronto) *Globe and Mail* (27 May 2010).
Maddy, Yulisa Amadu, and Donnarae MacCann. *Neo-Imperialism in Children's Literature about Africa: A Study of Contemporary Fiction*. New York: Routledge, 2009.
McGee, Celia. "'Ines' Captures Chile's Soul in 1500s," *USA Today* (9 November 2006).
Miller, Pamela. "Isabel Allende's New Novel Is Set in the 1500s, But the Parallels to Contemporary Issues Are Unmistakable," (Minneapolis) *Star Tribune* (31 October 2006).
Pabst, Georgia. "'Sum' Allows Spirited Look at Passionate Allende," *Milwaukee Journal Sentinel* (20 April 2008).
Perricone, C.R. "Allende and Valenzuela: Dissecting the Patriarchy," *South Atlantic Review* 67:4 (Fall, 2002): 80–105.
"Review: *Portrait in Sepia*," *Irish Times* (10 August 2002).
Schroeder, Shannin. *Rediscovering Magical Realism in the Americas*. Westport, CT: Praeger, 2004.
Shaw, Donald Leslie. *A Companion to Modern Spanish-American Fiction*. Rochester, NY: Tamesis, 2002.
Wilkinson, Marta L. *Antigone's Daughters: Gender, Family, and Expression in the Modern Novel*. New York: Peter Lang, 2008.
Zipp, Yvonne. "The Mother of Chile, Rescued from Obscurity," *Christian Science Monitor* 99:17 (19 December 2006): 17.

feminism

Isabel Allende's commitment to feminism yields "not a war against men, but ... definitely a war against patriarchy" (Richards, 2008). In *My Invented Country*, the author states that, despite her patriarchal stepfather, grandfather, brother, and uncles, independence has guided her from before memory. The dramatic ironies in the author's dogmatic ideas and outspoken pronouncement reside in the likeness of her temperament to that of her formidable grandfather. Critic Peter Cameron observed that, by definition of gender itself, the grandfather "was unable to foster or even condone such unfeminine characteristics" (Cameron, 2003, 19).

Allende's canon dramatizes the feminist philosophy through the assertiveness and chutzpah of the characters Nívea and Clara del Valle in *The House of the Spirits*, Iyomi and Kate Cold in *City of the Beasts*, White Owl in *Zorro*, and Pema in *Kingdom of the Golden Dragon*. Analyst Marta L. Wilkinson notes that women like the del Valles, "began making more progress, creating regulations for working women and allowing suffrage for all literate women" (Wilkinson, 2008, 151–152). For comic relief in *Of Love and Shadows*, Digna Ranquileo-Sánchez accepts the decision of her husband, Hipólito, "because he was the man and was always right," a tongue-in-cheek truism that belies the male villainy that foregrounds the tragic plot (Allende, 1987, 36). To the despair of critics and educators, Allende expresses the macha behavior of women through typically male faults, notably, in *Forest of the Pygmies*, Kate's reliance on vodka for a daily pick-me-up and Angie Ninderera's constant beer guzzling and spitting tobacco as a gesture of disgust. By co-opting male behaviors, notes critic Shannin Schroeder, Allende "wrests Adamic power" from males the likes of the strutting Esteban Trueba in *House of the Spirits*, roué Rafael Moncada in *Zorro*, and Commandant Maurice Mbembelé, a reputed cannibal in *Forest of the Pygmies* (Schroeder, 2004).

Critic Vincent Kling perceives Allende's narrative females as "forces of nature, earth mothers, regenerative bodies, earthy and earthly but also spiritual in their power to inspire," a description often associated with maids, cooks, and nannies, particularly Consuelo in *Eva Luna* (Kling, 2010, 248). Two additional feminists, Nadia Santos and journalist Kate Cold, insist on joining the men in nightly guard duty. Allende envisions a sharing of mortal powers through freedom, choice, sisterhood, respect, and equal opportunities for all, especially those women ensnared in patriarchal religious hegemonies. In *Forest of the Pygmies*, guide Michael Mushaha makes an obvious toast to gynocentric society in his description of pygmy chimpanzees, which enjoy cooperation and healthy offspring because they avoid the male tendency to fight. In agreement, Kate Cold adds, "There's hope that someday we may evolve like them" (Allende, 2005, 37).

The Female Consciousness

One element of human endeavor, intelligence, according to interpreter C.R. Perricone, lags behind because of "the widespread and long-standing reluctance ... to identify *Logos* with women as much as with men" (Perricone, 2002, 81). Allende balances female heart with mental powers and wisdom in *The House of the Spirits* by presenting history from a gendered perspective, beginning with the suffragism of Nívea del Valle, whose symbolic intellect survives her body after a bizarre car accident decapitates her. The matriarch's feminism underlies the self-empowerment of her daughter Clara, granddaughter Blanca, and great-granddaughter Alba, the story's narrator and the fourth del Valle female to bear a name resplendent with light and enlightenment. Through Clara's hovering beneficence, subversion of male hegemony extends from the big house on the corner to the plantation Las Tres Marías, and, by extension, across the police state. Critic Stephen Hart lauds the rebellious del Valle females for "(forging) an alternative way of being by rejecting the values associated with the masculinity Trueba upholds," a national *machismo* that asserts male dominance through violations of human rights (Kristal, 2005, 195).

It is Nívea's daughter Clara rather than the del Valle sons who takes responsibility for chronicling history and for rescuing the past from neglect. Allende indicates that the del Valle women equal in strength and vision the dominant patriarchy, beginning with Nívea's "new woman" example of chaining herself to the gates of the legislature and Supreme

Court and canvassing with posters and demands for woman suffrage and equal rights to a university education. Through atemporal journals organized by theme, Clara reflects on happenings and passes to her daughter Blanca and granddaughter Alba a reflection on a period of change that dislodges the patriarchal conservative party from power and elevates peasants to positions of self-government. Clara stands at the divide between chaos and survival, nursing Esteban to health after the earthquake and tending Amanda after an illegal abortion. Essential to Blanca's mental health, her mother welcomes her the day after Blanca's marriage to the perverse Count de Satigny and whispers "just like in old times" (Allende, 1985, 286).

Allende exhibits the male supremacy Esteban Trueba and his illegitimate grandson, Colonel Esteban García, as a violent deracination of women and their bodies from what analyst Amy Shifflet terms "the sacred circle of life," the source of female consciousness (Shifflet, 2000, 31). The del Valle family's growing defiance of social injustice extends over the anarchic behaviors of daughter Clara and granddaughter Blanca and concludes with the political force of Blanca's illegitimate daughter Alba, who develops a rebel's resilience in prison. To Grandfather Esteban, Alba possesses too much promise to waste on matrimony. He chooses to rear her like a man destined for the professions. Doris Meyer points out the significance of the arrangement: "The grandfather represents the internalized patriarchal culture and the granddaughter the newly born feminist," the first generation of women to think and act on their own (Faris, 2004, 172). The reclamation of Esteban Trueba from fascist patriarchy to egalitarianism enables Allende to end the novel with hope.

The remainder of the *House of the Spirits* trilogy—*Daughter of Fortune* and *Portrait in Sepia*–depicts women in feminist versions of frontier myth in the clutches of patriarchal and racial traditions. For the sixteen-year-old heroine Eliza Sommers, running away from a tightly controlled environment in Valparaíso, Chile, puts her in company with a different breed of women who "go to bed for money and have their big toes in hell" (Allende, 1999, 143). At a disreputable seaside bar, Eliza's effrontery startles Tao Chi'en, whose "initial surprise turned into frank amazement. This woman was actually planning to dishonor her family," an Asian perspective on her impulsive departure (*ibid.*, 147). At first fearful that "a devil had gotten into her body," he relents, abets her concealment in the ship's hold, and enables her to grow into womanhood on the California frontier (*ibid.*).

As described by Editor Michael Sollars, the novel's action chronicles Eliza's "difficult rite of passage into finding her own place in the world," a setting far removed from gentility and docility in Chile (Sollars, 2008, 199). The locale suits the heroine's plan to flee a repressive home life and trail her lover, the father of her stillborn child, in hopes of marriage. Miss Rose confirms the era's solution to unplanned pregnancies, even those sired by bounders and despoilers by plotting to "confront the accursed seducer, force them to marry" (Allende, 1999, 251). The unshaped milieu, which expands on serendipity and subterfuge on the frontier, welcomes pioneer skills that suit the moment, such as Eliza's piano playing for Joe Bonecrusher's troupe of prostitutes and Eliza's frying empanadas to earn enough cash to bankroll a meandering search for her love, Joaquín Murieta, who remains on the dodge.

By imparting positive energies to male characters, women like Eliza renew both personal relationships and community, an act accomplished by the title conquistadora in *Inés of My Soul* and Violette Boisier, the creative touchstone of *Island Beneath the Sea*. To ready the trio for authority, Allende equips Eliza, Inés, and Violette with self-control and gravitas, two traits essential to curbing the mayhem unleashed by violent males like bandit

Joaquín Murieta, Général Pedro de Valdivia, and Haitian liberator Toussaint L'Ouverture. Ironically, Eliza's training with a book on her head and a metal rod aligning her spine during piano practice proves less applicable to ladyhood than to her scheme to conceal her gender and flee to California. In contrast to Eliza's defiance of body-cramping conventions, Allende pictures Esther, an eighteen-year-old "soiled dove," who agrees to domestication by blacksmith James Morton, a charitable Quaker rescuer whose work at the forge embodies the concentrated effort of establishing a family in a fractious setting (Allende, 1999, 296). The unforeseen happy union counterbalances the raw, bohemian social order while auguring Eliza's acceptance of marriage to Tao and motherhood, both by choice, not by coercion.

Female Liberation

In a less dramatic depiction of femininity in *The Infinite Plan*, the text validates the powers of Joan and Susan to manage a vegetarian restaurant and of Olga, the fortune teller, who earns her place as a wonder worker by ridding a Chicana of facial hair, a source of male ridicule. Over much of the text, the novelist makes no issue of the stereotypical home training of little Hispanic girls to cook and serve tables while their brothers play. The decorous upbringing of women like Inmaculada Morales yields a wife who scrubs her husband's oil-stained overalls, the gendered order of daily life in a Los Angeles barrio. Instead of revolt, Inmaculada resigns herself to toil and female domestic labor, a situation she acknowledges "without a hint of self-pity" (Allende, 1993, 73). The next generation of American-born Chicanas dares to differ. Her daughter Carmen, who comes of age during first-wave feminism and alienates herself from her father, battles "the double standard that made prisoners of women but granted a hunting license to men," her metaphor for males constantly on the prowl for new conquests (Allende, 1993, 136).

The novel dramatizes the assumptions and instincts of Hispanic men and women. In times of threat, Allende describes men as either charging or fleeing, taking refuge in jobs, sports, bars, war, and gangs. Women, she explains, remain home centered, questioning the actions of gringos who "take their dogs to the beauty parlor and don't believe in the Virgin Mary," an apostasy to women reared under the orthodox Catholic model of pure, unattainable saintliness (Allende, 1993, 43). In domestic settings, Latinas "join hands and form a circle around their children and old people to protect them. That is our power posture" (Flores, 2002). The ideal result, Allende explains, is that "everybody benefits— individuals, family, community, society, and the world" (Richards, 2008). She leaves unsaid any blame to men for their failure to share domestic responsibility or for accepting color and "any wild stuff" in proper women who "trotted around balancing on stiletto heels, with their faces painted and their hair frizzled" (Allende, 1993, 226, 36).

By reclaiming female facility in generating change, the author not only valorizes women as historical figures, but also introduces to an entrenched male perspective the one-sidedness of reducing history to men's decisions and primacy. At a confrontation of male with female in the tent that Inés shares with Pedro de Valdivia, she acknowledges the consternation of male Spaniards unused to dining at the same table with a woman. Allende's logic calls on the past as witness to the faults of patriarchy: "Men have decided the destiny of this suffering planet, imposing ambition, power, and individualism as virtues" in matters as small as who shares a meal with whom (Axelrod-Contrada, 2011, 42–43). Of Tété, the disenfranchised protagonist of *Island Beneath the Sea*, Allende commiserates with a slave who struggles "just to be included in her own life — to have a say in how many children she has, where she lives, who she loves and how she makes her living" (May, 2010). In the text, the author words the patriarch's creed: "Women are never free.... They need a man to look after them," a dramatic irony following Tété's rescue of her master from attack by Maroons (Allende, 2010, 204).

In an address for the Babel Speakers series in Buffalo, New York, Allende promoted *machisma*, a feminine energy that values nurturing over the domination at the heart of male *machismo*. She cited two charitable women in Nepal and Guatemala who found joy in serving others afflicted by poverty and precarious times. For *Inés of My Soul*, Allende reprises the history of Peru and Chile to enlarge the scope of participants from "a purely male perspective" to include Indian and Spanish women and children (Haq, 2006). Her historical fiction lauds the title figure, Inés Suarez, as a heroine bolstered by qualities inherited from her mother and grandmother. Of the concept of "abundant love," Allende exclaims, "You have so much in you that you want to change the world," an indirect accolade to the female's eagerness to share affection (McNeil, 2009).

Perricone insists that Allende battles a social order based on biological determinism (Perricone, 2003, 84). *Portrait in Sepia* showcases progressivism in the form of protofeminism, a woman-centered power that transforms lives. Critic Philip Graham summarizes her feminist energy as "rage ... at the social conventions that trap women—and men—in constricted lives," particularly Diego Domínguez's sham courtship and marriage with Aurora del Valle and the immurement of singsong girls (Graham, 2001, 39). In addition to fostering runaway wives and mutually satisfying adultery, Allene introduces microfinancing, a progressive solution to female disempowerment introduced in thc 1790s by the Grameen Bank of Bangladesh.

The concept focuses on the will of third world females to uplift their families through microenterprise. Rather than risk the waste of funds on men, who tend to spend cash on alcohol and prostitutes, lenders focus on woman-owned business in developing nations. According to critic María Claudia André, Allende invents strategies for female characters to subvert patriarchal power to gain control of body, mind, fortune, and future. The concept of microfinancing loans for women draws on sisterhood for repayment. In the event of a default, another women provides funds for the one strapped for cash. To capture the labor and vigor of all social levels, Aurora photographs the gamut, all "indispensable parts of a vast fresco ... the very soul of reality" (Allende, 2001, 237).

Ironically, the author places in the words of a man, Riad Halabí, a feminist axiom: "Freedom begins with financial independence," demonstrated by Blanca and Aurora del Valle in *The House of the Spirits* trilogy and by Mimí, the newly created woman in *Eva Luna* (Allende, 1987, 212). Because women collaborate on creative expenditures to found start-up industries, their record of success earns them low-risk ratings and trust for repaying on time. Nívea, Paulina's kinswoman, supports the feminist concept of financing women's businesses as the beginning of a "more just and noble society" (Allende, 2001, 147). Paulina del Valle abandons the previous generations's distribution of handouts and begins supporting women's businesses in eggs, tailoring, laundry, and cartage, "whatever it took to rise out of the absolute poverty in which they and their children were living" (*ibid.*, 146). With her usual raffish humor, Paulina declares that microfinancing affords her "a good time, and I get to heaven" (*ibid.*). Critic Stella Clarke notes that Paulina becomes "so overblown and extravagant" in her entrepreneurial victories that the star character, Aurora del Velle, appears to "dwindle in her wake" (Clarke, 2001, R12).

See also female persona

• *References and Further Reading*

Axelrod-Contrada, Joan. *Isabel Allende.* New York: Marshall Cavendish Benchmark, 2011.
Cameron, Peter. "Review: *My Invented Country,*" *New York Times Book Review* (8 June 2003): 19.
Clarke, Stella. "Lie Back and Think of Chile," *The* (Sydney) *Australian* (6 October 2001): R12.
Faris, Wendy B. *Ordinary Enchantments: Magical Realism and the Remystification of Narrative.* Nashville, TN: Vanderbilt University Press, 2004.
Flores, Camille. "The Power to Transform," (Santa Fe) *New Mexican* (12 April 2002).
Graham, Philip. "A Less Magical Realism," *New Leader* 84:6 (November-December 2001): 38–39.
Haq, Amber. "The Mother of Chile: Isabel Allende's New Novel Celebrates the Spanish Conquistadora Who Helped Create a New Nation," *Newsweek* (13 November 2006).
Kling, Vincent. "Archetype, Not Ideology: Isabel Allende's Balance of Opposites," *Critical Insights* (October 2010): 239–257.
Kristal, Efraín, ed. *The Cambridge Companion to the Latin American Novel.* New York: Cambridge University Press, 2005
May, Meredith. "Allende Takes on Slavery," *San Francisco Chronicle* (28 April 2010).
McNeil, Harold. "Allende Urges Audience to Seek Life of Joy," *Buffalo News* (18 April 2009).
Richards, Jonathan. "Summing Our Mysterious Days," (Santa Fe) *New Mexican* (19 September 2008): PA-22.
Schroeder, Shannin. *Rediscovering Magical Realism in the Americas.* Westport, CT: Praeger, 2004.
Shifflet, Amy V. *Beyond Magical Realism: Magical Ideology as Political Resistance in Leslie Marmon Silko's Ceremony and Isabel Allende's The House of the Spirits.* Radford, VA: Radford University, 2000.
Sollars, Michael D. *The Facts on File Companion to the World Novel, 1900 to the Present.* New York: Facts on File, 2008.
Wilkinson, Marta L. *Antigone's Daughters: Gender, Family, and Expression in the Modern Novel.* New York: Peter Lang, 2008.

Flores-Ranquileo genealogy

An unusual expansion of a character into two personas, the mix-up at the birth of yields two daughters for Digna Sanchéz Ranquileo, one reared in the family home and the real daughter claimed by Antonio Flores and his wife. The two Evangelinas enable Allende to exonerate Pradelio for an incestuous relationship with his "sister" while providing a living champion in Evangelina Flores to decry the torture and murder of Evangelina Ranquileo-Sanchéz.

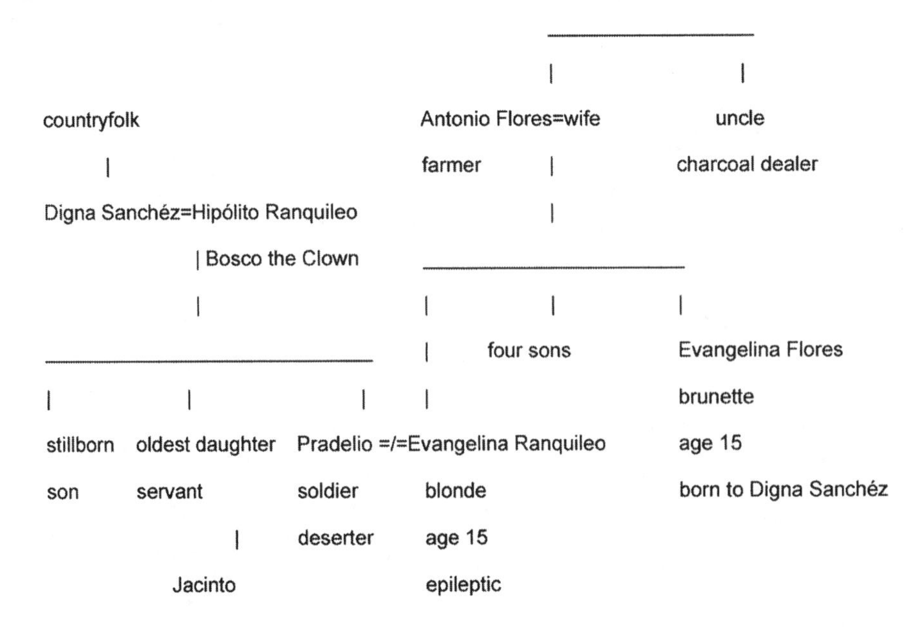

• *References and Further Reading*

Toomey, Mike. "Love and Chaos," (Melbourne) *Herald Sun* (7 August 2007).

food

Allende, a former secretary at the United Nations Food and Agriculture Organization in Chile, applies food service and the satisfactions of eating fresh crops to significant rituals in her works. Her literary menus accompany character events from family journeys and picnics, reunions, births, political dinners, and weddings to royal receptions, wakes, and funerals. Analyst Angel F. Méndez-Montoya corroborates the author's views on dining: "Matters related to food, such as eating and drinking, table fellowship, culinary traditions, the relationship between savoring and knowing, the esthetic, ethical, and political dimension of food ... are indeed vital and intimate" (Méndez-Montoya, 2012, 2–3).

For the political debut of Severo del Valle in *The House of the Spirits*, family and guests devour a pig roasted with plums and partridges, an internal stuffing that foreshadows the autopsy of Rosa, felled by rat poison in a gift decanter of brandy. The illicit transfer of food from Las Tres Marías enables Esteban Trueba to avoid his loathsome mother and sister by sending "crates of fruit, salted meat, hams, fresh eggs, hens, ... flour, rice, ... huge wheels of country cheese," guilt gifts that allow him to keep his distance (Allende, 1985, 83–84). The centrality of food to the del Valle matrilineage begins with the birth of Blanca, whose mother nurses her constantly rather than feed her "milk manufactured in some laboratory" from cow's milk diluted in rice water (*ibid.*, 124). Following episodes of household revolt, Esteban again distances himself from the female realm by retreating to a men's club, a male bastion that recurs in *Daughter of Fortune* for Jeremy Sommers's flight from female sanctuary in the kitchen, laundry, attic, sewing room, and servants' quarters.

Cooking and eating become problematic in *The House of the Spirits* after an earthquake that destroys the grandeur of Las Tres Marías. Tremors carry off china, servants, and the pantry of the elite, yet, ironically, restores the mother to the role of cook. In the place of staff, Clara labors in the kitchen to nourish Esteban back to health by "plucking chickens to make invalid soup and kneading bread" (Allende, 1985, 190). "Simplified to the point of frugality," post-earthquake plantation suppers of lentil soup, cheese, and quince jelly replicate the meals of country folk whom Esteban despises for their simplicity and poverty (*ibid.*, 196). In his lengthy tirade against the Bolshevik candidate preaching worker revolt, Esteban creates his own quake by shattering the soup tureen in Clara's hands, a symbolic gesture of his cane. For the first time, he directs an assault against their domestic union while epitomizing the potential of his party for violence against the innocent.

Table service takes on a regal air at Blanca's wedding, a phony spectacle of aristocratic traditions in a sacrament honoring an arranged marriage to a sham European count. Under duress, Clara puts in her false teeth and smiles briefly at guests in an expression of love for Blanca. Nicolás jumps into the fountain, an undignified baptism that mocks the ostentatious rite. Allende terms "scandalous" the amount of grilled beef, truffle-stuffed poultry, seafood and caviar, liquor, and champagne served to guests (Allende, 1985, 246). The desserts indicate Blanca roots with Western Hemisphere fruits—coconut, papaya, pineapple, and strawberries—and her intended's preference for fussy sweets—French éclairs, ladyfingers, and millefeuilles, a multilayered pastry implying the perverse strata that underlie Satigny's frothy courtesies. On an overdressed meringue cloud shading the

Acropolis, the wedding cake, a travesty of Greek mythology, mates the tragic lovers Venus and Adonis. Symbolically, Jean de Satigny assassinates the rosy Cupid, god of infatuation, with one slice of the ceremonial silver knife. The whole affair dramatizes a face-saving marriage doomed to failure.

Shared Meals

With less glamour, food brings the Truebas together over a plate of crackers, which Clara munches while keeping her chronicles. After she allows Esteban to enter her bedroom, the two share the snack while the ousted husband summons the nerve to ask about the future of his candidacy for the senate. Following Clara's death, Esteban loses his welcoming home to neglect. Allende describes the dietary decline from "roast pork and aromatic dishes" to "chick-peas and rice pudding" prepared by grumpy staff in abused cookpots, symbols of domestic discord (Allende, 1985, 339). Simple fare suits the egalitarianism of Alba and her anarchist father Pedro Tercero, who picnic on peasant fare—bread and cheese—while getting to know each other.

In the novel's resolution, food insecurity defines the country's distress. During the shortages and rationing under Marxism, Blanca develops a mania for hoarding by filling rooms with flour, dried fruit, cheese, rice, and sugar and locking the doors. Alba, the family altruist, learns from Amanda that the unemployed eat little—"barely a plate of corn mush every other day" (Allende, 1987, 432). Alba helps Miguel steal Blanca's cached goods to feed the poor. After the coup, the return of food to grocery stores reveals the method by which conservatives disrupt the economy to manipulate the citizenry. Party leaders debauch themselves on aphrodisiac quail eggs, a fragile snack suggesting the vulnerability of the underclass (*ibid.*, 471). In small increments, response to rampant hunger begins the reclamation of Trueba, who increases the household budget to feed beggars at his door. Méndez-Montoya honors such charitable gestures as divine evidence of redemption: "To share bread is to share God" (Méndez-Montoya, 2012, 3).

In *Eva Luna*, Allende echoes the theme of want among marginalized characters. The text stresses the nutrition of the poor in the orphan Consuelo's meals of fish and yucca and the hunger of prisoners who "lacked the strength to drag themselves across the courtyard" (Allende, 1987, 269). During Eva's scavenging in the streets, she learns that the best pickings appear "mid-morning on the garbage heap at the Central market and midafternoon in the garbage pails of hotels and restaurants" (*ibid.*, 66). Gift meals from El Negro tide her over with "more food than I could eat in two days" (*ibid.*, 116). Celebrations with Melesio, Eva's friend, "seemed like birthday treats, not ordinary everyday food" (*ibid.*, 126). Prosperity fails to relieve suffering during the joyous preparations of poultry and pigs for a Caribbean Christmas Eve feast, the cause of Consuelo's death from a chicken bone in her throat.

More detailed, the childhood foraging of Rolf Carlé, an Austrian survivor of World War II, contrasts the abundance he enjoys in his teens after his immigration to his Aunt Burgel and Uncle Rupert's home. Allende accounts for Rolf's contentment in the Western Hemisphere: "Food was central: their lives turned around the labors of the kitchen and the ceremony of the table" (Allende, 1987, 92). She describes a Caribbean version of a *chupe*, a stew built layer by layer of bacon, tomato, and onion seasoned with coriander, pepper, and garlic. For aphrodisiac effect, Rolf's aunt adds beans and corn, pimiento and cabbage, and a mix of beef, chicken, clams, fish, lobster, and pork. The grand dish is not complete until she stirs in herbs and beer. The family's rich diet includes sausage and ham, fruit and berry conserves, butter, cheese, and cream, foodstuffs common to country folk who raise livestock and vegetables.

Feasts and Famine

By learning to cook, Eva Luna cements her relationship with the Turkish peddler Riad Halabí. The arrival of his Palestinian nephew Kamal calls for a grand fiesta, a model of native reunions through Arab specialties so plentiful "it looked like a wedding feast in the courts of Baghdad" (Allende, 1987, 159). The author's indulgence in hyperbole—"fifty trays of Arabic and American dishes"—embellishes the fervor of family unity (*ibid.*). Emblematic meals continue in *The Stories of Eva Luna*, where the beneficence of kitchen aromas surrounds *niña* Eloísa, a Russian maker of bonbons in "The Little Heidelberg" who "smells of birthday parties" (Allende, 1991, 177). In a contrasting scene, El Benefactor, the "cold-blooded Andean" dictator of "Phantom Palace," lives the Spartan existence of a bandito, sleeping in his boots, drinking coffee, and eating corn and roast meat.

The edibles in *Of Love and Shadows* center on bread, eggs, mint tea, sugar lumps, and *maté* and the sale of pigs and honey to support the Ranquileo family. At the lowest socioeconomic stratum simmer the communal stewpots of the poor, a recreation of the folk fable "Stone Soup." At political extremes, lizards, rabbits, mice, birds, and roots nourish Pradelio after he deserts the military and hides in the mountains. For the meeting between Francisco Leal and Irene Beltrán, she guides him to a vegetarian restaurant that serves fruit juice and raisin and nut bread to "macrobioticists, spiritists, bohemians, students, and gastric-ulcer sufferers," a touch of humor in an otherwise terrorizing plot (Allende, 1987, 48–49). After the photographer completes a dangerous errand into the mountains, Irene rewards him with the mouth-to-mouth transfer of melon bites, a symbolic enhancement of her kiss that both refreshes and arouses.

For the Leals, immigrants from Spain, nostalgic dining relieves homesickness. A potato omelet recreates the southern European taste for a frittata, a hurry-up blend of vegetables and eggs for a light, satisfying meal. Francisco connects the family kitchen with after-school snacks, the service of real coffee, and the Spanish style recipes involving herbs and spices in pastries, potato cakes, and stews, which exude aroma, texture, color, and flavor. Hilda consoles her troubled son with a late-night cup of linden tea, a homestyle remedy for anxiety. At surprise arrivals, Hilda exclaims genially, "What feeds three will feed eight," a statement redolent with welcome (Allende, 1987, 26).

For Eliza Sommers in *Daughter of Fortune*, the dual parenting of the fastidious Englishwoman Rose Sommers and the Mapuche maid, Mama Fresia, enables the child to develop refined tastes for tea and "sweets prepared with recipes jealously guarded since the times of the colonies" (Allende, 1999, 24). Simultaneously, Eliza displays a "rare culinary gift" at age seven to "skin a beef tongue, dress a hen," grind maize and spices, and chop fruit and nuts (*ibid.*, 12). Eliza flourishes at frying empanadas, a common one-handed meal in Chile destined to earn her a living a decade later in Sacramento. Allende awards her protagonist a refined sense of smell that savors the kitchen for its aromas of chocolate, yeast bread, and caramel frosting. Outside the proper English dinner table at a coastal bar, bible salesman Jacob Todd consumes simple sailors' fare—conger eel fried with potatoes and eaten with a raw onion salad, the staples found in a ship's galley.

Less appealing, the hasty supplies of Joaquín Andieta—bacon, beans, flour, jerky, rice, and sugar—and the shipboard pantry of fish, hardtack, and salted meat epitomize the lack of forethought in bachelors and married men scurrying north to hunt for gold.

In like manner, Tao Chi'en survives on boiled crab, rice, tea, sugar, and opium while he builds his reputation as a healer. Aboard the *Liberty*, he cooks from a shipboard pantry that lacks fresh produce from the mainland, yet protects the crew from scurvy. In a blend of Western and Eastern fare, he boils oatmeal for breakfast and adds soy sauce; he also skins and cooks a fresh-caught shark and serves a pint of liquor to sustain sailors on the long passage. In a Chinese hotel, ethnic meals compensate for the loneliness and isolation inflicted on Asians.

Eliza's openness to food prefaces a career in cookery, a womanly fall-back common in women's history and key to female success on the California frontier. In Little Canton, bowls of green soup resemble "swamp water swarming with polliwogs," Eliza's first appraisal of a broth she finds delicious (Allende, 1999, 226). Over months of trail meals, she acclimates to Amerindian grasshoppers, seeds, and acorns. With genuine respect for frontier bounty, she turns bear, geese, hare, salmon, turkey, and venison into empanadas, a sure seller in the Sacramento mining camps. Her breakfasts and pastries draw hungry men who leave tips. On a grander scale, Paulina del Valle parlays fresh vegetables, eggs, fruit, and poultry into a fortune by packing them in glacial ice in the *Fortuna*, an apt name for her ship. Unlike scraggly sailors and miners, Captain John Sommers dines on oysters and doves flavored with pear preserves and almonds, the shore menu for a navigator willing to ferry Paulina's pantry to San Francisco.

The Colonial Menu

Allende's historical fiction dramatizes the role of food in the sixteenth-century conquest of the Americas. Cooking and feeding others in *Inés of My Soul* rids the quest novel of rigor brought on by failing pantries and street beggary. During the main character's three-month voyage from Cadiz, Spain, to the West Indies, she applies her skill at varying a recipe for empanadas with odds and ends from sailors' personal supplies, another sharing reminiscent of the folk story "Stone Soup." Upon arriving at an unidentified island, she samples cacao, manioc, fruit, and roast tapir, a respite from shipboard meals that restores vigor and hope. The menu reprises in little the commodity treasures that the New World offers Europe, but Allende freights the vast rewards of traversing "Satan's kingdom" with periods of starvation in which expeditioners eat raw monkey meat and survivors of the battle of Las Salinas "crept up to the patio door to ask for charity" (Allende, 2006, 61, 102).

Inés's skill at making meat and onion turnovers in Cuzco earns a sparse living on her patio oven and follows her on the long trek south from Peru to Chile. Allende pictures the flicker of life from "hundreds of little campfires where they cooked what food they had" (Allende, 2006, 122). At a campsite in Tarapacá, drinks of prickly pear *chicha* (beer) refresh diners; the aroma of corn, meat, and tortillas scents the air with the wholesome fare of South America. At the founding of Santiago, indigenous vegetables—beans, corn, potatoes—contribute to stews made from birds, rabbits, fish, and seafood. Allende credits communal dining in the Plaza Mayor with uniting spirits and silencing pettiness. More useful to Inés, a talent for communicating with Chilean Indians gains valuable gossip, which she shapes and dispenses to the benefit of her lover, Général Pedro de Valdivia. The shared pot returns to prominence at the end of the Siege of Santiago on September 11, 1541. Inés tackles ruined gardens and slain domestic animals by gathering herbs and tubers for a one-dish meal, a common make-do for survivors of war.

Allende characterizes two hard years of recovery by the dearth of edibles. Animals and humans share the bounty of nature—bitter fruit, piñon nuts, roots, and soup made from insects and mice. Only in the third year do colonists grow enough wheat for bread. Banditry against native villages supplies birds and grain, but Michimalonko's raids rob Santiagans of herd animals and harvests and murder the military parties foraging for water and food. The hardscrabble menus feature lizards, grass, dogs, the remains of dead domestic animals, and the quarry of Felipe, who hunts with his bow. The author touches on cannibalism, a source of protein to preserve the few souls strong enough to "eat the flesh of their fellows" (Allende, 2006, 216). In pity for the villagers, Inés places herself in the role of mother and dreams that her breast milk satisfies their hunger.

Overturning scenes of starvation with abundance, Allende dramatizes the joy of Santiagans upon their rescue by two ships from Peru. Full larders raise spirits; wine restores outriders. Inés celebrates with outings on the riverbank and a picnic at the pier. Cecilia, the Inca princess, treats her family to South American bounty in cinnamon and cocoa. Upon Valdivia's return from Peru, frenzies of making conserves and desserts from the summer garden prepare Inés for her lover's arrival. In the despair of Valdivia's delayed return, Inés stops eating until her nuptials with Rodrigo de Quiroga, for which she prepares garden vegetables, wine, and desserts, "a casserole of game birds, corn cakes, stuffed potatoes, beans with chili peppers, lamb and roast kid" (Allende, 2006, 257). The profusion contrasts the previous preparation for her mate, foretokening a bounty of love for both wife and husband.

The service of lavish meals returns to prominence in the novel's resolution, ten years after the founding of Santiago. Out of duty, Inés, wife of the lieutenant governor, prepares a victory banquet for Valdivia. Integral to the evening's ambience, the juxtaposition of fragrant candles and birdsong with seasonal fruit, roast fish and poultry, a symbolic empanada, and cups of wine pleases dignitaries and their wives, who sit at table alongside the men. In Renaissance style, Inés flavors "tortes, pastries, meringues, custards, puddings" and caramel with imported molasses and sugar, the popular spice of the era (Allende, 2006, 291).

Food and Riches

In the introduction to *Island Beneath the Sea*, Allende returns to historical research into eighteenth-century sustenance in Haiti. She lists the foods of the Columbian exchange—cassava, corn, gourds, peanuts, peppers, potatoes, and sweet potatoes, "never-before-seen plants" that conquistadors transport to Europe (Allende, 2010, 6). More vital to the economy, crops of cacao, cotton, indigo, sugar, and tobacco increase competition while demanding the unending toil of African slaves. For greedy French planters, sugarcane becomes the colony's "sweet gold" (*ibid.*, 6). Ironically, overseers deny slaves a taste of cane lest they gorge themselves on sweetness.

On Europe's tables, gradual acceptance of Latin American staples enhances menus with New World foods. In Haiti, a Senegalese grandmother scrapes a living from "a little fried food shop in the port" (Allende, 2010, 42). Simultaneous with her daily toil at "gutting fish amid fumes from rancid oil," a slave cook prepares meals for the privileged French (*ibid.*). She serves to Toulouse Valmorain and his noble Spanish wife, Eugenia García del Solar: "lamb cooked with chilies and spice ... beans, rice, salted maize cakes," the largess of the islands (*ibid.*, 54). At a significant point preceding the Haitian Revolution of 1791, Gambo, a kitchen boy working for Tante Mathilde, comforts recovered runaways with servings of bananas, corn, okra, sweet potato, and yucca. The menu reflects African and Latin

American contributions to world comestibles at the height of the slave trade. Tante Rose's curatives recipes turn bones, herbs, and liver into a curative soup, a source of iron to combat anemia. She also prescribes an Arawak nostrum, balls of quinoa ash and leaves to relieve pain and boost energy. Ironically, the Arawak and their indigenous cookery die out after European contact from contagion, enslavement, and violence.

Haitian food security determines the success of the island revolution as well as the bestowal of mercy on the cook, Tante Mathilde. As an uprising threatens among field crews, Valmorain treats mulatto militiamen to a bicultural fiesta of Creole stews, roast lamb, and European fruit tarts, a repast that acknowledges table traditions from both sides of biculturalism. Simultaneously, the distribution of meals to runaways in Zambo Boukman's camp revives stamina and ensures successful birthing and child health among those "with bloated stomachs and eyes from beyond the tomb" (Allende, 2006, 171). On the flight from Habitation Saint-Lazare to Toussaint's mountain compound, Gambo easily dislodges coconuts from a palm to ease his party's hunger and thirst. Feeding the Maroons, he and his five raiders return from forays on plantations with beans, cassava, corn, sweet potatoes, dried fish, flour, goats, hens, hogs, and mules. Of the availability of coffee and sugar, Allende notes that cane field workers had never tasted the products they harvested. Well fed and robust, the Maroons advance from bandits to warriors.

In contrast to the bare necessities of the flight from anarchy, Allende poses the dainties of New Orleans, a new jungle of rules and social codes that Valmorain learns from Sancho García del Solar, his sophisticated brother-in-law. The new cook, Célestine, earns her name, a French form of "heavenly," by ending meals of "leftovers of leftovers and crumbs of crumbs" (Allende, 2006, 273). She establishes her worth by plating garlic frog legs, roast chicken, gumbo, and crawfish in phyllo and wins the children's friendship with beignets, crêpes, mousse, biscuits, and caramel apples. For Valmorain's wedding to Hortense Guizot, a caterer showcases a marzipan and fruit wedding cake to conclude a dinner of crab, duck, fish, oysters, pheasant, turtle soup, cheese, and forty desserts. The extravagant courses indicate that the brush with death on Haiti fails to dim Valmorain's flair for elegant table spectacle.

Allende foregrounds female victories in terms of food. Before the faceoff between Hortense and Tété, the master's former concubine enjoys relative freedom from domestic supervision. At the Marché Français, where slaves spend the master's change for oysters with lime juice, Tété soaks up the ambience of fresh fruits and vegetables and spicy fried crawfish, the recipes that made New Orleans famous. A banquet sets the scene to welcome Hortense's first child, whose baptism the family celebrates with suckling pig, duck, shrimp, gumbo, oysters, pastries, and cake, a spread that contrasts the hunger of an infant who rejects breast milk. In defense of her child's inheritance, Hortense's hatred of her stepson Maurice immures him in a frozen hell in Boston, where cadets feed on chicken necks, boiled liver, cauliflower, rice, and oatmeal to condition them for the hardships of war.

The Meals of Nations

The author extends motifs of excess in her perusal of postcolonialism, in which evolving nations experience "the blooming shortage of food and supplies [and] the problems inherent in oceanic transit" (Allende, 2001, 42). For Paulina del Valle, the grande dame of *Portrait in Sepia*, self-absorption exonerates her for excessive weight from indulgence in pastries. By identifying the same psychological reliance on sweets in Chileans during the War of the Pacific, Paulina profits from speculation in sugar prices. Upon her return to Santiago, she distinguishes herself as a woman of the world by smoking slim Egyptian cigarettes and by deviating from common Chilean foods—beans, roasts, soup, stews, and colonial desserts—to servings of foie gras, camembert, and port-salut, the height of European table fare. During the evacuation of the del Valle mansion during the 1891 Civil War, Paulina fortifies her family with bread and cheese, cooked eggs, roasted fowl, and pastries, which they wash down with barley water and wine, appropriate travel food for flight to a rural family enclave.

For unique occasions, Aurora details the foods served, for example, Turkish coffee with cardamom seeds at the office of Gerald Suffolk at the Hobbs Clinic and *café con leche* with fresh bread after Christmas Eve mass. On the journey to Buenos Aires, Paulina revives her strength on stimulating sips of *maté* before distributing bread and cheese, roast pork, cake, champagne, and liquor. In the country, Aurora and her cousins enjoy the farm treats of *café con leche*, fresh dairy food, fruit, and preserves while the adults quaff red wine mulled with cinnamon, citrus peel, and sugar, an after-dinner beverage that dates to the Middle Ages. Dining becomes so elaborate that one meal extends into the next.

Allende fills in the privations of the world wars in *The Infinite Plan*, which surveys the second half of the twentieth century. While Bahai follower Nora Reeves mourns the deaths of thousands in the bombing of Hiroshima and Nagasaki, Japan, her pragmatic friend Olga rejoices in the end of war and food shortages. A peace treaty implies the end of rationing: "We'll have butter and meat and gasoline" (Allende, 1993, 31). After the Reeves' rescue by Hispanic immigrants from Zacatecas to a Los Angeles barrio, Inmaculada Morales, Greg's foster mother, welcomes guests to her patio, where she "stretched the food with the tricks of any hospitable woman—stirring a little more water in the beans" (*ibid.*, 36). A gathering of locals rebuilds the family shack while indulging in salsa, guacamole, tacos, fruit, tequila, and beer, celebratory foods of Latinos. Essential to traditional charity, the home builders pack up tools and tables and slip away before incurring thanks from the gringos.

At the next low point in the Reeves' fortunes, Charles's death leaves son Gregory hungry for comfort from Carmen Morales, who coats her finger with condensed milk for her friend to suck. Maternal generosity foretells Carmen's adult role as a female as generous as her mother. Just as Inmaculada adapts Mexican fare to suit the diabetic diet of her husband, Pedro Morales, Carmen encourages her adopted son Dai to abandon grieving for his birth mother and eat to survive. In another glimpse of the Vietnam War, food revives Greg on his return from combat to California. Before reuniting with wife Samantha and daughter Margaret, he wants San Francisco coffee, "the best in the world" (Allende, 1993, 220). The glimpse of his connection to place and flavor suggests a wartime experience that deprives Greg and his army buddies of the amenities of home.

Autobiographical Food

Allende depicts savored meals in her own life. In elevating the value of soup to diet, she compares it to peace for the soul. During her daughter's treatment in a Madrid hospital in the memoir *Paula*, the mother goes to dinner with Willie at Plaza Mayor and revels in foods that North Americans demonize—fried octopus and fatty roast pork, comfort foods banned by health activists. The revival conferred by meat and a jug of sangria remind Allende of life and libido, which she lavishes on her husband during his five-day visit. The connection between nourishment and carnal pleasure foretells the subject of her next publication, *Aphrodite*, an erotic cookbook. In the introduction, the author repents of dieting, "the delicious dishes rejected out of vanity," and cherishes her compilation of "one more collection of recipes" (Allende, 1998, 10, 11).

In the memoir *My Invented Country*, composed five years later, Allende uses food to differentiate classes and traditions. The table fare of society ranges from Christmas turkey, fried empanadas, and fattened goat to blackberries, quince, tin cans of milk for *dulce de leche* (blancmange), and bread from the corner bakery to the beans, lentils, and chickpeas of the poor. Nonetheless, Chileans compensate well for penury. She explains that the simpler the menu, "the more elaborate and spicy it becomes" (Allende 2003, 104). The text notes that, like Chileans, the cooks of India and Mexico follow a similar kitchen style of dressing up humble staples.

During a journey through the Atacama Desert to Bolivia, the author turns her travelogue into a food panorama. Train passengers buy leavened bread, black potatoes, ears of corn, and sweets, staples of the Western Hemisphere sold by Bolivia's Indian women. For ostentation, shoppers make a spectacle of filling carts with luxury groceries, then abandon the lot and creep out the door empty-handed. On a "true safari in my grandfather's automobile," her family ferries a carload of goods to the beach each summer, consisting of swimwear, roast chicken, and watermelon (Allende, 2003, 12). At rural stops along the way, innkeepers serve honey, risen bread, and "eggs the color of gold," the wealth of the countryside (*ibid.*, 13). Nearer the shore, cuisine features eels, fish cooked in butter and lemon juice, crabs, barnacles, oysters, abalone, langoustine, and sea urchins, the wealth of the sea, "including some with such a questionable appearance that no foreigner dares try them" (*ibid.*, 14).

Food Adventures

Throughout her fiction, Allende's selection of foods speaks in menu glimpses the status of her characters. Calamities remind the oligarchy of the pantry insecurity that daily besets the poor, such as the reduction of eggs, meat, and milk in the story "Ester Lucero," in which the title figure must subsist on protein-poor corn and plantains. For *City of the Beasts*, Allende demonstrates mother hunger in the absence of edible meals and the aroma of fresh cookies for the Cold family, who tiptoe around the day-by-day decline of mother Lisa into a "silent ghost" riddled with cancer (Allende, 2002, 6). Instead of mother-cooked food, the children subsist on tuna sandwiches, John's rubbery pancakes, and take-out pizza and Chinese food. On reaching New York City, Alex recoils from repulsive street garbage and the greasy noodles of an Asian restaurant endangering his stash of three twenty-dollar bills. Fear of hunger makes him identify with street beggars and the homeless, an essential of Allende's social message to middle-class readers.

The problem of food returns on Alex's journey along the Amazon, where he encounters the tedium of beans, dried beef, and coffee relieved by roasted monkey, anaconda, fish, and "things he couldn't even name" (Allende, 2002, 59). His pickiness limits him to bananas, condensed milk, and crackers. As primitive backdrops prove to be the norm, Allende stresses meals of beans, cassava, fish, tapir, toucan, and venison, all indigenous to South America, and the imported foods of villain Mauro Carías, who flies in extravagant choices—ice cream, shellfish, cheese, and cold cuts. Farther into the jungle, Alex ventures into unusual cuisine, including peach-like fruit retrieved from a palm tree and roast anteater, which he consumes "without noticing the dirt and without asking how it was made" (*ibid.*, 179).

The novel imparts inklings about food that Allende intends as instruction to readers. A mental Aha! strikes Alex after the group secures birds and fish for dinner. Because any more hunting would subject the kill to decay or infestation, he had no reason for accumulating more than the group can eat at one time. By the time that Alex mingles with Iyomi and the People of the Mist, he accustoms himself to specialties that combine sustenance with ritual. He accepts without complaint bread and a gourdful of a vinegary drink fermented from cassava that Indians reserve for men only and a sip of soup made from water, plantains, and the pulverized remains of the dead chief's bones, a native parallel of the Christian Eucharist. In a departure from cannibalism, the People of the Mist retain the "memory of the man, like the particles of courage and wisdom left in his ashes [which] passed on to his descendants and friends" (Allende, 2002, 227).

A bleaker existence in the Himalayas in *Kingdom of the Golden Dragon* depicts the Yetis as a dwindling race because of the devolution of a stout clan into small, nearly helpless beings with shortened life spans. Their flaccid bodies suffice on raw game and desperation meals of *chegnos* (herd animals) and corpses of their own kind. In Tunkhala, the capital of the Forbidden Kingdom, vegetarianism equates with Buddhist ascetism, an integral part of the preparation of a prince for ruling. At a group meal, the International Geographic group consumes spiced and peppered red rice along with a profusion of organ meats from goats, pigs, sheep, and yaks, which diners form into small balls and down with tearing eyes from the fiery flavor. The dinner precedes the royal birthday, which cooks celebrate with servings of sweets and rice liquor at tables where "everything was free" (Allende, 2002, 162).

The novel continues dotting scenarios with edibles, both good and bad. At the height of menace to Pema, Nadia, and four captive Tibetan girls, Allende associates the reek of garlic with the threat from black-toothed, Blue Horsemen, members of the scorpion sect. As a nemesis to evil, Allende contrasts the diet of destructive nomads with that of Master Tensing, a repository of goodness and strength. He shares with Dil Bahadur a tea flavored with salt and yak butter, a Tibetan staple that warms and energizes, especially when mixed with flour for *tsampa* and blessed "the brief ceremony of thanks they always performed before eating" (Allende, 2002, 214). After rescuing Pema, Tensing miraculously satisfies their hunger with standard trail food, cereal and vegetables, a magical meal that Alexander compares to Jesus's feeding of the five thousand with loaves and fishes. As in other episodes of implied sleight of hand, Allende undercuts the miracle by claiming that Tensing stole the supplies from the bandits' cave.

In the opening scenes of the sequel, *Forest of the Pygmies*, Allende describes the open-air market in Nairobi, where Kenyan street sellers offer corn cakes and fruit and butchers slaughter animals and sell the meat while buzzards eye the offal, a hint at the terrors to come. The meal of a healer on sour milk and fresh cow's blood typifies the diet of Masai herders. The feeding of tourists on bushmeat — roast antelope, carp baked in leaves, wild boar — lessens the problem of packing food while amplifying the thrill of camping in the wild. As a contrast to wealthy Westerners, Allende reminds readers that "half the people of Africa live below the subsistence level" and depend on food packages from donors like pilot Angie Ninderera, who flies in supplies to Ethiopia and the Sudan (Allende, 2005, 40).

Challenges to survival heighten in Central Africa, where a downed plane leaves passengers to feed themselves and to avoid being meals for termites and crocodiles. In a Pygmy village, visitors face a meal of cassava pudding, leaves, palm wine, and rats roasted in palm seed oil. A wedding calls for fruit pyramids and an assortment of antelope, lizards, hens, and rats along with cassava, corn, and palm wine. Allende contrasts the feast with the insects and partially decayed meat that the Pygmy hunters devour and a subsequent snack on raw monkey. Thematically, the author stresses the essentials of cooperation by which "people join together to build and plant and provide food and protect the weak ... all to better their conditions" (Allende, 2005, 136).

See also healing and health

• *References and Further Reading*

Feal, Rosemary Geisdorfer, and Yvette E. Miller, eds. *Isabel Allende Today: Anthology of Essays*. Pittsburgh, PA: Latin American Literary Review, 2002.

Gelman, Judy, and Vicki Levy Krupp. *The Book Club Cook Book*. New York: Penguin, 2012.

Méndez-Montoya, Angel F. *Theology of Food: Eating and the Eucharist*. Malden, MA: John Wiley & Sons, 2012.

Scott, Renée Sum. *What Is Eating Latin American Women Writers: Food, Weight, and Eating Disorders*. Amherst, NY: Cambria, 2009.

Forest of the Pygmies

In *Forest of the Pygmies*, the third of Allende's YA adventure trio, she resorts to an obvious ruse to involve the hero's grandmother in researching Kenya's elephant-led safari tradition, an element of east African life in history and literature, such as H. Rider Haggard's *King Solomon's Mines*. Reviewer Janet Hunt notes that the text opens on "an extraordinary melange of plot and character-type, with a nod along the way at just about every fashionable cause of recent years" (Hunt, 2005). In typical style, to build atmosphere, the author details secondary events and revelations—the disdain of a jealous bull elephant, an attack by an ostrich, demon possession, landing a small plane in a tropical rainforest, and boiling river water to purify it. Allende's research imparts facts about tiny mopani bees, monkey attacks, fermentation of palm wine, and the mating and family structure of the hippopotamus, details that validate the background and establish Allende's authority. Essential to characterization, the abiding friendship between Alex Cold and Nadia Santos relies on emails as well as telepathic exchange of "dreams, thoughts, emotions, and secrets," a postmodern touch that reminds the reader of conveniences the trekkers leave behind (Allende, 2005, 71).

Dedicated to Brother Fernando de la Fuente, an historic Marist missionary and martyr from Burgos, Spain, the novel incorporates the contemporary issues of savagery, hunger, poaching, and slavery alongside ongoing problems in the Central African Republic along with nature's poisonous snakes, swarms of cockroaches and bees, quicksand, and malaria. Allende develops the jungle trek episodically, presenting as vignettes forays against a wild boar and a crocodile "brazen enough to approach the faint glow of the coals and the oil lamp" (Allende, 2005, 88). For comic relief, brief clashes between Brother Fernando and the pilot, Angie Ninderera, air differences about religion and survival, a parallel to the greater conflict between that of the Pygmies (Aka) of Ngoubé village and a trio of villains, King Kosongo, the sorcerer Sombe, and Commandant Maurice Mbembelé, a reputed cannibal. The Aka describe the second-hand presentation of the king's commands through the "Royal Mouth," an enhancement of terror similar to the amplification of verbal commands in L. Frank Baum's *The Wizard of Oz* (*ibid.*, 119).

Allende turns the group's flattery of Kosongo into a gendered expectation that males are likely to respond to compliments. The subjugation of royal wives with a bamboo whip indicates the prominence and privilege of a king, which contrast the egalitarian Aka society and its lack of hierarchies. Evidence of structure in relationships takes shape during a communal entertainment, for which penned females enact an emotive dance to honor the king. Angie's contribution of the recruitment and mercenary tactics of the Brotherhood of the Leopard rekindles the fearsome camaraderie of the Scorpion sect in *Kingdom of the Golden Dragon*. Fernando summarizes the group's negative solidarity as an exoneration of Kosongo's evil and violence.

In the falling action, the author stresses an edenic cooperation between the Bantu and Aka in the past, before the enslavement of Africans to power the diamond, gold, and ivory trade. In a woman-to-woman exchange, the Aka prisoners reveal the savage method of their enslavers. If the men fail to track elephants and bring back the meat, skins, and tusks, Kosongo and Mbembelé sell the Aka children into slavery as domestics, circus exhibits, or entertainers of the rich. Village women make the most of their maid's work: "They know everything that goes on in the village ... they go into all the huts, they hear all the conversations, they observe," an empowerment of the lowly that Allende stresses in *Eva Luna* (Allende, 2005, 224). Female camaraderie increases in importance after a mother gorilla returns the favor of freeing her and her infant from a trap by protecting Alex and Nadia and leaving them food.

Central to the resolution, the Aka fear of ancestral spirits requires a test of courage by a meeting between Alex and Nadia and luminous, disembodied beings. Allende uses the ghosts to account for "imagination, dreams, creativity, and mystic or spiritual revelation" and solace to mourners (Allende, 2005, 208). She extends the concept of animism by revealing individualism and intelligence in trees and plants. The profusion of animals that engulfs the scene represents the "peaceable kingdom," a universal tableaux of the biblical Eden filled with energy and bound by harmony from the "mother planet" and an encompassing oversoul (*ibid.*, 210). The emergence of the goddess Nana-Asante resurrects a female cult of ancient times that espouses tranquility and benevolence, two qualities robbed from the Bantu and Aka by greedy, violent male smugglers. The author summarizes in the conflict the thuggery and manipulation of historic African dictators—Idi Amin, Robert Mugabe, Mobutu Sese Seko, and Moammar Qaddafi.

The orchestration of forces and loyalties in the resolution, similar in complexity to that of *Kingdom of the Golden Dragon*, illustrates Allende's faith in cooperation of the lowliest to unseat a single tyrant. *Kirkus Reviews* described as stiff and didactic the ensuing conflict, which reviewer Eva Mitnick summarizes as a "messy bit of business" (Mitnick, 2005, 147). At the dual royal nuptials and arrival of the Aka hunting party, hand-to-hand combat between Commandant Mbembelé and the Aka hunter Beyé-Dokou revives community spirit and faith in solidarity, the universal method of defeating repression. Reviewer Hazel Rochman affirms, "There is never any doubt that the amulets and totems will help the good guys win" (Rochman, 2005, 1284).

Allende worsens the chagrin of the overlords by sending Aka women into a foray against the Brotherhood of the Leopard, a gendered face-off in which the male taste for palm wine favors the sober female combatants. Nadia's shapeshifting into an eagle and Alex's appearance as a jaguar counterbalance the terrifying approach of the sorcerer Sombe, whose reputation derives more from legend and superstition than from actual magic feats. The convocation of powers from all three YA novels—Walimai and his spirit wife from *City of the Beasts*, Tensing and Yetis from *Kingdom of the Golden Dragon*, and gorillas and

Queen Nana-Asante on an elephant from *Forest of the Pygmies*—unmasks Sombe, one of Mbembelés three incarnations. When communal action performs the true conjuration by causing the Africans to rally, "all moved as one" (Allende, 2005, 286).

An obdurate critic, Donnarae MacCann, castigates Allende's "imperialist" plot for referring to the Aka as "Pygmies." More demeaning, MacCann claims, is the headlining of "indisputable greatness of Western wayfarers, colonizers, missionaries, and journalists" amid the terrors of "darkest Africa" (MacCann, 2007, 60). MacCann accuses Allende of xenophobic distortion and disparagement and finds the link between darkness and light "complex and disturbing" because of the intercessory status of the mostly white rescue effort (*ibid.*). The critique notes that, unlike Allende's standard commit to social betterment, her third YA novel opts to present the outsiders as "God-Sent Saviors of the 'Pygmies,' a denigration of a 'benighted' race through a rescue-the-missionaries tale" (*ibid.*). McCann aims lethal complaints against Brother Fernando, who poses as the only adversary to entrenched evil, his summation of native religion.

• *References and Further Reading*

Hunt, Janet. "Review: *Forest of the Pygmies*," *New Zealand Herald* (7 May 2005).
MacCann, Donnarae. "White Supremacy in Isabel Allende's Forest of the Pygmies," *Journal of African Children's and Youth Literature* 17–18 (2007): 60–75.
Mitnick, Eva. "Review: *Forest of the Pygmies*," *School Library Journal* (June, 2005): 147.
"Review: *Forest of the Pygmies*," *Kirkus Reviews* (15 April 2005): 467.
Rochman, Hazel. "Review: *Forest of the Pygmies*," *Booklist* 101:14 (15 March, 2005): 1284.

forgiveness

The tension between grievance and reconciliation colors Allende's character faceoffs with moral judgments and greatness of heart, as with the atonement of Juan José Bernal in "Wicked Girl." Frequent in her plots, the urge for vengeance clutches at the minds and spirits of troubled characters—Judy Reeves, the victim of a lustful father in *The Infinite Plan*, Diego de la Vega toward the womanizer Rafael Moncado in *Zorro*, and Eliza Sommers, victim of an obdurate society in *Daughter of Fortune*. In *The House of the Spirits*, Alba's reclamation of family history precedes rearrangement and editing of the journals of Clara del Valle, a responsibility that Alba takes personally. Through Alba, the author confronts her own contentious spirit toward the Pinochet regime and its murders and coverups. Analyst Hendrik Marthinus Viljoen explains Allende's compulsion to "take issue with the officially documented histories ... as recorded from a predominantly male perspective," one that the author identifies as vindictive and exultant in power on a par with the upheavals of Andre Brink's *Imaginings of Sand* (Viljoen, 2004, 84).

In a study of postcolonial literature, editor Susan VanZanten Gallagher depicts the resolution of *The House of the Spirits* as a "framework for conversion, a literal 'turning around,'" a basis in Christianity for a sincere change of heart (Gallagher, 75). Alba validates her grandmother's writings as a means to "see things in their true dimension," an application to historical outcomes that Clara foretells as crucial to a country overwhelmed by destructive intentions and actions (Allende, 1985, 490). Thus, forgiveness empowers Alba's optimism and her belief that a settling of grudges precedes harmony, both in her family and nation. Her adamant grandfather, Esteban Trueba, agrees, blaming "that damned agrarian reform" for luring peons from Las Tres Marías (*ibid.*, 474). He admits, "I've forgiven them and I'd like them to return," but his gesture makes no mention of a "turning around" through compensation for forced labor or the cyclical rape of peasant women (*ibid.*).

From a female perspective, Allende indicates a compelling incentive for Alba's reconstruction of history and Esteban's redress of faults and healing of hurts. As the result of positioning events in the order of cause and effect and redressing the gender imbalance, Alba achieves mastery of self by exterminating hatred, a responsibility that Viljoen calls "the dual task of overcoming and exorcising the past and constructing a new future," this time based on equality and mutual respect (Viljoen, 2004, 77). Alba exults at the extinction of hate: "I feel its flame going out as I come to understand" (Allende, 1985, 487). The triumph over vindication extends as well to her grandfather, who achieves redemption through his love and admiration of Alba and his grief at Clara's passing. An angelic death scene at Clara's bed depicts Esteban devoid of willfulness and rage. The return of Clara's spirit confers forgiveness on the virulent enslaver, rapist, and wife beater and enables him to complete the history of the Del Valle-Trueba clan on a positive note. Content in the arms of granddaughter Alba, Esteban summons his savior, "Clara, clearest, clairvoyant," his conduit to redemption (*Ibid*, 486).

Allende states in *My Invented Country* that "airing the truth is the beginning of reconciliation," which requires both admission of guilt and a request for forgiveness (Allende, 2003, 161). In her YA fiction, reconciliation counterbalances both alienation of tribes and the punishment of felons. Reviewers at *Publishers Weekly* praised the inclusion in Allende's YA quest novels of "compassion, forgiveness, and asceticism," an unusual trio in adventure literature ("Review," 2004, 75). Setting the tone, King Dorji identifies worthy strands in the character of villain Judit Kinski, a woman he had considered making queen of the Forbidden Kingdom until she revealed her part in grand larceny. After Prince Dil assumes his father's place on the throne, he offers Judit a Buddhist version of Christian conversion. She receives "the chance to improve her karma and evolve spiritually," the accepted progression to perfection in the Buddhist striving for nirvana (Allende, 2004, 436).

At the conclusion of *Forest of the Pygmies*, the third of Allende's trio of YA adventure novels, a host of repercussions against a tyrant result in a "fragile harmony" and restoration of peace between the Bantu and Pygmies (Aka) (Allende, 2005, 285). The author indicates a reconciliation based on forgiveness for a generation of mistreatment by the tyrant Maurice Mbembelé and his Bantu security force. Led by Nana-Asante, the elderly hermit queen — another version of the benevolent female rulers in *City of the Beasts* and *Kingdom of the Golden Dragon* — the Aka restructure a livable alliance, beginning with women. Nana-Asante chooses females as ambassadors of mediation and order because "They have more goodness within them," a belief that echoes throughout Allende's feminist canon (*ibid.*, 288).

On a grander scale, Allende neutralizes enmity between humans and beasts. The bush pilot, Angie Ninderera speaks through Nadia a pact of coexistence with crocodiles, who terrify Angie's fantasy of certain doom. The creation of a Peaceable Kingdom, a utopian archetype established in scripture as a reprieve from Earth's violence and mean-spiritedness, revives a times when "they had lived in harmony with nature for thousands of years, like Adam and Eve in Paradise" (Allende, 2005, 398). An equitable pact strips the Ngoubé village of a barbaric form of capital punishment, delivered by the snapping jaws of carnivores to hapless missionaries. The overarching symbol rids the third novel of nemesis or revenge, a divine retribution for sin. With a simplistic touch, Allende closes out the falling action with a prediction of a peace by which disparate spirits and divinities "share space in the human heart" (*ibid.*, 291).

See also betrayal; evil

• *References and Further Reading*

Gallagher, Susan VanZanten, ed. *Postcolonial Literature and the Biblical Call for Justice*. Jackson: University Press of Mississippi, 2007.

Klein, Kerwin Lee. "On the Emergence of Memory in Historical Discourse," *Grounds for Remembering* 69 (2000): 127–150.

"Review: *Kingdom of the Golden Dragon*," *Publishers Weekly* (15 March 2004): 75.

Schmidt, Siegfried J. "Making Stories about Story-Making, or Why We Need His- and Herstories: An Approach Towards a Constructivist Historiography," *Poetics* 28: 5/6 (2001): 455–462.

Viljoen, Hendrik Marthinus. *Storyscapes: South African Perspectives on Literature, Space, and Identity*. New York: Lang, 2004.

Gothic

Allende controls horrific details and dispenses them effectively throughout her canon. She magnifies the effects of fear in the execution of Tomás de Rameu in *Zorro* and the sinister mad scientists who treat Allende's daughter in the neurological ward in *Paula* to the splattered brains of the circus performer in *Of Love and Shadows* and the undulating serpent tattooed on Tránsito Soto's navel and the search for Nívea's decapitated head in *The House of the Spirits*. Her stories perpetuate grim scenarios—the beheading of a child murderer in "The Schoolteacher's Guest," the hermetic judge in "Clarisa," and the imprisonment of children for vivisection in "The Road North." The author's reflections on Chilean history mourn the ongoing mayhem of a country forever at odds with itself. According to critic Helen Falconer, the civil conflict reveals "highways ... heaped with the bashed-up, raped, and tortured bodies of its idealistic young" (Falconer, 2001).

Allende speaks from experience after her own viewing of chaos following the Pinochet takeover on September 11, 1973. On the positive side of horrific violence, Falconer credits experience that turns the author toward narrative as a means of recapturing grotesque hurts and of ridding them of their power to terrify. Of the universality of monstrous fears, the author declares terror to be "a black cloth that is always over us," a potential evil that could overwhelm a peaceful environment and turn it into a Belfast, Fallujah, or Pinochet's Chile (Wilson, 2002, 223). In a long line of narrative invention, notably in the survey of a morgue in *Of Love and Shadows* and of Amadeo Peralta's kidnap and imprisonment of Hortensia in "If You Touch My Heart," Allende turns edifices into chambers of horror, misbegotten marvels fraught with the sounds of vermin and spirits and the echoing moans of the dying. The locked doors and displays of grotesque bibelots within architectural labyrinths recur consistently in her long works and short stories as symbols of minds tormented by guilt and sadism and hearts unwilling to address the drain on health and sanity.

The author sets the tone of *The House of the Spirits* on mutilation and martyrdom by picturing Saint Sebastián, the suffering martyr "twisted in the most indecent posture, pierced by arrows, and dripping with blood and tears" (Allende, 1985, 12). The grotesque image, which recurs in *My Invented Country*, ushers in character torments, beginning with Rosa del Valle, who dies of male political treachery, an invention based on the author's actual Great-Aunt Rosa Barros. The poisoned brandy delivered by an enemy in the Conservative Party inadvertently stills the heart of the fictional Rosa with green hair, a suggestion of nature and fecundity destroyed by earthly corruption. The event turns the iconic Rosa into an elegant corpse, which Esteban and Jaime steal from the del Valle family vault in a bumbling, Laurel-and-Hardy tomb robbery.

Graceful as a water sprite under the knife of Dr. Cuevas, Rosa lies on the kitchen table in a grotesque scenario graphically disclosing her virginal young womanhood, "her intestines beside her on the salad platter," and her veins injected with embalming fluid (Allende, 1985, 53). Analyst Cherie Meacham describes the scene as "an abstract motif of truncated feminine creativity whose presence foreshadows the travails of the women who follow her," beginning with Nívea's beheading and concluding with Alba's imprisonment and rape (Meacham, 2001, 95). Contributing a grotesque touch, Dr. Cuevas's assistant remains behind to sponge the body clean of blood and kiss her pudenda, a gentle act of oral necrophilia.

The ghastly vision infects the novel, forcing young Clara to undergo a series of nightmarish fantasies, sleepwalking, and self-inflicted silence atoning for her guilt for predicting the assassination attempt, but not forestalling it. Esteban Trueba's gesture toward Rosa's poisoned remains foreshadows his adherence to a defunct economic system that poisons his values with greed and self-gratification. He displays a momentary regret for selfishness upon reuniting with his mother, Doña Ester Trueba, the death-in-life invalid infested with flies and worm, "two legs rotting alive" and toes puffed with an infected "death soup," whom the author based on her Grandmother Isabel Barros (Allende, 1985, 107, 108). A parallel leave-taking with Férula in the city slum emerges by candlelight in a dirty residence containing the corpse, her carnivalesque costume, and her digits nibbled by mice.

Blanca's expression of femininity takes a pagan form under the moon, where she meets Pedro García in a grove of trees, the ceremonial precinct of Wicca, Druidism, and pre–Christian nature worship. Meacham describes the carnal trysts as an "orgiastic dimension of ancient female rituals" providing outlets for the joy in pride and erotic pleasure, a feminist celebration pictured in Leslie Marmon Silko's *Garden in the Dunes* (Meacham, 2001, 99). The medieval punishment of Esteban's defiant daughter involves forced marriage to Count Jean de Satigny, a European gargoyle who installs his bride in a mansion with incongruous decor reminiscent of Edgar Allan Poe's horror story "The Fall of the House of Usher." Satigny drags Blanca through the Atacama Desert, a parallel of the god Hades abducting Persephone to the Greek nether world. The focus of the count's obsession, Incan mummies, allies his investment in smuggling antiquities with his interest in bizarre elements of death and burial and lurid pornographic photos of Indians cavorting in carnivalesque costumes. Like the decor of the Yugoslavian sculptor in *Eva Luna*, the dire surroundings predict Alba's eventual rape and torture by a sadist in a tomb-sized prison cell.

Revelation of the child whom Pedro sires with Blanca results in the primary infraction, Esteban's slapping his wife Clara for accusing him of the same breach of socio-racial standards by raping indigenous farm laborers. For the humiliation and loss of her front teeth, Clara condemns Esteban to loneliness by refusing to speak to him, a vow she carries out for nine years. Their residence, "as empty and lugubrious as a mausoleum," falls into decay (Allende, 1985, 239). In a subsequent nightmare, Esteban dreams of beating Rosa "the way I had Clara, and that her teeth also fell out" (*ibid.*, 233). Decades later, after Esteban places Clara's corpse in a grand salmon-colored monument, he attempts other acts of order to restore Las Tres Marías to its former glory and to influence Général Hurtado to release Alba from torture and cyclical rape in a punitive lockup called the "doghouse," an emblem of Colonel Esteban García's bestial treatment of inmates (*ibid.*, 466).

In expiation, a poignant example of Esteban's second loss of love appears in a macabre shape — the fetish the widower wears on his chest, a suede bag containing Clara's false teeth, a symbol of her gentle words that he treasures as a palpable apology for striking her. The image of a bridge of porcelain front teeth implies the vulnerability of Clara to a frustrated husband, the nine years of silence between them, and the burden of guilt, a mordant reminder of an unresolved marital fracture. Mouth imagery freights the text with the importance of communication to the del Valle-Trueba clan and the nation, where lies cloak the evil perpetrated by a fascist junta "armed to the teeth" (Allende, 1985, 453). Without Clara's conciliatory grace, the Trueba residence gradually founders, "swallowed up by oblivion" (*ibid.*, 338).

The resolution of *The House of the Spirits* requires extreme scenarios of the country beset by a vicious regime. As a model of the barbaric situation, Allende pictures a soldier "hanged from a post with his guts wrapped around his neck" (Allende, 1985, 449). The prison scenes of 200 captives plunged headfirst into excrement, zapped with electric wire, suspended by their arms, and run over by trucks. In a small sealed water tank, Alba joins five others in close confinement and wills herself to die. Allende's reduction of torment to three fingers mailed to Trueba ends the extended torment with a jolt to past cruelties committed against Pedro Tercero. The brief recital of Alba's sufferings in the infirmary recalls the medical experiments of the Third Reich on Jews and other detainees. Her return by horse cart through the huts of the poor contrasts the order of the High District, "everything clean, everything calm ... like another country" (Allende, 1985, 487).

A Pattern of the Grotesque

Allende maintains the motif of the outré juxtaposed with the mundane in *Eva Luna* and *The Stories of Eva Luna*, such as the passion of lonely shepherds in "Toad's Mouth" for sheep and seals skinned alive to emulate sirens and the ghostly presence of Indians in "Phantom Palace," a tumid symbol of colonial grandeur. In the house of Professor Jones, embalmed mummies share space with servants who listen to the radio and with the servant Consuelo, who conceals her pregnancy as the bloating of indigestion. After Eva departs at age seven to work, she encounters Elvira, a cook who keeps a coffin in her room "as a catchall for odds and ends" and a place for Eva to play-act at being dead (Allende, 1987, 57). To neutralize the evil of the mortuary bed, the maid chalks crosses on residential doors, "the meaning of which no one every deciphered" (*ibid.*, 70).

A discreet balance of horror with adventure and genteel city life sets the modified Gothic tone in *Of Love and Shadows*. Allende expresses mental terrors in families of the *desaparecidos* and indicates a resignation in those who accept that the abducted lie at rest, possibly in the hasty entombment at the Los Riscos mine, a symbol of postcolonial defeat of the El Dorado myth. Following a restrained revelation of skulls, dismembered limbs, maggot-ridden putrescence, and rag-wrapped torsos and the collection and tagging of remains in yellow bags, the text moves on to the unsatisfied curiosity of Irene. A crackerjack investigative reporter, she suffers nightmares of ashen cadavers in the morgue, where she searches for fifteen-year-old Evangelina Ranquileo, whose disappearance on a Sunday night worsens the crime to a violation of the Sabbath.

Oral imagery on a par with Allende's first novel embeds *Of Love and Shadows* with ghoulish metaphors. At Irene's loosening of the tongue of Corporal Faustino Rivera with roast pig and wine, she elicits a flow of testimony — an eyewitness account of a condemned man with crushed legs and an alleged rape of a moribund girl and the concealment of her remains. To exonerate the military, his chosen profession, Rivera excuses the events as "the worst of the dirty war they were all engulfed in" (Allende, 1987, 132). In Rivera's second testimony, the fiendish ravishing of a dying teenaged peasant resonates with necrophilia, a horrendous defilement against a girl the age of perpetrator Lieutenant Juan de Dios Ramírez's own daughter. Heightening the sacrilege of a young girl, the lieutenant tidies up the crime scene, where "a piece of the girl's white petticoat ... fluttered there like a wounded dove," a suggestion of her tender age (*ibid.*, 156).

The author moderates the atrocities and outrages in *Daughter of Fortune*, the second in her trilogy based on Chilean history. Her glimpses of port saloons and Chinese sickbeds fall within the normal limits of realism. The first breach of normality coincides with the shriek of grief from Tao Chi'en at the death of his wife Lin, a forewarning of Eliza's stillbirth of a "bloody little mollusk" in the hold of the *Emilia* (Allende, 1999, 205). In subsequent scenes, Tao fillets a shark that thrashes itself to death aboard the brigantine. The slaughter yields optimism in the fish heart that Tao cooks in soup to strengthen Eliza and the fins he dries to sell as aphrodisiacs. As the duo traverses California, they encounter bearbaiting, a pathetic show of a one-eyed bear marked with scars and dripping saliva before its barbaric pairing with a bull, emblems of frontier savagery that weight Pacific Coast history.

Colonial Gothic

For the opening of *Inés of My Soul*, Allende's retreat to the first encounter between Europeans and Chilean Indians, she introduces the insanity of Queen Juana, "the madwoman of Tordesillas" who kisses the reeking corpse of her husband, Philip the Handsome, over a period of two years (Allende, 2006, 188). The roll call of bizarre events includes the appearance of stigmata on the hands of Asunción, Inés's sister, and other holy week phenomena—levitation, the disembodied aroma of roses, and spontaneous generation of wings. The outré signs precede the immigration of Inés Suárez to the New World, where Europeans become "hidalgos of indomitable heart, with a sword in one hand and the cross in the other" (*ibid.*, 36). the height of Mesoamerican depravity derives from the Aztec religion, which demands blood sacrifice. To exacerbate the image of hearts torn from living chests, Allende pictures predatory birds too fat from flesh meals to fly and rats the "size of sheepdogs," one of the author's more memorable hyperboles (*ibid.*, 10).

The cost of crossing mountains and desert to reach Chile requires more grotesque scenarios. Before falling on hard times, Pedro de Valdivia's followers ransack Peruvian dwellings for beloved mummies, "dark and smelling of moss," to drag behind their horses, reducing their route to a bone-strewn horror (Allende, 2006, 136). To revive failing warriors, Catalina, Inés's native servant, administers a tonic of llama blood, milk, and urine. The failure of the water supply yields a madness that sends soldiers among the Indian bearers to seize their waterbags and to drink the urine of horses. Out of the rumors and legends of Chile, Peruvian accusers brand Inés as a vain whore who plied her trade in Spain and Cartagena and who revives her youth by drinking the blood of infants and "other horrors I blush to repeat" (*ibid.*, 247).

As *Inés of My Soul* dwindles into a gore-enriched epic struggle, Allende amplifies Gothicism to glorify the clash of colonial Spaniards with Indians who learned atrocities from their foe. For the 200 captives of Valdivia's riverside battle against Lautaro, the punishment of lopped Mapuche noses and right hands produces gory combat trophies. The Spanish toss basketfuls of human appendages into the river, "where they floated down to the sea, carried by the bloody current," a suggestion of the tales that swell colonial history and myth (Allende, 2006, 281). To the protagonist's denunciation of the amputations, Rodrigo de Quiroga replies with a warrior's stoicism, "War is war," a soldier's disavowal of personal roles in massacre (Allende, 2006, 282).

The novel's last battle begins with the reedy summons of battle flutes carved from human bones. Allende calls up more barbarity—the lopping of half a foot and seating a captive on a pike that pierced the entrails, a savage execution retrieved from ancient and medieval history. The trading of monstrous acts spirals: "Cruelty engenders more cruelty" (Allende, 2006, 305). The author builds suspense and fleshes out the text with unflinching commentary—"waving human heads and limbs," "avid for blood," "a quick and honorable death," "submerged ... in the putrid ooze," "nightmarish vision"—but refrains from overloading the narrative of a merciless war with purple prose (Allende, 2006, 306–309).

Poetic justice shapes a suitable end to *Inés of My Soul*. As a balance to Mapuche vengeance, Allende poses the thousands of deaths and corpses dishonored by the Spanish and awards Felipe/Lautaro the final insult to Général Pedro de Valdivia, his former master. By heightening the extravagances of cannibalism and molten gold poured down the throat, the text rewards a usurper with "his fill of the metal he loved so much, and that had caused the Indians so much suffering" (Allende, 2006, 313). The text leaps back toward grisly visual imagery to conclude the bloody career of Valdivia. In her concluding note, Allende exonerates herself for dramatic touches by picturing the narrative as a historic events "strung ... together with a fine thread of imagination" (*ibid.*, 317).

Caribbean Gothic

For *Island Beneath the Sea*, Allende enhances historical fiction with stark, macabre details, such as the filed teeth and bloody apron of a Congolese executioner and the burning of the martyr Macandal at the stake. The author places in the words of the slave girl Tété a description of the battle between the high priestess Tante Rose and the death god Ghede and his froglike lieutenant, Baron Samedi. The gestures, smoke, chalk circle, and amulets combine with Rose's whirling dance to create an aura of combat and virulent deal making, a parallel to the evil the French engender from their profiteering on sugar plantations where a cane mill crushes the forearm of Séraphine. Allende enhances the hellish scene with "a cloud of flies and the deafening noise of machines being pulled by mules," dumb animals as doomed to killing labor as slaves (Allende, 2010, 77). The text cloaks negotiations in a burst of Creole dialect, concealing from the reader the exchange of Séraphine's life for that of Eugenia as a gift to placate the god of death.

Gothic musings on death enhance the novel's approach toward the Haitian Revolution, with its reeking gallows and mass graves. After Eugenia dies quietly in her sleep in late 1789, Toulouse transports her in a "walnut and silver coffin" to Le Cap until he can decide where and how to inter her remains (Allende, 210, 284). At his rented abode, the coffin becomes hallway furniture, which Maurice and Rosette attempt to pry open with a kitchen knife. Like the deceased mother Addie Bundren in William Faulkner's *As I Lay Dying*, Eugenia becomes a family burden requiring explicit plans for burial in a Cuban convent graveyard. As a means of advancing the plot, Allende confides to the reader that Valmorain's intentions fail and that the coffin remains above ground until it is "consumed in flames two years later," a reference to the conflagration of Le Cap that follows the revolt of 1791 (*ibid.*, 151).

As in *The House of the Spirits* and *Of Love and Shadows*, monstrous crimes take on more realism as Allende approaches the historical climax. At the height of daring among Maroon rebels, gruesome evidence of brutality scents the island with carrion while death is "on the loose and lying in wait" (Allende, 2010, 178). Warriors brandish lances tipped with the remains of white infants; camp palings raise skulls and rotted carcasses. As whites retaliate and press the island colony toward catastrophe, the head of the Maroon leader Boukman joins the exhibits of savagery, an image of his plan still viable after his death at the stake. In the rescue of Valmorain, Tété struggles to save Maurice and Rosette from disemboweling, the torment exacted by Maroons on French planters. During a nighttime flight through the cane fields to Bois Cayman, Tété recoils from snakes, scorpions, and field rats, the terror that incites phobia in George Orwell's *1984*. The departure takes on the passage of a labyrinth, a Gothic convention derived from the maze encircling the Minotaur in Cretan mythology. Worsening the threats, the sucking mud and foul vapors of the swamp and the possibility of a "murderous mastiff" attack await the fugitives (*ibid.*, 187).

Allende pelts the reader with fearsome destruction. The end of Habitation Saint-Lazare typifies the end of colonialism, with lesser images of the fall of Habitation Lecroix and the skinning of the master as afterthoughts. In the rising dawn, hundreds of Maroons seize control of the Valmorain plantation, chopping a guard into "unrecognizable pulp" (Allende, 2010, 186). Destruction takes shape in the form of arson and a "saturnalia of revenge and devastation" wreaked by bayonet, chain, knife, machete, musket, and pole in a "hurricane of hatred," a suitable image for Caribbean colonialism extending over a century (*ibid.*, 186, 188). A "hair-raising saraband of howls" and hooting conches accompany the march of blacks on Le Cap, where marauders grip skulls by the hair (*ibid.*, 220). In terror for his life, Valmorain recognizes the scent of his sweat as the odor of martyred slaves, a sense impression equivalent to guilt. Allende turns the horrific scene into a second triumph for Tété, who leads the way toward the stampede of whites at the port. For effect, the presence of sharks devouring the slain heightens the fear of a no-win situation.

Allende tinges *Island Beneath the Sea* with terrifying females. The elevation of Hortense Guizot into the evil stepmother increases during the final trimester of her pregnancy. Like a black widow spider, she wallows in her confinement crocheting "webs like a tarantula" (Allende, 2010, 289). An exhibitionist, Sanité Dédé, the voodoo queen of place Congo, wraps herself in a snake to command attention and cast her subjects into a trance. Observers conclude that demonic possession fills her with the power to make worshippers foam at the mouth, drink animal blood, and wallow in the undergrowth in ritual "bacchanals" (*ibid.*, 326). The closing scene, a choreographic copulation between the voodoo god Erzulie and Tété, links the title with an imaginary retreat for the victims of bondage.

Terror and Adventure

For *City of the Beasts*, the first of a YA trilogy, Allende summons more mysticism than Gothicism for the tracking of a Yeti-like monster to the Upper Orinoco. Before Alex Cold departs from home, he spies on an emotional scene between his parents in which his father, Dr. John Cold, cuts the hair of wife Lisa to prevent a shaggy appearance during her chemotherapy. Analyst Elizabeth Gough connects Alex's terrifying view of something being "done to" his mother with other scenes in Allende's fiction of "female victimization and death" and the passivity of women dominated by patriarchal men, a misconception that Alex later corrects (Gough, 2004, 99). Subsequent terrors replace Lisa's cancer treatment with the immediacy of manta rays, caimans, an anaconda, and a boa constrictor, a house pet of the People of the Mist and reminder of the lifestyle of Amazonians compared with that of urban Californians.

Allende stresses the differences in settings by contrasting the perils of cancer to the American victim with an entire nation's endangerment from poaching and exploitation. Diane Roback, editor of *Publishers Weekly*, summarizes the author's blend of an "environmentalist theme, a pinch of the grotesque, and a larger dose of magic," the supernatural elements that empower the outsiders (Roback, 2002, 58). Like the ethereal presence in *The House of the Spirits*, the People of the Mist populate the rainforest with a graceful transformation at will from palpable to invisible. On a par with Rima in James Hilton's *Green Mansions* and the Eloi in H.G. Wells's *The Time Machine*, the lissome forest dwellers represent a peaceful extreme from the beasts of the title and a pocket of vulnerability in the path of loggers and miners.

Gothicism takes a more comic turn in *Kingdom of the Golden Dragon* with the creation of a Yeti society and a bumbling, muttering Yeti army that routs the dread Blue Brothers, members of the Scorpion sect. In *Forest of the Pygmies*, the final installment, Allende ramps up terror with rumors of cannibalism and a "macabre altar" featuring a gorilla skull adorned with hide, feathers, and dried monkeys' paws, a boundary marker for King Kosongo's territory that suggests beseeching hands (Allende, 2005, 102). The text enhances the dismaying welcome with leeches, worms, and monstrous rats and warnings of the power of Sombe the sorcerer. By focusing on his bestial gestures, Allende intensifies the man-versus-nature conflict that fuels literature about the African Congo.

See also superstition

• *References and Further Reading*

Falconer, Helen. "Colouring the Family Album," (Manchester) *Guardian* (17 November 2001).
Ford, Karen. "Triumph of Truth and Love," *The* (Melbourne) *Age* (23 September 2007).
Gough, Elizabeth. "Vision and Division: Voyeurism in the Works of Isabel Allende," *Journal of Modern Literature* 27:4 (Summer 2004): 93–120.
Meacham, Cherie. "The Metaphysics of Mother-Daughter Renewal in *La Casa de los espíritus* and *Paula*," *Hispanófila* 131 (2001): 93–108.
Roback, Diane. "Review: *City of the Beasts*," *Publishers Weekly* 249:25 (24 June 2002): 58.
Snodgrass, Mary Ellen. *Encyclopedia of Gothic Literature*. New York: Facts on File, 2005.
Wilson, R. Rawdon. *The Hydra's Tale: Imagining Disgust*. Edmonton: University of Alberta Press, 2002.

healing and health

Wellness and cures in Allende's writings derive from an easy alliance of medical and alternative treatments with magic, such as recovery from a scorpion's bite and the surgery that repairs the *madrina's* slit throat in *Eva Luna* and the merciful deaths of retarded siblings in "Clarisa." When narration calls for comedy, the author turns ignorance of anatomy and health into satire, as with Filomena's choice of chicken broth to overcome blindness in "A Discreet Miracle" and the wild dance and dried jungle herbs that restore the title figure from a puncture wound to the torso in "Ester Lucero." For "Simple María," the fable of a girl injured in a train wreck, the text satirizes the title figure's innocence and her treatment of constipation with "Agua de la Margarita," literally "daisy water," an astringent tonic intended to cure scrofula, a tubercular condition of the lymph glands (Allende, 1991, 155). Via hyperbole of María's purge and the added drollery of "perennial somnambulism," Allende compounds the outré qualities of the protagonist.

In *The House of the Spirits*, folk cures ally with current practice, such as eucalyptus plasters to ward off colds, blue methylene for mange, and hugs to quell asthma attacks. As evidence of megalomania, Esteban Trueba determines that local health providers offer less valuable advice than gringo doctors, to whom he turns for treatment of the effects of old age. Other futile medical treatments—borax and honey throat swabs, vitamin syrup—mark efforts by Dr. Cuevas to end ten-year-old Clara del Valle's silence. The intervention of the Rumanian quack Rostipov turns into hilarity after the dog Barrabás devours a bottle of lilac sugar pills with "no appreciable results," a contrast to the poisoning of Rosa with toxic brandy strong enough "to fell an ox" (Allende, 1985, 93, 40).

Allende illustrates the education in hygiene that lifts peons from squalor. In adulthood as mistress of Las Tres Marías, Clara views acts of charity as ineffective in relieving the misery of tenant farmers infested with lice and mange. Rather than follow the middle-class measures of her mother's generation, Clara institutes proactive health measures—bleaching laundry and boiling milk—and introduces treatments for diarrhea along with lessons on "the mysteries of the alphabet" (Allende, 1985, 123). Her skill at organization defeats some of the worst effects of the earthquake that destroys the country estate, bringing hoof-and-mouth disease to cattle and consumption to citizen survivors. A touch of humor relieves the terror of Blanca's simulation of tuberculosis symptoms by putting banana peels in her shoes and drinking chalky water. The ruse expands with hot brine, green plums, and a horse's girth cinching her waist, generators of exhaustion and sickliness that "transform the least ache or pain into a full-blown agony" to excuse Blanca from school (*ibid.*, 200).

At a dramatic impasse in *The House of the Spirits*, Nicolás cites brotherly loyalty as the reason for Jaime to abort Amanda's unborn child. Still a medical trainee, Jaime, a champion of liberalism based on the author's Tío Jaime, represents "certain alternatives to the status quo" (Perricone, 2003, 91). Jaime suffers both unrequited love for his patient and his first "moral conflict of helping a desperate woman" (Allende, 1985, 272). He fears causing "a river of blood and his science powerless to stop ... life from running out of that open faucet" (*ibid.*). The unprofessional surgery, which Allende compares to rape, concludes in 25 minutes with "bits and pieces in this sewer of a clinic," a ghastly conversion of clinical abortion to butchery and a cesspool (*ibid.*, 278). With a deft uptick in atmosphere, the text turns the abortionist/patient relationship into a tender love exchange that makes Amanda feel protected. The off-kilter romance foreshadows Jaime's haggard presence in the hospital and halls of the Trueba mansion, where he balances his career with tender nutritional supervision and parenting of Alba.

Healing the Poor

For *Of Love and Shadows*, Allende returns to nativist healing. She juxtaposes Mamita Encarnación's balms and compresses and Digna Ranquileo's linden tea for nerves, both folk treatments common to people who rely more on nature than pharmaceuticals. The notion of Evangelina Ranquileo's saintly intervention as a medium of assuaging the sick recurs at the home office of Don Simón, where "flasks, dried branches, herbs hanging from the rooftree" share space with printed prayers (Allende, 1987, 52). The suspicion of a curse on Evangelina begins with a visual urinalysis "to study the nature of her bodily fluids" (*ibid.*, 55). Treatment requires dosing with chestnut tea, chicory, aspen, gentian, gorse, holly, calcium, alum, and pine, but Don Simón leaves undisclosed the person who allegedly "evil-eyed" the innocent girl (*ibid.*, 54).

Allende's critique of the professions continues as the Ranquileos search for a cure. A modern physician diagnoses hysteria and prescribes a tranquilizer and electric shock, yet the intervention does nothing to halt the girl's noontime trances. Mamita Encarnación further muddies the intervention by connecting the carnivalesque fits with idleness and sexual awakening, a guess closer to the truth than other assumptions. The evangelist's linkage of Evangelina's spells with Hipólito's alcoholism indicates "sins of the fathers" as the cause of her gyrations and calls for communal prayer, also ineffective. Because Evangelina has made no First Communion, Father Cirilo blames Digna's faith in Protestantism and her lapse of worship in "the Holy Church" of Catholicism, an ineffectual splitting of hairs (Allende, 1987, 58). Allende turns the priest's counsel "a few 'Our Fathers' and a sprinkle or two of holy water" into evidence of the bumbling, Vatican-ridden philosophy that arouses enmity between the poor and orthodox Catholic prelates (*Ibid*, 62).

Cures in *Eva Luna* apply the same blend of curative herbs and edibles with common nostrums and the supernatural. Therapy begins early in the book with the lemon drops that missionaries trickle into the infected eyes of Consuelo, the title figure's orphaned mother. Folk cures permeate the text—sheep's tallow for chickenpox, fern root for tapeworm, and squash blossoms for parasites, a litany of natural elements. Consuelo's treatment of an Indian gardener for viper bite with turpentine poultices, herbal purges, and spiderwebs on the wound also incorporate lighting candles to saints, a last ditch effort she mistrusts. The ribald source of the Indian's recovery—regular intercourse with Consuelo—cloaks in wit the author's contention that an active sex life is conducive to wellbeing. She revisits the motif of carnal satisfactions in the adultery that alters Zulema's disposition. After the climactic seduction scene that releases her from a long period of discontent, lovesickness for her husband's cousin Kamal reduces her to a surly wraith. Neighbors in Agua Santa revere Zulema enough to suggest treatments with rue tea, syrups and vitamins, and chicken broth and the ministrations of a Goajiran healer, which make no headway against "the spell of Kamal ... his scent, his fire, his naked erect sex" (Allende, 1987, 189).

In *The Stories of Eva Luna*, Allende speaks more directly to the sufferings of a deaf-mute boy in Agua Santa and, in general, to the decline of the elderly, including Inés of "The Schoolteacher's Guest." For "Interminable Life," the author accounts for the compassion toward the dying of Dr. Roberto Blaum, an escapee from European anti–Semitism. From studies in public hospitals and the morgue, Blaum acquires knowledge to help critically ill poor, the people like Padre Miguel in "A Discreet Miracle" who rely on "herbs of poverty and poultices of humiliation" (Allende, 1991, 261). In a retreat to the grotesque, the author speaks knowingly of "fragile bodies chained to life-support machines, with all the torture of their needles and tubes," a status she later observes in the year-long illness of her daughter Paula from porphyria (Allende, 1991, 242). In Roberto's nightmares, the plight of the dying gives him no rest, especially the lethal cancer that overtakes his wife Ana.

Global Herbalism

An attack of traveler's illness in *Daughter of Fortune* extends the ongoing contrast between European and indigenous health philosophies. The bible salesman, Jacob Todd, stricken with intestinal complaint, surrenders to bloodletting, but continues to waste away from cramp and diarrhea, a familiar affliction to newcomers. Mama Fresia, the Mapuche cook, intervenes "with such assurance that the weakened man did not dare protest" (Allende, 1999, 29). She introduces a more sensible regimen of herb tea for pain, hot bricks and blankets for warmth, and massage and Mapuche incantations for sleep. Jacob's rapid recovery, hastened by chicken soup and Mama Fresia's commanding presence, precedes a reminder that unwashed fruit and polluted water carry the pathogen, a common sense instruction alerting newcomers to sources of gut distress. The servant's example prepares an apprentice, Eliza Sommers, for applying mustard and hydrangea to ripen tumors and for curing loneliness with violets and mood swings with verbena. To retain matriarchal wisdom, Eliza collects recipes in her notebook, a traditional female legacy similar to the cookbook in Kaye Gibbons's Civil War novel *On the Occasion of My Last Afternoon*.

Colonial gynecology, still shackled to misogyny as old as ancient Egypt and Greece, lacks the research and objectivity to treat women's ills effectively. As an abortifacient, Mama Fresia makes nostrums of borage, chicken droppings in black beer, mustard compresses, and sulfur baths, all insufficient to dislodge Eliza's fetus. A terrifying reminder of Victorian era treatment of "hysteria"—literally "wandering womb"—in single females requires cautery, a contrast to the Chilean application of holy water. A more effective treatment by German pharmacist for Rose's melancholy—"The Change" or menopause—consists of cod liver oil for anemia and valerian, a mild sedative and soporific, both more direct pharmaceuticals than Mama Fresia's pantry nostrums. Psychologically, the sudden sighting of Eliza in San Francisco works an immediate change in Rose, who needs hope to restore well being.

The shift in locale in *Daughter of Fortune* from Chile to California introduces an international flavor to healing and wellness. Tao Chi'en, a dealer in opium and rhinoceros horn, earns John Sommers's respect for skillful doctoring, which Tao learned by age nine from studying the plants around Kwangtung. Allende pictures the boy in a more aggressive medical apprenticeship than that of Eliza to Mama Fresia. By his teens, Tao observes the spread of cholera and typhus during a famine and the dangers of tuberculosis and venereal disease, major killers of the nineteenth century. In the hands of a skilled acupuncturist, Tao gains "a capacity for compassion and a sense of the ethical," a simplified statement of the Hippocratic oath (Allende, 1999, 158). Tao's patients present the ailments of sailors—venereal disease, scurvy, advanced alcoholism, and the bruises and cuts inflicted by port brawls. For their healing, he applies the philosophy that the most knowledgeable healer "has the greatest obligation toward humanity," a universal concept stated from the Confucian perspective (*ibid.*, 184).

A tricultural perusal of medicinal plants introduces Tao to unfamiliar cures, including coca leaves, a common palliative in South America; from books on Western medicine, he learns the source and prevention of contagion. He treats Eliza with Chinese nostrums, dragon bone and oyster shell, and with opium, a reducer of diarrhea, pain, and insomnia and a foundation of common nineteenth-century compounds. In Sacramento, he encounters acts of violence—cuts, dislocated bones, bullet and knife wounds, snakebite—and cholera, the lethal result of polluted water. Allende stresses the need for secrecy as Tao learns from Ebanizer Hobbs the basics of surgery, for "neither European nor Chinese patients admitted that the other race had anything to teach them" (Allende, 1999, 181). For Eliza, a return to Mama Fresia's cure for despair—raw egg with brandy—restores hope, but fails to quell a desire for a bath and conversation over tea, the longing for warmth and comforts common to females far from home. Allende demonstrates the value of folk medicine and surgical techniques in mining camps and brothels, where the sick, sad, drugged, and maimed accept whatever treatment they encounter.

Contagion and Violence

In *Island Beneath the Sea*, Allende pictures disease and fatigue as common killers. Island malaria, dysentery, dengue fever, cholera, yellow fever, and exhaustion carry off French colonists and cane field laborers without deference to race or class. The pustules, loose teeth and befogged mind bring retribution to the father of Toulouse Valmorain, one of the sybaritic colonizers of Haiti. For the unnamed father, "Dantesque treatments" turn bloodletting, mercury, and penile cautery into punishments rather than medical care. Without comment, the author pictures the 50-year-old victim lolling in a hammock with two black female teenagers, a reflection of sexual debauchery that infects Europeans in the Caribbean.

The novel describes a conventional decline in Eugenia García del Solar of Madrid, a planter's wife ill suited to the tropics. Saint-Domingue becomes "a purgatory of fatal illnesses" that kill more whites than people of color (Allende, 2010, 27). Allende mocks Dr. Parmentier, who pretends to visit Eugenia while actually he studies the herbal cures of Tante Rose, which he compiles in a manual. The text compares the ineffective mercury solutions and ice water baths of Europeans to the worthless snake oil, sage incense, and beneficent candles of island healers. More mysterious, the death of an infant from tetanus, a mysterious malady inflicted through the baby's fontanel, frees it from slavery.

Like the deceived husbands in Charlotte Brontë's *Jane Eyre* and *Wide Sargasso Sea*, Toulouse Valmorain courts Eugenia in Cuba without learning about "several lunatics in the García del Solar family" (Allende, 2010, 49). Of particular concern to Dr. Parmentier, the "hopelessly unhinged" Eugenia, a model of the Gothic "madwoman in the attic," despises Haiti for its vermin, humidity, and miasma and suffers miscarriages, dementia, and hallucinations (Allende, 2010, 66). Home treatments require "blessed candles, purification with sage incense, and rubdowns with snake oil," all prescribed by black doctors, and the ceremonial smudging of Tante Rose with cigar smoke to negotiate with death for the live birth of Eugenia's baby (*ibid.*, 66). Like the Hebrew shepherd-poet David, Eugenia's servant Tété sings and prays to dissipate hysteria and melancholia and to lull the patient to sleep. Parmentier induces drug addiction by keeping Eugenia sedated with opium, gradually turning her into a passive mute who communicates only through the rosary until her confinement to a convent, the standard lockup for the insane in Victorian fiction.

Allende accords to Tante Rose an understanding of island ills and the overarching syndrome of enslavement and dehumanization. Upon the arrival of the youth Gambo from a slave dealer, the aged healer prescribes only fat over the brand mark and poultices for the lashings, which must "close from inside out," an allusion to the captive's acceptance of ineluctable bondage, the "fire that smolders inside" (Allende, 2010, 111). Rose values her knowledge of curatives as a godly gift that she must share rather than hoard to keep the god's wisdom in circulation, even among whites. On a par with Rose, Tété dispenses understanding of all Gambo lost by abduction from Africa and confers love, which she describes as "good for healing," a common strand in Allende's writings (*ibid.*, 112). The author pictures the female dichotomy—Rose, the medicine women, and the affectionate handmaiden Tété—as stalwart antidotes for the despairing.

As the narrative progresses toward the Haitian Revolution of 1791, outbreaks of cholera, dengue fever, malaria, and yellow fever parallel the fever for liberation, a fervor as relentless and perilous as a bodily infection. Like Harriet Tubman, the heroine of the

American Underground Railroad, Tété reserves laudanum for quieting children during passage to freedom. Allende contrasts the sturdiness of the black servant Gambo from abduction and suffering with Valmorain, the soft-living planter whose "soft, rosy feet" become "nothing but raw flesh" and open sores from rubbing against boot leather, all emblematic of the effects of colonialism on the overlord (Allende, 2010, 188). Hyperbole castigates the Frenchman for looking like he has lived for a millennium as he degenerates from his former honor and manhood into bestial agony. Ironically, Dr. Parmentier treats the blistered feet with a native herbal treatment he learned from Rose.

In the ongoing debacle of Haitian politics, yellow fever settles the score between black rebels and Napoleon's French insurgents, who die by the thousands. In retreat from the newly declared republic of Haiti, refugees carry their epidemic to New Orleans. Folk medicine returns to respectability at Valmorain's new plantation outside the city. Treatments vary from boiled thorns and sliced potatoes to caiman grease and Indian roots, the nostrums of rural Louisiana. Dr. Parmentier retains the respect of patients despite his willingness to treat blacks and mulattos as well as elite whites. He succeeds using the herbal regimens of Tante Rose, notably soup, tea, and water to rescue the sick from cholera and poultices for scorpion bite and infected wounds. To those, Tété adds the simple concoctions to combat bladder and kidney stones, fever, infection, and migraines and potions to abort and quell hemorrhage.

More personal in *Paula*, Francisca offers her daughter blue pills to ease the distress of sitting in Paula's ward. Allende recovers slowly from the aftereffects of her mother's dosage and purchases less intrusive valerian, an ancient remedy for sleeplessness. In jubilation that Paula breathes on her own and opens her eyes, Allende and her mother celebrate signs of recuperation. An anecdote by Ernesto's father about an Indian muleteer in the Amazon who stanches bleeding with saliva indicates Allende's willingness to grasp any healing power. The event gives Allende hope that medical science can save Paula. As reality refutes baseless hopes, the author accepts that "there will be no miracle" (Allende, 2001, 315). Allende witnesses a failure of fairy tales for "Beauty in her glass coffin," where "no prince will come to save you with a kiss" (*ibid.*, 323).

Curing Despair

With authorial poetic justice, in *Portrait in Sepia*, Allende makes one of her humorous psychosomatic diagnoses in the case of Agustin del Valle, whose rage rots his liver. For *campesinos*, Aurora lists "secrets of nature, prayer, and the help of the *meicas*, the female Indian healers," who rely on local flora, the native antidote to ailments (Allende, *2001*, 237). Less amusing, Matías Rodríguez de Santa Cruz awaits the final stage of syphilis, a "slow calvary" for which "no cataplasm, poultice, or corrosive sublimate" exists to halt his mental vagaries and "putrefying," a corruption suited to a moral degenerate (Allende, 2001, 190, 185, 186). Unlike natives, who suffer external assaults to the body, both Agustin and Matías decay from the inside out, an appropriate end to colonialism and its depraved profiteering.

Allende offers an uplifting healing in the next generation of the del Valle clan. As a result of loving acceptance after Nívea belittles Severo del Valle's "butchered foot" as a mere inconvenience of a year's "rigor and stupidity" of war (Allende, 2001, 111, 21). To restore his "male attributes after the amputation, she proposes marriage, a more realistic stimulant than the liquor and gunpowder he drinks during combat (*ibid.*, 122). From days of delirium and despair, he revives from a single kiss, a fairy tale ending to a horrific battle and naval evacuation. Nívea's advance from quaking virgin to knowledgeable virago allows her to "infuse life into the man she loved," an erotic curative of his diminished self that Allende develops further in *Aphrodite* (*ibid.*, 120). Severo's rejuvenation from "making love like gypsies" attests to the author's belief in love and a fulfilling sexual relationship as essentials of wellness (*ibid.*, 122).

Allende extends her interest in healing throughout the novel. A view of Nívea's seventh birthing validates borage tea for circulation, chamomile oil for massage, and eucalyptus as aroma therapy to ease the passage of twin sons into the world. Postpartum treatment involves a tonic of red wine fortified with bull's blood. The text interweaves prayers and benisons, the religious adjuncts of herbalism and midwifery. The declining years of Grandmother Paulina del Valle requires a daily pose of vigor and a visit to Ebanizer Hobbs's clinic. Hobbs's practice of swift surgery "[diminishes] the risk of shock and blood loss"; aseptic conditions generated by phenol spray and lye scrubs and use of rubber gloves reduce infections. Upon recovery, Paulina bankrolls the clinic of Iván Radovic, an egalitarian who believes that "good health will be within reach of every Chilean" (Allende, 2001, 220).

Medicine and Culture

For *Inés of My Soul* and *City of the Beasts*, Allende orchestrates lush jungle fruits, medicinal plants, and aphrodisiac filters, the stuff of medieval and Renaissance romance. In the Panamanian jungle, bodies succumb to crushing by an anaconda, devouring by piranhas, and an unnamed illness— scurvy — which loosens the teeth and drains the body through hemorrhaging from every orifice. The swift death of Jerónimo de Alderete from "some tropical plague" sends him "to a better life," an admission by Inés Suarez that Panama's atmosphere dismays new arrivals (Allende, 2006, 293). While setting bones and binding wounds, Inés faces the imported European diseases—colds, influenza, syphilis, typhus, and smallpox — as well as rainforest fevers and insect bites. The text implies that Spaniards share the miseries that waylay aborigines, virgin soil populations that have no natural resistance to the contagions of Europe.

To the benefit of Spanish colonization of Chile, the Indian herbalist Catalina embodies the healing power of previous healers— Pedro García, Mamita Encarnación, Mama Fresia, and Tante Rose. Like her predecessors, Catalina applies age-old knowledge of aphrodisiacs, tonics and energizers, soporifics, and analgesics from the flora of Peru. In preparation for the role of healer to Valdivia's expedition to Chile, Inés and Catalina equip themselves with their individual curatives— herbs for Catalina and a lengthy list of Renaissance drugs for Inés. To German pharmaceuticals—"mercury, white lead, lunar caustic, powdered jalap, white precipitate, cream of tartar, salt of Saturn, basilicon, antimony, dragon's blood, silver nitrate, Armenian bole, cado, and ether"— Catalina merely shrugs her shoulders in scorn of chemical compounds and returns to natural remedies (Allende, 2006, 109).

Catalina continues developing her knowledge of plants by meeting secretly with Chilean aborigines to learn to identify and prescribe from the region's natural pharmacopoeia. Two folk curatives—*huella* (footprint) leaves and *oreja de zorro* (fox ears)— speed the healing of Cecilia after giving birth to Chile's first mestizo, Pedro Gómez. Bitter infusions of *maté* and doses of *latué* bark enable Général Pedro de Valdivia to withstand chronic pain of a broken leg and dispiriting predictions of doom. Catalina's hallucinogenics contain such power of communing with angels that Inés wisely conceals the results lest Catalina face witchcraft charges from the Inquisition, the iconic sixteenth-century arbiter of good and evil.

HEALTH IN THE WILD

Matters of health take prominence in *City of the Beasts* because of the clouds of Amazonian ants and mosquitoes, blood-sucking leeches, and the risk of intestinal illness, malaria, or typhus so far from Western medical care. On the Brazil-Venezuela border at Santa María de la Lluvia, nuns operate a hospital, a source of treatment for "miners crazed by mercury," the element used to extract silver from ore (Allende, 2002, 67). Without revealing her double-dealing in spreading smallpox as a source of genocide, Torres validates the skill of shamans at using medicinal plants for curatives. César Santos notes that Padre Valdomero, out of necessity, sets broken bones, extracts teeth, and removes cataracts from parishioners. To protect natives from infection, Dr. Omayra Torres travels as a representative of the National Health Service to inoculate remove tribes and airlifts patients to Manaus by helicopter, a service that alleviates native suffering through the intervention of modern technology.

Allende makes well being a priority to adventurers. Threats to life — electric eels, manta rays, fire ant stings, darts poisoned with curare — keep characters on edge. The rescue of photographer Joel González from an anaconda requires Nadia's knowledge of Indian body casts, formed of bark and mud and secured with vines. Without making a cultural judgment, Dr. Omayra Torres's report on the value of ground snake head to treat bone disease, baldness, and tuberculosis suggests her open-mindedness toward native curatives. More significant to the theme of survival, Alex's endurance of the fire ant test enables him to identify with the chemotherapy that floods Lisa's body to eradicate cancer. The strength of the boy's love and mental imaging communicates to Lisa a positive view of Alex as a man. Walimai's application of a curative paste to the ant stings stresses the reciprocal nature of indigenous poisons and antidotes. More precious to Alex, the water of health promises a cure for Lisa from what reviewer Carol Birch calls a "numinous realm" at the edge of a "new age paradise" (Birch, 2002).

For the suffering of nearly lifeless Yetis in *Kingdom of the Golden Dragon*, Allende depicts Tensing, the lama mentor of Dil Bahadur, as diagnostician, psychic healer, and nutritionist. Pity for infants dying from inadequate mother's milk inspires Tensing to pray for understanding of how to milk livestock and feed infants drop by drop. The sudden stomach discomfort and vomiting of bile that attest to poisonous mineral water that colors tongues purple require a simple substitution of potable water. After Nadia's appears in the guise of the white eagle, Tensing packs acupuncture needles and food suited to rescue her. He explains the tranquilizing power to halt pain from producing "tension and resistance, which blocks the mind and slows the natural ability to heal" (Allende, 2004, 247). The gold needles also activate the immune system. Allende tempers the implications of instant healing and suppression of pain with needles by reminders from Tensing that Nadia must rest to give her shoulder time to heal. The therapy retrieves Nadia from hypothermia and restore her damaged shoulder and stamina enough to make her useful for the attack in the falling action.

In the third installment, *Forest of the Pygmies*, the danger of mandrill bite takes on importance to safari members for causing fever and infection. Because the guide Michael Mushaha is unable to differentiate between a systemic sepsis and malaria, he takes the safe alternative of sending the patient, Timothy Bruce, to a physician in Nairobi. Contrasting modern medicine, the arrival of an herbalist to treat a Masai child interjects folk healing via amulets, gourd shakers, and feathered sticks. To an outsider's ridicule of traditional diagnosis and cures, Mushaha affirms ceremonial purgation of evil through the power of suggestion as both fast and effective. Allende corroborates native healing by affirming the relief of tubercular symptoms in Kate Cold from Amazonian powders and "an amulet of petrified dragon excrement," a talisman from the Forbidden Kingdom that knits broken bones and "wards off arrows, knives, and bullets" (Allende, 2005, 38, 39). From the trilogy's emphasis on therapy and wellness, Alex determines that "science and technology aren't enough to make someone well" and chooses medicine as his future career (*ibid.*, 201).

A Balance of Cures

Allende's interest in psychosomatic effects on health also colors therapies in *Zorro*. Examples perpetuate the mix of native superstition with scientific cure, such as the laudanum that soothes the left leg of Captain Santiago de León, the arnica that eases Nuria's bruised face, and the St. Christopher medals that accompany Bernardo and Diego on their voyage in 1810 from Alta California to Spain. In an extreme illness, the puerperal fever of Catherine Villars, even the combined strength of Christian prayer, African herbs, voodoo spells, and medical science fails to save the patient.

White Owl, the shaman/healer in *Zorro*, possesses intuitive diagnostic skills and years of experience with herbs and soporifics. Her talents fail Diego after pirates attack the hacienda, a turning point in the boy's coming of age. The assault leaves his mother Regina close to death from a dagger tip in her clavicle. At the beginning of his abandonment of boyhood, he punishes himself for wasting White Owl's painkiller, which might have saved Regina from the torment of cautery with a white-hot iron, a therapy that dates to prehistory. Priestly medicaments for Bernardo require gargling with communion wine and honey, borax lavage, warm throat poultices, and swallowing ground beetles, all methods of relieving the boy's muteness. The author stresses respect for these means of addressing the powers of evil. Ironically, after priests fail to cure Bernardo, it is White Owl's diagnosis that sorrow prevents him from speaking. Similarly all-knowing, she applies herbs that retrieve Diego from death by snakebite, which plunges him into a hallucination of death and heaven. The quelling of venom in his leg becomes a portent of the course of his future—like the rattlesnake, he will disguise himself, hide by day, and strike in the dark.

See also madness

• *References and Further Reading*

Birch, Carol. "Review: *City of the Beasts*," (Manchester) *Guardian* (30 November 2002): 33.
Davies, Lloyd. *Allende: La casa de los espíritus*. London: Grant & Cutler, 2000.
McGee, Celia. "'Ines' Captures Chile's Soul in 1500s," *USA Today* (9 November 2006).

The House of the Spirits

A postmodern metafiction told by a series of voices that prefigure history, Isabel Allende's *The House of the Spirits* (1982) displays a collective mission of self-writing through real experiences and the transcendence of spontaneous memory. Jennifer Gibb characterizes the text as a "progression down the colonial timeline into postcolonialism," a chronological ordering of events that kindred characters know only piecemeal or second hand, without linkage of cause with effect (Gibb, 2010, 240). Rather than reveal the history of

Latin America, the text focuses on what analyst Aníbal González calls "the private and subjective sphere" in the dictator novel, a uniquely Latin American genre pioneered by Miguel Angel Asturias and furthered by Allende (González, 2010, 42). The novel's success on the global fiction market compensates Allende for hurt and loss during exile, enabling her to transcend mourning for home by repairing the damage on a fictional stage where the dialogue between "two distinctly gendered voices ... allows the female narrator to face past trauma and to define herself within the context of her own family" (Wilkinson, 2008, 156, 153).

Alba, the chronicler, profits from the oral lore of her grandmother, one of what analyst Hendrik Marthinus Viljoen calls the "repositories and custodians of the past who, by recalling 'ignored' experience, are able to infuse it with meaning" (Viljoen, 2004, 74). Alba addresses her disillusion with her grandfather, Senator Esteban Trueba, and the government by searching the relationships and emotions of her family and its toxic secrets. González characterizes the flow of events as the result of "disenchantment, physical and spiritual wounds, and postrevolutionary fatigue" told through an "accumulation of genealogical and historical detail" (*ibid.*). According to critic Linda Maier, Allende wrote the book, from "an optimistic belief in the healing power of literature," a conviction that Allende shares with Cecilia Velastegui, author of *Traces of Bliss* (Maier, 2003, 237).

Followed by *Daughter of Fortune* (1999) and *Portrait in Sepia* (2000), the multigenerational saga grounds a complex account of six households in three continents over a span of 130 years of war, fascism, immigration, colonialism, feminism, racism, and bondage. In the words of reviewer John Moore, "The lineage goes: Nivea begat Clara begat Blanca begat Alba," a quartet of matrilineage that symbolizes the fate of Chile (Moore, 2010). Literary historian Donald Leslie Shaw summarizes the lineage as "generational steps towards ... the interlinked class, politics and women's struggles" (Shaw, 2002, 182). As a token of unique matrilineal traits, the green hair of Rosa del Valle recurs in her great niece, Alba del Valle, who rinses her hair in parsley water to heighten the "maritime color [in] its full leafiness," a symbol of life and sustained lineage to the del Valle-Trueba clan (Allende, 1985, 308).

Critic Karen Wooley Martin credits Allende with manipulating place and action to spotlight women, activists, and minorities in the socially and ethnically elastic frontiers of the New World, which are "constantly appearing, disappearing, and reappearing" in the Trueba mansion (Allende, 1985, 309). The story takes place in driving distance of natural obstacles, the Andes Mountains and the Atacama Desert, as well as socio-economic barriers. Through notebooks, begun when Clara is ten years old, she records significant subjects, organized by liberating events "that bore witness to life" (*ibid.*, 245). The transgression of Old World boundaries destroys myths of class privilege and racial purity and shrinks the power and influence in males sharing the aristocratic class with the reactionary Esteban Trueba, master of the plantation at Las Tres Márias.

Allende's matricentrism reflects a fictional version of Chile's history from 1904 to the 1970s, a text that critic Marketta Laurila calls a discourse of exile in a violent macho society, symbolized by Esteban's enraged swings of his cane at the telephone and inanimate objects that ignore his political clout. For material, Allende drew on "all the anecdotes my grandfather had ever told me, and lots of imagination" (Savio, 2002). She explains, "In the process of writing the anecdotes of the past ... I felt that my roots had been recovered and that during that patient exercise of daily writing I had also revered my own soul" (Teisch, November 2007). For its candor, reviewer Helen Falconer applauded the first of Allende's trilogy as a "remarkable must-read family saga" of the del Valles (Falconer, 2001).

The author structures her epic tapestry of history and female lineage with political allegory and insider knowledge of the bitter struggle of Chile's *campesinos* for democracy and self-actualization against a repressive oligarchy. She places Alba, the budding matriarch, as the mediator between Dr. Jaime's nonviolent plan for change and Nicolás's faith in a radical shift in the power structure, which "with a stroke of the pen ... changed world history" (Allende, 1985, 383). Disproving Trueba's predictions of terror and violence, the success for the left stirs the people to process "all night, beside themselves with joy" (*ibid.*, 389). Like the golden era of Roman literature—Ovid's *Metamorphosis*, Virgil's *Aeneid*—the collapse of a republic forced Allende to examine the source and spirit of Chile for evidence of the "right stuff," the makings of historic greatness. To pans of her novel as a pale copy of Gabriel García Márquez's allegorical *One Hundred Years of Solitude* (1967), critic Philip Swanson riposted that her fiction "enjoys sharper political focus precisely because it systematically subverts the magical dimension in order to confront the reader with harsh reality" (Swanson, 2006, 265–277).

The Gendered Perspective

The method of subversion, the remembering of past events and themes by a matrilineage of four women, predicates history from a female perspective. Susan R. Frick describes the circular narrative of Nívea, Clara, Blanca, and Alba as "an alternative to the male dominated world" that produces tyrants like Général Hurtado, Esteban Trueba, and his senatorial co-conspirators (Frick, 2001, 29). Alba, a leftist activist and the future of the del Valle-Trueba clan, revels in perusals of "a paradise of long forgotten objects" in the basement, which she reveres like artifacts from a sealed pyramid and uses to construct playhouses and stage dramas, miniatures of the life she will someday live (Allende, 1985, 309). Veneration for the past generates Alba's bedroom fresco and concludes with her writing of "metaphorical bridges" in prison, an "empowering cultural response to trauma" by tracing it to the roots of evil (Frick, 2001, 29). To inform Alba of "the opinion of the age (and regime) that Esteban embodies, according to Marta Wilkinson, he provides ten letters, a first-person testimony to amoral plots and despicable profiling of "decent women and all the rest," his discounting of worth in field laborers (Wilkinson, 2008, 158).

The author compensates for her time in exile by aggrandizing and adorning memories of home with fictional embellishments, which analyst Philip Graham calls "mansions that expand over the years with a kind of architectural improvisation" (Graham, 2001, 39). Allende chooses the unchronic city, a term that critic Daniel Noemi Voionmaa applies to an urban landscape unfixed in time, yet obviously mimicking the Chilean regime of Augusto Pinochet. The unnamed poet and country fit the background of Allende's homeland and Chilean love for the works of Nobel Prize winner Pablo Neruda. An earthquake sets in motion climactic events that reveal the cracks in the socioeconomic power structure and the wisdom of old Pedro García, who superintends Esteban's rescue and the setting of broken bones by touch. The author based the cataclysm on the undersea quake of April 6, 1943, a four-part catastrophe begun by an 8.3 quake that precipitates tsunamis, a volcanic eruption, and epidemics.

Clara's response to events sets the tone and direction toward amelioration and forgiveness. While nursing and feeding Esteban during his recuperation, his wife no longer channels clairvoyance. Instead, she anchors her energies in the earthly realm and rebuilds the family plantation. After 15 years of marriage, Esteban's pettish demands and tantrums end her affection for him much as Doña Ester's withering body had filled Férula with despair and seething anger at being the sole care giver. The animosity between husband

and wife remains civil, but obvious to the household and guests. As a widower, Esteban seizes the opportunity to restore marital intimacy and to lavish attention on Clara's remains, but brushing her hair and slipping on a tunic fail to restore her "luminous gaiety," the clear light that had first drawn him to her (Allende, 1985, 337). As a token of Clara's absence, Allende describes the withering of funeral bouquets, a natural attrition paralleling Clara's quiet departure from life.

The Male Hegemony

Allende's knowledge of Salvador Allende's Marxist regime and its replacement by Pinochet's military junta supply an insider's memories of idealism trounced by corruption and coercion. In the polemical discussion between Esteban and Hurtado, the latter attempts to disabuse Esteban of fears that Marxism can triumph. Hurtado belittles the Indians, peasants, and sailors whom Esteban expects to form a soviet and ridicules the Communist Party as "four bums without any statistical importance" (Allende, 1985, 347). The concerns still unrelieved, Trueba claims that radicals, Communists, Socialists, and other splinter groups can ally with the soviet, thus overthrowing conservative land holders, Chile's moneyed tyrants.

Significantly, Esteban Trueba, whom Allende describes as a "caricature of the picturesque, reactionary oligarch ... fanatical, violent, antiquated," seems unaware that women's political groups threaten male dominance (Allende, 1985, 351). Nívea, the godmother of suffragists, sets the example by "[chaining] herself with other ladies to the gates of Congress and the Supreme Court, setting off a degrading spectacle that made all their husbands look ridiculous" (*ibid.*, 81). The post–World War I campaign coordinates personal and media appearances, pamphleteering, and posters to fight for equal rights to the vote and education and an end to the shaming of illegitimate children. By conferring triumph on female characters, the author compensates initially for domestic sufferings—imprisonments, disappearances, torture, executions. Dramatic protest validates the role of all women—peons, servants, beggars, radicals, prostitutes, socialites—in the struggle for class and racial justice, a solidarity the author extends in *Of Love and Shadows*.

An influence on Maryse Condé's *Tree of Life*, Allende's saga, according to critic María Roof, redefines the family by the "reintegration of excluded members," a source of "unavoidable violence" (Roof, 2010, 79). Allende's gynocentric world illuminates empowerment in the so-called "weaker sex." The focus on *macha* women and an underclass willing to hold on through misery and terror forms the backdrop of a patriarchal triangle. Esteban Trueba, the privileged overlord, in a moment of lust, impregnates Pancha García, the grandmother of a hybrid monster, the bestial Colonel Esteban García, despoiler of the privileged, whom critic Christopher Hitchens describes as a "cold, plebeian, ambitious type" (Hitchens, 2011). As a parallel to violation of workers, the political allegory transforms the rape of Trueba's granddaughter Alba into the rape of a nation. In an era of ideological flux, Chile struggles to right ancient wrongs and to tap patriot strengths while negating prevalent weaknesses. Of the size of Allende's saga, playwright and adaptor Caridad Svich remarked, "It's massive, and it has so many subplots, all of which are tantalizing and could be plays in their own right" (Lengel, 2012).

Secret Sins

The saga frames hidden sins that interlace family heritage, the foundations for dynasty and longevity of people "still living exactly as they had in colonial times" (Allende, 1985,

83). Allende symbolizes the weight of past crimes in the "huge colonial pieces" that deck the plantation manse alongside "heavy wool carpets, and lamps of hammered iron and copper," a metal Chilean press gangs once mined at the direction of Hispanic overlords (*ibid.*, 205). The novelist's scrutiny of the family linkage of Esteban Trueba with Pancha García uses them as models of the change that the unnamed Latin American country must undergo to cleanse itself of colonial taint. Because Allende links Trueba with the del Valles and the Garcías, the convoluted lineage incorporates the strengths of aristocrats and peasants to produce a third generation endowed with spirit and promise. Allende enhances the saga by diminishing suspense and narrating the Truebas' efforts through unsettling times that test the mettle of its patriarchs and matriarchs.

At times disjointed, but well substantiated with alternating visions of family and nation, *The House of the Spirits* proceeds in an unusual order, leaping ahead by decades to predict hard times, good times, and continuity. Allende utilizes third-person omniscient point of view interspersed with first-person commentary by Alba and Esteban Trueba, progenitor of the del Valle-García-Trueba line. In describing Trueba's predations on female plantation works, then allowing him to speak his loneliness and misgivings, Allende reports on a tormented soul who "was not crying because he had lost power. He was crying for his country" (Allende, 1985, 443). Released at last of authoritarian extremes, he searches for "his fury and his hatred and was unable to find them" (*ibid.*, 446). Cleansed of emotional weakness, he foresees that the premise on which he builds a dynasty has already compromised the future.

The text applauds the courage that inspires Esteban to redeem himself through confession and a change of heart by ridding himself of "the rage that had tormented him throughout his life" (Allende, 1985, 489). His example buoys Alba and Miguel, the next generation, to strive for domestic and national stability. Through the acceptance of Pedro Tercero and Miguel, Allende's fictional Truebas reground their proud ancestry and revitalize inherent character traits, such as Pedro Segundo's ability to heal injured cattle, Clara's education of laborers in hygiene and literacy, Jaime's altruism toward the sick, Blanca's generosity toward retarded children, and Pedro García's establishment of plantation ethics and belief systems. The refinement process, like Darwin's survival of the fittest, supports an optimism for the nation's future and a belief that other families like Trueba's will undergo a similar purification to assure the nation a populace worthy of the cost of revolution.

In a model of toxic lust, the outsider, Esteban García, lives on hate and erotic vengeance. In the presence of six-year-old Alba, he holds her on his knee and presses her hand against his erect penis, a symbol of violence against the vulnerable, the true motivation for rape. A second encounter at Alba's fourteenth birthday party, revives his sadistic yearning for her and leaves her feeling sordid and humiliated. He compounds the degradation of a born blue blood by plunging her head into excrement "to avenge himself for injuries that had been inflicted on him from birth" (Allende, 1985, 464). Allende's explicit descriptions of the pedophile's gropings angered American evangelicals of Modesto, California, who objected to inclusion of *The House of the Spirits* on public school reading lists.

In a gesture to biological determinism, Allende reveals the blended virtues of Alba's ancestors, especially Uncle Marcos's adventurous spirit, Nívea's feminism, Clara's compassion and writing skills, Esteban's independence, and Blanca's creativity. As idealistic and resilient as her forebears, Blanca Trueba and Pedro Tercero, Alba rebounds from imprisonment and torture and adopts the role of family scribe. While awaiting the birth of her daughter, Alba interweaves the old ledgers, notebooks, and letters that hold her family's past. Like genes intermingling in a family bloodline, the resulting words "[bear] witness to life for fifty years" (Allende, 1985, 488). The saga concludes with a new vigor winnowed out of debauchery and classism. Through words, Alba can "reclaim the past and overcome terrors of my own" (*ibid.*, 7). The motif of new motherhood re-instills worthy traits in subsequent echelons of the matrilineage. In Alba and her unborn daughter reside these qualities and the energy to counter old faults and guide the family toward selflessness and charity.

Forgiveness abounds in the resolution, in which Alba acknowledges that "we cannot gauge the consequences of our acts," an aphorism that applies to the entire fictional cast (Allende, 1985, 490). The voice of Alba, looking ahead to her task as clan speaker and mother of Clara and Esteban Trueba's great-granddaughter, establishes balance. Her text assures the reader that Trueba's curse is exorcised and that his self-confidence, coupled with Clara's compassion and Alba's respect for family history, will pass into the next generation. Ensuring spunk, Pedro Tercero's idealism undergirds Miguel's revolutionary zeal. The author's variant points of view parallel the perpetual process of genetic fusion, a merger of human traits that renews and energizes society.

See also forgiveness; del Valle–García–Trueba genealogy

• *References and Further Reading*

Falconer, Helen. "Colouring the Family Album," (Manchester) *Guardian* (17 November 2001).
Frick, Susan R. "Memory and Retelling: The Role of Women in *La casa de los espíritus*," *Journal of Iberian and Latin American Studies* 7:1 (June 2001): 27–41.
Gibb, Jennifer. "Victory of the Ash Buttocks: The Role of Hybridity in Colonization, Decolonization, and Postcolonization," *Journal of the Utah Academy of Sciences, Arts & Letters* 87 (2010): 235–243.
González, Aníbal. *Love and Politics in the Contemporary Spanish American Novel.* Austin: University of Texas Press, 2010.
Graham, Philip. "A Less Magical Realism," *New Leader* 84:6 (November-December 2001): 38–39.
Hitchens, Christopher. *Arguably.* New York: Hachette, 2011.
Lengel, Kerry. "Playwright Tackles Big 'Spirits' in Own Way at ASU," *Arizona Republic* (31 March 2012).
Maier, Linda. "Mourning Becomes Paula: The Writing Process as Therapy for Isabel Allende," *Hispania* 86:2 (May 2003): 237–243.
Martin, Karen. "Mapping Ethnicity in Isabel Allende's *Daughter of Fortune* and *Portrait in Sepia*," *Grafemas* (December 2007): 1–8.
Moore, John. "A 'House' of Horror and Wonder," *Denver Post* (24 September 2010).
Roof, María, "Maryse Condé and Isabel Allende: Family Saga Novels," *Critical Insights* (October 2010): 74–85.
Savio, Anita. "A Teller of Tales: Isabel Allende," *Latino Leaders* (1 October 2002).
Shaw, Donald Leslie. *A Companion to Modern Spanish-American Fiction.* Rochester, NY: Tamesis, 2002.
Swanson, Philip. "Z/Z: Isabel Allende and the Mark of Zorro," *Romance Studies* 24:3 (November 2006): 265–277.
Teisch, Jessica. "Isabel Allende: Book by Book," *Bookmarks* (1 November 2007).
Viljoen, Hendrik Marthinus. *Storyscapes: South African Perspectives on Literature, Space, and Identity.* New York: Lang, 2004.
Wilkinson, Marta L. *Antigone's Daughters: Gender, Family, and Expression in the Modern Novel.* New York: Peter Lang, 2008.

humor

In interviews and print, Allende displays the infectious merriment of a stand-up comedian and the drollery of the fabulist. While presiding over lunch for Janet Hawley, a writer for *The* (Melbourne) *Age*, the author smirked, "Gluttony and lust are the only deadly sins worth the trouble, my dear. Please eat more" (Hawley, 2008). Spots of resistance to social and moral conventions arouse fun in Allende's stories, such as the flight of Elena Etxebarria from her wedding into the arms of a stranger in "The Guggenheim Lovers" and the retarded woman in "Simple María" who confuses sexual romps with a Greek sailor with "the blessing from heaven that the nuns in her school had promised good girls in the Beyond" (Allende, 1991, 159). As a result of the misperception, María enjoys the orgasmic stimulus of "her innermost grottoes," a double allusion to intimate, private satisfaction and the rural shrines of hermit saints (*ibid.*, 160). Similarly exuberant, the coupling of Elena with Pedro Berastegui satisfies the bride's longing for love and manages to lighten Detective Aitor Larramendi's "rusted policeman's heart" from the couple's magical night drinking the colors of the Guggenheim's art works (Allende, 2005, 111). For added zest, Allende depicts the museum caretakers deeply involved in a Vatican scandal exposed on television.

With the skill of Anton Chekhov, Allende crafts scenarios as satires on universal faults, such as the gullibility of the upper class in "The Proper Respect." According to critic C.R. Perricone, such wit becomes a function of theme in Allende's narratives, as with the local physician dancing naked around a patient in "Ester Lucero" and the frog convention and the frozen sheep donated to feed the poor in *Of Love and Shadows*. In *Aphrodite*, the author collects anecdotes and recipes intended to boost titillation from tasty bites and connubial intimacies. Allende appears no less waggish in *Eva Luna*, where the unwary succumb to the proselytizing of young Mormon evangelists. Text cites the contiguity of a seminary, brothels, the Opera House, and the city's best French restaurant as a kind of "topographic democracy" (Allende, 1987, 210). More satiric in the vein of Kurt Vonnegut's *Cat's Cradle*, the claims of the church on local power in *Eva Luna* overlooks male disdain for Mosaic laws and the position of atheism in *machismo*.

The author opens her first novel, *The House of the Spirits*, by ridiculing restrictive female clothing in Nívea del Valle's broken corset rib. The birth of Rosa del Valle rewards Clara with a rhapsodically lovely sister as perfect as a porcelain doll. To the midwife, however, Rosa's green hair and yellow eyes bear the stigma of "the days of original sin, as the midwife put it, making the sign of the cross" (Allende, 1985, 6). The gesture prefaces subsequent thrusts at Catholicism for its medieval superstitions. The motif of strictures on women includes daughter Clara's response to the sermon topic that hell awaits humankind: "We're all fucked, aren't we" (Allende, 1985, 17).

The opening chapter frolics through additional family tendencies, beginning with Uncle Marcos's carnivalesque crystal ball, flying machine, and a parrot that hawks nostrums to cure impotence, portents of Clara's immersion in spiritualism and caged birds and her son Nicolás's intent to fly north over the *cordillera* in a zeppelin. A grim sarcasm follows the months of restoring Las Tres Marías, when the sole pastime is "castrating pigs and bulls" and cockfighting, androcentric barbarisms that anticipate Esteban Trueba's moral decline in the glorification of "gunpowder and blood" and dreams of "blood, semen, and tears," an anticipation of catastrophes to come (*ibid.*, 70–72). No less farcical, the response of the dog Barrabás to treatments of Clara del Valle's speechlessness turn to hilarity after he consumes a bottle of sugar pills and quivers in teeth-chattering fear of Nana, who dresses in Halloween disguise to terrify Clara into speaking.

Didactic Comedy

Allende uses humor for subtextual commentary, for example, satirizing English schools that promote hymn singing, vegetarianism, and humility, "except those (vanities) in the realm of sports," a dig at male self-glorification through team competition (Allende, 1985, 343). She introduces venereal disease at the Christopher Columbus brothel as a token of allegations that the first Spanish explorers infected Indians with syphilis. Significant to the destruction wrought by the conquistadors, Esteban Trueba's uncontrolled rampages turn his cane into the weapon of a *patrón*, a title replete with colonial posturing and self-importance, but with no more significance than a wallop of his walking stick. Just as he impulsively assaults the mouth of his wife Clara for telling the truth, his cane obliterates two telephones during an operatic melodrama for bearing untenable news of Blanca's pregnancy with the child of Pedro Tercero, which Esteban calls "a monstrous folly" (Allende, 1985, 246). A third cane shatters during Esteban's tirade at Clara's door, which remains closed to a despicable proposition that Blanca marry Count Jean de Satigny, a fortune hunter and Inca antiquities smuggler. Esteban's attack on the radio at the sound of Pedro Tercero's singing dramatizes the protracted enmity between the *patrón* and Alba's father. Allende allegorizes Esteban's vicious canings by describing protection of a tender rubber plant, an anthropomorphic bit of flora that droops and exudes milky tears at the *patrón*'s approach.

Humor permeates the del Valle-Trueba saga at moments of strife, beginning with Clara's handy bouts of asthma to stop household chaos and her discussion of cross-stitching and "the hierarchy of sin" with nuns while they sip chocolate during ceramics classes for retarded children (Allende, 1985, 321–322). Surreal touches lighten the alien nature of the Blanca's honeymoon retreat, which Satigny adorns with dark drapery, leopard-skin upholstery, gold fixtures, baroque porcelain, and ornate tassels. The appearance of the hairless, coca-chewing Indian majordomo in Louis XV heels introduces a deepening incongruity, worsened by the groom's "secret revels," a sexual quirk the author dramatizes in Lukas Karlé in *Eva Luna* (Allende, 1985, 290). Allende draws the vision of men in heels from "two horrific French porcelain figurines" in her grandfather's mansion in Santiago (Allende, 2003, 31).

In *Of Love and Shadows*, Allende blends hurtful ironies with the laughable clichés of Rosa, the maid and nanny of the Beltrán household. The affectionate pairing of the Ranquileos contrasts the mismatch of the Beltráns. Eusebio Beltrán maintains a liberal philosophy of "help your friends, screw your enemies, and in all other cases be just" (Allende, 1987, 42). His lackadaisical air of *noblesse oblige* backfires in his marriage to Beatriz Alcántara, a social climber given to aristocratic posturing. For his error in bride selection, Allende notes, "a lifetime was not long enough to regret it" (*ibid.*, 43). Ironically, Eusebio, even with the offer of cash for a divorce, is unable to slip away from Beatriz until after he suffers a spate of nagging and quarrels.

Allende makes throwaway sallies throughout *Eva Luna*, in which the orphan Consuelo receives a cuff from missionaries after the child inquires which priest is her father, a subtextual rebuke of Catholic hypocrisy and pedophilia. The author extends her underhanded slaps at the church with the image of a flea-bitten parrot cursing while reciting the "Our Father," an echo of the unholy recitation of prayers by blasphemers (Allende, 1987, 3). Additional asides titter at praying at dawn for humanity, atoning for universal sin by kneeling on peas, female lust for St. Benedict, and misidentifying a bust of Beethoven on a home altar as St. Christopher. Eva's *madrina* creates anthropomorphic fund of worship by praying for hangover cures and by calling gods on the telephone and "interpreting the hum of the receiver as parables" (*ibid.*, 47).

For *Daughter of Fortune*, Allende enlarges on sanctimony and incongruence, especially in social behaviors and religious ritual, such as the prostitute Azucena Placeres's savings from her earnings to pay for church indulgences to spare her time in purgatory. The fellowship between Captain John Sommers and Jacob Todd, a false missionary and bible seller, invites irreligious outbursts from John, who declares that the poor "don't deserve the misery of being evangelized" (Allende, 1999, 68). Allende's models of bonhomie cloak barbs directed at self-important Europeans who promote exploitation of Indians while purporting to care for their souls.

As witty as her brother, Rose Sommers tosses out diatribes against social naiveté and hypocrisy, for example, her belief that women marry, not to be entertained, but to "be maintained" (*ibid.*, 74). The comment implies the feminist dictum that actualized women must have access to money and self-empowerment. The corollary, "the only good thing about marriage is becoming a widow," expresses the female need for an unfettered life, a liberation from patriarchy and the social yoke of the wife/mother/matron (Allende, 1999, 36). Similarly jubilation accompanies the freedoms of advanced years. Rose asserts, "Nothing is as liberating as age," a statement that acknowledges her loss of responsibility to brother Jeremy at his death (Allende, 2001, 13).

At a dismal point in *Portrait in Sepia*, the third installment in the *House of the Spirits* trilogy, Captain John Sommers, who is dying of a ruined liver, dreads the thought of reincarnation as a non-drinker. He smirks that he might return as a Muslim, who embraces sobriety as a religious duty. The author makes death jokes out of Aurora's fear that menarche will kill her and from the apoplexy of Feliciano Rodríguez de Santa Cruz, a fetching mate whom *Kirkus Review* labels "the robber-baron elite" ("Review," 2001). Feliciano's estranged wife mourns in comedic distress, "Don't die on me, Feliciano, you know widows never get invited anywhere" (Allende, 2001, 122). For comfort, she looks to "mountains of sweets and long baths," the self-indulgences suited to a self-absorbed survivor. Paulina's ability to reduce situations to their farcical bases reduces angst while lifting character spirits. Of her nephew Severo's growing family, in 1896, she reminds him that the income of a lawyer is inadequate "unless you steal twice as much as the others do" (Allende, 2001, 199).

Autobiographical Jest

In *The Infinite Plan*, a fictional biography of her husband, William C. Gordon, Allende reveals a private assessment of the American frontier. The text accounts for California's appeal to "adventurers, desperadoes, nonconformists, fugitives from justice, undiscovered geniuses, impenitent sinners, and hopeless lunatics" (Allende, 1993, 28). With deft wording, Allende also snatches pathos from comedy, as in the Vietnam combatants singing "A Mighty Fortress" while Gregory Reeves, a resident of Los Angeles, sings "O, Susanna," a paean to the frontier woman's tears at abandonment. Allende describes California as naturally agitating to the spirit and enticing to fortune hunters who lose their souls in the rush for wealth, a theme that foregrounds *Daughter of Fortune*.

Allende jests about the appeal of evangelism to people who have no background in scriptural history. Despite evangelist Charles Reeves's sincerity, lower-class followers attend lectures more out of curiosity and boredom than "reasons of faith" (Allende, 1993, 25). She further ridicules the ignorant for believing that Jesus wrote the Bible in English, a language unknown until 1385. From the same era, she satirizes the religious tent revivals that rely on fundamentalist scare tactics and prophesies of Jesus with "whip in hand" as the showmanship that lures churchgoers to a two-for-the-price-of-one viewing of "redemption and entertainment," an authorial dig at the melodrama of televangelism (*ibid.*, 26).

Allende wrings drollery from the actions of Padre Larraquibel, pastor at the Church of Our Lady of Lourdes and boxing coach of parishioner Gregory Reeves. To sway youth from sin, the priest flaunts "apocalyptic predictions about the consequences of sinful thoughts" and "accused communists of being the Antichrist incarnate" (Allende, 1993, 91, 96). At the parting of Greg from his pseudo-father Cyrus in the hospital, Greg stops Padre Larraquibel from administering last rites to "an unreconstructed agnostic" (*ibid.*, 124). Allende uses the standoff to illustrate Catholicism's immutability. Overriding Gregory's declaration that Cyrus is both unconscious and an unbeliever, Padre Larraquibel insists on performing priestly duties with holy water, "capitalizing on the dying man's inability to defend himself" (*ibid.*, 124). The diction depicts the padre as an opportunist who exploits unfair advantage over the moribund.

Allende thrives at angling humor to reveal its dark underside, for example, the emergence of Gregory Reeves from the confessional to the sacristy to learn to box. Critic Vincent Kling affirms the author's "study in hilarity" and characterizes as salutary the mockery of priestly judgment, which comedy strips of its moral impact (Kling, 2010, 241). With similar zest, Allende's characters speak witty, sometimes mordant truths at the expense of the pompous. From the paradox of pulpit thunderations and the humor they arouse, Allende "[draws] sustenance from a dynamic in which wisdom and healing emerge from the balancing of opposites" (*ibid.*, 242).

In a summary of the author's adventures, in 1996, Allende wrote of surviving "three revolutions, one invasion by the United States Marines, four earthquakes, a military coup, and Mexican food" (Allende, 1996, 21). After four decades of professional fictionalizing, she explained, "Now that I make a living with these lies, I am called a narrator" (*ibid.*). Miranda France, a reviewer for *New Statesman*, credits Allende with a keen sense of the ridiculous and a flair for anecdotal history, which complement her "gift for conversational writing" (France, 2003, 53). Joshing about the would-be Nerudas in Chile, Allende claims that, under every rock visitors find "a poet or a balladeer" (*ibid.*). Her admiration for Chilean women causes her to laud modesty, industry, and affection while admitting to the dominating, gossipy, and chauvinistic side as well. The balance of witticism with shrewd analysis rids Allende's writing of the edifying dogma common to less facile writers.

In *My Invented Country*, the author finds incongruity and reasons to chaff her grandmother's séances, devotees of the Virgin Mary, bus trips to holy sites, and prelates of all types. Of evangelical and Pentecostal worshippers, she describes as irritating their ability to bypass "the priestly bureaucracy" of Catholicism, which remains fixed in medieval principles (Allende, 2003, 60). She views Mormons as an "employment agency" on a par with the Radical Party, and a handful of other beliefs—Jewish, Muslim, New Age, ecological, Buddhist, Eastern, folkloric, herbalist, hypnotist, agnostic, animist, fundamentalist, and psychic—as variants of the same venality (*ibid.*). Leading to a witticism about Augusto Pinochet and priests, Allende describes his self-exonerating euphemism about blessing Chile with "a totalitarian democracy," a contradiction in terms that conceals the president's true aims (*ibid.*, p. 63).

Twenty-first Century Mockery

Timing enhances Allende's bon mots, for example, the priestly intonation in *Zorro* of the Latin phrase *sursum corda* (lift your hearts), "which had no bearing on anything but sounded impressive" (Allende, 2005, 345). With similar reductive logic, Isabel de Romeu, still innocent at age 16, stares her fill at naked Panamanian Indians and smirks that male genitals "could be tucked comfortably into her reticule" (*ibid.*, 326). The author tweaks the overly romantic Juliana de Romeu for her attraction to the cunning seducer Rafael Moncada. With a cynic's boldness, the text puns, "A man with good hair has a head start in this life" (*ibid.*, 180). Eulalia de Callís, Rafael's aunt, makes a subsequent thrust at his hauteur by commenting: "Even the most stupid man looked good in a uniform" (*ibid.*, 198). Subsequent jabs at Jean Lafitte and Diego de la Vega derive from the author's belief that philanderers base their woman chasing on vanity, which blinds them to the depth of women's character and passions.

Allende's young adult novels alleviate serious purpose with teen humor. Just as flute music allies Alex and Nadia with the People of the Mist in *City of the Beasts*, so too does shared laughter at Alex's imitation of Tarzan pounding his chest. In jest, the Indians imitate him and fall down laughing, concluding the episode by "(slapping) each other's backs like old friends" (Allende, 2002, 178). The allusion to the Tarzan films and television series subtly reminds the reader that the trio of Tarzan, Jane, and Cheetah form a pseudo-family in the same style as Alex, Nadia, and Borobá, a comical monkey.

Animal humor opens the third of the trio, *Forest of the Pygmies*, which reviewer Janet Hunt describes as "[swinging] wildly from comedy to tragedy and [hovering] unsettlingly between the fiction of its main storyline and the better realities of modern Africa" (Hunt, 2005). By showcasing the prejudice of the elephant Kobi against Alex, the beast of burden seeks a private alliance with Nadia, who speaks his language. Complicating the triangle, Borobá also seeks Nadia's attention and raises his fist in anger at Kobi's intrusions. Humorous elements dot the otherwise fearful clash in the jungle with insightful details, particularly pilot Angie Ninderera's reliance on a totemic lipstick and escapism through addiction to cigarettes, a parallel of Kate Cold's reliance on vodka pick-me-ups.

For a balance in *Inés of My Soul*, Allende pokes fun consistently at pompous priests and hidalgos, who charge underlings with indulging in "vices reserved for their masters" (Allende, 2006, 264), She characterizes Spanish humor as wry comments to lighten the misery of hunger and fear of Mapuche attacks. Using the values of Felipe, the mascot of Santiago, for contrast, she ridicules European superiority. In a verbal duel between the boy and Padre González de Marmolejo, Felipe counters the priest's judgment on native polygamy with a fair description of concupiscence among conquistadors. The unfavorable image of soldiers seizing Indian girls as concubines and abandoning them at will concludes with Felipe's musing, "Perhaps Spaniards and Mapuche would meet in hell" (*ibid.*, 221). Humor drains from the quip in the novel's resolution, in which Felipe reveals his true identity as Lautaro, the nemesis who savors the demise of his former master, Pedro de Valdivia.

For *Island Beneath the Sea*, Allende's ready quiver of quips serves well in small matters, for example, the setting of Madame Delphine's parlor. For courtesan Violette Boisier, Delphine pays the price of two goats. Background education came from Delphine "made me pray to the Virgin Mary, a goddess who doesn't dance, just weeps, because they killed her son and she never knew the pleasure of being with a man" (Allende, 2010, 40). On a visit, Violette and Delphine occupy fragile chairs near a clavichord "the size of a pachyderm" and sip coffee from "tiny flower-painted cups for dwarfs," a droll contrast of extremes in a womanly domain (*ibid.*, 35). During negotiations for the sale of Tété, Delphine displays a more niggardly control on largesse with "biddy-sharp" eyes that enable her to wrest a profit from the deal (*ibid.*, 26).

The author needles the arrogant French colonials with their need for exhibitionism at entertainments. To upgrade Tété's understanding of European refinements, Valmorain has her educated under the mentorship of Zacharie, majordomo of the Intendance. Zacharie demystifies the forest of wine glasses and silverware and teaches Tété how to remove chamber pots during grand dinners. During the 15-course dinner that Valmorain organizes for his own aggrandizement, guests ride a block or two in carriages, producing a wealth of horse manure that staff must shovel from the street. Allende notes the service as a means of preventing "stench from impinging upon the ladies' perfume" (Allende, 2010, 201). The subjects of sewage and nasal distress return to mock the protocols of newlyweds, Toulouse and Hortense Guizot-Valmorain. While immured for three days in the bridal chamber, Toulouse suffers a sneezing fit from contact with swan feathers on his bride's negligee. The only relief from boredom and stifling heat are the arrivals of meals and the removal of chamber pots.

See also hypocrisy; names

• *References and Further Reading*

France, Miranda. "Old Wives' Tales," *New Statesman* 132:4667 (8 December 2003): 53–54.
Hawley, Janet. "A Woman of Spirit," *The* (Melbourne) *Age* (15 March 2008).
Hunt, Janet. "Review: *Forest of the Pygmies*," *New Zealand Herald* (7 May 2005).
Kling, Vincent. "Archetype, Not Ideology: Isabel Allende's Balance of Opposites," *Critical Insights* (October 2010): 239–257.
Perricone, C.R. "Allende and Valenzuela: Dissecting the Patriarchy," *South Atlantic Review* 67:4 (Fall, 2002): 80–105.
"Review: *Portrait in Sepia*," *Kirkus Review* (15 August 2001).

hypocrisy

Hypocrisy deserves both indignation and satire in Allende's writings. In *Paula* in a lengthy discussion of the author's innocence at age 20, she tackles the subject of collective hypocrisy. In a few sentences, she captures the absurdity of sex education in the early 1960s that introduces young males to condoms but conceals birth control pills and other methods of contraception from females. The author jokes that girls in her generation "[pretended] that sex did not interest us because it was not good form to appear to be collaborating in your own seduction" (Allende, 1995, 102). She recalls parental warnings about drinks drugged with barnyard aphrodisiacs and about drives in the country that ended in fornication. A grief of her early womanhood, the freedom of the author's brothers Pancho and Juan to seduce the household staff and "to go out all night and come back at dawn smelling of liquor, with never a word of rebuke" offends Allende with the rampant "macho arrogance [and] abuse of class," prevalent themes in her canon (*ibid.*).

In *My Invented Country*, the author continues raging against "our rituals for maintaining appearances," a pretense that runs counter to her mother Francisca's open liaison with a married man (Allende, 2003, 103). Allende decries puritanical upbringing and cites euphemisms for breast feeding and torture, taboo terms among Chile's prudes. More unbearable, the scandals arising from "any little peccadillo someone else commits" coincide with the heaping up of the accusers' private sins that remain undisclosed to the public (*ibid.*, 121). Allende blames snobbery, conservatism and "the crushing authority of the Catholic Church" for violence and rancor (*ibid.*, 178). She derides the bride's haste to produce children "so no one would think I used contraceptives," which physicians prescribed only to married women (*ibid.*, 120). For the sake of public standing, individuals concealed abortions, transvestism, and AIDS. The author discusses at length annulment in Chile, where polite people avoid speaking of sexual proclivities and divorce law "is still pending" (*ibid.*, 77).

Fictional Hypocrites

Like the excesses of deceit in Emilia Pardo Bazán's social novel *The House of Ulloa*, Allende's fictional hypocrisies in *The House of the Spirits* range from the pulpit speaker pointing "a long incriminating finger" at "sinners in public" to the outbursts of Esteban Trueba about traditional values, both family and religious (Allende, 1985, 8). At a climactic point, Trueba ignores the source of Blanca's pregnancy and seizes Count Jean de Satigny, a passionless fop who courts Blanca only for her father's wealth. While denying intimacy with the "deflowered daughter," the count softens his denials at mention of "Blanca's dowry, her monthly income, and the prospect of inheriting" Trueba's estate, a topic limited to man-to-man discussions (*ibid.*, 247). For maximum irony, Trueba compares investment in an heiress to the operation of a chinchilla farm, which fails.

The wedding itself reaches a height of dissembling in Trueba's demand to have a bishop officiate at a cathedral service. The notion of an amply pregnant woman in a white dress with eighteen-foot train "fit for a queen" characterizes the father's insistence on show, however absurd. After her photo graces the society page, the term a "Caligulaesque party with sufficient fanfare and expense" alludes to the opulence of decadent Romans in the first year of the Empire, a period renowned for the flouting of republican tradition (Allende, 1985, 248). The trumped-up wedding ends appropriately with a check written to Jean de Satigny to finance his home and pottery business in the north, away from gossip and social approbation. To mock the ostentation, Blanca rebukes her father for siring bastards in the Trueba line, a foreshadowing of the tragic incarceration and torture of Blanca's daughter Alba by corrupt police.

The double dealing of police in *Eva Luna* involves a flaunted visit to the madam, La Señora, to negotiate a bottle of liquor and extort a portion of the proceeds from whoring. Allende speaks with a journalist's knowledge of the chain of graft reaching upward to the police chief and Minister of the Interior, "both [of whom] had been benefiting for years and therefore had a moral obligation to listen" to complaints from the underworld (Allende, 1987, 130). The precarious nature of hush money tips in favor of a new sergeant, who raids the red light district, accidentally killing a baby with tear gas. The arrests of people not a part of "elegant clientele" exacerbates the hypocrisy, which resonates with the vigor and street ribaldry of the *commedia dell'arte* (*ibid.*).

A break in the "tacit code of honor" resulting in the public shaming of police officers and a cabinet minister generates a "War on the Underworld," a ridiculous flap over an illicit business that had functioned with official backing for decades (Allende, 1987, 129, 132). Allende shapes "this stupendous brawl" into an exposure of tyranny resulting in torture, murder, and a civil uprising of students and workers requiring a military presence in tanks (*ibid.*, 134). As a four-day riot simmers down, the author honors participants for generating a "spark of democracy," a folk backlash against venality (*ibid.*, 135). While the demimonde again thrives after police return to the job of persecuting beggars, madmen, and political enemies, Allende satirizes the flexible nature of honesty among officials sworn to serve and protect.

HISTORICAL DISSEMBLING

Allende's historical fiction discloses the false attitude and principles that began during colonial times. The life of Inés Suarez in *Inés of My Soul* provides the author with details of a nation founded on usurpation, cant, and sanctimony. From the beginning Spaniards, who colonize tribes ostensibly to civilize and Christianize them, "raid Indian villages to steal grain, birds, blankets—whatever they could find—like bandits" (Allende, 2006, 213). Duplicity pervades the founding of Chile's capital city. After her second marriage, the protagonist ponders two-faced Santiagans, who gossip about her happy union with Rodrigo de Quiroga. With Cecilia, the Incan princess, Inés comments on the triumphs of bold women: "Courage is a virtue appreciated in a male but considered a defect in our gender" (*ibid.*, 265).

In *Island Beneath the Sea*, Allende extends her derision of imposture and cant. A prime example of smarmy sanctimony, the interest of priests in conducting mass at Habitation Saint-Lazare focuses on a plantation known for high quality rum squeezed from cane sugar by hapless field hands. Amid rampant venality among enslavers and their confessors, planter Toulouse Valmorain admires the restrained pose of his brother-in-law, the wastrel Sancho García del Solar, among the status-ridden clergy and matrons of New Orleans. Hypocrisy enables Sancho to curry favor for the sugar plantation and to buffer the slights of elite Louisiana Creoles toward French refugees from Haiti's revolution. In terms of searches for appropriate bachelors for unwed daughters, the author mocks the importance of uses of the table fork among the upper crust as opposed to the trivializing of moral virtues.

Allende grounds historical fiction about the rise of the slave trade in the principles of the French Revolution of 1789, a provocation to libertarianism around the globe. Critic Nina Sankovitch noted that the juxtaposition of colonialism with cries for freedom set "a course of hypocrisy and conflict whose legacy is still felt today" (Sankovitch, 2010). Allende extends her concerns to New Orleans society by picturing salon displays of a witty *mot juste* in an atmosphere redolent with suspicion of sincere intellectualism, such as that of Toulouse Valmorain, an enlightened reader of Rousseau. Critic Disha Mullick characterizes Valmorain's private hell as "arrogance undercut by jabs of guilt and lucidity about his actions" (Mullick, 2010). After Valmorain weds Creole conniver Hortense Guizot, she refuses to play the game of naive wife and easily manipulates her indecisive husband. To rid their union of opportunism and elevate herself as mistress of the manse, she compensates for Valmorain's background as a Haitian planter.

In *Daughter of Fortune*, Allende shames the atheism of the bible salesman Jacob Todd, the boldness of a Mormon polygamist who offers store credit and liquor to converts to his faith, and the head shaving of wayward girls. For protagonist Eliza Sommers, life in the stifling English-Chilean milieu of Valparaíso shackles young girls to class expectations as "impermeable and hypocritical" as the sale of singsong girls to brothels during the California gold rush of 1849 (Sollars, 2008, 199). Ostensibly fleeing home to follow her lover to California, Eliza evades social proprieties while learning to value freedom and self-fulfillment in the amorphous society of San Francisco. Allende mirrors Eliza's success in the death-bed conversion of Agustin del Valle, who comes to treasure Paulina, a daughter as willful and determined as Eliza to violate hypocritical standards that immure women in a Latino version of purdah.

For *Portrait in Sepia*, the upsurge of the 1891 Chilean civil war against President José

Manuel Balmaceda earns outrage at his employment of torturer Joaquín Godoy as head of political police to control the liberal clergy and Congresistas. Allende pictures jeering at monarchist Frederick Williams, who secures the del Valle household from attack by raising a British flag on the roof at Paulina's request to "counteract a little of the conservative and patriarchal hypocrisy of this family" (Allende, 2001, 145). On a more occluded plane, Williams joins Señorita Matilde Pineda and Don Pedro Tey in a secret operation to print revolutionary lampoons and propaganda to combat government corruption. At school, Sor María Escapulario violates a nun's vows of obedience by secretly teaching progressivism to schoolgirls and "sowing rebellion in childish minds" (*ibid.*, 147).

Hypocrisy and government censorship turn the gracious, overtly courteous Chileans into savages. Nívea declares the nation a seething revolution just waiting for an opportunity to unleash "our cruel streak," an undercurrent less praiseworthy than the rebels demands for social betterment (Allende, 2001, 176). In a mockery of pious notions of salvation, she chooses hell rather than a heaven that accommodates Godoy with his sackful of heinous crimes against liberal Chileans. The foxhole conversion of the reprobate Paulina to God's mercy revives the family's religiosity and encourages Paulina "to pray in her own way," an apostasy that avoids extreme Catholic dogma (*ibid.*, 165).

See also patriarchy

• *References and Further Reading*

Mullick, Disha. "Destiny's Slave," (Hyderabad, India) *Deccan Chronicle* (28 August 2010).
Sankovitch, Nina. "Out of the Hell of Haiti: *Island Beneath the Sea* by Isabel Allende," *Huffington Post* (26 April 2010).
Sollars, Michael D. *The Facts on File Companion to the World Novel, 1900 to the Present*. New York: Facts on File, 2008.

idealism

Allende approaches writing with a sense of wonder and a resolve to uplift the downtrodden. Idealists crowd her pages, including suffragist the life-giving physician Robert Blaum in "Interminable Life," who researches the nature of death and the mental strengths of cancer patients who are loved, and Nívea del Valle in *The House of the Spirits* and *Portrait in Sepia*. According to critic Linda Gould Levine, Allende's "female protagonists not only assume the right to speak, but also the willingness to accept dangerous political risks that further the cause of justice," a characterization of the storytelling protagonist of *Eva Luna* and of Inés, the wonder-working schoolteacher in *Eva Luna* and "The Schoolteacher's Guest" (Levine, 2002, 17). After retirement from teaching, Inés becomes an adviser and mediator in the village of Agua Santa, surpassing the priest in authority. As spokesperson for justice, she lops off the head of her son's murderer, an execution that places her "in the right" (Allende, 1991, 218).

In *The House of the Spirits*, a dangerous idealism takes the form of Clara's suffragist speeches to factory workers about rights and equality, an example of "flaming ideals" that spreads to university students (Allende, 1985, 101). Her son Nicolás sells Clara's diamond ring to finance a pilgrimage to "the land of Mahatma Gandhi," a journey intended to enlighten and instill virtue (*ibid.*, 271). A gullible idealist, Nicolás walks the martyr's way through India, where Gandhi promoted passive resistance to oppose British rule during the mid–1900s. On return home, Nicolás's version of asceticism yields humor when he bores his family with a vegetarian ritual of chewing each bite fifty times, going naked in winter, and holding his breath for up to three minutes. By turning his obsessions into sight gags, the text makes palpable the starry-eyed credulity of a dreamer.

The pontifical stuffiness of Jeremy Sommers, a merchant in *Daughter of Fortune*, accepts clichés wrapped in aphorism. Of his bachelorhood, he justifies cohabitation with sister Rose as a curb on natural male savagery. An adage explains that "it is woman's destiny to preserve moral values and good conduct," a dramatic irony on the fact that Rose conceals the scandalous affairs of her brother John and hoards pornography in a locked library (Allende, 1999, 13). Allende enlarges on idealism in the carnal wrestlings of Eliza with her lover, Joaquín Andieta, whose spirit is always "somewhere else" (*ibid.*, 119). To invest their weekly coitus with high romance, she glamorizes hasty, unsatisfying sex as the introit to a lifetime of wholehearted love. Joaquín compensates for haste by writing fulsome love letters, a skill that Eliza turns to profit on the California frontier.

Allende's theorizers lack self knowledge, the basis of philosophy in ancient Greece. In *Daughter of Fortune*, Utopian idealist Jacob Todd rants about communal society and perfect cities before wasting church money and fleeing from charges of embezzlement. After the cruelties of a sadistic father, Rolf Carlé, a photojournalist in *Eva Luna*, prides himself on a ruthless pragmatism without recognizing that, underneath a gruff exterior, he dreams of a just world. A similar idealogue, Professor Leal, a refugee from Franco's Spain in *Of Love and Shadows*, anticipates "a united world where all man's races, tongues, customs, and dreams are one" (Allende, 1987, 95). To Leal, boundaries and nationalism violate reason and humankind by supporting "the most outrageous abuses," the novel's controlling theme (*ibid.*).

The utopist's dream of El Dorado colors character foibles with age-old credulity. Allende's skill at drollery enlivens *The Infinite Plan*, in which the naive Chicano pictures success in California as "his own Cadillac and a blonde on his arm" (Allende, 1993, 41). In *Inés of My Soul*, the cause of Inés Suarez's dislocation, her husband Juan's pursuit of the land of gold, ends a first marriage and sets the grass widow on her own trek from Spain over the Atlantic toward something grander and more expansive than precious metals. Her second lover, Général Pedro de Valdivia, seduces her "by his courage and his idealism" (Allende, 2006, 99). He intends to "build a just society based on hard work and cultivating the land, not on the ill-gotten wealth bled from mines and slaves," the epitome of New World colonialism (*ibid.*, 104).

The author depicts the crumbling of utopianism in New World nation builders. Valdivia establishes the first laws of Santiago out of an idealistic attempt to govern a city through service and unity rather than greed, a concept the Spaniards share with the Puritan founders of New England. The author, according to reviewer Maggie Galehouse, peruses "the politics of domination and intimidation" in the colonization of Chile (Galehouse, 2007, 19). A subtle lesson in moral corrosion, the focus on the decline in probity in conquistador Pedro de Valdivia exposes the power of the edenic El Dorado to consume and destroy idealists, whom Allende pictures as vulnerable to their own dreams.

More powerful than the collapse of ideals in Chile's founding, the demise of idealism in *Island Beneath the Sea* derives from a conflagration fed by the complex social and racial antipathies of planters, working-class whites, freedmen, mulattos, and slave laborers. At the heart of the coming-to-knowledge by Antillean planters stands a dandy, Chevalier Toulouse Valmorain, a compound of what critic Marcela Valdes terms "vanity, selfishness, and self-deception" (Valdes, 2010). The twenty-year-old's misperception of the source of his wealth and leisure ends rapidly with the death of his father, the elder

Maurice Valmorain, from syphilis, a nemesis common to the debauched white investor. Rapidly, the former enlightened follower of Rousseau becomes what critic Naomi Daremblum calls a "ferocious defender of slavery, a coarsened man" (Daremblum, 2010).

As the Haitian Revolution takes shape, racial conflicts prove more complex than black versus white and rich versus poor. At the end of 1791, Major Etienne Relais observes the catastrophic hatred of lower tier whites for enfranchised blacks. Like the post–Civil War backlash of landless whites against newly freed slaves in the U.S. that resulted in formation of the Ku Klux Klan, jealousy fuels Haitian savagery. The loss of life to arson, rape, hangings, and slit throats raises a stench over Haiti that wafts out to sea, causing the idealist Parmentier to question planter Valmorain's notion of the "superiority of the white race" (Allende, 2010, 169).

Historically and fictionally, resettlement of Haitian refugees in Louisiana offers former slave tormenters a new slant on clemency. Valmorain, who carefully allots his fortune toward staffing a sugar plantation with 150 slaves, abandons his admiration of Rousseau. In the real world, Valmorain perceives that the high price of workers requires that he adopt humanitarian principles. After 23 years of mistreatment of workers in Haiti, he returns to the ideals of 1770, a forgotten zeal that Dr. Parmentier keeps alive with subtle verbal needlings. Meanwhile, to Capitaine Gambo La Liberté, an officer of Toussaint L'Ouverture, a utopian dream of Guinea remains whole, despite the destruction of the 1790s. He envisions music and fruit trees where his father awaits, fish leaping from waters, and vegetables growing spontaneously. To Gambo, the African paradise is "the island beneath the sea," the dream world of the title peopled by blacks who die in the conflict (Allende, 2010, 303).

- *References and Further Reading*

Daremblum, Naomi. "Not Magical, Not Realism," *New Republic* (28 April 2010).
Galehouse, Maggie. "Conquer and Convert," *New York Times Book Review* (14 January 2007): 19.
Levine, Linda Gould. "Weaving Life into Fiction," *Latin American Literary Review* 30:60 (July–December 2002): 1–25.
Valdes, Marcela. "Isabel Allende on Haiti's Slave Rebellion: A Lost Cause," *Washington Post* (8 June 2010).

Inés of My Soul

Allende's well-researched historical fiction *Inés of My Soul* follows a common narrative conceit, that of the elderly woman reciting the pinnacles of her life, in this case, the first Spanish woman in Chile. Called the female founder of Chile, diarist Inés Suárez became the legendary lover of Spanish conqueror Pedro Gutiérrez de Valdivia, builder of Santiago on February 12, 1541, and colonial governor in 1549 under Charles V. A widowed *conquistadora*, the historical Inés, at age 32, nursed fallen soldiers and, on September 11, 1541, donned armor and helmet to lead a charge that revived mettle among the Spaniards during an attack by indigenous Mapuche. To capture the vigor and resolve of Inés, the author embodied the heroine and composed a first-person narrative that "could only be told in her voice" (Block, 2006). Editor Andrea O'Really credits the historical and fiction Inés with being the "mother of the whole nation of Chile" (O'Reilly, 2010, 49).

In a fictional letter to her adopted daughter composed in 1580, Inés recognizes an evil that fuels the violence that saturates the 1540s. In acknowledgement of human frailties, she declares, "Nothing changes; we humans repeat the same sins over and over, eternally" (Allende, 2006, 245). The text, laden with minutia of sixteenth-century voyages and colonialism, flounders under the load of facts. To excuse the need to repeat vital information, the first-person voice apologizes for being elderly and forgetful. As the unnamed *Kirkus* reviewer notes, the gimmicky epistolary form breaks down from encyclopedic commentary and conversations the writer never heard. The analysis lobs harsh criticism—"Turgid and detached—homework masquerading as epic"—at passages in which the author lapses into stilted phrasing and bombast ("Review," *Kirkus*, 2006, 919). Spanish professor Joanna O'Connell refutes the *Kirkus* review with praise for Allende's theme: "Her works have grown more nuanced in showing what happens when forms of power, such as different cultures, intersect and clash," an apt description of the events following the Spanish push south from Peru down the Pacific Coast (Miller, 2006).

Like main characters in Amy Tan's *The Bonesetter's Daughter*, Laura Esquivel's *Malinche*, and Alison Wong's *As the Earth Turns Silver*, Inés lives multiple personas, first as a seamstress in Plasencia in Extremadura, Spain, then as an adventurer journeying from Cartagena, Panama, to Callao, Peru. Initially, she intends to locate her errant husband Juan de Málaga, a soldier under adventurer Francisco Pizarro, whom Inés identifies as "that fearless bastard" (Allende, 2006, 2). The retreat from the repressive Inquisition leads her to new possibilities in the Western Hemisphere, where "traditional laws have no bearing and society is completely scrambled" (*ibid.*, 2). She describes her duties as "taking care of my house and the colony, looking after the sick, the plantings and the animal pens, along with my reading lessons," even dowsing for water, welcoming settlers, beheading prisoners, and disposing of their remains (*ibid.*, 189). In the gamut of persecutions and mutilations, critic Maggie Galehouse identifies the protagonist's gravitas, the mark of the stateswoman devoted to charity and to the well being of servants and animals.

Galehouse applauds the novel's scope: "Allende's reach is broad, scooping up politics, history, romance and the supernatural" (Galehouse, 2007, 19). A harsh terrain intensifies the psychic despair of females then struggling under the Renaissance glorification of the male. As a widow, Inés exults, "Juan de Málaga was dead and I was free ... my life began that day" (Allende, 2006, 85). She tackles business management in the center of Cuzco, Peru, by selling homemade empanadas, embroidering cloths for sale and as gifts to the church, and doctoring the sick. During battles on the march south in February 1541, she organizes aid stations, turns rags into dressings, applies tourniquets, and cauterizes wounds with hot coals. For the dead, she confers absolution and last rites "that they might go in peace," a daring usurpation of man's work under the direction of the Vatican (*ibid.*, 156).

A more equitable situation to the south lures Inés to follow Yanacona guides across the *cordillera*, like soldiers during the 1891 Civil War in *Portrait in Sepia*. The only woman among 100 men, she treks inexorably through the Atacoma Desert toward an idealized colony. Amid the incursive Spanish and the brutal Mapuche, she witnesses an epic battle, which overwhelms Santiago on the significant date of September 11. She recognizes the clash of masculinities, white against Indian, that pits combatants in a fight to the death for liberty with "more cruelty than a Christian soul can tolerate" (Allende, 2006, 245). Reviewer John Freeman refers to the climate and hostile surroundings as "the creeper vine of mutiny," an apt description of undercurrents of disloyalty and jealousy (Freeman, 2006).

The list of atrocities in Allende's novel replicates in fiction the historical reports of Spanish decapitations, impalings, and "blood that makes monsters of the oppressors" (Allende, 2006, 110). The shocking beheading of shackled slaves to save the trouble of freeing them from their chains and the use of lactating women as sources of refreshment on the march charge soldiers with a loss of humanity. The protagonist's imposition of table courtesies restores some civility. She exults, "I poured them wine by my own hand, and served them food with the property hospitality" (*ibid.*, 132). To profit from the indigenous knowledge of the terror, Inés plants and cultivates her garden Indian style. As the wars of the 1540s increase in savagery, the depiction of Inés as a force for right and truth wears thin, especially after the defection of Valdivia for Peru and the codification of compassionate laws by Charles V to ensure fair treatment and pay for native workers. Allende depicts the legal free fall in the trial of Valdivia, whose quasi-licit endeavors incite envious Peruvians to charge him with usurping power, purloining colonial treasuries, and executing the innocent.

The novel's resolution draws on epic grandeur to adorn protracted clashes between Spaniards and Mapuche. Schooled in soldiery by Felipe/Lautaro, the spy turned commander in chief, the Indians press their home court advantage over the troops of Jerónimo de Alderete and Valdivia, who camp along the Bío-Bío River. Allende matches the aim of the harquebus against the accuracy of the *boleadoras*, a simple weighted stone that drops riders and their mounts within range of warriors with stone clubs. With a gesture of admiration toward native courage, Allende depicts Valdivia "stymied by savages," a consequence of Spanish arrogance and superiority (Allende, 2006, 279). The intervention of an apotheosis of the Virgin Mary or Santiago, "the apostle Saint James" summoned "during centuries of fighting the moors"—in reality, a meteor—delivers the *deus ex machina* to save the perplexed Spaniards from defeat (*ibid.*, 155). Allende's linkage of colonial wars with the Crusades suggests Catholicism's lengthy history as an abettor of murder and usurpation.

Details lessen as the action mentions in passing the founding of the Chilean cities of Concepción, La Imperial, Valdivia, and Villarrica to the south. As commerce replaces the communal behaviors from Santiago's early days, Allende curtails her previous noble tone and looks outward toward the natural wonders of rain, waterfalls, volcanoes, and the surrounding snow-topped mountains as well as the comforts of a satisfying marriage for the protagonist. In a salute to Chile, the author combines two literary utopias—El Dorado and the Garden of Eden—as paradigms of the region's glories. A wry rejoinder to self-awarded laurels, the Mapuche trick of showering Valdivia's patrol with gilded river rocks jerks the narrative back to reality. Lautaro reprises his audacity by stationing Mapuche sirens at the edge of a bog, where armored men and their mounts sink into mire.

Reviewer Celia McGee praised the epistolary novel for its feminism: "Leave it to Isabel Allende to write a novel of the conquistadors with a woman at its fast-pumping heart" (McGee, 2006). The stress on women's contributions corrects much frontier history that belittles or omits women's contributions to settling the Western Hemisphere. Additional literary devices dot the final pages of *Inés of My Soul*. To enhance the unknowns of period history, the author exploits legends of the wealth stolen by Juana Jiménez and Gothic touches in the arms, heads, and legs that Lautaro's warriors suspend from branches as "bloody fruit of the forest" (Allende, 2006, 303). The ignoble defeats of Spaniards spread thin over the colony serve the novel as reminders of the cost of building Chile into a Spanish state. For the role of Inés Suarez, María Claudia André and Eva Paulino Bueno acclaim the author for "wearing into the historical backdrop stories of passion, intrigue and the triumph of integrity over corruption" (André and Bueno, 2008, 15).

See also Chile

• *References and Further Reading*

André, María Claudia, and Eva Paulino Bueno. *Latin American Women Writers: An Encyclopedia*. New York: Routledge, 2008.

Block, Melissa. "Allende Reimagines Life of Conquistador 'Inés,'" *All Things Considered* (NPR) (6 November 2006).
Freeman, John. "Riot GIRRRLS," (Minneapolis) *Star Tribune* (29 October 2006).
Galehouse, Maggie. "Conquer and Convert," *New York Times Book Review* (14 January 2007): 19.
McGee, Celia. "'Ines' Captures Chile's Soul in 1500s," *USA Today* (9 November 2006).
Miller, Pamela. "Isabel Allende's New Novel Is Set in the 1500s, But the Parallels to Contemporary Issues Are Unmistakable," (Minneapolis) *Star Tribune* (31 October 2006).
O'Reilly, Andrea. *Encyclopedia of Motherhood*. Thousand Oaks, CA: Sage, 2010.
"Review: *Inés of My Soul*," *Kirkus* 74:18 (15 September 2006): 919.

The Infinite Plan

An *émigrée* author living outside her homeland, Allende wrote *The Infinite Plan* as a departure from her previous Latino-centered works. The result, a quest novel and neo-romantic *Bildungsroman*, features the maturation of her husband, William C. "Willie" Gordon, a San Francisco attorney. After reading her version of his life, he realized, "This is a map of my life; now I understand where I've been" (Correas de Zapata, 2002, 80). The protagonist's lengthy maturation allows the author to examine motivations and outcomes of American social development from the hippie era into the "me" generation of the 1980s. Literary historian Donald Leslie Shaw lauds Allende for her faith in love and reconciliation: "It is hard to think of a novel written after the end of the Boom which more explicitly replaces the Boom's disquieting metaphors of existence with a comforting one," especially the need for "blending cultures" (Shaw, 2002, 183, 184).

The text describes the peripatetic ministry of Charles Reeves, a self-made philosopher who simplifies a cosmic concept similar to the medieval Great Chain of Being. The structure places an omnipotent deity at top and lesser creatures in order of importance:

Supreme Intelligence, the creator
|
Logi, invisible messengers and supervisors of order in the universe
|
Master Functionaries, communicators of rules, including mentors like Charles Reeves
|
humans, composed of a physical body, mind, and soul

Reeves appears to predicate his philosophy on the *logos* of Heraclitus of Ephesus, (384–322 B.C.E.), an Ionian philosopher who used the Greek term to indicate reason, word, or plan to characterize and justify the ongoing changes in earthly life.

The text stresses the culture and values of Los Angeles Hispanics and the obstacles to their advance toward equality and self-fulfillment "on the other side," which Gregory epitomizes as Pershing Square, an urban nerve center dominated by affluent whites (Allende, 1993, 88). Allende commiserates with nonwhite newcomers who "would always be foreigners," a feeling she shares (*ibid.*, 44). She sympathizes with the naiveté of barrio inmates and with the large number who fail to thrive in the U.S. More than social failure, she stresses the loss of tradition and the corrosion of recollections, which would "leave them without memories," thus ending their reliance on cumulative wisdom (*ibid.*, 41).

A Man's Man

At the center of Allende's view of Latino culture lies *machismo*, the glorification of males. The automobile mechanic Pedro Morales epitomizes the idealist who batters at exclusion and employers' lies to establish citizenship in the new land. A fillip at cultural differences, Pedro's amazement at people who disbelieve in the Virgin Mary and whose women wear bras and short shorts in public accounts for the immigrants' intent to live apart from such a profane culture and to guard their daughters from social ruin. Allende notes the elements of Latino culture: "Men should be merciless, brave, dominant, loners, fast with a weapon, and superior to women in every sense" (Allende, 1993, 50). Pedro's veneration of womanly chastity illustrates both cultural identity with Mexico's gendered social order and his naiveté in a California fleshpot.

At a critical phase of Gregory's boyhood, Allende composes an internal monologue, a *tour de force* that summarizes his adventures and survivalist creed. To enhance the immature thought patterns, she resorts to frequent understatement and bathos, the fall from the grand to the mundane, such as Gregory's intent to die dramatically in front of a moving train and his rejection of the idea because of posthumous nausea at the thought of guts spilled by an engine "huffing like a stampeding dragon" (Allende, 1993, 101). The interplay of Arthurian grandeur with banality hinges on the boy's devotion to his dog Oliver, whose scruffy looks and raffish behavior parallel Gregory's ghetto identity. Allende maintains a facetious tone, a slant toward controlled humor that lifts the mood above any real suicidal intent to sustained amusement.

Key to the blend of despair with hijinks, Allende's admiration for her protagonist resounds with respect for a born entrepreneur. Not only does Gregory survive gang fights and sodomy by his nemesis Martínez, the hero bobs back from victimization with a money-making venture involving Carmen's juggling, Gregory's harmonica tunes, and Oliver's showmanship, which earn "as much as a laborer received for a full day's work in any of the area factories" (Allende, 1993, 87). In late adolescence, Gregory's rascality gives place to sexuality, the "brutal and incomprehensible ardor" that drives him into the tutelage of Olga, an older woman willing to redirect his blundering libido into manly self-control (*ibid.*, 91). His ardor satisfied, Gregory expends his intellectual curiosity on reading and education, the mental preparations suggested by Cyrus, an elderly Communist elevator operator.

Mature Satisfactions

According to analyst Louise M. Stone, central to Allende's "infinite plan" for Gregory, his many fumbles illustrate the pitfalls of the misdirected through "an array of desires, fantasies, and stupidities," (Stone, 2009, 13). In the chaos of the Vietnam War, he shares the squalor and pumped-up courage "as one man, a family of desperadoes" in a post-adolescence rite of passage (Allende, 1993, 198). After the hellish firefights that send him into drugged hysteria, he reposes in a Hawaiian rehabilitation center and turns into the path of selfishness and greed. His rage claws at "every single one of the corrupt bastards getting rich on this war" (*ibid.*, 209).

Sex replaces combat as the protagonist's next horizon. The next fictional stave finds Greg self-destructing from a merry mix of professional triumphs celebrated on his office couch with "various female fellow lawyers and an undermined number of secretaries, clients, and friends" (*ibid.*, 249). Willing females pass in and out of his little black book, leaving him susceptible to Samantha and Shannon, ill-chosen wives who achieve no hold on his heart. A more devastating female betrayal derives from the detachment of daughter Margaret from "daddy," a patronym that she withholds until too late in her decline into promiscuity and drugs. To his detriment, Gregory blames himself for the failures of wives, marriages, and daughter as well as the intractability of son David.

In an interview, the author admitted to liking Gregory Reeves more than her other male characters and that she chose from real adventures for his life story, even leaving out parts that sounded exaggerated. She summarized the resilience of Willie and Greg as "corks that sink and bob back up again and against; strong, formidable men filled with flaws, passions, and generosity" (Correas de Zapata, 2002, 81). According to literary historian Donald Leslie Shaw, Allende intends Greg's story to make sense of "lived experience" and to "interpret [humans] as social beings," a motivation not usually found in postmodernism (Shaw, 2002, 222). Greg's precipitous rush of life phases reaches middle age before Allende reveals self-discipline in her protagonist.

Maturity comes late to Greg, who, like Homer's Odysseus, makes the full circle back to the values of Inmaculada and Pedro Morales. Critic Beth W. Jorgensen characterizes the change in Greg as a rejection of individualism in favor of community and family. Near ruin from debt and despair at David's anarchy, Gregory profits from counseling, a life preserver that a friend tosses the drowning man. By accepting the massive job of restructuring outlook, home, and office, Gregory ironically achieves "the infinite plan" that his staid, orderly father outlined. Hinting at her role in the life of Willie Gordon, Allende implies that the aforementioned stages in maturity prepare him for living a less riotous existence and for a partnership with a realistic mate.

• *References and Further Reading*

Correas de Zapata, Celia. *Isabel Allende: Life and Spirits*. Houston, TX: Arte Público, 2002.

Jorgensen, Beth E. "'Un Punado de Criticos': Navigating the Critical Readings of Isabel Allende's Work," *Latin American Literary Review* 30:60 (July–December, 2002): 128–146.

Shaw, Donald Leslie. *A Companion to Modern Spanish-American Fiction*. Rochester, NY: Tamesis, 2002.

Stone, Louise M., and Troy Place. *Magill's Survey of World Literature*. Pasadena, CA: Salem, 2009.

injustice

Allende surveys much of the world's wrongs as a landscape on which to set such stories as the suffering of the Palestinian Kamal at the hands of Israelis in *Eva Luna*, the caging of Juana la Triste by Judge Hidalgo in the prophetic fable "The Judge's Wife," and the horse whippings and hangings perpetrated by vigilantes in *Daughter of Fortune*. Unlike most Hispanic-Americans, the author atones for the land theft and genocide that resulted from the European discovery of the Western Hemisphere, a topic prominent in much of her writing. She pictures peons as little more than slaves, whom *patróns* pay only with food and lodging in exchange for domestic service. She commiserates with the enslavement of indentured Chinese and Polynesians, a system that remains legal so long as their owners immure them on ships offshore. The author's outrage at the exploitation of Indians compares their subsistence to that of animals "sold or inherited with the property" (Allende, 1999, 42).

The survey of inequity throughout the *House of the Spirits* trilogy worsens when allied with greed. The first text depicts miner Esteban Trueba's intent to colonize both land and peasants and to force his workers into the role of what analyst Amy Shifflet calls a "commodity for personal gain" (Shifflet, 2000, 15). In *Daughter of Fortune*, Chilean peons pan for gold that they pass to their *patróns*. In *Portrait in Sepia*, the text casually introduces how easily the Domínguez family buys Mapuche land in exchange for liquor and how Don Sebastián treats his laborers like "slightly retarded children" (Allende, 2001, 231). At Christmas, free food lures Pehuenche Indians to Caleufú, the Domínguez plantation. Allende mentions without comment the injustice of landlessness to natives whose plight the government ignores.

In an overview of Spanish exploration of Peru and Chile in *Inés of My Soul*, Allende presses diction to extremes to characterize the motivation of soldiers of fortune. Among the crimes of conquistadors—rape, murder, arson, torture, theft—she pauses to list the literary misdeeds of warrior-poet Alonso de Ercilla y Zúñiga, the "runny-nosed boy" from Madrid who compiled an erroneous saga about Chile's conquest (Allende, 2006, 65). She damns him with an egregious misdemeanor—deviating from fact to force rhymes for *La Araucana* (1569–1589), the national epic of Chile. With the aplomb of a bicultural storyteller, she sets the story straight with the epic acts of Inés Suarez, a *conquistadora* who becomes Chile's founding mother.

In the style of the wise griot, in *The House of the Spirits*, Pedro García summarizes the standoff between overlords and peons in a beast fable, an allegory of colonial exploitation. By picturing men like Esteban Trueba as a fox stealing eggs and eating baby chicks, Pedro implies that the plantation system borders on cannibalism for devouring the indigenous young. By dramatizing a hen coterie launching a reprisal of cunning and cooperation and pecking the fox, Pedro predicts the socialist revolution, a source of cantina ballads for the storyteller's grandson, Pedro Tercero. Thus, the old man's story remains viable throughout the novel as a foreshadowing of the clash of socialism with the corrupt colonial establishment, an injustice that dates to the arrival of the predatory Spanish in the Western Hemisphere in 1492. Clara observes in liberal women an attempt to stanch unfairness through altruism, but she realized that "charity had no effect on such monumental injustice" (Allende, 1985, 97). The over-correction that places a dictator in power compounds oppression, which attempts to erase the past by prohibiting use of the words comrade, trade union, liberty, and justice.

Varied Prejudices

For *Eva Luna*, the author creates a procession of standard characters from fiction—cruel employers, greedy exploiters of children, and petty thieves on a par with Charles Dickens's Fagin and Oliver Twist. The transsexual Melesio, an unusual character growing up "in a climate of tragic opera," receives sympathetic narration for his bouts with a bullying father and for issuing self-clarifying proclamations, "I am not homosexual, I am a woman" (Allende, 1987, 121). A friendship with the prostitute La Señora introduces Melesio to a transvestite bar where notoriety enables him to live the pampered existence of a female singer. The author's empathy for misidentified gender takes the form of delighted Melesio's play with Eva Luna, who learns femininity from watching the performer put on makeup and sew beads on cabaret costumes. Allende pictures Melesio's arrest in "fake pearl-and-diamond bikini, pink ostrich tail, blond wig, and platform sandals," the accoutrements that create an illusion of femininity (*ibid.*, 207). At their meeting during gunfire outside the Church of the Seminarians, the two reunite with regard for each other's achievement of womanhood, two triumphs over adversity.

With a parallel respect for the demimonde, the evolution of San Francisco from the California gold rush in *Daughter of Fortune* builds a city on a dubious past. Editor Michael Sollars summarizes Allende's narrowed theme base as "social status and class struggle," two common attributes of frontier history (Sollars, 2008, 199). Cultural diversity pits American speculators against successful Chileans, rowdy Australians, shanghaiing sea captains, and Chinese tongs judged by the legal decisions of a "corrupt upstart become a judge" (Allende, 1999, 356). Racism ghettoizes blacks, Chinese, and Indians in lowly, ill-paid work and vigilantism.

On a baser level, the injustices in *Island Beneath the Sea* derive from colonial enrichment from a barbaric form of slavery. Slaveholder Toulouse Valmorain's reliance on overseer Prosper Cambray exonerates brutality to pregnant field hands, most of whose children succumb to abortion or death in infancy. After surviving the Haitian Revolution of 1791, in the estimation of critic Carolina De Robertis, Toulouse retreats into defensive resignation by considering himself a more equitable manager than Cambray has been. While rationalizing the theft of Lacroix's investments, Valmorain builds once more in Louisiana and congratulates himself for improving worker conditions for the 150 laborers who inhabit his new slave quarters. Owen Murphy, the Irish overseer, provides rest and recreation for his charges and concentrates on imposing Catholicism, a pervasive excuse for human bondage.

Wreathed in aristocratic privilege from his birth in France to the lace-cuff-and-powdered-wig set, Valmorain can't conceive of any other human social condition than the slave/master alliance that dominates profitable sugar planting in Haiti. He justifies an economy by which "a third of the wealth of France, in sugar, coffee, tobacco, cotton, indigo, and cocoa, came from the island" (Allende, 2010, 6). The fact that slaves died of exhaustion within eighteen months of purchase carries no import to Valmorain. Significantly, as Maroon rebels encroach on the new plantation, the owner sees no reason for slave unrest, given the cushy post and new slave quarters. To his concubine Tété's yearning for emancipation, Valmorain claims liberty as a white man's ideal and urges her to forget so vaporous a pipe dream. Allende stresses the Frenchman's social hypocrisy, which accords him "total freedom" (*ibid.*, 424).

Allende's creates a conundrum from the planter's bigotry. After Père Antoine engineers the legitimizing of Tété's manumission papers, Valmorain reverts to greed and execrates his former concubine for daring to abandon him, a betrayal of a white man who generously gave her a son and daughter. Allende envisions the white female as the more vicious of the set piece by describing the intimidation and baiting of Rosette, Tété's daughter by Valmorain, and the jailing that leads to the quadroon's death. By advancing Hortense Guizot's bloodlust beyond that of Valmorain, the author confers a small atonement and moral reclamation to the master shortly before his death, an exoneration similar in great-heartedness to the forgiveness of Esteban Trueba.

Allende juxtaposes lesser larcenies alongside the U.S. seizure of Pacific territory once owned by Spaniards. Egregious claim jumping worsens in the courts, where hidalgos witness the usurpation of land grants dating to Spanish colonialism. Outraged victims respond with the scrawled tocsin "Death to Yanquis" (*ibid.*, 340). Legal favoritism by the California legislature empowers sheriffs to discriminate against "dark-skinned foreigners" and to "hang them in the full majesty of the law" (*ibid.*, 329, 340). The stacked deck forces Latinos into outlawry such as that committed by Joaquín Murieta and Three-Finger Jack, the mythic scapegoats for unsolved crime.

Reprising the mystique of the unknown *bandito*, Allende returns to the rapacity of colonialism in Zorro in 1810, when Diego and Bernardo witness a greedy rancher's foray against an Indian village. The assault concludes in the dispersal of women, children, and elders, and the hanging of an elderly chief. The Monterey legal system ignores usurpation of Indian lands because justice to indigenous tribes holds a low priority. More damaging to the boys' youthful ideals, Alejandro de la Vega, the cynical alcalde, knows "the class system too well to harbor any hope of righting the wrong" (Allende, 2005, 84). Fortunately for Diego and the storyteller, the incident imprints on the future Zorro the need for intervention to forestall more theft of Indian lands. He develops what Allende calls "a disproportionate love of justice," an exaggerated evaluation of one man's ability to ensure equality (Allende, 93).

Twentieth-Century Wrongs

In *The Infinite Plan*, the twentieth-century war against racist injustice takes on the gritty reality of everyday life in a Los Angeles barrio. While Gregory Reeves practices the egalitarianism he learns from Cyrus, the library's elevator operator, the struggle of workers against ogreish overseers continues to favor whites over nonwhites. Cyrus insists that Gregory instruct fellow factory drones "to sacrifice self-interest for the common good," a noble act that Cyrus epitomizes as the birth of the New Man (Allende, 1993, 120). Fortunately, Gregory abandons Cyrus's communist orthodoxy for the pragmatism of the courts, in which the budding lawyer fights a legal system rigged against poor, illiterate nonwhite immigrants and illegals. In preparation, he joins Berkeley protesters in "denouncing the government, the military, foreign policy, racial abuses, ecological crimes—all the eternal injustices" (*ibid.*, 130). The ringing damnation captures the idealism of college students of the 1960s who undertake huge skirmishes against inequity. Their romanticism prefigures the errors of Gregory in manhood, when he risks health and fortune in a battle against American bias.

Allende organizes the psychic preparation of Gregory for law, thus explaining his peculiar skill at rescuing illegal aliens from unjust regulations. Fueling the crusade, his childhood of reverse discrimination as the only blue-eyed blond among Chicanos readies him for knighthood in the crusade for fairness. In his first position at a prestigious law firm, he focuses on "an aggregate of regulations so entangled they no longer served the purpose for which they had been created" (Allende, 1993, 249). The author's metaphor of a spider web accounts for the ensnaring of the poor in a mesh of governmental obfuscation. The scramble for toeholds exploits Gregory's cunning at surviving a jungle war, an extension of the web image that accounts for the protagonist's inability to make peace with his military experience in Vietnam. Allende leads the protagonist toward a more profound truism—that injustice at home warrants more of Gregory's energy and focus than the small fires he extinguishes in the barrio.

For the *City of the Beasts* triad, the author departs from realism to engineer a dramatic irony in the plan of the Beasts to rid themselves of enemies one by one. Through YA quest lore, Allende echoes the ongoing reprieve of Sudan, Rwanda, Iran, and Chile from warlords and political oppressors. Rather than lower the number of invasions, the huge size and fierce smell of the Beasts lures more adventurers to the Upper Orinoco to determine the truth about media myths of Amazonian Yetis. Injustice burgeons in the theft of an oracular statue in *Kingdom of the Gold Dragon* and in the enslavement of the Bantu and Aka in *Forest of the Pygmies* to provide gold, diamonds, and ivory to usurpers.

According to reviewer Janet Hunt, Allende places in the hands of teen sidekicks Alex Cold and Nadia Santos an opportunity "to deliver justice and restore peace [to] the nomadic and peaceful pygmies and the Bantu people who once lived in harmony in this harsh world" (Hunt, 2005). Thus, the reinstatement of order rids the People of the Mist, the Forbidden Kingdom, and Central Africa of greedy manipulators and environmental vandals, a fictional righting of wrongs on a par with ridding Uganda of Idi Amin, Iraq of Saddam Hussein, Zimbabwe of Robert Mugabe, and Libya of Moammar Qaddafi.

A fierce critic of Allende's idealized quest lore, Donnarae MacCann discredits the validation of white rescuers to the detriment of the Africans of Ngoubé and their culture. MacCann charges Allende with neo-imperialism for "shrewdly [reminding] Caucasian readers about their superiority, about the indisputable greatness of Western wayfarers, colonizers, missionaries, and journalists" (Maddy and MacCann, 2009, 56). Peter Nazareth enhances the charge of postcolonial imperialism as an effort "to steal the wealth generated by the people" (Nazareth, 2000, 80). A rejoinder from critic Don Latham, who applauds the use of magical realism in a merging of disparate realms. Janet Hunt further acclaims Allende for "[evoking] Joseph Conrad's *Heart of Darkness*," the touchstone of Western anti-imperialism (Hunt, 2005).

See also racism

• *References and Further Reading*

De Robertis, Carolina. "Review: *Island Beneath the Sea*," *San Francisco Chronicle* (25 April 2010).
Hunt, Janet. "Review: *Forest of the Pygmies*," *New Zealand Herald* (7 May 2005).
Latham, Don. "The Cultural Work of Magical Realism in Three Young Adult Novels," *Children's Literature in Education* 38:1 (2007): 59–70.
Maddy, Yulisa Amadu, and Donnarae MacCann. *Neo-Imperialism in Children's Literature about Africa: A Study of Contemporary Fiction*. New York: Routledge, 2009.
Nazareth, Peter. *Critical Essays on Ng-ug-i wa Thiong'o*. New York: Twayne, 2000.
Shifflet, Amy V. *Beyond Magical Realism: Magical Ideology as Political Resistance in Leslie Marmon Silko's Ceremony and Isabel Allende's The House of the Spirits*. Radford, VA: Radford University, 2000.
Sollars, Michael D. *The Facts on File Companion to the World Novel, 1900 to the Present*. New York: Facts on File, 2008.

irony

Allende's dexterous handling of irony extends its application to both tragedy and comedy, such as African slaves in *Zorro* who consider the white world "hostile and barbaric," Tao Chi'en's shanghaiing aboard the *Liberty* in *Daughter of Fortune*, and the image of title figure in *Inés of My Soul* as the *conquistadora* riding a white horse, the usual mount of the dashing hero (Allende, 2005, 317). For Inés Suarez, the royal imprimatur turns armed aggression into conquest, a point of honor too skimpy to conceal the murderous avarice of Spanish adventurers. At the trial of Pedro de Valdivia for a list of trumped-up charges, prosecutors damn him for falling under the power of his concubine, a betrayal of Spanish *machismo* that outranks his other alleged crimes. A more poignant irony in *The Stories of Eva Luna*, the increase of technological equipment to photograph Azucena in "Of Clay We Are Created" amplifies the plight of a dying child trapped in mud that a simple pump can alleviate. Of Allende's skill at unexpected twists, critic Clarence Major declares: "Allende's forte is irony and ambiguity, both usually rendered with wonderful subtlety ... restraint and grace" (Major, 2001, 179).

In *The House of the Spirits*, ironies emerge from the cataclysmic earthquake that destroys planter Esteban Trueba's petty fiefdom and leaves his body immobile from broken bones. In the heavy labor that follows, Pedro Segundo and Clara form an executive power structure to sort out losses and rebuild Las Tres Marías. Allende enhances irony from Esteban's toothless rages, Clara's realization of her mother's socialist cause, and the fantasies of Pedro Segundo about his esteem for his mistress. While Esteban watches from his cot, his foreman and wife fight epidemics and purchase the supplies for constructing new worker housing and shelters for farm animals. Clara, abandoning her extended childhood and supernatural protections, develops into "an efficient woman with callused hands," an achievement that privileged women view as a detriment to refinement (Allende, 1985, 196). From the smooth alliance of a female aristocrat with a peon, the estate arises once more on equitable foundations of cooperation and respect.

Allende's reliance on masking enhances incongruencies of action, a literary ploy her canon shares with Michel Faber's *The Crimson Petal and the White*. Allende creates a wry jest from the charade of the gift of fruit and vegetables from Las Tres Marías to the Papal Nuncio's residence, which conceals Pedro Tercero from notice by a tyrannical regime. As though reviving the protectionism of the Catholic hierarchy, the scene depicts Pedro in a bishop's cassock, the disguise that saves him from capture when he flees the country on the way to Canada. In *Daughter of Fortune*, the sequel to *House of the Spirits*, a disguise motif extends over half the action to cloak protagonist Eliza Sommers in men's attire, ironically, a façade for a girl searching for her lover, Joaquín Andieta. Editor Michael Sollars justifies Allende's choice of concealment in cross-dressing amid "the wild liberties available to all comers in gold-crazed California" (Sollars, 2008, 199).

More boldly, numerous ironies permeate the horrendous Haitian Revolution of 1791 and its aftermath, the focus of *Island Beneath the Sea*. The title refers to the slave myth of a mystical undersea afterlife, an Eden inhabited by Guinean slaves who died during the Middle Passage. Extensive hints at the coming conflagration derive from the shambles of a republic that replaces the fallen French monarchy after the revolution of July 14, 1789. For Major Etienne Relais, hopes of departing Haiti for retirement in Europe hinge on the arrival of the ship *Marie Thérèse*, which bears the name of the French dauphine whose mother, Marie Antoinette, meets her fate on the guillotine in October 1793, leaving Marie Thérèse an orphan.

Allende stresses the cost of liberty to black and white. In the estimation of reviewer Robin Vidimos, enslavement "not only denied the humanity of slaves but diminished the humanity of those who would own them" (Vidimos, 2010). A wise observer, Major Relais reports the December death count—2,000 whites, 10,000 blacks—of the revolt begun in Port-au-Prince and recognizes a fatal error in political backlash. Rather than strengthen the alliance between white planters and freedmen, the *Assemblée Nationale* strips the free blacks of their rights. The result, a catastrophe to whites, freedmen, rebels, mulattos, and slaves, continues to haunt lives long after escapees reach Havana before journeying northwest to New Orleans. Even in the Creole haven of Louisiana, French planters console themselves with dreams of returning to Haiti and reviving a lifestyle predicated on human bondage.

Allende's *Aphrodite* predicates her mirth on irony. She briefly slips the tether to humor and whimsy by envisioning a world without imagination, "a paradise of the military, fundamentalists, and bureaucrats" who direct their energies toward "more disciplined methods of killing one another" (Allende, 1998, 27). The abrupt pop-up of grim satire attests to the nearness of love and death, the two certainties that empower literature the intensity of *Paula*, *Zorro*, and *Of Love and Shadows*. In a later meditation, she satirizes American science for dismissing the occult as superstition at the same time that it condemns black magic as dangerous. The inconsistency illustrates uncertainty among empiricists concerning the actual powers of the paranormal.

• *References and Further Reading*

Major, Clarence. *Necessary Distance: Essays and Criticism.* Minneapolis: Coffee House Press, 2001.
Sollars, Michael D. *The Facts on File Companion to the World Novel, 1900 to the Present.* New York: Facts on File, 2008.
Vidimos, Robin. "Slave Uprising in Colonial Haiti at Heart of Isabel Allende's Latest," *Denver Post* (2 May 2010).
Weldt-Basson, Helene C. "Irony as Silent Subversive Strategy in Isabel Allende's *Cuentos de Eva Luna*," *Revista de estudios hispánicos* 31:1 (2004): 183–198.

Island Beneath the Sea

Allende's *Island Beneath the Sea* records the energies in a cultural milieu where whites work alongside blacks. The bloodletting, which reviewer Gaiutra Bahadur called a "fundamentally straightforward historical pageant," occurs amid silvery flashes of jungle cascades, macaw and parrot feathers, and orange and yellow toucan beaks, colors oblivious to the Gothic intent of slave overseers and revolutionaries (Bahadur, 2010, 26). Before Haiti becomes the "first independent republic of Negroes," the *grands blancs* function in a society undergirded by the talents of merchants and crafters, prelates and sailors, bureaucrats and soldiers, and a corrupt rabble of felons, pimps, and pirates (Allende, 2010, 157). The discontinuity of morals becomes grounds for enlightening discussions between Dr. Parmentier and his literary foil, the aristocratic Toulouse Valmorain, inheritor of Habitation Saint Lazare.

Committed to universal liberty, the novel opens in 1770 with riveting accuracy in pictures of luxury-loving whites learning up close the labors that produce sweet white crystals for the coffee of the rich and privileged. In her survey of colonialism, Allende dismisses justice and decency in a single phrase: "Vice was the norm, honor for sale, and laws made to be broken," a portentous description of France and its territories before the revolution of July 14, 1789 (Allende, 2010, 15). The polarizing effect of the Haitian caste system seizes the narrative momentum and holds in check any sympathy for the exploiters of African labor. By the 1690s, the demand for bondsmen populated Haiti with "hundreds of thousands" of black abductees, most of whom died before completing two years of membership in press gangs (*ibid.*, 6).

In a counterpoint of male and female perspectives, the text dramatizes the effects of plantation life on Valmorain, who becomes as enslaved to Habitation Saint-Lazare as his workers. Bored and isolated with only his son Maurice and blacks for company, he retreats into reading and a steady intake of wine and cognac. At age 40, he recognizes the signs of dissipation — wrinkles, double chin, and diminished energy and libido— and realizes "he detested the island" (Allende, 2010, 106). His insouciance in the face of mounting discontent among blacks epitomizes the failure of the ruling class to shore up their holdings against a future revolt. Men like Valmorain fall victim to the French Revolution, which cleaves *grand blanc* from *petit blanc*, a subclass supporting the peasant jacquerie of France in its drive for *liberté, égalité, fraternité*. For Toulouse, the vague hope of returning to his homeland ends with the realization that "his place was in the New World," an ominous resituation of hopes and destiny an ocean away from Europe and its appealing diversions (*ibid.*, 115).

Complex Choices

The dialect of *Island Beneath the Sea* serves the author's introduction to the African diaspora and the result of interracial sexual adventures that sire the protagonist, Zarité

Tété Sedella. In her first utterance, the patois for "my star or destiny," *mi z'étoile*, injects the liquid sounds for which the Caribbean is famous (Allende, 2010, 1). The term recurs at significant moments, especially those revealing the future of rebel Toussaint L'Ouverture and of Tante Rose and Gambo as well as Tété's daughter Rosette and her foster son Maurice. The phrase takes on distinct panache in dignifying fearful events that "we cannot change" (*ibid.*, 122).

The theme of subjugation overwhelms the text with longings and compromises. From her first lines, Tété exults that her living offspring live free, even as she serves Valmorain as bed slave. At the novel's climax, Allende pictures the planter examining by lamplight the parturient shape of Tété, "his most valuable possession," an ownership he takes for granted (Allende, 2010, 118). Still clinging to the notion that blacks have no emotions, he forbids her to mention her firstborn, who he indicates is still alive without revealing where he lives and under what name. By reducing his concubine to an object, he gives no thought to her humanity except when she serves him. After urging her to compete against him in evening games of cards, he discovers "logic, cleverness, and calculation" in a woman "as skilled as he" (*ibid.*, 106–107).

To disparage the notion that black field hands are simple witted, Allende exacerbates conflict in her bicultural cast. Significant to historical authenticity, the rise of Toussaint among Maroons in their mountain stronghold reveals the talents that turn a slave into the head of a revolt. Unlike strongmen Gambo and Boukman, Toussaint, a literate Catholic, bears the double role of minister of war, prophet, and *docteur-feuilles* (leaf doctor or herbalist). Modeled on the gifts of the Argentine physician Ernesto "Che" Guevara that benefited Fidel Castro and the Cuban Revolution in 1956, intellectual qualities that elevate Toussaint among blacks in 1791 also endear him to his master at Breda, where the slave takes charge of the fleeing white family. Historically, Toussaint earned respect during negotiations with the French for refusing to execute white hostages, a humanity unexpected in an upstart African.

In retrospect at Allende's perusal of character complexities, Michael Schaub, a reviewer for National Public Radio, avers that she "doesn't shy away from the florid and the dramatic," especially during the recovery from devastation in Haiti (Schaub, 2010). In the galloping, breathless style of Alejo Carpentier's *The Kingdom of This World*, Allende's text thrusts headlong into chaos. At the novel's climax, she elevates Tété to heroine over the choice of following her lover Gambo to freedom or leaving the Valmorains to die in a rush of Maroon savagery on Habitation Saint-Lazare. Skilled at white logic, Tété demands written manumission from Toulouse, which reassures her during a second decision to depart from Gambo and follow Valmorain across the plain to Le Cap. The decision leaves her vulnerable to the master's betrayals, repeated diminutions of Maurice's nanny by relegating her to a hotel slave quarters. More vile to Tété, the threat of the whipping post outside a Cuban jail precedes the terrorizing of a captive by the discharge of unloaded rifles, a Japanese ploy during World War II.

A surprising revelation in the falling action, Toulouse Valmorain's reunion with his mulatto son, Jean-Martin Relais, produces a contretemps with the foster parents, Etienne and Violette Relais, who rear the boy as their own. Even though the four-year-old presents good manners and a comely appearance, Valmorain thinks of the child as "that little mixed blood bastard," his son by mulatto handmaiden Tété and a mark on the planter's good reputation (Allende, 2010, 130). From nostalgic regard for Violette, Valmorain's former mistress, and Relais, an honored major in the militia, Valmorain chooses to surrender the child without fee. In adulthood, Jean-Martin's return to New Orleans presents Valmorain an opportunity to reclaim paternity, but Violette recognizes the scandal Valmorain faces by admission to fathering a mulatto.

CRITICAL EVALUATION

As in the case of *Portrait in Sepia* and *Inés of My Soul*, the text arouses differing critical take on the degree of success in Allende's historical *Island Beneath the Sea*. Marcela Valdes, a book critic for the *Washington Post*, admired most Allende's "amoral rogues," especially Uncle Sancho García del Solar, the womanizer who retains his humanity by extending affection and money to his biracial niece, Rosette (Valdes, 2010). Jennifer Levasseur, reviewer for the Sydney *Morning Herald*, charged the author with overstuffing a "historic bodice-ripper" with historical data covering the four decades from 1770 to 1810 (Levasseur, 2010). Betsy Willeford of the *Miami Herald* chastised Allende for bogging down the action in overwritten domestic detail, from cups of tea to minutia of costume for an afternoon out.

A repeated opinion characterizes slavery itself as the focus of Allende's historical novel. Canadian writer William Kowalski accorded kudos to prose of the Haitian half of the novel for its suspense and sadistic minutia of slow-roasting runaways for their crimes and the infection of infant fontanelles by slave mothers who would rather see their offspring dead than remanded to the Antillean cane fields. In contrast, the second half, in Kowalski's view, "offers Tolstoy-esque scenes of drawing-room intrigue that pale in comparison," a deliberate authorial contrast of rural and urban bondage (Kowalski, 2010). Olivia Barker cares less about the reversion to social satire than the attempt "to shoehorn in every milestone on the era's timeline, from the abolitionist movement to the Lewis and Clark Expedition" (Barker, 2010).

Gaiutra Bahadur, in a critique for the *New York Times*, came closest to identifying the novel's main flaw, the lack of "complex characterization and originality" and overuse of "melodrama and coincidence" (Bahadur, 2010, 26). By overreaching, Allende concludes with a sizable cast in the falling action, each of whom requires mention. Critic Margo Hammond describes the final chapters as crumbling under hasty resolution. The hurried dispatch of Maurice Valmorain to explore the hinterlands and Violette to expand on the annual *Bal de Cordon Bleu* leaves the reader uninformed of motivation and obstacles. Particularly perplexing, the offhand mention of Zacharie's wounding and the patching of his blinded eye lacks the finesse of Allende's previous plot and theme development.

• *References and Further Reading*

Bahadur, Gaiutra. "All Souls Rising," *New York Times Book Review* (2 May 2010): 26.
Barker, Olivia. "Allende's 'Island' Plunges into Some Troubled Waters," *USA Today* (10 June 2010).
Kowalski, William. "A Mixed Outcome," (Toronto) *Globe and Mail* (27 May 2010).
Levasseur, Jennifer. "Lost in a Sea of Clichés," (Sydney) *Morning Herald* (10 July 2010).
Schaub, Michael. "Dreams of Freedom in Allende's 'Island,'" www.npr.org/templates/story/story.php?storyId=126892427, accessed on April 4, 2010.
Valdes, Marcela. "Isabel Allende on Haiti's Slave Rebellion: A Lost Cause," *Washington Post* (8 June 2010).

Kingdom of the Golden Dragon

The second in Allende's YA adventure trilogy, *Kingdom of the Golden Dragon* follows a James Bond plot in vilifying the faceless, nameless Collector, the world's second largest moneybags while validating "compassion, forgiveness, and asceticism" ("Review," 2004,

75). The occluded villain plots sacrilege—stealing an oracular statue, a national symbol of the Tibetan soul that dates to 1200 C.E. In keeping with the trilogy's motifs, the author maintains an intergenerational, multinational, and multiracial arrangement of characters and cultures, who travel through India on their way to the Forbidden Kingdom of Tibet. The locations encourage geographical identification as well as what analyst Joan Axelrod-Contrada terms "a strong spiritual flavor" based on Hindu and Buddhist beliefs and practices (Axelrod-Contrada, 2011, 106). A *Publishers Weekly* review noted the neo-utopian creed of a "place where greed, hostility, and crime do not exist" ("Review," 2004, 75).

To link the first volume with the second, the author introduces the transcendent powers of the eagle and jaguar to an Asian locale. She opens on a framework adventure set among the Yetis of the Himalayas before reprising the events of *City of the Beasts*. The American investment of three valuable eggs to underwrite the Diamond Foundation rounds out the text of the previous novel and clears the way for the second stage of the trilogy. Alex Cold's grandmother, Kate Cold, rewards his courage and adaptation to danger by passing along a symbol of heritage, the "skin of a ten-foot-long python," an edgy Malaysian emblem of Kate's unconventional lifestyle and tentative relationship with relatives (Allende, 2004, 57).

BICULTURALISM AND STYLES

The text draws out differences in cultural and behavioral expectations, particularly the use of "cousin," "Little Grandmother," and "uncle" as respectful names conferred by the guide on tourists. On Alex's introduction to Asia, he experiences the Westerner's desire to uplift India's untouchables, the least honored caste. Allende speaks through Kate an unfortunate truth about guilt and charity: "You can't change anything with a few dollars" (Allende, 2004, 102). Additional events resonate with the Western concept of oriental inscrutability, a stereotype that marks Kate's interruption of cobra charming and Alex's intent to follow Tex Armadillo into the Red Fort, a structure begun by Shah Jahan and finished a decade later in 1648. More detailed, the need for proper attire, dining "using the three fingers of the right hand," and manners for an audience with the king of the Forbidden Kingdom reflects the range of Tibetan protocol (*ibid.*, 140).

The author appeals to young readers with the same skills she applies to adult fiction. Reviewer Lee Finkelstein locates in the YA text the standard elements of a good story: "intrigue, rogue characters, a valuable treasure to be found, heroes and heroines, magic and spiritual sacrifices" (Finkelstein, 2004, 20). Intercalary chapters return the reader to the Collector and his manic drive to amass more money than the world's richest person, a pointless competition illustrative of Western materialism. The Collector's petulance takes on so childish and calculating a tone and intensity that he becomes a laughingstock in contrast with the regal, impeccably mannered King Dorji of Tibet, guru Tensing, and polite guide Wandgi. Ironically, the Collector insists on shielding his reputation, a regard of questionable validity for a criminal who longs to be "richer than the ancient Egyptian pharaohs or Roman emperors" (Allende, 2004, 212).

In the return to the statue's repository, the text draws heavily on visual effects from Indiana Jones scenarios of skeleton, serpents, sinking floors above a void, mirrored walls, and lances from the ceiling. Allende dramatizes the plot to enrich the Collector through the step-by-step approach of Tex Armadillo and six Blue Warriors, a suspenseful clash of ancient security systems with a GPS and camera. Tex's identification of telepathy as "a psychedelic hell" implies that fail-safes from past centuries—a royal leopard, abysses under the floor, hidden trigger points, a round chamber with nine identical doors, weapons primed to strike intruders—equal in guile the technology of the twenty-first century (*ibid.*, 278). Allende's cliff-hanger method of disclosing the attack on King Dorji suits the tastes of young readers, who come of age amid electronic media that feed their appetites for danger and concealed surveillance. After the recovery of five kidnapped girls, Alex views the quick assault as "like something in an action film," a hint at the source of Allende's slapdash scenario (*ibid.*, 294).

YOUTHFUL COURAGE

The feats of daring that energize the escape from the mountains pit the ideas of male and female youths against sheer drops from the summit. As analyst Francis Sinclair explains, Allende applies contemporary fantasy by incorporating "a reality similar to our own, in which the impossible can occur without comment" (Sinclair, 2008, 34). The text expresses the humanistic concept of cooperative action in Alex's skill at rappelling and Pema's offering of long strands of hair to weave a third rope to complete the mission. To the tears of one girl for breaching female customs, Pema poses unheard-of logic—that the loss of hair will mark the rescuer as loyal to the king. Another contrast, the decking of Yeti warriors in horned helmets, places Dil and Tensing in the repugnant role of bloodletting. To the exclusion of Nadia, a Brazilian-Canadian teen, from the upcoming battle, she warns Alex that she will not accept a child's role nor will she take second place to a male. The mounting tension provides Nadia with a dramatic platform from which to declare herself equal to the challenge. Pema, equally liberated from gendered restraints, impresses General Myar Kunglung with her courageous resolve.

As the falling action pits rescuers against an unknown element in Chenthan Dzong, Allende again poses unrealistic strictures on females. Nadia, proposing to use invisibility as a means of reconnoitering the monastery, counters Alex's refusals with a sensible comment: "It's no more dangerous for me than it is for you" (Allende, 2004, 357). Tensing, the wise mentor, strips the argument of gendering by concluding, "We offer the talents we have" (*ibid.*). In the resolution, an initiation scene similar in gravity to the passage of power from the Siamese King Mongkut to Prince Chulalongkorn in *The King and I*, Nadia offers advice on Dil's return to the treacherous passage. The text acknowledges purity of heart in Alex and Nadia, who accompany Dil on a sacred mission to claim his throne.

Allende's solemn presentation of King Dorji lying in state in the ruins of Chenthan Dzong restores to the adventure novel a sense of mission and resignation at irreversible outcomes. Hallucinogenic dust confronts Dil, Alex, and Nadia with illusions of what each fears most—ruling the country, loss of a mother, and heights—a motif similar to the torment of Winston with rats in George Orwell's dystopian *1984*. The illusive Garden of Eden transforms one intruder by dissolving flesh from bone, another Indiana Jones scenario. In the style stereotyped by Tarzan movies of the 1930s featuring Tarzan, Jane, and the monkey Cheeta and reprised in later film convention, the quest novel concludes with laughter at cultural differences in language and courtesies and with the japes of the monkey Borobá.

In a reversal of transmission, the message to Prince Dil Bahadur in the final pages emerges from opaque quartz in the form of deep drum rolls, which Dil translates into Yeti ideograms. Language provides a jolly ending for the adventure as Alex restates American slang—"You bet!"—into the indirect and evasive language of polite Tibetan (Allende, 2004, 437). Critic Frances Sinclair notes that contemporary fantasy concludes with stipulations that protagonists keep secret the mysteries they have disclosed, as with the provenance of the dragon dung that may cure Alex's mother of cancer. By depicting some facts cloaked in obscurity under a curse, the author leaves undisclosed some ambiguities from a distant realm she peruses with what critic Susan L. Rogers calls "an intelligent, sympathetic look at cultures, customs, and creatures of a remote and fairly unknown area" (Rogers, 2004, 148).

• *References and Further Reading*

Axelrod-Contrada, Joan. *Isabel Allende.* New York: Marshall Cavendish Benchmark, 2011.
Finkelstein, Lee. "Older Readers," *Reading Time* 48:2 (May 2004): 20).
"Review: *Kingdom of the Golden Dragon,*" *Publishers Weekly* (15 March 2004): 75.
Rogers, Susan L. "Review: *Kingdom of the Golden Dragon,*" *School Library Journal* 50:4 (April 2004): 148.
Sinclair, Frances. *Fantasy Fiction.* Wanborough, UK: School Library Association, 2008.

language and silence

The significance of language in its myriad forms and in its absence impacts Allende's writing with anecdote, jest, dialogue, pun, satire, tale, proverb, and rumination, as with the unintelligible babble of a retarded child in "Clarisa," the futile preaching of Christianity to Indians in "The Proper Respect," and the grunts of Grr-ympr, the wise female Yeti in *Kingdom of the Golden Dragon.* For the fable "Two Words," Allende depicts Belisa Crepusculario discovering that "words make their way in the world without a master," a suggestion of the role of language in human liberty (Allende, 1991, 11). The ambiguity of Belisa's defeat of brutality derives from what critic Clarence Major terms "complex combinations of the symbolic and the mystical," the power of words to breach barriers that divide and alienate, a concept that Allende stresses in *Daughter of Fortune* and the YA trilogy begun by *City of the Beasts* (Major, 2001, 178).

In the opening lines of "Interminable Life," the author explains the basis of communication — how emotions pass into words and, from there, into narrative. Examples flourish in *The Stories of Eva Luna,* a collection of moral fables. For "Ester Lucero," Doctor Angel Sánchez restores his ideal woman through jungle herbs, which he reveres by "[speaking] with the stars in aboriginal tongues" (Allende, 1991, 147). The title figure in "Walimai" elevates words to elements of identity in the declaration that "to speak is also to be," a more complex utterance than conversation with the heavens (*ibid.,* 127). Out of respect for language, Walimai declares that oral tradition requires reverence and reason. His regard for language taboos recurs in *City of the Beasts,* in which indigenous people, according to cultural taboo, avoid citing the true name of an Indian or of the dead, who carry their names with them to the grave. The trilogy bases more mystical adventures in the Himalayas on the telepathic communication of the guru Tensing with outsiders and Yetis who speak unfamiliar languages.

For *Forest of the Pygmies,* Allende acknowledges a post-colonial polyglot, a lingual concurrence formed of Bantu, Swahili, and the English, Portuguese, and French of conquering nations. Kate Cold satirizes the ranking of tongues in her aphorism "We speak a language, anything else is a dialect," a rebuke of ranking languages according to colonial powers (Allende, 2005, 64). In one example of combined communications, Nadia Santos attempts to identify herself to prisoners as a friend by uttering positive messages "in Portuguese, her native language in Brazil, and then repeated ... in every language she knew" (*ibid.,* 141). Although Nadia's words fail, the captives deduce her intent through gestures, body language, and facial expression, all more trustworthy than foreign phrases. Language problems follow the trekkers from Kenya into Central Africa, where the Aka lack vocabulary to name the jaguar, Alex's totemic shape. The novel ends with a gesture of respect toward storytelling and honor to the three books compiled by Kate Cold summarizing an amazing three years of adventures.

In a departure from words, Allende depicts additional difficulties of communication that stymie human relations. She dramatizes the anger of grandfather for granddaughter in "The Road North" in the old man's silence and describes the disgust of Analía Torres for her duplicitous husband Luis in "Letters of Betrayed Love." The author reveals in "Our Secret" the post-coital silence that illustrates the Latin proverb, "Post coitum, omne animal triste est" (After sex, every animal is sad, reputedly confirmed by the Greco-Roman physician Galen of Pergamum around 189 C.E.). For the mannered story "The Little Heidelberg," a psychological presence replaces words with the gestures of the dance. The silence of El Capitán invites the myth-making of onlookers, who imagine reasons for muteness in a retired sailor. Chief among them, the nature of the establishment promotes silence, "for no one came there to talk" (Allende, 1991, 176). The emergence of a Scandinavian language from the old captain enlarges the group participation in food and music by wording his love for *niña* Eloísa in "the language of blizzards and forests," a territorial descriptor of northern Europe that foreshadows a chill, forbidding outcome (*ibid.*, 178). The reduction of his partner to a lacy, insubstantial memory and the fragrance of chocolate creates a melancholy atmosphere in which the captain welcomes a flesh-and-blood partner. Allende explained the conclusion as a twisted restoration of order.

Extremes of Expression

Allende's facility with language enlarges the range of her literary styles. She turns into humor in *My Invented Country* a childhood belief that Spanish is the universal language, with English and French merely irrational homework assignments for school. The author explained to interviewer Heather Knight, "Language is like blood, it is so yours," a tidy turn of metaphor from speech to an intimate heartbeat (Knight, 2001, 1). Allende's enthusiasm for words accounts for the urgency in her dramatic passages—terror in combat in *The Infinite Plan* and the sexual allure of teasing in *Aphrodite*—and the passion and intensity in love scenes and memories that root people into places, times, and communities, such her love for Willie Gordon in *The Sum of Our Days* and the lovelessness of Maya Vidal in *Maya's Notebook*. Through careful parsing, Allende strips layers of reality to get to the core meaning.

From an intellectual perspective in *Of Love and Shadows*, the author creates Hilda Leal, a Spanish refugee shielded from harm by a protective family. With the air purified of fearful events, Hilda appears to silence memories of "war, the dead she had buried, her accident, or that long march toward exile," a foretaste of the departure of Francisco and Irene from political corruption (Allende, 1987, 25). With the clever subversion of South American women under a tyrant, Hilda pretends to attend peaceful events while concealing her organization of an anti-government female coterie as adept at silent insurrection as she. Simultaneously, protagonists Francisco Leal and Irene Beltrán encounter another form of deliberate miscommunication. Against a barrage of bureaucratic obfuscation, seekers of truth about the nation's *desaparecidos* encounter pat excuses that toss worried families from the Ministry of Defence to the police station to the morgue. In the mode of Hatsue in David Guterson's *Snow Falling on Cedars*, a silent sufferer, Digna Ranquileo, creeps from her village under cover of night to tell Irene of the kidnap of fifteen-year-old Evangelina, whom the army silences permanently with a bullet. Like Hilda, Digna hesitates to mention the obvious crimes of the state in a gendered atmosphere that relegates women to the home.

As models of communication in *The House of the Spirits*, the author elevates Clara de Valle to a master of communication, both verbal and implied. Allende notes the perfect Spanish that Clara speaks to the infant Blanca and the natural language for speaking to birds that Clara teaches granddaughter Alba. More astonishing, the pagan tongues that Clara uses after meetings with the Mora sisters exemplify her command of the supernatural conversation of female mystics. According to Allende's gynocentric version of the Chilean revolution, women like Clara seized the public ferment as a logical historic moment to decry gender prejudice. During Chile's first-wave feminism, the pressure for change mobilized suffragists, the early protesters of the 1930s characterized by Nívea del Valle, the middle-class mother of Clara and Rosa. Historically, under the conservative aegis of the Christian Democratic Party, Chilean women warded off social opprobrium while verbally championing women's rights and banging on empty pots, an emblem of the food shortages that threatened their families.

The revival of feminism a generation later presses the fictional Clara into feminist mode as spokeswoman for peons at Las Tres Marías, her husband's plantation. Among her devices, Clara swings a Ouija pendulum to spell out words in Spanish or Esperanto, a source of communion with mystical elements. Out of respect for Esperanto, a universal Romance language, she suggests—tongue in cheek—that Esperanto be part of the school curriculum rather than English or French, an authorial tweak at the elevation of the two languages in contentious world affairs. Allende turns the question of a superior language into a connubial difference of opinion in view with her husband. From a *macho* perspective, Esteban insists that his granddaughter learn English rather than Spanish, "a second-rate language, appropriate for domestic matters and magic, for unbridled passions and useless undertakings" but worthless to the scientific community (Allende, 1985, 344).

Less fiery than the suffragists, Clara del Valle chooses altruism as a means of addressing lower-class misery and assaults on human dignity. With hyperbolic silence, she faces down her overbearing husband, whose egotism, rigid discipline, and violent swings of his cane echo the fascism of Augusto Pinochet and his henchmen. Ironically, Clara takes the postmodern tack of exaggerating the female convention of the passive matron, withdrawing from conversation and plunging into sewing and journaling, the conventional literary outlet for such silenced women as cloistered medieval nuns and the authors of Japanese pillow books. As Trueba chafes at his wife's withdrawal of affection, she worms her way wordlessly into his macho core, rapidly stripping him of effective verbal reproach, a model of female intrigue that Rose Sommers applauds in *Daughter of Fortune* as a neutralizer of male patriarchy.

Allende's spotlighting of Clara as communicator focuses on illusion, an impression that speaks truth. Analyst Lloyd Davies typifies the postmodern technique as a manipulation of the "slippery elusiveness of language," particularly Clara's choices of when to speak and when to remain silent as a defiance of male control (Davies, 2000, 43). Wendy B. Faris adds that the presence of the angelic Clara represents woman as "other," a differentiation from men who choose to split female flesh from spirit, a crime replicated in Amadeo Peralta's horrific immuring of Hortensia in the story "If You Touched My Heart." In disembodied form, Clara heartens Alba at the nadir of her courage to compose "without paper or pencil, to keep her thoughts occupied," a mental exercise that rids Alba of despair (Allende, 1985, 470). Alba extends the matrilineal respect for disclosure while confined by Colonel Esteban García in the "doghouse," where she resolves to testify against a lethal police state and its violations of human rights.

LANGUAGE AND ADVERSITY

Chauvinism toward Spanish, which pervades the author's canon, epitomizes the racism and classism of colonial South America, where Europeans abase indigenous culture and dialect. To enhance the religious tyranny of *Eva Luna*, Allende depicts the immurement of the child Consuelo in a city convent out of earshot of what nuns refer to as the "profane babel" of Indians (Allende, 1987, 7). For personal reasons, Zulema Halabí acquires facility in Spanish to absorb the stories of Eva Luna. For Rolf Carlé, acclimation to life in the Caribbean requires adding proficiency in Spanish and, for the sake of effect, some Latin phrases. Language takes on an intercultural subtlety after the arrival in Agua Santa of Kamal, the 25-year-old nephew. During Zulema's seduction of Kamal, a man more to her liking than her husband, she speaks in Spanish to avoid Arab social and gender taboos. Upon Kamal's departure, Zulema lapses into Arabic because her shame and dismay seems more suited to her native tongue.

An example of silent surveillance derives from Tété, a slave girl in *Island Beneath the Sea*, who hides understanding under a mute compliance. During negotiations for Tété's sale, Madame Delphine, her owner, declares that the child speaks only "the beautiful tongue of Molière" rather than black patois, which Allende acknowledges as "a tongue in a code that excluded whites" (Allende, 2010, 36, 75). Parallel with the girl's care for Maurice, the Valmorain heir, she avoids *parler nèg* (speaking black dialect), a devalued communication that Valmorain forbids (*ibid.*, 103). More discreet, the African vocabulary that Tété learns from her lover Gambo restores the tongue "my mother was not able to give me," a salve to mother hunger in the form of African words from a native speaker (*ibid.*, 111).

Allende shares with her heroine a need for research into discourse through English, French, and Spanish dictionaries that juxtapose her computer. The knowledge of Castilian Spanish that Tété must learn from her mistress, Eugenia García del Solar, proves frustrating on the Valmorain household's flight to Cuba. Tété finds the island accent "slippery and singsong," an elision of strict Castilian enunciation (Allende, 2010, 232). French, her second language, becomes the fallback for market and street exchanges. The round of lingual dominion shifts once more in 1803 with the Louisiana Purchase and the establishment of English as the dominate language in New Orleans.

In *The Infinite Plan*, variant dialects raise walls between cultures. Protagonist Gregory Reeves describes one aspect of his otherness in the Hispanic ghetto as "a strange language of rolled *r's* and rasping *h* sounds" (Allende, 1993, 53). In adulthood, his departure from the barrio and law school precedes training in Vietnamese and assignment to a mountain village. Fluent in musical Asian patois, he fits in with card players, jokesters, and a storyteller adept at transforming oral lore into "transport ... to heaven or hell" (*ibid.*, 201). At an epiphany of Gregory's turbulent life, he realizes that, in the midst of war, he communicates like a community member.

Allende's women possess powerful words that express healing strength and understanding, such as the oneness in *Zorro* of Isabel de Romeu with Bernardo, who teaches her Indian sign language as a means of bypassing Spanish. As Regina, Diego's mother, lies dying from the rigors of a 55-hour labor, White Owl strides directly toward her through a maze of unfamiliar hallways and calls "her true name, Toypurnia, and spoke to her in the tongue of their ancestors," the language of Regina's dreams (Allende, 2005, 32). By asserting aboriginal powers, White Owl restores health to her daughter and departs immediately from the Spanish-speaking household. By implication, the text pictures Regina slipping away from hacienda interests to uplift and protect the poor *indiada*. Her subversion of Spanish control takes the form of the language she teaches her son Diego, who speaks first in Indian before mastering his father's language.

At a pivotal moment in 1805, the rape and murder of Ana, Diego's wet nurse, leaves his milk brother Bernardo mute with terror and grief. Bernardo's comforter, a servant, rocks him like a baby and sings to him in the Indian language, a solace only his own race can croon. Bernardo learns from the shaman White Owl to contact his mother through astral communication and to console himself by playing a reed flute, a mathematical language based on aural intervals. Upon the reunion of Bernardo and Diego, the two boys renew their wordless thought reading, each content with knowledge of the other's mind, and practice Indian sign language "when telepathy and the flute failed" (Allende, 2005, 69). The three methods of wordless speech suggest that communication presses humankind to the extent of intelligence and ingenuity for methods of combating adversity.

Allende freights the return of speech in *Zorro* with mythic numerology and color symbolism. After three years of silence, Bernardo speaks to a motherless foal, a nurturing gesture that cleanses the boy of guilt, anger, and revenge at his mother's killers. After vomiting green mud, Bernardo and the foal wander for three days, during which the boy grooms the horse into a spirited mount he names Tornado. On the fourth day, Bernardo recognizes Tornado as a spirit guide, a model of "loyalty, strength, and endurance" indigenous to Native American mysticism (Allende, 2005, 76). Simultaneously, the number three confers protection on Diego, who sees three crows circling above and profits from surveillance by a watchful fox, which remains on guard for three days, a persistent number in folklore and scripture.

Language and Conquest

Language in *Inés of My Soul* presents obstacles to Spaniards, who must master the Quechuan tongue of Peru before tackling the musical Mapudungu of the Mapuche in Chile. For their aboriginal foe, conquistadors develop a curiosity about a preliterate people who gather to embroider news with clan histories "memorized from generation to generation" as part of worship of the god Ngenechén (Allende, 2006, 184). At a low point after the Mapuche attack on Santiago on September 11, 1541, Cecilia, the Inca princess, proposes tapping the female Quechua grapevine to pass through Mapuche lines and inform Pedro de Valdivia of the assault.

For similar needs, the blend of polyglot races in *Daughter of Fortune* and *Portrait in Sepia* leaves characters yearning for fluency in the languages of the powerful and for conversation in their mother language, a common source of homesickness throughout Allende's canon. For Rose Sommers, a scandal involving her with a Viennese tenor forces her into verbal silence and fervid journaling, a source of emotion similar to that of Clara and Alba del Valle. The dual mothering of Eliza Sommers instructs her in Rose Sommers's pristine English and Mama Fresia's Spanish and Mapudungu, the language for communicating with the local shaman. Eliza's facility with grammar and dialect serves her well in gold prospecting country, where she develops fluency in American English and the accents of Mexicans and Peruvians "to be accepted among them" (Allende, 1999, 273). Ironically, Spanish accents lead to persecution of anyone who might belong to the Murieta gang.

To elucidate the migration theme, Allende dramatizes the difficulties of outsiders. Jacob Todd, the bible salesman, suffers from lack of facility in any Chilean language, a dearth of skill that limits the completion of his mission. Tao Chi'en, a rising healer, pursues British English, the language of the winning side in China following the Opium War of 1839. He chooses English because the British "made the laws and administered them, and commanded the course of commerce and politics," a common rise in lingual favor following international conflicts (Allende, 1999, 177). As the two nations hammer out a commercial and diplomatic mutualism, Tao wishes for silence, an escape from the dissonance of the marketplace.

Critic Olga Ries commented that, on the American frontier, those not speaking English form an "obscure mass that is hardly noticed and certainly not treated as equals by the English-speaking population" (Ries, 2011, 6). Just as Uncle Jeremy predicts in *Daughter of Fortune*, Eliza Sommers Chi'en becomes the Spanish-speaking owner of a tearoom in San Francisco, where she addresses patrons in English and navigates Chinatown in Cantonese. For a refresher of Chilean Spanish, she walks several blocks to La Misión to listen to the language of her childhood, an extension of verbal power that leverages her skill in risky situations. Her daughter Lynn, steeped in all three languages, greets Aurora, her newborn, in Cantonese, English, and Spanish plus "invented words," the communication mothers share with their babes (Allende, 2001, 81).

Allende mocks snobbery in Santiago by picturing Frederick Williams, the former English butler of Paulina del Valle, as a newcomer to Chile. By speaking only four Spanish words, he cultivates an air of "wisdom, pride, and mystery," a cloaking of his lowly origins and his marriage of convenience to Paulina (Allende, 2001, 142). The illusion of style and high birth alongside Paulina's pose as a highly bred lady of charity further satirizes the class-crazed Santiagans, whom the author chaffs perennially in her works for their shallow view of human relationships and for grooming their daughters for an equally small-minded "matrimonial market" (*ibid.*, 143). In the resolution, Aurora del Valle deserts matrimony and language to succeed at photography, a method of perusing human relationships without the intervention of words.

See also humor; myth

- *References and Further Reading*

Davies, Lloyd. *Allende: La casa de los espíritus*. London: Grant & Cutler, 2000.
Knight, Heather. "Spinning Stories," *San Francisco Chronicle* (19 October 2001): 1.
Major, Clarence. *Necessary Distance: Essays and Criticism*. Minneapolis: Coffee House Press, 2001.
Ries, Olga. "Latino Identity in Allende's Novels," *Comparative Literature and Culture* 13:4 (2011): 1–8.
Weldt-Basson, Helene Carol. *Subversive Silences: Nonverbal Expression and Implicit Narrative Strategies in the Works of Latin American Women Writers*. Cranbury, NJ: Associated University Presses, 2009.

madness

The unanchored mind recurs in Allende's works in motifs of disorientation and mania, which she describes as wildfire, Golgotha, and calvary itself. In *The House of the Spirits*, Clara states that every family line contains "a fool or a crazy person" (Allende, 1985, 322). Insanity accounts for the hyperbolic fury of miner Esteban Trueba at the unforeseen poisoning of his fiancée, Rosa the Beautiful. Rosa's gift for stitching exotic animal shapes on a tablecloth for her trousseau returns in the family through niece Blanca's ceramic animals and great niece Alba's bedroom fresco. Clara values the exotic beasts in Blanca's crèches as evidence that "craziness can repeat itself in a family" in the creative germ passed from Aunt Rosa to niece Blanca to Blanca's daughter Alba (*ibid.*, 204).

To extend the motif of family eccentricity, Allende pictures Nicolás drawn to hashish and Jaime to Indian asceticism and charity on a par with the deluded saints of the Middle Ages. Esteban sums up the bizarre del Valle-Trueba household as the result of "marrying an eccentric and siring three good-for-nothing crazies," his dismissal of creativity and benevolence for their own sake (Allende, 1985, 256). His inability to value noncommercial traits in his family illustrate a soul immured by profit and loss. To Alba's herbal treatments of an invisible elephant at Jaime's direction, Esteban predicts, "This child is going to wind up stark raving mad!" (*ibid.*, 310). The family's eccentricities worsen after the rise of Marxism and rationing, when Blanca begins hoarding food behind locked doors.

Anomalies and Wonders

The author creates a feminist version of madness in *Eva Luna* from the collapse of a maid after giving birth to a two-headed baby. The pursuit of authorities and the media drives the servant to syncretic Catholic-Voodoo ritual and to a midwife to have her vagina stitched to prevent future anomalous births. Ragged and distraught, the maid "roamed the city streets mumbling unintelligibly" and measures the title figure's head with a knotted cord to determine virginity (Allende, 1987, 106). Obsessed with chastity, the madwoman insists that women lose their worth with the rupture of their maidenheads. In similar vein, Melesio thrusts himself into a physiological maelstrom to achieve partial femininity as Mimí. A series of macho lovers leaves him/her angry and depressed. The goal of becoming a woman scars Mimí, "(shattering) her dream of living in a fairy-tale world" (*ibid.*, 214).

The contrast of lunacies in *Of Love and Shadows* juxtaposes the noontime hallucinations of Evangelina Ranquileo with the idiocies of soldiers. Under Lieutenant Juan de Dios Ramírez, the infantry unloads a burst of gunfire at the Ranquileo adobe, "possessed with madness, beside themselves with power" (Allende, 1987, 70). Allende matches outburst with outburst by picturing the fifteen-year-old girl lifting her tormentor and hurling him to the patio along with his machine gun. In the grip of a military takeover, the Ranquileo family waited "motionless, terrorized ... for some atrocious response, some dark madness, some final calamity," the author's foretelling of the torture, rape, and murder of a *desaparecida* for violating the stature and command of an army officer (*ibid.*, 75).

The ostracism of eccentrics such as Evangelina questions glib definitions of sanity. In *Daughter of Fortune*, Rose Sommers and Paulina del Valle quail at the thought of a utopian colony based on "equality, free love, and communal labor" (Allende, 1999, 141). To Rose's diagnosis of madness in the utopist bible salesman Jacob Hobbs, her brother, John Sommers, a gallivanting sea captain, presents a worldly analysis of nonconformity: "People with original ideas always end up being considered mad" (*ibid.*). The adage tethers the novel's themes to events— risk-taking in the hunt for gold in California, rescue of tortured singsong girls, and investment in the North American frontier by a collection of whores, Quakers, miners, Indians, slaves, and outlaws. Of the search of the besotted Eliza for her lover, Joaquín Andieta, John recognizes his niece/daughter's ailment as simple infatuation. The eventual freeing of Eliza from an unpromising love match restores sanity at the same time that it satisfies the lengthy quest and enables the Anglo-Chilean cross-dresser "Chile Boy" to abandon men's attire and retrieve her femininity once more as Eliza.

THE BURDEN OF GUILT

For a Madrid beauty, Eugenia García del Solar, the plantation mistress in *Island Beneath the Sea*, insanity in the Caribbean follows the marital pattern that Charlotte Brontë set in *Jane Eyre* (1847) and Jean Rhys in *Wide Sargasso Sea* (1966). As wife to Antillean planter Toulouse Valmorin, Eugenia bargains for a privileged life based on the sin of black bondage to acres of sugar cane. Toulouse recognizes the basis for craziness in Haiti's "burden of temptations and degradation ... the climate that corroded health and dissolved man's most decent principles" (Allende, 2010, 241). Reviewer Margo Hammond itemizes the source of Eugenia's mental collapse as "enslaved by her own demons," an explanation of the plantation mistress's fear of insects and Guinea drumming, the long-distance communication method that eventually links rebel bands into an army (Hammond, 2010).

Symptoms take the form of nausea at meals and voices that impinge on Eugenia's sleep and, later, a "misty landscape" of amnesia that locks her away for four years (Allende, 2010, 117). After praying a rosary, she hears nonhuman voices, "from the shadows, the jungle, below the ground, hell, Africa," all jostling her serenity with wails and demonic laughter (*ibid.*, 57). The demented howls ally the Virgin Mary with the "Devil's whore," an unspecified female tormentor (*ibid.*, 58). Toulouse summarizes Eugenia's fears as reality in daylight and hallucinations in the dark that cause her to see an unborn fetus as a "child zombie, a living dead," a phantom that Eugenia conjures up from slave voodoo (*ibid.*, 70). As outsiders learn of Eugenia's quirks, gossip ridicules Toulouse because he is "married to a half mad Spanish woman" (*ibid.*, 48).

Until her death in late 1789, Eugenia's lapse into fits and delirium requires sedation with opium and nostrums brewed into tea by Tante Rose, a *docteur-feuille* (leaf doctor or herbalist) and *mambo* (high priest). The success of island botanicals intrigues Dr. Parmentier to test them in his laboratory and buy them in market stalls, an indication of the slow introduction of New World cures for such Caribbean ailments as fever and dysentery. Allende uses the open-mindedness of Parmentier to inject a note of acceptance to black spirituality, which he claims gives "a sense of meaning to the miserable existence of the slaves" (Allende, 2010, 68). Unfortunately, he predicts no cure for Eugenia's ravings, which, like those of Bertha Mason Rochester, the scorned wife in *Jane Eyre*, lead to immurement and oblivion. In decline, Eugenia becomes what Tété describes as an invalid "tame rabbit," an image that combines docility with vulnerability (*ibid.*, 135).

FAMILY TRAITS

In *The Infinite Plan*, mental imbalance threatens in two generations. The Reeves children watch their father decline from overt rationality to ravings and public masturbation, the result of post-traumatic war stresses that leave him fearful "of pain, of living as a paraplegic, of going crazy" (Allende, 1993, 208). In widowhood, his mother, Nora Reeves, takes an opposite route: she retreats from a tenuous intellectualism to a wraith "so insubstantial that it was difficult to remember her" (*ibid.*, 66). To amplify Nora's parasitic dependence on others, Allende juxtaposes the family boa constrictor, which retreats into its cage at a burlesque house to become "lethargic until the day it died" (*ibid.*, 67). Nora's example serves as both disappointment and tocsin to son Gregory Reeves, who chooses to take an active role in the ridding himself of mental torments.

A triumph of internal monologue, Allende's pacing of the mental anguish of Greg, veteran of the Vietnam War, suggests a universal trauma resulting from wholesale slaughter. During rehabilitation in Hawaii, Greg, like Tayo in Leslie Marmon Silko's *Ceremony*, grapples with the murkiness of his morals and aims. At last physically on the mend, Greg reveals his brain "at the boiling point" (Allende, 1993, 206). A list of terrors reminds the reader of the nightmare for the infantry in Vietnam and the looming risks of death, paraplegia, syphilis, imprisonment "in a cage for monkeys," and the living death—"if there is an afterward"—of a soulless killing machine unable to return to normality (*ibid.*, 208). The arrangement of torments from death to life calamities implies that, to the soldier, death seems preferable to ongoing pain, immobility, or madness.

An apt phrase sums up the scorpions in Greg's brain as "the fire of the end of the world," his image of the political sophistry that legitimizes a pointless war (*ibid.*, 209). The return to civilian squalor discloses fearful memories and sins, leaving Greg feeling "contaminated, dirty, dead tired" (*ibid.*, 221). Still indoctrinated to suspect Asians, Greg's brush with a Chinese man in San Francisco that triggers a reach for a sidearm illustrates the indoctrination that requires one race to suspect and kill another. The novel's downhill spiral sweeps into a mounting trash heap Greg's two marriages, an addicted daughter, and a monster son as well as the "benign madness" that wafts Nora from a graceful senility toward death (*ibid.*, 329). Always dependent on energy and wit, Greg, wearied by the fray, finds himself losing both vim and virility and sinking into a horrifying anxiety attack. At the hint of an upturn in his fortunes, Allende targets the demons that reduce him to "a cornered animal"—"uncertainty, restlessness, guilt, a sense of abandonment, and profound loneliness," a composite phantasm he calls "the Beast" (*ibid.*, 340).

See also health and healing

• *References and Further Reading*

Bahadur, Gaiutra. "All Souls Rising," *New York Times Book Review* (2 May 2010): 26.
Hammond, Margo. "A Slave Makes History in Allende's New Novel," *Pittsburgh Post-Gazette* (6 June 2010).

magical realism

Allende regrets that the term magical realism "follows me around" even though the supernatural occurs in only some of her works, such as the frog convention in *Of Love and Shadows*, the shipboard appearance of Lin's spirit to Tao Chi'en in *Daughter of Fortune*, magical dragon dung in *Kingdom of the Golden Dragon*, the door that magically swings open in "The Guggenheim Lovers," and the invisible floating Palace of the Poor in *Eva Luna* and "Phantom Palace" (Geracimos, 2002). The author differentiates between the real and imagined magic with a satiric jest in "Simple Maria" at "the five-peso consolations sold by the neighborhood fortunetellers and seers," obvious scams perpetrated against the gullible that recur in a Nairobi marketplace in *Forest of the Pygmies* (Allende, 1991, 151). An unusual example, cries from gallows ghosts in *Island Beneath the Sea*, settles on Maurice, a small boy who has no evil in his past. As planter Toulouse Valmorain struggles to rear his son in the style of French aristocrats, Maurice trembles from sightings of hanged men in his bedchamber, a warning of the extreme savagery of colonialism the child stands to inherit. The author turns the nightly terrors into symbols of the next generation of Haitian planters, who must absolve the colony of its bloody past. A subsequent scene depicts

Violette Boisier smashing the opal of her ring in Cuba and crying out for her husband, Etienne Relais, at the moment of his death in Haiti, a magical coincidence on a par with scenes from Rudolfo Anaya's *Bless Me, Ultima*.

In a style similar to that of Cecilia Velastegui's *Traces of Bliss*, Allende characterizes fiction as story-truth, a flexible substitution for happening-truth or absolute truth, as with Feliciano's liver rotting from rage in *Portrait in Sepia*, the coincidence of Carmen and Greg returning to Los Angeles at the same time in *The Infinite Plan*, the assistance of the bloody ghost of Juan de Málaga at the siege of Santiago in *Inés of My Soul*, Consuelo's ability to vanish in servant work in *Eva Luna*, and Regina's swimming in circles with the dolphins in *Zorro* to ensure world order. Through the epilogue of Isabel de Romeu in *Zorro*, Allende speaks her philosophy of truth: "There is no such thing as absolute truth ... everything passes through the filter of the observer" (Allende, 2005, 387). The author considers memory tricky and fragile and describes the human mind as fickle in choosing what to remember and what to forget, such as the ambiguous floating architecture in "Phantom Palace" and the return of spirits that critic Helen Falconer terms "personal hallucination" (Falconer, 2001). Of destiny, Allende admits, such "reality sometimes is as improbable" as a soap opera (Allende, 1993, 239).

Under the spell of the unlikely, the reader intuits startling truths not revealed in mundane affairs, for example, in *Eva Luna*, the mass burial of 15 Chileans slain under the preposterous claim of legitimate police business. John Flax, director of a stage adaptation of *The Stories of Eva Luna*, characterized the revelations as "a world that is larger than this pragmatic paradigm that we have bought into here" (Nott, 2005, 74). Choreographer Della Davidson added, "The tangible boundaries of the world are not quite as tangible as you think they are," his explanation of Allende's extension of events into a fourth dimension (*ibid.*). As critic Don Latham explains, magical realism transgresses reality to "undermine society's power structures," the purpose of supernatural interventions in Allende's *City of the Beasts* and *Forest of the Pygmies* (Latham, 2007, 61).

Allende's writing extends "an invitation to explore beyond the appearance of things," an opportunity to enhance memories with color and sparkle, hyperboles that ease earthly adversity, as displayed by Rosa's green hair in *The House of the Spirits* and the wings that sprout on the aged body of the protagonist in "Clarisa" (Allende, 1991, 28). Allende's canon resorts to larger than life characterization that draws on mythos, marvel, and religion for extremes of passion and retribution, the dominant responses of Spanish conquistadors to the unreality of the New World in *Inés of My Soul*. The ghosts of colonialism haunt the author's stories to bewail rape and genocide and to rally the living to a war on injustice. A gentler brush with spirits depicts Valdivia's ghost pulling Inés ears, a tug similar in meaning to that of Homeric spirits in the *Iliad*, where they communicate with the living by pulling their hair.

The author exploits extraordinary phenomena that violate physical rules of place and time with subtle nuances, such as character levitation, awareness of future outcomes, and communication with spirits, including the odor of orange blossoms that the spirit of Catherine Villars wafts over the sleeping Julianna de Romeu in *Zorro* and the camaraderie between Nana-Asante and the Aka dead in *Forest of the Pygmies*. Simultaneously, the descriptions traverse the real and the mysterious as though the two share the same dimension, as demonstrated by Regina's metaphoric third eye that enables her to keep tabs on her rambunctious son Diego, the future Zorro. The author instills in readers a trust of the supernatural phenomena that lie beyond empirical bounds and thus out of human control. Reviewer Saul Austerlitz acknowledges the author's command of magical elements and dubs her "the doyenne of the weird and wondrous" (Austerlitz, 2006).

In a departure from the more common pigeonholing of Allende's style, critic Patricia Hart labels her a magical feminist, a reclaimer of supernatural powers, notably prescience and telepathy, as substitutes for the enfranchisement and gender potency denied women by Chilean patriarchy. Unlike the superhuman women cloistered on Avalon in Marion Zimmer Bradley's *The Mists of Avalon*, the mystic seductress in Leslie Marmon Silko's *Ceremony*, or the fairy tale heroines of Angela Carter's carnivalesque Gothicism, Allende's women battle despoilers and persecutors on a human plane—on plantations, in prison, and in domestic scenarios. Throughout *The House of the Spirits*, the author creates a Gothic complex of behaviors that sets Clara del Valle apart from a macho Chilean cult of militarism and into the realm of pre–Christian aboriginal culture. In the early stages of spiritual hermetics, Clara absorbs instruction from "the magic books from Uncle Marcos's enchanted trunks" (Allende, 1985, 90). In "a universe of her own invention, protected from life's inclement weather," she can predict death and move a saltcellar or three-legged table by telekinesis, psychic exotica that prefigure her rise to clan matriarch (*ibid.*, 98).

In unpleasant situations—the confinement of the dog Barrabás in a cage and the poisoning and autopsy of her sister Rosa—Clara retreats into silence, eccentricity, trances, asthmatic seizures, and sleepwalking, a list of female escapist extremes dating to early medieval saints. Dependence on everyday magic enables Clara to slip through the house unseen and spy on Dr. Cuevas and his attendant as they prepare Rosa for burial. To shield the twins "at a safe distance from her magic," Esteban Trueba sends them to a no-nonsense English boarding school (Allende, 1985, 158). When Esteban upsets household peace, Clara's rubber plant droops and weeps a white fluid, a humorous flow of tears at the disrupter of family harmony. After Clara's death, Esteban and son Jaime exhume Rosa's remains, the two experience some of Clara's magic. Initially, Rosa retains "her orange-blossom crown, her green hair, and her unruffled beauty" until a breeze dissolves the corpse into "fine gray powder," a reduction to the elements that denies Esteban a reprieve from his loneliness and shriveled soul (Allende, 1985, 346).

Unlike Esteban's hurtful presence, the reality of Clara's life on earth and in the spiritual realm lies in her abiding love and comfort to others. Her marriage to a volatile miner who originally planned to marry Rosa produces an unsettled, unfulfilled family unit. Clara's obsessive recording of family history yields a heritage of narrative meant to prolong her beneficence in later generations. As an antidote to prison barbarities beyond her control, Clara's ethereal presence hovers above Alba's cell and entices her back to the task of the family scribe. The projection of courage from an elder to a neophyte predicts another extraordinary woman to arrive at a bleak historical moment when the family most needs her. Alba experiences an inexplicable linkage with her grandmother's writings "as if I had lived all this before and that I have already written these very words" (Allende, 1985, 487). The suggestion of "album" in Alba's name hints at the centrality of remembered and reorganized family events to clan solidarity and longevity.

Critics denounce Allende's magical realism as a duplicate of episodes from Gabriel García Márquez's *One Hundred Years of Solitude* and *Love in the Time of Cholera*. Opposing opinions reposition the implausible, unpredictable events within classic feminist fiction, notably, Toni Morrison's *Beloved* and Angela Carter's *Wise Children*. Unlike the maleficent wizardry of male writers, Allende's women wield power for the sake of good, as with White Owl's obedience to the mystic Indian grapevine communication system in

Zorro to rescue Regina from postpartum weakness and her appearance at the duel between her grandson and Rafael Moncada. White Owl continues destabilizing Spanish influence in her grandson's life by reciting legends, teaching symbol decoding and respect for religious sites, smudging with sweet grass, and picking magic plants.

In a 2002 interview with *Booklist* veteran reviewer Hazel Rochman, Allende defined magical realism as it compares to fantasy. In place of magic wands and fairy godmothers in *The Wizard of Oz*, magical realism probes real life mysteries—premonitions, dream prophecy, ESP, earth powers, and coincidence. Allende cites from *City of the Beasts* two examples—Alexander's location of an animal totem and Nadia's reliance on instinctual knowledge. A gentle hyperbole in *Inés of My Soul* confers on the native servant Catalina the power to "be in several places at the same time and disappear in a sigh," a flattering description of the worthy domestic (Allende, 2006, 86). An offhand reference to Catalina's spell that summons a two-headed llama illustrates the natural tone and atmosphere of Allende's more bizarre scenes of the arcane, which reviewer Celia McGee labels as surreal (McGee, 2006).

Human fortitude and mystic powers engulf *Inés of My Soul* at an historic turning point, the Mapuche attack on Santiago on September 11, 1541. Captain Aguirre, alert to the massing of Mapuche warriors "in the forests, in the hills, underground, in the clouds themselves," implies a mystic interpretation of a natural phenomenon—forces mustering on misty mountain tops (Allende, 2006, 182). The clairvoyance of the boy Felipe suggests a New World cliché, the ability of Amerindians to foresee the future. The wounding of so many and the slaughter of warhorses and farm animals prefaces the discovery of women and children unharmed in a cave. Inés hesitates to credit Our Lady of Succor or the layer of dirt that conceals the cave mouth. The understatement suggests how the terror of the moment can transform sensible self-protection into a miracle intervention by the Virgin Mary. The author restates the providential power of one Spanish woman in routing 8,000 invading Mapuche. To Rodrigo de Quiroga, war had turned Inés into a "demented basilisk"; Michimalonko, the commander in chief, rationalizes that Inés must be a witch for hurling human heads into the fray (Allende, 2006, 205).

Allende carefully centered Inés in the domestic realm, where feeding the hungry and healing hurts demands full attention. To the thriving legend of the Spanish valkyrie, Inés dismisses wild hero stories and turns her talents toward nursing the wounded. In later scenes, Allende credits the protagonist's mounting superstition with old age, which thins the "veil that separates this world from the next" (Allende, 2006, 229). Critic Celia McGee offers another perspective on a merger of supernatural elements: "a primitive, cruel Christianity, the Mapuche Indians' complex demonology, a devout New World nature worship and Inés' healing, a mystical mix of Catholicism and more ancient beliefs" (McGee, 2006).

See also Gothic; superstition

- *References and Further Reading*

Allende, Isabel. "*A Mule on a Piano*," *Newsweek* 134:3 (19 July 1999): 57.

_____. "The Short Story," *Journal of Modern Literature* 20:1 (Summer 1996): 21–28.

Austerlitz, Saul. "Chile's Colonial History Given Life," *San Francisco Chronicle* (7 November 2006).

Falconer, Helen. "Colouring the Family Album," (Manchester) *Guardian* (17 November 2001).

Geracimos, Ann. "Novel Views of Isabel Allende," *Washington Times* (19 January 2002).

Latham, Don. "The Cultural Work of Magical Realism in Three Young Adult Novels," *Children's Literature in Education* 38 (2007): 59–70.

McGee, Celia. "'Ines' Captures Chile's Soul in 1500s," *USA Today* (9 November 2006).

Nott, Robert. "Dancing Through Eva Luna's World," *Santa Fe New Mexican* (12 August 2005): 74.
Rochman, Hazel. "The Booklist Interview," *Booklist* 99:6 (15 November 2002): 591.

male persona

The male hegemony in Latin America figures large in Allende's writings, from her fictional settings to the personalized views of the Allende family. In short stories, she retains familiar profiles—the stout-hearted proletarian priest, the humble agrarian worker, and the blustering soldier or police official. With greater dependence on orientalist stereotyping, the author presents Asian kidnappers in *Kingdom of the Golden Dragon* as dark-toothed, garlic-breathed Blue Horsemen, members of the scorpion sect who value girls only as pawns, temporal amusements, and breeders of male children to enlarge the coterie. The threats of branding and tongue removal typify Gothic masculinity, which demands possession and silencing of females.

Critic C.R. Perricone categorized some of the male roles in the author's major works:

male	*title*	*role*
Alexander Cold	*City of the Beasts*	
	Kingdom of the Golden Dragon	
	Forest of the Pygmies	idealist, adventurer, rescuer
Babalú the Bad	*Daughter of Fortune*	bodyguard, pimp
Bernardo	*Zorro*	friend, husband
Brother Fernando	*Forest of the Pygmies*	missionary
Cyrus	*The Infinite Plan*	Marxist, laborer, mentor
Diego de la Vega	*Zorro*	rescuer, savior
Dil Bahadur	*Kingdom of the Golden Dragon*	ruler in training, ascetic
Doctor Parmentier	*Island Beneath the Sea*	philosopher, husband
Don Sebastián Domínguez	*Portrait in Sepia*	patriarch, planter
Esteban García	*House of the Spirits*	peon, police official, avenger
Esteban Trueba	*House of the Spirits*	patriarch, planter, senator
Eusebio Beltrán	*Of Love and Shadows*	aristocrat, desaparecido
Faustino Rivera	*Of Love and Shadows*	soldier, witness, diarist
Francisco Leal	*Of Love and Shadows*	psychologist, photographer, investigator
Gambo La Liberté	*Island Beneath the Sea*	slave, savior, guerrilla warrior
Gregory Reeves	*The Infinite Plan*	rebel, intellectual, sybarite
Gustavo Morante	*Of Love and Shadows*	career soldier, martyr
Hipólito Ranquileo	*Of Love and Shadows*	circus worker, wanderer
Huberto Naranjo	*Eva Luna*	rescuer, freedom fighter, mentor
Jaime Trueba	*House of the Spirits*	physician, surrogate father
Javier Leal	*Of Love and Shadows*	father, anarchist
Jean de Satigny	*House of the Spirits*	poseur, esthete, pervert
Jeremy Sommers	*Daughter of Fortune*	
	Portrait in Sepia	bachelor, merchant
Joaquín Andieta	*Daughter of Fortune*	
	Portrait in Sepia	idealist, bandit
John Sommers	*Daughter of Fortune*	
	Portrait in Sepia	sea captain, womanizer, adviser
Juan de Dios Ramírez	*Of Love and Shadows*	soldier, sexist
King Dorji	*Kingdom of the Golden Dragon*	ruler, savant
Lautaro	*Inés of My Soul*	slave, lover, warrior
Ludovic Leblanc	*City of the Beasts*	anthropologist, explorer
Lukas Carlé	*Eva Luna*	sadist, pervert

male	*title*	*role*
Pedro García	*House of the Spirits*	overseer, unrequited lover
Pedro de Valdivia	*Inés of My Soul*	conqueror, lover
Professor Jones	*Eva Luna*	esthete, intellectual, mentor
Professor Leal	*Of Love and Shadows*	father, propagandist
Riad Halabí	*Eva Luna*	
	Stories of Eva Luna	peddler, father, mentor, mediator
Rolf Carlé	*Eva Luna*	photojournalist, guerrilla warrior
Severo del Valle	*House of the Spirits*	soldier, dynast, politician
Tao Chi'en	*Daughter of Fortune*	
	Portrait in Sepia	student, healer, husband, father
Toulouse Valmorain	*Island Beneath the Sea*	planter, patriarch, enslaver
Walimai	"Walimai"	
	City of the Beasts	
	Kingdom of the Golden Dragon	shaman, healer, mediator

Allende's first novel, *The House of the Spirits*, makes an unmistakable parallelism between planter Esteban Trueba and the unnamed dictator, a fictional version of Augusto Pinochet. Critic Sara Cooper describes Trueba, an emotional cripple and prisoner of emotions, as a "hyperbolic macho-dictator in his home, patron and rapist on his estate, and bastion of 'democracy' in government" (Cooper, 2009, 22). A miner and land owner, he struggles with an unstable ego, producing angry outbursts and random violence toward anything violating his notion of machismo. At the death of his fiancée, Trueba cloaks himself in tragedy and claims all suffering for himself. In contrast to his self-aggrandizement, Clara falls silent and absorbs the emotional energy that marks her as the novel's dynamic center.

Analyst Renata Wasserman views Trueba as a defender of "values calcified into a complete inability to understand and guide events in the modern world" (Wasserman, 2007, 69). Trueba's bombast triggers retorts from his liberal daughter Blanca, who challenges his rhetorical question, "Do you know what would happen here without a *patrón*?" (Allende, 1985, 283). He believes that, without a tyrant at the head of a plantation, no one would establish order, sell crops, or take responsibility for laborers, a misperception that Clara disproves after the earthquake. He views early twentieth-century bolshevism as a formula for chaos, a collapse of control that would leave the sick, starving, orphaned, and widowed without aid. In Trueba's view, he treats laborers fairly and elevates their lives above ghetto dwellers in the city. The collapse of the ruling elite and of Trueba as benevolent/violent *patrón*, family controller, and elder statesman derives from poetic justice, the comeuppance to a "father who punished his children too severely," the *patrón* who chops off three of Pedro Tercero's fingers, and the patriot who seeks a true republic predicated on ethnic oppression "with a snakeskin whip and a silver cane" (Allende, 1985, 406, 408).

Allende showcases Trueba's manly passions in a subversion of the romantic ideal. Brash and powerful both socially and politically, he wins Clara's love, but not her admiration. At Las Tres Marías, he roars, "I'm the one in charge here and I have the right to surround myself with people I like," a childish self-affirmation the rids him of the need to win friends and cultivate workable relationships with peons (Allende, 1985, 160). His friendlessness leaves him "lonely and furious," an explosive combination as he advances toward a senate position (*ibid.*, 255). Further destabilizing Trueba's role as virile patriarch, the text poses as the choice mate for Trueba's daughter Count Jean de Satigny, bearer of Continental allure and precursor of the foppish alter ego of Diego de la Vega in *Zorro*. A dandified poseur, Satigny carries refinement into the feminine realm with blue eyewash and polished nails. The effete patois of the dynast annoys Trueba, a plain-spoken *patrón* who demands awe rather than the language of the European playboy.

In old age, Esteban changes little. He retreats to his hacienda at Tres Marías "to hold his meetings, weave his intrigues, forge his deals, and, in his lonely house, closet himself to release his rage, his frustrated desire, or his sorrow," all emotions that he mismanages (Allende, 1985, 324). Rescued by his beloved granddaughter Alba and her clarified family history, he achieves self-reclamation and a reunion with the spirit of the wife he abused. The epiphany of restored love of purity and understanding frees him from a grasping lifestyle punctuated by bouts of alienation and random violence against telephones and soup tureens. At peace with the afterlife, "more lucid than ever and happy conscious, and serene," Esteban exits a life of rapacity and coercion, an allegory of colonial Latin America (*ibid.*, 479).

Perricone notes that such men as the self-indulgent Esteban Trueba wield variant powers because "women willingly play a subservient role," the situation in the Clara del Valle's union with Esteban and in the brother-sister alliance between Lukas and Frau Carlé in *Eva Luna* and Violette and Etienne Relais in *Island Beneath the Sea* (Perricone, 2003, 90). Another male ill-suited to matrimony, Huberto Naranjo, the terrorist in *Eva Luna*, embraces a violent guerrilla band, brandishing his masculinity as a source of murder and tyranny of his lover, whom he pictures as disadvantaged by female birth. Eva realizes, "It was not likely that the Revolution was going to change those attitudes" (Allende, 1987, 233). The author assigns suitable ends to the worst of males, those guilty of disturbing incursions into the realms of women and the underclass, beginning with Esteban's rape of Pancha García. For punishment, the author ends Esteban's life in loneliness, frailty, and yearning. She extends the reprisals in *Eva Luna* by depicting Lukas in a noose rigged by vengeful schoolboys that first silences, then asphyxiates a brutal bully of a terrorized wife and retarded daughter.

Those nonconformists who elude the patriarchal construct—the elderly colonel in the nursing home in *Of Love and Shadows*; Macandal and Toussaint L'Ouverture, the mythic martyrs in *Island Beneath the* Sea; healer and sage Pedro García, the sympathetic Padre José Dulce María, and the daredevil and spiritual seeker Nicolás del Valle in *The House of the Spirits*; the lookout El Negro, the dying Indian gardener, and Mimí, the transsexual singer in *Eva Luna*; and Mario, the homosexual hairstylist in *Of Love and Shadows*—occupy satisfying social niches outside of politics, the Catholic hierarchy, and the military, the obdurate wielders of power in Latin America. For gentle males like Mario and Francisco Leal, Captain Gustavo Morante exhibits distaste and outright hostility, a conditioned response common to men locked into the macho mindset. Allende creates a special category for young men, including Felipe/Lautaro, the Indian warrior in *Inés of My Soul* and Alex Cold in the *City of the Beasts* trilogy. Both accept the strength of female companions who equal them in daring. Alex seems particularly eager to appear manly lest he "look like a coward in the eyes of the girl," a fear that appears to begin early in men (Allende, 2002, 83).

- *References and Further Reading*

Cooper, Sara E. "Family Systems and National Subversion in Isabel Allende's *The House of the Spirits*," *Interdisciplinary Literary Studies* 11:1 (Spring, 2009): 16–37.

McKale, Margaret A. Morales. Literary Nonfiction in Works by Isabel Allende and Guadalupe Loaeza. Columbus: Ohio State University, 2002.
Perricone, C.R. "Allende and Valenzuela: Dissecting the Patriarchy," *South Atlantic Review* 67:4 (Fall, 2002): 80–105.
Wasserman, Renata Ruth Mautner. *Central at the Margin: Five Brazilian Women Writers*. Cranbury, NJ: Bucknell University Press, 2007.

marginalism

In repeated interviews and written statements of intent, Isabel Allende has chosen to elevate peripheral or minority figures, the socially unacceptable who lurk on the rim of respectability. Because of her own marginalization as a Latina exile with a U.S. citizenship, the author readily claims a mixed heritage of "three-quarters Spanish-Basque blood, one-quarter French, and a tot of Araucan or Mapuche Indian, like everyone else in my land" (Allende, 1995, 14). Because of her own inclusive persona as Chilean, expatriate, American citizen, and world-class artist, she assigns importance to borderland characters—Joaquín Andieta and Mama Fresia in *Daughter of Fortune*, the prostitute La Señora and the Indian gardener in *Eva Luna*, Spanish neurologists and practitioners of alternative medicine in *Paula*, and Mapuche villagers and Princess Cecilia, the wife of a Spaniard in *Inés of My Soul*. In each case, the minority representative has something unique and worthy to add to Allende's canon, notably the infiltration of the ruling class with rancor, ambition, vigor, and genes.

Critic Shannin Schroeder credits Allende as well as Maxine Hong Kingston and Toni Morrison with rescuing "marginalized groups from social and historical amnesia," including the sexual deviates surrounding Count Jean de Satigny in *The House of the Spirits*, Mimí, the transdressing singer in *Eva Luna*, Mario the gay hairdresser in *Of Love and Shadows*, and Tété, a sex slave in *Island Beneath the Sea* (Schroeder, 2004, 129). Celia Correas De Zapata credits Allende with sympathizing with "the helpless, the orphaned, the uprooted" in unanticipated rescues that "can't be foreseen" (Correas de Zapata, 2002, 74). In *Of Love and Shadows*, the author's empathy for Digna and Hipólito Ranquileo and other families of the *desaparecidos* reclaims forgotten victims of history's dark chapters. By implementing these examples as well as indigenous Amazonians, Himalayans, Bantu, and Aka in the *City of the Beasts* trilogy and by conferring cultural status on disparate religions and customs, Allende revolutionizes literature by ushering readers into a broader world vision than previous literary giants have encompassed.

For infantryman Gregory Reeves in *The Infinite Plan*, the political result of depersonalizing takes pitiable form in the lives lost during the Vietnam War, both American and Asian. A "dyed-in-the-wool grunt," he regrets the governmental manipulation, hypocrisy, and deceit that forces him to "kill or be killed" (Allende, 1993, 208, 184). The racist front compares with his father's dismissal of the bombing of Hiroshima and Nagasaki as an extermination of Japs who "don't count" (*ibid.*, 31). The putrefaction of Vietnamese and American corpses stowed in helicopters lingers in the smell and "the screams; the dead aren't really gone" (*ibid.*, 188). The echo takes the form of post-traumatic stress disorder, a subconscious realization that the dregs of war clog the soul with regret and a too-late recognition that even "gooks" matter. Greg views the marginal losers as a wearying fact of consciousness: "I'm so used to atrocity that I can't imagine life without it" (*ibid.*, 194).

Literary historian Donald Leslie Shaw enumerates the outsiders—"women, young people, workers, homosexuals, Jews"—whom Allende and the Post-Boom coterie incorporate in fiction (Shaw, 2002, 179). The devalued peons in *The House of the Spirits* belie their relegation to sidelines by seizing the moment to rebuild Las Tres Marías after the earthquake and to rebel against colonialism. Pedro Segundo, the foreman, takes pride in his outcast son, Pedro Tercero, for avoiding the endless cycle of "planting potatoes and harvesting poverty" by distributing Socialist propaganda (Allende, 1985, 205). Pancha García, a peon embittered by rape, subverts sexual exploitation by her *patrón*, Esteban Trueba, by infecting the mind of grandson Esteban García with the injustice of cyclical violation. The seething nemesis disrupts Senator Trueba's idealized state with colonial sins that demand retribution.

The growth of an idea—the false premise of European superiority—results in a fascist backlash that tragically extorts recompense from Alba, Esteban's granddaughter. Critic Marta L. Wilkinson characterizes Alba as the child of miscegenation, "the mixed-breed product of the upper and lower classes, of the European whites and the indigenous people" (Wilkinson, 2008, 172). The innocent girl atones for the wrongs of her family and class through gang rape, solitary confinement in the "doghouse," and torture by electrocution. Her rescuer, a nameless female—"one of those stoical, practical women of our country"—represents the daring of faceless, marginalized women like those Esteban brutalizes (Allende, 1985, 429). Ironically, it is these witnesses—whom analyst Lloyd Davies credits as "the most potent agent of change"—who endure the patriarchal wrongs of the past and who excise the rot engendered by colonialism from their position on the margins (Davies, 2000, 45). As cited by analyst Margaret McKale, Allende's realistic sufferers "leave a legacy of conscience, clarity, responsible research, rhetorical power" (McKale, 2002, 156).

According to critic Karen Castellucci Cox, Allende ventures to the "edges of the story, at the margin where women, immigrants, and supplanted natives can have their stories told" (Cox, 2003, 26). In *Daughter of Fortune*, the author enlarges on the need for wit and guile in the life of the *huacho/huacha*, a Quechua colloquialism for kinless orphan, foundling, or bastard. In Argentina and Chile, speakers wield the term as a pejorative for a child of dubious parentage. Without thought to the birth and reclamation of Eliza in the Sommers household, Mama Fresia laments that Eliza's pregnancy by Joaquín Andieta will end in rejection for "a child of the gutter," the stereotypical classification of baseborn children in Victorian social novels (Allende, 1999, 128). To heighten the ill fortune of Eliza's fetus, the text reduces its stillbirth to a "bloody little mollusk," a dehumanization that ends Eliza's fears for her child (*ibid.*, 205).

In a secondary plot of *Zorro*, Allende examines the ability of Creoles to thrive within refined "white Americans only" society (Ries, 2011, 4). She pictures the Haitian buccaneer Jean Lafitte settling among bumptious Americans in the Territory of Texas, a region populated by proud dynasties as well as by misfits, transients, and ruffians like Jean's brother Pierre. Critic Olga Ries describes the successful adaptation of the pirate king to mainstream America as a national subversion of snobbery and racism, "an undercurrent since its very beginnings" (Ries, 2011, 4). Although Jean is a villain of "breathtaking vices ... a womanizer, a criminal, a smuggler, and slave trafficker," he changes his name and adopts the pose of respectable husband and father of eight (Allende, 2005, 323, 296). Thus, Ries concludes, Allende's canon and its staged marginality "represent products for an international market ... of interest to a large readership in several languages" (*ibid.*, 8).

For *Island Beneath the Sea*, Allende invests New Orleans with a similar ability to absorb varied social castes into a viable port city. She sets in the outer rim of respectability such minor figures as mulatta seamstress Adèle, casino owner Fleur Hirondelle, slave cook Loula, and voodoo priestesses Tante Rose and Sanité Dédé. Males, too, occupy unconventional social roles, from abolitionist Harrison Cobb to the historic figures of Toussaint L'Ouverture's brother Jean-Jacques and General François Dessalines and Portuguese pirate captain Romeiro Toledano, who officiates at the off-shore union of an incestuous couple. In each case, the outcasts perform some essential service, as with Toledano's rescue of runaway slaves by sea and Cobb's initiation of Maurice into abolitionist philosophy.

Key to the fictional accommodation of variant castes, Père Antoine, the Spanish Capuchin pastor of the New Orleans cathedral, becomes the city's adored saint and racial ombudsman. An aged prelate with rough features and soiled clothing, he resolves human dilemmas, notably, the inclusion of nonwhite worshippers in Sunday services, the feeding of the poor in hospitals and jail cells, counsel to orphans and the despairing, tolerator of Jews and heretics, and welcomer of whores and beggars at his ministerial abode. As valuable to interracial discourse as Dr. Parmentier to a host of multicultural patients, the priest ventures into social taboos brandishing an ecumenical spirit and the tolerance of a peacemaker. After a hurricane, he organizes "a procession with the Most Holy in the lead and no one dared make fun of that method for dominating the climate" to ward off epidemics (Allende, 2010, 280). His intervention in potentially explosive issues of emancipation enables Tété to force her owner, Toulouse Valmorain, into a public humiliation of signing her freedom papers. The act, for its chutzpah, equates with the force of Toussaint L'Ouverture in negotiations with the French for Haitian liberation.

See also prostitution

• *References and Further Reading*

Correas de Zapata, Celia. *Isabel Allende: Life and Spirits*. Houston, TX: Arte Público, 2002.
Cox, Karen Castellucci. *Isabel Allende, a Critical Companion*. Westport, CT: Greenwood, 2003.
Davies, Lloyd. *Allende: La casa de los espíritus*. London: Grant & Cutler, 2000
McKale, Margaret A. Morales. *Literary Nonfiction in Works by Isabel Allende and Guadalupe Loaeza*. Columbus: Ohio State University, 2002.
Ries, Olga. "Latino Identity in Allende's Novels," *Comparative Literature and Culture* 13:4 (2011): 1–8.
Schroeder, Shannin. *Rediscovering Magical Realism in the Americas*. Westport, CT: Praeger, 2004.
Shaw, Donald Leslie. *A Companion to Modern Spanish-American Fiction*. Rochester, NY: Tamesis, 2002.
Wilkinson, Marta L. *Antigone's Daughters: Gender, Family, and Expression in the Modern Novel*. New York: Peter Lang, 2008.

marriage

Allende's ideal pairings imply a transcendent union between a man and woman destined to complete each other's lives and balance their foibles with virtues, as with the fantasy romance created by Doctor Mario and Señora Tosca in the story "Tosca" and the ethereal union of a rainforest warrior and Ila woman in "Walimai." Happy unions echo similar strains, notably, the shipboard marriage of Ana to Roberto Blaum in "Interminable Life" and the tender alliances of Professor Leal with his injured wife Hilda and of Digna with Hipólito Ranquileo, whose clown costume she repairs in *Of Love and Shadows*. The ideal, however, founders under tyranny and patriarchy, which destroys the hopes of men like Javier Leal and negates freedom of choice to women like Blanca del Valle, the pregnant aristocrat whom her father trades to Jean de Satigny as damaged goods. In *Daughter of Fortune*, the author generalizes the failure of a union in a lifeless bond held firm by

Roman Catholic dogma. Allende depicts a faithless womanizer, Agustín del Valle, and his dowdy, respectable wife made "tremulous and hangdog" from a life of "virtue, faith, and abnegation" (Allende, 1999, 41). For their sons, destiny promises the carousing and indulgence that marks Agustín's life. For their daughters, the future holds out more of the same that his wife endures— the hypocritical "marriage of convenience and motherhood" (*ibid.*).

From a feminist perspective, Allende ponders the idealized union, a serene life of husband and wife that fills the fantasies of Tao Chi'en in *Daughter of Fortune*. The text predicates successful wedlock in the romance of Quaker blacksmith James Morton with Esther, an eighteen-year-old runaway from a fanatic father. Esther travels in Joe Bonecrusher's caravan, a rolling brothel modeled on the frontier prostitution in the short stories of Bret Harte, the film *Buffalo Girls*, and Larry McMurtry's novel *Lonesome Dove*. As a wife and future mother, Esther discovers that, with James as husband, "peace lighted her like a halo" (Allende, 1999, 354). The same contentment takes longer to ally Tao Chi'en with Eliza Sommers, who searches two years for her first love, "an increasingly improbable chimera" (*ibid.*, 360). The winsome relationship in the closing chapters predicts success to mates of disparate races far from what editor Michael Sollars calls "a society driven and governed by class consciousness in Chile," where families plot "advantageous marriage" based on social and economic suitability (Sollars, 2008, 1999). Instead, long shots like James's gamble on Esther and Tao's infatuation with Eliza produce viable unions unaffected by previous misalliances.

To eradicate the pat wedlock of romance novels, in *Eva Luna*, the text satirizes the *telenovela* for glossing over human differences and marital compromise. Allende reduces to sappy cliché "a single kiss that led to the ecstasy of the paradise of no return: matrimony" (Allende, 1987, 152–153). While learning to read, Eva compresses the elements of literary romance into plots revealed in full by page three. To dramatize more realistic obstacles to marital bliss, she conceives of a female gun runner and a man who goes to India to treat leprosy. The young storyteller's training ground, *A Thousand and One Nights*, presents modules of human behavior that she swaps and transfers from plot to plot, adjusting details and anecdotes to suit innovation for characters who "were neither good-looking nor rich" (*ibid.*, 256).

The Perfect and Imperfect

An essential of the popular romances in Linda Lael Miller's *Don't Look* series and Nora Roberts's *Bridal Quartet*, altar vows strip brutes of aggression and sexual adventuring and refine them for mating with appealingly spirited, intellectual women, for example, Alba with Miguel in *The House of the Spirits*, Juan de Málaga with Inés Suarez in *Inés of My Soul*, and Huberto Naranjo with the title figure in *Eva Luna*. Exemplary mating offers the flawed male an opportunity to develop commitment, loyalty, and fatherly concerns. Critic Vincent Kling pictures the optimal union as a spontaneous relationship, a mystic alchemical "fusion of opposites that must attract because neither can be complete without the other" (Kling, 2010, 250). Less sanitized than the impractical courtly love of medieval chevaliers and their ladies, the result of romantic alliance suits the intent of domestic writer to promote connubial love and family, held together by "the bonds of affection and mutual assistance" like that of herbalist Tao Chi'en and his wife/assistant, Eliza Sommers (Allende, 1993, 361).

Examples of unlikely matings in *Zorro* allow Alejandro de la Vega to make a life commitment to the Indian warrior Grey Wolf/Regina; similarly, in *Island Beneath the Sea*,

Major Etienne Relais amazes his comrades by wedding the former courtesan Violette Boisier, "one of questionable reputation" (Allende, 2010, 123). After the first glance at Violette, Etienne realizes "he could never tear that girl of honey and silk from his soul" (*ibid.*, 16). Regardless of racial or social disparity, he marries the "woman of color ... and went out with her on his arm with no concern for malicious tongues" (*ibid.*, 169). Less tidy, the union of Feliciano Rodríguez de Santa Cruz with Paulina del Valle in *Portrait in Sepia* results from mutual lust and unfettered passions. As a token of Feliciano's vigor, the text pictures an inverse of the guardian angel, the tattoo of a blue dragon on his shoulder that goads him to daring sensuality with Amanda Lowell. After years of marriage, Allende notes, at age sixty, his "aging scoundrel's heart still fluttered at the scent of a conquest" (Allende, 2001, 58).

The failure of the ideal in the marriage of Esteban Trueba and Clara del Valle in *The House of the Spirits* results from the pairing of a young girl with a rough miner fifteen years her senior and from her attempt to gentle a willful spirit coarsened by manual labor and masculine debauchery. After an earthquake destroys their country estate fifteen years into the marriage, Esteban observes Clara's distancing from intimacy, capped by the bolt she installs on her bedroom door. He notes that years of living together results in extensive awareness: "Each had the exact geography of the other at our fingertips" (Allende, 1985, 210). He admits that his "sour temper of the daytime" rules out nightly amour, but his yearning for physical contact perpetuates the ardor he felt on their honeymoon (*ibid.*, 211).

To enhance the disengagement of husband from wife, Allende describes Esteban's spiritual and physical shrinkage, a touch of magical realism easily explained by the knitting of broken bones and the normal skeletal settling brought on by aging. As remorse begins to dawn for his youthful sins, Esteban admits that "his ideas were also probably withering away," a preface to his reclamation in old age (*ibid.*, 282). With a disconcerting touch, he compares himself to Napoleon and Hitler, both great, but short politicians. In secret, Clara ponders a more distressing marital conundrum in the "commercial arrangement" that allies her firstborn with Jean de Satigny, a French schemer bearing a "silent-movie-idol manner" that the text implies is both ambiguous and decadent from his secretive photography and use of cocaine and opium (*ibid.*, 284).

In the background of working relationships, the author sympathizes with the battle-scarred wife, such as Doña Eulalia de Callís in *Zorro*, the devalued wife of Governor Pedro Fages "known as The Bear because of his bad temper" (Allende, 2005, 10). The governor proffers his own perspective on their union by describing the fits with which Eulalia torments him. The author chooses sides by having Pedro fly into a rage, "[collapse] like a sack," and die at her feet in a spontaneous act of poetic justice (*ibid.*, 40). As literary foils to the governor and his wife, the author admires the simple loyalty of Gypsies Amalia and Ramón, who share travel, hunger, and suspicion of *gadje* (outsiders). Allende recommends the high point of their union: "They celebrated at the slightest excuse" (*ibid.*, 151). In addition to affection and trust, the author poses fun as an additional requirement for marital longevity.

From experience, Allende must acknowledge the gradual dimming of passion as marriages weaken over time and distance. In picturing Regina and Alejandro de la Vega, the text blames separation by day for the cooling of intimacies by night. Further degrading the marital bond, Regina regrets her husband's "chiseled-in-stone ideas," particularly his distaste for mestizos, a pejorative that ironically describes their son Diego (Allende, 2005, 71–72). Less advisable, the union of tennis fanatic Samantha Ernst with law student Gregory Reeves in *The Infinite Plan* characterizes the failure of a self-absorbed socialite to appreciate the qualities of Greg, a war veteran and devoted father to their daughter Margaret. A more virulent pairing, Toulouse Valmorain with Hortense Guizot in *Island Beneath the Sea*, fails because the egotistical bride "never doubted that she would trap Valmorain," an attitude prefacing her paralysis of the household economy, Hortense's eavesdropping on Toulouse, and her dislike of Maurice, her stepson (Allende, 2010, 268). Even Sancho, the matchmaker, regrets that Toulouse marries a devious woman.

HISTORIC ARRANGEMENTS

At a coming to knowledge in *Inés of My Soul*, Allende dramatizes the Renaissance marriage of convenience as a sham imposed by Bishop Pedro de la Gasca, the mouthpiece for Charles V and a mockery of New Laws of 1542 to cloak the fornication and usurpation of conquistadors in South America. The text lauds Inés's flexibility in turning the debacle into a marriage for love. To attain affection, she trusts tasty food and satisfying sex, the mystic combination that Allende lauds in *Aphrodite*. Mutual affection awards Inés a blessing and the mature "joy of feeling loved," an abundance reflected in the 300 attendees at her wedding and the outlay of wines and foods on the reception tables (Allende, 2006, 256). Ensuing marital bliss derives in part from the need of Rodrigo de Quiroga for his wife's advice and counsel and for her training in carnal pleasures. With her innate sense of comic gender differences, Inés asserts that "men, like dogs and horses, have to be domesticated" (*ibid.*, 263). Her delight in sensuality mocks the prissiness of Marina, Valdivia's wife, who wears the traditional nightgown with a keyhole embroidered like a Christian cross over her pudenda.

Athwart the ridiculous mating rituals of Europe, Allende poses the pagan passions of Mapuche couples, Felipe/Lautaro with Guacolda and Caupolicán with Fresia. In place of gallantries and gift giving, the native Romeos impress their Juliets with hardihood and endurance. Under the guise of stableboy Felipe, Lautaro outrages the Spaniards and dashes naked into the river and through the forest to reunite with Guacolda, his long-time adviser and consort. Lautaro admits to mutual possession: "he belongs to her, just as she belongs to him" (Allende, 2006, 271). To win Fresia and unite his people, Caupolicán shoulders an oak trunk while reciting an incantation predicting the long Araucan War against the advancing Spaniards. Fresia washes her lover with wet rabbit hides and offers water and bites of chewed food, symbolic domestic aid to sustain him during the ordeal. The epic standards of these love stories puts to shame the political and economic betrothals of Europeans—Doña Eulalia de Callís and Governor Pedro Fages, Count Jean de Satigny and Blanca del Valle—based on financial and social advancement.

The complex social layering of *Island Beneath the Sea* bases the author's views of marriage on exigency. Despite critic Naomi Daremblum's complaint of a "Harlequin quality" to the gynocentric plot, Allende wins readers and critics to a sweeping saga that ventures two generations beyond the Haitian Revolution (Daremblum, 2010). In New Orleans, Dr. Parmentier allies openly with the seamstress Adèle, a mate whom law prevents him from marrying. He explains, "My wife's name is Adèle. She is not exactly my wife—you take my meaning, yes? But we have been together many years" (Allende, 2010, 169). Fortunately, upon relocation to New Orleans, Parmentier realizes he "did not have to resort to unworthy strategies" of living apart and creeping into Adèle's bed each night (*ibid.*, 350). More important to equity, the two share opinions and value each other's professions, a basis on which their marriage thrives.

The prevalent imbalance of whites and mulattos requires an intellectual solution. Upon the emergence of Rosette from the Ursuline convent, Violette, whom reviewer Corrie Pikul calls a "biracial Becky Sharp," determines to rescue the fifteen-year-old from a chancy alliance with a white lover (Pikul, 2010). With the help of seamstress Adèle, slave Loula, and heroine Tété, Violette readies Rosette for *plaçage*, an illicit arrangement, because she has "neither money nor good family" (Allende, 2010, 366). Plaçage teeters on a balance of needs and satisfactions of "young whites with a fortune, and those seriously interested" in "left-handed marriage" (*ibid.*, 368, 313). Allende compares the system to African polygamy and notes the priority of love for offspring over loyalty to mate. For scheming mulattas, the need to protect tender mixed-blood daughters from violence and rape takes precedence over alliances based on prestige or money.

Until national emancipation on January 1, 1863, the New Orleans's invitation-only *Bal de Cordon Bleu* suffices as an elegant debutante ball that secures introductions for proud quadroon girls to wealthy Creole males. The arrangement satisfies both parties, who were ambitious and "wanted their descendants to prosper" (Allende, 2010, 365). The ensuing cohabitation respects a contract of honor based on threats of social ruination if mulatta mothers discover their daughters abandoned to poverty. Although the system began in the 1740s, Allende situates the founding of the business arrangement in 1803 as a result of the Louisiana Purchase and incipient Americanization of a Creole society. From a mulatta's view, Violette validates the social covenant by commenting that "for once, the whites will have to accept our conditions" (*ibid.*, 367).

Balancing the cynicism of a parade of nubile girls for sale to white-gloved bidders, the novel accords respect to stable marriages, such as the ongoing love of Violette for her French husband, Major Etienne Relais, who died in the Haitian conflict. Tété's romance with Zacharie, the casino owner who previously taught her elegant manners, nearly capsizes after the author dims the husband's handsome appeal following a fight with street scrappers, who slice his face and blind one eye. In the novel's resolution, Tété, at age 40, continues to bear children for her mate as testimonials to their ongoing romance. More discreet, the longstanding relationship between the seamstress Adèle and Dr. Parmentier sets a stronger precedent for the biracial union so common in New Orleans society. Allende honors the couple's loyalty with Adèle's proclamation that she will never again endure separation from her white lover.

See also humor; women

• *References and Further Reading*

Daremblum, Naomi. "Not Magical, Not Realism," *New Republic* (28 April 2010).

Kling, Vincent. "Archetype, Not Ideology: Isabel Allende's Balance of Opposites," *Critical Insights* (October 2010): 239–257.

Pikul, Corrie. "Review: *Island Beneath the Sea*," *Elle* (9 April 2010).

Sollars, Michael D. *The Facts on File Companion to the World Novel, 1900 to the Present*. New York: Facts on File, 2008.

materialism

Allende's writings capitalize on the worst of human foibles, notably acquisitiveness and greed. Materialism motivates protectors of museum treasures in "The Guggenheim Lovers" and inspires the greeters of the Pope in "Clarisa" to sell T-shirts, plastic saints, and hair from the pontiff's head. The grifters Abigail McGovern and Domingo Toro perfect con games in "The Proper Respect"; Indians in the Amazon jungle lust after steel tools and weapons in *City of the Beasts.* In the latter work, money buys prestige and governmental influence, the protectors of Mauro Carías, an exploiter of the Amazon's gold, jewels, and lumber. The author silences him and ends his predations with living death, a convalescence on life support, a chilling retribution for an amoral predator.

In the sequel, *Kingdom of the Golden Dragon*, the description of the Collector revisits the vast acquisitiveness of villains in James Bond films. Allende slants the scenario of ownership for ownership's sake from condemnation to satire by ridiculing a list of treasures that include Einstein's brain and the famed Coca-Cola formula. Reverence for the *objet d'art* in the title discloses the fallacy in hoarding by depicting the bejeweled dragon jealously guarded by monarchs who deny access to their subjects. The author's condemnation of materialism finds voice in Nadia, who feels dizzy and asphyxiated in a palace, where a maharajah's ornamentation gives "no place for your eyes to take a rest" (Allende, 2004, 99). The theme of greed takes on theological significance in Alex's description of Buddhist self-denial, a practice with which Nadia instinctively identifies.

Allende allows characters to speak her loathing for greed. A Mapuche shaman in *Daughter of Fortune* describes avarice as the worst of obsessions, a psychological truth displayed by white usurpers of the jungle in "Walimai," in which the despoilers disrespect nature by amassing a fortune in minerals, rubber, and wood with the aid of press gangs. The story epitomizes oneness with living things in Walimai's release of the Ila concubine from torment to send her spirit to "the land of souls" (Allende, 1991, 133). The arrival of the former slave with the Ila woman's spirit into "the silence of time" precedes the release of her soul, a sacrificial act that Walimai endows with awe and veneration (*ibid.*, 134). A more ghoulish story of greed derives from "The Road North," a tale of a mother's wish for a comfortable life for her son Juan. The decline of the pipe dream into an horrendous example of North American inhumanity draws on media accounts of traffic in human organs removed from unwitting children.

After the death of her daughter Paula, the author began confiding to interviewers the importance of trust, conciliation, and acceptance of loss. The harrowing illness that Allende attempted to forestall taught her the importance of destiny. Her old friend and colleague John Rodden recognized that she embraced the long journey of her life as evidence that she "shouldn't cling to life and the world so much ... to the material aspects of the world" (Rodden, 2010, 185). From a mature perspective, the author became more detached from objects and less prone to live for the temporal world. Surrendering to eventual separation from loved ones, Allende accepted that all possessions, all ambitions remain behind when the spirit moves on to a higher plane.

Possessions and Spirit

From her first publication, Allende contrasts spirituality with materialism. In *The House of the Spirits*, the bewitching nature of luxury infects Esteban Trueba in young manhood. Like the misguided protagonist in Willa Cather's story "Paul's Case," Esteban longs for "the small comforts that made him feel rich" (Allende, 1985, 62). Beguiled by the dining room of the Hotel Francés, the boy risks 50 centavos for a Viennese coffee, served by waiters in a goblet and topped with whipped cream and a glazed cherry. His humiliation for destroying the thin glass with a tap of the spoon foreshadows his life's goal to mine for gold and enrich himself enough to pose as an aristocrat, a false persona that leads to disillusion and downfall.

In a pagan environment, Esteban's life at Las Tres Marías centers on his belief that land survives "when everything else is gone" (Allende, 1985, 60). His words prove prophetic as he tours the ruins of the house and resolves to press his tenants into the task of restoring grandeur to the Trueba name. Before marrying Clara del Valle, Esteban imposes elegant architectural standards—German stained glass, Austrian moldings, bronze faucets, Italian marble, American locks—on the home that will house his lineage. Luxury proves worthless in establishing happiness to a man who values only outward shows of columns, French topiaries, and Turkish rugs. The lighting, suitably called "teardrop chandeliers," like the ones in Allende's grandfather's mansion, later crashes during the earthquake, the crystal tears symbolically elicited to weep for mass destruction and death (Allende, 1985, 114). The loss includes the demise of Nana with her hair on end and eyes popped out and the end of Pedro Tercero's patience with peonage.

Allende foregrounds the fall of the Trueba ideal in the arrival of Clara and Blanca to their country home. After investing in a palatial town home on a corner lot in the capital, Esteban initiates a façade of middle-class gentility while maintaining his country manse, the setting dark with carnal sins. Blanca prefigures her eventual fall from grace by stripping naked to play outdoors in mud with Pedro Tercero, a prophetic alliance of the classes in innocent fun reminiscent of Adam and Eve in the Garden of Eden. The text marks the children's embrace and predicts their future fornication when "a whole lifetime would not be long enough for their atonement" (Allende, 1985, 127).

The author stresses the nature of change, which so alters the estate over its 18-month reconstruction that Esteban loses his former status as its builder and master. He admits that the gaudy furnishings he purchases fail to survive the earthquake, a divine intrusion in the plan of the *patrón* that makes way for modernism. In place of outworn European decor, Pedro Segundo and Clara oversee installation of modern amenities—hot water, kerosene heaters, and a telephone, technological advances that precede revolution. Troubled by the distancing of his wife and daughter during the rebuilding, Allende challenges Esteban faith that, by returning to the finery of his town home, his notion of civilized living will restore family harmony. Meanwhile, he orders replacement furnishings for Las Tres Marías, significantly "colonial pieces" that regenerate his arrogance (Allende, 1985, 205). More damaging to the del Valle-Trueba dynasty, Esteban arranges Blanca's marriage in the European manner, an acquisition of a titled aristocrat for Esteban's son-in-law. The deception of Count Jean de Satigny requires a variety of materialistic equipage, from his silk bathroom, velvet jackets, Tyrolean hats, and effete shoes to his Lebanese cigarettes and games of croquet, a term ironically derived from the peasant shepherd's crook. Blanca, at age 24, refuses to warm to a marriage proposal and goes through the motions of living large in Satigny's manse until the birth of her mestizo daughter, irrefutable proof that the marriage is a sham.

For *Of Love and Shadows*, Allende expresses Beatriz Alcántara's aristocratic notions through her exquisite taste in furnishing and Oriental rugs. As a touch of satire, the author pictures Beatriz's husband, Eusebio Beltrán, striving to maintain a lordly façade on the house to ensure respect from neighbors who might misjudge Beatriz for operating the Will of God Manor, a rest home for the elderly. As a token of public insult, the garbage and excrement dumped on Beatriz's bed expresses suspicion about the family's disgrace caused by Eusebio's disappearance. In secret, she affords the "airs of a duchess" by selling pieces of silver, paintings, and jewelry for needed cash (Allende, 1987, 40–41). To prepare daughter Irene for marriage, Beatriz stocks a hope chest with "English china with bird motifs, embroidered Dutch table linens, French silk lingerie ... Belgian laces, Japanese silks, Irish linens, Scottish wools" and other luxuries that have no bearing on the troubled relationship between the creative journalist and her fiancé, a strict warrior (*ibid.*, 100). For Irene, marriage to a pillar of militarism becomes unthinkable; to Beatriz, the fact that "the heroic military had been forced" to wipe out Marxism justifies the flow of goods and services to the elite (*ibid.*, 221).

Possessions as Symbols

Detailed descriptions of dwellings, food, clothing, and personal possessions texturize *Daughter of Fortune* with a contrast in status and economic levels. During the rise of Tao Chi'en to a respected acupuncturist, he invests in quality clothing as evidence of his serious purpose, but he avoids the acquisitiveness of whites, who lack "food for the spirit" (Allende, 1999, 319). Allende contrasts his frugality with the burst of British demand for Chinoiserie in screens, fans, porcelain, ivory, and Asian trinkets, a material appetite that fuels the East-West trade of Jeremy Sommers. The arrival of Paulina del Valle to San Francisco with 93 trunks precedes her dismantled house and its accoutrements—wallpaper, harp, lamps, porcelains, and piano, all setting an aristocratic tone in their new location in "the most important city of the Pacific" (*ibid.*, 323). She speaks the author's belief that disreputable founders have the most reason to revere respectability, a belief justified by the history of Australia.

Of the settlement of Chile in *Inés of My Soul*, the protagonist harbors no illusions of altruism in New World colonists. To her idealistic lover, Général Pedro de Valdivia, she asserts, "Men go where there is wealth, not glory alone" (Allende, 2006, 233). The text corroborates her statement with the enthusiasm of short-term colonists who long to take their gold and return to Spain to display New World fortunes. Among them, Padre González de Marmolejo amasses a treasure that breaches the priestly vow of poverty. Under the guise of employing a Quechuan servant, he also transgresses his oath of chastity by coupling with a concubine. Allende forgives in part the priest's avarice and concupiscence because he enriches himself on the crossbreeding of stout, resilient Chilean horses.

Portrait in Sepia expresses the author's flair for excess through the acquisitiveness of Paulina del Valle, the owner of a line of refrigerated ships and a carved Florentine bed. Under the name "Cross," which replaces Rodriguez de Santa Cruz y del Valle, the exhibitionist grandmother sets up a mansion on Nob Hill that Allende calls "a delirium" (Allende, 2001, 6). More insidious, the "fortune-grubbing" priest "sniffing out the wealthy on their deathbeds" unites Allende's distaste for avarice with her intolerance for religious hypocrisy, which reaches a height in "that old augurer of fatalities," a "grumbly old man with an odor of sanctity" (*ibid.*, 244, 190, 188). To protect Aurora del Valle from the clutches of church and family rivals, Matías Rodríguez de Santa Cruz works out a plan with Severo del Valle to ensure the child's inheritance of her just portion of the family fortune. The salvation of wronged females takes a more desperate tone in the description of singsong girls, the Chinese slaves salvaged from auctions through the monetary manipulations of Donaldina and Martha, Presbyterian missionaries. In contrast to the pernicious nuns and priests who filch from Paulina's house, the rescuers apply another type of guile to retrieve victimized Chinese girls "even if we have to hack down the doors of those dens of evil" (*ibid.*, 294).

The inheritance from a life of materialism freights the falling action of *The Infinite Plan*. After suffering a massive anxiety attack, attorney Gregory Reeves realizes how the excesses of the past leave him vulnerable to the emotional punishments that come late in life. Central to his regrets lie the fragmented lives of his addicted daughter Margaret and hyperactive son David. Through therapy with Dr. Ming O'Brien, Greg recognizes a destructive pattern in the upbringing of his children, who "had grown up like savages" (Allende, 1993, 373). Awash in money and privileges but deprived of parental affection, both Margaret and David require a late-in-life socialization to strip them of false values.

Colonial Values

According to critic Bernadette Murphy, *Island Beneath the Sea* "fully [penetrates] the world in which the slave rebellion took place" on Haiti in 1791 (Murphy, 2010). Allende uses characterization of a fictional cast to understand enslavers' mindsets and "to sense viscerally the drive for human dignity that impelled [slaves] to freedom" (*ibid.*) A minor figure, mentor Harrison Cobb, captures the moral tone of the era with his cynical belief that "decency quickly succumbs before greed," a mode of fortune hunting instilled by the French monarchy into speculators vying with the Spanish for New World treasure and real estate (Allende, 2010, 379). Central to the novel, the arrival of young Toulouse Valmorain to his father's plantation reveals how quickly the lust for wealth and social position seizes the mind and obliterates past loyalties, notably, Toulouse's interest in his mother and sister left behind in France.

At the destruction of Habitation Saint-Lazare, Allende reveals Valmorain's ornamental extremes acquired by an "orgy of spending" (Allende 2010, 33). As hundreds of Maroons assault by dawn light, they swarm the family manse, destroying Chinese screens, Dutch tapestry, Spanish chests, German clocks, Roman statues, and Venetian mirrors, the typical glut of exhibitionism in European plantations. Like the cavorting figures in Edgar Allan Poe's story "The Masque of the Red Death" and the self-pleasuring of Becky Sharp during the waning Napoleonic era in William Makepeace Thackeray's *Vanity Fair*, French islanders delude themselves that parties, bingeing, whoring, and evenings at the theater can restore the fading glory of colonial Haiti.

The text focuses on Valmorain's foppery in his effort to recover the illusion of nobility. After the United States invests in the Louisiana Purchase, he secures a French cook, viewing his investment as likely to yield returns. The planter dreams of restoring his wait staff to white gloves and his burned-out property to productivity. To ensure fastidious obeisance to European grandeur, he enrolls Tété under a mentor, Zacharie, majordomo at the Intendance, and hires Monsieur Adrien to superintend a fifteen-course dinner party. After seven years of servitude beyond the date of her manumission, Tété asks Père Antoine about the terms of her freedom from a sybarite. Faced with the implacability of a Capuchin saint, Valmorain attempts to discredit the document liberating Tété and her daughter Rosette. Allende pictures the Sunday morning discussion of rights as a model of "divine intervention" (Allende, 2010, 328). Ultimately, the church becomes the only power strong enough to disarm the vain, acquisitive Valmorain, whom *Kirkus Reviews* exonerates as "a man of his time" ("Review," 2010).

- *References and Further Reading*

Murphy, Bernadette. "Review: *Island Beneath the Sea*," *Los Angeles Times* (14 May 2010).
"Review: *Island Beneath the Sea*," *Kirkus Reviews* 78:7 (1 April 2010).
Rodden, John. "Isabel Allende, Fortune's Daughter," *Critical Insights* (October 2010): 184–194.

migration literature

Allende paints the global diaspora as a rush of "humans fleeing violence or poverty ... to start a new life," a description of her own self-exile from Chile to Venezuela in 1975 (Allende, 2003, 187). She studies the losses and gains of fellow travelers to new lands, whether a New World heir in *Zorro* journeying to tutelage in Spain and first wave Chinese in San Francisco in *Daughter of Fortune* or nomadic laborers supporting socialism in *The House of the Spirits* and conquistadors from Peru usurping Chile from Mapuche Indians in *Inés of My Soul*. In the story "A Discreet Miracle," the author characterizes a slow assimilation of the British Boulton clan from Liverpool, who cling to language and the custom of tea drinking and wearing tweed until "a commingling with local blood had diluted their arrogance" (Allende, 1991, 253). As a result of intermarriage, the Boultons accept local names— the widow Filomena, the poet Gilberto, and Padre Miguel, a priest — rather than their heritage of Anglo-Saxon Christian names. Of the trio, Miguel sympathizes with indigenous problems, notably, the loss of the *desaparecidos* and the hunger strikes of dissidents.

In the introduction to *My Invented Country*, Allende admits that she, too, has been "an exile and an immigrant," a personal experience with shifting places and cultures that strengthens her writing (Allende, 2003, x). After considering the role of nostalgia in her texts, she explained her purpose: "I write as a constant exercise in longing," the task of an outsider, a pilgrim trying to return home (*ibid.*, xi). In the story "Interminable Life," she remarks on the lasting effect of statelessness of Ana and Roberto Blaum, escapees from anti–Semitism in Europe, in "the feeling of insecurity so common among exiles" (Allende, 1991, 240). The statement echoes the sentiment of Professor Leal in *Of Love and Shadows*, where he is "able to express every passion except the one that clawed at his soul" (Allende, 1987, 125). His wife Hilda, however, chooses "not to burden herself with ancient woes" (*ibid.*, 27).

Victims and Exigencies

Allende weaves into fiction the departures and returns forced by circumstance. At the end of World War I in *The House of the* Spirits, trains bring the war dead as well as immigrants "fleeing the hunger back home, stunned by the roar of the bombs," a fearful diaspora reprised by the French from Haiti to Cuba and New Orleans in *Island Beneath the Sea* (Allende, 1985, 860). World War II brings an unusual outsider, Count Jean de Satigny, a foppish esthete who contrasts the ragged post-war arrivals from Central Europe, Armenia, and Turkey. In "The Proper Respect," the influx of outsiders erases the clear demarcation of social classes: "It was no longer possible to ascertain the ancestry of every individual" (Allende, 1991, 230). Analyst Mel Boland accepts the author's interest in the shuffling of world peoples as "an expected progression in her work" given her peripatetic life and experience with self-exile from terrorism (Boland, 2003, 477).

On the subject of nationhood and absolute borders, Allende agrees with author Leslie Marmon Silko that boundaries invite breaches. Allende promotes fictional "traversals of the boundaries [that] have traditionally separated people," whether caste, culture, gender, race, or religion, as with the successful travels of Muslim peddler Riad Halabí in *Eva Luna* and the flight of Francisco Leal and Irene Beltrán to Spain in *Of Love and Shadows* (Levine, 2010, 220). In the ship bound for Chile in *Inés of My Soul*, the text depicts a nomadic class occupying the second-class cabins and stocking their hearts with hope. Among them, critic Olga Ries singles out a Croatian doctor and his son who evolve into

Chile's "scientific elite" (Ries, 2011, 6). Ries identifies the emergent "urbanity and cosmopolitanism" for welcoming independent female entrepreneurs and adventurers (*ibid.*).

In *The Infinite Plan*, Allende's cultural reportage commiserates with socially excluded Central American and Mexican newcomers whom border patrols and police harass and employers exploit and persecute. Depicted as third-class undesirables, "wire-cuttin wetbacks" who swim the Rio Grande, they fantasize about reclaiming property lost to them by the 1848 Treaty of Guadalupe Hidalgo (Allende, 1987, 41). However, by migrating from lesser nations to an industrial superpower, "They are no longer anachronisms; by arriving in the United States, they have joined the future" (McKale, 2002, 151). Allende pictures the U.S. home territory of Chicanos as "a citadel within the city, a rough, impoverished ghetto born of spontaneous growth around an industrial zone where illegal immigrants could be employed without anyone's asking questions" (Allende, 1993, 69). Descriptive passages envision a barrio teeming with womanizing, gambling, substance abuse, labor infractions, and fatalism. Among the survivors, mechanic Pedro Morales embraces residency in southern California because "he did not want to retrace the footsteps of his father and grandfather, impoverished *campesinos* on a hacienda in Zacatecas" (*ibid.*, 42).

The author makes use of newcomers as witnesses to idiosyncrasies of a foreign clime. By selecting Jacob Todd as the perspective for scenes in *Daughter of Fortune*, Allende attunes the reader's impressions of Valparaíso, Chile, to those of a startled Englishman unaccustomed to humidity and intestinal complaints. Ironically, while Todd hobnobs with elite Englishmen at the Club de la Unión, he profits from his position as a newcomer proposing the rescue of heathen Chilean Indians. After Anglicans welcome him to their gatherings, Todd speaks of Jewish refugees in a strange land to preface an anecdote about proselytizing Patagonian natives, whom Jeremy Sommers describes as "ripe to be evangelized" (Allende, 1999, 18). Sommers rules out preaching to the Araucans, who have dwindled in number since the Hispanic conquest. He also comments on attempts of settlers to conceal shameful traces of Indian blood: "The government is trying to improve the race by importing European immigrants" (*ibid.*, 20). Sommers further makes light of Indian sufferings by describing murder as a "favorite sport" of colonists (*ibid.*).

Recovery in a New Land

After the chaos of the Haitian Revolution of 1791 in *Island Beneath the Sea*, migration rescues French colonists from hordes of black rebels. After the slave victory over Napoleon's troops, European émigrés, "shrunken and impoverished," keep arriving from Le Cap to Cuba and Louisiana "in a sad dribble" (Allende, 2010, 260). Buoyed or crushed by foreign news, they cluster at the Café des Émigrés for news of the status of the French monarchy, Napoleon's victories, and the progress of the revolt in Haiti, where they hope to return (*ibid.*, 284). Ill-gotten pesos keep Toulouse Valmorain in luxury, which he rationalizes as his due after he buries the remains of Lacroix, the rightful owner. Crucial to the sail from Cuba to the Mississippi Delta, new clothes present the Valmorain household as "investors, not refugees," a distinction that furthers the sewing career of Adèle while erasing from the planter the failures of the past (Allende, 2010, 232). To reinstate Valmorain's role as a successful French sugar planter, he funds a new plantation a day's drive from New Orleans, a second chance that allows him to atone for barbarities against Africans that he allowed under overseer Prosper Cambray.

Consistent with the aspirations of newcomers, Allende's émigrés long for a piece of the American dream. For slaves, a bit of garden outside the French quarter enables families to work for their own rewards. Leanna and Owen Murphy and their brood of seven children echo the aim of blacks and free mulattoes to save enough to buy land. For Dr. Parmentier, his concubine Adèle, and Violette Boisiers, life among scornful Havanans relegate the refugees to the French community, where survivors of mass murder make do on savings, renting out slaves, or working agricultural acreage. Allende pities the "ruined people" for their relegation to barrios, where they endure the harassment of Spanish officials and the disapproval of Cuban society (Allende, 2010, 309). The solution to the trio's quandary is emigration to the "flourishing society of free people of color in New Orleans," a multicultural, multiracial haven unique in North American history (*ibid.*, 312).

See also San Francisco

• *References and Further Reading*

Boland, Mel. "'Orienting' the Text: Eastern Influences in the Fiction of Isabel Allende" in *Cross-Cultural Travel*, ed. Jane Conroy. New York: Peter Lang, 2003.

Levine, Linda Gould. "Isabel Allende in Context: The Erasure of Boundaries," *Critical Insights* (October 2010): 220–238.

McKale, Margaret A. Morales. *Literary Nonfiction in Works by Isabel Allende and Guadalupe Loaeza*. Columbus: Ohio State University, 2002.

Ries, Olga. "Latino Identity in Allende's Novels," *Comparative Literature and Culture* 13:4 (2011): 1–8.

mothering

Allende awards praise and compassion to what editor Andrea O'Reilly terms the "mother knot [that] ties each woman to her children," a connection illustrated Juan's loving parent in "The Road North" and by Aka slave women and their families in *Forest of the Pygmies* (O'Reilly, 2010, 49). The author's fiction focuses on the beginnings wrought by mothers and mother figures. Critic Anne J. Cruz elevates familial elements of "the matrilineal story of the nation," a symbolism captured in the fable "Tosca," the revenge tale "The Schoolteacher's Guest," and autobiographical vignettes in *The Sum of Our Days* (Cruz, 2003, 215). A case in point, the large bosomed Nana in *The House of the Spirits* cures Clara's asthma with the warmth of her breasts much as seven-year-old Clara cuddles the scrawny pup Barrabás and restores him to health. Whether the author describes the amazon bodyguard Loula, the maternal elder Honoré, or the concubine Adèle in *Island beneath the Sea*, Paulina's tending of son Matías in the last stages of syphilis in *Portrait in Sepia*, or the letter from a stepmother to her stepdaughter in *Inés of My Soul*, Allende characterizes maternal instincts as the basis for women's relationships with family and self and a nation's hope for renewal.

O'Reilly reports that Allende's first writings "established a political stake in motherhood and a feminine genealogy that stands against patriarchal repression" (O'Reilly, 2010, 48). In the first novel, *The House of the Spirits*, Clara del Valle, the eternal mother figure, nurtures in a "feminine dyad" the infant Blanca simultaneous with Clara's altruistic outreach to refugees, peasants, and strangers (Allende, 1985, 15). Cruz declares that the author's method of legitimating female roles in history is "through their inscription in the family, as mothers and as the carriers of love and compassion," which spill over to the needy (Cruz, 2003, 216). A model of what critic Philip Graham calls "formidable parental figures," Clara manages to elicit the best from the younger generation without bulldozing them in the style of her tyrannical husband Esteban Trueba, who wants her to abandon all interest except her role as his wife (Graham, 2001, 39).

After death, Clara returns to earth as an effulgent spirit to revitalize granddaughter Alba from interrogation, gang rape, and immurement in a tomb-like cell. In the spirit of Demeter rescuing Persephone from Hades's dark world, Clara exerts maternal authority to undo despair and strengthen Alba to actuate her promise. The magical appearance of the mothering angel has its limits. Analyst Cherie Meacham stresses the boundaries of Clara's maternalism: "Not in historical reality, in the novel, nor in the myth, do women have the power to abolish the horrors of the underworld," a lesson that Allende learns from her year of nursing daughter Paula through terminal porphyria (Meacham, 2001, 98). Alba's identity restored, she shoulders what Cherie Meacham terms "the dignity, the burden, and the hope of humanity," an aim derived from a loving matrilineage (*ibid.*). Forever instructed by a brush with dehumanizing terror, Alba must retain the memory as a lesson for the future.

For Paulina del Valle in *Portrait in Sepia*, the maternal role defines her life. The summation of family and financial investments boils down to simple outcomes: "I had three sons and a granddaughter. All the rest was just trimming" (Allende, 2001, 198). In adulthood, Aurora, Paulina's beloved granddaughter, soothes mother hunger and the disappointment of a false marriage by sinking into the care of mother-in-law Doña Elvira Domínguez, whose "gentle and unconditional love acted like a balm" (*ibid.*, 266). Again, the myth of Demeter and Persephone holds true in that Elvira, for all her goodness, cannot undo the harm caused by her son Diego's adultery with his sister-in-law.

Allende stocks her casts of characters with exemplary mothers. In a brief sentence in *Zorro*, the text depicts an enslaved African woman howling for her dead baby while the island dogs of Barataria chorus their sympathy. The juxtaposition of human with animal implies that the capacity to nurture and love replicates bestial instincts for survival and reproduction that thrive in a broad range of maternal figures. For Eliza Sommers Chi'en in *Portrait in Sepia*, the moans of her daughter Lin/Lynn summons memories of giving birth and experiencing the wonder when a "child lets go and comes to light," a metaphoric description of Aurora's fetal advance from a water to a land animal with the first breath (Allende, 2001, 80). As a model of commitment in *Inés of My Heart*, protagonist Inés Suarez refers to stepdaughter Isabel de Quiroga as "the child of my heart," a loving differentiation between a child of the body and a stepchild (Allende, 2006, 66).

Contrasts in Parenting

In contrast to sterling parental material, in *The Infinite Plan*, Gregory Reeves recognizes the strangeness of his son-mother relationship. Because Nora Reeves remains distant and reserved, she chooses not to touch her son and ponders how to lessen her parental responsibilities from two children to one daughter by giving Greg away. Unlike Nora, older sister Judy fills the role of parent by nestling with Greg, providing "warmth and the rhythm of her breathing," a cadence instilled in creatures from conception (Allende, 1993, 55). Olga, Nora's opposite, showers Gregory with kisses, cookies, and dimes, a model of affection and monetary reward that corrupts his adult relationships. Another matriarch in the chain of maternal heroines, Daisy, an immigrant from the Dominican Republic, sails into harbor in time to rescue Greg from domestic insanity by calming his son David with affection and West Indian voodoo and cooking.

A pinnacle of Allende's maternal characters, Inmaculada Morales, the all-encompassing mom in *The Infinite Plan*, embraces the role of giver. Another literary foil, Inmaculada Morales, brings food and kindness as well as a "sharp eye for perceiving the needs of others," an integral skill of the barrio's matron in residence (Allende, 1993, 56). With an authorial smirk, Allende notes that Inmaculada's husband Pedro struts his paternity, but the community recognizes that his genial wife embodies family power. The return of Gregory Reeves to the Morales household contrasts the lukewarm emotion of Greg's birth mother, sister, wife, and daughter with the Chicana who graces him with the name "blond son," a gesture of acceptance to his gringo heritage and need for parenting (*ibid.*, 71).

Allende uses the Morales household as a model of matrilineal inheritance. Carmen, Inmaculada's frustrated daughter, displays her mother's acceptance of stray and needy children, but thwarts the maternal instinct by aborting a fetus, the offspring of selfish lover Tom Clayton. Allende depicts Carmen's child hunger through a labyrinth of cross-cultural paperwork and intrigue that nets her Dai Morales, the posthumous son of Carmen's brother, soldier Juan José, and Thuy, a dying Vietnamese mother. The new mother-son relationship between Carmen and Dai puts to rest the ghost that haunts Carmen since the day that Olga drops the aborted remains of Tom's child down the drain.

The author juxtaposes both the joys and hurts of parenting. In reference to sorrow for daughter Paula's suffering and death, Allende declares that "Children, like books, are voyages into one's inner self" (Allende, 1995, 10). Maternal emotions undergird the rescue of Eliza, a foundling in *Daughter of Fortune*, in the immediate grasp of Rose Sommers "clinging to the babe as if its mother" and the erasure of Eliza's abandonment through family myths of an elegant basket and a mink coverlet (Allende, 1999, 7). Contrasting the made-up background and idealized gentility, the mothering of Mama Fresia, the Indian maid, stands on tradition—goat's milk for nourishment, raw meat to prevent measles, and cinnamon tea for colic. In a witty side note, Allende comments on the goat's old age because killing it would be "like murdering one's mother" (*ibid.*, 24). In retrospect, Eliza recognizes the most liberating feature of an English upbringing—"large spaces of internal freedom," the independence that enables her to thrive in the helter-skelter milieu of the California gold rush (Allende, 1999, 12).

The dilemma of the pregnant teen poses the choice between abortion and the stigma and poverty of women like Joaquín's mother, the seamstress and model single parent left in poverty and loneliness to rear an illegitimate son. Perhaps because of the wealth of maternal affection that cushions her childhood, Eliza perceives "the voice of the baby in her womb" and ponders its right to survival, a tender moment that illustrates the prenatal formation of a mother-child bond (Allende, 1999, 134). Upon facing the seamstress, Rose exhibits a nobility of motherhood in blaming herself for self-absorption that kept her from recognizing her daughter's distress. The outpouring of maternal trials for "having been born a woman" unites Rose and Joaquín's mother over tea, a female palliative common to Victorian fiction and stage plays. Rose acknowledges that Eliza has followed her lover to California because Rose would have done the same.

The geniality of female groups takes shape in the rolling brothel of Joe Bonecrusher, a traveling madam with "a motherly heart" who rescues whores from addiction and adopts a pseudo-grandson named Tom No-Tribe (Allende, 1999, 301). In an egalitarian atmosphere, the four prostitutes and Eliza, disguised as Elías "Chile Boy" Andieta, travel the mining camps to sing, gamble, and entertain lonely males. Because of the madam's protection of her caravan of people "God had forgotten," Tom imagines that Joe is his grandma (*ibid.*, 332). Esther, the beautiful Mexican, and the other prostitutes heal from beatings, abortions, and venereal disease and reward Joe with "the loyalty of daughters" (*ibid.*, 297).

Free nurse care to miners ill with dysentery epitomizes the unique bond between males and the women who sell them love.

Mothers and Racism

Within *Island Beneath the Sea*, Allende juxtaposes protagonist Tété with Eugenia García del Solar, the Madrid beauty whose insanity renders her incapable of caring for the infant Maurice Valmorain. The text depicts Tété in mourning for her own unnamed son, lost to the impersonal workings of slavery, which the master compares to removing calves from cows and pups from a bitch, a husbandry that reduces blacks to the level of unsentimental livestock. Predictably, Tété, the birthing room attendant and nursemaid, adapts to the post of nanny with "stories, songs, laughs, kisses, and from time to time a swat" to discipline the heir to Habitation Saint-Lazare (Allende, 2010, 102). Her invaluable dominance of the house dramatizes the predicament of bondage — a domestic enslavement that gradually shackles master to slave.

Tété's second pregnancy places her in a dilemma of bearing a child that could be the master's or Gambo's. The text describes quickening, the first stirs of the fetus in her womb, which fill her with "affection and compassion," a reference to Tété's abandonment of abortion as a solution to her problem pregnancy (Allende, 2010, 117). She recalls carrying Maurice on her back African style, an extended period of mother-child contact with a "pale, silent little mouse" who thrives on mothering (*ibid.*, 136). The contact reflects anthropologist Ashley Montagu's premise in *Touching* (1971) that placing skin on skin confers "the most powerful means of establishing human relationships, the foundation of experience" (Montagu, 1971, xv).

At the novel's climax before the 1791 assault on Habitation Saint-Lazare, the invitation to join the Maroons in freedom places Tété in a dilemma of loyalties to her lover Gambo and her children, Maurice and Rosette, whom rebels intend to disembowel. The author exulted, "She does what any woman would do: She chooses her children" (Timpane, 2010). A mirror image of the scene occurs during a Maroon uprising in 1795, when the protection of slave children in Valmorain's house ensures that slave mothers will stay in the quarters.

The text wrings pathos from painful admissions of bicultural parentage. At Tété's reunion with her daughter Rosette, a student at an Ursuline convent, the mother ponders the dilemma of keeping Rosette and risking the child's sale or rape by her birth father. Long separated from her mother, Rosette stiffens at a welcoming hug. Allende lends operatic emotion to the auction scene at which Valmorain inadvertently reveals to Tété and Jean-Martin his inglorious conception and birth. In private, two mothers, Tété and Violette, devise a false lineage. By claiming that Violette conceals his birth into bondage, Tété hides the fact that she is the real slave mother. Tété's awareness that protection comes at a price resonates with the complexities of slavery, a cruel enemy of family unity.

See also female persona; feminism

• *References and Further Reading*

Cruz, Anne J., Rosilie Hernández-Pecoraro, and Joyce Tolliver, eds. *Disciplines on the Line: Feminist Research on Spanish, Latin American, and U.S. Latina Women*. Newark, DE: Juan de la Cuesta, 2003.

Graham, Philip. "A Less Magical Realism," *New Leader* 84:6 (November-December 2001): 38–39.

Meacham, Cherie. "The Metaphysics of Mother-Daughter Renewal in *La Casa de los espíritus* and *Paula*," *Hispanófila* 131 (2001): 93–108.

Montagu, Ashley. *Touching*. New York: HarperCollins, 1971.

O'Reilly, Andrea. *Encyclopedia of Motherhood.* Thousand Oaks, CA: Sage, 2010.
Timpane, John. "Isabel Allende's Heroines Are, Like Their Feminist Creator, Strong and Independent," *Philadelphia Inquirer* (5 May 2010).

music

As with other elements and motifs from classic literature, music figures in unexpected venues in Allende's writings, as with the surrounding birdsong in the jungle setting of "Phantom Palace," Dil Bahadur's song transposing Yeti ideograms in *Kingdom of the Golden Dragon*, and Eloísa and El Capitán's turn on the dance floor in *The Stories of Eva Luna*. In *City of the Beasts*, the absence of Lisa Cold's singing in Italian reminds the family of her suffering from cancer, which suppress joy in the household. Analyst notes that Allende "has articulated a plea for artistry and creative dreams in the face of political repression" (Feal and Miller, 2002, 156). For *The House of the Spirits*, the expected locations of song—Rosa's funeral, Blanca's cathedral wedding, Alba's seventh birthday—remain silent. Instead of traditional celebration, the author enlivens the return of Nicolás from Granada, where gypsies teach him the flamenco. Nicolás seizes the dining room table as a dance floor and, like Esmeralda in Victor Hugo's *The Hunchback of Notre Dame* (1831), taps out an Andalusian staccato that splinters the tabletop to the texture of a butcher's block, a meaningful reminder of Rosa's autopsy on the same spot. The success of flamenco instruction mirrors the growth of liberalism and free love, elements of modernity that defeat conservatism.

Esteban Trueba's stodginess symbolizes the cold-hearted venality of the ruling party. Adherence to colonial values causes him to rule out radios as "sinister influences" and to attend only opera and performances of lyric Spanish zarzuela, a colonial tie to the Spanish motherland (Allende, 1985, 263). Significantly, Allende links Old World music with winter, a season rife with loss and death that the author echoes in *Eva Luna* and "The Little Heidelberg." In true die-hard form, Esteban purports to represent the people, who know more about rising socialism than their newly elected senator. Popular among listeners, the music of folk singer Pedro Tercero spreads a version of the fox and hens story of his grandfather, a liberating beast fable that begins taking on a life of its own.

Music returns to the text during the rifling of the Trueba mansion by agents of the military junta, a sacking akin to cultural rape. Typically soulless, the troops burn books and opera scores, then "broke his classical records one by one," a methodical assault reflecting the vulnerability of an elder statesman and his granddaughter (Allende, 1985, 454). The author indicates that music lives, not in scores or on records but in the souls of survivors. As torturers carry out their round of cruelties on captives, women in the concentration camp sing hymns and Beethoven's "Ode to Joy," which uplift and stabilize captives against the terror of electrocution on bedsprings and repeated rape (*ibid.*, 480). Far from worthless, art energizes and confers hope on Alba, Adriana, Ana Díaz, and the compound of women and children.

The Music of Life

Allende positions music at significant passages in character lives, from birth to death. In *Zorro*, the antidote to maternal death and a hazardous flight by sea back to America lies in music. Bernardo first sits like a babe on an Indian consoler's lap and hears sweet music. As he revives from sorrow, he plays the reed flute, an instrument that produces sounds of the *vox humana*, and treasures the voice of Light-in-the-Night, which melts his glacial heart. A similar grim situation aboard the *Madre de Dios* [mother of God] in winter 1815 lightens on departure from Cape Verde as Captain Santiago de León plays his violin in accompaniment to Juliana de Rameu's harp. In spring, Madame Odilia orchestrates a Creole funeral for her daughter, Catherine Villars, which begins with mock Christian piety and concludes African style with "feasting, music, and dancing, as was fitting" (Allende, 2005, 318).

Allende values musical entertainment at significant religious and community celebrations. The role of rhythm and melody in *Inés of My Soul* begins in a tavern with the union of a stringed instrument with a drum, a universal pairing of entertaining and reassuring sounds. On arduous travel in the New World, travelers ask the protagonist to "sing them a song or tell them tales of Spanish when we camped at night and their hearts were heavy with nostalgia," a feeling the author knows from her own exile from Chile (Allende, 2006, 79). The long march south from Peru over the *cordillera* sets "fifteen hundred robustly singing soldiers" ahead of Yanacona on the way to Chile, marking time in the historic style of Roman legionaries and Christian crusaders advancing on the Holy Lands (*ibid.*, 114). Even at age eighty, conquistador Francisco de Aguirre continues singing "the risqué songs of his youth," a literary convention of the lusty soldier (*ibid.*, 135).

As Spaniards encounter foreign peoples, the text hints at a melding of races and cultures, beginning with camp sounds of Indian *quenas* (reed flutes), African drums, and soldiers' flutes and *vihuelas*, Renaissance guitars combining the vibrations of twelve pairs of strings. During the rise of Santiago from village to town, residents observe saints' days, a mark of the devout Catholic that divides colonists from aborigines. Indians speaking "their common language, Mapudungu" take opportunities to "tell stories, dance, drink, and arrange new marriages," Allende's acknowledgement of normal human rhythms (Allende, 2006, 176). More equitable, musicales "in which Spaniards, Indians, blacks, and mestizos participated equally" presage a democratization of Chile and, by extension, the Western Hemisphere (*ibid.*, 231).

Freedom and Musical Abandon

From the opening lines of *Island Beneath the Sea*, the author depicts African slaves bearing the music from home in their very fiber, another perspective introduced in the African godmother in *Eva Luna*. Drumming unites slaves into a pulsing clan of freedom fighters. In reference to the diaspora, Allende describes Honoré as permeated with Dahomean rhythm and dance, which he reveres as a source of worship, healing, and escape from bondage. The text connects freedom with dance, a luxuriant looseness of body in rhythm with music, "a wind that blows away the years, memories, and fear" (Allende, 2010, 1). At place Congo, Tété, the protagonist, eludes the crouching terror inside her by returning to childhood in Guinea and moving to the beat of drums to "[sweeten] my memory" and leave her "clean and happy," a spiritual cleansing of coercion via unfettered dance (*ibid.*). The spiritual thrust of cadences in her blood unites her with Erzulie, the love deity, in a whiplike apotheosis.

Allende returns Tété to joyful abandon at the celebration of her daughter Rosette's birth. After the sacrifice of a hen, the new mother, unlike sequestered white mothers, "danced and danced, breasts heavy, arms lifted high, hips crazed, legs independent of my thoughts, responding to the drums" (Allende, 2010, 136). The throbbing body welcomes the newborn at the same time that Tété lets go grief for her firstborn, lost to slavery without knowing his mother. The collapse of the plantation system sends mounted militia toward the north. Although the men bear European stringed instruments to accompany African drums, their music sounds "out of tune," a parallel to the discordance of plantation life in its death throes (*ibid.*, 165).

In non–African settings, music uplifts voodoo rituals of blessing and rescue. Beats of the *boula*, *seconde*, and *maman* and the joyous rhythm of maracas sustain Tété on the final hour of her flight through the jungle to Le Cap. At the extremes of exhaustion from heat and exertion, she dances into French territory in a trance induced by the compassionate goddess Erzulie, the patron *loa* of mothers. A subsequent image of rejuvenation sets Tété in search of drums beating in a Cuban plaza, where she yields to "the volcanic impulse to dance in a kalenda" (Allende, 2010, 233). Again revived by the throb to jubilation, she joins slave dancers in exaggerated motion, "legs and hips animated, buttocks gyrating provocatively, arms like the wings of the dove, breasts bouncing, heads in a fog ... a typhoon of skirts and arms" (*ibid.*). In imitation, her daughter Rosette performs for the throng with an enthusiasm born of the child's ignorance of bondage.

The importance of dance to Tété recurs on her first outing as a freedwoman. In the arms of Zacharie, her dashing date, she dances for a half hour at the Salon Orléans to "waltzes, polkas, and quadrilles" with the prissy restraint of white women (Allende, 2010, 344). At the second phase of their evening, she enters his casino, Chez Fleur, and the "merry music of two orchestras" (*ibid.*, 345). Free to be herself, Tété gravitates to the dance circle, where she rids herself of imitation of Europeans to "dance in my style" into the wee hours (*ibid.*, 346). West African music and dance carry her through the terrors of the falling action and, in the novel's conclusion, reunite her with Erzulie.

A similarly exotic setting in the Amazon jungle turns natural sounds in *City of the Beasts* into music. During the upriver journey, Alex plays the flute of his famous grandfather, Joseph Cold, a legacy that unites him with art and performance abandon. At peace with his music, the boy enjoys Lisa Cold's favorite romantic concerto, a singular European lyric suited to the leafy surrounding. The suitability of flute solos to Brazil reminds Alex of his grandfather's belief that "music is a universal language," a way of communicating with all sentient beings, including the ephemeral People of the Mists (Allende, 2002, 174). The assuaging of hostile spirits with music returns during a council with the Beasts, when Nadia dances in imitation of a dolphin, jaguar, and serpent, which Allende describes as a gift, "a grand offering" to sluggish animals (*ibid.*, 284).

Nadia's skill at free-form dance continues in *Forest of the Pygmies* as she follows the lead of a healer. Among the Aka saluting King Kosongo, drumming relieves the subject peoples of despair by releasing their spirits to perform figures and songs with tones from nature "that undulated on the air like a serpent" (Allende, 2005, 130). The outsiders respect the intensity and musicality of each cycle for its emotion and grace. The poignance of enslaved female Aka enacting their sufferings draws others into the circle and sets the king into rhythmic kinship with the people he stores in pens. In ceremonial dancing, the Aka petition "Ezenji and other divinities of the animal and plant worlds" for power to overcome tyranny (*ibid.*, 238). By the novel's end, the unified Africans "organized their own carnival" of drumming, singing, and dancing, a celebration of liberation (*ibid.*, 281).

• *References and Further Reading*

Feal, Rosemary Geisdorfer, and Yvette E. Miller, eds. *Isabel Allende Today: Anthology of Essays*. Pittsburgh, PA: Latin American Literary Review, 2002.

Murphy, Bernadette. "Review: *Island Beneath the Sea*," *Los Angeles Times* (14 May 2010).
Waldron, Linda. *Isabel Allende: Literary Inheritance and the Establishment of a New Dimension in Chilean Female Fiction*. St. Augustine, Trinidad and Tobago: University of West Indies, 2003.

My Invented Country

For a summation of the real and imaginary in her life, Allende composed *My Invented Country: A Memoir*, an etude on the union of geographical place and transcendent being. The text, a series of vignettes, identifies the self through self-invention, the private legend by which the individual records personal observations and experience. The construct typifies the title narratives of *The Stories of Eva Luna*, the photos of protagonist Aurora del Valle of *Portrait in Sepia*, wartime experiences in Vietnam in *The Infinite Plan*, and the mirrored reflection of a self-made knight errant in *Zorro* (2005). According to analyst Barbara Mujica, the author deliberately avoided an encyclopedic style to produce "an unsystematic, impressionistic, personal memoir" viewed by the heart (Mujica, 2003, 57).

Critic Gloria Maxwell admired the memoir's unflinching honesty about Chilean tendencies toward class pettiness, male domination, and "inherent conservatism and clannishness" (Maxwell, 2003, 115). To explain elements of background and personality, Allende lists the heritage of Spanish "passion and severity" as well as exuberance and the workings of destiny, a unified interpretation of what reviewer Lindsay Wright terms "the Chilean national psyche" (*ibid.*, 80; Wright, 2003, 18). For more aggressive female characters, the process of self-creation takes shape in the storied career of the title figure in *Inés of My Soul* and the corsetry, perfume, and sexual allure with which Violette Boisier transforms her orphaned self into a courtesan in *Island Beneath the Sea*. For a model, the author chooses her grandmother, Isabel Barros, and, in the same vein as Amy Tan's *The Hundred Secret Senses*, describes a life of telepathy and séances, psychic powers derived from the "multiple dimensions to reality" (Allende, 2003, 69).

Allende explains her personal involvement in self-fashioning: "Word by word I have created the person I am" (Allende, 2003, 180). Analyst Linda Gould Levine accounts for the flexible self-image of the creator and its influence on art in "enlarging life and making it immune to the passage of time" (Levine, 2010, 221). From a negative view, in *Daughter of Fortune*, Allende regrets the historical erasure of Californios, Indians, and, Mexicans on the American frontier and, in *The House of the Spirits*, the falsification of tyranny and atrocity in the dark times that assailed Chile. Similarly cataclysmic, the War of the Pacific, expressed through an eyewitness account in *Portrait in Sepia*, investigates the causes and outcomes of a border conflict so vicious as to arouse animosities that survive for decades. Analyst Patricia Soper admired the author for having "a hard look at a country that has endured much, yet tenaciously clung to the essence of self" (Soper, 2003, 35).

Out of affection for home, Allende wrote a gentle chauvinistic paean to Chile, with its magical Gypsies and tribal mentality. To center herself in the Santiago of the late 1940s, she compares herself to palm trees that survive the demolition of her grandfather's house because the trees cling to Chilean soil in their roots. Critic Roxanne Dunbar-Ortiz identified the text as a "nostalgic memoir of Chile and a farewell love letter to her motherland," which the author graces with apple orchards and vineyards in a Garden of Eden and the La Silla observatory, an eye on the heavens (Dunbar-Ortiz, 2003, 15). To compress the idea of home into text, she divides topics into factual and impressionistic chapters on terrain, Catholicism, Aymara and Mapuche Indians, history, and women. In one of her humorous conceits, she pictures the capital of Santiago, constructed on the Spanish plan of a plaza with streets radiating out from center, "like a demented octopus" (Allende, 2003, 11).

Allende returns to childhood memories of her grandfather, "authoritarian and machista," to stage a compulsory family reunion and to quell gossip and rumors (Allende, 2003, 112). She satirizes his insistence on stoic forbearance of "cold showers, food difficult to chew, lumpy mattresses, third-class seats on trains, and clunky shoes," all beneficial for the hardships they impose on the individual (*ibid.*, 96). Because of his superiority, her grandfather believes that he can negotiate forgiveness of sins without the intervention of priests. Under men like the grandfather, women may attend adult films—*Fiddler on the Roof, The Last Temptation of Christ*—only in the company "of a man of the family, who takes responsibility for the moral harm" of realism of the delicate female (*ibid.*, 74). Whereas the Chilean woman must be serious and industrious, "sloth is a male privilege," forgivable because it is inevitable, much like alcoholism and infidelity (*ibid.*, 82).

Central to the writings of a well-traveled author lies the concepts of class and nationality, which Levine connects with "ethnic cleansing and the destruction of minority cultures and religions" (Levine, 2010, 222–223). The Santiagan caste system separates walled and gated manses of the rich from the slums of the have-nots. Allende quotes an ironic comment on the divide: "When democracy gets democratic, it doesn't work at all" (Allende, 2003, 13). The house in which the author's mother was born differentiates areas by purpose—for guests, family, and maids. Similarly geometric, the author divides the nation according to Indian tribe—Aymara, Mapuche, Quechua, and Alacalufe—and denies that African blood mixes with Chile's Basque-Spanish genealogies.

The author's constant awareness of Chile's dictatorship draws repeated social and economic reminders of hardship during the 1970s. Her class distinctions cover those who fled, the conservatives who stayed, and the economic exiles who emigrated to seek work. The strong arm of Augusto Pinochet retains its power of coercion in the macho flavor of male-female relationships, which the author describes as "injurious" (Allende, 2001, 52). She credits the blithe abandonment of home and children to the polygamy of the Araucan and to the womanizing of Spanish conquistadors among Indians. As a comeuppance to the Chilean male, Allende describes him as "bad-tempered, unjust, master of all rights" (*ibid.*). For all the negatives—dictatorship, spousal and child abuse, disasters—the book earned a positive critique from *Kirkus Reviews*, which summarized the memoir as "dazzling as a kaleidoscope: an artful tumbling and knocking that throws light and reveals strange depths" ("Review," 2003, 514).

• *References and Further Reading*

Dunbar-Ortiz, Roxanne. "The First September 11th," *Women's Review of Books* 21:3 (December 2003): 15–16.
Levine, Linda Gould. "Isabel Allende in Context: The Erasure of Boundaries," *Critical Insights* (October 2010): 220–238.
Maxwell, Gloria. "Review: *My Invented Country*," *Library Journal* 128:17 (15 October 2003): 115.
Mujica, Barbara. "Review: *My Invented Country*," *Americas* 55:5 (September/October 2003): 57.
"Review: *My Invented Country*," *Kirkus Reviews* 71:7 (1 April 2003): 514.
Soper, Patricia. "Fascinating Look at Chile," (New Zealand) *Southland Times* (11 October 2003): 35.
Wright, Lindsay. "Home Is a Long, Thin Country," *Taranaki* (New Zealand) *Daily News* (30 August 2003): 18.

myth

The natural coalescing of myth from social tempest serves Allende's writings with the peasant lore of history, exemplified by the description of frog feet, fish gills, and caiman's teeth on Maroons in *Island Beneath the Sea*, the Indian legends and syncretic hagiography of Mama Fresia in *Daughter of Fortune*, and the ghost ship Caleuche and the author's recreation of Little Red Riding Hood in *My Invented Country*. Emblematic cobras and scorpions and a curse on a magical statue in *Kingdom of the Golden Dragon* contribute to the air of mystery and evil in India, where Alex and Nadia encounter a Blue Warrior, a member of a nomadic sect indelibly marked by indigo dye. Membership in the Sect of the Scorpion resonates with nineteenth-century glimpses of Thuggees, a vicious band of assassins immortalized in Rudyard Kipling's *Gunga Din* and the story "A Deal in Cotton" and in the film *Indiana Jones and the Temple of Doom*.

Additional aspects of legend and myth invest the Tibetan palace, topped with mythic figures in ceramics. Fabulous elements guide the prince, Dil Bahadur, who passed tests that include swimming icy waters and riding a wild stallion, a coming-to-power ordeal that dates to Plutarch's biography of Alexander the Great and the warhorse Bucephalus. Like the feat of the infant Hercules strangling serpents or Arthur pulling a sword from stone, Dil must ride the horse, which "will recognize his authority and be as tame as if it had been broken" (Allende, 2004, 133). To link ancient symbolism of Asia and South America, Allende installs in the Tibetan palace images of flying dragons that flourished among the People of the Mist in *City of the Beasts*. The combined effect drapes the palace in mystery and menace.

Visits to El Dorado and the fountain of youth and encounters with an invisible spirit wife of the shaman Walimai seem normal in *City of the Beasts*, where the primitive aura of the Amazon erases the normality of Alex Cold's life in urban California. Grandmother Kate's respect for experiential learning leaves Alex on his own to encounter firsthand the wonders of Brazil. Within a setting filled with the sounds of birds and insects and the lust green of lianas and ferns, he recalls his grandmother's statement that "spirits walked among the living," a Gothic presence enhancing the fears of a boy far from home (Allende, 2002, 90). In the land of the gods, he makes a connection with the Greek myth of Ariadne, Theseus, and the Minotaur in the maze, a setting that J.R.R. Tolkien mimics in the Mines of Moria in *The Lord of the Rings*. While following Alex's train of thought in a grotto on the route to El Dorado, Allende proposes historic explanations of dragons, which may have been Paleolithic reptiles that coexist with humankind. The author impresses Alex and Nadia with the surreal beauty of El Dorado before trouncing the Spanish myth with an ironic truth — the elegant city consists of mica and pyrite or fool's gold. With the insight of a Westerner, Alex thinks of the hollow mesa as "an ecological archive" lacking an "organized society" (*ibid.*, 267–268).

The Myth Makers

Throughout *The Stories of Eva Luna*, the author establishes the need of the populace to create myth from unique events. Examples range from inflations of the beauty of Dulce Rosa Orellano in "Revenge" and the rumors regarding the faked kidnap of Abigail McGovern in "The Proper Respect" to the surreal night of love in "The Guggenheim Lovers." For the story "Simple María," people feel obligated to provide mythos for the title figure, a scrappy prostitute known for trouncing pimps. To account for María's unusual career on the Calle República, stories award her a Spanish birth to aristocrats and a dignified death, two traits lacking in most urban brothel history. Because of María's ability to transmit feelings of love to her clients, her legends "circled the globe ... by sailors of all races," one of Allende's hyperboles that suggests a kernel of truth (Allende, 1991, 161).

For Allende's first novel, *The House of the Spirits*, the author shrouds in classic lore the folk elder, Pedro García. Like the archetypal Greek seer Teiresias, the epicist Homer, and the fallen king Oedipus Rex, stricken blind in punishment for hubris, Pedro suffers cataracts, a "milky film that had slowly screened out all light" (Allende, 1985, 218). For clarity, he looks inward for folklore and age-old herbalism to cure the sick. From the elder Pedro, Blanca and Pedro Tercero learn to protect themselves from scorpion bite and how to dowse for water with a stick. Essential to the grandson's edification, the old man tells the fable of the "hens who joined forces to confront a fox," a model for revolution that Pedro Tercero later reclaims as his literary heritage (*ibid.*, 163). Appropriately, old Pedro García escapes modernism by dying "a few days before the presidential elections" and continues to influence Las Tres Marías through an impressive funeral and the memories of his extended family (*ibid.*, 216).

With additional classic hints at the myth of Andromeda and the Minotaur, Allende imparts to *Of Love and Shadows* the task of the investigative reporter, Irene Beltrán, to follow the trail of a "long thread" into the dark cave of dictatorship to witness up close the terrors of a monster (Allende, 1987, 121). The text parallels the orderliness of the Beltrán household with the "dark unknown region" that the journalist first encounters at the municipal morgue, a dismal labyrinth cloaked in bureaucratic lies and evasions (*ibid.*). Peering into a tyrannical abyss at Los Riscos, she realizes that the bottomless hole contains the answers to locating *desaparecidos*, the unexplained disappearances that harry families to scrutinize a fiendish bureaucracy. The thread motif recurs in Irene's acceptance of a task, to cling to the "end of a long thread in her hands that when tugged would unravel an unending snarl of horrors" (*ibid.*, 127).

The Heroic Myth

For *Daughter of Fortune*, Allende supplies fictional protagonist Eliza Sommers with putative communication with the noted *banditos* of the California gold rush and the symbolic "Robin Hood of California" (Allende, 1999, 338). Critic Ignacio López-Calvo observes that the character, Joaquín Andieta/Murieta becomes "an absent being, like a fable, like a spirit, heard of, but never seen" (López-Calvo, 2007, 164). Trailing Joaquín to Sacramento and surrounding gold fields, Eliza searches for the slippery Chilean through queries and rumors, the half-truths that a pile of summer draperies foreshadows during the sexual adventures of her youth. While amputating gangrenous fingers from a criminal named Jack, she makes a tentative connection with Andieta, now known as Murieta. An offhand description of a mounting crime wave lists a likely pair — Joaquín Murieta and "Three-Finger Jack," a probable name for the patient whose hand Eliza saves (Allende, 1999, 329).

Allende turns to the frontier's spurious media as a source of the Murieta myth, which describes a superman who outlives gunfire until a silver bullet can fell him, a folkloric weapon against werewolves and enemies of the Long Ranger. [The term "silver bullet" appears to have derived from the invention of Salvarsen, the first cure for syphilis.] For Eliza, the phantom lover appears in her dreams with a star on his forehead, an obvious symbol of an ideal closer to fantasy than real life. With the "dual arrogance of an Englishman and a journalist," Jacob Freemont, a self-indulgent writer eager to inscribe Murieta's biography in period yellow journalism, resolves to interview the heroic criminal or to turn isolated scraps into a dime novel (*ibid.*, 339). Eyewitnesses describe the slippery Murieta as a noble/vulgar, handsome/scar-faced, oversexed/monogamous, savage/kind evader of constables who avenges oppressed Spaniards. The mystique of banditry and the manufacture of an ambiguous history from "some truths and a mountain of lies" attest to the elasticity of heroism myth to suit the *Zeitgeist* (*ibid.*, 341).

For the background of Haiti, like that of Edwidge Danticat's *Haiti Noir* and Alejo Carpentier's *The Kingdom of This World*, Allende orchestrates what reviewer Betsy Willeford terms island "vitality, her tragedy, her history, her mystery; all significant, all contradictory" (Willeford, 2010). The text of *Island Beneath the Sea* repeats the Guinean belief that slave catchers sell Africans to cannibals "who had crocodile claws and teeth like hyenas," a metaphor for the predations of slave dealers and masters (Allende, 2010, 120). With the same misperceptions of whites, the captive Gambo observes the first Caucasians at one of the forty slave castles on the Gold Coast in disbelief. He assumes that his hairy, ill-smelling captors lack human traits, a twist on the European stereotype of the apish black.

As a nemesis for enslavers, the text aggrandizes the person of Macandal, the one-armed leader of maroons, the martyr of Carpentier's impressionistic epic. As with the background of Bras Coupé in George Washington Cable's *The Grandissimes* (1879), the facts about the birth and emergence of the charismatic Macandal remain murky and clouded by hero worship. Allende pictures Macandal as the prince of Guinea, a literate Muslim herbalist and healer, a justification for fictional guile and strategy greater than that of whites. Like the physical assets of the monumental Kunta Kinte in Alex Haley's *Roots* (1976) and of Geronimo in the mythic lore of Laguna writer Leslie Marmon Silko, Macandal speaks wisely of the Mandingo ways of tracking and combat, swift of foot, and endowed with "eagle eyes" (Allende, 2010, 49).

In the pattern of both Kunta Kinte and Geronimo, Macandal resolves to free himself rather than remain confined by the French *grands blancs*, whom Louis XIV armed in 1685 with the Code Noir, a decree empowering whites over blacks. According to editor Prem Poddar, the code established a penal system that "reinforced the slave owners' powers by further commoditising slaves as human merchandise" (Poddar, 2008, 146). Unlike the earth-bound Kunta Kinte, Macandal shapeshifts into appropriate animals. His supernatural power requires knowledge of poisonous plants, which inflict a cattle murrain and human epidemic. The cost of revolt begins with the hundreds of slaves tortured for information about the poisoner. Like the Gaul Ariovistus before Julius Caesar, Macandal towers in chains like "the only truly free man in the throng" (Allende, 2010, 52). With the prophetic majesty of King Arthur, Macandal vows to return, a resurrection found in the myths of the Greek Aesclepius, Egyptian Osiris, Persian Damuzi, Indian Bodhidharma, and Hebraic Jesus.

At the beginning of the Haitian Revolution on the night of August 14, 1791, Allende dramatizes a nighttime voodoo summit, a primeval juncture of human powers surrounding a Santerian altar. Held in Bois Cayman (alligator woods), the growing assembly of rebels at the *hounfor* (temple) thrums to the beat of the drums and the voice of Boukman, "that giant with the voice of a tempest ... the spark that lighted the fire of rebellion" (Allende, 2010, 173). Magical realism reclaims Tante Rose from old age by giving her youth and a steady walk. Invisible to the mounted militia, she inspires beatification, marked by worshippers kissing the hem of her robe and her tinkling jewelry. Testimony to cruelties at Limbe and Le Cap precede an invocation to the divine protector Bondye and divine sorcerer Legba and to a rising star, Toussaint L'Ouverture, the legendary liberator.

Conflicting stories of assault and survival muddy the history of the Haitian Revolution and the charisma of Toussaint, the new chief with "the heart of a jungle dog" and his "z'etoile (star) the most brilliant in the sky," an astral trait he shares with Julius Caesar and King Arthur (Allende, 2010, 289). As Toussaint, the former coachman, achieves the position of slayer of Spanish troops and mediator of black-white negotiations in December 1791, Allende contrasts his elevation to power with the diminution of his enemy Valmorain. The freeing of the French planter from execution at Habitation Saint-Lazare forces him to tramp the harsh jungle to avoid Maroon incursions. At the end of strength, the Frenchman huddles in the underbrush from aching legs and bloodied feet, his manhood sapped by humiliation, loss, and thirst.

A rapid recovery of French arrogance on the ride to Le Cap shifts his story of the flight away from certain death and rescue by Gambo. Fortunately for history, Major Etienne Relais recognizes Valmorain's concocted tale as a deviation from the truth of Tété's version. Through rumors from Haiti, refugees in New Orleans piece together the rise of Toussaint L'Ouverture, the negotiator for the abolition of island slavery. From mulatto gossip in the Marché Français, Tété hears myths of the liberator's skill as a prophet and telepathic wizard. Impervious to bullets, he wins successive skirmishes under Jesus's protection. Simultaneously, a song circulates describing the heroism of Gambo La Liberté. A "model for courage," he shapeshifts into a wolf that haunts the infamous French general Dessalines (Allende, 2010, 443).

Educational Stories

In the United States, another historical giant, Père Antoine, the Capuchin friar and rector of Saint Louis Cathedral in New Orleans, assumes a more ingenuous fame. He earns regard for his tolerance of all sinners at Le Marais, where he ministers to felons and whores "protected by his inalterable innocence and his indistinct aureole" (Allende, 2010, 332). At a perilous moment, public reverence for Antoine's procession forestalls a post-hurricane epidemic. His saintliness as cook and nurse for prisoners precedes a rumor that "a luminous plate floated above his head," tangible proof of mythic beneficence (*ibid.*, 324). Allende compounds the iconic goodness with a comment that the aged prelate sees more clearly in the holy realm than in the earthly sphere.

Myth supplies educational material for the education of Bernardo and Diego de la Vega, the budding Zorro. Allende pictures the boys learning Indian language and philosophy from the stories they hear in childhood. As the two travel by sea to Acapulco, the author alludes to Herodotus's animal fable "Arion and the Dolphin," in which a dolphin saves a singer from drowning after sailors throw him overboard. In Diego's case, sailors suspicious that the boy's luck at cards is "a little double-dealing" consider the same end for Diego until whales gather nearby and distract them from plotting assassination (Allende, 2005, 95). The implied connection with Arion stresses Diego's innate talents and the charmed life that spares him hurt. Diego's plunge into the sea to save Bernardo reshapes the fable from animal rescue to an act of brotherhood, which Bernardo accomplishes "without thinking" (*ibid.*, 97). The dolphin motif returns in the epilogue at the tomb of Padre Mendoza, where Indians honor him by turning his discovery of pearls into a new legend to add to the mythos of Alta California.

In *Inés of My Soul*, the text outlines a lengthy worship service, which begins with clan histories and "feats of their heroes ... recorded in Mapudungu" and leading to a recitation of the Mapuche creation myth (Allende, 2006, 118). The familiar role of the serpent, an animistic element common to the Japanese *Kojiki* and Laguna and Navajo creation stories, rescues the Mapuche from a catastrophic flood, another motif found in Genesis and Gilgamesh. Mapuche invocations, reminiscent of Psalms 3, 37, 69, and 120 from the Old Testament, request a superhuman extension of mortal powers to shield the Mapuche from their invaders. Duplicating avian lore as a natural blessing on prayer, the worshippers view a condor gliding overhead, a symbol of majesty and grace.

• *References and Further Reading*

López-Calvo, Ignacio. *Alternative Orientalisms in Latin America and Beyond.* Newcastle, UK: Cambridge Scholars, 2007.

Poddar, Prem, Rajeef S. Patke, and Lars Jensen, eds. *A Historical Companion to Postcolonial Literatures: Continental Europe and Its Empire.* Edinburgh: Edinburgh University Press, 2008.

Willeford, Betsy. "Tete's (and Haiti's) Trials in *Island Beneath the Sea*," *Miami Herald* (25 April 2010).

names

Allende's fiction displays naming that initiates a metaphoric response to people and places, such as the homophone "my daughter" in the name of Elena Mejías in "Wicked Girl," the ship *Madre de Dios* (mother of God) in *Zorro*, and the seraphic "Uncle Angel" and the double light and star etymologies in the title figure of "Ester Lucero." For a transcendent scene of animism and the oversoul, Allende names the elderly queen Nana-Asante, a motherly combination in Swahili for Grandmother Thanks. Patronyms typify character behaviors, as with Judge Hidalgo (gentleman) and Juana la Triste (the sad) in "The Judge's Wife." The choice of Tex Armadillo, named for the "little armed" digger of the New World, arouses humor in the actions and attitudes of a middle-aged hippie in *Kingdom of the Golden Dragon*. For allegory, Allende chooses historic names—Tensing (holder of Buddhist doctrine), Dorji (true light), and Dil Bahadur (Brave Heart)—and the flower name Pema (lotus blossom) and the animal name Tschewang (empowered life) to identify characters invested with Asian ecological and theological significance. The humorous use of "Little Grandmother" for Kate demonstrates both respect and cultural denigration of women as vulnerable women made ineffectual by age.

Three symbols—Ampari (protection) in "The Road North," the warrior name Alexander (defender) in *City of the Beasts*, and Domingo Toro (bull), the massive bootlegger and arms dealer in "The Proper Respect"—confer strong images against the terrors of organ harvesting and the jungle dangers of the Amazon. One emblematic name, Patricia (upper class) Zimmerman, expresses the chief obstacle to the courtship of Horacio Fortunato (lucky) in "Gift for a Sweetheart." At a critical point in the search for kidnapped girls in *Kingdom of the Golden Dragon*, Alexander reminds himself "I'm not named Alexander, defender of men, for nothing" (Allende, 2004, 225). For the storyteller in "Two Words," Allende allows the girl to name herself "Belisa Crepusculario" (beauty and twilight), an appropriate empowerment of self by the child of "a family so poor they did not even have names to give their children" (Allende, 10). The author stresses that self-naming suits the longings of a girl for individuality and direction.

The selection of names sets the narrative tone in the Hotel Christopher Columbus, the autopsy conducted by Dr. Cuevas (caverns), and a dog named Barrabás (son of the father) in *The House of the Spirits*, an allusion to the criminal released from a death sentence preceding Christ's crucifixion. The fecundity of earth marks a resurrected plantation named Saint-Lazare, a planter of the Lacroix (cross) family in *Island Beneath the Sea* and Riad (garden) Halabí in *Eva Luna*. Another suggestion of plenitude lies in the choice of Diego de la Vega (St. James of the plain) for Zorro (Fox), who flourishes both as his father's heir to a plantation and as the sly requiter of injustice. For the reclaimed chauffeur Sebastián Canuto, bearing the name of Saint Sebastian, a martyr pictured in art pierced with arrows, the nickname El Cuchillo (the blade) instills a reverse image of cruel, clandestine assault. A touching conclusion to *The Stories of Eva Luna*, the naming of Azucena (lily) imposes a purity on the child who dies in the mud of an avalanche because of the ineptitude of Colombian bureaucracy.

NAMES AS EMBLEMS

In *Of Love and Shadows*, the author creates a cast of metaphorically named characters—the privileged Beatriz (blessed), the grieving Digna (worthy), the writer Irene (peace), Evangelina (messenger), Juan de Dios (John of God), and Hilda Leal (loyal protector), a socialist living in exile from Franco's Spain. For the hero, the author chooses Francisco (St. Francis of Assisi), a masculine version of her own pseudonym, Francisca Román (story), that Allende used while writing for the magazine *Paula*. In dramatic moments, the author speaks directly of the skills of Tránsito Soto, a prostitute at the Red Lantern and friend of the authoritarian Esteban Trueba. Tránsito succeeds at her trade through the "Tibetan gift" of "crossing over" from sex with clients into her imagination (Allende, 1985, 88). The name serves double duty by characterizing her ambition to advance from the brothel to fame and wealth in the capital. Likewise, the naming of the twins' automobile Covadonga revives a village where Iberians began the reconquest of Spain from the Moors. For Allende, the recovery of the unnamed nation from conservative colonialists, begun halfway through the text, boosts the tone to hope for freedom and equality.

Critics seize on the literary archetypes emerging from Allende's carefully crafted matrilineage within *The House of the Spirits*, in which characters replicate the waving of white handkerchiefs in defiance of the patriarchal Pinochet junta. The author compounds the elements of clarity and purity in a female lineage beginning with Niveá (snowy), the symbolic repository of female power and wisdom that shepherds the del Valle-Trueba family line toward egalitarianism. The color imagery extends over the next three generations to Clara (clear, bright), Blanca (white), and Alba (dawn, white). Analyst Susan R. Frick describes the family line as advancing from "from coolness to clearness to whiteness to the dawning of a new era of female experience" (Frick, 2001, 39).

Vincent Kling's critique accepts the matrilineal del Valle names as "an ascendancy of light ... a new beginning" (Kling, 2010, 244). The image of spirituai illumination precedes the cleansing and refinement of purification, a positive portent for the subversion of autocracy and violence in the nation and the clan of Trueba, a Basque scion who wanted a female child to perpetuate his patronym. The failure of Esteban's plans accord authority to Clara and the union of women who subvert the senator and his coterie of aristocratic males. The birth of twin males does nothing to oust Blanca, the blank page on which Clara inscribes her views on patriarchy and colonial tyranny.

Clara del Valle's literary foil, Rosa del Valle, the perpetual virgin, takes meaning from the fragrance of romantic flower that sets her apart from her clear-eyed psychic sister, the family knight errant. At a Gothic moment in the childhood of Clara, she watches Dr. Cuevas turn into a vampire by performing an autopsy on Clara's sister "la bella (beautiful)" Rosa, the fairy princess of the del Valle household whose purity suggests the rosary.

Analyst Elizabeth Gough highlights "the importance of getting outside a scene to understand its internal meaning, of standing on the sidelines in order to comprehend what is occurring within the borders" (Gough, 2004, 101). At the thematic center of the scene, the power of the male over the inert cadaver prefigures Clara's adult quandaries with male authority figures, from husband Esteban Trueba to son-in-law Count Jean de Satigny and the ultimate vampire, the dictator who seizes the country. The author regenerates the voyeuristic scene in *Eva Luna* with Jochen's interruption of his father's degradation of his mother, at Tao Chi'en's viewing of violence against slave masters and Jacob Todd's spying on the elusive Joaquín Andieta in *Daughter of Fortune*, in the coming to knowledge of Aurora del Valle (dawn in the valley) about her husband's infidelity in *Portrait in Sepia*, and in *City of the Beasts* as Alex watches his father cutting the hair or Alex's mother, a victim of cancer.

Establishing Character

Allende's skill at selecting subtle names focuses on both genders. The impudent Eva, mother of humanity, and the tender Consuelo (consoler) in *Eva Luna* contrast less noble character names. Over the radio come the characters Montedónico (lord of the mountain) and Salvatierra (save the earth), both males in melodramas. For *Daughter of Fortune*, Allende names the heroine after George Bernard Shaw's Eliza Doolittle and the upbeat seasonal surname of Sommers. As an appropriate pairing, the author identifies Eliza's lover, Tao Chi'en, by Chinese characters signifying energy and serenity, a gesture toward his patience during the lengthy search for Eliza's wayward love and toward Tao Chi'en's vigorous lovemaking after Eliza accepts him as husband in *Portrait in Sepia*.

In *Island Beneath the Sea*, the author creates irony out of the temporary success of overseer named Prosper Cambray, who later shoots himself in the mouth rather than die at the hands of rebel slaves. The text makes much of the confused family of Maurice (Moorish) Valmorain, a dying colonial bearing a darkling name that passes to his grandson, an abolitionist. Secretly adept at Creole as well as French, the boy suffers soap in the mouth for referring to Tété, his nanny, as *maman* (mama). He ceases insulting his father with the word, but refuses to stop calling Tété's second child *ma soeurette* (my little sister). The text implies that Maurice can surrender the name "mama" because Tété fosters him in place of Eugenia (noblewoman), the "ill lady," but Rosette, his true little sister, remains so in his thoughts and loyalties (Allende, 2010, 137).

Allende chooses as anarchist from Habitation Saint-Lazare the Guinean abductee Gambo, a proud warrior bearing a Hausan name and reduced to "the boy in the kitchen" (*ibid.*, 139). The name suits the rebel by naming Gambo, Central African Republic, a former French town at Africa's heart. Reminiscent of novelist Joseph Conrad's *Heart of Darkness* (1899), the character values freedom and honor above other earthly treasures. An incidental irony, the historical Vicomte Philippe Blancheland, governor of Haiti, bears the name "white land," a pun that would have elicited titters from pro-black forces. For maximum drollery, Allende pictures Blancheland attended by four servants, a steward to supervise a tray holder, a coffee pourer, and an extender of the sugar bowl. Meanwhile, the steward stands at attention. A subsequent summit of Maroons and rebels at Bois Cayman enhances the meaning of "alligator woods," the clearing that Boukman chooses for the nighttime consortium with voodoo deities.

See also Gothic; myth

• *References and Further Reading*

Frick, Susan R. "Memory and Retelling: The Role of Women in *La casa de los espíritus*," *Journal of Iberian and Latin American Studies* 7:1 (June 2001): 27–41.

Gough, Elizabeth. "Vision and Division: Voyeurism in the Works of Isabel Allende," *Journal of Modern Literature* 27:4 (Summer 2004): 93–120.

Kling, Vincent. "Archetype, Not Ideology: Isabel Allende's Balance of Opposites," *Critical Insights* (October 2010): 239–257.

Weldt-Basson, Helene Carol. *Subversive Silences: Nonverbal Expression and Implicit Narrative Strategies in the Works of Latin American Women Writers*. Cranbury, NJ: Associated University Press, 2009.

nativism

Allende infuses her fiction with a nonjudgmental revelation of cultural indicators, for example, Pedro García's understanding of ant behaviors and diagnoses of broken bones in *The House of the Spirits* and Tensing's lack of interest in materialism and comfort and Nadia's skill at identifying odors and marking the passage of time in *Kingdom of the Golden Dragon*. Allende catalogs native traits during the conquest of Peru and Chile in *Inés of My Soul* as a differentiation of Inca, Mapuche, and Spanish values. For focus, the author describes the customs and innate skills of Felipe, the stable boy and mascot of Santiago. By characterizing his ability to merge with a horse during a hunt, the text enriches the concept of animism and oneness with nature, a quality that transforms Felipe into Lautaro, the mature chief and nemesis of the Spanish Général Pedro de Valdivia.

Indigenous life forces and joy in sexuality and oneness with nature permeate Allende's text, from the curative jungle herbs in "Walimai" and "Ester Lucero," boys and girls enjoying nude bathing in *City of the Beasts*, and the lusty sex of Hermelinda and her Asturian lover in "Toad's Mouth" to the ghostly habitation in "Phantom Palace" and the devotion of Lautaro and Guacolda, an Indian couple in *Inés of My Soul*. In multiple examples, Allende rewards the poor and downtrodden with strong libido and a yen for shared entertainments and meals to assuage the hurts of poverty and authoritarianism, a theme in *Of Love and Shadows*. In the resolution of *Forest of the Pygmies*, the performance of the Ezenji, a sacred dance, readies the hunters for expeditions into the jungle after game. Allende describes how the ritual, under a tyrant's rule, "degenerated in Ngoubé to become a tourney of death," a destruction of Central African worship into a desperate grasp on life as they pray for a successful hunt of elephants for their ivory tusks to prevent the sale of Aka children into slavery. (Allende, 2005, 231).

In outlining the outdoor freedoms and respectful courtships in the first-person narrative "Walimai," Allende reveals the tribal unity of the Children of the Moon, Amerindians who live in the shadow of the rainforest in a pre–Columbian civilization within range of rumors of Europeans. At the first encounter with whites, natives scorn a people who survive "without skill or courage," a charge the shaman Walimai levies against men who move clumsily through the undergrowth and who boast of the superiority of their religion and education (Allende, 1991, 129). The text, as analyzed by Dana Del George, "criticizes modern white culture from the perspective of a supernaturalist one" (George, 2001, 120). The story contrasts the outsized verbiage of whites with the tender, clandestine communication between Walimai and the disembodied voice of the Ila woman's spirit, which lodges in his sternum after the custom of the "good death" found in premodern tribal beliefs. Critic Stephen M. Hart notes that "Allende's view of the supernatural is not one in which the dead need to be propitiated" (Hart, 2003, 65). Rather, Walimai reveres the eternal nature of the spirit and sets about reuniting it with the nether world.

Native Evaluation

The significance of native invisibility impacts *The House of the Spirits* with plantation peasants "still living exactly as they had in colonial times" in physical, economic, and political isolation from modernity, medicine, and technology (Allende, 1985, 68). Esteban Trueba maintains his suzerainty under a belief that indigenous people are incapable of thinking, making decisions, and caring for themselves. According to analyst Jennifer Gibb, Trueba cloaks his containment of workers under an altruistic myth. Rather than admit that he burdens them with a primitive lifestyle, he "takes great pride in the fact that he is educating the people of Tres Marías and encouraging their immersion into a more European cultural system," from which they eventual free themselves (Gibb, 2010, 241).

Trueba's daughter Blanca, a child reared each summer in nature, enjoys the woods and river in the company of her pal, Pedro Tercero. At a magical moment in their maturation, they creep to the pasture to observe at dawn the birth of a colt, a rather clumsy literary reminder that, after menarche at 14, Blanca becomes a young woman. Although Pedro is a year behind her maturation, the text implies an instinctive knowledge of male-female differences and the "ecstatic passion that would torment them for the rest of their lives" (Allende, 1985, 174). Symbolically, they part at summer's end with secret kisses in the granary, a phallic image bearing the seeds of an adult love. As the tenor of change overwhelms the colonial plantation of Las Trés Marías, Pedro Tercero and an onslaught of disgruntled laborers make the first landfall under Esteban's sweeping survey. Native restlessness advances and retreats in a peasant surge that threatens the established hierarchy. Gradually, the do-alls of labor and domesticity subsume visions of ease and satiety with cries for justice.

For *Eva Luna*, Allende creates a compassionate character in the Turkish peddler Riad Halabí. He enters an area marked by jungle roaming and colonial Spanish attitudes, where "people are generous and forgive easily" (Allende, 1987, 178). Upon his arrival at Agua Santa, he takes charge of a tragic scene, supervising a funeral and wake for a boy shot through the head by a greedy outsider. The mangoes that the boy pilfers become weapons of a folk community that doubts that authorities will seek justice. The author turns into magical realism the filling of the killer's house with mangoes, which the desert heat turns into marmalade, a sweet blend paralleling the good nature of inhabitants. After Halabí settles in Agua Santa, he welcomes the pathetic Indians who visit on Saturdays and channels garden produce and handicrafts to the city to benefit local sellers. Allende accounts for his native hospitality as a tendency "to take in anyone with a look of need" (*ibid.*, 150).

To understand Halabí's nativism, the author explains at length the female side of an arranged marriage to Zulema, a 25-year-old woman from the old country. Ministrations of Arab women prepare the bride with henna on her hands, honeyed slippers on her feet, and cream on her depilated skin. The heavy symbolism of veiling during ribald songs and hair braided with pearls suggests the folk link between Halabí and the country people he lives among in the Western Hemisphere. Central to Arabic foodways, Halabí's favorite dishes require Eva's willingness to prepare couscous, hummus, falafel, tahini, kibbeh, yogurt soup, tabbouleh, stuffed grape leaves, and baklava, the staples of Turkey.

Coming of Age

Allende promotes native ideals in the emergence of youth into adulthood. The native élan of *Zorro* takes hold of Diego and Bernardo as they reach early manhood. Under White Owl's direction, the boys undergo a vision quest in the wild, where "deer, rabbits, mountain lions, and bears nosed around the camp; and at night they heard the howls of wolves and coyotes" (Allende, 2005, 73–74). As though conferring blessing and protection, an eagle glides above the boys. Identification with the totemic black foal and fox extends the image of the Great Spirit shielding the two boys as they step over the threshold of adolescence into manhood. The theme of protection remains active into Diego's transformation into Zorro, a chancy disguise against skilled swordsmen.

For *City of the Beasts*, Kate Cold introduces her grandson Alex to alternate philosophies by defining death as less fearful to Amazon natives than theft of the soul or tyranny over dreams. At Santa María de la Lluvia, the influx of prospectors and poachers of jungle animals and exploiters of lumber threatens the customs and beliefs of Indians whom Allende identifies as scions of Chinese nomads who entered North America via Alaska thousands of years ago. Through Padre Valdomero, the author valorizes the independence of natives to whom "freedom is more important than life itself" (Allende, 2002, 72). The priest explains that, above materialism, Brazilians value "the mental plane" that connects them to the wild (*ibid.*). Costume extends the link between the People of the Mist and the outdoors by supplying colored mud and flowers for decorating naked bodies and yellow feathers to crown the leader, Mokarita.

Complex relationships deepen the significance of the quest motif in what reviewer Angela J. Reynolds typifies as an eco-thriller. The patronizing of Nadia Santos by villain Mauro Carías implies that no one with education or ambition should live in the Amazon and condone its ways. By offering to educate her according to European dictates of womanhood and "make a little lady of her," Carías faults Brazil and its rearing of children as subpar in a land that measures times in "dawns, tides, seasons, and rains" (Allende, 2002, 112). Allende extends the differences in perception through Nadia's communication with the monkey Borobá and other animals and her understanding of the local language through social affinity because "words are not that important when you recognize intentions" (*ibid.*, 202). Reviewer Jane P. Fenn notes that the layering of unlikely events involves Nadia and Alex more deeply with the People of the Mist, revealing social and survival traditions, as with the handholds that lead up the waterfall, the tunnels that link huts, and gendered rituals.

Nativism continues to separate Nadia from less intuitive people in *Kingdom of the Golden Dragon*. Her telepathy with two cobras in an Indian market and her rapport with Borobá and Tschewang, the royal leopard of King Dorji, indicate that animal communication applies worldwide. The king's respect for Nadia's skills reflects his reverence for nature, which he demonstrates in a gift of bird portraits that he photographed. Conjunction with beasts and their languages continues in *Forest of the Pygmies*, in which Nadia learns to communicate with Kobi, a bull elephant who displays his affection, and a female gorilla and her baby, whom Nadia and Alex rescue from a pit. Allende extends the thanks of natives after the adventurers free Aka women and their children from barracks. To celebrate, the liberated natives strike up a spontaneous dance to African drumming.

See also Zorro

• *References and Further Reading*

Fenn, Jane P. "Review: *City of the Beasts*," *School Library Journal* (February 2003): 77.

George, Dana Del. *The Supernatural in Short Fiction of the Americas: The Other World in the New World.* Westport, CT: Greenwood, 2001.

Gibb, Jennifer. "Victory of the Ash Buttocks: The Role of Hybridity in Colonization, Decolonization, and Postcolonization," *Journal of the Utah Academy of Sciences, Arts & Letters* 87 (2010): 235–243.

Hart, Stephen M. *Isabel Allende, "Eva Luna" and "Cuentos de Eva Luna."* London: Grand & Cutler, 2003.
Reynolds, Angela J. "Review: *City of the Beasts*," *School Library Journal* 48:11 (November 2002).

Of Love and Shadows

Allende's anti-authoritarian novel *Of Love and Shadows*, which critic Margaret McKale calls a documentary and testimonial discourse, invokes a subtle subversion engineered by victims of covert violence. The plot opens on a Latin American dictatorship five years after *The House of the Spirits*. Analyst Aníbal González characterizes the post-coup novel as the production of "amorous and sentimental elements [that] definitively triumph over violence and suffering" (González, 2010, 42). Allende states her promotion of hope through a revival of generosity, justice, and love, which she terms "old-fashioned" values that speak to "real dilemmas in the lives of the nation and of readers themselves" (Nelson, 2002, 196). Quiet acts of resistance emerge from solidarity, a peasant strength that draws men, women, and children into actions as simple as viewing police in coverups of crime. Critics damning the author with faint praise as an imitator of Gabriel García Marquez withdrew the charge in 1984 after the publication of *Of Love and Shadows*.

Allende's survey of the peasant underground and resistance to military rule speaks the truths of an eyewitness to what *Bookmarks* critic Jessica Teisch called "the often toxic mix of love and politics" (Teisch, 2007). Although schooled by Boom authors, Allende developed a unique style by melding chivalric storytelling with female empowerment in an era of individual heroism and transformative love. In contrast to desperate peasant actions, Beatriz Alcántara, a snobbish grass widow, cultivates the "golden and powerful elite" (Allende, 1987, 168). She conceals a search for her wandering husband Eusebio, assumed to be a *desaparecido*, by taking her query to the Archbishop, a more discreet venue than the police or media. She credits the Vicariate with defying the government and assisting "the persecuted, never stopping to inquire about their political hue" (Allende, 1987, 40). To regain social prominence, she escapes into "the orderly peaceful world of the fashionable neighborhoods, the exclusive beach clubs, the ski slopes, the summers in the country" that reassure her safety from the murderous dictatorship (*ibid.*, 111). The padding of materialism and patriotic passion shield Beatriz from the reality of indiscriminate abductions, book burnings, and corpses floating in the canals.

Allende builds the plot on urgency in identifying the significance of a teenage saint who possesses curative power and in clarifying a growing body of evidence against the militant dictatorship. She illustrates the value of community in what critic Alice Nelson calls "issues concerning the body as a real and symbolic terrain" (Nelson, 2002, 11). The abduction and murder of Evangelina Ranquileo and her brother Pradelio's flight to a mountain hideout create shock waves that rupture a dictator's silencing of horrific deeds to halt "subversive acts and fucking up the whole country" (Allende, 1987, 131). The evidence at the abandoned mine at Los Riscos refutes the martinet Beatriz, who values "law and order" at the cost of a few beggars' lives (*ibid.*, 168).

The novel's climax, the discovery of mass murder and a communal grave in the mine, vivifies the definition of "climax" as a point in the action beyond which nothing can return to its previous state of innocence or denial. The opening in the earth "drilled in the mountainside" becomes "a mouth shouting a soundless scream," a personification dramatizing the centrality of folk revolt and a free press to revealing the crimes of tyranny (*ibid.*, 178). Paralleling the humanoid mouth, a rumor spreads "like a fire storm, from mouth to mouth, house to house, valley to valley, until it was known everywhere" (*ibid.*, 228). The dismembered hand of a cadaver ensures the coming to knowledge of two investigators into national atrocities, an historical massacre that attorney Máximo Pacheco revealed in his documentary *Lonquén* (1983). Upon Francisco Leal's return to the mine shaft, it has become a sepulcher — the tomb of Evangelina.

The eternal pairing of love and death empowers the novel by supplying an antidote to terror and despair at the power wielded by the Political Police and torturers. Wedged in adjacent to a story of passion, the anarchist Leal deconstructs a soldier's indoctrination to an infantile pride in a uniform with regimental embellishments for "the thousand puerile ceremonies in which they waste their lives" (Allende, 1987, 195). The placement of diction — "perversion," "humiliating," "vanity," "passive obedience," "despotic discipline," "stupid order"—conveys a liberal rejection of brainwashing the young with militaristic myth. In the fulfillment of military order, Allende conveys the intent of the Political Police to subvert justice. The characters shift their publication of atrocities from the vulnerable press to the Cardinal, the local head of the only institution that can defeat a fierce junta.

A study of female silence in *Of Love and Shadows* reveals the physical interaction of male and female in situations in which women confront patriarchy with hyperbolic wordlessness, the investigative ploy of Irene and the necessary result of the murderous assault that nearly kills her. Digna receives the news of Evangelina's interment in the mine with stoic calm, an element that generates solidarity among the peasantry. A method of subverting the status quo, the refusal to engage in dialogue expresses more plainly than argument the female rejection of iniquitous values and norms. In the historic mode of Julia Alvarez's *In the Time of the Butterflies* (1994), Allende depicts female secrecy out of the mainstream as a means of concealing from a male-dominant society a folk conspiracy against a power-mad general, death squads, and mass graves.

• *References and Further Reading*

González, Aníbal. *Love and Politics in the Contemporary Spanish American Novel.* Austin: University of Texas Press, 2010.

McKale, Margaret A. Morales. *Literary Nonfiction in Works by Isabel Allende and Guadalupe Loaeza.* Columbus: Ohio State University, 2002.

Nelson, Alice A. *Political Bodies: Gender, History, and the Struggle for Narrative Power in Recent Chilean Literature.* Danvers, MA: Bucknell University Press, 2002.

Teisch, Jessica. "Isabel Allende: Book by Book," *Bookmarks* (1 November 2007).

order

Allende depicts Latin American society positioned on "three patriarchal bastions—church, state, and the military," often reduced to church and a military state (Perricone, 2003, 84). She maintains a tension between tradition and social and religious order and the inevitable changes that mark history, for example, the arrival of Spaniards in Chile and the establishment of Santiago in *Inés of My Soul*, the building of an Alpine Eden in the Caribbean in *Eva Luna*, and the establishment of Chinatown in San Francisco in *Daughter of Fortune*. In a brief set-to between old and young in the story "The Little Heidelberg," Allende pictures the exhibitionism of young motorcyclists with their boots, chains, and keys clanking to intimidate elderly guests. Without violence, the noise and derision give place to pleasure and amusement after members of the band intervene. The serenity implies that youthful intrusions lack the menace to rout the older generation from a country entertainment center. A more disastrous insurgency of guests in "Phantom Palace" reduces the palace to a shambles eventually overgrown with the disorder of the jungle. More dismaying, the volcanic mud that kills Avucena in "And of Clay Are We Created" pictures nature as the undeniable master of human disarray.

In the 1920s in *The House of the Spirits*, colonial order begins to crack and give place to democracy. While women embody intellectual and artistic values, members of the landed gentry, including reactionary Senator Esteban Trueba and his pals, plot to ensure control of peons by rigging elections. To certify the status quo, they court peasant voters with empanadas, barbecue, and wine and harangue the masses to support the conservative party, a contingent that "grew fat and old and spent their time in hair-splitting discussions" (Allende, 1985, 347). Additional chicanery involves the bribing of police and scare-mongering about job loss if the party loses the majority. More insidious, the use of the term "patriotic conscience" arouses homeland fealty and suspicions of liberals, radicals, Communists, and atheists (*ibid.*, 89). The multiphase plan results in "perfect order" free of the disruptions threatened by "Indians and Negroes," a stereotyping of nonwhites as the instigators of unrest and dictatorships (*ibid.*).

The grand disarrangement of the earthquake and its aftermath, like the Haitian Revolution in *Island Beneath the Sea*, generates a disorder that stymies Esteban. The whole concept of order shifts downward for the ruling class and upward for peasants, who use the disaster as an opportunity for revolt. After giving up estate management, he runs for a senate seat and further disarranges the household on the corner of the High District, where Clara and the Mora sisters summon spirits, Jaime collects the homeless for short-term residency, and Nicolás brings his girlfriend Amanda to add her dark presence to the chaos. Within the maelstrom of party platforms and hallway ghosts, an invisible no man's land separates Esteban's tidy political realm from that of his obdurate wife, who builds surreal "rooms, staircases, turrets, and terraces" to contain the mix (Allende, 1985, 259).

Creative Order

The unconventional lifestyle of Clara del Valle becomes the key to reordering both family and nation, a giving of self that Allende revisits in *Portrait in Sepia* in Doña Elvira Domínguez's sewing classes and schools for tenant children. Before Clara's death around 1958, she distributes clothes to the staff and jewels to Blanca and organizes her notebooks "that bore witness to life in minute detail" (Allende, 1985, 174). Esteban, the organizer of earthly order, prepares his wife for burial and determines that Clara's tomb should also give final rest to Nívea's head that has been "gathering dust down in the basement since God knows when" (*ibid.*, 333). Concluding the rites, streams of mourners bid farewell, including Pedro Segundo, the restorer of order to Las Tres Marías. The text pictures Esteban's design of a grotesque mausoleum, an overblown tribute out of proportion to Pedro's simple gift of wild flowers, a fitting reminder of Clara's unfettered spirit and gentle life.

Literary historian Donald Leslie Shaw cites the author's intent to strip reality of chaos by imposing the order of artifice and fictional patterns, even though "life is not that way" (Shaw, 2002, 181). For the creation of a stereotypical German village in *Eva Luna*, Rupert and Burgel apply industry to their tourist trap, which bears authentic touches in apple strudel and a handmade cuckoo clock. Their two daughters and nephew, Rolf Carlé, attack the day-to-day chores of training dogs for sale, fluffing eiderdowns, and gathering strawberries to add to desserts. Even Rolf's erotic night three to a bed with his cousins follows a prescribed order of preference as well as "techniques to ration his energy and pleasure" (Allende, 1987, 98). Rolf's presence in *The Stories of Eva Luna* perpetuates a realism that is both lyrical and sensuous. Editor Andrea O'Reilly reports that Allende's unique style imposes "fictional order on chaos by a long trancelike process," admirably demonstrated in the witty romantic romp "The Guggenheim Lovers" and the life-and-death fable "Interminable Life" (O'Reilly, 2010, 48).

Shaw characterizes Allende's portrayal of history as "straightforward, reader-friendly," yet it reveals underlying corruption through postmodern conventions of metafiction, feminist characterization of males, and circular narrative (*ibid.*). Key to her negotiation of truth lie mysteries that disclose hidden forces below their surface appearance, particularly the media's representation in *Of Love and Shadows* of walled-off slums that deserved invisibility because they "did not follow the order of time and the laws of God" (Allende, 1987, 168). To achieve a faux reality, a militaristic regime requires the complicity of the press to exalt consumerism and to acclaim "crime as achievement, lack of scruples as virtue, and selfishness as a natural requirement," a subversion of truth akin to the cockeyed principles of George Orwell's *Animal Farm* (McKale, 2002, 122).

The disorder in *Of Love and Shadows* stems initially from a display of hysteria in the peasant girl/woman Evangelina Ranquileo. By emulating passion in her bowed back and gyrations, the daily event presents to gawkers a physical anomaly set at the ambiguous stroke of noon, the divider between morning and evening. Critic Aníbal González interprets the seizures as evidence of the mystical and the diabolical, which merit variant interpretations from neighbors, a midwife, a physician, and a priest and Protestant minister. González associates the daily convulsions with "the biblical 'noonday demon'" mentioned in Psalms 91:6 and "the antinomies that divide Chile as a country" (González, 2010, 46, 47). By investing journalistic talents and curiosity in Evangelina's "dubious miracles," Irene Beltrán and Francisco Leal turn the girl's daily torment into the fulcrum for disclosing the atrocities of a corrupt government (*ibid.*, 127).

The Pre-Industrial Frontier

In *Daughter of Fortune* in episodes set in California, Allende indicates that the disorderly frontier prefaces a new state bound by law. For Eliza in the mining camps around Sacramento, freedom means a desertion of the "impenetrable armor of good manners and conventions," the routines and social manacles that bind her within the Anglo-Chilean norms of Valparaíso (Allende, 1999, 275). In place of the genteel parlor, Eliza discovers that "the vices of gambling, liquor, and brothels rule" (*ibid.*, 280). No longer afraid of the unknown or eccentric, she plays myriad roles as the deaf-mute Chinese boy and the ingénue of an acting troupe, switching to suit the need. Reflecting on the romance that forces her out of the Sommers home, she rejoices in a rebirth and the euphoria of nomadism among people who are inventing "absolute equality without authorities, police, or religion" (*ibid.*, 291).

For the *City of the Beasts* trilogy, Allende characterizes the order of closed preindustrial societies, which have only peripheral experience with industrialized states. In the first text, the People of the Mist go to extremes to protect privacy and security from poachers and exploiters. Because of the lack of interbreeding for animals, the sloth-like beasts in the title maintain prehistoric attributes, a defiance of Darwin's principles of evolution. For *Kingdom of the Golden Dragon*, the monarch's insistence on order and control wards off change in an effort to protect ecological balance within the Forbidden Kingdom, a nature sanctuary. Landscape artist Judit Kinski, in a bid to win the favor of King Dorji, dubs the monarch a "white knight for the ecology," a title rich in medieval gallantry (Allende, 2003, 105).

In the final sequel, *Forest of the Pygmies*, the destruction of Aka and Bantu symbiosis enables King Kosongo and his security force to undermine nature's balance. Through intimidation, the tyrant fleeces Central Africans of gold, diamonds, and ivory from the few remaining elephants. Allende turns the royal court into a comic shambles by having a sharpshooter disable a carrier of the king's portable throne. The unforeseen disorder strips Kosongo of pretensions after he "crashed, tangled in his mantle, hat askew and bawling with rage" (Allende, 2005, 261). Revelation of Commandant Maurice Mbembelé's pose as the king precedes the daring challenge of one-on-one combat with the hunter Beyé-Dokou, a resetting of the biblical battle of David with Goliath in I Samuel 17:1–58. With the dictator's demise, the Aka and Bantu restore their cooperative lifestyle and reclaim Aka families from slavery.

• *References and Further Reading*

McKale, Margaret A. Morales. *Literary Nonfiction in Works by Isabel Allende and Guadalupe Loaeza*. Columbus: Ohio State University, 2002.
O'Reilly, Andrea. *Encyclopedia of Motherhood*. Thousand Oaks, CA: Sage, 2010.
Perricone, C.R. "Allende and Valenzuela: Dissecting the Patriarchy," *South Atlantic Review* 67:4 (Fall, 2002): 80–105.
Shaw, Donald Leslie. *A Companion to Modern Spanish-American Fiction*. Rochester, NY: Tamesis, 2002.

patriarchy

Isabel Allende structures a series of political love stories within a governmental context to inform readers of the struggle of normal emotion to survive under tyranny. Her writings picture men who lord their power over women, a *modus operandi* that critic Stephen Hart calls "patrocentric political oppression" (Kristal, 2005, 197). A cartoonesque example, Ludovic Leblanc, the anthropologist in the *City of the Beasts* trilogy, propagates theories based on beliefs that the dominant man must commit atrocities "in order to transmit his genes," a concept skewed by his self-enlargement through grandstanding and fabricated acts of heroism (Allende, 2002, 138–139). His female nemesis, Kate Cold, easily defies Leblanc with frequent caustic asides and refutations.

Allende introduces the thundering masculinity of the womanizer in "The Gold of Tomás Vargas" and the strongman in "Two Words." In the latter story, just the sound of El Mulato's horses scares all citizens from the plaza except the storyteller Belisa Crepusculario, a match for the puffed-up bully who serves "the Colonel," a model of the military autocrat. According to critic Janice Radway, the author champions the self-fulfilled female protagonist as a mark of feminist achievement. Rechanneling romantic fiction from formulaic Cinderella wish fulfillment to subversion of the protective male, the renegade author became the first Latin American author to claim that regional class violence is an outgrowth of male obduracy.

Critic Donica Radulescu explains that "the more oppressive of women a given society or community is, the more women establish indelible ties with each other and learn to 'stick together,'" an element established in Amy Tan's *The Kitchen God's Wife* and Julia Alvarez's historical novel *In the Time of the Butterflies* (Radulescu, 2002, 477). For Eliza, the foundling mothered by Rose Sommers and Mama Fresia in *Daughter of Fortune*, the female realms of kitchen, laundry, sewing room, and bedrooms protect women from the stern supremacy of Jeremy Sommers. Rose, a skilled deceiver, retreats into headaches and migraine blindness to wrest from Jeremy promises of a proper dowry and marriage for

Eliza. In private, Rose admits that marriage enslaves the wife to the husband, who confers "fewer rights than those of a servant or a child" (Allende, 1999, 51). To ensure maximum independence for Eliza, Rose trains the teenager in "dissembling, manipulation, and cunning," the traditional methods by which repressed women elude patriarchal mastery (*ibid.*). The training prepares Eliza for a world where woman "could not travel, sign legal documents, go to court, sell or buy anything" (*ibid.*, 64).

Allende's work develops strategies for coping with a domestic and governmental oligarchy within a macho culture, such as the ridicule of female fantasy, the constraints of women's education, and the censorship of mail to women in *Daughter of Fortune*. A significant diminution of women, the marriage brokered by a bishop and the father of the bride, removes interference by the future wife, Paulina del Valle, and her future mother-in-law, the widow Rodríguez de Santa Cruz. Justification for a "man's affair," the protection of old family honor, requires an elaborate ruse that fools no one, especially the elite, who recognize common phases of social subterfuge (Allende, 1999, 56). Radway notes the significance of standard male-female situations in women's fiction and validates such recurring motifs as the kept woman and the silent and patient housewife. In a style reminiscent of Pearl Buck's classic mother O-lan in *The Good Earth* and the peasant woman in *The Mother*, Allende dramatizes the devalued female head of household in the marginal existence of Tao Chi'en's mother, whose life ends in Kwangtung with a simple funeral "because she was a woman" (Allende, 1999, 154). In streets and canals, baby girls lie like garbage "chewed on by dogs or rats" (*ibid.*, 162). Critic Tania Modleski adds to the survey of female double binds the fact that Allende's so-called chick lit "is as much a protest against as an endorsement of the feminine condition" (Lindsay, 2003, 121).

In *The House of the Spirits*, Esteban Trueba epitomizes the patriarchal ideology of the authoritarian husband, a defining presence in his home, plantation, and community in what analyst C.R. Perricone calls a "system based on false and illogical premises" (Perricone, 2002, 103). Esteban resolves on his honeymoon to abandon "rape and whoring" in favor of genteel seduction to envelope his young wife Clara body and soul (Allende, 1985, 118). Male control follows what critic María Roof calls "traditional oligarchical lines to exclude children sired by the patron with indigenous women" (Roof, 2010, 79). The ostracism of illegitimate offspring engenders a suppurating wound in the text, a running sore that initiates violent rebellion and payback. In addition to an unacknowledged lineage of angry illegitimate children, Senator Trueba enriches himself on acreage and mining, the era's sources of Chilean wealth, which he acquires through privileged loans. He wraps himself in the male mantles of "family, the fatherland, private property, and the Church," all of which validate only those children bearing the surname of legitimate fathers (Allende, 1985, 3).

Virility and Menace

In *Of Love and Shadows*, Allende continues to blame "the macho element" for creating a climate of evil in Latin America. The cause lies in corrupt governments guilty of random human rights violations, beginning with curfews and censorship and retrogressing into arrest, imprisonment, and execution without due process. Allende cites as a model of conservative profiling the belief of Captain Gustavo Morante that females fall into two distinct categories—whores and decent women. His blind allegiance to men like murderer and rapist Juan de Dios Ramírez crumbles after the Political Police gun down Irene Beltrán, forcing her to flee the country while still recuperating from bullets to the chest. In contrast to women idealized by Ramírez and her stodgy fiancé, Irene embraces sexuality as a human right for the expression of physical and emotional joy.

From the beginning of the picaresque novel *Eva Luna*, Allende stresses the power of Spanish friars over the orphan Consuelo. When she reaches adulthood at age twelve, the men gratefully confine her and five native girls to the Convent of the Little Sisters of Charity before the six virgins can express their womanhood and bring carnal shame to the mission. The immurement of females begins with a nun locking them into a cloister, a Gothic image that smacks of the labyrinthine enclosures of Victorian novels. In freedom at the home of Riad Halabí in Agua Santa, Eva Luna experiences opportunities at an unprecedented rate, notably "writing and a proof of existence" (Allende, 197, 158). From learning to read to cooking for the community as a gesture of friendship, she rids herself of the paternalism that had prevented Consuelo from developing into a whole person.

Nonetheless, Allende clings to established patriarchal patterns by revealing Halabí's relief that the arrival of a nephew ensures protection by a male while Halabí travels. The former relationship between Eva and Riad sours after Kamal replaces her in domino games and evenings at the movies. The androcentric traditions of Arabs place Riad in an untenable bind to observe "centuries of taboos ... and the bonds of blood," which demand a men-only audience for casual amusements (Allende, 1987, 162). The text indicates that Riad changes his social behavior to accommodate Kamal's gender expectations rather than to tyrannize his wife and Eva Luna, whom he compensates with small gifts.

Unlike social novelist Luisa Valenzuela, Allende extends sympathy to her patriarchs, especially those who destroy their own peace of mind. Esteban Trueba's conflicted *machista* attitudes and accounts by female narrators belie the air of confidence he flaunts in public before male peers who admire his willful fornication with female laborers. He creates incongruity by sitting at a desk before "a grandiose portrait of the Founding Father at some valiant battle," a general description that strips combat of glory and historical significance (Allende, 1985, 344). The scene alludes to Général José de San Martin, liberator of Argentina, Chile, and Peru from Spanish overlords. As patron of people in the south, San Martin freed Indians from bondage before deferring to Simon Bolivar, a more practical savior who suppressed the chaos that followed liberation. For Esteban, the job of king-maker slips from his hands, leaving him disillusioned with the forces that sweep conservatives back into power.

Medical Paternalism

In adulthood, the author guarded herself against the power and arrogance of authorities who resembled to her the Pinochet regime. After the death of daughter Paula Frías Allende in December 1991, in an interview with Alfred Starkman, Allende verbalized her fear of the male-dominated medical establishment. A bit of family history recalls the doctor who treated Allende's mother for hysteria by injecting her with a sedative that silenced her for half a day, a common quelling of women by male physicians. The diagnosis dramatizes the standard diagnosis for women's despair and anger as far back as classical Greek medicine, particularly during the nineteenth-century treatment of female depression, the subject of Charlotte Perkins Gilman's classic feminist story "The Yellow Wallpaper."

Like Dr. Henry Kelekian, the attendant ogre in Margaret Edson's Pulitzer Prize–winning play *Wit*, the stereotypical doctor appears as "a high priest, masked and robed in white" who "officiates" over birthing with arrogance and a demand for timing convenient with his calendar (Allende, 1999, 188). Paula's medical team pursues objectivity to the point of churlishness, leaving the patient's family bereft of hope or encouragement. Doctors spare no time for lengthy observation of Paula. Likewise, medical students and professors "pass through and examine her like some animal" (*ibid.*, 128).

As Paula's condition worsens into coma, technology and pharmacopoeia form the armor of the doctor-warrior. For the author, medical machines, probes, tubes, and syringes become a gauntlet to be "saved from" (Allende, 1999, 121). At first, the author accepted that "none of these strange doctors ... promised to restore my daughter's health" (*ibid.*, 237). The daily onslaught erodes Allende's heart with "pessimism and the sordidness of the ward," a Gothic atmosphere similar to the surroundings in Sylvia Plath's *The Bell Jar* (*ibid.*, 128). At a low point in Paula's care, the text pictures the medical staff as "vanquished," an appropriate descriptor for males who approach ailments as battles to be won or lost (*ibid.*, 93).

In contrast to Paula's neurologist, Tao Chi'en, the herbalist and acupuncturist in *Portrait in Sepia* takes an Asian approach to healing. With humility and concealed sorrow, he advises Captain John Sommers on giving up gin. Simultaneously, Tao hides "the feelings of terrible impotence that overcome him when he confronts "how limited the resources of his science were and how immense man's suffering" (Allende, 2001, 15). The cultural difference between Tao and the physicians in Madrid highlights alternate approaches toward helping the sick and disparate attitudes toward the conquest of disease. A more gendered view of diagnoses occurs during the treatment of Severo's war injury. Because the Vergara family doctor fails to halt "feverish paroxysms," Nívea supersedes the professional opinion with her own observation (*ibid.*, 117). She realizes that physical illness results less from the amputation than from a post-war sickness of soul, a complex sorrow she treats with affection, a womanly antidote reduced in slang to TLC.

Female Independence

Critic María Claudia André admires the author's skill at defeating patriarchy in *Portrait in Sepia* to allow female characters to control their actions, thoughts, fortunes, and destinies. Paulina del Valle, the matriarch and entrepreneur, defies the male hegemony that reduces her in girlhood to embroidery and the rosary, a symbolic bondage enforced by Roman Catholicism. Her father, Agustín del Valle, a crusty Valparaiso agriculturist confined to a wheelchair, acknowledges the repressive nature of rearing a girl and of controlling the poor. The pairing names a common linkage in Allende's fiction, which pictures women as compassionate to the underclass, where females like Amanda and Ana Díaz in *The House of the Spirits* and the Widow Andieta in *Daughter of Fortune* predominant solely because of gender restrictions. As a chastening to "the daunting Agustín del Valle" for his tyrannical hold on his daughter, the novel glories in Paulina's spiraling wealth as a result of shrewd investments in a man's world via her transport of produce on her shipping line and the ferrying of fresh water to the transcontinental railroad (Allende, 2001, 7). As a fillip to Agustín's patriarchy, Allende confines him "in the history books of Chile as the founder of a small and miserly, ultraconservative political party" that ultimately disappears (*ibid.*, 11).

In adulthood, Paulina maintains a womanly defiance of male control by marrying the mate of her choice, Feliciano Rodríguez de Santa Cruz. She extends her campaign for selfhood by dominating her husband, who shares Agustín's diminution of women from humans. Ironically, Feliciano, a womanizer for life, demeans females as capricious sirens, "delicious creatures with little moral fiber" (Allende, 2001, 10). At one point, Paulina slices the sleeves and legs from her husband's clothes and leaves the shreds at his office door as a symbolic dismemberment of his manhood. The symbolic gesture implies her willingness to immobilize any man attempting to bully her, particularly one involved in a public liaison with Amanda Lowell, a publicity-seeking courtesan.

Through deception, the novel develops female contrasts to Paulina's brash womanhood. Severo del Valle's unidentified mother finds herself with "no vote at the patriarchal table," yet conspires with the Virgin Mary to solve the coming-of-age problems of her gangly son (Allende, 2001, 21). A more shocking affront to *machismo*, Sor María Escapulario, a parochial school teacher, subverts church patriarchy by encouraging the feminism of Nívea del Valle rather follow the parochial school curriculum devoted to grooming docile girls. To train Severo's daughter Aurora, grandmother Paulina hires as the child's tutor an agnostic suffragist, a woman free of both church and governmental control. Paulina prefers a socialist to nuns to "counteract a little of the conservative and patriarchal hypocrisy of this family" (Allende, 2001, 145).

For *Island Beneath the Sea*, Allende draws an immediate contrast between courtesan Violette Boisier, a 15-year-old mulatta who negotiates with patrons her price and future, and Eugenia García del Solar, the 19-year-old Spanish beauty who obeys her irritable brother Sancho in matters of courtship. Before Eugenia can age out of the marriage market, Sancho shares refreshments with suitor Toulouse Valmorain in the garden pergola and resolves the issue of engagement and wedlock. The text notes that "Eugenia was not present for the final details," being left to decide matters of her trousseau (Allende, 2010, 27). Allende's mockery of the betrothal of a choice virgin and her brother's "charlatan eloquence" expends no compassion on a social milieu seriously lacking in true romance (*ibid.*). The joke ricochets against the patriarchal Valmorain, who misinterprets Eugenia's silence as modesty rather than ignorance of French. Male primacy continues to dominate thought and behavior. At the announcement of Eugenia's pregnancy, Valmorain exclaims, "A son!," his first thought (*ibid.*, 64).

See also male persona

• *References and Further Reading*

André, María Claudia "Breaking Through the Maze: Feminist Configurations of the Heroic Quest in Isabel Allende's *Daughter of Fortune* and *Portrait in Sepia*," *Latin American Literary Review* 30:60 (2002): 74–90.

Kristal, Efraín, ed. *The Cambridge Companion to the Latin American Novel*. New York: Cambridge University Press, 2005

Lindsay, Claire. *Locating Latin American Women Writers: Cristina Peri Rossi, Rosario Ferré, Albalucía Angel, and Isabel Allende*. New York: Peter Lang, 2003.

Perricone, C. R. "Allende and Valenzuela: Dissecting the Patriarchy," *South Atlantic Review* 67:4 (Fall, 2002): 80–105.

Radulescu, Domnica. *Sisters of Medea: The Tragic Heroine across Cultures*. New Orleans: University Press of the South, 2002.

Roof, María, "Maryse Condé and Isabel Allende: Family Saga Novels," *Critical Insights* (October 2010): 74–85.

Paula

By reliving the suffering and death of her daughter in the memoir *Paula*, Allende published an epistolary eulogy. The author anticipated the tender tone and terrorizing atmosphere by the agonizing death of Azucena in "And of Clay Are We Created" and the sufferings of Irene Beltrán from gunshot wounds in *Of Love and Shadows*. Critic Anita

Savio declared *Paula* Allende's "most powerful work to date ... published to huge literary acclaim" (Savio, 2002). In relating Paula's story, Allende took an urgent midlife trajectory across her own past and the final moments shared with her dying firstborn. In the analysis of Miriam Fuchs, Allende's choices boiled down to "no constructive or reconstructive narrative possibilities," only the events themselves (Fuchs, 2004, 9). In obedience to the dictates of separation, sorrow, and recovery, the author followed her mantra: Write what should not be forgotten. Through magical thinking, she envisioned a time when the composition revived her daughter, like Sleeping Beauty, from the evil of inherited disease. Fuchs labeled the unusual merger of memoir and autobiography a "biopathography ... a version of Paula from the outside" (*ibid.*, 164).

The result, a journalistic immediacy and interiority based on family dread of death, affirmed the humanity of a 28-year-old girl while speculating on her unfulfilled promise. Ironically, Allende recalled warning Paula about life's brevity and receiving a quippy reply from her daughter. As an extension of family loss, the isolated author put herself in Paula's place and merged into "the child and girl I was, the woman I am, the old woman I shall be ... all water in the same rushing torrent" (Allende, 1995, 23). Allende looked outward, connecting the crisis to Chile's political upheaval and exile, another situation over which the memoirist had no control. Unable to transmute the hospital scenes, the author advanced from the historical fiction of *The House of the Spirits* to a more painful nonfiction about what Fuchs called "a contested body or territory invaded by an invisible adversary" (Fuchs, 2004, 17). In so doing, the author transforms autobiography and family biography into "a maternal ethical activity" that restores equilibrium (*ibid.*, 22).

Although Willie Gordon advised suing the hospital for administering the wrong dosage, the author declined because "I couldn't go through the pain" (Moline, 2003, 89). To fill in the gestalt of lineage and family with memory, Allende wrote 190 letters to her mother and created a literary version of a baby book filled with anecdote, stories intended to jolt Paula to wakefulness. Like a quilt pieced from scraps of memorable events, the text articulated the generation that preceded Paula's birth to the Allende-Llona-Frías clan. Critic Isabel Dulfano explained: "To compensate for Paula's death, a state of voicelessness, Allende rekindles the rupture in the female genealogy and narrative by appropriating Paula's place" (Dulfano, 2006, 498). An I/thou narrative built along the Hebrew humanist lines of Martin Buber's philosophy, *Paula* filled in an eternal void created by an untimely physical collapse, which the mother euphemistically labels a long sleep. A broader community as far away as Madrid prayed for Paula, sharing "humanity's most ancient and inevitable sorrow" (Allende, 1995, 291).

Fuchs characterized the joint mother/grandmother effort at resuscitation as "feminine resolve and maternal solidarity ... powerful enough to vanquish death" and the possibility of amnesia or mental retardation (Fuchs, 2004, 175). With faith in the unfathomable Christian practice of laying on of hands, the mother placed her palms on Paula's head and chest in an effort to project energy and wellness. A short period of breathing without help from the respirator raised Allende's optimism that Paula maintained enough life to survive. Inconsistent with hope, Allende gave thanks for Paula's "absolute solitude": "It would be much worse if you understood how ill you are" (Fuchs, 171; Allende, 1995, 127).

While spooling out the family's beginnings, the author advanced from chronicler to analyst, the logician penetrating existential mysteries of family members long dead. Of necessity, she followed truth from observable fact into honest fiction to validate emotion.

The worst of her fixations, maternal love, overwhelmed her thoughts and broke her heart as Paula regressed into a pre-infantile fetus, silenced by a metabolic impairment. The author pictured her "absent, mute, paralyzed" (Allende, 1995, 162). The melodrama influenced Isabel's tone and cadence, freeing flow, then damming it with the unforeseen—Paula's transfer to the neurology ward, a heart attack, and dwindling hope of medical intervention and rescue. At a personal epiphany, Isabel turned motherhood to an emblem of "an enormous protective presence" (Allende, 1995, 30). Like a lioness, Allende commanded, "You are the star of this illness, you must give birth to your own health, fearlessly and with great fortitude" (*ibid.*, 189).

As Paula progressed from patient to comatose victim to subject of observation to corpse, Isabel retreated to "a time of immobility and meditation," a state of anticipation reversing the prenatal relationship between mother and fetus (Correas de Zapata, 2002, 75). The elegy followed an existential time framework of catastrophe followed by realization of the intractability of mortality and bereavement. In the no man's land of terminal illness marked by the hum of a respirator and pricks of neurology tests, the author joined a community of lab technicians, medical personnel, and the patients and families who shared Paula's room. Grappling for handfuls of hope, the author intended "to distract [death] so it [could] not find [her] door" (Allende, 1995, 82).

Wracked with guilt for trusting the medical establishment, the author imagined herself trapped in a blind alley or on a rudderless raft floating through the tides of pain. A vision of Paula jolted Isabel with the decrements of dying—of crossing from one world into another. The dream daughter stated her need to die to end the hurt and physical degeneration. Wearied by the struggle to survive, the apparition reassured her mother, "It's all useless now.... I have lived my time" (Allende, 1995, 315). Promising to communicate "as a constant, soft presence," the vision comforted her mother and enabled her to hold Paula as she expired with grace. Sapped by the year-long vigil, the author/mother declared herself a victim of trauma: "I'm lost. I don't know who I am" (*ibid.*, 319). In praise of the book, reviewer Ruth Behar asserted, "*Paula* is a heartbreaking lament, written with the charged poetry that emerges at those times when there is an urgent need to speak, though one knows that words, no matter how ravishingly spoken, will change nothing" (Axelrod-Contrada, 2011, 118).

After encountering death, the great humbler and equalizer, Allende accepted that "It was her karma to die young; mine is to live for her, remembering her" (Correas de Zapata, 2002, 88). The layering of fiction and reality informed the author of her reason for bearing in her heart the courage and death of Omaira Sanchez and for writing a fictional version in "And of Clay Are We Created." Allende summarized her need for a map to the underworld as well as "myths, stories, prayer, touching, visualization, rituals, and especially love" to reorder personal chaos (Bolen, 2007, n.p.). The mother/author vows "to examine my path through the world, to return to the true and the fantastic pasts, to recover memories others have forgotten" (Allende, 1995, 162). The finished pathography plus the epistolary collection *Cartas a Paula* (1997) restored Allende to resilience while offering readers a concrete glimpse of letting go. Similar in scope to Jamaica Kincaid's *My Brother*, a reprise of her brother Devon's death from AIDS, Allende's tender thanatography outdistanced a sibling's experience by reliving the birth and departure of daughter Paula from Earth, a beneficial catharsis for thwarted mother love. The rigorous writing left Allende "cleansed and naked" (Flores, 2008, 20).

• *References and Further Reading*

Axelrod-Contrada, Joan. *Isabel Allende*. New York: Marshall Cavendish Benchmark, 2011.

Bolen, Jean Shinoda. *Close to the Bone: Life-Threatening Illness as a Soul Journey*. 2nd ed. San Francisco, CA: Red Wheel/Weiser, 2007.

Correas de Zapata, Celia. *Isabel Allende: Life and Spirits*. Houston, TX: Arte Público, 2002.

Dulfano, Isabel. "The Mother/Daughter Romance—Our Life: Isabel Allende in/and *Paula*," *Women's Studies* 35:5 (2006): 493–506.

Flores, Camille. "Review: *The Sum of Our Days*," (Santa Fe) *New Mexican* (8 August 2008): 20.

Fuchs, Miriam. *The Text Is Myself: Women's Life Writing and Catastrophe*. Madison: University of Wisconsin Press, 2004.

Moline, Karen. "The Spirit of Love," *Australian Woman's Weekly* 73:8 (August 2003): 88–92.

Savio, Anita. "A Teller of Tales: Isabel Allende," *Latino Leaders* (1 October 2002).

Portrait in Sepia

A vigorous, rococo bridge novel filling in blanks in the del Valle family tree, *Portrait in Sepia* reflects on the open-ended genealogy that concludes *Daughter of Fortune*, the second novel in the *House of the Spirits* trilogy. Book editor Jeff Zaleski calls the third novel "a grand installment in an already impressive repertoire" of intergenerational sagas (Zaleski, 2001, 1142). According to reviewer David Walton, the novel excels at richness of "characters and story lines, skillfully told [with] breadth and the sense of scale needed to sustain a story that includes war, revolution and numerous family crises" (Walton, 2005). Covering 57 years from 1853 to 1910, the unfolding revelations about the life of Aurora del Valle take direction from a character/author mantra: "I want to elucidate the ancient secrets of my childhood, to define my identity, to create my own legend" (Allende, 2001, 314). She shares the aim with fictional heroines Alba del Valle in *The House of the Spirits*, the title figure in *Eva Luna*, and Eliza Sommers, the Westward seeker of *Daughter of Fortune* as well as with the author herself.

Critics applaud Allende's fresh, inventive writing, which balances what analyst Wolfgang Karrer refers to as *machismo* versus effeminacy. By picturing Lin Chi'en/Lynn Sommers as a transcendent beauty unlimited by racial or ethnic stereotypes, the text frees her to develop her "American-ness," a trait still undefined in her day by the arts and media. By passing for Caucasian, she breaches the ethnic divide of Chinatown and accepts the "enormous honor of modeling" for an iconic statue of the Republic, an emblem of the American melting pot (Allende, 2001, 52). Critic Karen Martin points out that such "access to the American dream requires ... the absence of any clearly indigenous, Asian, or Hispanic traits" (Martin, 2007, 5).

The denigration of people of color reaches dangerous proportions in San Francisco. The Chinese Exclusion Act of 1882 specified local abomination for Asians, who suffered more exclusion than Hispanics like Paulina del Valle, a widow ignored for "her Latin American origins and her kitchen maid's accent" (Allende, 2001, 124). During the search for a model for the statue of Republic in *Portrait in Sepia*, white residents rebuff the idea of a mixed blood image because they doubt that "people of another color were entirely human" (*ibid.*, 53). To the sculptor, Lynn Sommers answers his need for uniqueness, a sensuality he describes as "exotic." Unlike her brother Lucky, a resident of Chinatown ostracized by whites for his Asian looks, Lynn's acceptability as a national symbol derives from her features, the conventional facial markers labeled "classic" (*ibid.*, 53).

The novelist draws on the ambiguity of the sepia portrait as a symbol of dubiety of interpretation, a no-man's-land of indistinction that Allende introduces in the story "Clarisa." Although Lin/Lynn makes the break from biculturalism and passes for white, she pays for her accomplishment as a sculptor's model through rape, disillusion, and death in childbirth, a recompense centered on her femininity. Allende characterizes the unforeseen demise as the result of a violent patriarchy, an androcentric social order that awards rich womanizers like Matías Rodríguez de Santa Cruz unlimited power, both monetary and sexual. Lynn's reward, daughter Aurora, passes quickly to other hands as life drains away from the birth mother. The tragedy sets attorney Severo del Valle quaking from "a long howl surging from the center of the earth and passing through his body to his lips" from unrequited love for a ruined woman (*ibid.*, 84).

Allende leaves the multicultural clashes unsettled until the third generation of the Chi'en–del Valle–Sommers family line. The theme of rootlessness continues in the truncated upbringing of Aurora in Chinatown and her shuttling to Pauline del Valle, a proud Chilean determined to rid Aurora of Asian traits and leanings. The least actualized of the trilogy's females, Aurora struggles with a blurred, ill-defined self-image, a self obscured "as if I had popped up in the del Valle clan through parthenogenesis," the mythic conception of Athena, the Greek goddess of wisdom (Allende, 2001, 136). Allende risks swamping her third heroine in the misaligned cultural elements of her background. As though re-entering the lies surrounding Eliza's conception and adoption, Allende plunges Aurora into Chile's closed social world, a microcosm devoid of validation for Asian ethnicity. As a result, according to reviewer Karen Martin, Aurora "remains paralyzed by the truncation of two-thirds of her identity" (Martin, 2007, 7).

The scrambled social and racial elements of Aurora's birth and rearing incite her curiosity about her conception. More troubling, the recurring nightmares of Grandfather Chi'en's murder obscure the criminal tong angered by Chi'en's efforts to disband prostitution rings. After multiple evasions by Nívea and Severo del Valle, Aurora importunes Grandmother Paulina to ease the burden of "so much mystery" about Aurora's parentage (Allende, 2001, 153). The arcana of budding femininity send Aurora into dark visions, fervid masturbation, and wading into the pond, an image of brash steps among vulnerable fish and water lilies. Secretly, Aurora fears the female spasms that drive some girls to hysteria, but she conceals from Grandmother Paulina the eddy of emotions that disrupt her equanimity. In contrast to her sensitive granddaughter, Paulina remains the "Phoenician merchant," the powerhouse and foil of Charles Dickens's Miss Havisham by "becoming ever more corpulent, but no less vain" ("Review," 2001). Lavishing money on herself and others, Paulina enriches the clan with income from shrewd business speculation in ice and Chilean cheese and vineyards as well as modeling female self-empowerment for the good of Aurora.

Significant to the novel, mentoring and sources of information inform Aurora of her turbulent arrival in the short life of her mother, Lin/Lynn Sommers, a biracial beauty doomed by the effect of her magnetism on lustful men. A childhood with Tao and Eliza Chi'en ensures love and acceptance from people who honor a firm family and work ethic. From Paulina, Aurora learns the lessons of growing hardy grapes in stony ground: "The more difficult the circumstances, the better the fruit," an aphorism directed at Aurora's unconventional upbringing (Allende, 2001, 197). From Señorita Matilde Pineda come classes in research and logic and a personal model of courting risk to pursue liberal ideals, a preview of the theme of California xenophobia and the bludgeoning of Tao Chi'en. Photographer Juan Ribero's influence directs Aurora's attention to humanistic concerns and to making portraits that capture the uniqueness of individuals, like the actual photo of the author's Great-Aunt Rosa Barros. Thus, according to Allende expert John Rodden, Aurora becomes the "vocational and spiritual ancestor to Eva Luna, working with still images rather than the motion pictures of television" (Rodden, 2005, 62–65). Unlike the perverse poses arranged by Jean de Satigny in *The House of the Spirits*, Aurora's photos enhance the humanity of her subjects, much like the immortalization of events in Rolf Carlé's pictures in *Eva Luna* and Francisco Leal's study of Avucena's dilemma and death in "And of Clay Are We Created."

Allende rewards Aurora a serendipitous mothering and a second coming of age. Her mother-in-law, Doña Elvira Domínguez, discloses domestic power in the compassionate, understanding female head of household that promotes defiance in Aurora while melting "silent tantrums" and "placating my sometimes suffocating anxiety" (Allende, 2001, 253). Because of the opposition in their methods— Elvira's genteel discretion and Aurora's confrontation of her unfaithful husband Diego— a stasis emerges that protects Elvira from a family blowup while yielding a method of escape for Aurora. The daughter-in-law's respect for her long-suffering second mother creates a yearning for children. Aurora looks upon pregnancy as a reward: "I wanted nothing more than to offer it to Doña Elvira as a gift" (*ibid.*, 243). Love for Elvira eases the spite that severs Aurora's marriage to Diego and allows the wronged wife a measure of pity for a man who has no choice about whom he loves.

Allende carries literary foils to extremes, contrasting female characters as well as males crucial to the story, particularly the saintly Severo del Valle and his cousin Matías, whom *Kirkus Review* dubs "a bisexual roué and opium addict" who succumbs to syphilis ("Review," August 2001). Wedged between the vile Matías and the saintly Doña Elvira, the text creates a unique spot for Frederick Williams, whom reviewer Helen Falconer describes as "the transported convict turned Jeeves-type butler" (Falconer, 2001). The proficient do-all and calm "Uncle Frederick" in Aurora's troubled life, the former butler becomes her grandfather, adviser on the choice of beaux, comforter during Paulina's decline, and originator of Aurora's trust fund, kept "safe in various bank accounts" (Allende, 2001, 188). Of Allende's skill in narrating Aurora's good fortune and strong family backing, a reviewer for the London *Times* called the author "one of the finest and most entertaining novelists writing today" ("Review," 2005).

• *References and Further Reading*

Falconer, Helen. "Colouring the Family Album," (Manchester) *Guardian* (17 November 2001).
Martin, Karen Wooley. "Mapping Ethnicity in Isabel Allende's *Daughter of Fortune* and *Portrait in Sepia*," *Grafemas* (December 2007): 1–8.
"Review: *Portrait in Sepia*," *Kirkus Review* (15 August 2001).
"Review: *Portrait in Sepia*," (London) *Times* (16 April 2005).
Rodden, John. "Technicolored Life," *Society* 42:3 (March/April 2005): 62–65.
Walton, David. "Review: *Portrait in Sepia*," (Minneapolis) *Star Tribune* (18 December 2005).
Zaleski, Jeff. "Review: *Portrait in Sepia*," *Publishers Weekly* 248:29 (16 July 2001): 1142.

prostitution

Allende recognizes the self-empowerment of prostitution, which critic Kavita Panjabi lauds for affording marginal females monetary security and a modicum of political clout. In a salute to female entrepreneurship, Allende pictures the liminal success of leaders of the demimonde— the enterprising Tránsito Soto in *The House of the Spirits*, La Señora in *Eva Luna*, and the mulatta courtesan and entrepreneur Violette Boiser in *Island Beneath the Sea*. Tránsito displays the spunk of a pro by surrendering her body to the client and "transporting her soul to some distant place" (Allende, 1985, 87). Because the commodity — sex on demand — maintains market appeal, even during social and political upheaval, the two prostitutes wield more power than the wife and choose among more options than passivity and submission.

In times of peace or war, Allende pictures sexual commerce as an economic necessity, a position she maintained in 1972 while interviewing prostitutes for *Paula* magazine. Her depictions drew on a fictional convention in Latin American novels featuring nonerotic female sexuality as a form of capitalism like that depicted in *Of Love and Shadows*. Out of brotherly love for the protagonist of *Eva Luna*, her protector, Huberto Naranjo, strives to bar her from the street walker's pathetic existence. Analyst Diane E. Marting notes that Allende's descriptions of the whore/client relationship "still point to the problems of repressive societies where poverty and political repressions persist," a complex coercion that leaves unemployed females like Mapuche women in *Inés of My Soul* with few methods of escaping penury for themselves and their children (Marting, 2001, 30). The economic subjugation and lowering of dignity occurs in *Eva Luna* among camp followers who "in exchange for a little food, ... offer themselves, quietly, never raising their eyes," a modest exchange that Leslie Marmon Silko depicts in work camps in *Garden in the Dunes* and Toni Morrison at a pig slaughterhouse in *Beloved* (Allende, 1987, 36). Such women risk male aggression, pregnancy, death during illegal abortion, and disease as well as shaming by family, community, and clergy.

Unlike impoverished women who sell their bodies out of need, Allende pictures La Señora in *Eva Luna* as an investor who profits by paying hush money to the *guardia* (police), creating sex games for the General, and "illegally shipping prostitutes overseas" (Allende, 1987, 209). To Eva Luna, La Señora's bedroom capers "were simply a trade" (*ibid.*, 128). La Señora admits "she lacked the patience to earn a living through respectable means" (*ibid.*, 123). Another confident pro, Hermelinda in "Toad's Mouth," values offering quality services, the source of "sparks of pleasure she afforded" to clients (Allende, 1991, 64). In *Aphrodite*, the author marvels at the whore's game of "the silken muffler" and applauds the erotic writings of Anaïs Nin in the 1940s, which define the essence of libido (Allende, 1998, 98). Critic Karen Wooley Martin explains that, in the case of a proud sex worker, "Allende doesn't condemn prostitution itself," but she draws the line at intimacies that degrade or compromise the innocent, as in the case of child prostitution or coercion of the feeble minded, a felonious sex trade demonstrated by the kidnap and imprisonment of Aurora by a madam in *Portrait in Sepia* (Martin, 2010, 138).

The collusion of women enhances gender complexities in Allende's first novel, *The House of the Spirits*, in which an ambitious prostitute, Tránsito Soto, rescues Alba del Valle, the protagonist. Restrictively quartered, Tránsito, the brothel manager at the Hotel Christopher Columbus, navigates the fringes of tyranny. After leaving employment at the Red Lantern in San Lucas on a fifty-peso loan from Esteban, by restricting her domination to the demimonde, she grasps more power than the aristocratic Senator Esteban Trueba. She explains her business plan: "The thing to do is form a cooperative and tell the madam to go to hell," an application of Marxism to the bordello (Allende, 1985, 138). Her investment turns the Christopher Columbus into a city landmark, a "social event and a historic monument," a snide jibe at the role of illicit sex in Latin American history (*ibid.*, 315). In contrast to the del Valle women sequestered in the patriarchal mansion in the capital, Tránsito enjoys not only freedom of choice but also the control of her finances and investments arising from "her commercial vision," which includes repayment to Esteban in the rescue of Alba (*ibid.*, 470).

Allende ponders the pressures on sex workers in the restriction of La Señora to the red light district in *Eva Luna*, Margaret Reeves's sale of her body over nine years to pay for heroin in *The Infinite Plan*, and the immurement of enslaved Aka women in barracks in *Forest of the Pygmies*. In variant settings and relationships, according to reviewer Donald Leslie Shaw, Allende commits some females to "collaboration with the men they love," even when the pairing of mates results in Tránsito's feigned affection for Esteban Trueba and the longing for a wayward amour in "Simple María," the story of a popular port hooker whose "legend had circled the globe" on the tattoos of satisfied sailors (Allende, 1991, 161). Allende extends her empathy for prostitutes by disclosing the concealment of sex trafficking from the police in *Eva Luna* and Aurora's plight in the hands of a money-grubbing system. As a contrast to the self-liberating women like Tránsito Soto and La Señora, Allende pities the Chinese comfort girls of San Francisco who "served up to thirty men a day, and ... died of venereal diseases, abortion, pneumonia, hunger and rough treatment," a certain fate derived from lockdown in a man's world (Allende, 2001, 292–293). Equally reprehensible, Margaret Reeves's drug addiction and the female Akas' separation from male hunters in Ngoubé reflect the compromise of females under criminal control (Shaw, 2002, 182).

A more structured society in Le Cap, Haiti, in *Island Beneath the Sea* views female slaves as commodities intended to pay dividends to slaveholders, a situation similar in tone and poignance to Maryse Condé's *Victoire: My Mother's Mother*. Allende lauds mulatta courtesan Violette Boisier, a lush, sensual seductress, for lifting herself from an orphaned thirteen-year-old to the eye-catching mistress of Captain Etienne Relais, leader of an island militia. To the French officer, the crafty flirt becomes a "girl of honey and silk," a woman he pursues to the altar and loves to the end of his days (Allende, 2010, 16). Violette declares, "This is a long way from prostitution ... I can assure you, from personal experience, that protection by a white is indispensable" (*ibid.*, 365). Allende surprises the reader by picturing the widowed Violette at age 38 clinging to memories of a grand union that leaves her sorrowing for Etienne.

Violette's literary foil, Tété, lives the down side of bondage. She endures domestic seclusion as concubine of Toulouse Valmorain and continues service to a master who refuses to honor her emancipation after they immigrate to New Orleans. In the description of reviewer Disha Mullick, Tété "becomes the reflective surface on which the political, philosophical and emotional conflicts" take shape (Mullick, 2010). Tété lives the nightmare of concubinage, a perverted sexual relationship that produces biracial children — Jean-Martin and Rosette — who are doomed to an ongoing alienation for abducted West Africans. To assert the Guinean perspective on bondage, Allende gives Tété a series of first-person narratives, intercalary chapters that personalize a world of connivery and taboo loves. As a stamp on the harsh truth of bedroom slavery, Tété declares without judgment, "This is how it happened" (Allende, 2010, 157).

In *Daughter of Fortune*, Allende introduces a time when erotica and prostitution prosper "the longer the rigid Victorian moral code was imposed" (Allende, 1999, 324). The protagonist, Eliza Sommers, lives unaware of her conception by her drunken Uncle John and an unidentified Indian prostitute on the shores of Valparaíso. Allende expresses the value of such intimacies to maritime trade even before the arrival of the brigantine *Emilia* to San Francisco. The harbormaster admires the spunk of young Yankee females who brave the sex-starved males of California and who earn a year's pay within a few hours. Allende confers a beneficent role on the prostitute Azucena Placeres, who teams with herbalist Tao Chi'en in tending seasick passengers and saving the stowaway Eliza Sommers from blood loss following a miscarriage. The blurring of demarcation between whore and nurse returns to importance after epidemic dysentery strikes miners, whom Joe Bonecrusher and her girls treat and feed through recuperation.

The rapid growth of Sacramento includes a "madame with [her] gay-life girls," the necessary bawds in a land swelling daily with single men (Allende, 1999, 243). In urban slums, parents watch their daughters carefully lest they "disappear into the cracks of child prostitution" (*ibid.*, 130). The short span of life for a singsong girl seems deemed by ill fortune to the bottom of Chinatown's social hierarchy, where imprisoned females expire without pity. According to Tao Chi'en, the shanghaied girls change little in status because "in China more or less all women were slaves" (*ibid.*, 347). Allende enhances the contrast between Asian expectations and the equality of genders on the California frontier, where whites choose to ignore Chinese enslavement as they would "the insane and beggars and dogs" (*ibid.*, 351). Tao's ability to pity young prostitutes indicates a growth of character in a sexist Asian who becomes Americanized during the gold rush.

See also Eva Luna; injustice

• *References and Further Reading*

Martin, Karen Wooley. *Isabel Allende's House of the Spirits Trilogy: Narrative Geographies.* Rochester, NY: Tamesis, 2010.

Marting, Diane E. *The Sexual Woman in Latin American Literature: Dangerous Desires.* Gainesville: University Press of Florida, 2001.

Mullick, Disha. "Destiny's Slave," (Hyderabad, India) *Deccan Chronicle* (28 August 2010).

Shaw, Donald Leslie. A Companion to Modern Spanish-American Fiction. Rochester, NY: Tamesis, 2002.

Quiroga-Suarez-Valdivia genealogy

Inés Suarez, whom reviewer David Hendriks called "Chile's Eva Peron," tells her stepdaughter, Isabel de Quiroga, the story of founding a nation through the speaker's relationships with three men.

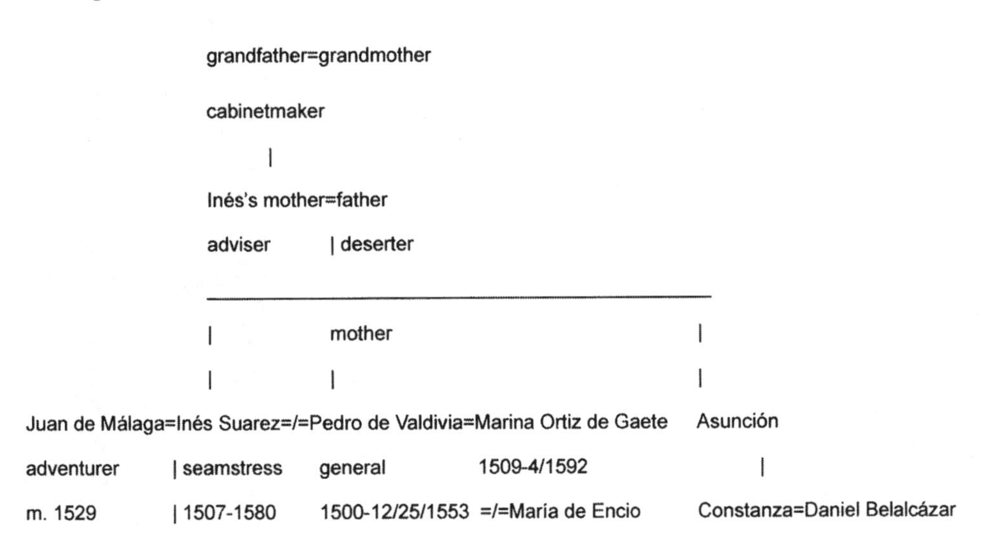

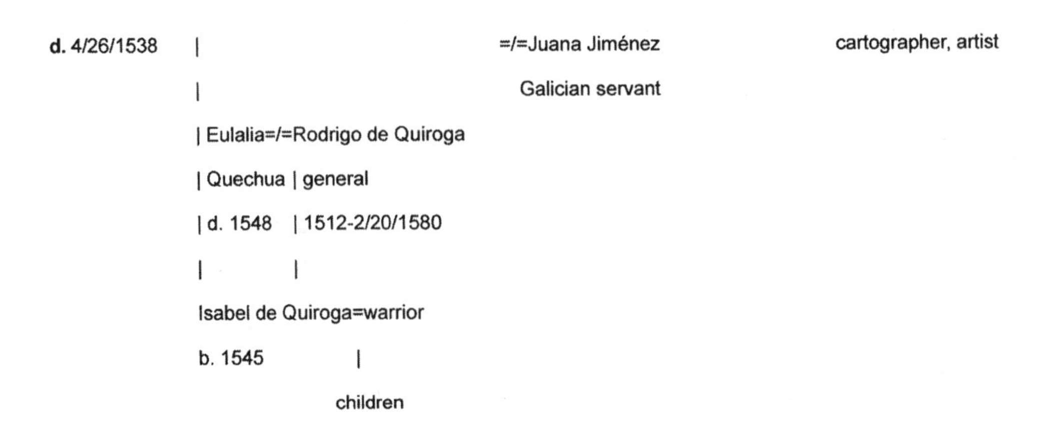

• *References and Further Reading*

Hendriks, David. "Allende's Latest Conquest No Small Feat," (Sydney) *Sun-Herald* (17 December 2006).
Ross, Veronica. "Sewing Didn't Cut It for Inés," *Guelph* (Ontario) *Mercury* (3 March 2007).

racism

Allende's experience with racism, both personal and historical, empowers her texts with the extreme contretemps that perpetuates tension and animosity among ethnicities. As she explains in *My Invented Country*, Chileans dismiss racism as an element of "the class system," as exemplified by a mestizo attorney who remains unemployed because he has a Mapuche surname and by the social climbers who identify themselves by two surnames as examples of lineage and good breeding (Allende, 2003, 34). Additional commentary about the "unbreachable barriers between the social classes" explains the *roto* (caste system) that flourishes in Allende's writings, mooring the snobbish old aristocracy at the top and the wealthy subclass of Arabs, Chinese, and Jews at the bottom with the Araucan, Aymara, Mapuche, and Quechua (*ibid.*, 45). When her texts enter international realms, such as the Upper Orinoco in *City of the Beasts*, the Himalayas in *Kingdom of the Gold Dragon*, and Ngoubé, Central Africa, in *Forest of the Pygmies*, bigotry worsens.

Clara del Valle, the seer in *The House of the Spirits*, serves Allende as witness to racial hypocrisy. Clara possesses the inner eye that penetrates a domestic reality. Her political awareness enables her to assess the wrongdoing of Esteban Trueba, her husband, the sexual predator whom Lloyd Davies views as a "fiery Old Testament patriarch through his moral posturing and his uncompromising defense of the status quo" (Davies, 2000, 43). Allende pictures him in negative terms: "His voice very hard, his beard very scratchy, and his habits of rape and whoring very deeply ingrained" (Allende, 1985, 114). By viewing the invisible relationship between Esteban and the angry laborers he controls by coercion and random rape, Clara correctly interprets "the workers' resentment, fear, and distrust" at Las Tres Marías (*ibid.*, 127). To ensure a fair representation of outside opinions on colonial injustice, she welcomes other perspectives on the underclass and outrages Esteban by "[running] around ministering to the poor behind my back" (Allende, 1985, 472). The magical realm enables her to survive and heal racist divisions, even after death, when she returns as an invisible force for good.

Racial superiority seizes the thematic high ground in *Daughter of Fortune* in the first chapter with a contrast between the Mapuche maid, Mama Fresia, and the Anglo-Chilean householder, Rose Sommers. Both provide mothering, culture, and language instruction to the foundling Eliza, but Rose insists on a fiction of breeding in the child that ignores Eliza's dubious parentage and Indian hair. A subsequent discussion of a waitress at the Hotel Inglés introduces assumptions about cannibalism and superstition among the Araucan Indians and the Patagonians of Tierra del Fuego. Captain John Sommers justifies savagery as a human response: "You and I would do no less if someone slaughtered our family, burned our village" (Allende, 1999, 18). He ridicules his effete brother Jeremy and Jacob Todd for harboring notions of proselytizing Indians into Protestantism and forcing the naked to wear britches, a concession to English notions of modesty. To the captain, missionaries replace nativism and innate goodness with "the designs of a tyrannical god," an image depicting a pagan civilization victimized by Christian orthodoxy (*ibid.*).

In a segue to Chinese history, the novel depicts the superiority of the English over Asians following a triumph in the Opium War of 1839. In new enclaves at Macao, Hong Kong, and Peking, whites demean "a land of dirty, ugly, weak, noisy, corrupt, and savage people" (Allende, 1999, 178). The fastidious dismissal of Asians, notes critic Ignacio López-Calvo, ignores the Chinese "use of writing many thousands of years before the British" (López-Calvo, 2007, 161). To justify racism, the English degrade Confucianism below Christianity, the "one true faith," and accuse the Chinese of eating cats and snakes and of killing newborns (*ibid.*). The notion of racial supremacy pervades San Francisco, where prostitutes reject blacks and Chinese in a segment of history freighted with "concessions, intimidations, lies, and deceit" (Farr and Harker, 2008, 203). Tao regrets that "to white people I am just a revolting Chinese pagan, and Eliza is a greaser" (*ibid.*, 363). The situation worsens in Sacramento, where Indians live in abject need at the fringes of society, where vigilantism scapegoats them as perpetrators of crime.

Racism and Bondage

Allende reserves some of her most pointed denunciations for enslavers. *Island Beneath the Sea* opens on a typical separation of classes and races by depicting elite *grands blancs* students playing their own musical instruments rather than "the ones the mulatta girls touched" (Allende, 2010, 2). A multi-layered social structure divides castes according to percentage of white blood, education, and land ownership. The elevation of mulattos fosters the spite of low-level whites that fueled social crises in the post–Civil War South and empowered the Ku Klux Klan. At bottom, the brutalized slaves "counted for nothing," a decimation of worth that festers before rebellion secures liberation (*ibid.*, 9).

Field work on sugar plantations kills off laborers in eighteen months. Replacement requires boatloads of "fresh meat from Africa," a description rife with disparagement of black humanity (Allende, 2010, 261). At a slave auction outside New Orleans, potential buyers check teeth, eyes, scrotum, and anus for proofs of health. Planter Toulouse Valmorain justifies the concept of human bondage as a series of "categories ... necessary for the equilibrium of society," his euphemism for colonial exploitation of blacks (*ibid.*, 263). He struggles to convince Maurice, his libertarian son and heir, that the unfairness of racism actually hinges on the complexities of nature. One of the complexities concerns Maurice's blood kinship to Rosette, the half-sister with whom he shares a bed.

To the mulatta courtesan Violetta Boisier, African slaves become mere "merchandise," objects for sale to the highest bidder (Allende, 2010, 34). Close relationships with masters demand immediate concessions of custom and language. The body servant must learn to communicate in the master's language, which is French with Toulouse Valmorain and

Spanish in the case of his wife, Eugenia García del Solar. Of the slave's lowliness before her mistress, Tété, a "café au lait slave" mutters, "No one cared what I felt" (*ibid.*, 322, 43). For such dehumanization of dark-skinned people, Allende describes a hatred "that floated in the island's air like clouds of mosquitoes and April pestilence," a denunciation rife with potential for violence and death (*ibid.*, 45).

The text contrasts male authority figures in terms of aptitude for slave management. The overseer, Prosper Cambray, "looked after the interests of Saint-Lazare better than the owner ... with firmness and few inhibitions" (Allende, 2010, 162). Allende remarks that Cambray trains and grooms Congo and Mandingo slaves like fighting cocks, feeds them gunpowder and hot chili, and awards their victories with females, a regimen paralleling the training of Roman gladiators in Howard Fast's *Spartacus*. In contrast to Cambray, Valmorain feels out of place in a colonial structure "soaked in blood" and regards his plantation as though he is "only passing through," a rationalization of his culpability for the crimes of bondage (*ibid.*, 163).

The physician, Dr. Parmentier, occupies a professional niche apart from plantation hierarchies. In the chapter "A Being Not Human," Allende places in the dialogue between Valmorain and Parmentier a discussion of the human qualities of Africans. To Valmorain's assertions that blacks suffer less physical pain and exhaustion and work harder and better than whites because "they lack ambition and noble sentiments" (Allende, 2010, 81). Parmentier retorts, "the same could be said of a white brutalized by slavery" (*ibid.*). Valmorain's argument iterates the contentions of apologists who believe that plantations necessitate enslavement and that humanitarianism absolves enslavers of sin. The master asserts that buyers of plantation cigars and sugar perpetuate the system, a charge that inflamed American abolitionists. Allende alludes to anti-slavery stores that boycotted plantation coffee, cornmeal, cotton, grits, molasses, rice, sugar, tobacco, or slave-produced pharmaceuticals as a protest of the flesh trade.

In the tense scenes preceding a massacre at Habitation Lacroix, Parmentier views the peculiar power shifts at Habitation Saint-Lazare from Valmorain to his manager. The master's unease with slave infractions results in a rise in the liberties that the overseer Cambray takes with Valmorain's liquor and household. In an extension of the plantation hierarchy, the superior attitude of Haiti's mulattos becomes a tool in the hands of the French, who appoint freedmen as army officers. The three-layered impasse strengthens the military with freed blacks, but causes white racist soldiers to desert rather than serve under non-white leaders. In the author's estimation of a complex island society, antipathy reaches "biblical proportions" (Allende, 2010, 175). The precarious nature of reshaping island politics results in the guillotining of Gouverneur Blancheland, a Caribbean execution on a par with the French regicide of Louis XVI and Marie Antoinette.

The reminder to Valmorain that Tété and Rosette are technically free makes no difference to the aggrandized Frenchman. After escaping black invaders and re-installing himself in luxury, he rapes his concubine at will to restore her obedience to white mastery. A greater betrayal of his rescuer, Valmorain lodges himself and his son Maurice in a balconied hotel room in Cuba while relegating Tété and Rosette to a windowless, dirt-floored slave quarters. At the signing of manumission papers in New Orleans, Valmorain dismisses both women from thought. Although Père Antoine counsels Tété to forgive, she "dug very deep into her soul, but could not find the slightest spark of generosity" toward the white man who stole her virginity and sired Rosette (Allende, 2010, 440).

Racism Against Aborigines

In *Inés of My Soul*, Allende describes Spanish conquistadors and the dehumanization of indigenous peoples in Latin America. At an early triumph in the life of Général Pedro de Valdivia, Francisco Pizarro awards him a hacienda in La Canela Valley, the Porco mine, and, as though in afterthought, hundreds of Incan laborers to unearth silver ore. Valdivia acknowledges the worth of native slaves, without whom "the mines and the land have no value" (Allende, 2006, 101). In exchange for loyalty and military brilliance, Pizarro expects the establishment of a two-level society consisting of an aristocracy of Spanish overlords and a subcaste of newly baptized Indians. With the sexual carelessness of Toulouse Valmorain, the conqueror makes no social provision for a third layer comprising mestizos, the result of colonial coercion and dalliance across caste lines.

In token of the monstrous injustice to natives, the novel honors New World aborigines for pride and patriotism and characterizes the Mapuche of Chile as "defending to the death" their native land (Allende, 2006, 233). For good reason, the Mapuche refer to Spaniards as *huincas*, which translates as "lying thieves." For a tally of loss during a march across the desert, the author slips in informal racist comments to illustrate how natural the caste system seems to Renaissance Spaniards. After listing the deaths of "three soldiers, six horses, one dog, and thirteen llamas," Catalina indicates that no one bothers to count the deaths among the Yanacona, the original servants of the Inca (Allende, 2006, 134). Catalina's estimate of "thirty or forty" Indian casualties indicates two factors in the social order of New World conquest: that natives suffer ten times or more the fatalities of Europeans and that the loss of the Yanacona ranks in importance below that of four-legged animals.

The historical novel develops an alternative to either-or racism by authenticating the growing mestizo population, the result of rape and cohabitation between soldiers and Chilean Indian girls. The author identifies with biculturalism and asserts: "I am mestiza by culture ... so I can understand both and I feel entitled to speak for both" (Block, 2006). To esteem people of mixed heritage, Allende turns the first Inca-Spanish birth into an omen of vigor and direction by describing the breech birth of Pedro Gómez, who is "born on his feet" (Allende, 2006, 139). Through the musings of Inés on the scrambled society of "saints and sinners, whites, blacks, browns, Indians, mestizos, nobles, and peasants," the text dramatizes the democratizing of New World colonies (*ibid.*, 2). The idealist, Pedro de Valdivia, proposes an end to European caste systems by promoting a nation of mestizos, a blend of aboriginal and colonial strengths. However, lodged in the vision of Santiago's future stands the physical divide, a segregated housing system that portends ongoing racism, with full-blood Spaniards lording their ancestry over people of mixed heritage.

In *Zorro*, Allende takes a gentle approach to the elitism of Alejandro de la Vega, the alcalde in Pueblo de Los Angeles, who ignores the snubs that blue bloods direct toward his Shoshone wife, Toypurnia/Regina. His lack of vision allows him to leave unquestioned "the ideas he had inherited from his ancestors, even though sometimes they were not appropriate to the reality of America" (Allende, 2005, 35). More essential than evenhandedness, Alejandro intends to be a Christian royalist "wealthier than any of his relatives had ever been," a New World aim that dated to the arrival of Christopher Columbus to the West Indies and subsequent seekers of El Dorado (*ibid.*). With the insouciance of the privileged, Alejandro dreads the thought of Spain undergoing an upheaval like the French Revolution, upsetting the "absolute superiority of his race, his nation, and his faith" (*ibid.*, 41).

In Spain, Diego not only learns swordsmanship, but also gains a clearer understanding of his father. Upon arrival in Barcelona, Diego encounters another father figure in Tomás de Romeu, who considers servants like Bernardo invisible. Other incidents of racism occur quite naturally among the superior European Christians, who banish Bernardo from the captain's table aboard the *Madre de Dios*, force Manuel Escalante's family to abandon Jewish surnames, and accuse Gypsies of being the sons of Cain. For educational purpose, Allende broadens the mind of Diego via the skepticism of Captain Santiago de León, a libertarian "weathered by many seas" (Allende, 2005, 101). The older man, a member of the secret society La Justicia, reveals that other nations nurture the same delusion of primacy over lesser peoples and of worshipping "the only true God" (*ibid.*, 105). The mentoring in free thought appears to derive from a seagoing life that introduces Santiago to more cultures and ethnic variables than Diego's parochial experience in Alta California. The Captain leaves Diego with a new perspective on racial superiority: "Every nationality suffered from the same delusion" (*ibid.*).

See also language

• *References and Further Reading*

Block, Melissa. "Allende Reimagines Life of Conquistador 'Inés,'" *All Things Considered* (NPR) (6 November 2006).

Davies, Lloyd. *Allende: La casa de los espíritus*. London: Grant & Cutler, 2000.

López-Calvo, Ignacio. *Alternative Orientalisms in Latin America and Beyond*. Newcastle, UK: Cambridge Scholars, 2007.

reading

In an essay for *American Libraries*, Allende lionizes books as a source of comfort and edification, a fount of inspiration, and a vector pointing away from ignorance toward insight. In reflection on her childhood in *My Invented Country*, Allende accords respect and thanks to Tío Pablo, the bachelor book hound who opened his library to his seven-year-old niece. With his blessings, she read *War and Peace* and circumvented her grandfather's curfew with a flashlight to extend the evening's pleasure. She lists her interest in fairy tales, Pablo Neruda's verse, didactic novels, classic writings of Sor Juana de Inés de la Cruz, and the weekly *El Peneca*, a Chilean comic book series, but extends her range to European classics—*Anna Karenina* and *Les Miserables*—and Latin American works, José Donoso's *The Obscene Bird of Night* and Jorgé Luis Borges's *The Aleph*. Allende listed as her favorite authors Hispanic giants García Márquez and Vargas Llosa, classic Russians Fyodor Dostoyevsky and Leo Tolstoy, French sci-fi master Jules Verne, and English novelists Walter Scott, Jane Austen, Charlotte and Emily Brontë, and Charles Dickens. Among mystery writers, she preferred Agatha Christie and Conan Doyle. As a model of characterization and plot, she chose *To Kill a Mockingbird*, a thematic study of racism that affirms her own views on freedom and obligations to the oppressed.

Reading becomes a significant accomplishment for her unschooled protagonist Eva Luna, a fan of Harun al-Rashid's *A Thousand and One Nights*. Books provide a medical education for Tao Chi'en in *Daughter of Fortune* and a comfort to Jacob Todd, an English outsider in Valparaíso in *Daughter of Fortune*. For the stuffy Gilberto Boulton in "A Discreet Miracle," regular perusal of the London *Times* asserts Anglophile tastes for an émigré to a Latin American country. In descriptions of the reading of Pradelio Ranquileo in *Of Love and Shadow*, Allende stresses that he devours sports magazines in solitary confinement. Hiding in the mountains, he reads cowboy novels about Hopalong Cassidy and the Lone Ranger, North America's "mythic defenders of justice" (Allende, 1987,190). The choices imply the pathetic idealism of peasants to counter the monstrous power of a dictator with the mythic weapons of "comic-book heroes, the magical elements that could turn a nobody into a master of life and death" (*ibid.*). In contrast to Pradelio's superman fantasies, Francisco Leal chooses psychology texts and Latin American authors, an indication of professional and nationalistic interests.

The author's love of books includes suggestions for readers, notably, prognostications in the *I Ching* and readings of Thomas Mann's *The Magic Mountain*, Hermann Hesse's *Steppenwolf*, novels by Henri Troyat, Alexandre Dumas's *La Dame aux Camélias*, and *The Count of Monte Cristo*, Dumas's Christian fable mentioned in *My Invented Country*. By preferring abstracts from journals to daily newspapers, Jones epitomizes the tunnel vision of the scientist out of touch with the world. For satire, Allende presents the downside of indiscriminate reading, such as Professor Jones's faulty conclusions about creating geniuses from idiots with a thump on the head, as stated by a single model in *The Physician's Friend*. A similar naive interpretation occurs in *Of Love and Shadows* when a protestant preacher picks at random from the bible the debauchery of Holophernes from wine and deduces a divine message about alcoholism.

In an interview for *Writing* magazine, Allende summarizes her varied tastes as "young-adult books ... Shakespeare, Russian novelists, a lot of science fiction, and all the great writers of the boom of Latin American literature of the '60s and '70s" ("Everything," 2006, 10). Above didactic themes, Allende validates storytelling as the purpose of fiction. Of intellectualism and scholarly analysis, she commiserates with university students "tortured during the semester looking for symbols and metaphors" rather than encouraged to read for pleasure (Axelrod-Contrada, 2011, 11). Her works dramatize aspects of learning in the intellectual awakening of Eva Luna and of Gregory Reeves in *The Infinite Plan*. Both characters revere film stars, one through reading movie magazines and one from attending the cinema. Upon realizing the possibilities of a world outside the Los Angeles barrio, Gregory resolves to live the adventures of his movie-stoked fantasies.

Allende dramatizes the mind enlarged by reading in the cerebral advancement of Dr. Parmentier in *Island Beneath the Sea*, Alex Cold in the *City of the Beasts* trilogy, sea captain Santiago de Léon and Agnès Duchamp, a French aristocrat marred by a gunman's bullet in *Zorro*. Five-year-old Alba del Valle, a family chronicler in *The House of the Spirits*, rapidly advances to discussions of the newspaper with her grandfather and readings in her uncle's medical treatises. Uncle Jaime holds a liberal attitude toward free-wheeling autodidacticism and maintains that Alba will not read anything uninteresting. If material absorbs her, she is "sufficiently mature to read it," an open-minded approach to a child's free adventuring in books (Allende, 1985, 311).

Post-colonial Literacy

Prefatory to the del Valle–Trueba family's inception, literacy anticipates the power of knowledge to engender progress. Esteban Trueba, the *patrón*, overcomes a limited selection of old magazines and English grammars by ordering books from town to teach him practical skills of building a radio, giving injections, and practicing homeopathy. For backup, he shelves an encyclopedia, readers, and notebooks. His literary foil, the peasant boy Pedro Tercero, learns vicariously from Blanca, who edifies him with world classic accounts of Robin Hood and Sinbad. Pedro peruses drawings of the cardiovascular system, and within weeks, "learned to read voraciously," a suggestion of his openness to ideas (Allende, 1985, 165). Under the influence of union organizers and the socialist priest José Dulce María, Pedro advances to "the forbidden pamphlets of the unionists, the teacher's political newspapers," polemics that shape his natural defiance of authority (*ibid.*, 189). At a defining moment in Pedro's education, he realizes that, because of their illiteracy, "peasants are always the last to understand" world change (*ibid.*, 201).

The del Valle-Trueba clan incorporates books as an impetus to eccentricities, as with the Mora sisters' reading of mystic poets and study of the occult. Jaime, the family recluse, creates a labyrinth of books in his room, including love sonnets ostensibly by Neruda; his twin Nicolás, the family genius, stores information for use in debate, at which he trounces Jaime. During a period of interest in clairvoyance and telekinesis, Nicolás studies secret societies, tarot cards, Chinese horoscopes, and the *I Ching* and tries to verify mystic hagiography in Alban Butler's *The Lives of the Saints*, a Catholic reference work. The Mora sisters lend books on divination, but the lack of inborn proficiency at the supernatural defeats Nicolás's efforts to follow in his mother's avocation. In contrast, Nicolás's brother-in-law, Count Jean de Satigny, distributes heroic wartime booklets, reads the Marquis de Sades's *La Philosophie dans le boudoir* (Philosophy in the Bedroom), and passes sentimental novels to Blanca. The hackneyed texts suit Satigny, a deceiver whose elegant fabrication of "his splendid past, his incalculable fortune, and his noble origins" cloaks a cunning fortune hunter and pervert (Allende, 1985, 226).

In the cellar, a symbolic debasement of arcana, Great-Uncle Marcos's trunkfuls of maps, vampire stories, and fairy tales survive neglect, a forgetting that Allende counters through family journals. Although Alba, a prodigious reader, scans her father's Liberal Party documents, she chooses to return her family to its supernatural origins by sinking into the magic books and entering "the world-without-return of the imagination" (Allende, 1985, 305). Her mother's feminist transformation of family fairy tales subverts "Sleeping Beauty," "St. George," and "Little Red Riding Hood" into "a prince who slept a hundred years, damsels who fought dragons single-handed, and a wolf lost in a forest who was disemboweled by a little girl for no reason whatsoever" (*ibid.*, 347). Because Alba records the feminist narratives, the stories become a woman-to-woman heritage.

In a post-coup sacrilege, Alba destroys any books from Jaime's library that might compromise the family. The crimes of the fascist regime take the forms of citizen murders, textbook censorship, alterations to films and songs, and the erasure of history and maps. The military invasion of the house of the Poet "who had sung to life" causes his heart to fail (Allende, 1985, 440). To revive sanity and hope, Blanca conceals Pedro Tercero in an empty room, where he reads Jaime's books. The ransacking of the Trueba residence and burning of the books of magic from Uncle Marcos's trunk include a bonfire of the works of Marx and Trueba's opera scores," a destruction of titles spanning the humanities, from polemics to music (*ibid.*, 456).

The motif of bibliophiles surrounded by personal libraries continues in *Of Love and Shadows*, in which Irene Beltrán "read any book that came to her hands," concealing them from her mother by reading by flashlight under the blankets, an action presaging her revelations of police corruption (Allende, 1987, 144). Countering the intellectual stimulus of reading, the dictatorship holds book bonfires to rid the fatherland of censored materials. In a learned home, Francisco Leal grows up hearing poetry recitation and the classics read aloud. Unlike his brothers, Francisco writes verse and stockpiles books in his room. His rival, Captain Gustavo Morante, spends dreary hours in the Antarctic region immersed in history books, "adding a new dimension to his thought," a clue to the motivation for his martyrdom (*ibid.*, 99).

Rose Sommers, a secret pornographer in *Daughter of Fortune*, satisfies her urge for naughty books from gifts imported by her sea captain brother. Without revealing their content, Allende pictures Rose securing her library with lock and key. The image of closeted reading recurs in the teen years of Eliza, who lives "the eternal illusion of being in England," the putative fount of refinement and knowledge, which the family follows in out-of-date English newspapers (Allende, 1999, 44). For escape, she crouches behind the drapes to consume at random classics, romances, a Spanish bible, and newspapers. Like Alba's retreat to trunks filled with books in the cellar, Eliza studies Captain John's stored writings—travelogues, maps, and ships' logs, tokens of his adult journeys and omens of her adventures in California. As a guide to her wanderings around Sacramento, she rereads Joaquín's love letters, a false testimonial to love and loyalty.

For *Eva Luna*, Allende describes a cache of works—romances, encyclopedia, dictionary, maps—similar to those of Uncle Marcos and Jaime. In the home of Professor Jones, Consuelo dusts the shelves, treasuring each work for the magic of story within. After the professor's paralysis from stroke, Consuelo's daughter, Eva Luna, attends the old man by holding books for him to read. As a reward, he translates for her the Latin phrases. Eva's education increases from perusals of pornography and, in her mid-teens, turns to writing as an outlet for "yearning and restlessness" and a basis on which she builds a career in writing *telenovelas* (Allende, 1987, 187).

In *Zorro*, a crate of books, an unforeseen gift from the sea, broadens the horizon of Bernardo and Diego, pre-teens who memorize texts that Diego's father dismisses as inconsistent, error-filled, and too personal. In *Inés of My Soul*, the text esteems pleasure reading as an alternate to lovemaking in the intimate moments the protagonist shares with Pedro de Valdivia. Secretly, Inés studies literacy with a priest, Padre González de Marmolejo, as a surprise for her lover, and reads *Amadis of Gaul*, a post–Arthurian volume of knight errantry and influence on Miguel de Cervantes's Don Quixote. Inés looks forward to reading less bellicose texts, even titles banned by the Inquisition, which become "a sinful pleasure, and for that reason much requested," a testimony to her defiance of male control (Allende, 2006, 188).

For *Island Beneath the Sea*, Allende applauds the writings of the liberal humanists—Denis Diderot, Jean-Jacques Rousseau, and Voltaire—for introducing readers to speculations about humankind and its capabilities, notably those of non-whites. For Toulouse Valmorain, philosophical treatises do nothing to alleviate the suffering on his Haitian plantation, where he and his overseer regularly work slaves to death. Ironically, his insistence that his son Maurice receive a gentleman's education forever separates father and son. At a private school in Massachusetts, Maurice chooses readings from *The Interesting Narrative of the Life of Olaudah Equiano, Or Gustavus Vassa, The African*, a late eighteenth-century slave autobiography detailing the damage done to West Africans in bondage to whites. In the novel's closing chapter, Maurice flees the Antilles to make a new life for himself on the American frontier, a raw, unliterary assuagement of his disillusion and grief. The journey, like that of Eliza Sommers, holds out hope for his re-education in ambition and democracy.

• *References and Further Reading*

Allende, Isabel. "*My House Is Full of People*," *American Libraries* 27:4 (April 1996): 42–43.

Axelrod-Contrada, Joan. *Isabel Allende*. New York: Marshall Cavendish Benchmark, 2011.
"Everything Is Possible," *Writing* 29:2 (October 2006): 8–10.

realism

A former journalist and respecter of sense impressions, Allende embodies a link with the Latino Boom begun by Gabriel García-Marquez. Literary historian Donald Leslie Shaw maintains that she "has taken on board the Boom's questioning of our ability to observe and report reality," which she tames and orders by imposing startling conceits and narrative patterns on the history of Chile, China, Africa, the Himalayas, the Amazon, California, Venezuela, and Haiti (Shaw, 2002, 181). In the same vein as war reporters Walt Whitman and Ernest Hemingway, she navigates the connection between memory and oblivion by immortalizing the legendary tones of Hispanic storytelling in *Eva Luna*, human rights violations in *Inés of My Soul* and *Of Love and Shadows*, Vietnam War impressions in *The Infinite Plan*, the study of photographs in *Portrait in Sepia*, and the *vaquero's* skill during roundup and the immurement of illicit slave coffles in *Zorro*. By resurrecting tales, testimony, and anecdotes and ordering them into sense impressions, dialogue, and conceits, she forestalls the gradual obliteration of the individual that follows physical death.

Critic Stephen Hart notes that, in *The House of the Spirits*, Allende gradually dismisses fantasy and replaces it with "a kind of harsh realism following the harrowing political realities of the coup" (Kristal, 2005, 95). For focus, Allende imagines herself writing for her mother, who also lived Chile's nightmarish departure from colonialism. Fictional recompense repays patriarchal violence, as with the rapes Esteban Trueba inflicts on Pancha García and other female peons. Critic John Moore characterizes retribution for the cycle of the master's violences: "Insurrection and payback are inevitable" for "populating his fields with bastard children like litters of dogs," the subjects of Allende's revolutionary clashes (Moore, 2010). In more ethereal scenes, her characters experience the nearness of wraiths who smudge the barriers between ongoing lives and ancestry. For the author, the recording of interaction between worlds presses her into action to find the narrative thread that awaits telling. Passion tethers her to the job until its end, which reviewer Moore describes as "transforming Esteban into a grotesque, Greek-scale monster, before necessarily shriveling away" (Moore, 2010).

Allende illustrates the collection of inklings from disparate sources that contribute to truth. During the Great Depression, Clara's immersion in daydreams and unreality relieves her of the stress of fighting a typhus epidemic. Allende speaks the truth about contagion that thrives in "the poorest quarters of the city, because of the harsh winter, the malnutrition, and the dirty water and it joined forces with the unemployment" (Allende, 1985, 156). To scenes of fever, sores, bloody stools, and hallucinations as fearful as Daniel Defoe's *Journal of the Plague Year*, Clara "took everybody else's suffering onto her own back" (Allende, 1985, 426). Just as she did in childhood, she begins sleepwalking and consulting with spiritualists—"the Rosicrucians, the Theosophists, the acupuncturists, the telepathists, the rainmakers, the peripatetics, the Seventh-Day Adventists," any source of healing or comfort to the terrified peasant population (*ibid.*, 243).

Motherly example sets the tone of coming of age in the del Valle-Trueba clan, who ignore Esteban's conservatism and rantings about tradition. While Clara oscillates between distributing clothing and food to the poor and conferring with the mystic world, her daughter Blanca follows her to the ghetto. Son Nicolás turns to adventure; his twin Jaime, the family idealist, reads the works of Karl Marx and contemplates what Esteban terms "Bolshevik ideas" (*ibid.*, 163). A side episode, the beating death and hanging of the corpse of a revolutionary by the Sánchez brothers foregrounds the virulence of the coming revolt, which Allende describes in journalistic detail. The brothers pursue the hapless distributor of leaflets to his grave, dig up his remains, and display the rotting body as a tocsin to fomenters of socialism.

Textual Testimony

To charges that Allende writes sappy chick lit, she bridles and ripostes with facts about the marginal characters who defy a corrupt system. Unlike the melodrama of *telenovelas*, her realistic conflicts picture poverty and the struggles that empower and ennoble characters, such as the squatters who make a home in the Palace of the Poor and the women who earn a living at the military factory in *Eva Luna* and the peasant defiance of fascism by spying on a military coverup at the Los Riscos mine in *Of Love and Shadows*. At a momentary struggle between mother and child in *Daughter of Fortune*, Rose Sommers drags Eliza twelve blocks to a convent and dramatizes the ill fortune of orphans in contrast to lucky babes like Eliza, whom a refined English family grooms and educates "like a little lady" (Allende, 1999, 11). The lesson in the whims of destiny impact Eliza, following her to California mining camps, where she turns cooking and piano playing into useful skills much as Eva Luna soothes her audiences with the plot of *Bolero*.

Time and maturity replace romantic ideals with actions suited to needs. Editor Michael Sollars describes Allende's shift in style from the magical elements of *House of the Spirits* to "a more immediately realistic style" (Sollars, 2008, 199). In her twenties, Eliza wanders among the miseries of the gold fields before turning to San Francisco to help Tao Chi'en operate a medical clinic and rescue and treat moribund Chinese singsong girls, who die in their teens. Struggle and disappointment disengage Eliza from a romantic fantasy of lover Joaquín Andieta and turn her mind and heart toward Tao, an available man who adores her. Allende pairs the coming to knowledge of Eliza with a similar awakening in Tao, who heeds the advice of Lin's ghost, which visits him "in his bosom, in the very core of his tranquil heart" (Allende, 1999, 348). The mystic visitation, a magical version of the dawning of good sense, injects his spirit with an appreciation for Eliza, a homemaker more suited to "gather his dirty clothes, sew on his buttons, brush his suits" than the ethereal first wife. Thus, pragmatism relieves both Tao and Eliza of unrealistic dreams of the past and thrusts them into the ebullient lifestyle and ambitions of the American frontier.

To claims that the author rights wrongs with happy endings, Allende refutes criticism with examples from *The House of the Spirits*, in which the perverted fascist remains in power, and from *Of Love and Shadows*, in which slayers of peasants receive military promotions. In *The Stories of Eva Luna*, Allende reveals forced prostitution, lethal cancers, intimidation by warlords, and the criminal traffic in children for use as organ donors. Her often-taught story "And of Clay Are We Created" pictures a child trapped in mud while surveying the media cameras that record her dying moments. Scenes in *Daughter of Fortune* capture the fetid belowdecks of the brigantine *Emilia* and the tumult of the ports of Valparaíso, Chile, Hong Kong, and San Francisco, where pimps take command of incoming prostitutes and singsong girls. Without deviation for romantic illusions, Allende's social fiction connects ghettos and flophouses with stench and contagion and records without flinch the demise of the poor from hunger, dysentery, hanging, knifings and gunshot wounds, and exhaustion.

Feminist Realism

An ongoing misery in *Portrait in Sepia*, the Catholic boarding school for girls promotes "submission and ugliness" for children of aristocrats, who come of age under false notions of femininity (Allende, 2001, 143). The text pictures a daily hell of joyless activities, prudery that requires full covering of the body, and brainwashing through Satan lore and penance spent kneeling on pebbles, a reprehensible atmosphere that Jean-Martin Relais endures in *Island Beneath the Sea*. Not only do the girls' hands chap from cold water and their braids inflict pain from so tight a plait that "sometimes their scalps bled," but the inmates ponder an eternity of punishment after a lifetime of torment (*ibid.*, p. 144). The horror tales of parochial school convince Paulina to rescue Aurora from fanatic nuns and to replace sadistic Catholic training with liberal tutoring.

The hyperbole rampant in *Inés of My Soul* enhances realism with visual imagery. On a seven-week voyage from Panama to Callao, Peru, the title character faces a familiar menace, lustful sailors long deprived of female companionship. To dramatize the threat, Allende pictures Inés surrounded by "panting wolves, tongues hanging out and fangs dripping blood, ready to pounce on me — all of them at once," a hyperbolic recreation of gang rape (Allende, 2006, 75). The scenario recalls another assault, the nighttime attack of Sebastián Romeo, whom Inés stabs in the back before leaving Panama. The progression from men to wolves to a would-be rapist reinforces the realism of a woman's life in sixteenth-century colonial Latin America, where gender determines fate.

For female strength, Allende injects her heroine with feminist resolve. During serious decision making regarding the march south from Peru through Chile, Inés admits an age-old female ploy of manipulating her opinions to make Général Pedro de Valdivia think the ideas came from him. With a subdued smirk, Inés explains: "A man does what he can, a woman does what a man cannot," a summation of social, nursing, and home-making skills (Allende, 2006, 134). At an upsurge in the fortunes of Santiagans, Inés abandons her spartan appearance and embraces a womanly hairdo and face cream "to cultivate the feminine graces I had discarded" (*ibid.*, 224). For the sake of realism, Allende balances Inés's liabilities with her assets as the only Spanish female on the expedition and the object of desire who ignites Pedro de Valdivia's jealousy. The author creates irony that the crime of Escobar, Inés's would-be seducer, takes the form of dishonor to Valdivia rather than attempted rape of Inés, a lopsided triangle that provokes honor killings in the Arab world and India.

In *Island Beneath the Sea*, Allende surveys at close range the horrific island conditions in Haiti beginning in 1770 with the arrival of a fop, Toulouse Valmorain, the heir to a sugar plantation. As the job of commanding slaves to work the family cane fields introduces him to the overseer's perspective, Valmorain reassesses his humanistic beliefs gained from reading Enlightenment philosophers Denis Diderot, Jean-Jacques Rousseau, and Voltaire. The planter admits to Dr. Parmentier, "Life on this island has hardened me," for example, in the matter of treating Séraphine's amputation and saving her unborn child (Allende, 2010, 83–84). From witnessing the cyclical demise of slaves from exhaustion and fever, Valmorain admits he no longer believes that Africans possess human traits. In counterpoint, Allende reminds the reader of slave suicides in vats of boiling molasses and of Séraphine's plea that Tante Rose kill Séraphine and her unborn child and send them to the land of the dead, a reprieve from earthly bondage.

See also racism; violence; war

• *References and Further Reading*

Kristal, Efraín, ed. *The Cambridge Companion to the Latin American Novel.* New York: Cambridge University Press, 2005.

Moore, John. "A 'House' of Horror and Wonder," *Denver Post* (24 September 2010).

Shaw, Donald Leslie. *A Companion to Modern Spanish-American Fiction.* Rochester, NY: Tamesis, 2002.

Sollars, Michael D. *The Facts on File Companion to the World Novel, 1900 to the Present.* New York: Facts on File, 2008.

reclamation

In part because of Allende's peripatetic life and experiences with loss and disappointment, she distributes scenes of retrieval and restoration within her works, as in her biography of her daughter in *Paula*, a restatement of family history and the dead woman's role in redefining membership and impacting future achievements. Allende's fictional reclamations of deeds and oral tradition take shape in the Indian reclamation of El Benefactor's palace in *Eva Luna*, Diego's retrieval of the hacienda and de la Vega family honor in *Zorro*, efforts to recover plantations lost to black rebels in *Island Beneath the Sea*, and Greg Reeves's retrieval of his soul from crass materialism in *The Infinite Plan*. In *My Invented Country*, the author explains that rootlessness forces her to "trust in memory to give continuity" to her life, a philosophy she projects onto characters Aurora del Valle in *Portrait in Sepia* and the title figure in *Zorro* (Allende, 2003, 79).

By mastering what Toni Morrison calls "rememory," Allende injects feminist interpretations into events previously distorted by male chroniclers and historians, including the causes and outcomes of the War of the Pacific and the California gold rush of 1849. In *Daughter of Fortune*, Allende's version of the search for gold, runaway Eliza Sommers reinvents herself by dressing first as a Chinese boy, then as "Chile Boy," the cook for a brothel on wheels. The freedom from confinements of ladyhood confer invisibility. Editors Feal and Miller observe that Eliza can "reclaim the rights only men enjoyed, those of embracing the spirit of adventure and forcing their own destiny" (Feal and Miller, 2002, 56). In the resolution, she opts to iron her dresses and deck herself once more in the accoutrements of a woman, a choice that strips of the phony English mannerisms she learned in girlhood. As a reward, she releases both soul and body, "the fearsome beast that after years of hibernation was roaring back, filled with demands" (Allende, 1999, 387).

Post-colonial Remastering

In *The House of the Spirits*, according to analyst Sara E. Cooper, "both the Trueba family and Chilean politics are shown to be systems in which each event or action requires a change or reaction from within the system," which remains mired in colonial philosophy and expectations (Cooper, 2009, 16). After Clara's self-silencing at age ten, Nívea and Nana devote themselves to restoring the child to normalcy from the medical regimens of Dr. Cuevas and from tender devotion to the child's needs. For nine years, Nana baths and powders her charge, brushes her hair, and treats her to breakfasts on a tray. The folk remedies—linden tea, chamomile, lemon, rue, and mint—fail to lift Clara from enclosure in a fantasy world and immersion in taking notes "to reclaim the past and overcome terrors," a feminist restatement of history from an eyewitness view (Allende, 1985, 7). Until the writing succeeds in lifting the family curse, according to analyst Marta L. Wilkinson, "Personal experiences are repeated and revisited on succeeding generations, forcing a confrontation between the individual, family, society and trauma" (Wilkinson, 2008, 151).

Overt religiosity involves Jaime Trueba in rescuing the destitute and Esteban in fabricating the aura of a blessed nuptial for his pregnant daughter Blanca. In rebuttal of orthodox faiths, Jaime speaks for the author the contention that organized "religion was the cause of half the world's misfortunes," a restatement of Karl Marx's contention that "religion is the opium of the people" (Allende, 1985, 255). Jaime equates Christianity with superstition, a depression of the human spirit that inhibits spontaneous charity to widows, orphans, and stray dogs. His twin, Nicolás, takes action to destroy ineffectual piety by organizing hippies into a carnivalesque clique, parading the streets, and stripping "naked as a baby" to lie down in a cross shape in the midst of traffic (*ibid.*, 339). Esteban's promotion of the status quo prevails after he scatters the flaky assembly and dispatches Nicolás out of the country to reclaim the dignity of the Trueba escutcheon. The scene presents a stop-gap in the del Valle-Trueba fortunes from a temporary flourish of outdated colonial traditions.

After the national coup, Allende illustrates the need for a personal redemption. Esteban's reclamation requires a face-to-face encounter with the military junta that replaces the senate. After the confiscation of his car and driver, he views the status of his nation from sidewalk level. Although the conservative leader shouts: "I'm Senator Trueba! For God's sake don't you recognize me?," the mantra of wealth and officialdom fails to restore his prestige and power (Allende, 1985, 457).

The concealment of his old enemy Pedro Tercero in the basement of the Trueba residence forces Esteban to examine his motivation for spite: "He tried to summon up his fury and his hatred and was unable to find them" (*ibid.*, 446). The ironic delivery of Pedro in the trunk loaded with lettuce and tomatoes to the Papal embassy reconnects the Truebas and their former worker with the plantation and the foodstuffs that originally enriched Esteban and his peasant workers. More poignant to the departure scene, Esteban's entrusting of Blanca to Pedro brings tears to Blanca, who reclaims her father as the man she admired in childhood. At the moment of parting, Esteban admits his failure as a father. In writing family history, according to critic Karen Castellucci Cox, "Alba separates herself from a masculine interpretation of the past and a need to blame," a tradition she gains from both Grandmother Clara and Grandfather Esteban (Cox, 47).

Re-entering the Self

Allende's celebration of redemption invests *The Stories of Eva Luna.* Renewal energizes the mystic pilgrimage of the title figure in "Walimai" and enables two women to revive love in their hearts in "The Judge's Wife" and "Phantom Palace." New directions for the wife and concubine in "The Gold of Tomás Vargas" rely on the complicity of feminist sisters in overthrowing a bully. More powerful, the reclaiming of humanity in photojournalist Rolf Carlé in "And of Clay Are We Created" requires his identity with a dying girl and a lengthy review of the nightmares that haunt his soul. Rolf's apotheosis introduces him to episodes that live on from the past, tormenting his mind with his father's sadism to Rolf's mother and retarded sister Katherina. By confronting the worst that can happen, Rolf experiences a problematic change in perspective that Allende leaves undefined, yet tinged with self-enlightenment.

In *Portrait in Sepia*, investor Paulina del Valle mellows distinctly from the wheeler-dealer of San Francisco to the adoptive mother of her granddaughter Aurora. By accepting the five-year-old from her maternal grandmother Eliza Sommers, Paulina rescinds the animosity of a veritable lioness among the social elite and offers respect to Aurora's maternal grandmother. A similar scene involves Paulina's renewal of concern for her wayward son, Matías Rodríguez de Santa Cruz. Upon his return from Europe in the last throes of syphilis, Paulina recoils from his caregiver, Amanda Lowell, Paulina's onetime rival for her husband Feliciano. The reunion animates life-long hatred for the courtesan. At Matías's request, Paulina not only forgives and reclaims Amanda as a friend, but also sets off a round of laughter that rescinds "years of futile jealousy, shattered rancor, marital deceit, and other abominable memories" (Allende, 2001, 184). The refreshing elation restores for the del Valle family a hospitality and unites members against Matías's grave illness. For Allende, the scene depicts one of womanhood's enduring strengths, the ability to share with other women the absurdities of cherished animosities and vendettas.

See also vengeance

• *References and Further Reading*

Cooper, Sara E. "Family Systems and National Subversion in Isabel Allende's *The House of the Spirits*," *Interdisciplinary Literary Studies* 11:1 (Spring 2009): 16–37.

Cox, Karen Castellucci. *Isabel Allende, a Critical Companion*. Westport, CT: Greenwood, 2003.

Feal, Rosemary Geisdorfer, and Yvette E. Miller, eds. *Isabel Allende Today: Anthology of Essays*. Pittsburgh, PA: Latin American Literary Review, 2002.

Wilkinson, Marta L. *Antigone's Daughters: Gender, Family, and Expression in the Modern Novel*. New York: Peter Lang, 2008.

Reeves genealogy

The textured family tree of Gregory Reeves depicts a wider than usual variety in influences and perspectives, from criminal to saintly as he rids himself of childhood misperceptions and establishes his own family.

English horse thief
imprisoned in Sydney Russian Jews mother
| | died at 105
Greg=/=Olga Reeves=/=Charles Reeves=Nora Reeves |
Russian | Australian | immigrant teacher Pedro Morales=Inmaculada
sibyl | pedophile | Bahai pacifist mechanic | mother figure
| d. 1946 | d. ca. 1985 dies of |
Margaret=movie producer | diabetes |
Virginia| bankrupt | |
aristocrat| ______________________________(blood brother)__________
| | | | |
Samantha=Gregory =Shannon Jim Morgan= Judy Thui =/=Juan José Tom Clayton=/=Carmen
Ernst |Reeves | b.1937 Nguyen | war casualty | "Tamar"
| b. 1939 | __________ cancer | | jewelry
______________ | | victim | | maker
| | son seven others | aborted fetus
Margaret David Dai Morales
addict hyperactive mathematician

• *References and Further Reading*

Swanson, Philip. "California Dreaming: Mixture, Muddle, and Meaning in Isabel Allende's North American Narratives," *Journal of Iberian and Latin American Studies* 9:1 (2003): 57–67.

religion

Allende wields a consistent doubt about the worth of organized faiths, such as anti-woman Dutch Lutheranism and the wisdom of Quaker and Buddhist philosophy in *Daughter of Fortune*, eccentric holy men and cows in *Kingdom of the Golden Dragon*, and the staunch Catholicism of the title figure in "Clarisa." For the medical crisis in "A Discreet Miracle," Padre Miguel, a Marxist priest, spews his distaste for angel lore, hospitals for the rich, military facilities, and the Opus Dei, a lay brotherhood he accuses of materialism in embroidering the chasubles of priests with gold thread. In reference to empty religious gestures, Miguel snorts, "Heaven is not won with genuflexions," his term for gestures of piety (Allende, 1991, 262). Based on an actual event, the miracle of Juana of the Lilies that returns sight to both Miguel's eyes alters his opinion of folk saints. The phenomenon stirs doubts in the Vatican about the votive practices—flowers, processions, medals, plaques, candles, orthopedic prostheses, thanksgiving songs— revering a non-canonized saint for her divine intervention.

In an interview with Jonathan Richards for the Santa Fe *New Mexican*, Allende expressed a wry skepticism about orthodoxy, the scripted religious purity that balances the upper class taste for perverted sex. She noted, "When ... beliefs belong to the patriarchy, they are called religion. When they belong to women of the so-called 'primitive people,' they are superstition" (Richards, 2008). She accused power mongers of perpetuating organized faiths as a source of control of women and gullible males. In place of rigid religious canons, she professed animism, a belief in spirits in mind, body, and inanimate objects. By taking elements of varied faiths, she created a designer faith, one that sanctions a healthy quantity of mysticism.

The author's canon illustrates her devotion to a peaceful ecumenism that suppresses the obligatory childhood training she received in Catholic piety and cant. In a fillip toward pietists, Allende joked that Evangelicals and Pentecostals believe themselves directly in touch with the almighty while the rest of the world must negotiate "through the priestly bureaucracy," her summation of the orthodox hierarchy (Allende, 2003, 60). At her wedding at age 20, she chose a civil service that ignored a faith she compared in *Paula* to a millstone about her neck. Images of sexually repressed women permeate *Inés of My Soul*, an historical novel that opens in a region of Spain "steeped in war and religion," an ironic pairing suggesting that combat precedes and exacerbates Catholicism's colonial violence (Allende, 2006, 6). Additional repudiation of Catholicism in *My Invented Country* states the church's unilateral condemnation of the Mapuche for polygamy. Simultaneously, church authorities overlook the bands of women held captive by colonial Spanish womanizers, who bred "more souls for the Christian religion" (Allende, 2003, 53). In both instances, Allende sides with women against the enforcement of religious dogma dominated by men.

Spirituality and Activism

During the Pinochet regime, which undergirds the novel, Allende worked through the church because of its survival of fascism and its channeling of aid to "the most needy, the ones in prison, families of the disappeared, the widows and the orphans, especially in marginal areas where unemployment reached eighty percent" (McKale, 2002, 117). She outlines the progressive liberalization of the clergy in *The House of the Spirits*. At first, Catholic attitudes emerge from a staid tradition of sermons and confessions and the prejudices of people like Nana, who does not want to be buried among Protestants and Jews. As the political situation heightens postcolonial intolerance, populist priests shift their mission to the working class. The passive kindness of Father Anthony toward the poor in the slums anticipates the activism of José Dulce María, a priest with a mission to spread socialist doctrine among indigenous laborers to relieve them permanently of want and tyranny. Father José speaks a Marxist faith that "In union there is strength," a philosophy that echoes the slogans of the Russian Revolution (Allende, 1985, 179).

Allende extends a fine line separating ignorance and symbolic insight. At a serious conflict to Esteban Trueba's pretensions, Count Jean de Satigny, a pompous peacock of questionable ancestry, derides provincial behavior, particularly reverence toward religiosity and virginity. His sneers generalize the "vulgarity of these stale, out-of-date families, whose daughters were still chaperoned," a demonstration of values abandoned by the decadent rich (Allende, 1985, 252). He mocks the wearing of scapulars, a set of religious badges strapped over the heart on the chest and back with tapes, strings, or cloth bands to bind symbolism to flesh to symbolize allegiance to a religious sodality or saint. In an era of strife between liberals and conservatives, Satigny's apostasy parallels that of Severo del Valle, a bohemian son of aristocrats in *Portrait in Sepia* who feels like a "prisoner in a thicket of dogmas and prejudices" in an extended family that deems itself above "the common people" (Allende, 2001, 22). Unlike Satigny's dismissal of religious metaphor, Severo denounces the aristocracy and declares that conservatives "belonged to the hordes of the devil," a personification that brands the upper classes with the worst of sins (*ibid.*, 23).

The differentiation between empty ritual and the war against iniquity lies at the heart of *Of Love and Shadows*. The author derides unsubstantiated miracles, but applauds efforts of the church to rescue victims of the police. She depicts a priest allying with a Protestant evangelist to suppress pilgrimages to Evangelina Ranquileo's noontime contortions, which produce a "carnival of insignificant wonders" (Allende, 1987, 60). To reset the Evangelina mystery, Allende strips the oracle of her mysticism by revealing her torment of her brother Pradelio, a subtextual comment on the real lives of people adored as saints. Following Evangelina's arrest and disappearance, the Cardinal, "a Prince of the Church," wisely contains his rant at the breach of human rights and applies "strategy, backed by two thousand years of prudence and acquaintance with power," a subtle summation of Vatican influence (*ibid.*, 208). The church's defense of victims of "unspeakable evil" breaks Allende's pattern of mocking Catholicism and honors the Cardinal's cautious intervention against a pernicious government (*ibid.*, 209).

More frequently, Allende satirizes hypocrisy among the devout. In *Eva Luna*, casual mention of the peddler Riad Halabí's success in army barracks notes that he sells both prints of Saint Gabriel and girlie photos of film stars, a ribald juxtaposition. Humor at the expense of religious exhibitionism continues in *Daughter of Fortune*, where homes of English immigrants display "a court of blood, crucified Christs, plaster virgins, and saints dressed in the mode of ancient Spanish noblemen," a jab at Renaissance religious art and its fascination with suffering (Allende, 1999, 40). Protestant missionaries arrive in Chile untutored in Spanish or Mapuche to preach "the true faith" and die of exposure or "devoured by their own flock," a grim death joke at the expense of inept evangelists (Allende, 1999,

14, 28). At chapter's end, the author dramatizes the momentary sanctity as church bells chime noon. Instantly, the community returns to its former divisions—English exploiters and beggars at the church door—as though faith makes no lasting inroads against racism and class distinctions.

In *Inés of My Soul*, Allende describes a tyranny of adamant, dogmatic confessors as "an assembly of corrupt and odious men," a charge laden with gendered implications (Allende, 2006, 104). Piety destroys the illusions of Général Pedro de Valdivia about chaste, thirteen-year-old Marina Ortiz de Gaete, whom the text dismisses as "a quiet sheep" (*ibid.*, 33). As a bride, she expends her energies embroidering chasubles with gold and praying "rosary after rosary in a never-ending litany," an obvious postponement of marital obligations to her husband (*ibid.*, 34). For Pedro, his body meets "an insurmountable obstacle" in Marina's soulful rituals (*ibid.*, 25). The author, a defender of human sexuality, sides with Pedro and awards Marina a boring old age marked by officious church duties, "wrinkles, and silly affectations" that end in disillusion and penury (*ibid.*, 227). The connection between stitchery and devotion returns in *Portrait in Sepia*, in which Aurora del Valle refuses to cave in to an onerous, medieval faith that reduces female education to "embroider and pray," a witty putdown repeated in *Island Beneath the Sea* in the education of Eugenia García del Sola (Allende, 2001, 197). Allende enlarges on ridicule by picturing old maids as the dressers of saints' statues.

Conquest and Syncretism

The waste of energy on tedious devotions contrasts the spirit of conquest that lures Pedro from his saintly wife to adventure in the New World. Ironically, conquistadors justify their savage wars against Indians as the duty of European Catholics to win New World heathens to Christianity, a faith that one cynic reduces to "a couple of crossed pieces of wood" (Allende, 2006, 47). Before an all-out battle between the armies of Francisco Pizarro and Diego de Almagro on April 26, 1538, Chile's Quechua noncombatants view ritual "magic with crosses and silver vessels," which priests conclude with little chunks of bread and blessings on warriors readying for a two-hour mass killing (*ibid.*, 68). The disconnect between pious posturing and the bloodbath and mass rape and pillage that end the Battle of Las Salinas puzzles the Quechua, who witness no beneficence in Spain's Christian armies. Valdivia, the honorable leader of Pizarro's forces, suffers nightmares from so shameful a triumph, a torment amplified by the author's denunciation of Spanish combat methods.

At a height of suffering from the army's lack of water, the text describes the first efforts at syncretic worship. Into the desert, Inés advances muttering Ave Marías to the "Virgencita ... Nuestra Señora del Socorro" (the little virgin, our lady of succor) while she dowses for underground streams (Allende, 2006, 128). The antiphonal Quechua invocations of Catalina echo Inés's supplications in an Indian version directed at an animistic deity. Into old age, Inés continues interweaving the faiths of Old World and New. She explains, "I confuse the Virgen del Socorro with the blessed Mother Earth of the Mapuche," but quickly adds that she is still a staunch Catholic, as though words alone can exonerate her for reverencing an animistic spirit (*ibid.*, 208).

A study of layered godhood reprises a description of Eliza and Lynn Sommers' theology in *Portrait in Sepia*, in which she accepts Jesus as "a reincarnation of Buddha" and pictures a rural Virgin Mary as a doll that the devout dress weekly in new raiments (Allende, 2001, 51). At a tense pass in Lynn's labor with Aurora, Lynn's mother Eliza retreats to an altar dedicated to three powers—Buddha, Christ, and Lin Chi'en, Tao's deceased wife who died in childbirth and returned to earth as a beneficent spirit. The triad demonstrates a mother's mustering of any source of comfort and understanding, especially a female spirit who had suffered a similar trial. Like Inés Suarez's fusion of deities in Santiago, Eliza and Lynn choose an amalgam of spiritual traditions as a means of honoring the blended society of San Francisco's Chinatown. By merging faiths, all three women circumvent the need to embrace one theology at the expense of the other.

For *Island Beneath the Sea*, Allende maintains an evenhanded respect as she examines the indigenous gods of West Africa in new settings in colonial Haiti and their contrast with French Catholicism. According to reviewer Carolina De Robertis, Allende affirms African faith "to lift up what has been trodden down, to expose its beauty to the light" through bizarre episodes of biting off chicken heads and turning trances into sexual debauchery with the god Erzulie, the loa (spirit) of beauty, dance, and mother love (De Robertis, 2010). The heroine, Tété, concubine of colonial sugar planter Toulouse Valmorain, reaches beyond the physical for spiritual empowerment against rape and lashings through "a rich mystery tradition [of] spiritual sustenance" indigenous to Guinea (*ibid.*). Pleading to Erzulie, Tété grapples with the reform of the Code Noir and the promise of the abolitionist movement, which advances with "anti-size steps" (Allende, 2010, 446). The precipitous Haitian Revolution of 1791 resonates with divine damnation of bondage and blessing on unfettered lives in New Orleans. Through it all, Tété remains true to Erzulie, "whose name becomes a melodic refrain throughout the book" in rhythm with the Guinean dance jubilees (De Robertis, 2010).

In celebration of emancipation, Tété dances the kalenda, a black jubilee derived from Guinea, through which she escapes trauma into transcendent joy. Allende restructures voodoo from exotic worship to the fulfillment of everyday spiritual need. Like Sufist ecstasies, the pulsating rhythm fills participants with divinity: "It mounts them. It empowers them. They won because of the coherence of their spiritual beliefs" (Timpane, 2010). Rapture returns at the mid–August beginning of the Haitian Revolution, when blacks ally with "spirits of nature and of dead slaves who have not found the way to Guinea" (Allende, 2010, 157). The black victory accords a triumph to voodoo, which convinces Toulouse Valmorain, an atheist who "believed in nothing," of the aid of the dead (*ibid.*).

Allende pictures the beliefs of black Haitians following them to Cuba and New Orleans in a perpetuation of African ritual. The culture clash in Cuba caused by General Galbaud's retreat with Haitian whites besets Tété in her dealings with islanders. Incarcerated for abandoning Maurice Valmorain in the street while she enters the "vortex of the dance," Tété spends the night in jail with a Spanish-speaking female convict (Allende, 2010, 234). Although the two speak different languages, when the inmates separate the next day, Tété mentally recites an invocation to Erzulie while the Spaniard calls "*Virgen María, madre de Dios, ruega por Nosotros pecadores*" (Virgin Mary, mother of God, pray for our sins, *ibid.*, 235). Allende illustrates that, through parallel orisons, the inmates achieve oneness in their reliance on deities that empower mothers.

Tété's perceptions of syncretism account for Louisiana-style voodoo, which blends with Catholicism and Baptist singing and dancing until the original parameters no longer apply. The performance of an invocation to the Virgin Mary at Valmorain's open house suggests that slaves know how to mimic religious fervor to the master's tastes. In a subsequent scene of god against god, Tété achieves status among plantation slaves by delivering an endangered slave fetus. At the height of the birthing struggle, she draws on the combined strength of Erzulie and Saint Raymond Nonatus (the unborn), the thirteenth-century Catalonian patron of midwifery and infants revered by the Irish overseer's wife, Leanne Murphy. Allende acknowledges syncretism through the beneficence of Père Antoine de Sedella, the pastor and peacemaker of the cathedral in New Orleans. He legitimates the merger of Guinean *loas* with the Almighty and his saints and issues a welcome "for all the divinities" (Allende, 2010, 277). His encouragement of ecstatic dancing at the place Congo indicates an ecumenical spirit toward Guinean worship styles, which are more cultural than religious.

The non-judgmental inclusion of greater New Orleans, promoted by Père Antoine, encourages a less plangent atmosphere than that of Haiti. For contrast to his ministry of goodness and service, Allende characterizes black orgies at the place Congo under the spell of Sanité Dédé, New Orleans's first voodoo queen, who wraps herself in a snake, a pagan symbol of sensuality and power. To Tété, the fatalism of voodoo makes more philosophical sense than "the virtue of resignation" or anticipation of equality in heaven, which promotes complacency toward bondage (Allende, 2010, 298). Over time, her attitude drifts toward the white faith from observations of Père Antoine, whose superintendence of the New Orleans cathedral enables him to bring together all races in a holy atmosphere, the "most tolerant place in Christianity" (*ibid.*, 325). Allende stresses that the daily example of kindness to prisoners, orphans, and the undeserving wins Tété to a religion expressed in actions rather than platitudes.

Revelations of Theology

With a similar emphasis on action rather than dogma, Allende uses her YA trilogy to describe young adventurers discovering foreign religious ritual. The native philosophy in *City of the Beasts* corresponds with African voodoo in suiting the needs and lifestyle of Amazonians, including the asking of permission to spear a fish and the eating of a soup made from the chief's bones, a form of initiation for neophyte tribe members. Guide César Santos validates animism as the belief in a universal soul that exists within matter, a transcendental cosmology that the shaman Walimai later explains in the use of clay and the blood of the moon in creation. Lacking concepts of materialism, guilt, shame at nudity, and set creeds, the Indians have no understanding of Christian martyrdom, prudery, or unvarying invocations. After the death of a native, the group creates an *ad hoc* service comprising Kate's prayers, a tree platform, and carved crosses. In similar makeshift fashion, Walimai prepares Jaguar and Eagle to take his position as shaman, a grooming of the young in the style of Lois Lowry's coming-of-age fable *The Giver*, in which wisdom passes to the next generation.

In the sequel, *Kingdom of the Golden Dragon*, Allende presents Buddhism and Hinduism from a tourist's perspective. Reviewer Susan Carlile identifies in Alex and his grandmother, Kate Cold, an embrace of mysticism: they "find a certain peace that neither expected," the result of Buddhist traditions and pacifism among Himalayans (Carlile, 2004, 170). For Alexander, reared by agnostics, the spirituality of "even the most trivial things" demonstrates how religion can permeate the nativist mindset (Allende, 2004, 312). He ponders an enigma in so peaceful a land, the fortified monasteries that hold contrasting populations—peaceful monks and soldiers, who guard king and country. The juxtaposition of contemplative monks alongside enforcers of law explains itself during the chaotic attempt to rescue kidnapped girls and the abducted king. Participants in the struggle "learn of their own inner strength; the value of humility; and most important, an appreciation of those who are very different from themselves," a tolerance that encompasses an inquisitive Bhutanese pilot, the felonious Judit Kinski, and a phalanx of bumptious Yetis (Carlile, 2004, 170).

In the second sequel, *Forest of the Pygmies*, Allende details opinions on religious differences. She introduces variant religious responses to Brother Fernando's scapulary, a Catholic "holy object, blessed by the pope" that Fernando kisses (Allende, 2005, 63). Angie Ninderera, the African pilot, wears an amulet that Fernando arbitrarily denounces: "One represents the power of Christ, and the other is pagan superstition" (*ibid.*, 64). Allende uses the ensuing discussion as a platform for ironic presentation of racism and ethnocentrism. Kate, a Protestant amulet wearer, attempts to make peace by declaring Catholicism "as picturesque as African religious ceremonies" (Allende, 2005, 63). The most pointed comments, Angie's comparison of African theology with Christianity, refutes the logic of Jesus's martyrdom and of "a hell where souls suffer for all eternity," an endless punishment that Angie finds incomprehensible (*ibid.*, 186). Alex wisely avoids siding with white religion because he wears an amulet under his shirt, a concealment that keeps his faith private and unobtrusive to doubters.

In a chapter of *Neo-Imperialism in Children's Literature about Africa: A Study of Contemporary Fiction* (2009), co-editors Yulisa Amadu Maddy and Donnarae MacCann accuse Allende of valorizing Western religion by stripping African spiritualists and healers of authenticity. The critics state that Allende defames African practitioners as "dangerously malicious, power-hungry witch doctors," a charge that denigrates Allende's novel for xenophobia and imperialist distortion (Maddy and MacCann, 2009, 25). However Maddy and MacCann overlook the healing power of a witch who relieves a small boy from internal rigidity and of the Aka amulet Ipemba-Afua, which cures the insect bite that bedevils photographer Joel Gonzalez. In the resolution, before Alex returns to the white world, he requests "a few grams of the miraculous green powder" to ensure that his mother continues to defeat cancer, a secondary conflict that binds the three novels (Allende, 2005, 289). His discretion suggests a respect for individuals and cultures on a par with that of Confucius, who advised followers to avoid displays of ritual, religious superiority, or proselytizing.

See also healing and health; wisdom

• *References and Further Reading*

Carlile, Susan. "Review: *Kingdom of the Golden Dragon*," *Journal of Adolescent & Adult Literacy* 49:2 (1 October 2005): 170.

De Robertis, Carolina. "Review: *Island Beneath the Sea*," *San Francisco Chronicle* (25 April 2010).

Maddy, Yulisa Amadu, and Donnarae MacCann. *Neo-Imperialism in Children's Literature about Africa: A Study of Contemporary Fiction*. New York: Routledge, 2009.

McKale, Margaret A. Morales. Literary Nonfiction in Works by Isabel Allende and Guadalupe Loaeza. Columbus: Ohio State University, 2002.

Richards, Jonathan. "Summing Our Mysterious Days," (Santa Fe) *New Mexican* (19 September 2008): PA-22.

Timpane, John. "Isabel Allende's Heroines Are, Like Their Feminist Creator, Strong and Independent," *Philadelphia Inquirer* (5 May 2010).

San Francisco

As the obverse of traditional, class-conscious Santiago and stodgy Valparaíso, Allende endorses San Francisco for being "happy, tolerant, open, and cosmopolitan" (Allende,

2003, 186). In contrast to the manginess of New York City streets in *City of the Beasts*, San Francisco appeals with its seaside amenities and inclusive citizenry. Other depictions admit faults. In *The Infinite Plan*, Gregory Reeves gauges summer weather as typically cloudy and gusty with a winter wind. In *Daughter of Fortune*, Allende summarizes the port's beginnings as a "sophisticated and diverse city," a nexus for the slave trade "with no legal tie-ups and in full light of day" (Allende, 1999, 410, 349). Nonetheless, she pictures the pier overlooking "the most beautiful bay in the world," a compliment that Allende corroborates with her exuberant love of Sausalito, a community to the south of San Francisco's city center (*ibid.*, 133).

Allende's fictional version of San Francisco teems with hundreds of immigrants arriving daily. The area becomes "an enormous camp for men on the move" (Allende, 1999, 223). Makeshift dwellings suit the work of adventurers, merchants, preachers, and prostitutes, all drawn west over the frontier to live in huts and tents and enrich themselves on the California Gold Rush of 1849. From its close ties to sea travel and trade, the city's fame spreads around the globe. Because of the hopes of youth to wrest wealth from the earth, the economy thrived on an energetic populace, both male and female, decent or criminal, "strong, noisy, and brimming with health" (*ibid.*, 356). Critic Karen Cox viewed the newcomers as "a greedy, chaotic band developing a haphazard government in which frontier justice rules" (Cox, 2003, 131). The prediction of an agricultural bonanza correctly foresees the region's future in what editor Michael Sollars terms "a land of possibilities, both real and imagined" (Sollars, 2008, 199).

The polyglot mix encompasses speculators, local tribes, freedmen, and veterans of European wars. Among prospectors come pushy Yanquis, former slaves, drunken and argumentative Oregonians, Russian mountaineers, Peruvian merchants, Australian roughnecks and felons, Hawaiian gamblers, Chileans in Chilecito, and Tasmanian and New Zealand ruffians. Whites slam Mexicans as "greasers [who] looked alike," a faulty perception that prevents posses from identifying and capturing the bandit Joaquín Murieta (Allende, 1999, 264). Below Latinos at the bottom of social status live frugal Chinese in Little Canton, the "lowest among the undesirable foreigners," all residents of tents, shacks, or cardboard and sheet metal hovels in identifiable barrios along "the muddy alleyways of San Francisco" (*ibid.*, 223, 344). Despite racial antipathies, critic Ana Patricia Rodríguez maintains that the contiguity of cultures illustrates the capacity of cities "to 'Americanize' and acculturate people by force" out of the necessity to communicate and conduct everyday business (Farr and Harker, 2008, 193).

Californian Identity

Allende describes the exigencies and materialism that alter people so rapidly that "no one was who he seemed" (Allende, 1999, 320). Of the moiling, greedy masses, women earn their keep by cooking and tending the sick, a service provided by Joe Bonecrusher's prostitutes during a dysentery epidemic. A photographer captures the milieu in facial expressions, portrait groupings, and costumes. The Chinese profit by spending little while doing laundry, cooking, and performing acupuncture and herbalism. Jacob Todd, under the name Jacob Freemont, sells tales of the frontier "including Indian massacres, immigrants flooding in..., uncontrolled price gouging" and the details of vice and vigilantism, the stuff of dime novels sold in Boston, New York, and England (*ibid.*, 292). Among Freemont's florid compositions, he demeans Hispanics with racial profiling based on the embroidered myth of Joaquín Murieta, Three-Finger Jack, and their cutthroat gang.

Tales told in Valparaíso, Chile, compare California's wealth to that of Aladdin and Sinbad's treasures. Thus, expectations based on myth and legend begin the 7,000-mile journey for plucky Chileans. Less memorable, stories of crime, illness, and accidents make no dent in the yearnings of dreamers. By tackling the layered historical foundation of San Francisco history, the author salutes multiculturalism, the philosophy that undergirds the city's global success, and specifies the adaptive power of Latino culture. She hyperbolizes that "the entire world passes through San Francisco, each person carrying his or her cargo of memories and hopes" (*ibid.*, 196). The mix yields an urban tolerance of foreign and disparate cultures, each contributing religion, language, costume, medical theory, and foodways.

For Eliza Sommers in *Daughter of Fortune*, a biracial outcast reared among elite English whites—Anglo-Spanish with Mapuche upbringing—San Francisco offers what critic Olga Ries characterizes as "a new beginning, a clean page, a complete reconstitution of identity" (Ries, 2011, 5). The action, set on the bay overlooking the Pacific, introduces urban growth through the eyes of two immigrants, one Chinese and one Anglo-Chilean disguised as an Asian boy, both arriving by sea. Through their encounters with xenophobia, the reader vicariously experiences what critic Mel Boland describes as a microcosm of "global concerns, from factionalism and ghettoization to ambition and greed" (Boland, 2003, 479). Boland further credits Allende's friendship with novelist Amy Tan for the emerging stress on the Chinese-American's role in migration history and their inclusion of Asian wisdom, healing, and cookery on Western society.

A Moneyed Metropolis

In Allende's writings, San Francisco coalesces into a city at the inception of corporate globalization and industrial capitalism, a view of urban creativity expressed by critic Z. Nelly Martínez. Ries credits California with "a state of constant un-readiness, a mixture of ambition and restless energy" that result in instant wealth for pimps, bandits, and pornographers and penury for scraggly, underweight miners and singsong girls (*ibid.*). In the milieu of the Gold Rush, Eliza finds opportunities to develop the person she wants to be by dressing in men's clothing and braiding her hair into a queue. Through picaresque exploits with an acting troupe, she remains on the trail of a wayward love, the legendary Joaquín Murieta, a literary foil of the serene herbalist Tao Chi'en and kindly Quaker James Morton. The contrast of aims and expectations suits the ebullience of a city still in the formative stage and a citizenry that contributes the multiple talents essential to a coastal metropolis.

In the opening lines of the sequel, *Portrait in Sepia*, the Chinese ghetto runs on its own reality in two languages, Cantonese and Mandarin. At daybreak, Allende declares, "The clocks obey no rules, and at that hour the market, the cart traffic, the woeful barking of caged dogs awaiting the butcher's cleaver, was beginning to heat up" (Allende, 2001, 3). The image of the vulnerable awaiting the *coup de grâce* from the captor expands on the nature of conquest, a theme that began with the arrival of Spaniards in 1492 and continues into the settlement of Alta California by its new owners, the Americanos. The author holds in abeyance the raised cleaver until the speaker, Aurora del Valle, fishes from her repressed memory the murder of her Chinese grandfather, Tao Chi'en. The gentle herbalist succumbs to racist tongs for his campaign "on behalf of the horrible fate of the tiny slaves (singsong girls) right in the heart" of the city (Allende, 2001, 296). *Portrait in Sepia* pictures the city at the height of the American Civil War, when art shops, book stores, theaters, and bars display West Coast fresco, tableaux, and paintings. Far from combat, San Francisco becomes "a hornet's nest of corrupt politicians, bandits, and loose women," but still a proving ground for ambitious males (Allende, 2001, 5). By emphasizing the entrepreneurial success of men during the Gilded Age, the story anticipates first wave feminism by exalting Paulina del Valle, a female investor who bests males at astute guesses on how to make money from an expansive era. By ferrying ice and fresh produce north by steamer, her shipping line contributes to the city's reputation for good food and modernism.

• *References and Further Reading*

Boland, Mel. "'Orienting' the Text: Eastern Influences in the Fiction of Isabel Allende" in *Cross-Cultural Travel*, ed. Jane Conroy. New York: Peter Lang, 2003.

Cox, Karen Castellucci. *Isabel Allende, a Critical Companion*. Westport, CT: Greenwood, 2003.

Farr, Cecilia Konchar, and Jaime Harker, eds. *The Oprah Effect: Critical Essays on Oprah's Book Club*. Albany: State University of New York Press, 2008.

Ries, Olga. "Latino Identity in Allende's Novels," *Comparative Literature and Culture* 13:4 (2011): 1–8.

Sollars, Michael D. *The Facts on File Companion to the World Novel, 1900 to the Present*. New York: Facts on File, 2008.

secondary characters

Much as Shakespeare uses Father Laurence in *Romeo and Juliet* and Polonius in *Hamlet*, Allende assigns perceptions and insights to lesser characters at crucial points for the edification and instruction of primary figures, for example, the kindness of the teacher Inés in "The School Teacher's Guest" and the saintly ministrations of the title figure in "Clarisa," two stories based on characters in *Eva Luna*. Through creations as disparate as the eccentric traveler Uncle Marcos and the fanatical Padre Restrepo in *The House of the Spirits*, journalist and cinarist Aravena in *Eva Luna*, Babalú the Bad and gambler Joe Bonecrusher in *Daughter of Fortune*, and overseer Owen Murphy in *Island Beneath the Sea*, Allende excels at making her supporting cast meaningful in dialogue and action. To enhance the value of minor characters, the author maintains personal engagement with the least involved, including maids, vendors, guards, and street figures, such as the uniformed security force in the palace in *Kingdom of the Golden Dragon* and Cubans in Havana and the superior old guard in early nineteenth-century New Orleans in *Island Beneath the Sea*.

In *The House of the Spirits*, the action fleshes out a mélange of social levels and relationships, particularly Father Antonio, the voyeuristic priest who hears Férula's confessions; Amanda, an unmarried woman living a lower middle-class nightmare of genteel poverty; and Count Jean de Satigny, the high-flown grifter posing as a French aristocrat investing in Western Hemisphere fauna. Nicolás observes both Amanda and Satigny, displaying his naiveté by accepting the count at face value and loving Amanda without pondering how deprivation diminishes her and her brother Miguel in their private lives. The shallow summation of acquaintances reveals Nicolás's frivolity as a boy from a wealthy background with a "bird-of-passage heart" (Allende, 1985, 272). He has no notion of socioeconomic truths or co-dependent love like that between Miguel and his older sister. Fortunately, Nicolás realizes, "I have a lot to learn" (*ibid.*). Tragically, his twin Jaime suffers his own mental hell from idealizing a secret love for Amanda, whose name in Latin means "she who should be loved." With maternal insight, Amanda highlights the difference between Nicolás and a mature lover: "Can't you see my soul is very old and you're still a child? You'll always be a child" (*ibid.*, 267).

The paralleling of family faults and transgressions in *Daughter of Fortune*, the sequel to *The House of the Spirits*, underscores mortal weaknesses, both in clans and passing acquaintances. For Rose Sommers, the eighteen-year-old seduced by the roué tenor Karl Bretzner in London, history repeats in the misjudgment of her adopted daughter Eliza. In 1848, sixteen-year-old Eliza's affair of the heart with Joaquín Andieta mirrors in passion and recklessness Rose's misstep in 1830. At the first evidence of Eliza's deception and flight from Valparaíso, Rose relives the "pitfalls of forbidden love" (Allende, 1999, 250). Spared a teen pregnancy and humiliation by a married bounder with two children, Rose acknowledges that youthful indiscretions "had shaped her destiny" (*ibid.*). Mindful of the compromises and social masks necessary to restoring Eliza's position in the family, Rose takes action while her stodgy brother Jeremy does nothing. Overdressed for a meeting with Joaquín's mother, Rose feels ridiculous in addressing the sexual peccadilloes of young lovers, yet she recognizes that, given the options, she would have followed her seducer to California.

A Human Procession

For *Eva Luna*, the passage of people through the lives of an orphan juxtaposes friars with nuns, an Indian gardener with embalmer Professor Jones, Eva's African godmother with Elvira, a Caribbean cook, and the scruffy con artist Huberto Naranjo with the prostitute La Señora and the transdresser Mimí, Eva's *ad hoc* family. Allende expresses through cyclical life changes the character maturation Eva undergoes, from her mother Consuelo's death to dealings with the priest who comforts the old professor and the faceless authorities who dispose of the professor's goods. After joining the household of Riad Halabí in Agua Santa, Eva draws support and learning from Inés, the village schoolteacher, and a community welcome from citizens who leave their doors open to drop-ins. In brief exposition of secondary figures, Allende pictures need in Indians, who "came in single file, ragged, followed by a pack of dwarf dogs, the children naked, the old worn by time, the women pregnant" (Allende, 1987, 145). Eva's skill at interacting with Indians and guerrilla warriors dramatizes critic Domnica Radulescu's vision of "the disturbing and often inseparable bond between female creativity, the creativity of the heroine, and the violence of which she is a victim" (Radulescu, 2002, 137).

In more alarming realism, secondary characters provide perceptions on the dictatorship and the plight of Latino poor in *Of Love and Shadows*. In a turmoil of battered lives, the maid Rosa conceals the stillbirth of an illegitimate child, Digna Ranquileo suffers conjugal beatings from husband Hipólito, and their daughter Evangelina dies of rape and murder by a police official. In the breakdown of military indoctrination, Lieutenant Juan de Dios Ramírez discovers that "the world was spinning backward," causing the officer to humiliate himself before his squad (*ibid.*, 127). Sergeant Faustino Rivera, an Indian and soldier under the command of Ramírez, recognizes the decline of police pride and patriotism wrought by the torture and execution of prisoners. Through Rivera's memory of the shooting death of a boyhood companion, Irene Beltrán realizes the insidious nature of clichés as prevalent as "kill or be killed, this is war" (Allende, 1987, 126). The stark pain of loss takes shape in the duties of morgue attendants and the martyrdom of Gustavo Morante, whom Francisco mockingly names "the Bridegroom of Death" (*ibid.*, 64).

In *Daughter of Fortune*, secondary characters provide Allende with juxtapositions of opposites, a literary ploy as old as Aesop's fables. To Tao Chi'en's serene, unassertive demeanor, English surgeon Ebanizer Hobbs launches laughter and gestures that preface an unlikely friendship between East-West students of herbalism. Lacking subtlety and poise, Hobbs introduces the studious Tao to dissection and autopsy, two medical regimens forbidden in Chinese training. The exchange of Asian and European ideas enlarges Tao's initial education with greater awareness of organ function and disease. More revealing of Tao's character, his marriage to Lin surprises him that women can be more than workhorses, mothers, and ornaments, the three stereotypes he learns in Canton during his apprenticeship. To his false assumptions, he adds "the natural joy" of marital bliss, which he enhances with knowledge of human anatomy and pleasure points (Allende, 1999, 182). Through Hobbs, Tao realizes that Lin's tuberculosis cannot be cured. Hobbs favors his colleague with bittersweet advice, "You must enjoy her while you have her" (*ibid.*, 184). Hobbs lacks familiarity with animistic tradition that enables Lin to remain hovering as a spirit when Tao most needs her.

Gauging Character

For *The Infinite Plan*, based on the life of Allende's husband, William C. Gordon, the author uses characterization as a means of expressing California's duality in its Anglo and Latino environments. The text draws on an extended supporting cast that particularizes settings and events as well as the hopes of the immigrant male to "become an impresario with his own Cadillac and a blonde on his arm" (Allende, 1993, 41). For the reality of the California barrio, Allende focuses on the Morales family, especially Gregory Reeves's friendship with Carmen and his filial love for Inmaculada and Pedro. Away from home, Greg struggles with daily battles with the gangbanger Martínez, who teaches him escape and avoidance strategies. The dysfunction of Greg's mother and sister, Nora and Judy Reeves, contributes motivation and response in a son who rejects a dead-end existence among "the lowest of the low" (*ibid.*). For learning, Greg draws on college pal Timothy Duane, mentor Cyrus the elevator operator, and army buddy Leo Galupi, who expedites Carmen's adoption of a son in Vietnam. To express Greg's missteps in designing his own family, Allende creates wives Samantha and Shannon. By injecting life into the supporting cast, the text contends that Greg has ample opportunity to find happiness, but poor choices muddle his thinking well into middle age.

The lengthy list of secondary figures in the *City of the Beasts* trilogy indicates a widespread indigenous influence on villages and cultures, notably the People of the Mist in the Upper Orinoco region, the Yetis of the Himalayas, and the Bantu in Ngoubé, Central Africa. The partnering of primary and secondary casts enables the People of the Mist to protect their prehistoric lifestyle with the aid of teen adventurers Alex and Nadia and the wise woman Iyomi, a delicate, but decisive "chief for the chiefs" (Allende, 2004, 230). Allende activates a range of female strengths to combat the problems of incursions into closed societies in Brazil and, in the Forbidden Kingdom, the weakening of Grr-ympr, the leader-mother of Yetis in *Kingdom of the Golden Dragon*. For the Brazilian natives, Iyomi responds to the need to protect a people who "could not hide forever in the trees, like monkeys" (Allende, 2002, 380). For the Yetis, the promise of Tensing to pose as ruler *pro tem* relieves Grr-ympr of her fear of death and subsequent chaos among semi-human beasts "only slightly more intelligent than a chimpanzee" (Allende, 2004, 331). In both cases, Allende equips the mother-leader with wisdom and patience to survey future needs.

In the introduction of African mysticism in *Forest of the Pygmies*, Allende continues creating peripheral females who impact the direction of the novel's conflict. In Nairobi, Kenya, the outré garb and mysticism of Má Bangesé creates both suspense and humor in the inability of Alex to break the hold of the seer on his person. Allende expands the cast with Angie Ninderera, an African bush pilot, and Nana-Asante, a hermit who receives the dead at the cemetery of Ngoubé. Through concerted female action of the oracle Má Bangesé, Angie, writer Kate Cold, enslaved Aka domestics, and teen adventurer Nadia Santos, the Aka of Ngoubé free themselves of a male tyrant. In the resolution, Nana-Asante becomes the reconciler who revives a symbiotic relationship with the neighboring Bantu, one of Allende's pervasive visions of community cooperation in secondary characters.

• *References and Further Reading*

McKale, Margaret A. Morales. *Literary Nonfiction in Works by Isabel Allende and Guadalupe Loaeza.* Columbus: Ohio State University, 2002.

Radulescu, Domnica. *Sisters of Medea: The Tragic Heroine across Cultures.* New Orleans: University Press of the South, 2002.

Weldt-Basson, Helene Carol. *Subversive Silences: Nonverbal Expression and Implicit Narrative Strategies in the Works of Latin American Women Writers.* Cranbury, NJ: Associated University Presses, 2009.

Sedella-Valmorain genealogy

The complex family tree of slaveholder with concubine tangles ethnically and socially with successive births of mixed blood scions. For concubine Tété Sedella and her master, Toulouse Valmorain, the knotty relationships reach a precarious accord in the birth of their granddaughter, Violette Solar, the offspring of an incestuous marriage of brother with sister.

```
                              wife=Maurice Valmorain          Senegalese=/=Frenchman-wife
African queen=/=white sailor  exiled  | sugar planter         grandmother |
leaps from a    |             in Italy| dies of syphilis                  |
cliff           |                  | ca. 1770             ______________________________
                |             ______                          |                        |
Guinean=five    |             |    |       courtesan=/=white soldier      freed children
father  wives   |             |    two     killed  | murderer              ________
      |         |             |    spinsters       |                       |      |
Gambo=/=Zarité "Tété" Sedella=/=Toulouse Valmorain=/=Violette Boisier=Major Etienne Relais   brother
La Liberté  slave housekeeper  | sugar planter   free courtesan   French soldier
slave       b. ca. 1770        | b. 1750         orphaned at 13     1738-1793
runaway     freed 11/30/1800   |                 m. 1779
rebel                 _______________            foster mother
b. 1774               |              |     |              religious fanatic grandmother
            Rosette             Jean-Martin Relais                    |
            1789-1804           b. ca. 1785              father=hysterical mother
                                                                      | suicide
            =/=Zacharie                                               |
```

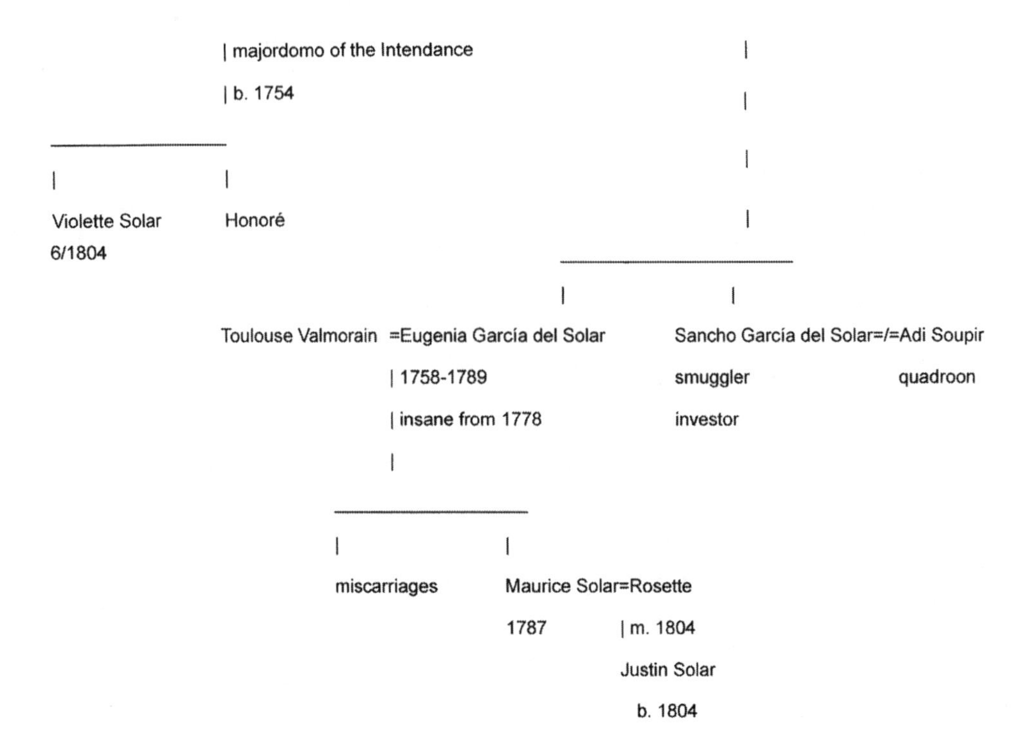

The second family of Toulouse Valmorain, born in New Orleans:

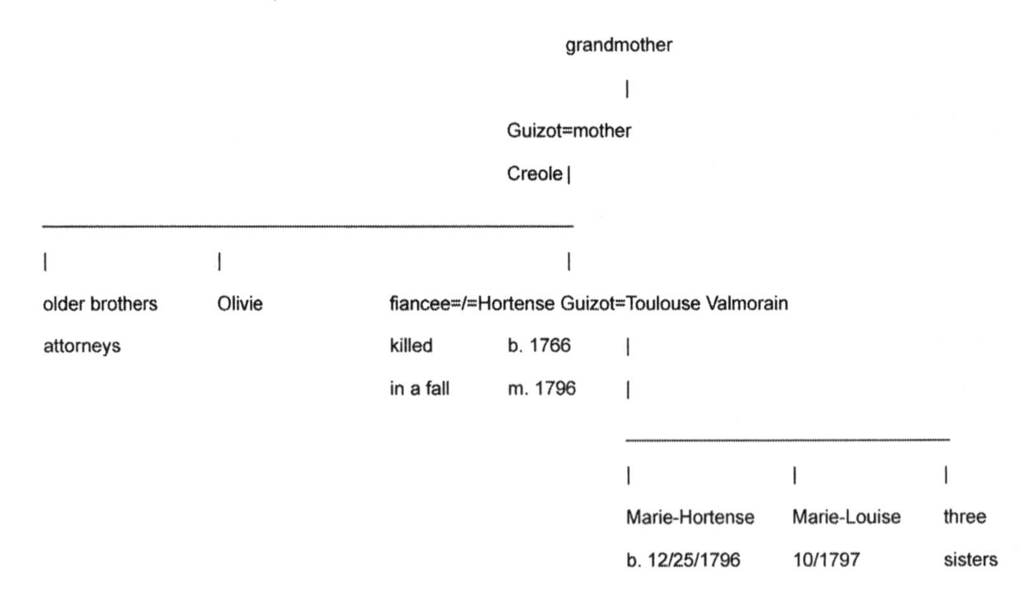

• *References and Further Reading*

Barker, Olivia. "Allende's 'Island' Plunges into Some Troubled Waters," *USA Today* (10 June 2010).
De Robertis, Carolina. "Review: *Island Beneath the Sea*," *San Francisco Chronicle* (25 April 2010).
Timpane, John. "Isabel Allende's Heroines Are, Like Their Feminist Creator, Strong and Independent," *Philadelphia Inquirer* (5 May 2010).

sex

Passion is never far from Allende's thoughts. In the author's summation of writing method, she compares narrative to tantric sex, a languorous coupling enhanced by long delayed climax, a storytelling ploy that enhances the significance of choices and actions. She pictures her work station as a private temple, "a sacred place to perform the ceremonies or sexual love of writing," an immersion of mind in body (Allende, 1996, 25). Clearing her thoughts through meditation, she begins searching for character secrets by penetrating "the darkest caverns of the human psyche," a metaphor enriched by coital innuendo (*ibid.*, 26). Sinking into physical awareness, she enjoys "the sensations of the body and the expansion of the spirit," a whole body wresting of consequence from character behaviors and insights (*ibid.*).

Allende explores variant forms of sex, from the lesbianism of Férula Trueba and Esteban's tumbles with Tránsito Soto at the Red Lantern and the Christopher Columbus in *The House of the Spirits* to the birth of Rosa's baby-that-fell-through-the-skylight in *Of Love and Shadows* and the one-night stand of Zulema with Kamal in *Eva Luna*. Sensitivity toward gendered behaviors begins in the young, as with Nadia Santos, who refuses to stay apart from her father to be near Mauro Carías, a menacing male who disturbs her with his touch and smarmy solicitude. To account for the arousal of libido in a widow in "Simple María," Allende explains the appeal of male "voices, their fresh-shaved cheeks, and the smell of tobacco," which the widow's family disdains as "frivolous temptations" (Allende, 1991, 156, 157). Allende builds on María's lack of sex education by thrusting her into a momentary coupling with "an insatiable Greek Sailor" following "several weeks of oceanic chastity," the author's excuse for the seaman's vigorous coitus (*ibid.*, 158).

As literary historian Donald Leslie Shaw explains, Allende's lively interest in coition infuses the Post-Boom literature with such satisfying romps as the naked groom chasing his bride in "The Guggenheim Lovers" as well as the troubling sexual temptations in "Revenge" and "Wicked Girl." Her dramatizations of sexual liaisons contrast "the relative absence of love as a possible solution to some of life's problems in the Boom" begun by the works of Gabriel García-Marquez (Shaw, 2002, 174). The author's sure-footedness along routes to heterosexual fulfillment enables her to blend romantic ideals with feminist values, including those that move the gutsy entrepreneur Hermelinda to solace lonely shepherds in the story "Toad's Mouth" and enlighten the speaker in the bedroom parable "Our Secret." In *The House of the Spirits*, sexual infractions define a postcolonial abasement of women and, by extension, their illegitimate offspring. Esteban Trueba, the patrón of Las Tres Marías and a frequenter of the prostitute Tránsito Soto, debauches his farm women and those of neighboring haciendas. His brutal acts constitute sexual imperialism in the "tumbling girls in the wheatfields," a casual approach to rape that results in the "bullet-riddled bodies of peasants" and the birth of a monster, Esteban García (Allende, 1985, 127, 81). For justification, the *patrón* excuses multiple bastardies as "progress" and basks in the envy of males of the landed gentry (*ibid.*, 77). Esteban Trueba's dismissal of carnal sins hastens his enlightenment to the solidarity of angry peons.

Similarly powerless to a patriarchal society, the del Valle women surrender themselves to passion and commitment, but elude the traditional life in domestic chains. At the dawning of suffragism, Nívea, the fount of the del Valle matrilineage, demands freedom of self and beliefs through what French feminist Simone de Beauvoir described as "mutual recognition of two liberties" (Abao, 2000, 88). For Nívea's daughter, Clara del

Valle, the next generation of liberalized women, the sexual awakening of her children causes no alarm, even the cushioning of the twins behind the garbage dump on the bovine breasts of a woman who replicates in softness the mothering of Clara, Férula, and Nana. The fatal breakdown of Clara's marital commitment to Esteban Trueba results in the twentieth year of the marriage from an abrupt slap by which he dislodges her front teeth and bloodies her nose. Always capable of retreating into clairvoyance, Clara retaliates by removing her wedding ring, reverting to her maiden name, and escaping into silence, three gestures negating the marital bond. Her reluctance to laugh and to kiss Esteban hurts him "like a slap across the face," an emotional blow he deserves (Allende, 1985, 205). For Esteban, the only revival of his marital relationship occurs when he carries his wife's teeth in a suede pouch, sniffs Clara's clothes, and embraces her pillow, a disembodiment of sexuality that solaces him after her death.

Second-Generation Sexuality

In the ensuing generation of del Valle children, Allende destabilizes romantic convention with deft twists on stereotypes of women's emotional and economic dependence on men. Prominent in relationships, the coital partnering of Nicolás/Amanda, Blanca/Pedro Tercero, and Alba/Miguel excites paired participants to heights of intimacy and ecstasy. To Nicolás's jealous brother Jaime, Amanda is a free spirit who embodies "the essence of everything feminine ... of everything forbidden," an omen of her suffering during an abortion of the fetus Nicolás sires. Contributing drama to the scene, Jaime performs the surgery while concealing his unrequited love for the patient. Nicolás discloses his naiveté by begging for forgiveness "to let them go on as if nothing had happened," an immature dismissal of her life-threatening operation and of the poverty that burdens her daily life (*ibid.*, 267).

In another episode transgressing moral boundaries, Blanca copulates with a peasant, Pedro Tercero, her childhood companion. After Esteban disowns her, forcing Blanca to earn her keep, the ouster from Las Tres Marías liberates her physically and emotionally from a bleak atmosphere of male dominance. Freed of aristocratic prudery and snobbery, she adapts to the self-empowerment of working for a living and of reveling in Pedro's body and scent, an olfactory delight identical to Esteban's embrace of Clara's pillow. Personal and financial independence increases the likelihood that Blanca's affair will last. Caste-free, she accepts the conditions of loving Pedro—exile from the hacienda class as well as displacement among plantation peons. Committed to the impermanence of her amour, she prefers "furtive hotel rendezvous with her lover to the routine of everyday life, the weariness of marriage" that destabilized Clara's union with Esteban (Allende, 1985, 311).

Allende's scrutiny of family sexual proclivities continues with Alba's attachment to a student rebel, Miguel, a second love match based on attraction and desire rather than class dictates. Like Blanca, Alba overturns the Cinderella motif by "sleeping down" with a man from a lower class and by creating her own castle, a funhouse bedchamber in the Trueba basement from oddments of cloth, books, and mattresses, where they "played like children" (Allende, 1985, 376). Alba mirrors her mother's illicit love by precipitating a pregnancy that Alba treasures as the next link in the del Valle matrilineage. Far from the romanticizing that critics claim infantilizes her fictional couples, Allende places sexual relationships in realistic settings. The text mirrors liberation in the future after Alba survives rape in a torture chamber. Bearing the next generation of del Valle womanhood, Alba rids herself of elitism and despair and cherishes the future of her own daughter.

Sexuality and Innocence

In *Eva Luna*, the author reprises the advancement of Tránsito Soto in the demimonde through a childish story by Eva Luna. From a nine-year-old's perspective, the protagonist turns her house into "a place for parties and good times," a child-sized vision of a bordello selling ice cream and malted milk and the habitation of women who refuse to cower before bullies (Allende, 1987, 65). By age fifteen, Eva outgrows sexual fantasy. She spies on Zulema's blatant seduction of Kamal, which Allende glorifies as "absorbing him in her quicksands, devouring him, draining him, and leading him to the Gardens of Allah" (*ibid.*, 165). The carnal hyperbole scrolls on, describing a coital smell that infiltrates the house until it is "transformed into a lewd beast," an omen of Zulema's suicide and the vicious interrogation of Eva (*ibid.*, 166). Her experience at police headquarters introduces her to the collateral damage of adultery.

To the gentle coupling of Tao Chi'en and Eliza Sommers in *Portrait in Sepia*, the text contrasts delicacy with the acrobatic positions employed by Nívea and Severo del Valle, who, despite birth control with gall and vinegar, conceive fifteen children during their "play in the dark" (Allende, 2001, 173). Reviewer Helen Falconer credits Nívea with violating Victorian standards through the power of "pure lust and uncrushable willpower," a beacon of feminism during the enlightenment of Aurora del Valle (Falconer, 2001). Aurora, like her mother Lynn, develops urges that no anatomical training explains. In anticipation of her wedding in September 1898, she yearns for Diego Domínguez, her beloved, but "didn't know exactly for what," a witty authorial explanation of edginess in adolescent maidens (Allende, 2001, 222). Because of her lack of background, Aurora falls victim to the privileged male, a gender hierarchy that oppresses the wife, denying her autonomy and carnal pleasure. In reference to Aurora's insecurities and self-doubts, the author credits feminism with updating women on their needs and capabilities.

In lieu of sex education, Aurora envisions "a cottony sugary future through which we would float" (Allende, 2001, 223). Her disillusion with an unsatisfying wedding night coupling derives from ignorance of anatomy and Diego's haste in producing "love without pleasure," a nightly drudgery that leaves Aurora blaming herself because "something basic was lacking in my womanhood" (*ibid.*, 230, 255). For a year, she drags frustration "like a heavy bridal train," an overt criticism of her unfulfilling wedlock, marked by Diego's purchase of twin beds separated by a table (*ibid.*, 253). Sensibly, she accepts responsibility for her own carnal delight, a duty anticipatory of first wave feminism of the 1960s. After watching the languorous lovemaking of Diego and his sister-in-law, Aurora nurtures pity for Diego and Susana for the charade of their days among family members and the reduction of their trysts to stolen moments in the barn, a suggestion of the animal nature of their lust for each other.

Sex and History

The violence and audacity of Renaissance love permeates Allende's recreation of the founding of Chile. In the approach of the title character to Chile in *Inés of My Soul*, the author investigates the motivation for Christian license in the New World, where "men needed immediate love, or a substitute for it" (Allende, 2010, 101). As Inés Suarez increases the distance between herself and church and parental authority in Extremadura, Spain, she reassesses traditional virtues and their applicability in the Western Hemisphere. Inés questions the presence of God in a land where men take their pleasure among native women. She rationalizes that her own straying from chastity ranks below the self-pleasure of dissolute conquistadors, who "take Indian and black women at will" and abandon them without thought of their mestizo offspring (*ibid.*, 78). In the anonymity of Latin America's Pacific coast amid fragrant flowers and lush fruits, she wonders, "Who was there to judge me" for yielding to extramarital temptation with a gusto equivalent to that of Spanish men (*ibid.*, 76).

In her first satisfying amour, Inés speaks the Renaissance image of coital climax as "to die and die again," an image for the "little death" of sexual orgasm that the author introduced in the coupling of Tao Chi'en and Eliza Sommers in *Portrait in Sepia* (Allende, 2006, 97). Inés credits herself with intimate knowledge of Francisco Pizarro's field marshal, Général Pedro de Valdivia, whom she knows "in a way history could never know him: what he feared and how he loved" (*ibid.*, 99). The need for a complete love life follows Inés to age 70, when she ponders the mechanics of geriatric sex by which she and second husband Rodrigo de Quiroga "could have loved as in our best days" (*ibid.*, 226). While the *Chicago Sun-Times* reviewer dismisses the musings of the *gobernadora* as a "historical bodice-ripper," more tolerant critiques value the novel as a revelation of female contributions to colonialism, which range from cooking, sewing, nursing, and wielding a spear to coupling with the great men of the era.

In a view of late eighteenth-century war in *Island Beneath the Sea*, Allende indulges in contrasts of secondary characters, beginning with the voluptuous courtesan Violette Boisier, the toast of Le Cap, Haiti. Like lush fruit, she captures Captain Etienne Relais, eliciting a marriage proposal to the fifteen-year-old mulatta within the first night of sexual dalliance at her three-room lair at place Clugny. Despite the depth of his love, she finds romance irrelevant to a career based on Moorish tricks and rapidly compromised by hard living and occasional bruised eyes. Shrewd to the parameters of prostitution, she saves gold and jewels for the day when she narrows her mates to Relais alone, a lover who proposes marriage and stability. During their wedlock, Violette maintains her egalitarian view of males, whom she imagines naked and bereft of "titles, power, fortune, ... (and) race" (Allende, 2010, 128).

Equally quelled in her youth, Eugenia García del Solar loses her girlish figure and charm after numerous miscarriages. Unlike the lascivious Boniface, Jr., in Maryse Conde's *Victoire*, Allende's Toulouse Valmorain ceases the niceties of courtship and attacks Eugenia "without preamble, with the urgency of a sailor," an ironic duplicate of the fornications between enslavers and Guinean girls bound in ships' holds during the Middle Passage (Allende, 2010, 69). At the far end of the sexual continuum, Lacroix, the neighboring planter, reduces sex to animal mating with a "seraglio of girls chained in a barracks," where guests and black studs take their pleasure (*ibid.*, 104). Wisely, Valmorain distances himself from Lacroix and predicts that the sadist will pay for "fundamental crimes" of inhumanity to black females (*ibid.*). For the sake of poetic justice, Allende pictures Lacroix slaughtered, skinned, and left for Valmorain to bury. Meanwhile, Valmorain's predictable mountings of slaves, like bulls on cows, produce more mulatto livestock for the plantation.

Allende contrasts concubinage with the derailed love of African captives. As a symbol of the surge of freedom in the hearts of enslaved lovers, the kitchen boy Gambo and Tété, she feels her lover "embedded in her heart," a phallic image faithful to the classical myths and Renaissance paintings of Cupid's arrow implanting a lasting emotion in the beloved's chest (Allende, 2010, 197). When Gambo flees to the mountain hideout, he "found relief" with camp women, a release of ejaculate that leaves him emotionally unsatisfied (*ibid.*, 177). Upon the reunion of Gambo with Tété, the couple reignite their fervid passion. A night of coitus in an empty bedroom at the Habitation Saint-Lazare precedes a lengthy flight through swamp and enemy territory of Tété and Toulouse Valmorain with Gambo as their guide. Within earshot of the grim-faced master Valmorain, Tété frequently couples with Gambo, a forest assignation as fraught with demonic omens as the forest tryst of Aeneas and Dido in Virgil's *Aeneid.*

Both act and memory shape Allende's slave era triangle. On cyclical nights, the sounds of joyous intercourse between Gambo and Tété strip Valmorain of manhood, forcing out sobs of humiliation. Upon return to Le Cap, the master finds himself ensnared by jealousy because he both desires and hates Tété for imaginings of her "familiar body, her walker's legs, her firm rump, her narrow waist, her generous breasts, her smooth skin" in fornication with Gambo (Allende, 2010, 190). A welter of emotions forces Valmorain to impose his will on the concubine who saved him and Maurice from the black mobs' machetes. A symbol of the perversity of master-slave relations, the master's nightly beddings with Tété become one more household chore, which she describes as "dark and shameful" and which Valmorain recalls as "nostalgic unburdenings" (*ibid.*, 112, 117). During her second pregnancy, she describes the nightly servicing as "[doing] it like dogs," a verbal diminution of human sex into animal coupling for which the slave curses the master "in her heart" (*ibid.*, 131).

The private lives of Tété and Valmorain envelope the action, producing what critic Bernadette Murphy calls "a lifelong dance of control and manipulation, sharing children, houses, even a harrowing escape" (Murphy, 2010). A contrast to the sensual "prickling of pepper over all our bodies" when the handmaiden escapes to Gambo's arms, Tété's coitus with Valmorain requires a mental disembodiment that frees her spirit of the depravity borne by her body (*ibid.*, 122). In the year following her lover's flight to the Maroons in the mountains, she attempts to hold his shape by imagining that the hairy, alcohol-breathed Valmorain is Gambo. Under the brief imaginary coitus with her lover, she feels her body "open and sway, remembering pleasure" (*ibid.*, 158). Long after the brief affair of Gambo with Tété, she "resigned herself to sending messages to Gambo in my thoughts," a fantasy romance that gradually fades (*ibid.*, 212). Allende awards Valmorain a similar sexual abandon in the arms of his second wife, Hortense Guizot. The Creole mistress of Valmorain's second plantation outside New Orleans uses intimate caresses and shocking displays of libido to overpower Valmorain and displace him as financial controller of a vast estate. To grasp both money and cane fields, she needs a son to supersede Maurice, but produces five daughters.

A complex coital arrangement between slave and master produces the off-kilter household in which Valmorain grooms his son Maurice for inheritance of an Antillean sugar plantation. Contemporaneous with Maurice's coming of age, his half-sister Rosette, child of Valmorin and Tété, illustrates the disparities of bondage. The two, literary foils in character and physical makeup, become fast friends, with Rosette defending the effeminate heir. Powerless to intervene in bedtime cuddling, Tété observes forced training of the two, Maurice in a merciless Massachusetts military school and Rosette among the Ursulines at a New Orleans convent school, neither of which intervenes in a true love match. The eventual marriage of Maurice to his taboo bride on a pirate ship forces a choice: either give up loving his sister, or move her to Boston, a stronghold of New England abolitionism far from the castigation of New Orleans Creoles.

In defiance of a worldwide horror at incest, Allende condones the brother-sister union. She allows the love match to fuel a romantic tragedy, begun by separation of the newlyweds and Tété's consolation of Rosette. In the style of the Victorian domestic novel, at the boiling point of antipathy toward Maurice, his stepmother precipitates a slap fest on Chartres Street. The fallout from a quadroon striking a white *grand blanc* jeopardizes Rosette's survival in prison. The text leads inexorably to the bride's demise and the near death of her newborn son Justin, whom his grandmother rescues and rears. Allende names the babe as a reminder of the ongoing struggle for justice in a world fraught with racial hostilities and social hierarchy. As though passing sexual triumphs from the enslaver to his victim, the text awards Tété a satisfying relationship with her lover Zacharie and a daughter, Violette Solar, as well as Justin Solar, the motherless grandson.

Twentieth-Century Dissatisfaction

To dramatize the 1970s and the "me" generation, Allende surveys periods of abstinence and separation in a fulfilling sex life wrought by what literary historian Elliott Robert Barkan calls moral disconnection and spiritual disadvantage. Upon the return of Gregory Reeves from the Vietnam War in *The Infinite Plan*, he finds no warmth or even welcome from his mother, wife, daughter, or sister, a rebuff he counters with a frantic erotic hunt for the perfect woman. Only the embrace of his blood sister, Carmen Morales, enables him to abandon himself to unfettered carnality. His lovemaking, desperate and engulfed in solitude, reveals to Carmen that strife has claimed her childhood blood brother. In part because of his bizarre upbringing by a monomaniac father and incommunicative mother, Greg "had grown up without water or care," like a devalued weed (Allende, 1993, 244). The spontaneity of Greg's coital reunion with Carmen leaves them uncomfortable in each other's company. Greg blames combat for subsuming his emotions in "a malignant form of contact that in the end left me with a terrible emptiness" (*ibid.*, 255).

The novel illustrates the echoes of the past in the dissatisfactions of the present. Carmen blames the unsuitability of their sexual encounter on Greg's drift from war to capitalism. Their two-year separation stymies spontaneous intercourse that leaves untouched two souls now nearly unrecognizable to each other. Without discerning the role of post-traumatic stress disorder in her old friend's ongoing unhappiness, Carmen misses the mark and avoids regular communication. Greg realizes that "neither of us was ready to lead the other along the paths of love" (Allende, 1993, 256). Rudderless amid a sea of willing females, he attacks the field with the resolve of warrior rather than a lover. During his "years of libertinism," he wastes opportunities for intimacy on acquisition of power through conquest, literally killing the prize he seeks to possess (*ibid.*, 256). When he tries to describe his series of private office orgies, he recalls only "blank pages" (*ibid.*). Significantly, after counseling, Greg achieves self-renewal during which his "little black book with its list of ladies got lost," leaving him cleansed for a more mature love life (*ibid.*, 374).

- *References and Further Reading*

Abao, Frances Jane P. "The Power of Love: Rewriting the Romance in Isabel Allende's *The House of the Spirits* and *Eva Luna*," *Humanities Diliman* 1:2 (July–January 2000): 87–99.

Barkan, Elliott Robert. *Making It in America: A Sourcebook on Eminent Ethnic Americans*. Santa Barbara, CA: ABC-Clio, 2001.

Murphy, Bernadette. "Review: *Island Beneath the Sea*," *Los Angeles Times* (14 May 2010).

Shaw, Donald Leslie. *A Companion to Modern Spanish-American Fiction*. Rochester, NY: Tamesis, 2002.

social class

The benefits and deterrents of birth and caste permeate Allende's writings in a variety of situations, as with Beatriz Beltrán's yearning for upper-class respectability in *Of Love and Shadows*, Horacio Fortunato's wooing of the haughty Patricia Zimmerman in "Gift for a Sweetheart," and the social revolt against colonial values in *The House of the Spirits* that ends the predations of conservatives like Esteban Trueba in a phallocentric capitalist society. The feudal division of the landed class from miners and laborers allots to the rich imposing town mansions, country villas, foreign travel, and private schools, all bought with the profits from nitrate and copper mines, vineyards, and plantations. The proletariat makes do in rural adobes and shanties or in ghettos that ring cosmopolitan areas and work as laborers and service personnel. As in the social milieu of Iris Anthony's *The Ruins of Lace*, the poor incur a disproportionate amount of suffering from food shortages and rationing, epidemics, and fascist scapegoating of females, sexual deviates, and non-whites.

In the latter title, the del Valle women create methods of ridding themselves and the underclass of machismo tyranny, a holdover from colonial brutality. For Nívea and Clara, populist activism becomes a tactic for subverting patriarchal social and religious discord that are at once anti-intellectual, anti-woman, and anti-family. Allende notes that the landed class remains "unaware of the danger that threatened the fragile equilibrium of their position" until too late to stop a revolt (Allende, 1985, 82). Trueba, the loser as a result of a workers' insurrection, grouses that "agrarian reform ruined things for everybody," an "everybody" constituted of the rich and influential (*ibid.*, 64). Although the fictional laboring class maintains its hospitality and gratitude, two traits it shares with the peasantry of the author's homeland before her exile, *campesinos* depart from rural traditions and uplift themselves through education. Critic Olga Ries notes the back country's "slow disintegration ... as the heart of Latin American society," a loss to nationalism and industrialization common to agrarian societies worldwide (Ries, 2011, 7).

In *Island Beneath the Sea*, the panoply of conflicted relationships—slaves/*grands blancs* (French slaveholders), freedmen/*petits blancs* (white middle class), rebels/monarchists, French/Creoles, slave owners/concubines—builds a tension similar to the simmering fury in Alejo Carpentier's *The Kingdom of This World* and Madison Smartt Bell's *All Souls' Rising*, both steeped in Antillean anarchy. Reviewer Margo Hammond defines Allende's orchestrated lawlessness as the result of a "carefully calibrated—and explosively precarious—racial hierarchy" (Hammond, 2010). Because of the role of slaves in generating wealth from Haitian cane fields, the French elite maintains that "work was for a different class of people" (Allende, 2010, 8). However, the landed class cannot avoid living within sight and sound of bondsmen.

For Madrid-born beauty Eugenia García del Solar, marriage to Toulouse Valmorain and elevation to mistress of his plantation plunges her into back country paganism punctuated by drumming and ecstatic dance and worship. To buoy her spirits, she flaunts her pedigree from "the best society of Madrid, from a noble Catholic family," a designation that gains her no peace or escape from the surroundings of Habitation Saint Lazare (Allende, 2010, 55). Because her son Maurice befriends his mulatto sister Rosette and cuddles with her for naps, Valmorain sets the parameters of privilege, which discredit fraternizing with the lower class. The father's summation—"male ... white, free, and rich"—characterizes the pecking order of Maurice's era (*ibid.*, 164). To the boy's demands for justification of his privilege, his black nanny redefines the island hierarchy as "twisted and unfair" (*ibid.*, 164–165).

Allende pictures the reordering of reality as the islanders' method of defining themselves. Social-climbing mulattos own slaves and mimic the drawing room manners and Catholic fervor of whites. The incongruity of blacks owning blacks derives from the denial of light-skinned Haitians of "the African blood of their mothers" (Allende, 2010, 124). To mixed-blood strivers, black heritage stigmatizes them with the mark of Cain, which relegates island mulattos to less than full citizenship among land owners like Eugenia and Toulouse. For social betterment, Violette Boisier, a mulatta courtesan at place Clugny, plots to escape the "hierarchy of class" (*ibid.*, 307). She hedges her commitment to her white husband Etienne Relais by conniving with her bodyguard Loula in smuggling and usury. Allende indicates that hard cash hidden "in a hole in the patio" outweighs a rise in class by marriage for women like Violette, a hard-edged capitalist bent on buying her way out of Haiti's social web (Allende, 2010, 126).

The move of the Valmorain household to New Orleans demands compliance with insular social standards. Avoiding the ostentation of the nouveau riche, Valmorain purchases a sedate residence in the quarter and cultivates musicales and dance lessons for Maurice and Rosette as evidence of refinement. Valmorain follows Sancho García del Solar, his brother-in-law, to bars and cafés and endures the chitchat of the city's "mean-minded society" (Allende, 2010, 95). The result is ennui at "the same faces with nothing new to say" (*ibid.*, 243). Despite boredom and distaste for cockfighting and gambling, Valmorain abides by the dictates of the elite, a code that Allende satirizes for its aridity and predictability, particularly the urbane style of duels to the death, a "favorite pastime" (*ibid.*, 259). While men like Valmorain and García del Solar live in leisure, Valmorain's plantation slaves share small quarters and eat from troughs like pigs. The conditions indicate that Valmorain learned nothing from his experience with wrathful leaders of the Haitian Revolution who slew and skinned fellow planter Lacroix and ransacked island plantations.

Lineage and Mixed Blood

For characters with Guinean lineage, class distinction hinges on the degree of blackness and West African traits. Social matrons weigh the birth gift of one-half, one-fourth, or one-eighth European blood, an obvious typology among the nubile females who process at the Bal de Cordon Bleu. Encased in cotillion gowns, the girls display a variety of pigmentation from almost white to café au lait and darker, coloration that they pass to their offspring. Female social clout rests on the honor of their beaux and a benign form of blackmail: "If a man violated his given word, the women would make sure his reputation was ruined" (Allende, 2010, 368). In the estimation of critic Carolina De Robertis, the social order following the Louisiana Purchase derives from the couplings and birthings of the next generation, who "define and culminate ... their unprecedented attempts to transcend societal limitations" (De Robertis, 2010).

In *Zorro*, where "pure-blooded Spaniards" rank above other racial groups, Allende explains the success of New Orleans's quadroon balls, a socially approved method of finding mates for Creole concubines, like the sweet, submissive Catherine Villars (Allende, 2005, 45). By merchandising beautiful mixed-blood girls to wealthy males, mothers find a way around Louisiana laws that forbid interracial marriage. Training of young mulattas offers them "domestic skills and arts of seduction that no white woman even suspected existed, to create the rare combination of mistress of the house and courtesan" (*ibid.*,

302). The social mixers preserve the caste system, bolster white power over intimate relations, and keep nonwhite women subjugated, yet secure with pensions and stylish cottages. As a "mark of distinction for a caballero," men provide their bedroom companions with slaves, elegant wardrobes, and a Continental education for the resultant offspring (*ibid.*). French privateer Jean Lafitte, Catherine Villars's husband, notes an irony: the manipulation of social rules affords Creole girls more choice in mating than that enjoyed by white belles.

The example of proud New Orleans quadroons introduces a new layer of society and a reorganization of who outranks whom. Don Sancho, who admires the high-stepping mixed-blood Louisiana blacks, compares them to "fine fillies," a left-handed compliment that denigrates mulattas as race horses, another bibelot of the wealthy French (Allende, 2010, 252). Sancho dramatizes his interest in curvaceous quadroons by fighting a duel over Adi Soupir, a "frivolous, greedy" woman reputed to have "plucked the fortunes of several suitors" (*ibid.*, 275). The sudden shift in the ownership of Louisiana in 1803 injects anxiety into the quaint layered society of New Orleans with its snooty Creoles and mulatta cotillion planners. After Napoleon sells the 828,000 square miles to the United States, refined urbanites fear control by coarse Kaintucks, their term for backwoodsmen given to "drunkenness, killings, and whoring," the incivilities that Bal de Cordon Bleu planners intend to stymie (*ibid.*, 241).

In *Portrait in Sepia*, the interbreeding of disparate races provides Allende with a controlling theme similar to that of Emile Zola's family saga and in Dolen Perkins-Valdez's *Wench*. Paulina del Valle, a Spanish aristocrat, looks askance at Eliza Sommers, the allegedly Anglo-Chilean-Mapuche owner of a pastry shop in San Francisco. Paulina charts the social hierarchy in her mind, but, because of her own reputation as a businesswoman, hesitates to comment on a woman's need to earn a living by serving the public tea and sweets. Paulina also takes stock of Eliza's "devastating indiscretion," her common law marriage to Tao Chi'en, a Cantonese herbalist (Allende, 2001, 20). Miscegenations, a serious racial gaffe, presents problems of acceptability for the couple's biracial son Lucky, who is, nonetheless, "proud of his origins and had no intention of ever leaving Chinatown" (*ibid.*, 50). For Lucky's sister Lynn, beauty transcends caste, yet predisposes her to ruin by the moneyed gentlemen who eye her with lust, an ungovernable libido that ignores racial boundaries.

Class Accommodation

Allende's dramatic irony, the fathering of Eliza's granddaughter by Paulina's wayward son Matías Rodriguez de Santa Cruz, generates the first layer of class nemesis for Paulina. As a result, she must share with Eliza their mutual granddaughter Aurora, the child of a matrilineage tangled by interbreeding. More devastating to Paulina's snobbery, the marriage of nephew Severo del Valle to Lynn to give her illegitimate baby a patronym installs the child in the proud del Valle matrilineage. Paulina's castigation —"Nephew, those people are not of our social class"— earns from Severo a sensible retort (Allende, 2001, 83). He claims that Lynn, Eliza, and Tao are "the most decent family I know," a moral judgment that disregards caste considerations (*ibid.*). Feliciano Rodriguez de Santa Cruz, Paulina's fractious husband, compounds the uproar over Severo's "unpardonable" sin of marrying a mixed-race women, a breach of class that "betrayed this family" (*ibid.*, 82). Significantly, the most damning clan shame falls on Paulina for her "flood of joy" after Lynn's death from blood loss during childbirth (*ibid.*, 85).

For the sake of plot and comedy, the devolution of friendship between Eliza and

Paulina results in a Chinatown version of the eighteenth-century stage bitch fight. Wisely, Eliza allows Paulina's rage to blow away like an ocean storm and promotes familial unity on Aurora's behalf. Eliza contends, "The more people who love [Eliza], the better it will be for her" (Allende, 2001, 88). Paulina's riposte that the Chi'ens "would see who the Rodríguez de Santa Cruzes were, how much power they had in this city, and how they could ruin Eliza ... and her Chinaman" expends the paternal grandmother's trump card, leaving her deflated and sobbing in her carriage (*ibid.*, 89). Allende honors Eliza for saying little and graciously sharing Aurora with her paternal grandparents.

In an exercise of identifying her origins, Aurora overrides the spat of grandmothers by declaring Tao her favorite and most reliable grandparent. In adulthood, Aurora absorbs her father's dictum: "Dirty linen is washed at home," a reminder that family discord remains private amid the prudish, petty del Valle clan (Allende, 2001, 97). Allende develops the contretemps after Tao's death by picturing Paulina in widowhood accepting a granddaughter to rear and by joining her butler, Frederick Williams, in a marriage of convenience to provide a father figure. Paulina eases Aurora's way among Chilean snobs by concealing with half-truths the child's bastard birth to a working-class biracial mother. Paulina emphasizes the girl's ancestry from "the best people" and her step-grandfather's alliance with "men of position" in the Club de la Unión, an enclave of "well-known families" (Allende, 2001, 140, 148). Adjustments to social and racial identity increase the likelihood that Aurora will grow up with stable notions of her place in Chilean society as an heiress with Anglo-Chilean-Mapuche and Chinese heritage. She develops objectivity in photographic portraiture and focuses on all classes, including plantation Indians and *campesinos* and third-class travelers during an Atlantic crossing from Europe to Buenos Aires. The affixing of poses to platinum prints retrains to eye away from "seeing only what we want to see" (*ibid.*, 257).

See also racism

• *References and Further Reading*

Gray, Herman, and Macarena Gómez-Barris. *Toward a Sociology of the Trace.* Minneapolis: University of Minnesota Press, 2010.

Hammond, Margo. "A Slave Makes History in Allende's New Novel," *Pittsburgh Post-Gazette* (6 June 2010).

Wilkinson, Marta L. *Antigone's Daughters: Gender, Family, and Expression in the Modern Novel.* New York: Peter Lang, 2008.

The Stories of Eva Luna

Yoking tales by a framework reflecting the ordering of *A Thousand and One Tales of the Arabian Nights*, Allende envisions twenty-three short narratives linked by humanistic themes. The fictional Eva Luna selects and arranges the stories and fables to entertain her lover, Rolf Carlé, a photojournalist. Confident in the role of Scheherazade, she introduces the anthology with a tribute to a life thread woven into patterns of memory and sense impressions. The text incorporates "all we have lived and have yet to live, all times in one time, without beginning or end" (Allende, 1991, 4). The hypnotic flow of stories gains reader involvement through what critic Gloria Konig Fiero describes as the interlacing of "terse, straightforward narrative and sensuous allegory" (Fiero, 2002, 172).

Essential to each dramatic situation, the illuminations and contradictions reveal a shared humanity in disparate lives and social levels. The contrast in willful characters juxtaposes the hagiography revealed to Padre Miguel in "A Discreet Miracle" with the carnivalesque ending to "Gift for a Sweetheart," the story of Horacio Fortunato's courtship of Patricia Zimmerman, a haughty aristocrat, with circus acts. Allende foregrounds plot with universal themes, as with the perversion of the Cinderella motif in "Toad's Mouth," the overturn of the romantic tradition in "Tosca," and the colonial dehumanization of rubber workers and supernatural solace to a widower in the tale "Walimai." Through psychological insight and satire like that of English author Geoffrey Chaucer and Italian raconteur Giovanni Boccaccio, Allende's stories delve into memorable emotions ranging from despair and regret to maternalism. Acmes of personal triumph produce a pivotal moment for Dulce Rosa Orellano in "Revenge," Analía Torres in "Letters of a Love Betrayed," and Inés in "The Schoolteacher's Guest."

Over a varied terrain of situations—provocative women, sex slaves, press gangs, euthanasia, tyranny, adoption fraud, May–December unions—Allende manages to shape a cohesive text. Threads of intimacy and heartbreak tether "If You Touched My Heart" to "The Gold of Tomás Vargas," stories of self-indulgent males who objectify women as sources of pleasure and who suffer for their sins of abusing and silencing their mates. In the latter story, paired victims, wife Antonia Sierra and concubine Concha Díaz, conspire to better their lives and rid themselves of patriarchal violence by outsmarting a bullying wife beater. The horrific details of bondage and retribution in "If You Touched My Heart" serves college literature classes with a frequently anthologized model of Gothicism and female silencing. Of the totality of longing, regret, and frustrated love, critic Joan Axelrod-Contrada pictures the stories forming a "greater meta-narrative" of postmodern self-awareness (Axelrod-Contrada, 2011, 115).

Amorous Powers

The collection opens on a fable, "Two Words," a playful tribute to storytelling as a bearer of news and views. With the universal elements of a happily-ever-after tale and carefully placed silences, Allende counters the warrior, hardened by years of civil war, with the magic of language, which his career has ignored. Wrapped in the mesh of a hammock, his face in shadows, the Colonel lives a solitude that denies him love. The touch of Belisa Crepusculario on his hand casts a spell on a grizzled spirit, conferring the gentility and female warmth of a survivor of poverty and hard luck. The balance of powers—Belisa's femininity and the Colonel's ferocity—neutralizes her need for safety and his longing for the people's love. According to critics Joseph O'Beirne Milner and Lucy Floyd Milner, the story "projects the power of language to answer the power of guns," a global issue that took on greater urgency after 9/11 (Milner and Milner, 2003, 212).

Based on unlikely love plots, Eva Luna's stories demonstrate forms of abuse and sexual empowerment. Analyst Patricia Hart asserts that Allende emphasizes the risks incurred by women like Eva Luna to control their bodies and futures. A case in point in "Wicked Girl," the childish fantasy of Elena Mejías about a romance with singer Juan José Bernal traces the brief physical contact in two minds. Elena summons him via prayers and dreams, "all her magic ceremonies contrives to draw him to her" (Allende, 1991, 29). While Bernal's awakening to a tender, semi-nude eleven-year-old turns his mind toward schoolyards and fetishism with girls' panties, over the next eleven years, Elena outgrows her fixation on her future stepfather and forgets his role in her advance to puberty. The irony that illicit love between an adult and a child "fired [Bernal's] blood and poisoned his mind," not the girl's, overturns the more common depiction of a young female enamored of a first embrace and the fantasies it engenders (Allende, 1991, 34).

Allende's limited subjectivity aroused in critic Clarence Major a tribute to her "refusal to channel the reader in a single emotional direction" (Major, 2001, 179). In contrast to the normal mating of Bernal and his wife in "Wicked Girl," Allende reveals a whore's skills in "Simple María," a story that director Cora Bissett adapted for stage in 2007, and in "Toad's Mouth," a narrative named for the toss of coins at Hermelinda's vagina. The randy tale of the Asturian's romance with Hermelinda derides the English colonists, who lack the vivacity and sexual pleasures of their native employees. Similar validation of tribal animism dramatizes events in "Walimai" and "Ester Lucero," both of which accept at face value the beliefs of jungle denizens that earth's powers can delight, sustain, and heal. More intense, the shared healing in "Our Secret" generates sympathy and catharsis between lovers who suffer post-traumatic stress from memories of torture in Chile, a political time and place suggested by a map on the wall. Allusions to crucifixion exonerate the characters for their sexual needs, which assuage the hurts of martyrdom suffered by "Ana Díaz and the other betrayed *compañeros* being led in one by one with their eyes blindfolded" (Allende, 1991, 169).

WORD PICTURES

Allende's literary acumen emerges in her ability to express a controlling theme in a single metaphor, archetype, hyperbole, allegory, or testimonial. In mythic telling, a rich description of conquistadors as centaurs in "Phantom Palace" alludes to the duplicity of the conquerors of Venezuelan Indians, whom the Spanish insurgents tortured under the guise of Christian indoctrination. In "Tosca," the metaphoric shadow of a macaw that follows Maurizia Rugieri freights the scene with symbolic regret that she has lived a fantasy. For "Walimai," the author's honorarium to words illustrates her faith in language as the conduit of culture and identity. Carnivalesque elements enhance her fables, introducing "the only hermaphroditic and ventriloquist dwarf in history" in "Gift for a Sweetheart" and the retrieval from a cage and revival of Hortensia in "If You Touched My Heart." The double screening of Analía Torres in "Letters of Betrayed Love" in the "garret of the forgotten saints" at the Sisters of the Sacred Heart convent introduces a surprising story of repressed love (Allende, 1991, 289). Parallel in action and theme to Edmond Rostand's *Cyrano de Bergerac*, the masking of a worthy love match heightens the satisfaction of a happy ending.

Essential to the magnetic appeal of Eva Luna's stories, her characterizations make short work of uniqueness in primary and secondary figures, such as the celibate life of *niña* Eloísa and her mother in "The Little Heidelberg" and the filth-caked shaman and crazed Doctor Angel Sánchez in "Ester Lucero." For the *bandito* Nicolás Vidal in "The Judge's Wife," the cost of the criminal's life in exchange for the momentary delights of Doña Casilda Hidalgo's body balances the exchange with "intimacy, tenderness, secret laughter, the celebration of the senses, a lover's joyful pleasure" (Allende, 1991, 193). Some characters recur from *Eva Luna*—Uncle Rupert and Aunt Burgel in "The Little Heidelberg" and Riad Halabí and Inés in "The Schoolteacher's Guest"—and Eva herself. Others replicate stereotypical behaviors, notably, the rebel warrior Tadeo Céspedes in "Revenge," a "man habituated to violence" like Eva's friend, Huberto Naranjo (*ibid.*, 274). The use of Dulce Rosa (sweet rose) for the heroine exhibits Allende's reliance on hyperbole, a common element of fairy tales and parables that awards the girl "magnified charms" (*ibid.*, 277).

In the background of "A Discreet Miracle," Allende positions hints of the savage

Chilean regime she castigates in *The House of the Spirits* and *Of Love and Shadows.* Padre Miguel, a veteran of random searches and senseless inquisitions at police headquarters, speaks the language of the people, the victims of a corrupt junta. In discussion of his ophthalmic treatment, the text blames the dictatorship for making medical care "a privilege of caste," a discriminatory situation that the author hints at with mention of public hospitals in "Interminable Life" (Allende, 1991, 260). Sensory perceptions of trickery alert Miguel to the elevator music of the German Clinic and cause the snit that nets Miguel a four-hour wait at a Southside waiting room, a common deterrent to the well being of the poor. Through an unforeseen rescue of Miguel's vision, the inconveniences enhance his dedication to the underdog and instill a greater dedication to his savior, Juana of the Lilies, a rescuer endowed with the purity of fragrant white blossoms.

The pictorial horrors of the final story, "And of Clay Are We Created," derive from a news event that haunted the author six years after it filled headlines with the slow death of Omaira Sánchez. The text, which editor Patrick A. Smith calls "psychologically taxing and poetic," examines the subjectivity of a photojournalist who allows himself to pity a thirteen-year-old girl trapped in a mud avalanche, a cataclysm that occurred in Colombia on November 13, 1985, from the eruption of the volcano Nevado del Ruiz (Smith, 2002, 12). Throughout the revealing three days of suffering, the story allies viewer and viewed in a shared humanity, a vulnerability to pain and mortality that locks the fictional Azucena in the sucking mire while cloaking Rolf Carlé in the toxic memories of his cruel father, symbolized by vultures and helicopters that hover overhead. The story concludes on a catharsis so overwhelming that Rolf loses himself in contemplation of the apotheosis—he and Azucena merge into one example of the human condition. Analysts Robert Rubenstein and Charles R. Larson view the effects of Azucena's slow death on Rolf as "the power of events to overtake their observers" (Rubenstein and Larson, 2002, 46). The story serves as a coda for the collection and a gesture toward the cumulative might of narrative to reveal fundamental truths that create irrevocable change in the reader.

See also language; storytelling

• *References and Further Reading*

Axelrod-Contrada, Joan. *Isabel Allende.* New York: Marshall Cavendish Benchmark, 2011.
Fiero, Gloria K. *Modernism, Globalism, and the Information Age.* Boston: McGraw-Hill, 2002.
Major, Clarence. *Necessary Distance: Essays and Criticism.* Minneapolis: Coffee House Press, 2001.
Milner, Joseph O'Beirne, and Lucy Floyd Morcock Milner. *Bridging English.* Upper Saddle River, NJ: Merrill/Prentice Hall, 2003.
Rubenstein, Roberta, and Charles R. Larson, eds. *Worlds of Fiction.* Upper Saddle River, NJ: Prentice Hall, 2002.
Smith, Patrick A. *Thematic Guide to Popular Short Stories.* Westport, CT: Greenwood, 2002.

storytelling

More storygiver than novelist, Allende recognizes the strength of narrative to ease tensions and effect socio-political change, as with the amusing anecdotes of Count Jean de Satigny in *The House of the Spirits* and the story of David and Goliath by which Alex Cold encourages the minuscule hunter Beyé-Dokou in *Forest of the Pygmies.* During the year-long vigil over her daughter, Allende envisions a realistic "Sleeping Beauty in her glass coffin, except that no prince will come to save you with a kiss" (Allende, 1995, 323). Through magical thinking, Allende deflates the notion of privilege and equates all people, even her moribund daughter. As the ventriloquist for characters, she reveals emotion as a source of character and reader coming to knowledge. A model of storytelling as a respite from tragedy and death in "And of Clay Are We Created" earned critic Clarence Major's regard for "Allende's ability to create and to sustain suspense" (Major, 2001, 179). Major extends his admiration by acknowledging the skill of Allende's allegories, which "recall the narrative force of ancient storytelling" (*ibid.*). The author reverences verbal recitals as what analyst Amy Shifflet calls "a sacred gift that forms the nexus among people, thus binding one another to the divine energy within," a community builder in Agua Santa in *Eva Luna* and Ngoubé, Central Africa, in *Forest of the Pygmies* (Shifflet, 2000, 36).

Allende depicts narrative as truer than truth, a revelation in fiction that she honored in a speech in March 2007 to a consortium dedicated to "Ideas Worth Spreading" through Technology, Entertainment, Design (TED). In search of verities, the author evokes in *My Invented Country* the passions she has lived. The autobiography anticipates the title character of *Inés of My Soul*, who requites the homesickness of Spaniards in Peru with tales from their mother country and organizes evening tale telling and poetry recitation in Santiago to satisfy a hunger for narrative structure. Spanish soldiers work their own oral magic with "tales of womanizing and ... risqué soldier ballads," which yield "sinful pleasures" by breaching the Inquisition's black list (Allende, 2006, 188). Allende creates magnetism in her characters from Eva Luna and Clara del Valle in *The House of the Spirits* to the narrative talents in *Zorro* of White Owl, relayer of Indian myth, and Diego de la Vega, spellbinder of sailors with tales of sirens and the living dead. Critic Debra Dean awarded Allende a left-handed compliment: "Skimming has proved impossible. She pulls you right in and doesn't let go" (Mabe, 2012).

The author makes no secret of her joy in composing plots. She informed Lynn Neary, interviewer for National Public Radio, of the aim of the oral performer: "I want the highlights, the lowlights. I want the tension, the rhythm, the tragic" found in the bittersweet love story of survivors of tyranny in "Our Secret" and the cautionary tale of the greedy boy who falls into the pot of *dulce de leche* in *My Invented Country* (Neary, 2008). The delving into human troubles requires "a silent introspection, a journey into the dark caverns of memory and the soul," as with the author's survey of her own sorrow in *Paula* (*ibid.*). In the end, the author realized that the peeling back of layers of truth, such as Matías's reminiscences of Lynn Sommers to his daughter Aurora in *Portrait in Sepia*, teaches the hearer more about self than about other people.

Modes and Genres

Allende specializes in varied narrative genres, from beast fable, prognostication, secrets, history, and anecdote in *the House of the Spirits* to elegy, vision, and epitaph, the three literary modes that round out *Paula*. For her first novel, female narration, organized by subject in Clara's notebooks rather than chronologically, expresses what critic Susan R. Frick calls "women's time," a gendered text that passes on truths omitted or corrupted by male storykeepers (Frick, 2001, 41). Analyst Anne J. Cruz notes that Alba, the female protagonist has "the power to tell a version of the story that opposed the official story of the dictatorship" (Cruz, 2003, 217). The reconstruction of events in Alba's notebook begins with mental composition during solitary confinement in the "doghouse," a framing of Alba's encounter with Colonel Esteban García that inflicts on her his animosities toward the postcolonial ruling class as far back as the rape of his grandmother, Pancha García. The flow of events continues in the women's concentration camp and the refurbished Trueba town house, gradually cleansing Alba's spirit of vengeance and replacing it with understanding of how her family advanced from colonial miners and planters to include radicals, suffragists, and reformers.

The use of personal narrative to flesh out and elucidate history permeates the rest of Allende's canon. In *The Stories of Eva Luna*, short fiction records the exploitation of miners by British colonists in "Toad's Mouth" and the unpredictable raids of bandits, the conflict in "Revenge" and "Two Words." In *Island Beneath the Sea*, Allende sketches the volatility of French colonial history during Napoleon's wars, a backdrop that also impacts shifts in loyalties in *Zorro*. The author breaks the tension at Diego de la Vega's cheating at cards with a fool tale about gullible drunks who gamble five dollars each on their ability to split the presbytery door with a single head-butt. For *Aphrodite*, the raconteur dredges up outré recipes, kitchen lore, and bits of legend about two historic figures, erotic painter Giulio Romano and dancer Lola Montez. In each telling, Allende frames action and cast to suit a particular mood or atmosphere, as with the dreamy romance in "The Guggenheim Lovers" and the threat of death to Nicolás Vidal, the love-besotted bandit in "The Judge's Wife."

Allende introduced to post-boom literature the female perspective of a Latin *Scherezada* (Scheherazade), a "prodigious storyteller of Araby" (Allende, 1998, 16). More than an alluring seducer, Scheherazade boldly shaped narrative intended to extend a lifeline to the audience in the same way that the Arabian bride "saved her neck from the scimitar" wielded by a jealous husband (Allende, 1998, 17). Romance writing—that of Allende and the Arab survivor—obeys instinct to navigate events that expose gender imbalance. In the tradition of collective memory in oral dream interpretation, oracle, song, story, and verse, the novelist allows the actions of her cast to speak for them, as with the assuaging coitus of torture survivors in "Our Secret" and Horacio Fortunato's wooing of Patricia Zimmerman with circus performances in "Gift for a Sweetheart." Like the set-up of Horacio's "outrageous circus," each story carries character intent to an appropriate, but often unforeseen, conclusion (Allende, 1991, 108). Allende stated her faith in the "patient craft" of artists, "each one imagining reality and re-inventing the past in original ways" (Allende, 1996, 23). Her description of literary progress in women's writing extols the shift in fictional outcomes from the predictable *novela rosa* (fairy tale) to the "new woman" novel and the novel of ideas, both rooted in sociocultural amelioration.

In practice, Allende imagined her craft in the mode of the African griot, the teller of stories who migrated from village to village. She pictured that she would "sit in the middle of the plaza and tell a story and the people gather around and listen," much as Captain John Sommers instructs daughter Eliza with seagoing tales and world maps in *Daughter of Fortune* and the religious "stories of gods and demons, and spirits of sky and earth" that captivate the People of the Mist in *City of the Beasts* (Lindsay, 2003, 138; Allende, 2002, 81). Of minor importance, Allende added, the reviewer's attention rated far below that of her audience, who treasure recitals of human truths. To critic Nuala Finnegan's devaluation of Allende's canon as "crude, sentimental pulp," the novelist retorted that scholars reinforce male literary discourse and denigrate women's contributions to literature for their inclusion of emotion (*ibid.*, 117). She listed herself among the chief subversive writers of the 1990s, the marginalized women (Patricia Cornwell, Barbara Kingsolver, Kaye Gibbons, Kathy Reichs, Nora Roberts), blacks (Maya Angelou, Paula Marshall, Toni Morrison, Alice Walker), chicanos (Julia Alvarez, Rudolfo Anaya, Sandra Cisneros, Laura Esquivel, Esmeralda Santiago), Indians (Sherman Alexie, N. Scott Momaday, Leslie Marmon Silko), Asians

(Amy Tan, Maxine Hong Kingston, Gish Jen), and immigrants (Peter Carey, Jamaica Kincaid, Doris Lessing, Salman Rushdie) who succeeded in the popular market.

REVEALING NARRATIVES

In *Eva Luna*, Allende creates the fictional rudiments of the orphan Consuelo, who rebels silently against religious coercion by blending jungle adventures with the martyrdom and miracles of saints, sources of a "prodigious flow of fables" that train Eva for her career as a writer (Allende, 1987, 8). For satire, the text tweaks the nuns' misinterpretation of Consuelo's unpredictable compositions as evidence of "heavenly visions," a two-edged jest that simultaneously degrades and sanctifies the teller's talents (*ibid.*). In midlife, the author colors Eva Luna's world with "the treasures of the Orient, the moon, and beyond," evidence of the worth of free-flowing words to people poor in earthly wealth (*ibid.*, 22). In preparation for her own life of "one long series of farewells," the child follows Consuelo and tracks household smells, by which she identifies places and objects (*ibid.*, 70). As though training Eva Luna in sense impressions, Allende advocates living through the eyes, ears, nose, mouth, and touch.

The use of prophecy, oration, and cautionary tales takes prominence in *City of the Beasts* as a counter measure to the deliberate fabrications of the anthropologist Ludovic LeBlanc, a facile liar and poseur. Lowland Indians spread to the People of the Mist in the Upper Orinoco a warning of white people in planes, which Indians call Rahakanariwa, the "spirit cannibal-bird" (Allende, 2002, 87). Eased by a visit from the shaman Walimai, the secretive People of the Mist sit in a circle to listen, chant to defy ghosts, and prepare themselves for "times in which the boundary between this world and the world of the beyond was unclear" (*ibid.*, 221). Walimai's denunciation of unfit, greedy whites mocks the arrogance of outsiders who "speak to us of their gods but ... do not want to hear of ours" (*ibid.*, 222). The events and challenges that adventurer Alex Cold faces form narrative strands long before he has a home audience to tell them to. He realizes that the eccentricities of his resilient grandmother set him on a path toward success. The juncture of life stories implies that Alex will profit from them and use their wisdom in plotting his medical career.

Allende warns the unwary of the foolishness of ignoring or discounting oral wisdom. In a recreation of Guinean community life in *Island Beneath the Sea*, she introduces Parisian Toulouse Valmorain as an outsider who "had paid very little attention" to his father's stories of colonial life in Haiti. Thus, Toulouse must suffer anew the hardships faced by the previous generation. Narrative from the perspective of Tété presents the free time of the plantation quarter, when slaves cook, sew, and garden for their own profit and assemble for stories. For amassed residents, listening trains young slaves to survive. Religious songs and retellings of the episodes of Bras Coupé from the 1830s express hope in a Louisiana escape artist, "a gigantic man with one arm" who eludes death in the swamps "more than a hundred times," a hyperbole based on repetitions of his story rather than cyclical deeds of strength (Allende, 2010, 297). Like the Norse Jötunn and the Welsh Bran the Blessed, king of the Island of the Mighty, Bras Coupé symbolizes the universal powers that overwhelm evil and imbue a minority race with courage and forbearance. Islanders infuse their own heroes—Boukman, Macandal, Toussaint L'Ouverture, Gambo La Liberté—with the awesome traits of storybook giants and invoke their ego ideals at the historic moments when blacks demand emancipation. Thus, by identifying with legends, Haitians become the first slaves to establish a government of freedmen.

See also language; myth

• *References and Further Reading*

Allende, Isabel. "The Short Story," *Journal of Modern Literature* 20:1 (Summer 1996): 21–28.
Cruz, Anne J., Rosilie Hernández-Pecoraro, and Joyce Tolliver, eds. *Disciplines on the Line: Feminist Research on Spanish, Latin American, and U.S. Latina Women*. Newark, DE: Juan de la Cuesta, 2003.
Frick, Susan R. "Memory and Retelling: The Role of Women in *La casa de los espíritus*," *Journal of Iberian and Latin American Studies* 7:1 (June 2001): 27–41.
Lindsay, Claire. *Locating Latin American Women Writers: Cristina Peri Rossi, Rosario Ferré, Albalucía Angel, and Isabel Allende*. New York: Peter Lang, 2003.
Mabe, Chauncey. "A Few Words with FIU Honoree Isabel Allende," (South Florida) *SunSentinel* (29 February 2012).
Major, Clarence. *Necessary Distance: Essays and Criticism*. Minneapolis: Coffee House Press, 2001.
Neary, Lynn. "In Memoir, Allende Reveals Life to Late Daughter," *Weekend Edition (NPR)* (13 April 2008).
Shifflet, Amy V. *Beyond Magical Realism: Magical Ideology as Political Resistance in Leslie Marmon Silko's Ceremony and Isabel Allende's The House of the Spirits*. Radford, VA: Radford University, 2000.

The Sum of Our Days

More expansive and self-critical than *Paula*, Allende's reminiscences in *The Sum of Our Days* evaluate her life as a 65-year-old matriarch for quality of wisdom and engagement. Chronicling from 1993 in panoptic style, she validates humor and skill by documenting human entanglements in her extended family following attendance at her daughter Paula's bedside during a year-long coma and death from porphyria on December 6, 1992. The immediacy of Allende's devotion to her children and grandchildren sets an upbeat tone and an atmosphere that invites reader complicity in authorial snooping, prying, and micromanaging lives. Editor Andrea O'Reilly admires the author's candidate for son Nico's second wife, "a woman so perfect for him that the two fell in love at first sight" (O'Reilly, 2010, 49). The author's role as yenta parallels her adroit mating of fictional characters for lifelong companionship. The most true-hearted pairs mirror Isabel's romance with Willie Gordon, her second husband, who enables her to write in "silence, being alone, and feeling warm and bundled" (López, 2008, 106).

By examining episodes told in her witty, self-deprecatory style, the reader discerns how Allende shapes fictional plots from a mélange of missteps and impressions, notably, visions that she experiences from ingesting the hallucinogen ayahuasca in South America and inklings of "the ugliness of old age," which she combats with cosmetic surgery to "trick time" (Allende, 2008, 150). The texture of the Allende-Gordon household management is serendipitous, a "dirty, disorderly, quick process filled with unforeseen events" (*ibid.*, 236). Much like the unpredictability in Allende's *Eva Luna* and "Gift for a Sweetheart," everyday reality requires counseling and compromise to cope with the death of Willie Gordon's daughter Jennifer, the fostering of premature granddaughter Sabrina, the scattering of Paula's ashes, daughter-in-law Celia's choice of a female life partner, Nico's divorce, and the demands of rearing the Allende-Gordon grandchildren. As in the charged atmosphere of *The House of the Spirits*, the memoir features spectral visions and the fragrance of jasmine that reveals the presence of Paula's spirit, still active in family life. Allende justifies the retreat into the nether world as a necessary escape from earthly pain.

Key to Allende's success at personal monologue, the abundance of detail and frank self-analysis draw on the author's journals and fifteen years' worth of daily correspondence with her 87-year-old mother, Francisca Llona Barros. With the admission "I was born to tell and tell and tell," Allende welcomes the reader into the clan like a guest and accounts for spiritual transformation in herself and her loved ones, whom she calls a "tribe" (Allende, 2008, 367, 41). The author speaks of sorrow as a learning experience in how "to manage sadness, making it my ally" (*ibid.*, 96). In publishing a third memoir, she admitted to workaholism: "My superego is always standing next to my computer with a whip, demanding more and more of me. I have become very critical of my own work," which she typically loads with passion, melodrama, and the wisdom derived from hard knocks (Cruz-Lugo, 2008, 55). From a colorful, at times painful life of abandonment by her father, divorce from her first husband, and exile in Caracas, Venezuela, Allende extracts a personal code: "Never do harm, and whenever possible do good" (Allende, 2008, 37).

Critical response maintained Allende's reputation for rebellious characters and provocative decisions, particularly her receipt of a rejected female baby in India and the subsequent donation of royalties to save the lives of unwanted and abused girls. Analyst Sarah Vine described the candid anecdotes as "hugely entertaining shenanigans of her family life ... where happiness is shared and suffering divided — all suffused with benign elements of the supernatural" (Vine, 2008, 10). *Booklist* reviewer Joanne Wilkinson remarked on Allende's "contentment and gratitude for the abundance in her life" (Wilkinson, 2008, 4). Toronto critic José Teodoro contrasted the lack of urgency in the sequel to *Paula*, a faulty judgment of a memoir based on his perceptions of the preceding thanatography. Teodoro declared the second volume "a baggy, unfocused affair" but acknowledged that the "long-bubbling stew" evolves into an "unexpectedly endearing" read (Teodoro, 2008, D7).

See also Paula

• *References and Further Reading*

Cruz-Lugo, Victor. "The Love That Binds," *Hispanic* 21:4 (April 2008): 54–56.
López, Adriana V. "Exclusive: Chilean Novelist Isabel Allende on Her New Tell-All Memoir" *Latina* 12:10 (28 February 2008): 106.
O'Reilly, Andrea. *Encyclopedia of Motherhood*. Thousand Oaks, CA: Sage, 2010.
Teodoro, José. "Review: *The Sum of Our Days*," (Toronto) *Globe and Mail* (28 June 2008): D7.
Vine, Sarah. "Humanity Laid Bare," (London) *Times* (12 April 2008): 10.
Wilkinson, Joanne. "Review: *The Sum of Our Days*," *Booklist* (1 February 2008): 4.

superstition

From a personal stance, Allende handles the supernatural with care. She stated, "I'm very superstitious. I think [the occult] will turn against me like a boomerang!" (Wilson, 2002, 71). Cautiously, she weaves into her writing the animism and folk wisdom of her characters, as with Elena Etxebarria selection of Pedro Berastegui as her lover in "The Guggenheim Lovers" and Loula's divination by cowrie shells and Prosper Cambray's fear of zombies in *Island Beneath the Sea*. In *Inés of My Soul*, the author incorporates a prediction of long life by the Quechuan Gypsy Catalina alongside warnings of "sea serpents..., monsters, tritons, the sirens that drive sailors mad, the ghosts of the drowned, phantom ships, and St. Elmo's fire," dangers that threaten sea-goers (Allende, 2006, 47). The balance of positive with negative implies that the wise believer must be wary of overconfidence, the fate that entrapped Odysseus and Oedipus in ancient Greek lore.

Allende's writings picture the occult in common human acts. In *Paula*, the author recounts the application of a foul-smelling liquid to the school floor to draw more student applicants and to Michael Frías to boost his construction business. She recalls an Indian healer who can "staunch a stream of blood with saliva" and "a few crosses in the air," an everyday miracle among the Guajiros (mountain folk) (Allende, 1995, 130). In more poignant moments, Dr. Miki Shima, a Japanese acupuncturist, experiences visits from

Paula's spirit, which "points out places where she has pain, suggests changes in the medicines" (*ibid.*, 293). Although not in the usual pattern of fame, Paula's posthumous notoriety fulfills the prediction of a seer, María Teresa Juarez, whom Allende meets at the embassy in Buenos Aires. In death, the daughter's significance to her mother and family takes on meaning in author-reader exchanges, fan letters, and responses to Allende's books *Letters to Paula* (in Spanish) and *The Sum of Our Days.*

In her first novel, *The House of the Spirits*, Allende sets apart Clara del Valle from an early age via the child's precognition and telekinesis of furniture, saltcellars, and "piano keys with the cover down" (Allende, 1985, 92). After marriage, Clara continues her ventures into the spiritual realm by consorting with Luisa Mora and the other two Mora sisters, a trio as disengaged from earthly realism as Clara. The foursome dines together and alternates between "urgent consultations with the spirits of the three-legged table and reading the verses of the latest mystic poet" (*ibid.*, 158). The need for communication with supernatural creatures arises in Clara after her husband assaults her and Blanca. In the retreat of mother and daughter to the town house, "spiritual counsel" and cold compresses from the Mora sisters rehabilitate the "bruised bodies and grieving souls" (*ibid.*, 242). Her confidence shaken, Clara advances into the realm of extraterrestrials and, for the first time, doubts her powers to breach boundaries of another dimension. Her wanderings into the supernatural express dismay with the real world, where husbands lash their daughters and strike their wives for speaking truth to colonial sexual excess.

Real and Fake Omens

In the comparison of the real occult with commercial spiritualism, in *Zorro*, Allende dredges up humorous and bitter beliefs based on ignorance and prejudice, such as the Catalan Juanillo's contention that Gypsies had forged nails that held Christ's hands to the cross. The author tweaks naval superstitions in the departure of the *Madre de Dios* (mother of God) from Portobelo, Panama. Fearful sailors delay the voyage on Good Friday and on the next day, when they encounter two portents, a redheaded man and a dead pelican landed on the bridge, an omen similar to the ominous albatross in Samuel Taylor Coleridge's *The Rime of the Ancient Mariner*. The crew also suspects a female passenger of attracting rough weather and calamity, a charge they repeat after the escape of Juliana and Isabel from Spain. In the Azores on the island of Flores, the men encounter islanders who suspect an extreme interpretation of the annual running of the bulls, in which "no one died of being gored ... for the first time in history" (Allende 2005, 110). Without specific omens, the people expect either an abundant year or disaster, a humorous commentary on the folk need to interpret mundane events in terms of blessings or catastrophe.

For *The Infinite Plan*, Allende milks Hispanic superstitions that explain the monetary success of Olga, a Russian immigrant in Los Angeles. In a barrio teeming with easy marks, Olga dispenses medicine and magnetized water, performs abortions and massages, and fleeces the gullible through tarot readings, divination, and spiritualism, typical cons pursued by flimflam artists. The source of her success remains the "clients' boundless credulity" toward sorcery (Allende, 1993, 238). Similarly attached to the ghetto, Nora Reeves refuses to sell her house lest she lose contact with the ghost of Charles, her deceased husband. She rationalizes, "The dead need a permanent hearth; they can't be moving from one place to another," an assumption based on centuries of specter study and interpretation (*ibid.*, 98).

The author illustrates the cunning of educated people in manipulating the gullibility of the ignorant. At a highly charged execution scene in *Inés of My Soul*, the apparent intervention of the Almighty in the hanging of the boy Escobar for attempted rape sends a frisson among the Indians and Spaniards as "the rope parted and the youth fell to the ground" (Allende, 2006, 148). The momentary mass hypnosis allows Constable Juan Gómez to whisk away the noose, which he appears to have severed in advance. As though knocking over ten pins, a wave of sanctity forces soldiers to their knees at the priest's cry of "God's judgment!," an on-the-spot interpretation of trickery by a church authority (*ibid.*). Unstated in the aftermath, Allende's suspicions about Catholic miracles connect them directly with chicanery.

Throughout *Island Beneath the Sea*, Allende pursues what Michael Schaub of National Public Radio calls "a kind of Day-Glo version of magical realism" akin to the fake gallows escape in *Inés of My Soul* (Schaub, 2010). Events emphasize the hold of religion over Haitians, both white and nonwhite, including the Catholic and voodoo fetishes that Jean-Martin wears under his coat on the departure from Haiti to Cuba and the *gris-gris* amulet that Toulouse Valmorain clutches after a stroke paralyzes one side of his body. During Eugenia Valmorain's labor, she sips miracle water from Cuba and receives the aid of Tante Rose, the voodoo mambo who battles the invisible Baron Samedi for the unborn child. The extended ceremony involves "filling the air with [cigar] smoke," encircling the bed with a chalk outline, and building an altar before arranging with the voodoo god for the death of Séraphine, a sacrifice of life for life (Allende, 2006, 89). An intercultural irony grips the welcome to the Valmorain heir, who bears a proud patronym in violation of Guinean custom. Upon the naming of Eugenia's son Maurice for his deceased grandfather, slaves fall silent in fear that the old man's spirit will emerge from the grave to wrest the child from his parents and carry him to the underworld. In later marvels, Tante Rose terrifies the overseer Prosper Cambray by gathering dust from graves and toxic flora and fauna for her rituals, which reduce human victims to zombies, a manipulation of death that strips the body of self-awareness while unleashing evil.

Theatrical elements anticipate the coming bloodbath that frees Haiti from bondage. The voodoo terrors of the "crossroads of the dead" divert fugitives from parts of the path to freedom where the lands of the living meet the nether world (Allende, 2010, 141). Along the route, Gambo avoids "lethal mushrooms, trees whose leaves rip off skin, anemones that hide toads" that blind with their saliva, all three exaggerations of the natural dangers in mangrove swamps (*ibid.*, 143). To heighten the dread of blacks, the text details "a cross formed of two poles, a human skull, bones, a handful of feathers and hair, another cross," perverse charms that battle the *ti-bon-ange*, a miniaturized version of a guardian spirit (*ibid.*, 145). For atmosphere, Allende adds the cry of wolves and hovering vultures, omens of the rebel Gambo's meeting with the lord of the dead and his lieutenants.

Nature's Wonders

In the same vein as Haitian voodoo trinkets and practices, the aura of natural myths and beliefs cloaks *City of the Beasts* with a philosophy suited to the unexplored regions of the Upper Orinoco. With an acquiescence similar to that of Gambo, Nadia Santos accepts a talisman from the clairvoyant shaman Walimai, who foresees danger in the International Geographic foray along the Brazil-Venezuela border. The text invests the cannibal bird Rahakanariwa with the deaths prophesied by Walimai, who speaks in metaphor of airplanes and helicopters that bring exploiters from the Western world. At Alexander's mystic trance at sight of a caged jaguar, Allende embeds the scene with six gyrating moons "like the heads of medusae," a black sky, and phosphorescent sand before unleashing mayhem as the jaguar slays a monkey and César Santos shoots the big cat (Allende, 2002, 104). Nadia needs no explanation of the dramatic face-off between Alex and the jaguar, his totemic animal, or of Alex's mental transportation to his mother, a telekinesis that awards him with the sight, touch, and smell of the patient in a Texas hospital. Nadia claims that precognition of other parts of the world requires looking "from afar, with the heart," a term that Allende repeats, but leaves undefined, much to the annoyance of critics (*ibid.*, 140).

Allende extends the tone and atmosphere of *City of the Beasts* in its sequel, *Kingdom of the Golden Dragon* in a style that analyst Frances Sinclair describes as "magical elements ... usually unknown to all but a small number of people," in this case, the miracles in the valley of the Yetis (Sinclair, 2008, 34). In the falling action, a series of superstitious beliefs invests a chaotic scene energized by the passage of power from one rescuer to another. The fear of incurring the curse of an oracular statue pales beside the fear of Blue Warriors toward Yetis armed with clubs and topped with horned helmets smeared with blood, a stagy costume suggesting depiction of Norsemen in Wagnerian opera. Contributing to the anarchic scene, the actions of the Yeti horde, who "shouted and leaped about like crazed orangutans," arouses primal terrors in the enemy toward "the forces of hell" (Allende, 2004, 378, 379). Allende turns superstition into a comic chase gag as the Yetis rout the Scorpions down the mountain.

The occult takes on a commercial air in the shopping scene of *Forest of the Pygmies*, in which Kenyan wonder workers in Nairobi sell dried reptiles, amulets and love charms, and medicines for ailments and dreams. Allende predisposes her adventurers to inexplicable African terrors only steps away from "tall buildings and bustling traffic" (Allende, 2005, 56). In the clutches of the "marketplace diviner," Má Bangesé, who reads the heart, Alex and Nadia hear her emit "a guttural sound that came from deep in her belly, a long, hoarse lament" (*ibid.*, 88, 15). The teenagers experience a vision of terrors to come from a "three-headed monster ... waiting for us" (*ibid.*, 146). To Nadia, the paranormal experience becomes less a prophecy than a "source of information, a way of learning," an interpretation suggesting the value of the Pythia, the Delphic oracle, to ancient Greeks (*ibid.*, 19). In less mercantile settings, Angie Ninderera displays a stellate birthmark, a sign of good fortune, and corroborates the accuracy of Má Bangesé's predictions.

In the jungle of Central Africa, a lifestyle bound by threats and ghosts separates free territory from taboo areas, which nature makes more forbidding with vines and close-packed greenery, the nightmarish fauna of Edgar Rice Burroughs's colonial Tarzan series. The leading Aka hunter, Beyé-Dokou, claims that the Ipemba-Afua amulet, the "soul of their people," is a human bone that protects and heals (Allende, 2005, 113). The return of the amulet to the tribe invigorates and heartens the Aka to throw off suppressors and embrace a normal life in cooperation with the Bantu. At a telling moment in the hunter's duel with Commandant Mbembelé, the tyrant's fear of Alex in the form of a jaguar strips the Commandant of courage and sends him fleeing into the jungle, an appropriate haven for a bestial military oppressor. For the sake of atmosphere, Allende leaves unexplained the coalescing of forces in a "fight to the death" that rescues the adventurers from man-made evils (*ibid.*, 269).

See also Gothic; magical realism; myth

• *References and Further Reading*

Schaub, Michael. "Dreams of Freedom in Allende's 'Island,'" www.npr.org/templates/story/story.php?storyId=126892427, accessed on April 4, 2010.

Sinclair, Frances. *Fantasy Fiction*. Wanborough, UK: School Library Association, 2008.

Wilson, R. Rawdon. *The Hydra's Tale: Imagining Disgust*. Edmonton: University of Alberta Press, 2002.

symbolism

Allende's braiding of female lives into expansive narrative relies heavily on motif and image. The literary elements emulate women's fiber work, cooking, and ceramic artistry. Suspense mimics the patience of a suppressed gender, characterized by the vulnerability of the storyteller in "Two Words," the weeping bride in "The Guggenheim Lovers," and the fatalism of Azucena in "And of Clay Are We Created." Azucena's story depicts the ineluctable flow of mud from an avalanche in contrast with the bureaucratic muck that prevents her rescue. The alternation of diction between "mud" and "clay" reflects the theme of media coverage of catastrophes and the counter issue of the sympathies of photojournalist Rolf Carlé, who shapes reportage with his camera much as the potter molds clay. The regenerative power of clay—the substance of the biblical creation story—vanquishes "the vast swamp of corruption and laments" that has saddened Rolf from boyhood (Allende, 1991, 330). Consoled by the dying girl, Rolf feels himself freed of despair that lies at the foundation of his determination to cover the news with photographic evidence of evil and destruction.

For symbolic reasons, Allende opens *The House of the Spirits* with the arrival of the dog Barrabás, "a hapless, utterly defenseless prisoner" in a cage (Allende, 1985, 7). His retrieval on Maundy Thursday, the beginning of Passion Week, concludes with the Easter Sunday affirmation of faith in regeneration. Rosa's green hair serves multiple purposes—individuation between sisters, redefining female beauty, and representing the vitality of earth from which the rose springs. At Rosa's death from poisoning, Barrabás mourns her all day with "shipwrecked howls," a wordless lament parallel to Clara's muteness. Analyst Vincent Kling notes that Rosa's example and Clara's reappearances among the living as a "mystic guide" justifies the logic of magical realism because the deceased "remain vividly in the memories of those around them," as resilient as the rug fashioned from Barrabás's hide (Kling, 2010, 253). Kling explains that Rosa's ghostly visitations represent an alternate strategy of experiencing a beloved relative. For language in Clara's farewell, the author quotes from the farewell address of Salvador Allende, who promised "I will always be with you" and to return from death to aid Chileans, a leave-taking like King Arthur's "Rex Quondam, Rexque Futurus" (Allende, 1985, 416).

The Christian implication that a three-day mourning period precedes human reclamation prepares the reader for the violence and terrorism that sweep the state clean of corruption. To infest the text with sinister foreshadowing, Allende pictures a plague of ants at Las Tres Márias, where gasoline, pesticides, and quick lime do nothing to deter the procession of insects. As importunate as women and the underclass, the ants grow "daily more impudent and more decisive" until Pedro García directs the swarm off the property (Allende, 1985, 133). Similar Gothic portents interlayer the novel with multiple impressions, signally, the severed head of Niveá, Férula's curse on her brother, the edenic scene at the river where Blanca meets Pedro Tercero, Alba's birth feet first, and the monstrous shapes that Blanca adds to her crèches to prefigure the worst of the revolution. Like a resurrection, the "mysterious glow" that coalesces into Clara "as she had been at her best" confers blessing on the del Valle-Trueba family and on Alba's efforts to reclaim the past (*ibid.*, 489).

More tangible miracles impel the del Valles and Truebas toward modernization and salvation from colonial sins. In a rural example, Pedro Segundo, the cowed manager of Las Tres Marías, lifts Esteban from entombment after the "death-rattling shudders" of the earthquake (Allende, 1985, 188). His father, Pedro García, sets broken bones, a suggestion of the true-hearted peasant attempting to resurrect and restructure the frame of an unstable head of household In covert support of Clara's charities, Pedro Segundo helps her ship cheese, eggs, fruit, chicken, and smoked meat to the victims of an exanthemic typhus epidemic, which, "like any other calamity that strikes the poor" resembles a punishment from God (*ibid.*, 156). Pedro treats the plantation mistress like the elevated lady of medieval romance. To her role as hacienda materfamilias, Pedro becomes the knight pledging fealty and willing to risk all in her defense. As though shielding the Madonna, Pedro rescues Clara from spousal abuse, drives her to San Lucas depot, and places a chaste kiss on her cheek. The old retainer completes a lifetime of devotion at Clara's funeral, where he carpets her burial site with wildflowers, an appropriate floral tribute to a free spirit, with the blessing and farewell of the flowers strewn on Ophelia's grave in *Hamlet*.

Entrapped in the Labyrinth

In a study of Allende's fiction, critic Maria Odette Canivell discloses a maze motif, "a locus of spiritual growth, magical quests and representations of human struggle where past, present, and future conflate into a single unit, an archetype for the inner world," such as the mishmash of hovels and tents at Sacramento in *Daughter of Fortune* and the underground passages in Diego de la Vega's Barcelona in which Jews hide from agents of the Inquisition in *Zorro* (Canivell, 2009, 71). Like the Gothic labyrinth in the Greek myth of the Minotaur and in Ariana Franklin's *The Serpent's Tale*, confusion and reorientation precede arrival at a destination. Within the interwoven layers, Canivell discerns safe passage, a hopeful journey illuminated by the del Valle family's communication via precognition. The seeker's journey into hideous secret sadism redeems and uplifts, saving Blanca from the mansion of Count Jean de Satigny, where, like Ariadne, she turns to knitting to dispel homesickness. Similarly, Diego and Bernardo in *Zorro* slither through sacred caves in Pueblo de Los Angeles and emerge through the hearth in the hacienda, a breakthrough representing Diego's eventual nativist discernment of Spanish values via his boyhood instruction in Indian lore and sacred rites.

Based on the medieval notion of the maze as citadel or refuge, Allende's applications of safe conduct take the form of Alba's flowered yellow car ferrying refugees to embassies in the capital city, a savior's task that the author herself performed in Santiago from 1973 until 1973. Like Theseus traversing the labyrinth to the Minotaur's lair, Alba narrates the events of her jailing, torture, starvation, and rape at the command of General Esteban García, a Chilean monster born of an Indian victim and a Latino overlord. By linking the family's individual connections to a revolution, at the urging of an apparition of Clara, her great-grandmother, Alba forms a comprehensive narration, a tether to the core of evil and an escape from self-pity back to the light of day. The act of will forces the prisoner beyond the physical torments of filth and coercion into a secret passageway to enlightenment, by which she fuses "people, freedom, and *compañero*," her passwords to liberation (Allende, 1985, 460).

In writing her family's history, Alba transforms Allende's historical novel into prison/entrapment literature, a *Bildungsroman*, a saga of the del Valle family, and a collective witness to Chile's struggle to throw off the corrosive sin of colonialism. By identifying with Clara's resilient spirit, Alba reclaims womanhood and del Valle determination, the resolve that keeps her sane when scream and moans invade her ears during blindfolding and the "stench of sweat, excrement, blood, and urine" assault her nose (Allende, 1985, 461). Her hellish imprisonment parallels Rosa's ghastly poisoning, Clara's nighttime rambling through the dark town house, Jaime's self-expatriation in books and fantasies of Amanda, Nicolás's sanctuary for the abused, and Férula's web of gossip. The mental effort to retell Alba's story of incarceration and brutalization carries her beyond survival to identity with the suffering nation and all Latin America. Like the colored ribbons that bind Clara's journals, Alba manages tangled strands, some corrupt with age and basement storage, and sets into chronological order the story of her family.

For the repressive regime in *Of Love and Shadows*, Allende returns to the labyrinth to describe a search through hidden atrocities. She manipulates metaphors of light and shade to delineate freedom and authoritarianism, in particular, the fate of the *desaparecidos* cached in mining runnels. In the opening chapter, she pictures crusading journalists breaching "the frontier of shadows," the hidden felonies researched by writer Irene Beltrán and photojournalist Francisco Leal (Allende, 1987, 51). To express the outmoded intellectualism of Professor Leal, the text focuses on his brass telescoping slide rule, a reminder of passé forms of calculation that he keeps on the bedside table. For Irene, an on-site investigation of "shadows" at the morgue strips her of naïveté, the innocence of the elite class that separates them from the everyday suffering of Latin Americans dumped onto slabs in the intricate halls of a city building. Her dreams snarl with memories of the morgue, Javier Leal's hanging, and "the endless lines of women inquiring about their *desaparecidos* (*ibid.*, 152). Irene realizes how worthless logic is to victims: "Reason has nothing to do with my nightmares, or with the world we're living in" (*ibid.*). In flight, the maze encases them once more, "a tunnel, a green labyrinth in which they were the only adventurers" following a trail to freedom (*ibid.*, 288).

The Seeker's Passage

In *Daughter of Fortune*, another story of twisting routes, tangible evidence of pursuit, detour, and rerouting embroider the text, grounding a lengthy overview of history in realism. For Tao Chi'en, the ideal of the Cantonese male resides in the woman with bound feet, emblems of "'bound' lives" that restrict them from full personhood (López-Calvo, 2007, 319). Like wise survivalists, Tao joins other Asians in a Chinese hotel, an existence that emulates "the life they had back in China ... isolated from the mainstream" (*ibid.*). Withdrawal, like Eliza's stowage in the hold of the *Emilia*, allows privacy and a modicum of safety while modeling the confinement of Joe Bonecrusher's prostitutes in retreat to a barn and the caging of singsong girls in cells of Ah Toy's bordello. The lopping of Tao's queue replicates actual attacks on Chinese-Americans during the California labor wars, ironically, setting him free of Cantonese bias to evolve a multicultural world view and medical practice under the tutelage of British physician Ebanizer Hobbs.

Gains and losses through fire and water elucidate California's frontier history. The loss of brothel finery in a fire limits the opportunity for prostitutes to continue their westward caravanning and begins their adaptation to a more settled, respectable life. The rescue of singsong girls from a subterranean hell ennobles Tao Chi'en and restores his sense of mission. A melodramatic ending — the shrinking of Joaquín Murieta's head "in a jar as a western artifact"—frees Eliza, the wandering picara, from a foolish quest for an idealized love (Dyck and Ruetter, 2009, 202). With her lover diminished from the outsized memories of her teen years, Eliza departs the public sideshow to begin a realistic future as Tao's wife, the situation that begins *Portrait in Sepia*. For the heroine's series of hardships, analysts Reginald Dyck and Cheli Reutter accord Eliza the respect of nation builders, "the strong pioneer women" created by Willa Cather, O.E. Rolvaag, and Laura Ingalls Wilder (*ibid.*, 203).

For *Portrait in Sepia*, the author makes the most of what reviewer Julie Dam calls "a vision rich in tones, shadows and light" (Dam, 2001). Aurora del Valle, a 30-year-old photographer reflecting on the lacuna in her lineage, learns to trust the camera, an objective recorder of memory. Allende stresses the emergence into light with "experimenting in the darkroom with different techniques for developing film and by photographing the family" (Allende, 2001, 237). At a turning point in Aurora's compliance with household and social obligations, she studies a series of poses for evidence of infidelity between sister-in-law Susana and Aurora's husband, Diego Domínguez. The obvious gestures, touches, glints of eye, and body language, "stark in the prints," overwhelm Aurora with the camera's ability to clarify a mounting conundrum (*ibid.*, 257). The symbolic device that rends the Gordian knot, the camera allows Aurora to conceal her face while surveying her marriage with a voyeur's eye. For reviewer Philip Graham, in apotheosis, the novel "catches the fire in its author's heart" (Graham, 2001, 38–39).

The opening of *City of the Beasts* with a nightmare of a black vulture invading the house energizes the first paragraph with evidence of a teenager's wrestling with a mature terror, Alexander Cold's fear of the cancer in the body of his mother, Lisa Cold. Subsequent images — airlessness, drowning, falling — contrast Alexander's sister Andrea's escape in costumes and witch fantasies and Nicole's collection of raccoons, kittens, a bird, and skunks, animals that encourage maternalism. On Alex's journey into the earth for healing water, Allende depicts him returning to the womb, a "closed, hot, dark, throbbing world," an existential impression that resembles a birth/death experienced "absolutely alone" (Allende, 2002, 300–301). In the two sequels, *Kingdom of the Golden Dragon* and *Forest of the Pygmies*, symbolic procurement of the magical water of health, amazonian medicinal plants, and petrified dragon excrement reminds the reader that the fear of death lurks in the boy's subconscious. The author returns to Ariadne's lifeline through Alex's rappelling and threading his way through corridors of the Forbidden Kingdom and pathless stretches of Central African jungle. By concluding with his enrollment in medical school, the YA series readies Alex for a career that centers on healing, the original quest that took him to the Upper Orinoco.

• *References and Further Reading*

Canivell, Maria Odette. "Of Labyrinths in Isabel Allende's *The House of the Spirits*," *The Labyrinth*, ed. Blake Hobby. New York: Infobase, 2009.

Dam, Julie K.L. "Review: *Portrait in Sepia*," *People* 56:22 (26 November 2001).

Dyck, Reginald, and Cheli Ruetter. *Crisscrossing Borders in Literature of the American West.* New York: Palgrave Macmillan, 2009.

Graham, Philip. "A Less Magical Realism," *New Leader* 84:6 (November-December 2001): 38–39.

Kling, Vincent. "Archetype, Not Ideology: Isabel Allende's Balance of Opposites," *Critical Insights* (October 2010): 239–257.

López-Calvo, Ignacio. *Alternative Orientalisms in Latin America and Beyond.* Newcastle, UK: Cambridge Scholars, 2007.

vengeance

Allende's lengthy survey of human spite covers historical violence and martyrdom from the sixteenth to the twenty-first centuries. With the anti-fascist testimonial novel *The House of the Spirits*, Allende resets the medieval *droits de seigneur* among racially diverse settlers of South America. In actions that fracture society, Esteban Trueba, the tyrannical planter of Las Tres Marías whose "bad temper became legend," indulges in tantrums and tirades (Allende, 1985, 76). Like the speaker of Robert Browning's "My Last Duchess," Trueba spews free-floating hostility at anyone who violates his concept of the ideal home or wins Clara's gentle attentions. To ward off his ill humor, she interprets the "colors of his rays" and defuses his rage before he can explode (*ibid.*, 154). Scenarios of Clara's reverse psychology applaud the clever passive wife for anticipating and evading temper eruptions without resorting to sarcasm or payback. Instead, she allows her rampaging husband to incur poetic justice arising from his own virulence, a subtle reminder that colonialism ultimately wreaks vengeance on itself.

Trueba's defense of the law of the jungle accounts for his fear of Communism and his "apocalyptic predictions" (Allende, 1985, 347). He rationalizes that colonial exploitation rewards the strong for dominating the weak, who "live or die on the dark side" of *machismo* (*ibid.*, 414). The concept of strong over weak determines Trueba's relationships with Clara, daughter Bianca, son Jaime, and his elder sister Férula. His rivalry with Férula for Clara's affection activates fury that destroys the serenity of Las Tres Marías, a source of what analyst Domnica Radulescu calls "the roots of the solidarity established between women in tragic predicaments" (Radulescu, 2002, 477). The earthquake that prefaces Trueba's fulmination over Férula's bedroom intimacy with Clara results in a double calamity—Trueba's threat to murder Férula and her curse on him, body and soul. Within hours of her death, Trueba execrates her memory with "Go to hell, bitch!," his attempt to rid his own heart of guilt for her narrow sanctimony and sacrifices for the poor (Allende, 1985, 180).

The *patrón*'s corrosive hate and disrespect of indigenous people corrupts Esteban García, the barefoot grandson of Pancha García, victim of white lust and depersonalization by Trueba, her despoiler. Esteban's hatred of his aristocratic grandfather seeks retribution for what analyst Marta L. Wilkinson terms "the culmination of the crimes and violence that have accumulated in both the private and public spheres," notably, the first Esteban García's illegitimate birth and for Trueba's discarding of Grandmother Pancha (Wilkinson, 2008, 167). Without the blessing of the Catholic Church and the Trueba name, Pancha feels devalued enough to twist Esteban García's thinking about "his cursed bastard fate" (Allende, 1985, 413). On a tip from the younger Esteban García, the *patrón* manages a murderous attack on Pedro Tercero by rifle and axe. Allende stretches the impressionistic scene into a face-off between age-old enemies too surprised by juxtaposition to achieve a kill. The gathered-up fingers that Trueba receives from the snitch generate revulsion in the *patrón*, whose vomit alleviates the desperation and terror out of reducing Pedro Tercero's right hand to one finger and a thumb.

The passage of power from colonists to the military restructures the García-Trueba family, placing the embittered Colonel Esteban García in control of his niece Alba and her unborn child for sheltering rebels and aiding citizens to flee the country. Trapped in his torture chamber, she recognizes that he persecutes her "to avenge himself for injuries that had been inflicted on him from birth," a series of crimes the predates her own birth and his by two generations (Allende, 1985, 411). Alba's great-heartedness, spawned by grandmother Clara and mother Blanca, rescues her from spite and enables her to tell the whole truth of the del Valle-García-Trueba family, including the patriarch's shameful fornication with peasant girls. Her pledge confers blessing on her own fetus, the daughter fathered either by Esteban García or by Alba's lover Miguel. Alba's love for a child of uncertain paternity symbolizes the female role in strengthening clan values by exorcising the ghosts of past sins.

Allende returns to Chile's sixteen years under Augusto Pinochet in *Of Love and Shadows*, a text marked by what critic Alice Nelson calls "the Popular Unity Experience and by the coup" (Nelson, 2002, 11). In token of the role of *machismo* in the deaths of Evangelina Ranquileo for embarrassing Lieutenant Juan de Dios Ramírez, Allende remarks, "Vengeance is a man's business." (Allende, 1987, 172). By collecting various responses to deception, arbitrary arrest, and brutality in the Latin America, the author surveys methods of combating tyranny, from Digna Ranquileo's quiet storytelling to the erosive hatred that forces Pradelio Ranquileo to force Ramírez to atone for the murder of his sister Evangelina. Unlike Padre José Leal, who intercedes for the poor with corrupt authorities, Javier Leal, who commits suicide in despair, and Francisco Leal, who investigates and records evidence of civil lawbreaking, Pradelio falls back on the all-or-nothing military training that teaches him to rely on his gun for requiting injustice.

The Code of Vengeance

For *Eva Luna*, vengeance takes both familiar and exotic forms, again in the hands of angry males. The raid of vice squads on a Caribbean demimonde serves the outrage of officials "notorious for slipping weapons and drugs into pockets to implicate the innocent" rather than for following the dictates of the law (Allende, 1987, 130). More bizarre, in Agua Santa, Riad Halabí's anguish at his wife Zulema for seducing a relative follows an Arabic code that requires him to lop his wife's breasts, to emasculate Kamal "in keeping with the traditions of his ancestors," and to stuff Kamal's genitals into his mouth, a graphic recompense to the despoiler of a marriage (*ibid.*, 170). Implied in the text, Halabí's vengeance stems less from violation of his wife than from Kamal's infractions of desert conventions of hospitality by the male head of household.

In the same vein, *The Stories of Eva Luna* bear witness to the endurance of retribution in fables, as with "The Schoolteacher's Guest," the tale of a whole town's complicity in the beheading of a villain. One of Allende's more grotesque models of vengeance, the punishment of the mobster Amadeo Peralta in "If You Touched My Heart" renders poetic justice to a prominent male for ravishing and sequestering Hortensia, a simple-minded fifteen-year-old virgin. The Gothic details of her immuring in an abandoned sugar mill, based on a crime against a real Venezuelan woman, connect Hortensia with scaly, clawed, and twisted forms from Greek mythology. From her hell in a ruin dating to colonial times, she emerges with the aid of neighbors. Attacks by masses of enemies against "the former caudillo" and his imprisonment begin the process of turning the perpetrator into a version of Hortensia's entombed self (Allende, 1987, 90). For good measure, Allende has Hortensia serenade Amadeo daily with the despairing plaint of her psalter, an antique instrument that links Amadeo's punishment with Old Testament reprisal.

The racial standoff in *Inés of My Soul* dramatizes a New World nightmare, the rage of natives at the usurpation of their lands. The novel stresses the smoldering vengeance of Michimalonko, the Mapuche chief who bides his time and marshals his forces to inflict the most damage. The protagonist invests her hatred for violence in the denunciation of conquistador Francisco de Aguirre, a "blustering and bellicose" military backer and buddy of Chilean governor Pedro de Valdivia (Allende, 2006, 19). Allende describes Aguirre as "a huge, extravagant man, loud, tall, strong," a singer of racy military ballads (*ibid.*, 134). The stereotypical self-promoter and womanizer dates to the braggart soldier of Aristophanes and the Plautine *miles gloriosus*, the glory hound of Roman theater. The abrasive figure regained favor during the Renaissance as Il Capitano, a stock character in *commedia dell'arte*, and in Shakespeare's Falstaff, the comic blusterer of *Henry IV* and *The Merry Wives of Windsor*, forerunner of pop culture heroes in the *Rambo* film series, *Patton*, and *Ronin*.

Allende's text builds the case for native vengeance. She summarizes Aguirre's activities as "eating, fornicating, and killing" (Allende, 2006, 142). In the years following the siege on Santiago on September 11, 1541, the action pictures Aguirre as a man without a conscience "impatient to stir up a skirmish with the Indians" (*ibid.*, 154). He awaits an opportunity to attack Indian villages and "give free rein to his impulsive and cruel temperament" (*ibid.*, 245). Inés recoils from the merciless burning alive of males, "from children to elders," in wood barracks (*ibid.*). The reduction of the Mapuche to women only invites his boast that he alone will repopulate the tribe by impregnating all female survivors.

The novel saves to the revolution the rise of Lautaro, a cunning student of European war tactics and of Spaniards who "eat and ... drink too much" (Allende, 2006, 273). By dramatizing his boyhood in Santiago under the name Felipe, Allende lauds a crafty infiltrator who absorbs the mindset of Spanish colonists and studies their use of the warhorse, newly introduced to New World stockmen. The narrative spools out enough mayhem on the Mapuche to warrant Lautaro's grand return as a despoiler of the conquistadors at "the disaster at Tucapel ... that Christmas Day" (*ibid.*, 310). The operatic reunion of Général Pedro de Valdivia with Felipe/Lautaro justifies the ensuing vicious torments reserved for Lautaro's vengeance. Reviews vary in their acceptance of the historical firestorm. Critic Saul Austerlitz contrasts Allende's skill at magical realism with her advance to an "historical re-creationist," a reinvention of style that he declares "not encouraging" (Austerlitz, 2006).

War and Destruction

The clash of liberal and conservative during the 1891 Civil War reprises the retributions recorded in the history of Valdivia's colonial contention against Lautaro and the Mapuche in *Inés of My Spirit*. For *Portrait in Sepia*, Allende finds little to honor on either side of the rebellion, an uprising that reviewer Helen Falconer terms "violence turned in on itself, as conservatives and liberals slug it out" (Falconer, 2001). On return of rebels to Santiago after the defeat of President José Manuel Balmaceda, the text pictures squads calling methodically on selected residences to sack "with malevolence and vengeful spirit" the homes of aristocrats (Allende, 2001, 177). Anti-presidential forces find the requital "entertaining" and "boisterous" in its controlled payback through theft, vandalism, and arson, which precipitate Balmaceda's suicide (*ibid.*, 178).

More virulent than civil war, the fulminating hatred that colors black-white relationships in *Island Beneath the Sea* infects even the serene scenarios of childbirth and celebration at Habitation Saint-Lazare, a more humane environment than the hellhole operated by the sadist Lacroix. Fed by the public burning of maroons, fever for the rebel Macandal's ideals of black liberation heats the hidden germ of insurrection. In the chapter "Turbulent Times," Allende pictures the revolutionary seed shapeshifting into "a serpent, a beetle, a monkey, a macaw, ... the whisper of the rain" and the mosquitoes that spread disease (Allende, 2010, 113). From the jungle susurration, the sound inflates into thunder, a howling gale. Mathematically, the author credits the storm's strength to the resentment of Haiti's Africans, two-thirds of whom — the *bozales* (literally "muzzled") — seek revenge for their abduction from Guinea. Allusions to the undersea kingdom of blacks drowned during the Middle Passage, a motif of playwright August Wilson's *Gem of the Ocean*, reflect the power of myth to nourish the will to be free and to blight the colonists beyond their ability to recover.

See also violence; war

• *References and Further Reading*

Austerlitz, Saul. "Chile's Colonial History Given Life," *San Francisco Chronicle* (7 November 2006).
Falconer, Helen. "Colouring the Family Album," (Manchester) *Guardian* (17 November 2001).
Nelson, Alice A. *Political Bodies: Gender, History, and the Struggle for Narrative Power in Recent Chilean Literature.* Danvers, MA: Bucknell University Press, 2002.
Radulescu, Domnica. *Sisters of Medea: The Tragic Heroine across Cultures.* New Orleans: University Press of the South, 2002.
Wilkinson, Marta L. *Antigone's Daughters: Gender, Family, and Expression in the Modern Novel.* New York: Peter Lang, 2008.

violence

In answer to the world's bent for greed and brutality, Allende writes of violence and redemption as a means of exorcising residual harm. She chooses scenes of cruelty or mayhem to heighten character traits, for example, a police lieutenant's battery of the title figure in *Eva Luna*, a fight to the death for prisoners in *Forest of the Pygmies*, and the burn that Charles Reeves inflicts on Greg's hand in *The Infinite Plan* as punishment for stealing a pencil. In the story "Ester Lucero," a single hyperbole captures the debilitating effects of unseating a dictator on Doctor Angel Sánchez, who "[returns] from the last Glorious Campaign, aged a thousand years," forever bearing a bullet in his groin, a token of war (Allende, 1991, 139). His appearance before Ester raises fear for a single reason — he "wore boots," an indication of military hardihood and potential for coercion (*ibid.*, 140). Worse than the soldier, Tadeo Céspedes, the career revolutionary in "Revenge," bears lasting memories of rape, dynamited walls, burned residences, hangings, and massacres long after he becomes a respected gentleman and mayor.

Allende's first novel, *The House of the Spirits*, depicts the unbridled vituperations of Esteban Trueba, the *patrón* of Las Tres Marías, replicated in guile and rages by Agustín del Valle, the planter in *Daughter of Fortune*, and in the atrocities committed by General Pedro de Valdivia in *Inés of My Soul* and sugar planters Lacroix and Toulouse Valmorain in *Island Beneath the Sea*. Critic Shannon Schroeder affirms Allende's depiction of "the violence men visit upon the female form," the cause of Clara's silence after viewing the autopsy of Rosa and after Trueba knocks out Clara's teeth, a direct aggression against her powers of speech and ability to protest spousal abuse (Schroeder, 2004, 139). More disruptive expressions of truth exacerbate Trueba's reactions. At the first sign of socialism in Pedro Tercero, Trueba lashes the boy with a snakeskin whip and promises worse if Pedro continues disseminating Marxist leaflets. Critics recognize the author's courage in confronting "the system through images of those who have had power over [women]" (Perricone, 2002, 81). A more terrifying anti-female scene, the entrance of Esteban García to the Trueba library, allows him to fantasize how easily he could strangle Alba and violate her naked body, a pedophilic dream state "poised on the edge of a bottomless pit" (Allende, 1985, 328). A composite of nativist unrest and perverse vengeance, according to critic Helene Carol Weldt-Basson, Esteban develops into "a hyperbolic portrait of social resentment and evil" (Weldt-Basson, 2009, 118).

In the final scenes, sadistic torment of the adult Alba among two hundred other captives reflects Chile's Colonia Dignidad, an authentic torture center begun in 1973 in Maule. Marta L. Wilkinson comments that "the problems, biases, and concerns of both the public and the private are literally revisited in the form of trauma on the last generation, the granddaughter Alba" (Wilkinson, 2008, 19). Fictional suffering begins with psychological isolation from tape over her eyes, a blinding that reduces "all sense of time and space," a disorientation useful to tormentors (Allende, 1985, 458). Thus begins the sexual savagery — groping, pummeling, dragging. Moans and screams terrorize Alba before the worst of her torture by Colonel García, which begins with smells of "sweat, excrement, blood, and urine," proofs of previous sufferings by other of his victims (*ibid.*, 461). Pain on Alba's nipples and slaps to her face alternate with a cup of coffee and a humiliating bathroom break, a rotation of kindness/mistreatment meant to break her spirit with the anticipation of more pain to come. The binding of Alba to a metal cot with springs for electric shock produces the illusion of dying "if she was not already dead," an indication of a battered, hopeless spirit (*ibid.*, 466).

Battery of the Innocent

Allende prefaces unthinkable human slaughter in *Of Love and Shadows* with the preparation of a pig for the spit, a foreshadowing of the atrocities committed inside "the barbed wire circle" of citizens' lives (Allende, 1987, 240). The horrendous bawling and bloodbath that sends journalist Irene Beltrán into a faint relieves her with a cup of "dark-clotted vampires' soup" simmered from the entrails, one of the many allusions to Christ's martyrdom (Allende, 1987, 105). That same night, the loss of vivacity in Irene signals her realization of terrors suffered by the *desaparecidos*, who include Evangelina Ranquileo, an innocent fifteen-year-old dumped into a mine tunnel with fourteen other cadavers. For the sake of focus and control, Allende limits detailed post-mortem evaluation of Evangelina's hand, a pervasive stench of putrefaction, and the tattered attire and corpses interred in the tunnel with bullet holes through the crania, blank eye sockets, and "fleshless hands," emblems of powerlessness (*ibid.*, 202).

Of the rise of martinets to power, Allende speaks through Professor Leal, a survivor of Francisco Franco's tyranny in Spain. Leal maintains a belief that "power is perverse, and that it always falls into the hands of the dregs of humanity" (Allende, 1987, 92). The proof of Leal's maxim begins with Irene's inspection of a corpse on a meat hook and her encounter with a battered, charred cadaver, a horror that lives on in nightmares. Because memory echoes the atrocity, Irene acknowledges, "Something had shattered in her soul," an innocence of atrocity that sets the privileged class apart from harried peasants (Allende, 1987, 112).

Analyst Aníbal González notes the revelation of Christian *agape* in the public reaction to the massacre. Amid streams of people seeking lost relatives, Irene and photographer Francisco Leal also encounter the solidarity by which mourners solace each other in the face of heartless, indifferent bureaucrats. Allende turns to remains in the morgue for evidence of "fingers amputated at the knuckles, bodies bound with wire, faces burned by blowtorches or beaten beyond recognition" and amputated hands (Allende, 1987, 109). After sharing the terror with Francisco, Irene recognizes in Captain Gustavo Morante, her fiancé, the source of militarism and the terrorizing of the citizenry. After Morante attempts to arouse outrage in the military, his research into "illegal acts of the regime" leads him to a chilling conclusion, that "the essence of the armed forces will never change" (*ibid.*, 275, 276).

Allende pictures the courageous, but ineffectual people's mutiny against military in *Eva Luna*. The overthrow of a Caribbean dictatorship derives from aristocratic privilege that allows a Country Club class of thugs to commit outrages as reprehensible as carving the faces of prostitutes with knives and raping homosexuals. The vengeful Huberto Naranjo counters by organizing a chain-armed street gang, La Peste (the scourge), a virtual children's crusade against repressive government. Huberto joins the guerrillas in warring on "the schisms that determine men's lives from birth" (Allende, 1987, 181). The author later resets the rebel band in the story "Ester Lucero" with "their belts stuffed with bullets, their knapsacks with poems, and their heads with ideals" and bound by demands for "Liberty or Death!" (Allende, 1991, 143, 144). However well intentioned, the insurrection lacks the clout to defeat a corrupt army.

For *Daughter of Fortune*, Allende has only to recite the atrocities of California history, a frontier rife with claim jumping, backstabbing, and on-the-spot vigilantism "waged against the Hispanics," Indians, Chinese, blacks, and other disenfranchised groups (Allende, 1999, 239). The scramble for instant wealth exposes characters to the luckless singsong girls abducted from China and the racist backlash against Cantonese and Chilean laborers. The text enlivens pages with the mischance of victims and closes on a horror, the heads of Joaquín Murieta and Three-Finger Jack, along with Jack's maimed hand, displayed to the public. Historian Bruce Thornton accounts for the attraction to the Murieta myth as a combination of "revolution and romance in the assertion and creation of the self" (Thornton, 2003, 128). The totality of crime and roguery characterizes an era of Western history from 1848 to 1854, when California becomes a state and San Francisco develops the attributes of a global port despite its cutthroat gangs, posses, and anti-vagrancy and racist labor laws.

Critic Jonathan Yardley characterizes the transformation of frontiersmen into criminals as "the virus of megalomania," a motif that returns in *Portrait in Sepia* (Yardley, 2006). Allende speaks of combat from the perspective of attorney Severo del Valle, who joins the Chilean army to fight in the War of the Pacific. Bolivians and Peruvians learn of "carnage and cruelty" from bloodthirsty Chileans and from Indian mercenaries "recruited at gunpoint" (Allende, 2001, 104). Reviewer Helen Falconer labels the war a form of "ghastly aggression against its South American neighbours," which begins on February 14, 1879 (Falconer, 2001). Trained by Prussians, Chilean soldiers also learn vicious tactics from Araucano warriors, a designation for the Mapuche who survive conquest. Applying aboriginal tactics, Chile's military earns a reputation for "shooting or knifing wounded and prisoners" (Allende, 2001, 103). Over the army and navy, the authorities elevate José Francisco Vergara, the historic lieutenant colonel whom Allende connects to the fictional del Valle family by marriage. Under Vergara's management of the fighting, Severo sinks into the barbarity of filth and gore, a result of exploding land mines, the rape of women, and bayoneting of children.

Allende describes Chile's military advantage as soldiers "drunk with violence" who dash head-on toward the Peruvian lines yelling "Gut them" (Allende, 2001, 107). The clash results in "bellies slit open, the entrails scooped out, ... and viscera roasted on sticks" (*ibid.*, 116). Severo, motivated by "fury and horror," devolves into a bestial "killing machine" (*ibid.*, 108). In semi-consciousness at a field hospital on January 16, 1881, he experiences Allende's touch of magical realism, the vision of Nívea, his beloved, caressing and reassuring him. The image indicates the author's separation of male and female during war, with men pressing the limits of humanity while women retain civility and grace amid the carnage of Lima's ruins. Into the mouth of a female surgical aide, the author places a sober adage about violence: "Killing is easy; surviving is the hard part" (*Ibid*, 114).

During the Chilean Civil War of 1891, episodes of beheadings, impaling, and cattle slaughter precede "arrests, sacking, tortures, and regulations," which target Don Pedro Tey, the bookseller at the Siglo de Oro (age of gold), an ironic minder of the colonial past (*ibid.*, 159). Tey abets the printing of propaganda for which "so much blood had been spilled" (*ibid.*, 184). Reviewer Saul Austerlitz extends the image by charging Spaniards as "less able to escape the bonds of the desires, re-creating the murderous passions of Europe in a new land, with a new enemy" (Austerlitz, 2006). In the aftermath of military martyrdom of young would-be sappers, family members discuss the extremes of ferocity in rebels and soldiers. Grandmother Paulina tries to shield Aurora from "such barbarity," but the attempt is a futile gesture to halt the snoopy preteen from observing all that occurs in the del Valle clan (Allende, 2001, 176).

Bloodletting and History

Without the patriotic fervor of *Portrait in Sepia*, Allende's *Inés of My Soul*, an historical novel of Chile's founding, links violence with the subjugation of women and Indians. In the scramble for land and power, the text exonerates the title character for arming herself with a Moorish dagger and plunging it into the vitals of Sebastián Romero, a sordid lecher. Of warding off potential rape, Inés Suarez remarks on victimization of females: "I find no fault in myself other than being a woman, but it seems that is crime enough" (Allende, 2006, 141). The incident prefaces Inés's extraordinary combat with pestilence, swamps, quicksand, caimans, piranhas, snakes, red ants, poisonous toads, and Mapuche Indians armed with lethal darts, the daily fare of her march south to Chile. The list of menaces supplies the quest novel with proof that Inés deserves honor for facing an unnerving milieu as asphyxiating as the anacondas and relentless as mosquitoes. Without challenge to Spanish insurgents, the founding of Santiago would lack the grandeur of epic courage.

The author's gift for reducing a people's culture to choice scenes of ruthless butchery opens her historical fiction to criticism. Of the kingdom of Atahualpa, she pictures uncontrolled fornication, sodomy, torture, and slaughter amid hyperbole that describes the palace compound as "Babylonian splendor" (Allende, 2006, 63). The reward for Général Pedro de Valdivia remains "glory, always glory, that was the lodestar," an aspiration that sets him apart from men like Romero, who live for rapine and sexual savagery (*ibid.*, 64). Additional hyperbole describing Valdivia's defeat of Diego de Almagro characterizes the fortune hunter and his nemesis, Francisco Pizarro, as excelling at plunder in Peru that left them "richer than King Solomon," additional links to Old Testament rivalries (*ibid.*, 70). In the building phase of colonialism, the swaggering Lieutenant Nuñez trains mastiffs to terrorize Indians until a mysterious contagion fells the hounds, a suggestion that indigenous people are capable of their own menace.

The crafting of images in *Island Beneath the Sea* begins with the title, a reference to the colonial burden of murdered slaves who die on the sea route from Africa to the New World. The mounting spite of Haitian slaves attests to recompense for the capture and shackling of Guineans. The newly enslaved undergo lifetimes of atrocities inherent in the master-slave relationship in a climate leaving them "gasping in the boiling humidity of the Caribbean while slaves thin as shadows cut the cane to ground level," an ominous image of blacks lurking out of the view of whites (Allende, 2010, 10). As a backlash rises toward revolt, Allende pictures the Valmorain property closing from outside turmoil like a fist, an appropriate foreshadowing of events to come. Allende personalizes the clash of men like sadistic overseer Prosper Cambray with the laborers who made Haiti the world's largest grower of sugar. He relies on whips, pistols, and fists to subdue and brutalize field hands, whose wounds require treatments of salt and vinegar for healing. Echoing his brutal regimen, cane falls into "toothed machines, crushing them in the rollers and boiling the juice in deep copper cauldrons to obtain a dark syrup," the distillate of black labor that frequently crushes the bodies of laborers whose loss owners factor in as normal plantation attrition (*ibid.*).

Little suspecting the image of the martyred Macandal burned alive at Le Cap, planters delude themselves about the power of myth to desperate blacks. Planters trust a French militia and "imaginative methods of repression," which range from lashings, slave tournaments, fornication, and sodomy to red ants swarming over molasses-coated torsos (Allende, 2010, 114). Cambray's pride in fear instilled in the workers at Habitation Saint-Lazare inspires a cockiness that betrays him. While bedeviling Tété, the master's concubine, Cambray threatens with words and gestures of his braided whip, a penile image enlarging on his reputation for raping slaves.

According to reviewer Gaiutra Bahadur, Allende encompasses "republicans versus monarchists, blacks versus mulattoes, abolitionists versus planters, slaves versus masters" (Bahadur, 2010, 26). The text begins the "orgy of blood" with a second-hand description of massacre at Habitation Saint Lacroix, a plantation suitably named for the Holy Cross, one of Europe's justifications of colonialism (Allende, 2010. 166). For his thick-headedness, Toulouse Valmorain, according to a Kirkus review, is "less a villain than a man of his time" ("Review," *Kirkus*, 2010). He subdues his concubine with cigar burns on her thighs, yet lacks enough experience with slavery to recognize a mounting defiance of casual atrocities. Valmorain's literary foil, Dr. Parmentier, anticipates a comeuppance to white arrogance, which he describes as a "logical response" to colonial savagery (*ibid.*, 167). Tragically, violence begets violence: the white backlash against black rebels calls for cannon and 1,500 dogs to track runaways, whom whites flay alive for burning cane fields and plantations. For a banner, slaves brandish a white baby speared by a lance, a gesture of rage at the next generation of masters.

For the aggression in youth, Allende depicts the inchoate assault on inescapable situations. For Alexander Cold in *City of the Beasts*, striking out at his posters, videos, and antique cars and planes suffices as a means of combating the lethal cancer that weakens his mother. In the aftermath, Alex words his motivation as a question, "Is Mom going to die?" (Allende, 2002, 11). A more tempered view of violence in the sequel, *Kingdom of the Golden Dragon*, dramatizes the guru Tensing's Buddhist approach to martial arts, which allows an attack on another person if there are no alternatives.

In *Zorro*, the text elevates fencing instruction to youths as an introduction to formal duels governed by rules and civility. To Manuel Escalante, the fencing master, the purpose of swordsmanship is "to confront death with nobility and thereby gauge the quality of the soul ... [and] gauge the measure of a man," one of Allende's unsubtle links between masculinity and violence (Allende, 2006, 152). In 2011, she met with leaders of the Global Fund for Women to state her philosophy that feminism is an antidote to brutality and war: "Bold women are a threat to a world out of balance in favor of men," a fact emphasized in the kidnap of six girls by a sect of assassins in *Kingdom of the Golden Dragon* and by the enslavement of African women in *Forest of the Pygmies* (Sohrabji, 2011, A21). Key to female resilience is the indestructibility of women's solidarity, despite the fact that "Violence against women is so ingrained in our cultures" (*ibid.*).

See also vengeance; war

• *References and Further Reading*

Austerlitz, Saul. "Chile's Colonial History Given Life," *San Francisco Chronicle* (7 November 2006).
Bahadur, Gaiutra. "All Souls Rising," *New York Times Book Review* (2 May 2010): 26.
Falconer, Helen. "Colouring the Family Album," (Manchester) *Guardian* (17 November 2001).
González, Aníbal. *Love and Politics in the Contemporary Spanish American Novel*. Austin: University of Texas Press, 2010.
Perricone, C. R. "Allende and Valenzuela: Dissecting the Patriarchy," *South Atlantic Review* 67:4 (Fall, 2002): 80–105.
"Review: *Island Beneath the Sea*," *Kirkus Reviews* 78:7 (1 April 2010).
Sohrabji, Sunita. "Writer Allende, Global Fund's Ramdas Discuss Militarism," *India-West* (28 January 2011): A21.
Thornton, Bruce S. *Searching for Joaquin: Myth, Murieta, and History in California*. San Francisco, CA: Encounter Books, 2003.
Weldt-Basson, Helen Carol. *Subversive Silences: Nonverbal Expression and Implicit Narrative Strategies in the Works of Latin American Women Writers*. Cranbury, NJ: Associated University Presses, 2009.
Wilkinson, Marta L. *Antigone's Daughters: Gender, Family, and Expression in the Modern Novel*. New York: Peter Lang, 2008.
Yardley, Jonathan. "Review: *Inés of My Soul*," *Washington Post* (12 November 2006).

vulnerability

A humanist devoted to uplift for the unfortunate, Allende composes speeches, novels, stories, and autobiography that resonate with hope. Her frailest characters—Azucena in "And of Clay Are We Created" and Hortensia in "If You Touched My Heart"—resonate with meaning, even in the extremes of physical need. Her most touching tribute to the vulnerable derives from the illness and death of daughter Paula. In the thanatography *Paula*, the author speaks of the first of twelve months of unconsciousness, when Allende calls Paula's name, which disappears "in the nooks and crannies of this hospital" as elusive as the Greek myth of Echo (Allende, 1995, 9). At the end of the second month, the comatose patient resembles a "sleeping bride," an image that captures Paula's youth and promise (*ibid.*, 94). By the time that death approaches, Allende describes Paula's soul as resilient, a contrast to the body weakened by porphyria that relinquishes its hold and slips into the light. The text refutes despair by welcoming Paula as an ever-present spirit.

In "The Guggenheim Lovers," Allende returns to a set piece—the adamance of the security guard juxtaposed against the fragility of lovers awakened at 5 A.M. in Bilbao's Guggenheim Museum. The text applies a humorous touch of magical realism toward Pedro Berastegui, whom the media dub "the magus of love," and Elena Etxebarría, his Helen of Troy with Cleopatra's green eyes (Allende, 2005, 105). Allende extends hints of the supernatural in the couple's arrival at the museum, a shelter that Pedro calls a miracle. The story turns love itself into magic, a transformation of a failed nuptial into a spontaneous union that seems like the continuation of a past life. As insubstantial as the camouflaged People of the Mist in *City of the Beasts*, Elena and Pedro inhabit human bodies as light as flies. Shielding the vulnerable youths from the heavy foot of Detective Aitor Larramendi, the building takes shape in Elena's memory as a crystal palace filled with art scenes in which the couple drink color, a whimsical kinesthesia that turns visual stimuli into a beverage. As a token of youthful passion, the author closes the story with a clean wedding dress and a bouquet of roses, repositories of love's delicate scent.

Social Extremes

In Allende's first novel, *The House of the Spirits*, her skill at balancing opposites enables her to survey the terrible without overwhelming the reader's sensibilities. Numerous examples fill events in the trilogy, such as the lovebirds, finches, parakeets, and canaries that Clara and Blanca release from cages as they close the family home in the capital. Analyst Diana Loevy describes the background as "fragile, vanished worlds filled with family secrets" (Loevy, 2006, cover). Similarly fragile, the keepsakes that Nana stores in her room —finger-nails, ribbons, locks of hair, baby shoes, and photos— remind Clara of the fragility of a kind family retainer who had loved each new life and her role in childhood and maturity. Ironically, Nana, the servant who had tried to scare Clara out of speechlessness, dies of fright, a frail old woman whose death alone in bed replicates the demise of Doña Ester Trueba and Férula. Allende's commentary on life's end stems from the existential belief that humankind faces the end alone.

Amid great strides at planting and harvesting, Allende commiserates with the downtrodden. Pedro Tercero views the *patrón*, Esteban Trueba, as "an angry giant ... at whose step the tenants trembled," an image laden with a disproportionate menace (Allende, 1985, 360). Trueba acts like a self-adulating lord, the medieval landholder whose "feudal arrogance made all of nature quake" (*ibid.*, 408). Under his sway, the del Valle-Trueba clan possesses huge tracts of acreage at Las Tres Marías and occupies a stronghold at the center of activity. Ranging outside the mansion, servants, the lowest class, inhabit and till small holdings, the pittance that Trueba allots to peons. The plantation system resembles a feudal fiefdom in that the *patrón* carries the responsibility for housing and feeding workers and for investing and earning enough to support the extended peasant family and his own aristocratic household. The text stresses that, under a fascist regime, the situation worsens: laborers could be "thrown in jail for the slightest protest," a loss of civil rights that leaves them "reduced to slavery" (*ibid.*, 435).

Central to Allende's feminist prose lies faith in egalitarianism, an element squelched by Latin American patriarchy. The paranoia of surveillance by uniformed officers, a given in the demagoguery and power mania of fascism, dramatizes the author's shudder at the threat to freedom for the underclass. A model of vulnerability in old age, Esteban Trueba reflects simultaneously the obduracy and fragility of a man "recognizing how worn out he was" (Allende, 1985, 446). His youthful impulses return to punish him and helpless family members, whom history entraps. More pathetic, the lives of peons remain as laborious as they had since the Spanish conquest, filled with "resentment, fear and distrust" (*ibid.*, 127). The author notes, the voiceless workers "had not heard of unions, or Sundays off, or the minimum wage," small gestures from the wealthy that could relieve suffering and threats to health and longevity (*ibid.*, 87).

Female Daring

In brash macho settings, Allende validates the courage of her heroines. Eliza Sommers, the protagonist of *Daughter of Fortune*, presents a split image of the fragile Anglo-Chilean girl dressed in Chinese garb and posing as Tao Chi'en's deaf-mute brother. The impression of defenselessness covers a stout heart and daring that overwhelms Tao, but can't conceal her trembling knees and the pain of long rides on horseback. Still weak from a traumatic stillbirth, she requires nutrition, yet aids her companion in medical work by stitching wounds. As evidence of their affinity as pals and traveling companions, they turn to each other in sleep and savor the fantasy of Tao with his deceased wife Lin and Eliza with Joaquín, the wayward lover. The safe harbor of friendship contrasts the frontier reality for women, which analyst Ignacio López-Calvo reduces to "prostitution, abuse, and the trafficking in women," the trio of anti-woman crimes that gives Tao a new mission in life and further endears him to Eliza (López-Calvo, 2007, 161).

Like the intrusion on Eden in Evelio Rosero's *The Armies*, the play of individual destinies in *Inés of My Soul* illustrates the soulless exploitation of natives and their salubrious community during the settlement of Chile, which concludes with treachery and atrocities. Before setting out from Cuzco, Peru, the protagonist, Inés Suarez, discusses with Cecilia, an Inca princess, the question of chaining ten thousand Yanacona Indians for the journey as bearers and military aides to five hundred Spaniards. Because of caprices of destiny, the text remarks on the diminution of Indians: "Any one among us can find himself in chains, branded with red-hot iron" (Allende, 2006, 2). Allende implies a gendered compassion in the disparate women, both of whom seek to lift the natives from ignominy and certain death, which occurs at "the disaster at Tucapel" (*ibid.*, 310). As a gesture to Cecilia's regard for the Yanacona, Allende honors her as mother of Pedro Gómez, Chile's first-born colonial child.

For the ongoing hell of agricultural slavery in *Island Beneath the Sea*, Allende draws on allusion and image to enlarge on confinement in Haiti, a failed Antillean haven. The lives of Guinean abductees revolve around the planting, cutting, and refinement of sugar cane, the source of French riches. As profits rise, so does black rage at a luxury food they never taste. Their traumas, according to analyst Marta L. Wilkinson, "are not fully grasped as they occur, but return later in repeated flashbacks, nightmares, and other repetitive phenomena" (Wilkinson, 2008, 154). The undercurrent inspires men like Macandal, Boukman, Toussaint L'Ouverture, and Gambo La Liberté to reclaim their humanity from the overlords. The uprising of blacks under leadership of Toussaint L'Ouverture resounds across the Western Hemisphere until the last slave enclave achieves emancipation. According to reviewer Marcel Valdes, the implosion of the white hegemony in Haiti "kept neighboring Cuba clinging to Spain for more than one hundred years" (Valdes, 2010).

Once more, Allende sympathizes with the victimized female. After Tété dooms herself to field labor as punishment for defying her owner's second wife, a date with the lash resounds in her gut and soul. Rows of sugar cane, the source of white wealth and privilege become a reptilian maze. As she navigates a path, "the spine chilling hiss of the cane blown by the wind" echoes amid "demons hidden in the tall stalks, snakes, scorpions, a labyrinth in which sounds are distorted and distances curl and twist" (Allende, 2010, 183). Tété envisions herself lost in the green monster, her voice powerless to summon rescue. Allende subverts the danger in the skill of Gambo to lose himself in viny jungle paths, his route camouflaged from the mounted patrol dispatched by enslavers. The snaky maze morphs into a hope-enriched green heart abundant with nourishment for spindly runaways and for a rebellion that turns the tide in favor of dark-skinned Haitians.

Subsequent novels depict at-risk communities fending for themselves, beginning with the People of the Mist in *City of the Beasts*, a young adult novel fraught with the dangers of exploitation and industrialization by the white world. The natives, perplexed by whites, describes them as "so crazed that they try to take with them the stones of the earth, the sand of the rivers, and the trees of the forest," leaving behind white diseases that kill a virgin soil population" (Allende, 2002, 222). In the sequel, *Kingdom of the Golden Dragon*, Allende demonstrates the harm of impure water on a community of Yetis. By forbidding consumption from polluted sources, Tensing rapidly restores health and vigor to a dying race. Allende saves for the last of the trilogy, *Forest of the Pygmies*, the most vulnerable of Aka women, who live the horror of enslavement and the sale of their children. As Aesop displays in his fable of the elephant and the mouse, the psychological restoration of self-esteem and dignity retrieves from bondage to tyrants the small Africans the text describes as "the poorest, most defenseless, and vulnerable" (Allende, 2005, 259). In each novel, an endangered people revive faith in communal strength and rid their communities of subjugation and theft of resources.

See also racism; violence; war

• *References and Further Reading*

Allende, Isabel. "The Guggenheim Lovers," *Virginia Quarterly Review* 81:3 (Summer 2005): 102–111.
Loevy, Diana. *The Book Club Companion: A Comprehensive Guide to the Reading Group Experience.* New York: Berkley Books, 2006.
López-Calvo, Ignacio. *Alternative Orientalisms in Latin America and Beyond.* Newcastle, UK: Cambridge Scholars, 2007.
Valdes, Marcela. "Isabel Allende on Haiti's Slave Rebellion: A Lost Cause," *Washington Post* (8 June 2010).
Wilkinson, Marta L. *Antigone's Daughters: Gender, Family, and Expression in the Modern Novel.* New York: Peter Lang, 2008.

war

Allende depicts war as an inevitable clash of males bent on the "Saint Vitus' dance of politics" and vengeance (Allende, 2001, 184). The military gives passion and meaning to men like the Greek warriors mentioned in *Aphrodite*, Juan de Dios Ramírez and Lukas Carlé in *Of Love and Shadows*, and Toulouse L'Ouverture and Major Etienne Relais, a militia officer in *Island Beneath the Sea*. From service during the civil war at Le Cap, Haiti, Relais maintains a reputation as a merciless, medal-winning "centaur of many battles," but admits his misunderstanding of the many-headed social beast that Haiti becomes (Allende, 2010, 124). As vengeful African captives spur the enslaved caste to anarchy, Relais studies the making and breaking of alliances when the social classes define and redefine their vision of a liberated island. Accustomed to the black versus white of battle, he misperceives the governmental hassles that follow a truce, a veering away from militarism to diplomacy that stymied the likes of George Patton, Black Kettle, and Poncho Villa.

Allende's contribution to the literature of dictatorship justifies combat as an unavoidable human endeavor, even in books for young readers. Malevolent scenes emerge from insurgencies and conquests in her YA trilogy *City of the Beasts*, where the People of the Mist fight for their existence against white invaders stealing Brazilian diamonds, gold, cattle, rubber, and lumber. Of the exploiters who fly in by helicopter, the shaman Walimai charges, "Their appetites are unbounded, like the caiman's" (Allende, 2002, 222). The visual representation of ravagers with toothy jaws wide open raises the question of which faction is more primitive, foreigners or aborigines.

In the second installment, *Kingdom of the Golden Dragon*, the battle against the Scorpion sect from India and their plan to abduct King Dorji from the Forbidden Kingdom in the Himalayas demands the alliance of Tensing and his band of ferocious Yetis with a multinational teen coterie consisting of Alex Cold, Nadia Santos, Pema, and Prince Dil Bahadur. To lessen the potential for destruction and death, Allende turns the confrontation of Scorpions by ten Yetis into a comic rout equipped by "the armory of the famous warrior monks who had lived in the fortified monastery," a security force that keeps watch on the royal family (Allende, 2002, 378). To restore sober emotions in the falling action, the plot characterizes grief in the nation's heir, Prince Dil, who must abandon his moribund father and return alone from combat to secure the throne and assume rule. Allende stresses that wartime exigencies leave little opportunity for personal emotion.

A prophecy of war returns in the last of the triad, *Forest of the Pygmies*, through a Herculean hallucination brought on by the fortune telling of Má Bengesé. In her booth in Nairobi, the clairvoyant visualizes a hydra, a three-headed ogre depicting "death, blood, war, and a destroyed forest," Allende's YA version of the biblical Four Horsemen of the Apocalypse from Revelation 6:1–8 (Allende, 2005, 17). Two insiders translate the apparition into real African horror stories. Pilot Angie Ninderera expresses concern for Ethiopia, another African hot spot. Starvation among Ethiopians requires air drops to relieve the privations of "colonization and war and disease," a truth that raises the death count on Africa's Horn (*ibid.*, 40). From another perspective, the missionary Brother Fernando corroborates the misery of war in Rwanda that generated refugees as well as hunger and fields gore-strewn from wounds and limbs mutilated by machete. Angie speaks for the author a message to the reader: "The world doesn't seem to care" how vulnerable Africans survive internecine brutality (*ibid.*, 49).

South American Struggles

For her first novel, *The House of the Spirits*, Allende explores the internal conflicts between Chilean conservatives and radicals that, on September 11, 1973, give rise to Santiago's urban war. Analyst Gwynn Thomas accounts for the roots of violence in "young adults in the 1960s and 1970s [who] were challenging their parents' social and political values," a persistent scenario in the homes of the García and del Valle-Trueba clans (Thomas, 2011, 71). Contributing external viewpoints, Iberian immigrants fleeing Federico Franco's Spain and Turks eluding Middle Eastern conflicts enlighten idealists. Behind barricades in the streets, students continue "celebrating in a festive spirit and singing that the people united would never be defeated," a university pipe dream dispelled by the crushing of Jaime under a tank and the arrest of Alba (*ibid.*, 394).

The cease-fire between generations yields an in-house reconciliation between Blanca and her elderly father, Esteban Trueba. Before yielding his fascist views, Trueba must witness the extremes of totalitarianism in a home invasion at his town house and the rape and torture of his granddaughter Alba via electrocution on a metal cot and the lopping of three fingers. The text depicts a civil muddle, "whether war against international Communism or its own people it's hard to tell, but war one way or the other" that lasts for sixteen years (Allende, 1985, 472). Through a feminist lens, Allende resets the parameters of human tolerance for what critic Karen Castellucci Cox terms "a universal cycle of war and terror that can only be broken through a new vision of the masculine and feminine" (Cox,

2003, 23). Analyst Nora Erro-Peralta restates the feminist view as "the transforming power of love and its ability to withstand the vicissitudes of war" (Smith, 2008, 98).

In the sixteenth-century assaults on Peru and Chile underlying *Inés of My Soul*, the novelist explores Renaissance philosophies of militarism, from savage slaughter to the science of strategy and conquest recommended in Niccolò Machiavelli's *The Prince*. Allende's text stresses the most pressing motivation to Général Pedro de Valdivia, his boredom with raising goats and sheep and growing cork and olives in Castuera. By juxtaposing Valdivia with a companion officer, Francisco de Aguirre, Allende contrasts Pedro, the educated warrior, with Francisco, the mercenary womanizer, exterminator of Mapuche, and stealer of horses. Refusing Francisco's taste for bluster, boasting, "eating, fornicating, and killing," Pedro governs his courage with dignity and respect for adversaries (Allende, 2006, 142). The elevation of Pedro over Francisco provides a memorable footnote to colonial history.

Experience at the 1525 battle in Pavia, "the beautiful city of a hundred towers," destroys Valdivia's self-esteem, the punishment of victory for a soldier who realizes the thrill of bloodlust (Allende, 2006, 22). At the turning point in Valdivia's career, Aguirre's letter nudges Pedro toward the idealized portrait of the conquistador "hidalgos of indomitable heart, with a sword in one hand and the cross in the other eager to discover and conquer," the pose of the Christian warrior during the Crusades and colonial wars of the New World (*ibid.*, 36). In idle moments, the iconic warrior slips from Valdivia's memory, leaving him "haunted by demons and ... beset with premonitions and regrets," the post-traumatic terrors that devour honor and decency (*ibid.*, 286).

The extremes of Chile's founding remain virulent in the minds of revolutionaries and conservatives in *Portrait in Sepia*. Allende examines the War of the Pacific, a conflict between Chile and the united front of Bolivia and Peru from 1879 to 1883 that leaves "ruin and twisted iron where once there had been a peaceful holiday resort" (Allende, 2001, 110). Critic Olga Ries describes the clash as "a dark shadow ... a trauma on all sides and an open wound (still)" (Ries, 2011, 7). Analyst Celia Correas de Zapata calls the war segment "one of the most moving parts of the novel" (Correas de Zapata, 2002, 183). Allende returns to the sacking of the city of Aria in *My Invented Country*, in which she pits the Peruvian account of a massacre against Chilean histories that dismiss incredible savagery as an occupation of the "city in an orderly fashion" (Allende, 2003, 156). She concludes, "The victors write history in their own way" by concealing mistakes and downplaying atrocities, a chronicling of lies common to all nations (*ibid.*).

The text of *Portrait in Sepia* depicts extensive face-offs and secret torture of captives in police lockups in Santiago. At a meeting of naive rural sappers before they blow up a bridge, an infantry contingent swoops down to break up the secret confab in a herder's shack, a symbolic assembly point for agrarian amateurs. In the aftermath, Allende glosses over backshootings, assaults, executions, and bayoneting that reduces one victim to "chopped liver" (Allende, 2001, 175). During the 1891 Chilean Civil War, an "orgy of blood," the author expresses her belief that war inflames bestiality in men by inciting drunkenness, rape, and arson, evidence of "the fever of violence" that mirrors the military intemperance of Francisco de Aguirre and the Haitian Revolution (*ibid.*, 175, 180). Dividing mourners into gendered responses, Allende pictures women sobbing and praying while men plot vengeance, an extension of the cycle of violence. The eerily genteel conclusion reveals President José Manuel Balmaceda trading places with his adversary at the gate of the North American embassy, a civil end to war's incivility.

MORE RECENT CONFLICTS

Allende excels at conveying the spiritual malaise and terror that overcome Vietnam War participants in *The Infinite Plan*. To achieve the realism of American struggles during jungle warfare from 1963 to 1975, she relies on interviews with her husband, William C. "Willie" Gordon, the prototype for her protagonist, Gregory Reeves. From combat, Greg learns that "to survive you had to break many rules ... in real life the villain fared better than the hero" (Allende, 1993, 245). Wrecked, disillusioned spirits turn into soulless zombies solely on what reviewer Philip Graham terms "harrowing immediacy" (Graham, 2001, 38). On stakeout, the wrung-out patrol ruminates over snatches of truisms like the hard wisdom that Domingo acquires in Cristina Garcia's *Monkey Hunting* or that the author/veteran ponders in Timothy O'Brien's *The Things They Carried*. On mustering out of the army, Greg shoulders the onus of shame, "like getting out of jail" (Allende, 1993, 247). To interviewer John Rodden, Allende regretted her inability to "get inside the humiliation that millions of Americans felt" about a war that the author never experienced (Rodden, 2001, 225).

Through *The Infinite Plan*, Allende stresses the irreparable damage that war does to the human spirit. Upon the recuperation of Greg from intestinal infection and drug addiction in Hawaii, he perceives an incorrigible weakness of body and will. His joyless safe return home to California fails to alert his mother, sister, wife, and daughter to the strain of surviving Asia's killing fields. However, under the keen perceptions of Olga, his pseudo-aunt, he discloses "a shattered soul" (Allende, 1993, 238). She interprets his unfeeling eyes and harsh voice as desolation and reconnoiters "the impenetrable wall" that encases him (*ibid.*). Through reverse psychology, she compares him to her frightened, suffering patients and offers assistance. With the self-preserving instincts of Pedro de Valdivia, Greg zeroes in on war disease, which he implies is incurable, a dour but realistic assessment.

See also madness; vengeance; violence

• *References and Further Reading*

Correas de Zapata, Celia. *Isabel Allende: Life and Spirits*. Houston, TX: Arte Público, 2002.
Cox, Karen Castellucci. *Isabel Allende, a Critical Companion*. Westport, CT: Greenwood, 2003.
Graham, Philip. "A Less Magical Realism," *New Leader* 84:6 (November-December 2001): 38–39.
Ries, Olga. "Latino Identity in Allende's Novels," *Comparative Literature and Culture* 13:4 (2011): 1–8.
Rodden, John. *Performing the Literary Interview: How Writers Craft Their Public Selves*. Lincoln: University of Nebraska Press, 2001.
Smith, Bonnie G. *The Oxford Encyclopedia of Women in World History*. Oxford, UK: Oxford University Press, 2008.
Thomas, Gwynn. *Contesting Legitimacy in Chile: Familial Ideals, Citizenship, and Political Struggle, 1970–1990*. University Park, PA: Pennsylvania State University Press, 2011.

wisdom

Allende adheres to intuitive wisdom, an inner guidance that bubbles up from an invisible spring fed by experience and a knack for satiric humor. She focuses on the role of women in negotiating differences and suppressing vengeance, controlling themes in the *House of the Spirits* trilogy, and the Americanization of clashing cultures in personal encounters, the focus of *Daughter of Fortune* and the *City of the Beasts* trilogy. Analyst Karen Castellucci Cox notes that marginal characters, both female and male, serve Allende's search for voices that "exhibit a wisdom their more gender-bound peers lack" (Cox, 2003, 23). By escaping the constraints of convention and social approbation, knowing speakers— Pedro García, Clara del Valle, Tensing, Mama Fresia, Hilda Leal, Tao Chi'en, Dr. Parmentier, Kate Cold, William Frederick, White Owl, Père Antoine, Riad Halabí, Cyrus the elevator operator, Walimai, Azucena — express worthy views that uplift and solace others during difficult times.

The source of Allende's astute purview comes at a price — the reliving of adversity and self-exile. She admits, "It has always been my fortune to sail on stormy seas," a complex insight into the wisdom that arises from challenge (Allende, 1987, 212). Appealing aphorisms segue into dialogue and description, contributing worthy perceptions about loss and disillusion. At the heart of her gendered comprehension lies a willingness to learn from the actual and the spiritual: "My mind and my heart are open to the mystery" (Allende, 2006, 6). In a brief aside on the role of women in settling the American frontier in *Daughter of Fortune*, she observes, "Where there are women, there is civilization," an authorial truism that also directs the casting of characters (Allende, 1999, 141). Faith in female acumen enables the author to shape native traditions and judgments into bases for the plot resolutions to "The Gold of Tomás Vargas," "Two Words," "And of Clay Are We Created," and "Phantom Palace."

In more personal realms in *Paula*, Allende plunders her store of wisdom to make sense of the death of a young, talented woman. The text expresses a pragmatic notion of time: "The future does not exist ... we can only be sure of the present — a brief spark that at the instant it is born becomes yesterday" (Allende, 1994, 147). Significant to her talent, patience allows the free flow of cognitions to come to fruition, including those that "can be interpreted in contradictory ways" (*ibid.*, 237). To interviewer Catherine Keenan, Allende explained, "If I allow the time and the silence — that is very important — to just be with a story, it will happen" (Keenan, 2005). Allende compared the wordless incubation of narrative to birthing, a singular effort that only a mother can complete.

Allende's writings battle the insubstantial nature of insight. She describes in *The Sum of Our Days* how memories become what reviewer Camille Flores terms "that ephemeral mist in which recollections dissipate, change and blend together" (Flores, 2008, PA-20). With similar mistrust, in *Inés of My Soul*, the title character recalls being gulled by infatuation. From the perspective of old age, the heroine, Inés Suarez, declares, "How accommodating love is; it forgives everything," a summation that requires intervening years to clarify (Allende, 2006, 10). Also susceptible to fantasy, explorers along the Orinoco discover that "things decay very quickly, especially the soul," which savant Daniel Belalcázar, a "chronicler and sketch artist" describes as a victim of the greed already present in their character (*ibid.*, 50, 45).

Examples from Fiction

After publishing *The House of the Spirits*, the author confided the importance of storytelling: "Actually, it is not telling the truth that makes us vulnerable, it's keeping secrets" (Cruz-Lugo, 2008, 55). By ridding a fictional house and nation of hurtful concealment, Allende neutralizes the toxic atmosphere and rids the country of hidden gulags. Alba, the survivor of torture and detention in a women's concentration camp, records in her notebooks the harm that dictatorship has wrought on the del Valle-Trueba clan and on the citizenry, "an unending tale of sorrow, blood, and love" (Allende, 1983, 453). In retrospect to the many deaths, she concludes with a respectful epilogue, "Memory is fragile and the space of a single life is brief," a maxim that honors the efforts of grandmother Clara to preserve family history as a warning to future generations (*ibid.*, 487).

In *Daughter of Fortune* and *Portrait in Sepia*, the frequent adages of wealthy investor Paulina del Valle reveal less of sagacity than the motivations of a cagy observer. As a manipulator, Paulina pledges to "rule from behind the throne" (Allende, 2001, 185). Her surmise about the settlement of San Francisco reveals a shrewd perception of the human needs for fresh produce, eggs, and ice as well as clothing and musical entertainment. To her nephew Severo's arrangements for an inheritance for his daughter Aurora, Paulina reminds him, "You can never have too much money," an apt motto for Paulina's life (*ibid.*, 84). In contrast to her crass materialism, her kinswoman, Nívea del Valle, supports the liberal cause during the 1891 Civil War, when she asserts, "Nothing's as dangerous as power with impunity" (*ibid.*, 160). The two aphorisms summarize the forces that drive an era of explosive growth and social restructuring.

Alongside Western sagacity, Allende places the thoughts of Tao Chi'en, who advances from apprentice to an herbalist in Canton to a *zhong yi* (practitioner) on South American sailing vessels and in California. From the master, Tao receives his name, which can mean direction, harmony, sense, or way, a reference to "the narrow path of wisdom" (Allende, 1999, 160). Lessons in "the norms of good behavior and respect for hierarchies" precede instruction in compassion, ethics, and joy (*ibid.*, 157). The master warns against pitfalls that Tao encounters in San Francisco: "The wise man desires nothing; he does not judge, he makes no plans" (*ibid.*, 164). At a turning point in medical practice, Tao incorporates the skills of Ebanizer Hobbs, who presents surgery and autopsy as methods of locating the source of affliction. Allende notes that each physician acknowledges "the limitations of his calling," a sage admission that no single philosophy suffices in itself (*ibid.*, 180).

In *Zorro*, the protagonist, Diego de la Vega, like Tao Chi'en, makes use of sea travel. On the voyage from the Western Hemisphere to Spain, Diego learns acrobatics in the ship's rigging, map reading from the captain, and sleight of hand from the cook, Galileo Tempesta. The author speaks through the wise Captain Santiago de León an egalitarian view of colonialism. To Diego, the old man imparts a simple truth: "All tyranny is abominable," a remark on the excess of New World conquest and on the Napoleonic era (Allende, 2005, 105). Further challenging Diego's childhood training in Amerindian beliefs, Santiago refutes the notion of divine right of kings and the existence of God. At age twenty, Diego recalls Santiago's beneficent reminder, "If a man lives long enough, he will come to revise his convictions and mend some of his ways," a prediction that describes Alejandro de la Vega's revived humanism in El Diablo prison (*ibid.*, 350). In Barcelona, Diego learns from fencing master Manuel Escalante an essential of dueling, "equanimity of mind," a control of anger that gives the fencer an advantage over an aggressor (*ibid.*, 120). In rebuttal to Escalante's idealistic devotion to justice, the author inserts Chevalier Roland Duchamp, who doubts that justice exists. The balance of opposing views alerts Diego to adult quandaries that require careful consideration before he takes action.

At the poignant falling action of *The Infinite Plan*, Allende's protagonist, Gregory Reeves, lacks Tao Chi'en's self-control and Diego's hard-won balance. Greg retreats from a brash attorney and champion of the underdog into a debt-laden ex-husband and father chilled by dwindling manhood and troubled children. His first self-criticism pictures his life in the mode of Pisa's Leaning tower, "my axis is off true" (Allende, 1993, 337). Outside the logic of white professionals, Greg's friend Carmen Morales intuits truth with the inborn discernment of the illegal aliens she knew in childhood. She urges Greg to pursue no grand exit plan but to live "the best you can, a little every day," advice that echoes the tenets of Alcoholics Anonymous (*ibid.*, 337). Her belief that crises offer new beginnings encourages Greg to "grow and change" from an idealistic transient like his father to a friend of the self (*ibid.*). Carmen's workable axioms enable Greg to tackle the huge task of reshaping his outlook in small, managcable increments.

In *Island Beneath the Sea*, the author advances from incremental change in individuals to grand revolutionary ideals that launch the Haitian Revolution of 1891. In superb dialogue, the dispensers of wisdom personify world views on the Western Hemisphere and the institution of slavery. Dr. Parmentier, the Haitian humanist, inserts noble, but feeble advocacy of human rights. In Boston, his peer, Harrison Cobb, promotes complete abolition of slavery and a new world order in Maurice Valmorain, a pupil endowed with "a fervent heart in which ... humanitarian arguments immediately took root" (Allende, 2010, 319). More effective at applied wisdom, Père Antoine, the Capuchin priest at the New Orleans cathedral, works toward community accord by welcoming all comers to Sunday worship and acting as ombudsman between quarreling parties. His gifts of healing, food, and tolerance comfort the lowly at the asylum, brothels, hospital, prison, and streets and swamps, where he attempts to "bandage knife wounds, separate the violent, prevent suicides, succor women, collect corpses," and rescue orphaned children (Allende, 2010, 332). At fearful confrontations, he states his creed: "Have faith in God, who never abandons us" (*ibid.*, 341). His winsome ministry, devoid of dogma, instructs through example, a parallel to the acts of Jesus and the saints, an august company that includes Antoine.

Allende elevates a more mundane sage, Sancho García del Solar, whose generosity to Tété and Rosette extends over much of the novel's action. During Tété's transition to freedwoman, Sancho explains why a hireling works harder than a slave, thus saving the employer money and frustration. Of the type of forced labor Tété performed in Haiti, Sancho observes that terror soon defeats itself, as proved by the violent overthrow of bondage enforced by French planters and their overseers. Into Tété's thoughts, Allende places wisdom concerning gender differences: whereas men value honor above love, women "love more and for longer" (Allende, 2010, 122). The statement encompasses Allende's memorable female characters, particularly the courtesan Violette Boisier, a businesswoman who models good sense and survivalism during the horrific turmoil wrought by civil war.

Instructing Youth

The expression of experience and logic in the *City of the Beasts* trilogy illustrates Allende's view of education as an ongoing process. Grandmother Kate piques Alex Cold's curiosity with a variety of commentary on native wisdom. She reminds her grandson, "With age, you acquire a certain humility," a contrast to his snide remarks and mockery, which she terms "the sin of arrogance" (Allende, 2002, 50). The motif of the older mentor and young apprentice continues in *Kingdom of the Golden Dragon* in Tensing's education of Dil Bahadur, prince of the Forbidden Kingdom, as well as in Alexander's recall of advice from his father, Dr. John Cold, a "cautious and methodical man" (Allende, 2004, 301). In daily exchanges involving food, rest, meditation, and exercise, conversations reveal Dil's weaknesses and immaturity. Tensing cites a Confucian principle of strength by contrasting the uprooted oak to the reed that bends in a storm. A universal concept, the pliant reed supplies Dil with a physical method of deflecting the attack of Tensing, a seven-foot martial arts expert who weighs 300 pounds. The exchange recalls the Emmy-winning TV series *Kung Fu*, in which David Carradine learns from his Shaolin master how to avoid or deflect adversaries with minimum effort.

In the leave taking at Dil's initiation into the rule of the Forbidden Kingdom, Allende illustrates the mechanisms by which tradition gives place to change. Attacked by the outside world for the first time since China invaded Tibet in 1950, Dil's nation loses its oracular statue as well as King Dorji, who dies of a bullet to the lungs. Tensing, fighting the urge to retain his young apostle, wills himself free of separation anxiety and ponders the truism that "every being is a part of a single whole" (Allende, 2004, 394). The final admonition invokes tiger-like strength from intuition and instinct and "trust in the virtues of your heart," a reference to Dil's goodness and benevolence (*ibid.*). The repeated wisdom of Tensing in *Forest of the Pygmies* comes from the mouth of Má Bangesé, a seer in Nairobi, but in so abstruse a form that it means no more to Alex than the words of the Pythia at Delphi to Greek seekers of truth. The action illustrates how guidance and direction emerge at opportune times from a subconscious store of truth.

• *References and Further Reading*

Cruz-Lugo, Victor. "The Love That Binds," *Hispanic* 21:4 (April 2008): 54–56.
Cox, Karen Castellucci. *Isabel Allende, a Critical Companion.* Westport, CT: Greenwood, 2003.
Flores, Camille. "Review: *The Sum of Our Days,*" (Santa Fe) *New Mexican* (8 August 2008): PA-20.
Keenan, Catherine. "The Legend Writes Again," (Sydney) *Morning Herald* (30 April 2005).

writing

Isabel Allende's writing exudes the sure-footedness of experience. The contention that memory equals action justifies her addiction to overt and subtle autobiography: "By writing about my life I can live twice" (Rennison, 2008, 1). She replicates her belief in *Inés of My Soul* by declaring through the main character, Inés Suarez: "As long as I have breath I will have memories to fill pages" (Allende, 2006, 260). Allende's individual situation growing up in "a family of secrets" motivated her to use composition as "a quest for identity," a motif she perpetuates in *Portrait in Sepia* and *Zorro* (Teisch, 2007). The job of translating experience into prose fills her day with research and recreation of facts and details, such as the security system that fails in "The Guggenheim Lovers" and religious processions during "animal sufferings" caused by floods in *Daughter of Fortune* (Allende, 1999, 34). She admits, "Many times what I write is useless and it goes in the trash," but she stays with the task to shape the beginnings into works that have popularized her around the globe (Donegan, 2008).

From the beginning, according to critic Margaret McHale, the novelist has applied the journalistic ploy of seizing reader attention in the first few lines, a method that serves "Gift for a Sweetheart" and "The Schoolteacher's Guest." In *The House of the Spirits* and its two sequels, Allende develops historical verisimilitude from a small seed of personal experience. In telling the story of Clara del Valle, the author becomes what critic Stella Clarke describes as "a rampant Scheherazade, writing for dear life.... Life in all its treacherous, baroque complexity is dear to her" (Clarke, 2001, R12). In an interview for the *Manchester Guardian*, Allende accepted criticism from reviewers who objected to sweeping romance and macabre details as female fluff. She refuted the notion that "the more hermetic and the more difficult your book is, supposedly it's better," her jab at the self-serving complexities of academia (Edemariam, 2007).

Authorial Techniques

Allende's controlling sense impressions contain the manifold meanings that require little explication. In the third generation of del Valle women, Alba thrives on female nurturance and emotional support. On the day of Alba's birth, Clara superintends amid "the shrieks of [Alba's] mother and the cries of the women bustling around her" (Allende, 1985, 281). To protect Alba from Blanca's husband, Clara destroys photos of Satigny and pretends he has no role in the family, an erasure certified by the del Valle chronicler and authenticator. The wails and levity foreshadow the joy of female captives in a concentration camp who revive Alba from torture and the solace of Clara's ghost, which prevents Alba from willing herself to die in prison. Through women's hope and resilience, Alba manages to regroup and rejoin her grandfather for the composition of her family's story. In *My Invented Country*, Allende accounts for Alba's intent "to understand one's own circumstance and to clarify the confusion of existence" (Allende, 2003, xiv). The resulting opacity, a gift from Grandmother Clara and from introspection, builds on notebooks from the previous generations that continue the nation's history with eyewitness details that dispel insecurity and relieve the compulsion for vengeance.

Proof of Allende's command of humanism lies in the immediacy of her prose, as with the noontime seizure of Evangelina Ranquileo and Irene Beltrán's love of riding Francisco Leal's motorcycle in *Of Love and Shadows.* The speed and "seismic shuddering between her legs" foreshadows sexual stimulus, Allende's summation of the appeal of cycling to couples (Allende, 1987, 60). A subsequent justification for the career of Mario the hairdresser, the forerunner of Mimí in *Eva Luna*, accounts for talent dedicated to color and frivolity, a profession that allies Mario with models and actresses and introduces him to the "feminine soul" and the "inner circle of art and culture" (*ibid.*, 83). By creation Mario as a secondary character, Allende dramatizes the role of disparate figures in the rescue of Irene and Francisco from death threats.

In an interview in 2011, Allende declared, "Writing is like breathing" (Hannau, 2011). Instead of weighty themes, she chooses characterization like that of Mario as a means of connecting with readers and stresses the consolation of secondary figures in the cyclical losses and tragedies that permeate a life. By shaping conflict and tragedy, Allende curbs pain and sorrow and makes it more tolerable, a task performed by the title character in *Eva Luna* and *The Stories of Eva Luna.* As demanding of excellence as Aurora del Valle, the photographer in *Portrait in Sepia*, the novelist searches past events and personalities for clues to her identity. From ancestral loves and betrayals, both character and author create their own legends and battle what the author once called "the dragons of our own souls" (Allende, 1996, 22). Her flair for conquest lore returns in *Inés of My Soul*, in which she describes an epic triumph over an allegorical monster who liberates Spain. As a balance to Gothic terrors, Allende intersperses clement impressions in the cool water of Santiago's Mapocho River and the fragrance of bay, rosemary, and *quillay* (soapbark), the natural gifts of the New World.

Readers and Reviewers

Allende resists the imposition of interpretations that she never envisioned. An example in the critique of *Inés of My Soul* by Jonathan Yardley for the *Washington Post* illustrates interpolated themes. The reviewer turns the title figure's desire for Juan de Málaga, her first husband, passion for Pedro de Valdivia, and mature love for second husband Rodrigo de Quiroga into an allegory of Chile's three-stage history. Yardley construes the three amatory states as parallels to Chile's advance from unspoiled native paradise to a wrenchingly subjugated colony to a sovereign nation. His pan of the novel for failure to make the case misjudges Allende's intent, which avoids turning history into allegory.

In the style of Djuna Barnes, Dorothy Allison, and James Baldwin, Allende enlists creative expressions as means of overcoming sorrow, including the grief of the protagonist in *Eva Luna* over the disappearance of Kamal and the sorrow of Rolf Carlé for Azucena, a victim of a mud slide in "And of Clay Are We Created." In a reflection over a period of silence and despair, Allende described composition as a blessed portal that granted entrance into a separate realm. During her self-exile from Chile to Venezuela, she affirmed fiction as a coping mechanism that "created artificial order in chaos. It set limits to the sorrow" engendered by Augusto Pinochet's 1973 disruption of democracy in Chile (Deiner, 2006). However, to dismissive academics seeking a straight path through emotion, the author retorted, "Life is not like a German essay. Memories are circular, not linear," an explanation of the circuitous route to understanding in *Portrait in Sepia* and *Maya's Notebooks* (Ojito, 2003, 1).

Beginning each January 8 on a new project, the author opens on a first sentence arising from deep within. Without an outline, she continues drawing on her past by peeling away layers and discovering the core within. Reviewer Peter Cameron justifies her method of examining the past: "Often it is only in novels, in art, where what has been irreparably sundered can be made whole" (Cameron, 2003, 19). Allende jokes about the profundity of details: "I am not a minimalist writer!" (Allende, 2006, 5). She credits quality of literary elements to learning "to research, to be disciplined, to meet deadlines, to be precise and direct, to keep in mind the reader," a command of composition she acquired during her work in journalism (*ibid.*). Crucial to the ordering of action, the mastery of the reader's attention comes first. An effective method of reeling in the audience, Allende's creation of winsome, sometimes startling conceits jolts the reader with their accuracy, for example, a comparison of first love to smallpox scars in *Daughter of Fortune* and the connection between memory and blindfolded eyes in "Our Secret."

After pouring out events and loose connections in some four months of free-form composition, the author advances to the "straightening out" of text. Key to her skill at storytelling, pacing metes out events and commentary along with standard oral transition phrases. In one instance Inés's discovery of water during a five-month slog over the Atacama Desert, the author enhances the jubilation of thirsty men by affirming the miracle with "and so it was," an understated gesture to a turning point in New World history (Allende, 2006, 128). The last stage of writing involves fine tuning diction, as revealed in the description in "A Discreet Miracle" of the Catholic Opus Dei as "reactionary Pharisees" and "a nefarious organization more concerned with soothing the conscience of the upper classes than with feeding the starving" (Allende, 1991, 261). Following textual tweaks, Allende's mother makes the first read and challenges Isabel with criticism and suggestions, especially about explicit sexuality and criticism of the Vatican and Catholicism.

Consistent throughout Allende's works, the dialogue relates realism from a personal perspective. In an interview with Michele Norris of National Public Radio, the author described the channeling of a protagonist's voice. For *Inés of My Soul*, Allende revealed, "I felt that I was her and that the story could only be told in her voice" (Norris, 2006). By internalizing historical episodes in the body of a *conquistadora*, Allende creates immediacy in the actions of the only Spanish woman to accompany the 110 founders of Santiago, Chile, then known as "the cemetery of Spaniards." The brash journey of a lone women to retrieve an errant husband suits the author's preference for risk takers on a par with fictional Blanca and Alba del Valle, Eva Luna, and Eliza Sommers. In summation of the long trek and longer wars, Inés concludes that the seven decades are "years well lived" (Allende, 2006, 3).

Analyst C.R. Perricone applauds Allende's eagerness to "defy the patriarchal law that imposes silence on women," particularly females of color (Perricone, 2002, 82). In a discussion of the slave heroine Tété in *Island Beneath the Sea*, the author asserted, "I can understand how she feels, I know her heart, I know her body," a writer's motherly embrace of her fictional creation (Gill, 2010). The character serves as a Greek chorus that presents the black perspective on the French Revolution, piracy, abolitionism, the rise of Napoleon, collapse of the Haitian colony during the Napoleonic era, and the sale of New Orleans to the Americans. Reviewer Marlon James describes Allende's passages as "striking ... making her as much conduit as storyteller" (James, 2010). Without the viewpoint of the underdog, the novel becomes a staged enactment of horrific scenes involving the immolation of a rebel slave and the skinning of Lacroix, the aptly martyred planter who deserves to be left hideless and dead in the ruins of his sugar plantation. Off the totality of suffering and death, reviewer Disha Mullick surmises that "there is something impressionistic about it, and that is its beauty" (Mullick, 2010).

The author's uncanny recreation of some of history's horrific scenes—the Inquisition, colonial genocide against Amerindians, the Middle Passage, the Vietnam War—elevates her works to classic identification with the victims of the past. In following Gambo La Liberté through the war, capture, sale, and transport of Guineans from Africa, she ennobles the survivors of shark baiting and a "stench so bad that it reached the world of the dead," the mythic "island beneath the sea" where Gambo's deceased family resides (Allende, 2010, 121). At the rebel seizure of Habitation Saint-Lazare, the last plantation to fall to the Maroons, Allende pictures a trail of torches as "a resplendent comet's tail," the portent promising freedom to field laborers and death to whites (*ibid.*, 186). The stream of light embodies the glow of Allende's classic canon, a contribution to world literature like no other.

See also Allende, Isabel

• *References and Further Reading*

Allende, Isabel. "The Short Story," *Journal of Modern Literature* 20:1 (Summer 1996): 21–28.

Cameron, Peter. "Review: *My Invented Country*," *New York Times Book Review* (8 June 2003): 19.

Clarke, Stella. "Lie Back and Think of Chile," *The* (Sydney) *Australian* (6 October 2001): R12.

Deiner, Paige Lauren. "Author Allende Speaks at Utpa," (McAllen, Texas) *Monitor* (25 April 2006).

Donegan, Lawrence. "This Much I Know," (Manchester) *Guardian* (12 July 2008).

Edemariam, Aida. "The Undefeated," (Manchester) *Guardian* (27 April 2007).

Gill, Harbant. "Freedom's Dream," *The* (Cairns) *Weekender* (1 May 2010).

Hannau, Lucia. "'Telling Stories Is the Only Thing I Want to Do,'" *Latin American Herald Tribune* (23 December 2011).

James, Marlon. "Review: *Island Beneath the Sea*," *Publishers Weekly* 257:14 (4 May 2010).

McKale, Margaret A. Morales. *Literary Nonfiction in Works by Isabel Allende and Guadalupe Loaeza*. Columbus: Ohio State University, 2002.

Mullick, Disha. "Destiny's Slave," (Hyderabad, India) *Deccan Chronicle* (28 August 2010).

Norris, Michele. "Allende Reimagines Life of Conquistador 'Ines,'" *All Things Considered (NPR)* (6 November 2006).

Ojito, Mirta. "A Writer's Heartbeats Answer Two Calls," *The New York Times* (28 July 2003): 1.

Perricone, C. R. "Allende and Valenzuela: Dissecting the Patriarchy," *South Atlantic Review* 67:4 (Fall, 2002): 80–105.

Rennison, Nick. *100 Must-Read Life-Changing Books*. London: Bloomsbury, 2008.

Teisch, Jessica. "Isabel Allende: Book by Book," *Bookmarks* (1 November 2007).

Zorro

Isabel Allende embraced her fictional Zorro with gusto. She chose to write *Zorro: A Novel* as a pastiche or literary afterlife, the extension of character and action originated by a previous author, Johnston McCulley, in *The Curse of Capistrano* (1919). Through disguise and duplicity, Zorro achieves a dual version of self as Diego de la Vega, the contemplative man, and Zorro, the vulpine man of action. As a result of Allende's venture, reviewer Allen Barra referred to the twenty-first century version as "one of those rare and perfect matches of subject and author" (Barra, 2005). Reviewer Melanie Milgram perceived in the adaptation a universal appeal from a "metaphor for the issues of identity that haunt him" and all humankind (Milgram, 2005, 5).

The text teems with details, such as the diseases emerging from a Panamanian miasma, the sage scent of the mesa, the mysterious "Indians' communication system," and the languages and costumes of the metropolis of Barcelona where Zorro studies swordsmanship (Allende, 2005, 31). In an essay for the London *Times*, Allende summarized the ideal of the Latin icon, "a masked lover, a defender of justice, romance, sword fights, family secrets, hidden identities ... all the stuff I love in theatre" (Allende, 2008). She found her hero vibrant, playful, and relevant to the Hispanic imagination as a weapon against "the xenophobic sentiments of many people in the United States" (*ibid.*). Her descriptors paired opposites: fun, yet arrogant; athletic, but nonviolent. The result yields a blend of Robin Hood's panache, the boyish bravado of Peter Pan, and the single-mindedness of Che Guevara, a mix of global heroism that incorporates brash courage with the activist's devotion to worthy causes. The cautious layering of self-restraint over derring-do rids the Zorro legend of taints of cruelty that mar the mythic crusaders in the Holy Lands, the Texas Rangers, and mercenaries hired by the CIA.

A Woman's Narrative

Through the voice of narrator Isabel de Romeu, the third member of Zorro's trio, Allende peruses the nature of heroism, which she allots to zealots and people fascinated with death. The results are what the *Los Angeles Times Book Review* calls "discreetly subversive" ("A Foxy," 2005). For those obsessed with the romantic notion of hero, Allende observes that idealists face poor remuneration and an early demise. The two liabilities echo events introduced by character originator Johnston McCulley, who drew on John Rollin Ridge's book *The Life and Adventures of Joaquin Murieta, the Celebrated California Bandit* (1854), the story of a bandit killed at age twenty-four by Mexican War veteran Harry Love. Another aspect of Allende's Zorro, the split personality of aristocrat/caballero and Latino/Californio sets the model of the campaigner who transgresses caste norms to right wrongs committed by the elite against Indians and Gypsies, the repositories of European hatred and vengeance. To prevent the hero tale from becoming too iconic, Romeu inserts a storyteller's aside that Zorro "tends to exaggerate his feats," a foible forgivable in one so handsome and charismatic (Allende, 2005, 379).

According to reviewer Lucy Clarke, Zorro's mixed Latino-Gabrieleno-Shoshone parentage symbolizes "the myriad influences that make him the man he becomes," one of the commanding mestizos of the New World (Clarke, 2005). Before studying in Spain, Diego de la Vega gains honor from his father Alejandro, spirituality and courage from his mother Toypurnia, loyalty from friend Bernardo, and gymnastics from Gypsies. The iconic boy/mentor relationship of the biblical Samuel/Eli and Arthur/Merlin the Mage influences the studies of fifteen-year-old Diego in Barcelona under Manuel Escalante, the wise grand master of nobles and knights. Introduced to La Justicia, a secret brotherhood akin to the Knights of the Round Table and Amerindian warrior fraternities, Diego shapeshifts into *el zorro* (the fox), his totemic self. With "ears pricked and snout trembling," the sly, lithe deceiver acts under cover of night and dark places, "the fox's elements," to right social wrongs (Allende, 2005, 79, 260).

THE DASHING ILLUSIONIST

Integral to Allende's version of Zorro, a cinematic brio draws on past screen models for the posture of actor Tyrone Power and Anthony Hopkins and the dash of Antonio Banderas and Douglas Fairbanks, the hero of *The Mark of Zorro* and *Don Q, Son of Zorro.* For racial complexity indigenous to North America, Allende's text elucidates brotherhood in the relationship between Diego de la Vega and his milk brother, Bernardo. The boys share Ana's breast milk as well as dog bites, bee stings, mock sword fights, and measles. The duo absorbs Indian training in following prey and the European skill at wielding the epée, a weapon less devastating than the six-gun. While Diego excels in the classroom, Bernardo outpaces him in swimming and at horse whispering, a nativist skill. A major division between Indian boy and his biracial blood brother occurs first during a drought, when Diego joins ranchers in pursuing wild horses to their death over a cliff. Bernardo's refusal to help suggests a nativist allegiance to nature and to respect for animal life. Allende develops the scene with more intense differences, notably, Bernardo's loyalty to a friend he assumes will be a mythic warrior, quick witted and extraverted. In the dual coming of age, Allende separates the boys after Bernardo experiences sexual bliss with Light-in-the-Night. Neither his sign language nor words can express to Diego a manhood ritual that Diego has yet to experience.

Allende intensifies Zorro's convoluted nature by revealing his choices. On return to Alta California in spring 1815, Diego parts forever from his love, Juliana de Rameu, who remains behind to rehabilitate her husband, freebooter Jean Lafitte, the novel's secondary warrior figure. In Allende's typical circular pattern, she pictures Diego resuming "his dangerous way of life" in the guise of Lafitte, a courtly combatant who dresses all in black (Allende, 2005, 324). Humorously indulgent in mirror gazing, Diego admires perfect teeth and a magnificent costume and regrets that he has trapped himself in duality that prohibits wearing the costume every day. By renavigating the boyhood cavern at his hacienda, Diego undergoes a second initiation, this time into the brotherhood devoted to "honor, justice, respect, dignity, and courage" (*ibid.*, 335). Dedicated to bamboozling Rafael Moncado, the novel's villainous roué, Diego recedes in the falling action under the manipulations of his second lieutenant, Isabel, who safeguards her heart from falling for the colorful fencer. Allende's deft elevation of Isabel creates a feminist twist on hero worship that limits Diego's power and range, at the same time rendering him more lovable for his faults.

• *References and Further Reading*

Allende, Isabel. "Zorro—My Ultimate Hero," (London) *Times* (3 March 2008).
Barra, Allen. "Zorro Meets Isabel Allende," *Chicago Sun-Times* (1 May 2005).
Clarke, Lucy. "Allende Unmasks Legend of Zorro," (Adelaide) *Sunday Mail* (22 May 2005).
Murray, Yxta Maya. "A Foxy Hero Returns to Duel with His Inner Selves," *Los Angeles Times* (1 May 2005).
Milgram, Melanie. "Who Was That Masked Man," *Read* 55:4 (7 October 2005): 4–5.

Zorro's genealogy

The defender of Alta California, Diego de la Vega undergoes training by his maternal Indian family and, in Barcelona, under mentors Jean Lafitte and sword master Manuel Escalante to become the Clark Kent/Superman liberator known as Zorro. Diego's affinity for the underdog allies him with the Indians on his maternal side and, in Barcelona, with Gypsies, the victims of age-old European prejudice and superstition.

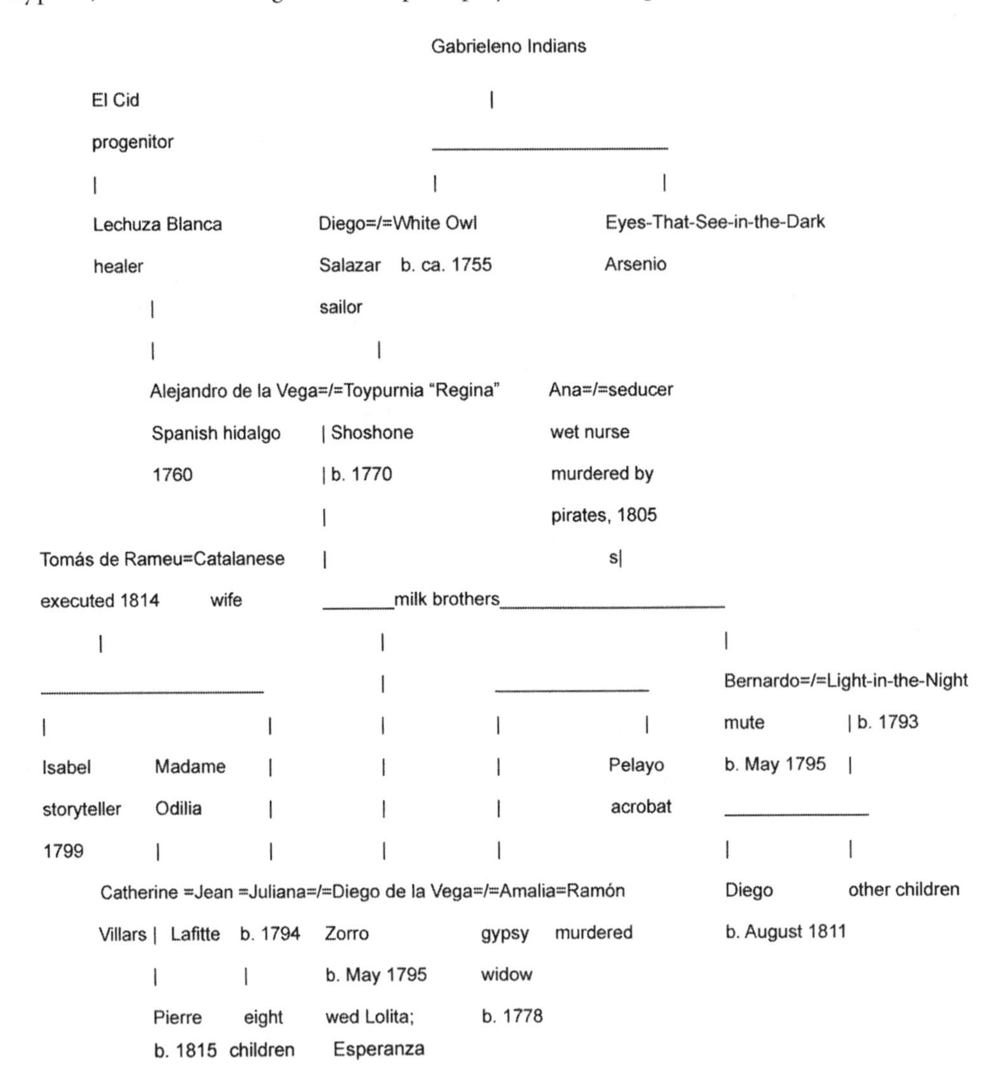

• *References and Further Reading*

Bauers, Sandy. "Isabel Allende Makes the Mark of Zorro," *Philadelphia Inquirer* (6 June 2005).
Cheuse, Alan. ""Review: *Zorro*," *World Literature Today* 80:1 (January-February 2006): 27–28.

Glossary

abuela (EL, pp. 70–73, 107, 193, 258–259, 265, 289; MN, pp. 13–18, 28, 37, 41–47, 54–60, 70–100, 111–125, 139–142, 154, 159, 166, 176–193, 207–219, 244, 262–266, 285, 290, 298, 305–323, 330, 350–366, 379–380, 387–393, 405–408, 416–422, 439–443; SOD, p. 282) grandmother.

acontecer (OLS, p. 214) to happen.

affranchi (IS, pp. 9, 45, 51–52, 60, 77, 94–95, 115, 124, 132, 139–140, 154, 168–170, 175, 196, 206–207, 212–213, 216) *fem. affranchie; pl. affranchis* emancipated slave, freedman.

agape (A, p. 28; P, p. 95) love that expects nothing in return.

ajoupa (IS, pp. 113, 158, 179) lean-to.

alcalde (Z, pp. 27, 32, 33, 34, 35, 39, 45, 71, 81, 82, 84) mayor.

Alta California (Z, pp. 5, 6, 10, 20, 21, 25, 33, 35, 45, 56, 68, 72, 238, 262, 285, 326, 330, 385) a province of New Spain that existed from 1769 to 1850. It consisted of Arizona, California, Colorado, Nevada, Utah, and Wyoming.

altiplano (CB, pp. 199, 242, 250, 370, 398; P, p. 127; PS, pp. 116, 159) high plains.

asson (IS, pp. 89, 159–160) ritual gourd rattle used to summon voodoo spirits.

ayahuasca (CB, pp. 224, 298, 333) an hallucinogenic alkaloid brewed from *Banisteriopsis* or "spirit vine."

bai yao (DF, p. 157) a Chinese coagulant that stops bleeding.

barranca (EL, pp. 67, 157, 278) ravine.

barrio (DF, pp. 225, 231, 375, 382; EL, pp. 6, 67, 116, 124; IP, pp. v, 23, 33–35, 44–77, 87–101, 107, 112–121, 126, 134–150, 163–193, 198–200, 206–229, 236, 239, 244, 251, 255, 271, 274, 300, 320, 343–344, 378–379; IS, 45, 95, 124, 307–309; MIC, pp. 18, 29, 88; OLS, pp. 21, 194, 219; P, pp. 85, 74; PS, p. 317; SEL, pp. 151–152, 160, 165, 231, 240–241, 268; SOD, p. 13; Z, pp. 145, 156, 177, 182, 186, 191, 221) a culturally cohesive residential district.

beignet (IS, pp. 128, 245; Z, p. 308) delicate fried bun topped with powdered sugar.

bolas (P, p. 228; SEL, p. 59) a weapon that entwines weighted ends of a cord around a target.

bolero (A, pp. 15, 78; EL, pp. 50, 72, 120, 296–299, 301, 306; HS, p. 250; MN, p. 249; OLS, p. 143; P, p. 65; IP, p. 299; SEL, pp. 25, 256) slow Latin dance music.

Bondye (IS, pp. 1, 41, 111, 159, 172, 277, 323) see *loa.*

bonze (OLS, p. 196) martyred Buddhist priest.

bota (Z, pp. 12, 43) leather or skin bags.

boula (IS, p. 192) a Caribbean drum that dominates the sounds of multiple instruments.

bozales (IS, pp. 113, 135) African-born slaves.

bracero (IP, pp. 13, 42, 110, 357–358) guest agricultural laborer from Mexico working in the U.S.

caballero (A, p. 60; DF, p. 32; El, p. 267; IMS, pp. 5, 19, 23, 61, 93–94, 132, 170; MN, pp. 42–43, 121, 346–354, 435; OLS, p. 50; P, p. 180; Z, pp. 112, 119, 126, 131–142, 159, 163, 172–179, 271, 300–302) gentleman.

caboclo (CB, pp. 53, 58, 61, 117–118, 139, 141, 147–148, 283) a mulatto of Brazilian Indian-African or Indian-European ancestry.

cacique (IMS, pp. 83, 151, 152, 157, 172, 199, 201, 245, 268, 272, 281; IS, p. 146; SEL, p. 84; SOD, p. 101) chieftain.

Calvario (SEL, pp. 198, 201, 204–205) a crucifixion scene.

camanchaca (IMS, p. 72; PS, p. 110) impenetrable fog.

camino real (Z, pp. 24, 55, 78, 86, 99, 327, 343, 365) royal highway leading from mission to mission in California.

campesino (CB, p. 52; DF, pp. 9, 60, 306; EL, p. 62; IP, p. 42; MIC, pp. 2, 14, 15, 22; P, pp. 184, 281; PS, pp. 155, 163, 171, 175, 198, 231, 235–237, 242, 250–252, 254, 265; SOD, pp. 19, 138, 197; SEL, pp. 198, 201, 265, 300; Z, pp. 134, 153, 169, 171, 175, 231, 235, 237, 242, 250, 253) *fem. campesina* farmer.

carabinero (MIC, p. 42; OLS, p. 281; P, pp. 192, 312) Chilean police.

caramba (DF, p. 123; MN, p. 120; P, p. 28) an interjection of surprise.

caudillo (EL, pp. 14, 135; MIC, pp. 146, 155, 169; OLS, p. 23; PS, pp. 103, 155, 184; SEL, pp. 90, 306, 309) warlord.

cazuela (IMS, pp. 195, 297; KGD, p. 176; MIC, pp. 87–88; MN, p. 418; P, p. 95) a hearty soup made from a hodgepodge of meats and vegetables.

charro (EL, p. 63) cowboy.

chasqui (IMS, pp. 117, 125, 136) runner, messenger.

chinero (MIC, p. 26) a man drawn to mixed-race women.

chingada (IP, pp. 37, 39, 40) fuck (n.), fucking (adj.).

chulo (IMS, pp. 8, 14) a dandy, overdressed peacock.

chupe (IP, p. 65; MIC, p. 88) meat stew.

Clarisas (HS, p. 11) nuns of the Poor Clares, a Franciscan order that Spain installed in Alta California, Chile, Ecuador, Mexico, and Peru

Code Noir (IS, pp. 54, 68, 75, 327) royal strictures on colonial slaves enacted by Louis XIV in 1685.

coligüe (DF, p. 129) bamboo.

comadre (EL, p. 46; IP, p. 36; MN, p. 136; OLS, pp. 28, 107, 113) godmother.

comandante (EL, pp. 180, 235–241, 262–274, 281–283, 295, 298–305; MIC, p. 151; MN, pp. 28, 378; SEL, pp. 144–145; SOD, p. 35; Z, p. 162) commander in chief.

compañero (EL, pp. 180–184, 232, 236–240, 269–271, 282, 295; HS, pp. 391–392, 403–404, 406, 410, 414–415, 432, 438, 457, 461–462; OLS, p. 36; P, pp. 184, 196, 214, 274; SEL, pp. 140, 169) *fl. compañera* comrade, companion.

comptoir (IS, pp. 33, 232) sales counter.

cordillera (DF, p. 75; HS, 22, 87, 100, 115, 149, 168, 261, 263; IMS, pp. 4, 72, 240, 283; MIC, pp. 2, 11, 21, 82, 119, 164, 177, 186; OLS, pp. 146–151, 159, 164, 190, 201, 287, 288; P, pp. 38, 184, 312; PS, 159, 162, 199, 206, 255; SEL, p. 55; SOD, p. 102) a complex of mountain ranges.

corrida (FP, p. 86) bullfight.

Covadonga (HS, pp. 141, 241, 306) a village in Asturias, Spain, where Iberians began the reconquest of land usurped by Moors.

cuchillo (SEL, pp. 257–259, 262, 266, 268) knife, blade.

cuchitril (SOD, pp. 3, 67, 194, 286) hut.

cumbia (EL, p. 50; HS, p. 86; SEL, p. 119) a slave dance popular in Chile and Peru.

curandera/curandero (CB, pp. 212, 219; HS, pp. 66, 219; IP, pp. 24, 39, 49, 129, 190, 249, 273; MIC, p. 61; Z, p. 48) native healer, shaman.

curanto (A, pp. 84–87) traditional Argentinian and Chilean spiced clambake.

Damballah (IS, p. 157) see *loa.*

derecho a pernada (MIC, p. 54; PS, p. 266) literally the "right of the first plunge," a feudal custom by which the lord of the manor has a right to deflower a virginal female subject.

desaparecido (OLS, pp. 40, 115, 144, 201, 212, 220, 233, 272; P, pp. 199, 224, 233, 246, 258; SEL, p. 255) a victim whom corrupt officials secretly abduct or imprison.

djembe drums (IS, p. 2) Malian goatskin hand drums that call people to peace rituals.

docteur feuille (IS, pp. 66, 189, 251, 302, 304, 352, 403) herbalist.

drabardi (Z, pp. 146, 262, 265) Gypsy fortuneteller.

dragoon (Z, pp. 7, 45) armed horseman.

dulce de leche (DF, pp. 136, 310; IMS, pp. 300, 336; MIC, pp. 10, 88; MN, p. 204; PS, p. 28) caramel.

efrit (EL, p. 168) an evil specter or genie in Arab literature.

eggfruit (EL, p. 147; HS, p. 126) lúcuma, a tropical fruit.

El Dorado (A, p. 244; CB, pp. 86, 88, 120, 246, 248, 249, 262, 280, 307; DF, pp. 121, 269; HS, p. 17; IMS, pp. 14, 48, 49, 61, 82, 283; SEL, p. 300; Z, p. 101) a mythic city or empire of gold that lured explorers to the New World.

éminence grise (Z., pp. 126, 195) counselor or brains of a group.

empanada (A, p. 38; DF, pp. 12, 244; HS, p. 421; IMS, pp. 13–15, 45–49, 52–53, 88–93, 97, 164, 257, 292; MIC, pp. 9, 87, 174; PS, p. 148) fried turnover stuffed with meat, seafood, and vegetables.

ensalmo (OLS, p. 54) incantation, counter-spell.

Erzulie (IS, pp. 1, 40–41, 57, 74, 110, 112, 134, 136, 159–160, 184–185, 192–193, 203, 231, 234–235, 269, 277, 295, 297, 323, 332, 346, 452, 457) see *loa.*

fan wey (DF, pp. 167, 172, 177–179, 185, 189, 195–197, 205, 225, 229, 244, 316–317, 334, 344, 363–366; PS, pp. 295, 297) Cantonese for "white person."

garçonnière (IS, pp. 34, 41, 42, 381; PS, pp. 38, 59, 60) bachelor's quarters.

garimpeiro (CB, pp. 99, 242) prospector.

gaucho (P, pp. 37, 228) cowboy.

Ghede (IS, pp. 88, 143, 146) see *loa.*

Goajira (EL, p. 170) a peninsula extending from Colombia into the Caribbean Sea.

grands blancs (IS, pp. 2, 8–9, 31, 34, 45, 51, 63, 115, 123, 128, 139, 163, 168, 174, 206,208, 214, 216, 228, 239, 308–309) the richest, most prominent tier of Haiti's white colonists. *See also petits blancs.*

gringo (CB, p. 366; DF, p. 333; EL, pp. 47, 74–76, 241; HS, pp. 85, 129–130, 160, 279, 387, 473, 485; IP, pp. 43, 60, 69–76, 82, 99–109, 120, 137, 157, 166, 185, 212; MIC, pp. 41, 106, 187–188; P, p. 90; SEL, pp. 117, 207, 226) *fem. gringa, pl. gringas* or *gringos* Spanish for "white person" or "native of England."

gris-gris (IS, pp. 276, 341, 404) a voodoo charm.

guardia (EL, pp. 13, 16, 63–64, 77, 104, 125, 137, 144, 174; MN, pp. 198, 269, 301, 377, 418; SEL, pp. 90, 186, 190–193, 241) civil patrol; national militia.

guacharo (SEL, p. 84) nocturnal bird.

guajiro (P, p. 130) mountain man.

guayabera shirt (EL, pp. 136, 154, 200, 273) a pleated men's shirt with straight hem made from white or pastel batiste.

hermano (IMS, p. 65; IP, pp. 35, 192) brother.

hidalgo (SEL, p. 183; Z, pp. 25, 35, 40, 71, 333) nobleman, gentleman.

hija (EL, p. 136) daughter.

hombre (CB, pp. 91–93, 102–104; HS, p. 347) man, buddy.

homme du monde (IS, p. 13) worldly man.

hounfor (IS, pp. 75, 136, 157, 159) a voodoo temple.

houngan (IS, pp. 74–75, 158–159, 172, 276) a voodoo priest.

houri (A, pp. 116, 158; EL, p. 163; SOD, p. 59) a temptress who awaits the heroic male Muslim in paradise.

huacho (DF, pp. 128–129) bastard, waif.

huinca (IS, pp. 118, 152, 155, 174, 181, 186, 268, 271–277, 298; MIC, p. 35) a non–Indian; a white person.

I Ching (DF, pp. 181, 318; HS, p. 216; MIC, p. 67; P. pp. 293–294, 320; SOD, p. 65) a Chinese system of divination.

imbunche (PS, pp. 165–167) the Chilean monster that guards the entrance to the cave of Brujo Chilote, a warlock with forked tongue.

indiada (Z, p. 34) a pejorative term for the Indian population.

inverti (IS, p. 396) homosexual.

joropo (CB, p. 283) Venezuelan folk waltz.

kalenda (IS, pp. 67, 70, 92, 132, 136, 157, 163, 193, 212, 233, 251) a ritual African dance accompanying drumming and stick fighting.

Kalfour (IS, pp. 143, 146) see *loa.*

kata (KGD, pp. 129, 141, 146) a silk scarf, usually white to emphasize sincere welcome to guests arriving in Tibet.

khamsin (EL, p. 147) dry, dusty wind blowing over northern Africa and Saudi Arabia.

Legba (IS, pp. 111, 159) see *loa.*

Les Morts et les Mystères (IS, pp. 85, 135, 157, 160) "The Dead and the Mysteries," a voodoo concept of an oversoul to which the spirits of the deceased return.

lettre de marque (IS, p. 394) official authorization of piracy by a government privateer.

loa (IS, pp. 1–2, 40, 41, 47, 74–75, 88–90, 110–112, 116, 134–136, 142, 146, 157, 159–160, 172, 184–185, 192, 203, 234–235, 251, 269, 276–277, 295, 298, 322–323, 346, 427, 452–453, 457) the animistic spirits of the voodoo religion, including Papa Bondye, the beneficent protector of life; Legba, aged god of sorcery; Kalfour, Legba's youthful twin; Damballah, god of creation and nature; Ghede, lord of the dead; Erzulie, the maternal god of love and music; and her husband, Ogoun or Ogu-Fer, the masculine spirit of war and iron.

machi (DF, pp. 83–84, 127–129; IMS, pp. 172, 276; MIC, p. 61; MN, pp. 51, 107, 347, 375) Mapuche shaman.

machista (MIC, p. 112) male authority.

madrina (EL, pp. 44–56, 62, 66–68, 103–111, 133, 136, 157, 162, 225–227, 273, 298; MN, p. 215; SEL, p. 241) godmother.

mahuang (DF, p. 369) ephedrine, a standard treatment for respiratory congestion.

mambo (IS, pp. 68, 72, 74–75, 89, 159–160, 163, 304) a voodoo priestess.

maréchaussée (IS, pp. 41, 44, 46–47, 135, 152, 155, 158–162, 167, 187, 192) mounted militia.

maroon (IS, pp. 40, 42, 44, 46–50, 53–54, 60–61, 64, 72, 101, 113, 146–147, 155, 158, 165, 171) a member of a colony of fugitive slaves.

masato (CB, pp. 180, 212–216) a mildly alcoholic drink fermented from cassava and offered as a token of hospitality and a ritual beverage.

maté (A, p. 97; DF, pp. 112, 261, 262; IMS, p. 249; MIC, pp. 119, 126; OLS, pp. 15, 18, 31; P, p. 37; PS, pp. 201, 251) a bitter South American tea infused in hot water from *Ilex paraguariensis.*

mea culpa (OLS, p. 59) a formal confession of "my fault."

mestizo (DF, p. 14; IMS, pp. 2, 79, 119, 135, 139, 256, 257, 264, 265, 268; IP, pp. 36, 166; MIC, pp. 34, 35, 39, 49, 53, 189; PS, p. 235; SEL, p. 219; Z, pp. 20, 25–28, 71, 94, 123, 135, 331) person of mixed race.

Migra (IP, pp. 42, 121) immigration officers; border patrol.

mistela (DF, p. 26) an aperitif fortified by alcohol.

moai (A, p. 85; MIC, p. 7) *pl. moais* monolithic human portrait statues.

mole (A, p. 280, Z, p. 86) sauce.

mondongo (OLS, pp. 87–88) soup made from the stomach of a cow.

muló (Z, pp. 152, 262) Gypsy revenant or vampire.

nahab (CB, pp. 109, 179, 213–214, 221–223, 230, 243, 274, 276–277, 280, 295, 307, 318, 323–350, 376–394, 403; KGD, p. 84) outsiders, non–Indians.

naiad (PS, pp. 4, 31, 129; Z, p. 214) river nymph.

namaste (KGD, p. 379) a Sanskrit greeting meaning "I bow to you."

neophyte (Z, pp. 6, 7, 8, 9, 11, 12, 17, 19, 24, 29, 34, 43, 47, 48, 49, 61, 65, 70, 81, 90, 327, 337, 362) recent convert to Christianity.

nganga (FP, p. 205) the Bantu name for a spiritual healer or herbalist.

niña (DF, pp. 134, 143–151; P, p. 56; PS, p. 209; SEL, pp. 173, 177–180; SOD, p. 295; Z, p. 191) *masc. niño* little one.

nono (SEL, p. 103) Italian for "grandfather."

odalisque (A, pp. 45, 52, 78, 143, 145, 152, 261; DF, pp. 88, 325; EL, pp. 76, 165, 195; HS, p. 356; IMS, p. 45; IP, p. 241; IS, pp. 20, 290; PS, pp. 57, 241; SEL, p. 312; SOD, p. 257) handmaiden, chambermaid in a harem, a common subject of erotic art.

Ogoun (IS, pp. 160, 185, 220) see *loa*.

okahué (Z, pp. 37–39, 62, 69, 159, 335, 384) an Indian concept of virtue comprised of courage, dignity, honor, justice, and respect for life.

onoto (CB, p. 344) a red berry that Yanomami women use to dye cloth and paint their bodies.

Opus Dei (MIC, p. 57; SEL, pp. 261, 266; SOD, pp. 27, 46–49) a spiritual fraternity of Catholic laity who carry out "God's work."

pachuco (IP, pp. 72, 99, 193, 334) sharp dresser, strutter.

Papal Nuncio (A, p. 48; HS, p. 444; P, p. 10) Vatican legate or ambassador.

pampa (A, pp. 96, 97; EL, p. 255; MIC, pp. 3, 6; PS, pp. 107, 159; SEL, pp. 56, 58) *pl. pampas* plain, grassland, prairie.

pariade (IS, p. 37) the pairing of male with female.

paseo (IMS, p. 231; Z, pp. 46, 81) promenade, stroll.

paso doble (IP, p. 299) Spanish dance replicating the moves of bullfights.

patrón (DF, pp. 4, 9, 34, 42–48, 127–128, 145, 257, 261; EL, pp. 44, 52–62, 67–72, 103–112, 126, 151–152, 157–170, 185–198, 279; HS, pp. 61–76, 84–87, 123–124, 130, 135–138, 159–163, 179, 186, 189, 214–220, 233, 244, 258, 323–326, 349, 356–357, 401–403, 407, 436–437, 470–475; OLS, pp. 9, 19, 59, 157, 169, 178; P, p. 184; PS, pp. 30, 155, 163, 235–236; SEL, pp. 38, 49, 56–57, 185; Z, pp. 34, 60, 199, 216, 221) *fem. patrona, pl. patrones* boss, landlord.

pernada (MIC, p. 54; PS, p. 235) the feudal right of an overlord to bed virgin peasants.

petits blancs (IS, pp. 8, 45, 51, 115, 124, 168, 216) the second and less prominent tier of Haiti's white colonists. *See also grands blancs.*

picaro (EL, p. 256) rascal, rogue.

picoroco (A, p. 138; MIC, p. 14) a giant barnacle eaten like shellfish.

pirarucú (CB, pp. 60, 139) fish.

piripicho (IMS, pp. 193, 234; SOD, p. 134) penis.

pisco (A, p. 84, 138, 230; MIC, pp. 4–5, 88; P, pp. 95, 179) grape variety in Peru and Chile.

plaçage (IS, pp. 313, 365–367, 369, 387, 390–391, 405, 408, 418–420, 423–424, 434, 456) biracial common law marriage.

place (IS, pp. 13, 40, 51–52, 125–128, 140, 173, 210, 219, 251, 271, 277, 326, 329, 333, 342, 357, 423, 457) town square.

placée (IS, pp. 365–367, 415) a girl entering a biracial common law marriage.

plátano (CB, p. 96) plantain, a tropical staple in the banana family.

poule (IS, pp. 23, 398) hen, a slang term for "prostitute."

poteau-mitain (IS, pp. 136, 146, 159) a post representing the conjunction of sky and underworld.

pythoness (OLS, p. 50; SOD, p. 34; Z, p. 312) priestess, seer.

Quechua (IMS, pp. 2, 38–39, 68, 78, 93, 128, 166, 213, 225, 240, 243, 254, 265, 294; MIC, pp. 3, 34, 38, 108) an indigenous people of Argentina, Bolivia, Chile, Colombia, Ecuador, and Peru; also, their language.

qi (DF, pp. 153, 203, 209, 237, 315) the Chinese concept of a life force; libido.

quillay (DF, p. 119; IMS, p. 131) soap bark.

rada (IS, p. 136) blessing.

ramblas (IP, p. 218; SOD, pp. 33, 39; Z, p. 191) gullies, side streets.

ranchera (EL, pp. 50, 120; IP, pp. 70, 77, 120; MIC, p. 52; MN, p. 417; OLS, p. 143; SOD, p. 78) popular Mexican country ballads.

rebozo (SEL, p. 197; SOD, p. 138) shawl.

riata (Z, p. 42) lasso.

roto (IMS, pp. 102, 108, 171, 282; MIC, pp. 45–46, 150; P, p. 6) low-class Chilean.

sang-mêlé (IS, p. 408) mixed blood.

santería (EL, p. 106) voodoo worship of Catholic saints.

sarao (Z, p. 86) party, fiesta.
scapular (FP, pp. 63, 296; HS, pp. 22, 287; IP, pp. 43, 102, 103, 189, 207, 233, 237; OLS, p. 229; PS, pp. 244, 268) a pair of devotional cloths suspended from the shoulders as symbols of fealty to a saint or religious principle.
semana (OLS, p. 214) week.
señorito (EL, p. 181) rich kid.
shabono (CB, pp. 55, 109, 117, 120, 129, 143, 157, 174, 200, 202–205, 222–228, 248, 382, 425) hut of a Yanomami Indian.
Société du Cordon Bleu (IS, pp. 366, 368, 371, 382, 391, 405, 407, 412, 456) the closed community of upper class free blacks, typically quadroons.
stupa (KGD, pp. 157, 258) a mounded or heaped reliquary housing Buddhist religious treasures.
sursum corda (Z, p. 345) lifted hearts.
surucucú (CB, pp. 95, 134; EL, pp. 17, 50, 226; KGD, p. 109) poisonous snake.
taffia (IS, pp. 2, 53, 92–93, 111, 141, 217) low-grade rum.
tangkuei (DF, pp. 208, 211) a nutritional tonic beneficial to women.
Tantra, Tantrism (A, pp. 10, 14, 153, 180) Sanskrit scriptures compiled during India's Gupta dynasty.
Tao-shu (KGD, pp. 73, 215–218, 240, 256, 285, 375) a Chinese text from around 960 A.D. that summarizes the effects of nutrition and wellness on anatomy and martial arts based on resolve and instinct.
tepui (CB, pp. 220, 226, 242 ff.; KGD, pp. 145, 196) mesa, tableland above steep escarpments.
tercio (IMS, pp. 19, 25, 154, 270) regiment.
ti-bon-ange (IS, pp. 103–104, 112, 145, 159) Creole for "little good angel" or guardian spirit.
tignon (IS, pp. 102, 184, 199, 233, 305, 314, 335, 343, 454) headscarf worn by West Africans and Louisiana Creole women as a badge of race and social class.
timbales (IS, p. 2) shallow Cuban drums.
toloache (Z, p. 73) datura or moonflower, a decorative plant that produces a seed used in ritual to produce amnesia and delirium.
tong (DF, pp. 44, 55, 56, 76, 131, 243, 292, 344, 352; PS, pp. 55, 131, 292, 294–295) a secret society or criminal brotherhood.
toqui (IMS, pp. 73, 173–176, 186, 269, 270, 273, 274; MIC, p. 36; PS, pp. 176, 247) field marshal among the Mapuche.
torero (FP, pp. 85–86; MN, p. 15; OLS, p. 165; Z, pp. 86, 180, 378) bullfighter.
tsampa (KGD, pp. 212–214, 233, 250, 299, 320, 333) a Tibetan convenience food formed of roasted flour kneaded into a dough with the addition of buttered and salted tea.
tulku (KGD, pp. 248, 353, 381) among Tibetan lamas, a spiritual master of the highest rank and supernatural power.
vaquero (Z, pp. 28, 42, 43, 44, 49, 50, 52, 54, 78) cowboy.
vévé (IS, pp. 136, 160) a cosmographic symbol in voodoo ceremonies.
yopo (CB, pp. 210, 216–218; SEL, p. 132) an hallucinogenic substance extracted from acacia beans for healing rituals.
z'étoile (IS, pp. 1, 122, 134, 185, 190, 348, 399, 416) Haitian Creole for "the star," meaning "destiny."
zhong-yi (DF, pp. 157–176, 181–183, 188–193, 201–208, 234–235, 240, 243, 246, 315, 319, 343–344, 347, 351, 365–367; PS, pp. 14, 43, 45, 46, 52, 68, 69, 80, 132, 188, 288–300) acupuncturist, healer.
zorro (Z, pp. 77, 79, 80) fox, a totemic animal.

Appendix A: Historical Timeline from the Allende Canon

Aphrodite (A)	*Kingdom of the Golden Dragon* (KGD)
Daughter of Fortune (DF)	*My Invented Country* (MIC)
Eva Luna (EL)	*Of Love and Shadows* (OLS)
Forest of the Pygmies (FP)	*Paula* (P)
The House of the Spirits (HS)	*Portrait in Sepia* (PS)
Inés of My Spirit (IMS)	*Stories of Eva Luna* (SEL)
The Infinite Plan (IP)	*The Sum of Our Days* (SOD)
Island Beneath the Sea (IS)	*Zorro* (Z)

ca. 563 B.C. Siddhartha Gautama is born in Lumbini, Nepal. (KGD, p. 162).

ca. 534 B.C. Siddhartha encounters suffering. (KGD, p. 163)

ca. 528 B.C. The Buddha begins a period of meditation. (KGD, pp. 163–164)

October 12, 1492 Christopher Columbus discovers the New World. (IMS, p. 9)

December 5 Columbus's arrival at Haiti brings death to the native Arawak. (IS, p. 5)

November 8, 1519 Hernán Cortés reaches Mexico City. (IMS, p. 9)

1526 Francisco Pizarro encounters the Inca of Peru. (IMS, p. 37)

July 26, 1529 Charles I of Spain names Francisco Pizarro the governor of New Castile, Peru. (IMS, p. 2)

June 23, 1531 Diego de Ordaz navigates the Orinoco River of Venezuela and Colombia in search of El Dorado. (SEL, pp. 299–300)

July 26, 1533 Francisco Pizarro arranges the execution of Atahualpa, the last ruler of the Inca Empire. (IMS, pp. 40, 117)

1534 Emperor Charles V proposes digging a canal across Panama. (Z, p. 98)

1536 Diego de Almagro becomes the first European to explore Chile. (DF, p. 41; IMS, p. 62)

July 8, 1538 Hernando Pizarro orders the garroting of Diego de Almagro. (IMS, p. 73)

February 12, 1541 Conquistadors under Pedro Gutiérrez de Valdivia, founder of Santiago, begin the conquest of Chile. (DF, pp. 52–53; EL, p. 1; IMS, p. 19; MIC, p. 5; SOD, p. 266)

September 11, 1541 Mapuche Indians, led by Michimalonko, besiege and burn the new settlement of Santiago, Chile. (IMS, pp. 193, 202, 268)

November 20, 1542 Charles V codifies the New Laws, a legal structure ostensibly preventing exploitation of American aborigines. (IMS, pp. 245–246, 252)

December 25, 1553 The Battle of Tucapel, Chile, concludes with Lautaro's torture and execution of Pedro de Valdivia. (IMS, pp. 221, 227)

1560 Lope de Aguirre sails to Brazil to search for El Dorado. (CB, pp. 273–274; HS, p. 29)

1569 Alonso de Ercilla publishes the first of the tripartite *La Araucana,* the epic of Chile. (IS, pp. 64–65, 118, 176, 228, 320; MIC, pp. 35, 63, 199)

October 1704 Alexander Selkirk is stranded on Juan Fernández island until rescue on February 1, 1709. (MIC, p. 8)

February 12, 1733 General James Oglethorpe establishes Savannah, Georgia. (IS, p. 378)

1735 The arrival in Chile of Francisco Errázuriz establishes a lengthy Basque dynasty of politicians and churchmen. (MIC, p. 80)

January 20, 1758 French Haitian planters burn at the stake François Macandal, leader of maroon rebels and poisoner of whites. (IS, pp. 45, 47–53, 56, 61, 64, 348)

November 2, 2769 Spaniards explore Yerba Buena, the basis for San Francisco. (DF, p. 223)

April 19, 1775 The American Revolution influences rebels in France. (IS, 83)

January 1775 Louis XVI appoints mulatto conductor Joseph Bologne as director of the Paris Opéra. (IS, p. 344).

October 25, 1785 Tongva/Gabrieleños shaman Toypurina leads a revolt against Mission San Gabriel. (Z, p. 12)

March 1789 Former slave Olaudah Equiano publishes his autobiography. (IS, p. 319)

July 14, 1789 The French Revolution overturns the nation's class system and spreads the spirit of insurrection over Haiti. (DF, p. 91; IS, pp. 115, 351–352, 442; SOD, p. 270; Z, pp. 41, 105, 144, 398)

August 26, 1789 The French Declaration of the Rights of Man and of the Citizen proclaims human liberty as a universal right. (IS, p. 132)

October 28, 1789 Haitian freedmen Vincent Ogé and Jean-Baptiste Chavannes launch a month-long revolt against white colonial authority. (IS, p. 139)

1790 Père Antoine de Sedella arrives in New Orleans as an authority of the Inquisition. (IS, p. 280)

August 14, 1791 Rebel François-Domingue Toussaint L'Ouverture heads the Haitian Revolution. (IS, pp. 161, 172–174, 178, 185, 189–190, 196–197, 199–200, 219, 226, 260–261, 284, 301–304, 347–348, 350–352, 442).

Boukman Dutty, a Jamaican voodoo priest, leads the blacks at Bois Cayman in a pledge to win freedom. (IS, pp. 158–161, 171–173, 189, 202)

April 4, 1792 Sonthonax heads the French Republican commission that controls Haiti. (IS, pp. 175, 200, 205–207, 212–219, 226)

January 21, 1793 Louis XVI goes to the guillotine. (Z, p. 36; IS, p. 202) [Note that Allende mistakenly sets the execution earlier and as well as the beheading of Marie Antoinette, who died on October 16, 1793.]

August 24, 1793 General Galbaud heads a retreat of Haitian whites to Cuba. (IS, pp. 224–225, 228)

September 20, 1793 England invades Haiti. (IS, p. 260).

late March, 1794 Jean-Pierre Toussaint dies in an ambush from a bullet wound. (IS, p. 301)

July 28, 1794 Jacobin executioner Robespierre dies on the guillotine. (IS, 239–240)

July 1795 Père Antoine de Sedella takes episcopal duties in New Orleans. (IS, pp. 240, 266–267, 276–277, 280, 291, 314, 320, 324–333, 341, 346, 352, 355, 366, 403, 427–429, 437–457)

August 19, 1796 Spain signs the Third Treaty of San Ildefonso, returning Louisiana to France. (p. 354)

May 19, 1797 Toussaint L'Ouverture becomes commander in chief in Haiti. (IS, pp. 283, 347)

November 10, 1799 The French proclaim Napoleon a consul of the republic. (IS, 300)

December 1801 General Charles Leclerc lands in Haiti to retake the island for France. (IS, p. 347)

April 30, 1802 Yellow fever kills 15,000 French troops in Haiti. (IS, p. 348)

May 27, 1802 French forces arrest and deport Toussaint L'Ouverture. (IS, 348)

October 1802 Jean-Jacques Dessalines commands Haiti's rebel forces. (IS, p. 352)

November 2, 1802 General Leclerc dies of yellow fever. (IS, p. 348)

April 7, 1803 Toussaint L'Ouverture dies in prison in the Jura Mountains. (IS, p. 350)

April 30, 1803 The Louisiana Purchase doubles the size of the United States. (IS, pp. 354–356)

May 18, 1803 The Napoleonic Wars begin on the seas. (DF, p. 91)

December 19, 1803 Ursuline nuns depart New Orleans for Cuba. (IS, p. 357)

December 20, 1803 Americans take control of Louisiana. (IS, p. 356)

January 1, 1804 Haitians declare an island republic. (IS, p. 356)

May 14, 1804 The Lewis & Clark expedition sets off to explore the Missouri River. (IS, p. 446)

December 2, 1804 Napoleon crowns himself emperor of France. (IS, p. 383)

1805 In the last five years of the Inquisition in North America, there is no priest who can exorcise demons. (Z, p. 65)

October 20, 1805 Horatio Nelson dies after his navy defeats the French at the Battle of Trafalgar. (IBS, p. 384)

1807 Jean and Pierre Lafitte set up smuggling operations in Barataria Bay, Louisiana. (Z, pp. 282, 285, 294, 300, 316)

July 7, 1808 Napoleon forces the Spanish king Ferdinand VII to abdicate in favor of Joseph Bonaparte, Napoleon's brother. (Z, pp. 82, 85, 105, 115–117)

March 11, 1810 Napoleon marries Marie-Louise of Austria. (Z, p. 128)

September 18, 1810 Chile becomes a republic under the Spanish crown. (DF, pp. 13–14, 15; MIC, p. 143)

November 16, 1811 José Miguel Carrera presides over Chile's first governing council. (EL, p. 190, 284, 291; MIC, p. 21)

March 19, 1812 Spain adopts a liberal constitution. (Z, pp. 144, 195, 197)

October 19, 1812 Napoleon's army marches home from Russia in defeat. (Z, pp. 170–171)

May 23, 1813 Venezuelans declare Simon Bolivar *El Libertador*. (Z, p. 194)

December 11, 1813 Ferdinand VII returns to power in Spain. (Z, p. 195)

April 6, 1814 Napoleon abdicates his French throne and enters exile at Elba. (Z, pp. 196–197)

January 8, 1815 Andrew Jackson defeats the British at the Battle of New Orleans. (Z, p. 283)

February 26, 1815 Napoleon escapes from Elba. (Z, p. 271)

February 12, 1818 Chile declares its independence from Spain. (MIC, p. 65)

July 24, 1823 Chile abolishes slavery. (DF, p. 42)

winter, 1833 Flooding overwhelms Chile. (DF, pp. 31–34)

March 18, 1839 The First Opium War pits China against the British. (DF, pp. 165–166)

October 16, 1840 The British Navy harbors a fleet at Valparaíso, Chile. (DF, 15).

1842 French portrait artist Raymond Monvoisin arrives in Chile. (DF, p. 31)

August 29, 1842 The Treaty of Nanking ends the First Opium War. (DF, pp. 167, 195)

May 23, 1844 Baha Ullah founds Bahaiism in Shiraz, Iran. (IP, p. 21)

September 11, 1847 Stephen Foster first performs "Oh! Susanna." (DF, pp. 234, 270)

January 2, 1848 Sam Brannan's publication of the discovery of gold at Sutter's Mill, California, begins a gold rush. (DF, pp. 120, 337, 408, 410, 420; MIC, p. 70; PS, pp. 7, 40, 284; SOD, pp. 196, 322)

February 2, 1848 The Treaty of Guadalupe Hidalgo ends the Mexican-American War. (DF, pp. 120, 329)

late 1848 Ah Toy becomes San Francisco's first Cantonese prostitute. (DF, pp. 293, 324–330, 348–359, 368–369; PS, pp. 44, 293, 299)

1849 Joaquín Murieta heads a criminal gang in California. (DF, pp. 310, 314, 328, 337–342, 357–360, 371–372, 384–386, 389, 396–398; PS, p. 40–41, 45–47)

Singsong girls arrive from China to San Francisco's Barbary Coast. (DF, pp. 345, 351–352, 364, 376; PS, pp. 34, 44, 56, 292–293)

James E. Birch operates California's first stage line. (DF, p. 330)

December 24, 1849 Fire destroys three blocks of San Francisco. (DF, p. 320)

September 9, 1850 California becomes the 31st U.S. state. (DF, p. 318)

July 5, 1851 Vigilantes hang Josefa of Downieville, California, for defending herself against a rapist. (DF, pp. 340–341)

1853 Levi Strauss sells blue jeans to miners. (DF, p. 319)

April 7, 1853 Queen Victoria gives birth to Prince Leopold under chloroform. (DF, p. 26)

May, 1853 Dancer Lola Montez arrives in San Francisco. (DF, pp. 389–391)

July 25, 1853 California State Ranger Harry Love kills and decapitates outlaw Joaquín Murieta. (DF, pp. 385, 396–399; PS, pp. 40–41, 45, 47)

1854 John Rollin Ridge publishes California's first novel, a biography of Joaquín Murieta. (DF, pp. 337–343)

December 1862 Peruvians enslave residents of Easter Island, who suffer from epidemics. (HS, p. 96; MIC, p. 7)

May 10, 1869 The Union Pacific joins the Central Pacific Railroad at Promontory Summit, Utah. (PS, p. 8)

June 25–26, 1876 Plains Indians massacre General George Armstrong Custer and his soldiers at the Little Bighorn River, Montana. (PS, p. 28)

February 14, 1879 The War of the Pacific breaks out between Chile and two foes, Bolivia and Peru. (PS, pp. 65, 70–72, 103; MIC, p. 156)

1880 Chile pacifies the Mapuche Indians. (MIC, p. 37)

January 17, 1881 Chilean forces occupy Lima, Peru. (PS, pp. 105–115)

May 8, 1882 The Chinese Exclusion Act banned Chinese immigration to the U.S. (PS, p. 49)

1884 Ottmar Mergenthaler invents the linotype. (MIC, p. 44)

1886 Sarah Bernhardt performs "La Dame aux Camelias" in Chile. (PS, p. 127)

September 18, 1886 Reformer José Balmaceda becomes president of Chile. (MIC, p. 144)

September 9, 1888 Chile annexes Easter Island. (MIC, p. 6)

October 1888 The National Geographic Society publishes the first issue of its magazine. (KGD, p. 146)

January 16, 1891 The Chilean Civil War results from conflict between legislators and President José Manuel Balmaceda over constitutional powers. (MIC, p. 144; P, p. 129; PS, pp. 153–160, 176, 184).

1908–1935 El Benefactor, the nickname of General Juan Vicente Gómez, rules Venezuela as a dictatorship. (EL, pp. 6, 10, 14–16, 26, 135–137; SEL, pp. 65, 121, 300–301, 306–312)

July 28, 1914 World War I envelopes Europe. (EL, p. 27; HS, p. 78)

late 1917 Venezuelans begin exploiting the nation's oil reserves. (SEL, p. 300)

July 17, 1918 Vladimir Lenin engineers the execution of the Romanovs, Russia's ruling family. (KGD, p. 47; IP, p. 96; SEL, p. 105)

November 11, 1918 World War I ends. (HS, p. 85; SEL, p. 300)

August 9, 1919 California author Johnston McCulley creates Zorro as hero of a pulp novel. (SOD, p. 268; Z, p. 400)

May 10, 1920 President Arturo Alessandri begins strengthening executive powers in Chile. (MIC, p. 144)

October 29, 1923 A Broadway song "The Charleston" popularizes a dance by the same name. (HS, p. 86)

May 10, 1927 General Carlos Ibéñez becomes dictator of Chile. (MIC, p. 145)

1930 The Great Depression seizes Chile's economy. (HS, p. 155)

April 1932 The Chilean Nazi Party forms in support of Adolf Hitler. MIC, pp. 39–40)

August 1933 Santiago, Chile, suffers a typhus epidemic. (HS, p. 1956)

July 17, 1936–April 1, 1939 The Spanish Civil War installs General Francisco Franco as dictator. (MIC, p. 43; OLS, pp. 93, 89, 166, 243; P, p. 129)

Thousands of refugees flee Spain for Chile. (MIC, p. 43)

December 25, 1938 Populist Pedro Cerda becomes president of Chile. (MIC, 145)

September 1, 1939 World War II breaks out in Europe. (EL, pp. 29, 108; SEL, p. 241)

September, 1939 Nazi concentration camps begin imprisoning millions of Jews, intellectuals, Communists, and Gypsies. (HS, p. 201, SEL, p. 238).

December 7, 1941 After the Japanese attack on Pearl Harbor, the United States joins Britain and the Soviet Union to form the Big Three allies. (HS, p. 209; MIC, p. 71).

April 6, 1943 An 8.2 earthquake strikes south central Chile, killing 50,000. (HS, pp. 186–192; MIC, p. ix)

1945 Padre Hurtado opens the Home of Christ in Chile to aid the poor. (MIC, p. 63)

March 29, 1945 Russian forces occupy Austria. (EL, p. 30)

May 8, 1945 World War II ends in Europe. (EL, pp. 29, 75)

August 6, 9, 1945 The dropping of atomic bombs on Hiroshima and Nagasaki, Japan ends the Pacific half of World War II. (IP, pp. 29–30; MIC, p. ix)

April 28, 1947 Anthropologist Thor Heyerdahl pilots the *Kon-Tiki* toward Tahiti. (MIC, p. 8)

August 15, 1947 India obtains independence from the British Empire. (KGD, p. 111).

October 7, 1950 The Chinese army invades Tibet. (KGD, pp. 19, 30, 67, 369)

August 31, 1951–January 1, 1958 Pedro Estrada serves Venezuela's National Security as torturer. (EL, pp. 69, 100, 133, 135, 175–177)

April 19, 1953–January 23, 1958 Marcos Pérez Jiménez serves Venezuela as president. (SEL, pp. 301–302)

July 26, 1953 Che Guevara joins the guerrilla warfare led by Fidel Castro. (EL, p. 179)

1955 The power of Senator Joseph McCarthy and the House Un-American Activities Committee peaks. (IP, p. 96)

November 4, 1956 Soviet Russia invades Hungary. (OLS, p. 93)

summer 1957 An H2N2 virus spreads Asian flu in a global pandemic. (EL, p. 173)

November 3, 1957 Russia's Sputnik 2 launches the dog Laika into space. (EL, p. 172)

July 15, 1958 A Lebanese political crisis requires U.S. intervention by Marines from the Sixth Fleet. (MIC, p. 110)

January 1, 1959 The Cuban Revolution ousts dictator Fulgencio Batista. (EL, 179, 241)

March 31, 1959 The Dalai Lama flees Tibet and seeks asylum in India. (KGD, p. 67)

1960 The University of California at Berkeley gains a reputation for tolerance and student activism. (IP, pp. 125–128)

May 2, 1964 Students in San Francisco launch the first major march against the Vietnam War. (IP, pp. 148–149, 155, 168, 179, 199, 222, 233, 245, 247, 252, 266, 270, 271, 320, 363, 378; SOD, pp. 33, 206).

October, 1965 A violent anti–Communist purge kills 500,000 citizens of Djakarta. (HS, p. 413)

October 9, 1967 Bolivian soldiers execute Che Guevara. (P, p. 143)

August 21, 1968 2,000 Soviet tanks invade Warsaw, Poland. (EL, p. 256)

July 20, 1969 U.S. astronaut Neil Armstrong becomes the first human to walk on the moon. (HS, p. 379; SEL, pp. 37, 45)

November 3, 1970 Salvador Allende becomes the first popularly elected Marxist president in history. (HS, pp. 380–381; MIC, pp. 105, 127, 129, 148–151; P, pp. 137, 163)

December 1, 1971 Right-wing Chilean women conduct the March of the Empty Pots in support of Agusto Pinochet. (HS, p. 362)

December 13, 1971 Pablo Neruda receives the Nobel Prize for Literature. (HS, p. 323; P, p. 166)

September 11, 1973 A military coup topples the Allende government and forces his alleged suicide. (HS, pp. 415–420, 422–423, 425, 427, 441; MIC, pp. xii, xv, 46, 106, 129, 142, 157–164; P, p. 192; SOD, pp. 213, 241).

Bombardment decimates La Moneda Palace in Santiago. (HS, pp. 417, 460, 472; MIC, p. 157; OLS, p. 237)

September 23, 1973 After the military rifles his home, Pablo Neruda dies. (HS, pp. 437–439).

September 30, 1974 A car bomb kills General Carlos Prats González. (P, p. 223–224)

December 11, 1974 Augusto Pinochet seizes the Chilean presidency. (HS, pp. 420–421, 425–4261 MIC, pp. 166–171, 181–182)

November 30, 1978 The discovery of 26 corpses in the limestone ovens in Lonquén, Chile, precedes a public indictment of Augusto Pinochet. (OLS, pp. 202ff)

August 1981 The CIA unites anti–Sandinista factions into the Nicaraguan Democratic Force to rid the country of tyranny. (IP, p. 363)

April 2, 1982 Argentina begins the Falklands War by occupying British territory. (MIC, p. 41)

November 13, 1985 An eruption of the Nevado Ruiz volcano in Colombia buries a girl in mud. (P, p. 309; SEL, pp. 319–331)

April 106, 1987 Pope John Paul II visits Chile. (EL, p. 94; MIC, p. 151; SEL, pp. 45–46)

October 5, 1988 Chile revives its republic by ousting Pinochet. (MIC, pp. xv, 92–93, 164, 191–192)

December 3, 1988 San Francisco suffers an earthquake. (MIC, p. 87)

April–July 15, 1994 Genocide in Rwanda kills 800,000 people. (SOD, pp. 75–76)

November 1994 California Proposition 187 proposes limitations on the use of public education, health, and welfare services by illegal aliens. (SOD, p. 137)

April 19, 1995 Timothy McVeigh and Terry Nichols detonate a bomb at the federal building in Oklahoma City. (SOD, p. 114)

October 17, 1998 Spanish agents arrest Augusto Pinochet in London. (MIC, pp. 194–195)

April 20, 1999 Two students murder twelve students and one teacher at Columbine High in Columbine, Colorado. (CB, p. 15)

March 11, 2000 Ricardo Lagos takes office as Chile's president. (MIC, p. 83)

September 11, 2001 Islamic terrorists guide planes into the World Trade Center in New York City. (MIC, pp. xi–xii; SOD, pp. 213–214)

May 27, 2002 A flood initiates mud slides in Chile. (MIC, pp. 85–86)

March 20, 2003 George Bush launches an invasion of Iraq. (SOD, p. 293)

February 12, 2004 San Francisco begins issuing marriage licenses to same-sex couples. (SOD, p. 260)

Appendix B: Writing and Research Topics

1. Contrast two love relationships from Allende's writings, for example Diego de la Vega/Juliana de Rameu, Adèle/Dr. Parmentier, Eva Luna/Riad Halabí, Irene Beltrán/Francisco Leal, Nadia Santos/Alex Cold, Allende/Willie Gordon, Tété/Gambo, Paula/Miguel Frías, Prince Dil/Pema, Greg Reeves/Carmen Morales, Hortensia/Amadeo Peralta, Aurora del Valle/Diego Domínguez, Pedro Berastegui/Elena Etxebarria, and Lin/Tao Chi'en.

2. Summarize the significance of these terms to Allende's canon: Alta California, *code noir, barrio, tignon, zorro, mestizo, desaparecidos, compañero, grands blancs, loa, patrón, zhong yi, cordillera, conquistadora,* El Dorado, and tong.

3. Characterize the motivation and purpose of ecofeminism in the works of Allende and those of Leslie Marmon Silko, Mary Hunter Austin, Rachel Carson, Marjorie Stoneman Douglas, Kathy Reichs, Marjorie Kinnan Rawlings, Willa Cather, Ursula Le Guin, Starhawk, Octavia Butler, or Barbara Kingsolver. Which authors valorize women's efforts at the peasant level? Which authors predict vengeance on the desecrators of Mother Earth? What works depict women as healers and saviors of earth's wonder and fecundity?

4. Summarize the effects of coercion, torture, intimidation, or military occupation in *Of Love and Shadows* and one of these works: Iris Anthony's *The Ruins of Lace,* J.R. Moehringer's *Sutton,* Margaret Atwood's *The Handmaid's Tale,* Marlon James's *The Book of Night Women,* Madison Smartt Bell's *All Souls' Rising,* Alejo Carpentier's *The Kingdom of This World,* Leslie Marmon Silko's *Almanac of the Dead,* Orson Scott Card's *Ender's Game,* Marge Piercy's *Woman on the Edge of Time,* Nevil Shute's *A Town Like Alice,* or Susan Straight's *I Been in Sorrow's Kitchen and Licked Out All the Pots.*

5. Summarize deathbed attitudes and instructions in the death scene of Clara del Valle Trueba and in similar views of the moribund in Margaret Edson's *Wit,* Katherine Anne Porter's "The Jilting Granny Weatherall," Leslie Marmon Silko's "Lullaby," Michael Ondaatje's *The English Patient,* Velma Wallis's *Two Old Woman,* Alan Gurganus's *Oldest Living Confederate Widow Tells All,* Kaye Gibbons's *On the Occasion of My Last Afternoon,* Rudolfo Anaya's *Bless Me, Ultima,* or Winnie Smith's *American Daughter Gone to War.*

6. Propose the choice of Allende's *Paula* or *Maya's Notebook* as a community read or a celebration of multicultural literature. Suggest an annotated character web, taped readings, improvised dialogue, historical timelines, or the use of fiction to clarify family concerns and actions during periods of change. Provide a list of alternate texts by Rigoberto Menchu, Kazuo Ishiguro, Mary Hunter Austin, Salman Rush-

die, Jamaica Kincaid, Gary Soto, Cathy Song, Peter Carey, Yoko Kawashima Watkins, Simon Joseph Ortiz, Gayle Ross, Joseph Bruchac, Carmen Deedy, Navarre Scott Momaday, Nora Ephron, Khaled Hosseini, or Joy Harjo.

7. Compare the turmoil of political and socio-economic change at Las Tres Marías with one of these literary settings: Robin Oliveira's *My Name Is Mary Sutter,* Dolen Perkins-Valdez's *Wench,* Esmeralda Santiago's *Conquistadora,* August Wilson's *Gem of the Ocean,* Barbara Kingsolver's *The Poisonwood Bible,* Stephen Ambrose's *Band of Brothers,* Jean Rhys's *Wide Sargasso Sea,* Peter Carey's *The True History of the Kelly Gang,* or Marlene Banks's *Son of a Preacherman.* Include music and dance, food, superstition, religion, learning, daily labor, ritual, fear, betrayal, love, and child rearing.

8. Analyze dangers to marginalized people in *Eva Luna,* particularly Consuelo, Mimí, Elvira, and La Señora. Contrast the fears and strategies of survivors with the post-war trauma in Toni Morrison's *Home,* Gayl Jones's *Corregidora,* E.L. Doctorow's *The March,* Ruth Prawer Jhabvala's *Heat and Dust,* Umberto Eco's *The Name of the Rose,* Harriette Arnow's *The Dollmaker,* Carlos Fuentes's *Old Gringo,* Virginia Ellis's *The Wedding Dress,* Thomas Keneally's *Schindler's List,* or Gish Jen's *World and Town.*

9. Account for variant images of confrontations in Allende's writing, particularly the Detective Larramendi's investigation of a breakup in "The Guggenheim Lovers" and the acceptance of death in *Paula* or *Letters to Paula.* Draw parallels from the arrival of slave catchers in Toni Morrison's *Beloved,* battle terrors in Nick Stafford's *War Horse,* demands for human rights in Rigoberto Menchu's *I, Rigoberto,* discussions of royal succession in James Goldman's *The Lion in Winter,* formation of an exploratory party in Ursula K. LeGuin's "Sur," clashes between white and black South Africans in Nelson Mandela's *The Long Walk to Freedom,* the captain's departure in Sena Naslund's *Ahab's Wife,* and Donald Davidson's advice in the poem "Sanctuary."

10. Contrast types of revolt in several of Allende's works. Include the following models:

- against crime in "Clarisa"
- against poaching in *Forest of the Pygmies*
- against concubinage in *Island Beneath the Sea*
- against convention in *Portrait in Sepia*
- against gender restrictions in *Aphrodite: A Memoir of the Senses*
- against arranged marriage in "The Guggenheim Lovers"
- against secret murder in *Of Love and Shadows*
- against natural disaster in "And of Clay Are We Created"
- against Napoleon in *Zorro*
- against tyranny in *Eva Luna*
- against patriarchal religion in *The Sum of Our Days*
- against in humanity in "If I Tell You My Name"
- against gentrification in *Daughter of Fortune*
- against snobbery in "Gift for a Sweetheart"
- against illegitimacy in *The House of the Spirits*
- against fear in Esteban Trueba with corrupt characters in Nora Roberts's *Sacred Sins,* Ron Rash's *Serena,* Michel Faber's *The Crimson Petal and the White,* Amy Tan's *The Hundred Secret Senses,* Henry James's *The Wings of the Dove,* Emilia Pardo Bazan's *The House of Ulloa,* Kate Chopin's *The Awakening,* Gabriel García Marquéz's *Love in the Time of Cholera,* Edith Wharton's *The Buccaneers,* or Jim Harrison's *Legends of the Fall.*

13. Summarize Allende's views on the disenfranchisement of nonwhite peoples in Valparaíso, Santiago, and New Orleans with the same theme in David Guterson's *Snow Falling on Cedars,* Leslie Marmon Silko's "America's Iron Curtain: The Border Patrol State," Dee Brown's *Bury My Heart at Wounded Knee,* Jamaica Kincaid's "Ovando," Alex Haley's *Roots,* Leslie Marmon Silko's *Garden in the Dunes,* Sherman Alexie's *The Lone Ranger and Tonto Fistfight in Heaven,* and Maryse Conde's *I, Tituba.*

14. Determine the source of trust in Allende's *The Stories of Eva Luna.* Compare the solidarity of strong women with similar bonding in Charles Frazier's *Cold Mountain,* Dorothy Allison's *Bastard Out of Carolina,* John Fowles's

The French Lieutenant's Woman, Marilynne Robinson's *Home,* Peter Carey's *Oscar and Lucinda,* Anita Diamant's *The Red Tent,* Robert Harling's *Steel Magnolias,* Terry McMillan's *Getting to Happy,* Kaye Gibbons's *Charms for the Easy Life,* Randall Jarrell's *The Woman at the Washington Zoo,* and Cecilia Velastegui's *Traces of Bliss.*

15. Account for humor in desperate situations in Allende's *The Infinite Plan* and in one of the following works: Frankk T. Hopkins's "Hidalgo," Anna Quindlen's *One True Thing,* James Clavell's *Noble House,* Marjane Satrapi's *Persepolis,* Tim O'Brien's *The Things They Carried,* Maya Angelou's *Now Sheba Sings the Song,* Tennessee Williams's *Cat on a Hot Tin Roof,* or Mariama Ba's *So Long a Letter.*

16. Compare gendered rules for behavior or career advancement in Allende's *Daughter of Fortune* with similar obstacles in Paolo Coelho's *The Alchemist,* Hannah Pakula's *The Last Empress,* Douglass G. Brinkley's *Cronkite,* Rita Dove's *Thomas and Beulah,* James Michener's *Chesapeake,* Jessamyn West's *The Friendly Persuasion,* Bernard Malamud's *The Fixer,* and Eve Ensler's *The Vagina Monologues.*

17. Discuss the tone and atmosphere of supernatural intervention in character action, particularly prescience and prophetic dreams. How does Allende present foreknowledge in Paula and Má Bangesé, telekinesis in Clara del Valle and the Moira sisters, instinct in Eva Luna and Nadia Santos, and age-old wisdom in Catalina, Walimai, Nana-Asante, Pedro García, Sanité Dédé, Tante Rose, Tao Chi'en, Iyomi, Cyrus, Tensing, and White Owl?

18. Summarize the traits of a good soldier in *Of Love and Shadows* or *Portrait in Sepia,* Mariano Azuela's *The Underdogs,* and Tim O'Brien's *The Things They Carried.*

19. Account for positive images of the grandmother, including Clara in *The House of the Spirit,* Francisca Llona Barros in *Paula,* Tété in *Island Beneath the Sea,* Isabel Allende in *The Sum of Our Days,* Kate Cold in the *City of the Beasts* trilogy, Eliza Sommers and Paulina del Valle in *Portrait in Sepia,* and Madame Odilia and White Owl in *Zorro.* How does Allende's personal life validate close relations among three generations of a clan?

20. Select contrasting scenes and describe their pictorial qualities, for example:

- rest in a hammock in "Two Words"
- commiserating with a slave in "Walimai"
- organizing a search in "The Proper Respect"
- courting a beautiful woman in "Phantom Palace"
- treasuring a handicapped child in "The Road North"
- praying for a criminal in "Clarisa"
- dancing in "The Little Heidelberg"
- concealing terrors in "Our Secret"
- entertaining a rich woman in "Gift for a Sweetheart"'
- mourning a deceased father in "Revenge"
- concealing love in "Letters of Betrayed Love"
- meeting a stranger in "The Guggenheim Lovers"

21. Discuss the suppression of cultural and familial values in the dictator novels of Isabel Allende, Julia Alvarez, Augusto Roa Bastos, Julio Cortázar, Mario Vargas Llosa, Gabriel García Marquez, and Robert Bolaño.

22. Contrast flaws and strengths in two of these secondary characters: Romás de Rameu, Kamal, Amanda, Pedro Tercero, Consuelo, Charles Reeves, Pema, Gustavo Morante, Toypurnia, Professor Leal, Férula Trueba, Rafael Moncado, Judy Reeves, Pedro Berastegui, Babalú the Bad, and Elvira Domínguez. Which characters recognize weaknesses? faults? inescapable dilemmas? temporary obstacles?

23. Write an extended definition of *conflict* using as examples Irene Beltrán's flight to Spain, Nico's divorce, Greg Reeves's drug addiction, Zulema's adultery, Lautaro's siege, Dorji's death, Jaime's performance of an abortion, Huberto Naranjo's prison break, Eusebio Beltrán's disappearance, Juliana de Rameu's wedding, Rosette's marriage to Maurice Solar, and Nicolás Vidal's capture.

24. Compare male and female nurturing in these scenes: Digna Ranquileo's receipt of the wrong baby, Bernardo's romance with Light-in-the-Night, Kate Cold's preparation of Alex for

travel, Tao Chi'en's care for his first wife, Nana's scaring of Clara de Valle, Esteban Trueba's forgiveness of Blanca, White Owl's Indian stories, Pedro Segundo's offerings at Clara's grave, Mama Odilia's care of her daughter, Walimai's final moments with his wife, Claveles Picero's long walk, Beatriz Alcantára's purchase of a trousseau for Irene, Elvira Domínguez's love of her daughter-in-law, and Tensing's treatment of Nadia.

25. Compare shifts in the family power structure in *Island Beneath the Sea* or *Maya's Notebook* with scenes from Alice Sebold's *The Lovely Bones*, James Agee's *A Death in the Family*, Sandra Cisneros's *Caramelo*, Peter Carey's *True History of the Kelly Gang*, Kaye Gibbons's *Ellen Foster*, August Wilson's *Fences*, Marion Zimmer Bradley's *The Mists of Avalon*, Khaled Hosseini's *A Thousand Splendid Suns*, Ann Petry's *Tituba of Salem Village*, or Pat Conroy's *The Great Santini*. Emphasize the compromises that allow individuals to cope with unlovable people.

26. Improvise a dialogue among the Yanacona, Araucani, and Mapuche on the subject of conquest and dispossession as determiners of vulnerability. As a model, explain through character speeches by Lautaro, Catalina, Guacolda, and Michimalonko the Amerindian attitude toward home, food, clothing, children, healing, storytelling, land, spirits, nativism, and personal belongings.

27. Contrast the use of the supernatural in "Phantom Palace" or *Forest of the Pygmies* to Lois Lowry's *Messenger*, Rudolfo Anaya's *Bless Me, Ultima*, Leslie Marmon Silko's *Almanac of the Dead*, Ray Bradbury's *Something Wicked This Way Comes*, J.K. Rowling's *Harry Potter*, William Shakespeare's *Midsummer Night's Dream*, Paula Gunn Allen's *Spider Woman's Granddaughters*, or Hugh Leonard's *Da*.

28. Cite occasions for storytelling in Allende's works, such as educating children about language, comfort to Spaniards marching from Peru to Chile, preserving Amazonian history, entertaining in public plazas, presenting models such as David's battle with Goliath, introducing recipes, singing subversive lyrics on the radio, recovering African culture at Guinean kalendas, expressing sorrow, composing *telenovelas*, and urging peons to unite against *patróns*.

29. Discuss the repeated motif of colonialism in Allende's works. Explain how she applies the setting and themes of infringement on the sovereignties of the Western Hemisphere through young adult quest novel, song, fable, bildungsroman, satire, jeremiad, polemic, dictator novel, cautionary tale, dreamscape, vignette, anecdote, short story, personal essay, fantasy, speech, travelogue, biography, and autobiography.

30. Account for the significance of secondary characters, such as Lisa Cold in *Forest of the Pygmies*, Iris the schoolteacher in *Eva Luna*, Adèle and Justin in *Island Beneath the Sea*, Ana Blaum in "Interminable Life," English investors in "Toad's Mouth," Blue Horsemen in *Kingdom of the Golden Dragon*, Hipólito Ranquileo in *Of Love and Shadows*, Inmaculada Morales in *The Infinite Plan*, Celia in *The Sum of Our Days*, Miguel and Ester Trueba in *The House of the Spirits*, and César Santos in *City of the Beasts*.

31. Contrast the sources of drama in these situations: securing children for human organ harvesting, rescuing a woman from a stillbirth, looking for a *desaparecida* in a morgue, locating a hermit queen in a cemetery, burning a rebel alive, creating sensual meals to enhance sex, recovering sight by a miracle, making a career out of jewelry, observing a failed hanging, dispelling an invasion of ants, avoiding an arranged marriage, and posing as a stable boy to learn Spanish secrets. Which provide visual effects for film or stage? Which suit oral storytelling, radio *telenovela*, or pantomime?

32. Characterize the importance of setting to these scenes: cooking empanadas, Javier's hanging, Zorro's first costume, Susana's meeting with her lover, building a Spanish city, soothing a coma victim with massage, making a tunnel of books, learning to speak Vietnamese, teaching mulattas to please their lovers, training a prince, immigrating to an English-speaking country, studying autopsy and surgery, and traveling with prostitutes.

33. Compose an annotated global map featuring these landmarks in Allende's life:

Caracas, Chiloé, Sausalito, Barcelona, Atacama Desert, Santiago, Beirut, Isla Negri, San Rafael, Madrid, Andes Mountains, the *cordillera*, Switzerland, Easter Island, Valparaíso, Juan Fernandez, Brazil, Argentina, San Francisco, and Lima. Why do Camino Real, Senegal, Haiti, New Orleans, and El Dorado belong on this list?

34. Explain the significance of the following names and terms to Allende's works:

euthanasia	"Wicked Girl"	Joe Bonecrusher
Tapestries of Hope	plaçage	Tamar
The Infinite Plan	War of the Pacific	*Island Beneath the Sea*
"Civilize Your Troglodyte"	Three-Finger Jack	totemic animal
the Collector	Evangelino Flores	widowhood

35. Locate examples of journeys as symbols of ambition, vengeance, and healing, particularly Blanca del Valle's return home after her marriage, Ludovic Leblanc's expedition to the Upper Orinoco, Allende's transfer of Paula from Madrid to California, Eliza Sommers's visit to the corpses of Three-Finger Jack and Joaquín Murieta, Irene Beltrán and Francisco Leal's interest in the Los Riscos mine, Allende's escape from Santiago to Caracas, Diego de la Vega's sea journey to Madrid, Eva Luna's departure from Agua Santa, Tété's flight from Habitation Saint Lazare, Inés Suarez's search for water in the Atacama Desert, Prince Dil's residence with Tensing in the Himalayas, and Carmen Morales's journey to Vietnam.

36. Debate the wisdom of the following choices: Juliana de Rameu's marriage to Jean Lafitte, Pema's escape from the Blue Horsemen, Nicolás Vidal's tryst with Casilda Hidalgo, Esteban Trueba's investment in chinchillas, Aurora del Valle's formal study of photography, Allende's search for Nico's second wife, Mario's assistance to Francisco Leal and Irene Beltrán, Nana-Asante's hermitage in the cemetery, Lautaro's plot against Pedro de Valdivia, Esther's marriage to James Morton, Allende's decision to write a book about food and sex, and Eliza Sommers's return to dresses.

37. Discuss the role of history in Allende's works. Include the Treaty of Guadalupe Hidalgo, Vietnam War, Francisco Pizarro's conquest of Peru and Chile, Macandal's execution, Louisiana Purchase, Siddhartha Gautama's birth, Napoleon's capture, Harry Love captures Joaquín Murieta, Chile elects José Balmaceda president, the First Opium War, Jean-Jacques Dessalines's command of Haitian rebel forces, Père Antoine de Sedella's transfer to New Orleans, Mapuche Indians' burning of Santiago, Allende's American citizenship, and Salvador Allende's death.

38. Discuss the effectiveness of the following rhetorical devices:

- *euphony* "one of those towns drowsing in the doldrums of the provinces, washed by rain, radiant in the incredible tropical light" (*Eva Luna*)
- *sense impression* "the stench of death clinging to his skin" (*Portrait in Sepia*)
- *alliteration* "I love you too much to lie to you, Isabel" (*Paula*)
- *foreign terms* "he never appears to the *nahab*" (*City of the Beasts*)
- *hyperbole* "buried himself alive in a room at the back of the patio" (*The Stories of Eva Luna*)
- *humor* "the Adventists, who served lemon pie on Sundays" (*The Infinite Plan*)
- *confessional* "I was transformed into a complex-ridden girl" (*My Invented Country*)
- *image* "the shaggy meadows, the golden wheatfields, and the far-off purple mountains disappearing in the clear morning sky" (*The House of the Spirits*)
- *aphorism* "no one is carried off to the other world before the appointed hour" (*Inés of My Soul*)
- *euphemism* "she isn't fat, she's ... robust" (*Forest of the Pygmies*)
- *sobriquet* "the multibillionaire called himself the Collector" (*Kingdom of the Golden Dragon*)
- *dialogue* "It isn't your fault, it's mine" (*Of Love and Shadows*)
- *romanticism* "a stream surrounded with tall redwoods whose tops formed the dome of a green cathedral" (*The Sum of Our Days*)
- *repetition* "Dance, dance, Zarité, the slave who dances is free" (*Island Beneath the Sea*)
- *allusion* "Amazons like herself reigned" (*Daughter of Fortune*)
- *personification* "Death laid its hands on you Monday" (*Paula*)

- *double entendre* "I'll pay you back someday. With interest." (*The House of the Spirits*)
- *pun* Tex Armadillo (*Kingdom of the Golden Dragon*)
- *myth* "every unpunished crime and excess in California was attributed to Murieta" (*Daughter of Fortune*)
- *detail* "the story tells that she lived five hundred years" (*Aphrodite*)
- *invocation* "Come, Erzulie, mother, beloved" (*Island Beneath the Sea*)
- *simile* "Silence, or you will die like a rat, Excellency" (*Zorro*)
- *parallelism* "divides the individual into body and soul, and love into profane and divine" (*Aphrodite*)
- *inversion* "It was the shock, the schoolteacher says" (*Eva Luna*)
- *visual image* "I look like a terrified mouse, black on black" (*The Sum of Our Days*)
- *vernacular* "except this leg. It is rotten" (*Zorro*)

39. Survey the rewards and recriminations of old age in two of Allende's characters. Consider the actions of White Owl, Pedro Garcia, Josefina Bianchi, Isabel Allende, Elvira, Toulouse Valmorain, Iyomi, Francisca Llona Barros, Paulina del Valle, Simple Maria, Nora Reeves, Professor Leal, Kate Cold, Tao Chi'en's mentor, Walimai, Agustín José Llona Cuevas, Ester Trueba, and Tensing.

40. Summarize the following feminist situations in Allede's works: womanizing males, intimidation by the military police, harassment of sex workers, forced marriage, women's role in tribal warfare, abduction and rape, disagreements between siblings, biracial children, public sexual harassment, limited education for women, devaluation of infant girls, concubinage, and illegitimate birth.

41. What are Allende's strongest comments about tyranny? *machismo*? underclass health care? child endangerment? poverty? racism? devaluation of the aged? slum housing? urban crime? student rebellion? war? female creativity? colonialism? Catholicism?

42. Describe how Allende presents social issues in fiction, such as spousal abuse, prostitution, suffrage, child abandonment, patriarchy, police corruption, banditry, post-traumatic stress disorder, gang violence, alienation, amputation, exile, religious fanaticism, and the extermination of Indian culture.

43. Arrange a literature seminar to compare the mothering instincts of Clara and Blanca del Valle in *The House of the Spirits* with biological and foster mothers in Marsha Norman's *'night, Mother,* Laura Esquivel's *Like Water for Chocolate,* Adrienne Rich's *Of Woman Born,* William Styron's *Sophie's Choice,* Barbara Kingsolver's *The Bean Trees,* Cristina Garcia's *Monkey Hunting,* Leslie Marmon Silko's *Ceremony,* Cormac McCarthy's *The Road,* Beth Henley's *Crimes of the Heart,* William Faulkner's "The Rose of Lebanon," or Tillie Olsen's "I Stand Here Ironing." Focus on shared elements, including gender restrictions on power and the willingness of mother figures to risk loss and alienation to give their children a worthy start.

Bibliography

Primary Sources

"An Act of Vengeance," *Short Stories by Latin American Women: The Magic and the Real,* ed. Celia Correas de Zapata. Houston: Arte Publico, 1990, 11–17.

"Afterward," *Tales of Zorro,* ed. Richard Dean Starr (2008).

"The Amazon Queen," *Salon* (25 March 1997); *San Francisco Examiner* (15 March 1998).

Aphrodite: A Memoir of the Senses. New York: HarperCollins, 1998.

Book Thieves and Literary Spirits. Berkeley, CA: Bancroft Library Press, 2007.

"Breath of Hope: On the Writings of Eduardo Galeano," *Monthly Review* 48:11 (April 1997): 1–6.

Cartas a Paula. Barcelona: Plaza & Janés, 1997.

"Christmas, Chilean American-Style," *Sunset* 225: 6 (December 2010): 54.

City of the Beasts. New York: HarperCollins, 2002.

Civilize Your Troglodyte. Santiago, Chile: Editorial Lord Cochran, 1974).

Daughter of Fortune. New York: HarperCollins, 1999.

Eva Luna. New York: Knopf, 1987.

Forest of the Pygmies. New York: HarperCollins, 2005.

"Foreword," *Imagining Ourselves: Global Voices from a New Generation of Women,* eds. Paula Goldman and Hafsat Abiola. New York: Taylor & Francis, 2007.

"Foreword," *In Praise of Women,* ed. Jonathan Meader. Berkeley, CA: Celestial Arts, 1997.

"Foreword," *Letters from a Stranger.* Crested Butte, CO: Conundrum Press, 1999.

"Foreword," *Tapestries of Hope, Threads of Love,* ed. Marjorie Agosín. 2nd ed. Lanham, MD: Rowman & Littlefield, 2008.

"Foreword," *Waiting to Be Heard: Youth Speak Out About Inheriting a Violent World.* San Francisco: 826 Valencia, 2004.

Giving Birth, Finding Form, with Alice Walker and Jean Shinoda Bolen. Boulder, CO: Sounds True, 1993.

"The Guggenheim Lovers," *Virginia Quarterly Review* 81:3 (Summer 2005): 102–111.

The House of the Spirits. New York: Plaza & Janés, 1982; Knopf, 1985.

Inés of My Soul. New York: HarperCollins, 2006.

The Infinite Plan. New York: HarperCollins, 1993.

The Island Beneath the Sea. New York: Harper, 2010.

"Just Back," *Travel & Leisure* 28:5 (April 1998): 239.

Kingdom of the Golden Dragon. New York: HarperCollins, 2004.

Maya's Notebook. New York: Harper, 2011.

"A Mule on a Piano," *Newsweek* 134:3 (19 July 1999): 57.

"My House Is Full of People," *American Libraries* 27:4 (April 1996): 42–43.

My Invented Country: A Memoir. New York: HarperCollins, 2003.

Of Love and Shadows. New York: Knopf, 1987.

Paula. New York: HarperCollins, 1995.

"Pinochet Without Hatred," *New York Times* (17 January 1999): 24–27.

The Porcelain Fat Lady. Madrid: Alfaguara, 1984.

Portrait in Sepia. New York: HarperCollins, 2001.

"Sacred Stillness: Spirit in Everyday Life" (speech), Institute of Noetic Sciences, (16 May 1996).

"The Short Story," *Journal of Modern Literature* 20:1 (Summer 1996): 21–28.

"Speech," TED conference, March 2007.

The Stories of Eva Luna. New York: Atheneum, 1991.

The Sum of Our Days: A Memoir. New York: Harper, 2008).

"This I Believe," *National Public Radio* (4 April 2005).
"This Much I Know," *San Francisco Observer* (12 July 2008).
"Toad's Mouth," *A Hammock Beneath the Mangoes: Stories from Latin America*, ed. Thomas Colchie. New York: Plume, 1991, 83–88.
"Tosca," *Latin American Literary Review* 19:37 (January–June 1991): 34–42.
"2010 National Book Festival," www.youtube.com/watch?v=61RL2aiuLi4, accessed May 29, 2012.
"Two Words," *The Year's Best Fantasy and Horror*. New York: St. Martin's Press, 1989).
"What You Have Is What You Give," *AARP Modern Maturity* 34:3 (May/June 2002): 58–60.
"Writing as an Act of Hope," *Paths of Resistance*, ed. William Zinsser. New York: Houghton Mifflin, 1989.
Zorro. New York: HarperCollins, 2005.
"Zorro— My Ultimate Hero," (London) *Times* (3 March 2008).

Secondary Sources

General

Acampora, Christa Davis, and Angela L. Cotten. *Unmaking Race, Remaking Soul: Transformative Aesthetics and the Practice of Freedom*. Albany: State University of New York Press, 2008.
Agósin, Marjorie. *Writing Toward Hope: The Literature of Human Rights in Latin America*. New Haven, CT: Yale University Press, 2007.
Anzaldúa, Gloria, and analouise keating, eds. *this bridge we call home: radical visions for transformation*. New York: Routledge, 2000.
Armstrong, Piers. "Reading the Ethnic Other: Representational Legitimacy and Shifting Genre Boundaries," *Textual Practice* 24:1 (2010): 69–91.
Arvide, Cynthia. "Author Isabel Allende Proves Strategic Funding Changes Lives for the Better," *Women News Network* (16 April 2012): 1–2.
Axelrod-Contrada, Joan. *Isabel Allende*. New York: Marshall Cavendish Benchmark, 2011.
Barbas-Rhoden, Laura. *Writing Women in Central America: Gender and the Fictionalization of History*. Athens: Ohio University Press, 2003.
Bird, Stephanie Rose. *Light, Bright, and Damned Near White: Biracial and Triracial Culture in America*. Westport, CT: Greenwood, 2009.
Blancpain, François. *La condition des paysans haïtiens: du Code noir aux codes ruraux*. Paris: Karthala, 2008.
Boland, Mel. *Displacement in Israel Allende's Fiction (1982–2000)* Dublin: University College, 2010.
Bollmann, Stefan. *Women Who Write*. London: Merrell, 2007.
Bortolussi, Marisa. "Implausible Worlds, Ingenuous Narrators, Ironic Authors: Towards a Revised Theory of Magic Realism," *Canadian Review of Comparative Literature* 27:2 (June 2000): 349–370.
Bowers, Maggie Ann. *Magic(al) Realism*. New York: Routledge, 2005.
Bridge, Gary, and Sophie Watson. *The Blackwell City Reader*. Malden, MA: Wiley, 2010.
Bronfen, Elisabeth, and Misha Kavka. *Feminist Consequences: Theory for the New Century*. New York: Columbia University Press, 2001.
Brown, Joan Lipman. *Confronting Our Canons: Spanish and Latin American Studies in the 21st Century*. Danvers, MA: Bucknell University Press, 2010.
Burns, John H. "Latin American Writers," *Feminist Collections* (1 January 2010).
Burstein, Julie. *How Creativity Works*. New York: Harper, 2011.
Caminero-Santangelo, Marta. *On Latinidad: U.S. Latino Literature and the Construction of Ethnicity*. Gainesville: University Press of Florida, 2007.
Carvalho, Susan E. *Contemporary Spanish American Novels by Women: Mapping the Narrative*. Rochester, NY: Tamesis, 2007.
Classe, Olive, ed. *Encyclopedia of Literary Translation into English*. Chicago: Fitzroy Dearborn, 2000.
Colby, Georgina. "Unfamiliar Crossings," *Contemporary Literature* 51 (20 June 2010): 438–448.
Cox, Karen Castellucci. *Isabel Allende, a Critical Companion*. Westport, CT: Greenwood, 2003.
Cávila, Arlene. *The Marketing and Making of a People*. Berkeley: University of California Press, 2001.
Cruz, Anne J., Rosilie Hernández-Pecoraro, and Joyce Tolliver, eds. *Disciplines on the Line: Feminist Research on Spanish, Latin American, and U.S. Latina Women*. Newark, DE: Juan de la Cuesta, 2003.
Dávila, Arlene. *Latinos Inc.: The Marketing and Making of a People*. Berkeley: University of California Press, 2001.
Day, Frances Ann. *Latina and Latino Voices in Literature: Lives and Works*. Westport, CT: Greenwood, 2003.
DeSalvo, Louise A. *Writing as a Way of Healing: How Telling Our Stories Transforms Our Lives*. Boston: Beacon Press, 2000.
Devlin-Glass, Francis, and Lyn McCudden. *Feminist Poetics of the Sacred: Creative Suspicions*. New York: Oxford University Press, 2001.
Donoso, José. "Interview: José Donoso: Revisiting Carlos Fuentes and the World of Latin American Literature," *Literature and Arts of the Americas* 80:43:1 (2010): 116–121.
Faris, Wendy B. *Ordinary Enchantments: Magical*

Realism and the Remystification of Narrative. Nashville, TN: Vanderbilt University Press, 2004.

_____. "The Question of the Other: Cultural Critiques of Magical Realism," *Janus Head* 5:2 (Fall 2002): 87–126.

Farr, Cecilia Konchar. *Reading Oprah: How Oprah's Book Club Changed the Way America Reads.* New York: SUNY, 2005.

Feal, Rosemary Geisdorfer, and Yvette E. Miller, eds. *Isabel Allende Today: Anthology of Essays.* Pittsburgh: Latin American Literary Review, 2002.

"Flash Backs: Looking Back on Literary History," *Book* (1 January 2003).

Fuchs, Miriam. *The Text Is Myself: Women's Life Writing and Catastrophe.* Madison: University of Wisconsin Press, 2004.

Gallagher, Susan VanZanten, ed. *Postcolonial Literature and the Biblical Call for Justice.* Jackson: University Press of Mississippi, 2007.

Giles, Paul. *Virtual Americas: Transnational Fictions and the Transatlantic Imaginary.* Durham, NC: Duke University Press, 2002.

Goldberg, Elizabeth Swanson. *Beyond Terror: Gender, Narrative, Human Rights.* New Brunswick, NJ: Rutgers University Press, 2007.

Gough, Elizabeth. "Vision and Division: Voyeurism in the Works of Isabel Allende," *Journal of Modern Literature* 27:4 (Summer 2004): 93–120.

Grover, Mark L. "Conversations with Isabel Allende," *Chasqui* (1 November 2005).

Hart, Stephen M., and Wen-chin Ouyang, eds. *A Companion to Magical Realism.* Woodbridge, U.K.: Tamesis, 2005.

Herrera, Adriana. "And God Made Me a Woman," *Americas* 61:6 (November/December 2009): 48–51.

Huggan, Graham. *The Post-Colonial Exotic: Marketing the Margins.* London: Routledge, 2001.

Jaggi, Maya. "The Guardian Profile: Isabel Allende, A View from the Bridge," *Guardian Unlimited* (5 February 2000).

Jorgensen, Beth E. "'Un Puñado de Criticos': Navigating the Critical Readings of Isabel Allende's Work," *Latin American Literary Review* 30:60 (July–December, 2002): 128–146.

King, John, ed. *The Cambridge Companion to Modern Latin American Culture.* New York: Cambridge University Press, 2004.

Klein, Kerwin Lee. "On the Emergence of Memory in Historical Discourse," *Grounds for Remembering* 69 (2000): 127–150.

Kling, Vincent. "Archetype, Not Ideology: Isabel Allende's Balance of Opposites," *Critical Insights* (October 2010): 239–257.

Kristal, Efraín, ed. *The Cambridge Companion to the Latin American Novel.* New York: Cambridge University Press, 2005.

Lambright, Anne, and Elisabeth Guerrero, eds. *Unfolding the City: Women Write the City in Latin America.* Minneapolis: University of Minnesota Press, 2007.

Langdon, Jo. "Magical Realism and Experience of Extremity," *Current Narratives* 3 (2011): 14–24.

Lavery, Jane Elizabeth. *Ángeles Mastretta: Textual Multiplicity.* Woodbridge, UK: Tamesis, 2005.

_____. "Locating Latin American Women Writers," *Modern Language Review* (1 January 2007).

Levine, Linda Gould. *Isabel Allende.* New York: Twayne, 2002.

_____. "Isabel Allende in Context: The Erasure of Boundaries," *Critical Insights* (October 2010): 220–238.

_____. "Weaving Life into Fiction," *Latin American Literary Review* 30:60 (July–December 2002): 1–25.

Lindsay, Claire. *Locating Latin American Women Writers: Cristina Peri Rossi, Rosario Ferré, Albalucía Angel, and Isabel Allende.* New York: Peter Lang, 2003.

Linning, Lyn. "Isabel Allende," *Magpies* 19:2 (1 May 2005): 20–21.

Luebering, J. E. *The Literature of Spain and Latin America.* New York: Rosen, 2010.

Mabe, Chauncey. "A Few Words with FIU Honoree Isabel Allende," (South Florida) *SunSentinel* (29 February 2012).

Macpherson, Heidi Slettedahl. *Women's Movement: Escape as Transgression in North American Feminist Fiction.* Amsterdam: Rodopi, 2000.

Main, Mary. *Isabel Allende: Award-Winning Latin American Author.* Berkeley Heights, NJ: Enslow, 2005.

Marting, Diane E. *The Sexual Woman in Latin American Literature: Dangerous Desires.* Gainesville: University Press of Florida, 2001.

Masiello, Francine. *The Art of Transition: Latin American Culture and Neoliberal Crisis.* Durham, NC: Duke University Press, 2001.

McCann, Janet. *Critical Survey of Long Fiction.* 4th ed. New York: Salem, 2010.

McKale, Margaret A. Morales. *Literary Nonfiction in Works by Isabel Allende and Guadalupe Loaeza.* Columbus: Ohio State University, 2002.

McNeese, Tim. *Isabel Allende.* New York: Chelsea House, 2006.

Metcalfe, Anna. "Small Talk," (London) *Financial Times Limited* (24 May 2010).

Meza, Laura E. "Mapuche Struggles for Land and the Role of Private Protected Areas in Chile," *Journal of Latin American Geography* 8:1 (2009): 149–163.

Milgram, Melanie. "Who Was That Masked Man," *Read* 55:4 (7 October 2005): 4–5.

Moore, Charles B. "Review: *Conversations with*

Isabel Allende," *South Atlantic Review* 68:4 (1 October 2003): 116–118.
Nelson, Alice A. *Political Bodies: Gender, History, and the Struggle for Narrative Power in Recent Chilean Literature.* Danvers, MA: Bucknell University Press, 2002.
Norat, Gisela. *Marginalities: Diamela Eltit and the Subversion of Mainstream Literature in Child.* Cranbury, NJ: University of Delaware Press, 2002.
Ocasio, Rafael. *Literature of Latin America.* Westport, CT: Greenwood, 2004.
Park, James. "Geopolitics and Historicism in Mapuche Poetry of Chile," *Latin American Indian Literatures Journal* 17:1 (Spring 2001): 1–19.
Payne, Judith A. "Latin American Women Dramatists: Theatre, Texts & Theories," *Canadian Journal of Latin American & Caribbean Studies* (1 January 2000).
Pearl, Nancy. *Now Read This II.* Westport, CT: Libraries Unlimited, 2002.
Perricone, C.R. "Allende and Valenzuela: Dissecting the Patriarchy," *South Atlantic Review* 67:4 (Fall, 2002): 80–105.
Pitman, Thea. "Introduction: Latin American Women's Writing, Then and Now," *Journal of Iberian and Latin American Studies* 14:2–3 (2008).
Poddar, Prem, Rajeef S. Patke, and Lars Jensen, eds. *A Historical Companion to Postcolonial Literatures: Continental Europe and Its Empire.* Edinburgh: Edinburgh University Press, 2008.
Postlewate, Marisa Herrera. *How and Why I Write: Redefining Hispanic Women's Writing and Experience.* New York: Peter Lang, 2004.
Ramblado-Minero, María de la Cinta. *Isabel Allende's Writing of the Self: Trespassing the Boundaries of Fiction and Autobiography.* Lewiston, NY: E. Mellen Press, 2003.
Riascos, Jaime. "Ancient and Indigenous Stories: Their Ethics and Power Reflected in Latin American Storytelling Movements," *Marvels & Tales* 21:2 (2007): 253–267.
Ries, Olga. "Latino Identity in Allende's Novels," *Comparative Literature and Culture* 13:4 (2011): 1–8.
Rodden, John. *Critical Insights: Isabel Allende.* Pasadena, CA: Salem, 2011.
_____. "Isabel Allende, Fortune's Daughter," *Critical Insights* (October 2010): 184–194.
_____. "Technicolored Life," *Society* 42:3 (March/April 2005): 62–65.
Rodriguez, Franklin. "Unsettledness and Doublings in Robert Bolaño's *Estrella distante,"* *Revista Hispánica Moderna* 63:2 (December 2010): 203–218.
Roof, María, "Maryse Condé and Isabel Allende: Family Saga Novels," *Critical Insights* (October 2010): 74–85.
Rosendo González, Pablo. "Isabel Allende: Secretos de Mujer," *3 Puntos 4* 4:203 (17 May 2001): 61–70.
Rub, Martha Lorena. *Politically Writing Women in Hispanic Literature.* Bloomington, IN: Xlibris, 2011.
Rubenstein, Roberta. *Home Matters: Longing and Belonging, Nostalgia and Mourning in Women's Fiction.* New York: Palgrave, 2001.
Rudge, Ian. "Magical Realism in Children's Literature: A Narratological Reading," *New Review of Children's Literature & Librarianship,* 10:2 (2004): 127–140.
Schmidt, Siegfried J. "Making Stories About Story-Making, or Why We Need His- and Herstories: An Approach Towards a Constructivist Historiography," *Poetics* 28: 5/6 (2001): 455–462.
Schwalm, Tanja. "'Relax and Enjoy the Show': Circensian Animal Spaces in Australian and Latin American Magical Realist Fiction," *Journal of Commonwealth Literature* 41:3 (2006): 83–102.
Serrano, Nancy, and Barrie Wharton, eds. *Crossing Boundaries: Spanish Across Cultures.* Limerick, Ireland: Limerick University Press, 2000.
Shaw, Donald Leslie. *A Companion to Modern Spanish-American Fiction.* Rochester, NY: Tamesis, 2002.
Simon, Sherry, and Paul St.-Pierre. *Changing the Terms: Translating in the Postcolonial Era.* Ottawa: University of Ottawa Press, 2000.
Sinclair, Frances. *Fantasy Fiction.* Wanborough, UK: School Library Association, 2008.
Smith, Bonnie G. *The Oxford Encyclopedia of Women in World History.* Oxford, UK: Oxford University Press, 2008.
Smith, Verity. *Concise Encyclopedia of Latin American Literature.* New York: Taylor & Francis, 2000.
Snodgrass, Mary Ellen. *Encyclopedia of Gothic Literature.* New York: Facts on File, 2005.
Solé, Carlos, ed. *Latin American Writers.* New York: Charles Scribner's Sons, 2002.
Sollars, Michael D. *The Facts on File Companion to the World Novel, 1900 to the Present.* New York: Facts on File, 2008.
Stack, Michael B. *Toussaint of Haiti.* Victoria, Canada: Trafford, 2003.
Swanson, Philip. *Latin American Fiction: A Short Introduction.* Oxford: Blackwell, 2005.
Tafolla, Carmen, and Martha P. Cotera. *Great Lives from History: Latinos.* Hackensack, NJ: Salem, 2012.
Tagore, Proma. *The Shapes of Silence: Writing by Women of Colour and the Politics of Testimony.* Montreal: McGill-Queen's University Press, 2009.
Taylor, Claire. "Latin American Feminist Criti-

cism Revisited: Helena Araújo's *La Scherezada criolla*," *Journal of Iberian and Latin American Studies* 14:2–3 (2008): 93–100.

Teisch, Jessica. "Isabel Allende: Book by Book," *Bookmarks* (1 November 2007).

Tseëlon, Efrat, ed. *Masquerade and Identities: Essays on Gender, Sexuality, and Marginality*. New York: Taylor & Francis, 2001.

Valdés, Mario J., and Djelal Kadir, eds. *Literary Cultures of Latin America: A Comparative History*. New York: Oxford University Press, 2004.

Vallejos, Alice Ruth Reckley. "Wild Violets: Agency in Latin American Women's Narrative," *Chasqui* 40:1 (May 2011): 195–199.

Varona-Lacey, Gladys M. *Contemporary Latin-American Literature*. Chicago: McGraw Hill, 2001.

Viljoen, Hendrik Marthinus. *Storyscapes: South African Perspectives on Literature, Space, and Identity*. New York: Lang, 2004.

Waldron, Linda. *Isabel Allende: Literary Inheritance and the Establishment of a New Dimension in Chilean Female Fiction*. St. Augustine, Trinidad and Tobago: University of West Indies, 2003.

Walter, Roland. *Narrative Identities: (Inter)cultural In-Betweenness in the Americas*. Bern: Peter Lang, 2003.

Wasserman, Renata Ruth Mautner. *Central at the Margin: Five Brazilian Women Writers*. Cranbury, NJ: Bucknell University Press, 2007.

Weldt-Basson, Helene Carol. *Subversive Silences: Nonverbal Expression and Implicit Narrative Strategies in the Works of Latin American Women Writers*. Cranbury, NJ: Associated University Presses, 2009.

Wellington, Ann M. *Flannery O'Connor and Isabel Allende: A Meeting of the Americas*. Lincoln: University of Nebraska Press, 2003.

Williams, Raymond L. *The Columbia Guide to the Latin American Novel Since 1945*. New York: Columbia University Press, 2007.

_____. *A Companion to Gabriel García Márquez*. Rochester, NY: Tamesis, 2010.

_____. *The Twentieth-Century Spanish American Novel*. Austin: University of Texas Press, 2003.

Wilson, R. Rawdon. *The Hydra's Tale: Imagining Disgust*. Edmonton: University of Alberta Press, 2002.

Wirshing, Irene. *National Trauma in Postdictatorship Latin American Literature: Chile and Argentina*. New York: Peter Lang, 2009.

Wood, Jamie Martinez. *Latino Writers and Journalists*. New York: Facts on File, 2007.

Young, Richard A., and Odile Cisneros. *Historical Dictionary of Latin American Literature and Theater*. Lanham, MD: Scarecrow, 2011.

Biography

"Author Isabel Allende Says Chile Should Clear Up Mystery of Salvador Allende's Death," *Canadian Press* (8 June 2011).

Ball, Heather. *Women Writers Who Changed the World*. New York: Rosen, 2011.

Barkan, Elazar, and Alexander Karn. *Taking Wrongs Seriously: Apologies and Reconciliation*. Stanford, CA: Stanford University Press, 2002.

Barkan, Elliott Robert. *Making It in America: A Sourcebook on Eminent Ethnic Americans*. Santa Barbara, CA: ABC-Clio, 2001.

Beaubien, Jason. "Chile's Edge over Haiti When It Comes to Quakes," (NPR) *Morning Edition* (8 March 2010).

Benatar, Raquel. *Isabel Allende: Memories for a Story*. Houston, TX: Piñata, 2004.

Bloom, Harold, ed. *Isabel Allende*. Philadelphia: Chelsea House, 2002.

Booker, M. Keith. *Encyclopedia of Literature and Politics*. Westport, CT: Greenwood, 2005.

Boss, Pauline. *Loss, Trauma, and Resilience: Therapeutic Work with Ambiguous Loss*. New York: W.W. Norton, 2006.

Correas de Zapata, Celia. *Isabel Allende: Life and Spirits*. Houston, TX: Arte Público, 2002.

Cruz, Barbara. *Triumphs and Struggles for Latino Civil Rights*. New York: Enslow, 2008.

Deiner, Paige Lauren. "Author Allende Speaks at Utpa," (McAllen, Texas) *Monitor* (25 April 2006).

Dempsey, Beth. "One Great Idea," *Library Journal* 134:14 (1 September 2009): 19–22.

Diebel, Linda. "Politics and Sex Both on the Lunch Menu for Isabel Allende," *Toronto Star* (23 October 2007): L1.

Elsworth, Catherine. "Isabel Allende: Kith and Tell," (London) *Telegraph* (21 March 2008).

Gebara, Ivone. *Out of the Depths: Women's Experience of Evil and Salvation*. Minneapolis, MN: Augsburg Fortress, 2002.

Geracimos, Ann. "Novel Views of Isabel Allende," *Washington Times* (19 January 2002).

Gilmore, Sue. "Isabel Allende Carries Her Torch to Set "Feminine Energy" Ablaze," *Oakland Tribune* (25 February 2009).

González, Gustavo. "Environment-Chile: Isabel Allende Backs Cause of Native Forests," *Global Information Network* (26 July 2002).

Gray, Herman, and Macarena Gómez-Barris. *Toward a Sociology of the Trace*. Minneapolis: University of Minnesota Press, 2010.

"The Guardian Profile: Isabel Allende, A View from the Bridge," (Manchester) *Guardian* (5 February 2000).

Hawley, Janet. "A Woman of Spirit," *The* (Melbourne) *Age* (15 March 2008).

"Isabel Allende," *Granta* 100 (1 December 2007): 208–209.
"Isabel Allende Named to Council of Cervantes Institute," *Latin American Herald Tribune* (23 October 2009).
"Isabel Allende on Hallucinogens," *Meanjin* 67:3 (2008): 10–11.
Knight, Heather. "Spinning Stories," *San Francisco Chronicle* (19 October 2001): 1.
Lamolinara, Guy. "San Antonio ALA," ALA Bulletin (19 February 1996).
Lannom, Gloria W. "Voices of Chile: Gabriela Mistral and Isabel Allende," *Faces* 19:4 (December 2002): 44–45.
Larrain, Jorge. "Changes in Chilean Identity: Thirty Years After the Military Coup," *Nations and Nationalism* 12:2 (April 2006): 321–338.
Levine, Linda Gould. *Isabel Allende.* New York: Twayne, 2002.
Lugo-Ludo, Carmen R. "'So You Are a Mestiza': Exploring the Consequences of Ethnic and Racial Clumping in the U.S. Academy," *Ethnic and Racial Studies* 31:3 (2008): 611–628.
McNally, Frank. "An Irishman's Diary," *Irish Times* (8 January 2010).
McNeil, Harold. "Allende Urges Audience to Seek Life of Joy," *Buffalo News* (18 April 2009).
Montagu, Ashley. *Touching.* New York: HarperCollins, 1971.
Mooney, Jadwiga E. Pieper. "Forging Feminisms Under Dictatorship: Women's International Ties and National Feminist Empowerment in Child, 1973–1990," *Women's History* 19:4 (2010).
Moran, Maria-Belen. "Isabel Allende," *AP Online* (27 September 2000).
Nagy-Zekmi, Silvia, and Fernando Ignacio Leiva. *Democracy in Chile: The Legacy of September 11, 1973.* Portland, OR: Sussex Academic Press, 2005.
Nava, Yolanda. *It's All in the Frijioles.* New York: Simon & Schuster, 2012.
Nogales, Ana, and Laura Golden Bellotti. *Latina Power!* New York: Simon & Schuster, 2003.
Ojito, Mirta. "A Writer's Heartbeats Answer Two Calls," *The New York Times* (28 July 2003): 1.
Power, Margaret. *Right-Wing Women in Chile: Feminine Power and the Struggle Against Allende.* University Park, PA: Penn State University Press, 2002.
Rodden, John, ed. *Isabel Allende.* New York: Salem Press, 2011.
Saenz, Rogelio, and Aurelia Lorena Murga. *Latino Issues: A Reference Handbook.* Santa Barbara, CA: ABC-Clio, 2011.
Savio, Anita. "A Teller of Tales: Isabel Allende," *Latino Leaders* (1 October 2002).
Sohrabji, Sunita. "Writer Allende, Global Fund's Ramdas Discuss Militarism," *India-West* (28 January 2011): A21.
Taylor, Tracey. "Nurturing Her Family and Her Tribe," *The New York Times* (11 April 2010: 25A.
Thomason, Elizabeth. *Nonfiction Classics for Students.* Detroit: Gale, 2001.
Timpane, John. "Isabel Allende's Heroines Are, Like Their Feminist Creator, Strong and Independent," *Philadelphia Inquirer* (5 May 2010).
Tompkins, Cynthia Margarita, and David William Foster, eds. *Notable Twentieth-Century Latin American Women.* Westport, CT: Greenwood, 2001.
Warren, Michael. "Chile's 2 Isabel Allendes, Author and Senator, Join President in Supporting Trapped Miners," *Canadian Press* (19 September 2010).
"A Writer's Magical Muse: Isabel Allende Mines Her Memory for the Crystals of a Greater Truth," *Washington Post* (24 November 2001).

Interviews

Berson, Misha. "This Old 'House' Opened a Lot of Doors for Isabel Allende," *The* (Washington) *Times* (1 June 2007).
Block, Melissa. "Allende Reimagines Life of Conquistador 'Inés,'" *All Things Considered* (NPR) (6 November 2006).
Cruz-Lugo, Victor. "The Love That Binds," *Hispanic* 21:4 (April 2008): 54–56.
Donegan, Lawrence. "This Much I Know," (Manchester) *Guardian* (12 July 2008).
Edemariam, Aida. "The Undefeated," (Manchester) *Guardian* (27 April 2007).
"Everything Is Possible," *Writing* 29:2 (October 2006): 8–10.
Fish, Peter. "Isabel Allende," *Sunset* 217:5 (November 2006): 182.
Flores, Camille. "The Power to Transform," (Santa Fe) *New Mexican* (12 April 2002).
Goodman, Amy. "Chilean Author Isabel Allende on Her New Novel 'Island Beneath the Sea,'" *Democracy Now* (3 May 2010).
Hannau, Lucia. "'Telling Stories Is the Only Thing I Want to Do,'" *Latin American Herald Tribune* (23 December 2011).
"Isabel Allende on Her Magical Adventures," *School Library Journal* (December 2002): 58.
Neary, Lynn. "In Memoir, Allende Reveals Life to Late Daughter," *Weekend Edition (NPR)* (13 April 2008).
Ojito, Mirta. "A Writer's Heartbeats Answer Two Calls," *The New York Times* (28 July 2003) .
Queirós, Carlos J. "Leading Lady," *AARP* 50:1C (January/February 2007): 12.
Quistgaard, Kaitlin. "Isabel Allende," *Salon* (5 March 2001).
Richards, Jonathan. "Summing Our Mysterious Days," (Santa Fe) *New Mexican* (19 September 2008): PA-22.

Rochman, Hazel. "The Booklist Interview," *Booklist* 99:6 (15 November 2002): 591.
Rodden, John, ed. *Conversations with Isabel Allende.* 2nd ed. Austin: University of Texas Press, 2004.

Aphrodite, a Memoir of the Senses

Anderson, Ross. "Erotic Culinary Activities," (London) *Times* (13 September 2005).
Bach, Lisa. *Her Fork in the Road: Women Celebrate Food and Travel.* San Francisco, CA: Travelers' Tales, 2001.
Breathnach, Sarah Ban. *Moving On: Creating Your House of Belonging with Simple Abundance.* Des Moines, IA: Meredith, 2006.
Deiner, Paige Lauren. "Reading in the Kitchen," (McAllen, Texas) *Monitor* (17 May 2006).
Dennis, Abigail. "From Apicius to Gastroporn: Form, Function, and Ideology in the History of Cookery Books," *Studies in Popular Culture* 31:1 (Fall 2008): 1–18.
Diebel, Linda. "Politics and Sex Both on the Lunch Menu for Isabel Allende," *Toronto Star* (23 October 2007).
"Eat This Book: Devouring the Literature of Food," *Cincinnati Magazine* 40:2 (November 2006): 294.
Fallis, Catherine. *Erotic Foods: Grape Goddess Guides to Good Living.* Lincoln, NE: iUniverse, 2004.
Méndez-Montoya, Angel F. *Theology of Food: Eating and the Eucharist.* Malden, MA: John Wiley, 2012.
Pérez González, Beatriz. "Filtering the Desire: The Effects of Time and Space," *Nómadas* 26:2 (2010).
Scott, Renée Sum. *What Is Eating Latin American Women Writers: Food, Weight, and Eating Disorders.* Amherst, NY: Cambria, 2009.
Waxman, Barbara Frey. "Food Memoirs: What They Are, Why They Are Popular, and Why They Belong in the Literature Classroom," *College English* 70:4 (March 2008): 363–383.
Zubiaurre, Maite. "Culinary Eros in Contemporary Hispanic Female Fiction: From Kitchen Tales to Table Narratives," *College Literature* 33:3 (Summer 2006): 29–51.

City of the Beasts

Acle-Menendez, Ana. "On the Shelves," *Hispanic* 16:1/2 (January/February 2003).
"Allende Is All Sbout Storytelling," *Toronto Star* (23 October 2002).
Austin, Patricia. "Review: *City of the Beasts*," *Booklist* 99:14 (15 March 2003): 1340.
Baker, Deirdre F. "Musings on Diverse Worlds," *Horn Book* 83:1 (January/February 2007): 41–47.
Beckett, Sandra L. *Crossover Fiction: Global and Historical Perspectives.* New York: Routledge, 2009.
Birch, Carol. "Review: *City of the Beasts*," (Manchester) *Guardian* (30 November 2002): 33.
Bradford, C. *Unsettling Narratives: Postcolonial Readings of Children's Literature.* Wilfred Laurier University, CA: Wilfred Laurier University Press, 2007.
Campbell, Patty. "Drowning in Success," *Horn Book* 82:1 (January/February 2006): 61–65.
"La ciudad de las bestias, by Isabel Allende," *Hispanic Outlook in Higher Education* (8 March 2004).
"Everything Is Possible," *Writing* 29:2 (October 2006): 8–11.
Fenn, Jane P. "Review: *City of the Beasts*," *School Library Journal* (February 2003): 77.
Fichtelberg, Susan. *Encountering Enchantment: A Guide to Speculative Fiction for Teens.* Westport, CT: Libraries Unlimited, 2007.
Haase, Donald. *The Greenwood Encyclopedia of Folktales and Fairy Tales.* Westport, CT: Greenwood, 2008.
Hammer, Yvonne. "Conflicting Ideologies in Three Magical Realist Children's Novels by Isabel Allende," *Papers: Explorations into Children Literature* (2009): 41–47.
Hannold, RoseMary. *The Teen Reader's Advisor.* New York: Neal-Schuman, 2006.
Heppermann, Christine M. "Review: *City of the Beasts*," *Horn Book* 79:1 (January-February, 2003): 65.
Houtchens, Bobbi Ciriza. "English in the News," *English Journal* 92:4 (March 2003): 84.
Keenan, John. "Novelist Allende Playful with Book for Young Adults," *Omaha World-Herald* (24 November 2002): 8.
Knight, Heather. "Review: *City of the Beasts*," *San Francisco Chronicle* (19 October 2001): 1.
Krug, Nora. "Review: *City of the Beasts*," *The New York Times* (9 February 2003): 21.
Latham, Don. "The Cultural Work of Magical Realism in Three Young Adult Novels," *Children's Literature in Education* 38:1 (2007): 59–70.
Miller, Lia. "Walden Acquires Film Rights to a Trilogy by Isabel Allende," *The New York Times* (16 January 2006).
Misani. "Go Get a Book in Your Hand," *New York Amsterdam News* 100:42 (15 October 2009): 18.
"A New Realm for Isabel Allende: Juvenile Trilogy Under Way," *Hispanic Outlook in Higher Education* (20 October 2003).
"Now!—Picks," *Teen People* 5:9 (November 2002): 80.
Ott, Bill. "Books Are Back at BookExpo America in New York," *American Libraries* 33:7 (1 August 2002): 40.

Renner, Coop. Review: *City of the Beasts,*" *School Library Journal* 51:7 (July 2005).
"Review: *City of the Beasts,*" *Chicago Tribune* (21 October 2002).
"Review: *City of the Beasts,*" *Kirkus Reviews* 70:19 (1 October 2002): 1462.
"Review: *City of the Beasts,*" *Publishers Weekly* (30 June 2003).
Reynolds, Angela J. "Review: *City of the Beasts,*" *School Library Journal* 48:11 (November 2002).
Roback, Diane. "Review: *City of the Beasts,*" *Publishers Weekly* 249:25 (24 June 2002): 58.
Rochman, Hazel. "Review: City of the Beasts," *Booklist* 99:6 (15 November 2002): 592.
Stableford, Brian. *The A to Z of Fantasy Literature.* Lanham, MD: Scarecrow, 2005.
Swanson, Philip. "Latin Lessons for Young Americans: Isabel Allende's Fiction for Children," *Revista de Estudios Hispanicos* 41:2 (May 2007): 173–189.
Weisman, Kay. "Review: *City of the Beasts,*" *Booklinks* 13:6 (July 2004): 40.

Daughter of Fortune

André, María Claudia "Breaking Through the Maze: Feminist Configurations of the Heroic Quest in Isabel Allende's *Daughter of Fortune* and *Portrait in Sepia,*" *Latin American Literary Review* 30:60 (2002): 74–90.
Badger, Robert L. *Ideas That Work in College Teaching.* Albany: State University of New York Press, 2008.
Bauers, Sandy. "Blair Brown's Narration Is Isabel Allende's Good 'Fortune,'" *Philadelphia Inquirer* (19 January 2000).
Boland, Mel. "'Orienting' the Text: Eastern Influences in the Fiction of Isabel Allende" in *Cross-Cultural Travel*, ed. Jane Conroy. New York: Peter Lang, 2003.
Campbell, Neil, Jude Davies, and George McKay, eds. *Issues in Americanization and Culture.* Edinburgh: Edinburgh University Press, 2004.
Carvalho, Susan. "Transgressions of Space and Gender in Allende's *Hija de la fortuna,*" *Letras Femeninas* 27:2 (Fall 2001): 24–41.
Dickson, E. Jane. "Word of Mouth," (London) *Times* (3 February 2001): 13.
Dyck, Reginald, and Cheli Ruetter. *Crisscrossing Borders in Literature of the American West.* New York: Palgrave Macmillan, 2009.
Farr, Cecilia Konchar, and Jaime Harker, eds. *The Oprah Effect: Critical Essays on Oprah's Book Club.* Albany: State University of New York Press, 2008.
Gelman, Judy, and Vicki Levy Krupp. *The Book Club Cook Book.* New York: Penguin, 2012.
Hoffert, Barbara. "Review: *Daughter of Fortune,*" *Library Journal* (15 October 2001): 105.
Kushigian, Julia Alexis. *Reconstructing Childhood: Strategies of Reading for Culture and Gender in the Spanish American Bildungsroman.* Danvers, MA: Bucknell University Press, 2003.
Lopez, Ruth. "Left on a Genteel Doorstep," *New York Times* (24 October 1999).
López-Calvo, Ignacio. *Alternative Orientalisms in Latin America and Beyond.* Newcastle, UK: Cambridge Scholars, 2007.
Macpherson, Heidi Slettedahl. *Transatlantic Women's Literature.* Edinburgh: Edinburgh University Press, 2008.
Martin, Karen. "Mapping Ethnicity in Isabel Allende's *Daughter of Fortune* and *Portrait in Sepia,*" *Grafemas* (December 2007): 1–8.
Maryles, Daisy, and Dick Donahue. "Fortunate Daughter," *Publishers Weekly* (21 February 2000): 20.
McClennen, Sophia A. "Isabel Allende: *Daughter of Fortune,*" *Comparative American Studies* 3:4 (December 2005): 184–185.
_____. "Review: *Daughter of Fortune,*" *Review of Contemporary Fiction* (Summer 2000): 184.
Meacham, Cherie. "Resisting Romance: Isabel Allende's Transformation of the Popular Romance Formula in *Hija de la Fortuna,*" *Latin American Literary Review* 35:69 (January–June 2007): 29–45.
Milanich, Nara B. *Children of Fate: Childhood, Class, and the State in Chile, 1850–1930.* Durham, NC: Duke University Press, 2009.
Pollack, Sarah. "Latin America Translated (Again): Robert Bolaño's *The Savage Detectives* in the United States," *Comparative Literature* 61:3 (2009): 346–365.
Pratt, Mary Louise. *Imperial Eyes: Travel Writing and Transculturation.* New York: Routledge, 2000.
Radulescu, Domnica. *Sisters of Medea: The Tragic Heroine Across Cultures.* New Orleans: University Press of the South, 2002.
"Review: *Daughter of Fortune,*" (London) *Times* (10 September 2005).
Rivero, Eliana. "Of Trilogies and Genealogies: *Daughter of Fortune* and *Portrait in Sepia,*" *Latin American Literary Review* 30:60 (2002): 91–111.
Rodden, John. "*Isabel Allende, Fortune's Daughter,*" *Hopscotch* 2:4 (2001): 32–39.
Stolley, Kathy Shepherd. *The Praeger Handbook of Adoption.* Westport, CT: Praeger, 2006.
Swanson, Philip. "California Dreaming: Mixture, Muddle, and Meaning in Isabel Allende's North American Narratives," *Journal of Iberian and Latin American Studies* 9:1 (2003): 57–68.
Tatsumi, Takayuki. "Literary History on the Road: Transatlantic crossings and Transpacific Crossovers," *PMLA* 119:1 (2004): 94.
Thornton, Bruce S. *Searching for Joaquin: Myth,*

Murieta, and History in California. San Francisco, CA: Encounter Books, 2003.

Eva Luna

Buedel, Barbara Foley. "Magical Places in Isabel Allende's Eva Luna and Cuentos de Eva Luna," *West Virginia University Philological Papers* (22 September 2006).

Cruz, Anne J. *Approaches to Teaching Lazarillo de Tormes and the Picaresque Tradition.* New York: Modern Language Association of America, 2008.

Gregory, Stephen. "Scheherazade and Eva Luna: Problems in Isabel Allende's Storytelling," *Bulletin of Spanish Studies* 80:1 (January 2003): 81–101.

Hart, Stephen M. *Isabel Allende, "Eva Luna" and "Cuentos de Eva Luna."* London: Grand & Cutler, 2003.

Lutes, Leasa Y. "Allende, Buitrago, Luiselli" in *Currents in Comparative Romance Languages and Literatures.* New York: Lang, 2000.

Reisman, Rosemary M. Canfield. "Eva Luna" in *Masterplots II: American Fiction Series.* Hackensack, NJ: Salem Press, 2000.

Sollars, Michael D. *The Facts on File Companion to the World Novel, 1900 to the Present.* New York: Facts on File, 2008.

Forest of the Pygmies

Carlile, Susan. "Y en Español: *Forest of the Pygmies,*" *Journal of Adolescent & Adult Literacy* 49:4 (1 December 2004): 357.

Cruze, Karen. "Audio for Youth," *Booklist* (15 October 2005): 87.

Hanke, Diana H. "Review: *Forest of the Pygmies,*" *Library Media Connection* 24:4 (1 January 2006): 69.

Harmanci, Reyhan. "Review: Forest of the Pygmies," *San Francisco Chronicle* (29 May 2005): E3.

Hunt, Janet. "Review: *Forest of the Pygmies,*" *New Zealand Herald* (7 May 2005).

Linning, Lyn. "Review: *Forest of the Pygmies,*" *Magpies* 20:2 (May 2005): 40.

MacCann, Donnarae. "White Supremacy in Isabel Allende's Forest of the Pygmies," *Journal of African Children's and Youth Literature* 17–18 (2007): 60–75.

Maddy, Yulisa Amadu, and Donnarae MacCann. *Neo-Imperialism in Children's Literature About Africa: A Study of Contemporary Fiction.* New York: Routledge, 2009.

Mitnick, Eva. "Review: *Forest of the Pygmies,*" *School Library Journal* (June, 2005): 147.

Moore, Claudia. "Review: *Forest of the Pygmies,*" *School Library Journal* 51:11 (November 2005): 87.

Nazareth, Peter. *Critical Essays on Ng-ug-i wa Thiong'o.* New York: Twayne, 2000.

Renner, Coop. "Focus On: Hispanic Heritage," *School Library Journal* 51:7 (July 2005): 44.

"Review: *Forest of the Pygmies,*" *Kirkus Reviews* (15 April 2005): 467.

Rochman, Hazel. "Review: *Forest of the Pygmies,*" *Booklist* 101:14 (15 March, 2005): 1284.

Rohrlick, Paula. "Review: *Forest of the Pygmies,*" *Kliatt* (May 2005): 6.

Schroeder, Shannin. *Rediscovering Magical Realism in the Americas.* Westport, CT: Praeger, 2004.

Ward, Elizabeth. "Review: *Forest of the Pygmies,*" *Washington Post Book World* (24 July 2005): 11.

Zachary, Nancy. "Review: *Forest of the Pygmies,*" *VOYA* 28:2 (June 2005): 141.

The House of the Spirits

Abao, Frances Jane P. "The Power of Love: Rewriting the Romance in Isabel Allende's *The House of the Spirits* and *Eva Luna,*" *Humanities Diliman* 1:2 (July-January 2000): 87–99.

Adcock, Joe. "It's Version of 'House of the Spirits' Offers Insights into Chile's Own 9/11," *Seattle Post Intelligencer* (7 June 2007).

Aparicio, Alfredo. "'The House of the Spirits": A Multi-Layered Saga," *Florida International University Student Media* (31 October 2011).

Bennett, Caroline. "The Other and the Other-Worldly: The Function of Magic in Isabel Allende's *La casa de los espiritus*" in *Isabel Allende.* Philadelphia: Chelsea House, 2003.

Berson, Misha. "This Old 'House' Opened a Lot of Doors for Author Allende," *Seattle Times* (1 June 2007): H44.

Bowman, Andrea Michelle. *Mirror, Mirror?: Vision of the Man in Isabel Allende's La Casa de Los Espiritus.* Charlottesville: University of Virginia, 2004.

Canivell, Maria Odette. "Of Labyrinths in Isabel Allende's *The House of the Spirits,*" *The Labyrinth,* ed. Blake Hobby. New York: Infobase, 2009.

Cooper, Sara E. "Family Systems and National Subversion in Isabel Allende's *The House of the Spirits,*" *Interdisciplinary Literary Studies* 11:1 (Spring 2009): 16–37.

Cruz, Anne J., Rosilie Hernández-Pecoraro, and Joyce Tolliver, eds. *Disciplines on the Line: Feminist Research on Spanish, Latin American, and U.S. Latina Women.* Newark, DE: Juan de la Cuesta, 2003.

Davies, Lloyd. *Allende: La casa de los espíritus.* London: Grant & Cutler, 2000.

Evans, Everett. "House of the Spirits Finds a Home at MST," *Houston Chronicle* (11 September 2009).

Faris, Wendy B. *Ordinary Enchantments: Magical Realism and the Remystification of Narrative.* Nashville, TN: Vanderbilt University Press, 2004.

Frame, Scott Macdonald. "The Literal and the

Literary: A Note on the Historical References in Isabel Allende's *La casa de los espíritus,*" *Studies in Twentieth Century Literature* 27:2 (Summer 2003): 279–289.

Frick, Susan R. "Memory and Retelling: The Role of Women in *La casa de los espíritus,*" *Journal of Iberian and Latin American Studies* 7:1 (June 2001): 27–41.

Garrett, Mary, Heidi Gottfried, and Sandra F. Vanburkleo. *Re-Mapping the Humanities.* Detroit: Wayne State University Press, 2008.

Gates, Anita. "A Tumultuous and Supernatural Family Saga," *New York Times* (9 March 2009).

Gibb, Jennifer. "Victory of the Ash Buttocks: The Role of Hybridity in Colonization, Decolonization, and Postcolonization," *Journal of the Utah Academy of Sciences, Arts & Letters* 87 (2010): 235–243.

Helsper, Norma. "Binding the Wounds of the Body Politic: Nation as Family in *La casa de los espíritus,*" *Critical Approach to Isabel Allende's Novels.*

Hitchens, Christopher. *Arguably.* New York: Hachette, 2011.

Honeycutt, Britt Elizabeth *An Annotated Bibliography of Four Novels by Isabel Allende, 1982–2007: The House of the Spirits, Of Love and Shadow, Eva Luna,* and *The Stories of Eva Luna.* Wilmington: University of North Carolina Press, 2009.

Kelton, Peter. "When Isabel Allende Speaks, Albuquerque Readers Savor the Writer's Humor" *Albuquerque Examiner* (30 October 2009).

Lengel, Kerry. "Playwright Tackles Big 'Spirits' in Own Way at ASU," *Arizona Republic* (31 March 2012).

MacAtir, Patrick. "The House of the Spirits," *Tribune Magazine* (18 March 1994): 9.

MacGwire, Scarlett. "A Spiritual Politics," *Tribune Magazine* (30 August 1985): 23.

Maik, Nwosu. "'Barrabás came to us by sea': Absence and Presence in Isabel Allende's The House of the Spirits," *Transnational Literature* 1:2 (May 2009).

Martin, Karen Wooley. *Isabel Allende's House of the Spirits Trilogy: Narrative Geographies.* Rochester, NY: Tamesis, 2010.

Meacham, Cherie. "The Metaphysics of Mother-Daughter Renewal in *La Casa de los espíritus* and *Paula,*" *Hispanófila* 131 (2001): 93–108.

Molton, Mary Dian, and Lucy Anne Sikes. *Four Eternal Women: Toni Wolff Revisited — A Study in Opposites.* Carmel, CA: Fisher King, 2011.

Monteón, Michael. *Latin America and the Origins of Its Twenty-First Century.* Santa Barbara, CA: ABC-Clio, 2010.

Moore, John. "A 'House' of Horror and Wonder," *Denver Post* (24 September 2010).

Pearlman, Cindy. "Casting Catcalls: Hit or Miss," *Chicago Sun-Times* (8 April 2001).

Pela, Robert L. "*The House of the Spirits*: No Apologies Needed," *Phoenix New Times* (12 April 2012).

Preston, Rohan. "Tapping a Vein of Grace and Pain," (Minneapolis) *Star Tribune* (21 October 2010).

Punter, Alfred. *A New Companion to the Gothic.* Malden, MA: Wiley, 2012.

Rennison, Nick. *100 Must-Read Life-Changing Books.* London: Bloomsbury, 2008.

Rohter, Larry. "Staging Latin American Magical Realism, Complete with Songs," *New York Times* (17 February 2009): 1.

Rolston, Bill. "Hasta la Victoria!: Murals and Resistance in Santiago, Chile," *Identities* 18:2 (2011): 113–137.

Rosendo González, Pablo. "Isabel Allende: secretos de mujer," *3 Puntos* 4:203 (17 May 2001): 61–70.

Sánchez, María Ruth Noriega. *Challenging Realities: Magic Realism in Contemporary American Women's Fiction.* Valencia, Spain: University of Valencia, 2002.

Serrano, Cristina Ruiz. "Patriarchal Paradigms in Magical Realism: Feminine Otherness and Magical Feminism in "La casa de los espíritus" by Isabel Allende and "Los recuerdos del Porvenir" by Elena Garro," *Bulletin of Spanish Studies* 88:6 (September 2011): 863–885.

Sheffield, Carrie. "Voices from the Political Abyss: Isabel Allende's *The House of the Spirits* and the Reconstruction and preservation of History and Memory in 1970s Chile and Beyond," *Proteus* 19:2 (Fall 2002): 33–38.

Shifflet, Amy V. *Beyond Magical Realism: Magical Ideology as Political Resistance in Leslie Marmon Silko's Ceremony and Isabel Allende's The House of the Spirits.* Radford, VA: Radford University, 2000.

Svich, Caridad. "The House of the Spirits, a New Play," *TheatreForum* 36 (Winter/ Spring 2010): 76–104.

_____. "Re/Constructed Acts: Capturing the Spirit of a Novel," *TheatreForum* 36 (Winter/Spring 2010): 73–75.

Thomas, Gwynn. *Contesting Legitimacy in Chile: Familial Ideals, Citizenshp, and Political Struggle, 1970–1990.* University Park: Pennsylvania State University Press, 2011.

Wilkinson, Marta L. *Antigone's Daughters: Gender, Family, and Expression in the Modern Novel.* New York: Peter Lang, 2008.

Wright, Emma. "Subversive Size," *Tribune Magazine* (14 May 1993): 9.

Inés of My Soul

André, María Claudia, and Eva Paulino Bueno.

Latin American Women Writers: An Encyclopedia. New York: Routledge, 2008.

Austerlitz, Saul. "Chile's Colonial History Given Life," *San Francisco Chronicle* (7 November 2006).

"Author Allende Finds Kindred Spirit with 'Ines,'" *Oakland Tribune* (25 November 2006).

Bleiberg, Larry. "Review: *Inés of My Soul,*" *Dallas Morning News* (24 April 2007).

Block, Melissa. "Allende Reimagines Life of Conquistador 'Inés,'" *All Things Considered* (NPR) (6 November 2006).

Burstein, Julie, and Kurt Andersen. *Spark: How Creativity Works.* New York: HarperCollins, 2011.

Edgell, Zell. "Chile con Mujeres," *Ms.*, 17:1 (Winter 2007): 75–76.

Ellwood, Carlene. "Allende Loses Her Magic," (Hobart) *Sunday Tasmanian* (17 December 2006).

Ewan, John. "Tragic, Bloodstained Trek Cleverly Portrayed," *Nelson* (Australia) *Mail,* (14 February 2007).

Freeman, John. "Riot GIRRRLS," (Minneapolis) *Star Tribune* (29 October 2006).

Galehouse, Maggie. "Conquer and Convert," *New York Times Book Review* (14 January 2007): 19.

Gambotto-Burke, Antonella. "Putting the Romantic Before the Authentic," *The Australian* (23 December 2006).

Gillespie, Kellie. "Review: *Inés of My Soul,*" *Library Journal* (1 October 2006): 56.

Goddard, Susannah. "The Woman Who Built a City," (Melbourne) *Herald Sun* (25 November 2006): W26.

Haq, Amber. "The Mother of Chile: Isabel Allende's New Novel Celebrates the Conquistadora Who Helped Create a New Nation," *Newsweek* (13 November 2006).

Harvey, Tamara. "Women in Early America: Recharting Hemispheric and Atlantic Desire," *Legacy* 28:2 (2011): 159–176.

Hendriks, David. "Allende's Latest Conquest No Small Feat," (Sydney) *Sun-Herald* (17 December 2006).

Hooper, Brad. "Advance Reviews," *Booklist* 103:1 (1 September 2006): 8.

"Ines Suarez a Hot Topic: Allende's Latest Is a Historical Bodice-Ripper," *Chicago Sun-Times* (31 December 2006).

Jones, Lewis. "More Cartland Than Márquez," (London) *Daily Telegraph* (29 May 2010).

Keates, Jonathan. "Review: *Inés of My Soul,*" *Times Literary Supplement* 5429 (20 April 2007): 20.

Kessel, Joyce. "Review: *Inés of My Soul,*" *Library Journal* 132:9 (15 May 2007): 128.

Loohauis, Jackie. "Isabel Allende Wields a Mighty Pen in Epic Tale of Chile's Founding Mother, 'Inés of My Soul,'" *Milwaukee Journal Sentinel* (16 November 2006).

McGee, Celia. "'Ines' Captures Chile's Soul in 1500s," *USA Today* (9 November 2006).

McMichael, Barbara Lloyd. "'Inés of My Soul': Isabel Allende's Story of a Real-Life Conquistadora," *Seattle Times* (24 November 2006).

Meade, Teresa A. *A History of Modern Latin America: 1800 to the Present.* Malden, MA: John Wiley, 2010.

Miller, Pamela. "Isabel Allende's New Novel Is Set in the 1500s, but the Parallels to Contemporary Issues Are Unmistakable," (Minneapolis) *Star Tribune* (31 October 2006).

Nicolopulos, James. *The Poetics of Empire in the Indies: Prophecy and Imitation in La Araucana and Os Lusíadas.* University Park: Pennsylvania State University Press, 2000.

Norris, Michele. "Allende Reimagines Life of Conquistador," *All Things Considered* (NPR), (6 November 2006).

O'Keeffe, Alice. "Myths of Conquest," *New Statesman* 136 (9 April 2007): 58–59.

Olvera, Javier Erik. "Allende, Heroine 'Inés' Are Kindred Spirits," *Inside Bay Area* (California) (25 November 2006).

On, Thuy. "The Victors' Tale of Freedom," *The* (Melbourne) *Age,* (30 December 2006).

Park, James Barnhart. "Geopolitics and Historicism in Mapuche Poetry of Chile: Lorenzo Aillapan and Rayen Kvyeh," *Latin American Indian Literature Journal* 17:1 (Spring 2001): 1–19.

Pena, Beatriz Carolina. *Images of the New World in the Travel Narratives (1599–1607) of Friar Diego de Ocana.* Ann Arbor, MI: ProQuest, 2008.

"Review: *Inés of My Soul,*" *Kirkus Reviews* 74:18 (15 September 2006): 919.

"Review: *Inés of My Soul,*" *Publishers Weekly* 253:33 (21 August 2006): 46.

"Review: *Inés of My Soul,*" *Publishers Weekly* 254:9 (26 February 2007): 86.

Ross, Veronica. "Sewing Didn't Cut It for Inés," *Guelph* (Ontario) *Mercury* (3 March 2007).

Saricks, Joyce. "Review: *Inés of My Soul,*" *Booklist* 103:12 (15 February 2007): 94.

Shires, Ashley Simpson. "A Conquistadora Comes to Life," *Rocky Mountain News* (10 November 2006).

Smith, Wendy L. "Isabel Allende's 'Inés of My Soul' Has the Soul of a Mediocre Romance Novel," (San Diego) *Union-Tribune* (19 November 2006).

Smyth, Amanda. "Isabel Allende's Powerful, Satisfying Haitian Saga," *Irish Times* (5 June 2010).

"Tragic, Bloodstained Trek Cleverly Portrayed," *The Nelson* (New Zealand) *Mail* (14 February 2007).

Wides-Muñoz, Laura. "A Tale of Love and Conquest," *The Gold Coast* (Australia) *Bulletin* (25 November 2006): 22.

Yardley, Jonathan. "Review: *Inés of My Soul*," *Washington Post* (12 November 2006).

Zipp, Yvonne. "The Mother of Chile, Rescued from Obscurity," *Christian Science Monitor* 99:17 (19 December 2006): 17.

The Infinite Plan

O'Neil, Patrick M. *Great World Writers: Twentieth Century*. Tarrytown, NY: Marshall Cavendish, 2004.

Peck, David R., and Tracy Irons-Georges. *American Ethnic Writers*. Pasadena, CA: Salem, 2009.

Rodden, John. *Performing the Literary Interview: How Writers Craft Their Public Selves*. Lincoln: University of Nebraska Press, 2001.

"Soapy Operation," *Tribune Magazine* (30 July 1993): 5.

Sollars, Michael D. *The Facts on File Companion to the World Novel, 1900 to the Present*. New York: Facts on File, 2008.

Stone, Louise M., and Troy Place. *Magill's Survey of World Literature*. Pasadena, CA: Salem, 2009.

Swanson, Philip. "California Dreaming: Mixture, Muddle, and Meaning in Isabel Allende's North American Narratives," *Journal of Iberian and Latin American Studies* 9:1 (2003): 57–67.

Island Beneath the Sea

"Allende's Latest Set in Haiti," (Batavia, NY) *Daily News*, (23 July 2010): 3B.

Alter, Alexandra. "Isabel Allende on Superstition and Memory," *Wall Street Journal* 255:94 (23 April 2010): W4.

Astor, Michael. "Isabel Allende Weaves Rich Tale of Colonial Haiti in 'Island Beneath the Sea,'" *Canadian Press* (26 April 2010).

Bahadur, Gaiutra. "All Souls Rising," *New York Times Book Review* (2 May 2010): 26. Barker, Olivia. "Allende's 'Island' Plunges into Some Troubled Waters," *USA Today* (10 June 2010).

Clark, Lucy. "Allende Back with Rich Melodrama," *Northern Territory News* (6 June 2010).

Daher, Anita. "Allende Uses Broad Focus to View Haitian Slave History," *Winnipeg Free Press* (1 May 2010).

Daremblum, Naomi. "Not Magical, Not Realism," *New Republic* (28 April 2010).

Dempsey, Dianne. "Zarité Stuff for Story of Slavery," *The* (Melbourne) *Age* (15 May 2010).

De Robertis, Carolina. "Review: *Island Beneath the Sea*," *San Francisco Chronicle* (25 April 2010).

Ewan, John. "Gripping Mix of Class, Children and Cruelty," *The Nelson* (New Zealand) *Mail* (26 May 2010).

Garwood, Sasha. "Review: *Island Beneath the Sea*," *TLS* 5595 (25 June 2010): 21.

Gill, Harbant. "Freedom's Dream," *The* (Cairns, Australia) *Weekender* (1 May 2010).

Green, Paula. "Review: *Island Beneath the Sea*," *New Zealand Herald* (31 July 2010).

Gumbrecht, Jamie. "Isabel Allende to Discuss New Novel, 'Island Beneath the Sea,'" *Atlanta Journal-Constitution* (4 May 2010).

Hammond, Margo. "A Slave Makes History in Allende's New Novel," *Pittsburgh Post-Gazette* (6 June 2010).

Harvey, Tamara. "Women in Early America: Recharting Hemispheric and Atlantic Desire," *Legacy* 28:2 (2011): 159–176.

Hendricks, David. "Review: *Island Beneath the Sea*," (San Antonio) *Express-News* (25 April 2010).

Hoffert, Barbara. "Review: *Island Beneath the Sea*," *Library Journal* 135:1 (1 January 2010): 70–74.

James, Marlon. "Review: *Island Beneath the Sea*," *Publishers Weekly* 257:14 (4 May 2010). Jones, Lewis. "More Cartland Than Márquez," (London) *Daily Telegraph* (29 May 2010).

Kelton, Peter. "Isabel Allende's 'Magical Feminism' Yields to Historical Pageant in 'Island Beneath the Sea,'" *Albuquerque Examiner* (2 May 2010).

Kowalski, William. "A Mixed Outcome," (Toronto) *Globe and Mail* (27 May 2010).

Leggatt, Johanna. "Revolting Times in Paradise," (Sydney) *Sun-Herald* (23 May 2010).

Levasseur, Jennifer. "Lost in a Sea of Cliches," (Sydney) *Morning Herald* (10 July 2010).

May, Meredith. "Allende Takes on Slavery," *San Francisco Chronicle* (28 April 2010).

Mullick, Disha. "Destiny's Slave," (Hyderabad, India) *Deccan Chronicle* (28 August 2010).

Mulligan, F. "A Rich and Heady Blend," (New Zealand) *Southland Times* (31 July 2010).

Murphy, Bernadette. "Review: *Island Beneath the Sea*," *Los Angeles Times* (14 May 2010).

Patterson, Leslie. "Review: *Island Beneath the Sea*," *Library Journal* 135:7 (15 April 2010): 72.

Pikul, Corrie. "Review: *Island Beneath the Sea*," *Elle* (9 April 2010).

Popkin, Jeremy D., ed. *A Concise History of the Haitian Revolution*. London: Blackwell, 2012.

Ratner-Arias, Sigal. "Isabel Allende Sets New Book in Haiti with Theme of Slavery and Regrets Timing," *Canadian Press* (18 May 2010).

"Review: *Island Beneath the Sea*," (Hobart) *Sunday Tasmanian* (25 April 2010).

"Review: *Island Beneath the Sea*," *Jordan Times* (23 August 2010).

"Review: *Island Beneath the Sea*," *Kansas City Star* (12 May 2010).

"Review: *Island Beneath the Sea*," *Kirkus Reviews* 78:7 (1 April 2010).

Ritchie, Harry. "Literary Fiction," (London) *Daily Mail* (14 May 2010).

Sankovitch, Nina. "Out of the Hell of Haiti: *Island Beneath the Sea* by Isabel Allende," *Huffington Post* (26 April 2010).

Schaub, Michael. "Dreams of Freedom in Allende's 'Island,'" www.npr.org/templates/story/story.php?storyId=126892427, accessed on April 4, 2010.

Seaman, Donna. "Review: *Island Beneath the Sea,*" *Booklist* 106:13 (1 March 2010): 5.

Smyth, Amanda. "Isabel Allende's Powerful, Satisfying Haitian Saga," *Irish Times* (5 June 2010).

Staskiewicz, Keith. "Review: *Island Beneath the Sea,*" *Entertainment Weekly* (28 April 2010).

Terrazas, Beatriz. "Review: *Island Beneath the Sea,*" *Dallas Morning News* (2 May 2010).

Valdes, Marcela. "Isabel Allende on Haiti's Slave Rebellion: A Lost Cause," *Washington Post* (8 June 2010).

Vidimos, Robin. "Slave Uprising in Colonial Haiti at Heart of Isabel Allende's Latest," *Denver Post* (2 May 2010).

Viramontes, Helena María. "The House of the Slaves," *Ms.* 20:2 (Spring 2010): 56–57.

Willeford, Betsy. "Tete's (and Haiti's) Trials in *Island Beneath the Sea,*" *Miami Herald* (25 April 2010).

Kingdom of the Golden Dragon

Carlile, Susan. "Review: *Kingdom of the Golden Dragon,*" *Journal of Adolescent & Adult Literacy* 49:2 (1 October 2005): 170.

Cox, Marge, Carl A. Harvey, and Susan E. Page. *The Library Media Specialist in the Writing Process.* Santa Barbara, CA: ABC-Clio, 2007.

Cox, Ruth. "YA Fiction: Wishful and Willful," *Teacher Librarian* 31:4 (April 2004): 21.

Finkelstein, Lee. "Older Readers," *Reading Time* 48:2 (May 2004): 20).

Renner, Coop. "Review: *Kingdom of the Golden Dragon,*" *School Library Journal* 51:7 (July 2005): 44.

"Review: *Kingdom of the Golden Dragon,*" *Kirkus Reviews* 72:7 (1 April 2004): 323.

"Review: *Kingdom of the Golden Dragon,*" *Kliatt* 39:1–6 (May 2005): 46.

"Review: *Kingdom of the Golden Dragon,*" *Publishers Weekly* 251:11 (15 March 2004): 75.

Rochman, Hazel. "Review: *Kingdom of the Golden Dragon,*" *Booklist* 100:12 (15 February 2004): 1050.

_____. "Review: *Kingdom of the Golden Dragon,*" *Booklist* 100:12 (15 March 2004): 75.

Rogers, Susan L. "Review: *Kingdom of the Golden Dragon,*" *School Library Journal* 50:4 (April 2004): 148.

Maya's Notebook

Álvarez, Marcela. "Isabel Allende Returns with 'El cuaderno de Maya,'" *La Prensa San Diego* 35:31 (5 August 2011): 4–5.

Kerrigan, Michael. "Two Worlds Together," *Times Literary Supplement* 5687 (30 March 2010): 20–21.

My Invented Country

Arnold, Lee. "Down South America Way," *Library Journal* 131:4 (1 March 2006): 59–61.

Askeland, G.A. "You Will Never Again Be a Chilean Like the Others: From Diaspora to Diasporic Practices among Chilean Refugees Returning from Exile," *Journal of Comparative Social Work* (2011): 1–18.

Ayala, Elaine. "Defining Moments for Isabel Allende," *San Antonio Express* (2 May 2007).

Billen, Andrew. "With a Family Like Mine You Don't Need an Imagination," (London) *Times* (14 October 2003).

Burns, Ann. "Review: *My Invented Country,*" *Library Journal* 129:3 (15 February 2004): 45.

Cameron, Peter. "Review: *My Invented Country,*" *New York Times Book Review* (8 June 2003): 19.

Dunbar-Ortiz, Roxanne. "The First September 11th," *Women's Review of Books* 21:3 (December 2003): 15–16.

France, Miranda. "Old Wives' Tales," *New Statesman* 132:4667 (8 December 2003): 53–54.

Gold, Sarah F. "Review: *My Invented Country,*" *Publishers Weekly* 250:17 (28 April 2003): 57.

Gómez-Barris, Macarena, and Herman Gray, eds. *Toward a Sociology of the Trace.* Minneapolis: University of Minnesota Press, 2010.

Kasperek, Sheila. "Review: *My Invented Country,*" *Library Journal* 128:10 (1 June 2003): 118.

Larson, Jeanethe. ""Review: *My Invented Country,*" *Booklist* 100:3 (1 October 2003): 340.

Maxwell, Gloria. "Review: *My Invented Country,*" *Library Journal* 128:17 (15 October 2003): 115.

Mujica, Barbara. "Review: *My Invented Country,*" *Americas* 55:5 (September/October 2003): 57.

Polanco, Marcela. "Autoethnographic Means to the End of a Decolonizing Translation," *Journal of Systemic Therapies* 30:3 (2011): 42–56.

Reed, Kay. *New Directions in Social Theory: Race, Gender and the Canon.* Thousand Oaks, CA: SAGE, 2006.

"Review: *My Invented Country,*" *Kirkus Reviews* 71:7 (1 April 2003): 514.

Seaman, Donna. "Review: *My Invented Country,*" *Booklist* 99:15 (1 April 2003): 1354.

Soper, Patricia. "Fascinating Look at Chile," (New Zealand) *Southland Times* (11 October 2003): 35.

Wright, Lindsay. "Home Is a Long, Thin Country," *Taranaki* (New Zealand) *Daily News* (30 August 2003): 18.

Of Love and Shadows

Bickford, Donna M. "Using Testimonial Novels to Think About Social Justice," *Education, Citizenship and Social Justice* 3:2 (July 2008): 131–146.

Clancy, Laurie. "Isabel Allende's 1988 Novel Looks Again at Love and Dictators," *The* (Melbourne) *Age* (11 February 2008).

Danow, David K. *The Spirit of Carnival: Magical Realism and the Grotesque.* Lexington: University Press of Kentucky, 2004.

Ford, Karen. "Triumph of Truth and Love," *The* (Melbourne) *Age* (23 September 2007).

González, Aníbal. *Love and Politics in the Contemporary Spanish American Novel.* Austin: University of Texas Press, 2010.

Hague, Angela. *Fiction, Intuition, & Creativity: Studies in Brontë, Woolf, and Lessing.* Washington, DC: Catholic University of America Press, 2003.

Hayes, Michael A. *Truth and Memory: The Church and Human Rights in El Salvador and Guatemala.* Herefordshire, UK: Gracewing 2001.

Kohut, David R., and Olga Vilella. *Historical Dictionary of the "Dirty Wars."* Lanham, MD: Scarecrow, 2010.

Kristal, Efraín. *The Cambridge Companion to the Latin American Novel.* New York: Cambridge University Press, 2005.

Pendergast, Sara, and Tom Pendergast. *Reference Guide to World Literature.* Detroit: St. James, 2003.

Stanley, Maureen Tobin, and Gesa Zinn. *Female Exiles in Twentieth and Twenty-First Century Europe.* New York: Macmillan, 2007.

Tolchin, Karen R. *Part Blood, Part Ketchup: Coming of Age in American Literature and Film.* Lanham, MD: Lexington, 2007.

Toomey, Mike. "Love and Chaos," (Melbourne) *Herald Sun* (7 August 2007).

Weldt-Basson, Helene Carol. *Subversive Silences: Nonverbal Expression and Implicit Narrative Strategies in the Works of Latin American Women Writers.* Cranbury, NJ: Associated University Presses, 2009.

Wright, Thomas C. *State Terrorism in Latin America: Chile, Argentina, and International Human Rights.* Lanham, MD: Roman & Littlefield, 2007.

Paula

Carvalho, Susan. "The Craft of Emotion in Isabel Allende's Paula," *Studies in Twentieth Century Literature* 27 (Summer 2003): 223–238.

Crosby, Margaret. "The Voyage Through Pain: Conceptualizing Illness in Isabel Allende's *Paula,*" *Hispanofila* 147 (May 2006): 83–98.

Dulfano, Isabel. "The Mother/Daughter Romance—Our Life: Isabel Allende in/and *Paula,*" *Women's Studies* 35:5 (2006): 493–506.

Feather, Jacqueline. "Re-Imagining Hekate: Muse for Memoir," *Psychological Perspectives* 54:1 (2011): 7–18.

Fowler, Kathleen. "'So New, So New': Art and Heart in Women's Grief Memories," *Women's Studies* 36:7 (October/November 2007): 525–549.

Fuchs, Miriam. *The Text Is Myself: Women's Life Writing and Catastrophe.* Madison: University of Wisconsin Press, 2004.

Grover, Robert J., and Susan G. Fowler. *Helping Those Experiencing Loss.* Santa Barbara, CA: ABC-Clio, 2011.

Hopkinson, Amanda. "Isabel Allende" in *Contemporary Literary Criticism.* Farmington Hills, MI: Gale Cengage, 2003.

Jolley, Jason R. "Mother-Daughter Feminism and Personal Criticism in Isabel Allende's Paula," *Revista Canadiense de Estudios* 30:2 (1 January 2006): 331–352.

Levine, Linda Gould. "Defying the Pillar of Salt: Isabel Allende's *Paula,*" *Latin American Literary Review* 30 (2002): 29–50.

Kennedy, Alexandra. *The Infinite Thread: Healing Relationships Beyond Loss.* Hillsboro, OR: Beyond Words, 2001.

Kiser, Laurel J., Barbara Baumgardner, and Joyce Dorado. "Who Are We, but for the Stories We Tell: Family Stories and Healing," *Psychological Trauma* 2:3 (September 2010): 243–249.

Maier, Linda. "Mourning Becomes Paula: The Writing Process as Therapy for Isabel Allende," *Hispania* 86:2 (May 2003): 237–243.

McCracken, Anne, and Mary Semel, eds. *A Broken Heart Still Beats: After Your Child Dies.* Center City, MD: Hazelden, 2000.

Moline, Karen. "The Spirit of Love," *Australian Woman's Weekly* 73:8 (August 2003): 88–92.

Mooney, Jadwiga E. Pieper. *The Politics of Motherhood: Maternity and Women's Rights in Twentieth-Century Chile.* Pittsburgh: University of Pittsburgh Press, 2009.

Myers, Linda. *The Power of Memoir: How to Write Your Healing Story.* San Francisco: Wiley, 2010.

O'Reilly, Andrea. *Feminist Mothering.* Albany: State University of New York Press, 2008.

_____. *Encyclopedia of Motherhood.* Thousand Oaks, CA: Sage, 2010.

Taylor, Martha A., and Sondra C. Shaw-Hardy, eds. *The Transformative Power of Women's Philanthropy.* San Francisco: Jossey-Bass, 2005.

Vazquez, Carmen Inoa, and Dinelia Rosa. *Grief Therapy with Latinos: Integrating Culture for Clinicians.* New York: Springer, 2011.

Wile, Richard. "Review: *Paula,*" *Fourth Genre* 10:1 (1 March 2008): 189–191.

Portrait in Sepia

Arrington, Teresa R. "Isabel Allende: Retrato en sepia," *World Literature Today* (1 January 2002): 115.

Brice, Chris. "Entrancing Family Portrait," *The* (Adelaide) *Advertiser* (20 October 2001); M23.
Castro, Jan Garden. "Review: *Portrait in Sepia*," *St. Louis Post-Dispatch* (28 October 2001): G11.
Changnon, Greg. "Review: *Portrait in Sepia*," *Atlanta Journal-Constitution* (2 December 2000): C4.
Clarke, Stella. "Lie Back and Think of Chile," *The* (Sydney) *Australian* (6 October 2001): R12.
Dam, Julie K.L. "Review: *Portrait in Sepia*," *People* 56:22 (26 November 2001).
Dinnison, Kris. "Review: *Portrait in Sepia*," (Spokane) *Pacific Northwest Inlander* (21 February 2002).
Ervin, Andrew. "A Woman's Reconstruction," *The New York Times* (4 November 2001): 32.
Falconer, Helen. "Colouring the Family Album," (Manchester) *Guardian* (17 November 2001).
Graham, Philip. "A Less Magical Realism," *New Leader* 84:6 (November-December 2001): 38–39.
Heredia, Sylvia. "Retrato en sepia," *Library Journal* 126:4 (1 March 2001).
Hoffert, Barbara. "Review: *Portrait in Sepia*," *Library Journal* (15 October 2001): 105.
Hooper, Brad. "Review: *Portrait in Sepia*," *Booklist* (1 September 2001): 3.
Hoult-Saron, Stacy. "Review: *Portrait in Sepia*," *Valparaiso University Books and Coffee* (Spring 2002).
"Isabel Allende Just Keeps Them Coming," *Philippine Daily Inquirer* (27 May 2002).
Kephart, Beth. "Review: *Portrait in Sepia*," *Book* (November-December 2001): 60–61.
Lagos, María Inés. "Female Voices from the Borderlands: Isabel Allende's *Paula* and *Retrato en Sepia*," *Latin American Literary Review* 30:60 (2002): 112–127.
Martínez, Z. Nelly. "Isabel Allende's Fictional World: Roads to Freedom," *Latin American Literary Review* 30:60 (2002): 51–73.
McCartney, Jenny. "Review: *Portrait in Sepia*," (London) *Times* (14 October 2001).
Mujica, Barbara. "Review: *Portrait in Sepia*," *Americas* 53:5 (October 2001): 63.
"Picture Imperfect," *New Straits Times* (15 November 2001).
Pohlad, Mark B. "Contemporary Fiction and the History of Photography," *History of Photography* 26:3 (Autumn 2002): 178–191.
Ratcliffe, Sophie. "Branching Off," (London) *Times* (1 December 2001).
"Review: *Portrait in Sepia*," *Hispanic Outlook in Higher Education* (14 February 2005).
"Review: *Portrait in Sepia*," *Irish Times* (10 August 2002).
"Review: *Portrait in Sepia*," *Kirkus Reviews* (15 August 2001).
"Review: *Portrait in Sepia*," (London) *Times* (16 April 2005).
"Review: *Portrait in Sepia*," (London) *Times* (11 June 2005): 8.
"Review: *Portrait in Sepia*," *Publishers Weekly* (16 July 2001): 1142.
Rivero, Eliana. "Of Trilogies and Genealogies: *Daughter of Fortune* and *Portrait in Sepia*," *Latin American Literary Review* 30:60 (2002): 91–111.
Santiago, Sylvia. "Portrait in Sepia," *Herizons* 16:2 (22 September 2002): 44.
Stavans, Ilan. "Do You Remember?" *Times Literary Supplement* 5140 (5 October 2001): 26.
Walton, David. "Review: *Portrait in Sepia*," (Minneapolis) *Star Tribune* (18 December 2005).
Wood, Michael. "Girls with Green Hair," *New York Review of Books* (14 March 2002).
Zaleski, Jeff. "Review: *Portrait in Sepia*," *Publishers Weekly* 248:29 (16 July 2001): 1142.

The Stories of Eva Luna

Amago, Samuel. "Isabel Allende and the Postmodern Literary Tradition: A Reconsideration of Cuentos de Eva Luna," *Latin American Literary Review* 28:56 (July–December 2000): 43–60.
Berliner, Janet, and Joyce Carol Oates. *Snapshots: 20th Century Mother-Daughter Fiction*. Boston: David R. Godine, 2000.
Carpi, Daniela, ed. *Bioethics and Biolaw Through Literature*. Berlin: William de Gruyter, 2011.
Chandran, K. Narayana. *Texts and Their Worlds II*. New Delhi: Foundation Books, 2005.
Devine, Rachel. "Passion, Betrayal and Love in a Hot Climate," (London) *Sunday Times* (15 November 2009): 15.
Díaz, Cassandra Shannon. *Feminism and Human Rights in the Short Stories of Isabel Allende*. Waco, TX: Baylor University, 2000.
Fiero, Gloria K. *Modernism, Globalism, and the Information Age*. Boston: McGraw-Hill, 2002.
Gaudet, Marcis G., and James C. McDonald. *Mardi Gras, Gumbo, and Zydero: Readings in Louisiana Culture*. Jackson: University Press of Mississippi, 2003.
George, Dana Del. *The Supernatural in Short Fiction of the Americas: The Other World in the New World*. Westport, CT: Greenwood, 2001.
Gregory, Stephen. "Stories as Aphrodisiacs: The Price of Seduction in Isabel Allende's Storytelling," *Journal of Iberian and Latin American Studies* 8:2 (2002): 225–240.
Hooper, Brad. *The Short Story Readers' Advisory: A Guide to the Best*. Chicago: American Library Association, 2000.
Laurie, Victoria. "Songs Bring Allende's Tales to Life," *The* (Sydney) *Australian* (12 February 2001): 14.
Lindsey, Claire. "Re-reading the Romance: Genre and Gender in Isabel Allende's 'Niña perversa,'" *Romance Studies* 19:2 (2001): 135–147.

Major, Clarence. *Necessary Distance: Essays and Criticism.* Minneapolis: Coffee House Press, 2001.

May, Charles Edward, ed. *Critical Survey of Short Fiction.* Pasadena, CA: Salem, 2001.

McClennen, Sophia A. "Teaching Bad Books," *American Book Review* 31:2 (January/February 2010): 7–8.

Milner, Joseph O'Beirne, and Lucy Floyd Morcock Milner. *Bridging English.* Upper Saddle River, NJ: Merrill/Prentice Hall, 2003.

Moser, Robert Henry. *The Carnivalesque Defunto: Death and the Dead in Modern Brazilian Literature.* Athens: Ohio University Press, 2008.

Nott, Robert. "Dancing Through Eva Luna's World," *Santa Fe New Mexican* (12 August 2005): 74.

Rubenstein, Roberta, and Charles R. Larson, eds. *Worlds of Fiction.* Upper Saddle River, NJ: Prentice Hall, 2002.

Schwartz, March. "The Right to Imagine: Reading in Community with People and Stories," *PMLA* 126:3 (May 2011): 746–752.

Smith, Patrick A. *Thematic Guide to Popular Short Stories.* Westport, CT: Greenwood, 2002.

Spargo, R. Clifton. *The Ethics of Mourning: Grief and Responsibility in Elegaic Literature.* Baltimore: Johns Hopkins University Press, 2004.

Umpierre, Luz María. "Unscrambling Allende's 'Dos palabras': The Self, the Immigrant/Writer, and Social Justice," *Melus* 27:4 (Winter 2002): 129–136.

Weldt-Basson, Helene C. "Irony as Silent Subversive Strategy in Isabel Allende's *Cuentos de Eva Luna,*" *Revista de estudios hispánicos* 31:1 (2004): 183–198.

The Sum of Our Days

"Allende Spins More Family Tales in New Memoir," *Northern Territory News* (23 September 2007).

Barbassa, Juliana. "Isabel Allende's Latest Book an Invitation into Her Family and Her Writing," *Canadian Press* (28 March 2008).

Basu, Chitralekha. "Review: *The Sum of Our Days,*" *TLS* 5481 (18 April 2008): 32.

Clark, Lucy. "Reading Room Reviews," (Brisbane) *Sunday Mail* (20 April 2008).

Donahue, Deirdre. "'Sum of Our Days' Another Invitation into Allende's Life," *USA Today* (27 May 2008).

Ewan, John. "Allende Family Memoir Entertains," *The Nelson* (New Zealand) *Mail* (4 June 2008).

Flood, Alison. "Allende Memoir in April," *Bookseller* 5304 (26 October 2007): 13.

Flores, Camille. "Review: *The Sum of Our Days,*" (Santa Fe) *New Mexican* (8 August 2008): PA-20.

Gambotto-Burke, Antonella. "Novelist's Purest Symphony of Being," *The* (Sydney). *Australian* (5 April 2008): 15.

Harbant, Gill. "Sharing an Amazing Life," (Melbourne) *Herald Sun* (28 June 2008).

Kessel, Joyce. "Review: *The Sum of Our Days,*" *Library Journal* 133:14 (1 September 2008): 178.

Locke, Michelle. "Author Isabel Allende Chronicles Her Own Real-Life Drama in New Book," *Canadian Press* (28 March 2008).

López, Adriana V. "Exclusive: Chilean Novelist Isabel Allende on Her New Tell-All Memoir" *Latina* 12:10 (28 February 2008): 106.

Miller, Pamela. "The Stories She Can Tell," (Minneapolis) *Star Tribune* (30 March 2008).

"Mistress of the Castle: Isabel Allende Continues Her Chronicle of Dysfunctional Family Life," *Washington Post* (13 April 2008).

O'Connor, Shaunagh. "Layers of Lessons in Soap-Opera Family," *The* (Melbourne) *Age* (10 May 2008).

Pabst, Georgia. "'Sum' Allows Spirited Look at Passionate Allende," *Milwaukee Journal Sentinel* (20 April 2008).

Parks, Tim. "The Knife by the Handle at Last," *The New York Review of Books* 55:14 (25 September 2008): 18–22.

"Review: *The Sum of Our Days,*" *Kirkus Reviews* 76:3 (1 February 2008): 123.

"Review: *The Sum of Our Days,*" *Publishers Weekly* 255:7 (18 February 2008): 146.

"Review: *The Sum of Our Days,*" *Quill & Quire* 74 (2008): 35.

Sparrow, Joyce. "Review: *The Sum of Our Days,*" *Library Journal* 133:7 (5 April 2008): 84–85.

Teodoro, José. "Review: *The Sum of Our Days,*" (Toronto) *Globe and Mail* (28 June 2008): D7.

Valby, Karen. "Motherly Love," *Entertainment Weekly* 985 (4 April 2008): 66.

Vine, Sarah. "Humanity Laid Bare," (London) *Times* (12 April 2008): 10.

Wilkinson, Joanne. "Review: *The Sum of Our Days,*" *Booklist* (1 February 2008): 4.

"Writing About the People She Loves," *Northern Territory News* (20 April 2008): 47.

Zipp, Yvonne. "An Author Shares the Real Drama in Her Life," *Christian Science Monitor* 100:103 (22 April 2008): 14.

Zorro

Allen, Brooke. "Adventures in Pop Culture," *New Leader* 88:3 (May/June 2005): 36–38.

Barra, Allen. "Zorro Meets Isabel Allende," *Chicago Sun-Times* (1 May 2005).

Bauers, Sandy. "Isabel Allende Makes the Mark of Zorro," *Philadelphia Inquirer* (6 June 2005).

Benjamin — Labarthe, Elyette. "American Cinema: *The Mask of Zorro* and the Chicano Canon" in

U.S. Latino Literatures and Cultures: Transnational Perspectives, ed. Francisco A. Lomelí and Karin Ikas. Heidelberg: Carl Winter, 2000.

Bennett, Steve. "Legend of Zorro Retold in Rollicking Adventure Yarn, *Guelph* (Ontario) *Mercury* (11 June 2005).

Brown, Georgina. "The Lark of Zorro," (London) *Mail on Sunday* (20 July 2008): 13.

Burke, Wendy. "Fresh Approach to Adventure," *Winnipeg Free Press* (8 May 2005): 7.

Byrd, Max. "'Zorro': Man in Black," *New York Times* (15 May 2005).

Charles, Shaun. "Marking Zorro's Place in History," *The* (Brisbane) *Courier Mail,* (23 April 2005): M8.

Cheuse, Alan. "Review: Isabel Allende's *Zorro,*" *NPR All Things Considered* (10 May 2005).

_____. ""Review: *Zorro,*" *World Literature Today* 80:1 (January-February 2006): 27–28.

_____. "The Female Pen," *Chicago Tribune* (8 May 2005).

Clark, Lucy. "Allende Unmasks Legend of Zorro," (Adelaide) *Sunday Mail* (22 May 2005).

de Kosnik, Abigail. "Should Fan Fiction Be Free?," *Cinema Journal* 48:4 (Summer 2009): 118–124.

Drew, Bernard A. *Literary Afterlife: The Posthumous Continuations of 325 Authors' Fictional Characters.* Jefferson, NC: McFarland, 2010.

Falconer, Crystal. "Enchantment and Adventure Meet Feminism: Isabel Allende," *Boulder* (Colorado) *Examiner,* (17 September, 2010).

Gill, Harbant. "From Zero to Zorro," (Melbourne) *Herald Sun,* (7 May 2005): W29.

Glaister, Dan. "Zorro and Me," (Manchester) *Guardian* (18 May 2005): 6–7.

Griffin, Michelle. "Z Marks the Spot for a Dull Blade," *The* (Melbourne) *Age* (7 May 2005): 4.

Hart, Christopher, Louis Wise, and David Dougill. "Rest of the Week's Theatre," (London) *Sunday Times* (20 July 2008).

Hicks, Ian. "Sword Proves Mightier Than the Pen," (Sydney) *Morning Herald* (18 June 2005).

Jury, Louise. "Zorro Cuts a Dash on Stage," (London) *Evening Standard* (28 April 2008).

Keenan, Catherine. "The Legend Writes Again," (Sydney) *Morning Herald* (30 April 2005).

Leen, Catherine. "The Caballero Revisited: Postmodernity in "The Cisco Kid," "The Mask of Zorro," and "Shrek II," *Bilingual Review* 28:1 (January-April 2007): 23–35.

Matthews, Charles. "Zorro Rides Again," *The* (Hobart) *Mercury* (21 May 2005).

Memmott, Carol. "'Zorro' Gets Behind the Mask," *USA Today* (12 May 2005): 5.

Mujica, Barbara. "Zorro and the Zahir," *Américas* 57:6 (November-December 2005): 62–63.

Murray, Yxta Maya. "A Foxy Hero Returns to Duel with His Inner Selves," *Los Angeles Times* (1 May 2005).

"Mystique of the Masked Avenger," *Nelson* (New Zealand) *Mail* (26 July 2006): 25.

Review: *Zorro,*" *Publishers Weekly* (28 February 2005): 39.

Stone, Micha. "Review: *Zorro,*" *Library Journal* (1 March 2005): 74.

Swanson, Philip. "Z/Z: Isabel Allende and the Mark of Zorro," *Romance Studies* 24:3 (November 2006): 265–277.

Wides-Munoz, Laura. "Concubines and Queens Inspire Scribes Isabel Allende, Gioconda Belli," *Canadian Press* (11 November 2006).

Wright, Lindsay. "Masked Fighter for Justice," *Taranaki* (New Zealand) *Daily News* (11 June 2005).

Index

Numbers in **boldface** refer to main entries. Letters in parentheses refer to works from Isabel Allende's canon: *Aphrodite* (A); *The City of the Beasts* (CB); *Daughter of Fortune* (DF); *Eva Luna* (EL); *Forest of the Pygmies* (FP); "The Guggenheim Lovers" (GL); *The House of the Spirits* (HS); *Inés of My Soul* (IMS); *The Infinite Plan* (IP); *Island Beneath the Sea* (IBS); *Kingdom of the Golden Dragon* (KGD); *Maya's Notebook* (MN); *My Invented Country* (MIC); *Of Love and Shadows* (OLS); *Paula* (P); *Portrait in Sepia* (PS); *The Stories of Eva Luna* (SEL); *The Sum of Our Days* (SOD); *Zorro* (Z)

abolitionism (IBS) 161, 181, 204, 207, 230, 245, 259, 287, 301
abortion 9, 54, 96, 101, 125, 129, 143–144, 155, 194, 225, 226, 256, 273, 317
achievement **29–33**, 41–42, 55, 62, 72, 85, 89, 91, 117, 152–154, 158, 170, 178, 204, 214–215, 239, 245, 260, 280, 290, 294, 302
"An Act of Vengeance" (opera) 24
acupuncture 16, 127, 131, 188, 218, 236, 248, 272
adaptation 15, 19–24, 30, 31, 32, **33–37**, 39, 42–45, 49, 55, 57, 74, 111, 162, 173, 180, 195, 249, 256, 266, 278, 302
Adèle (IBS) 34, 95, 181, 184–185, 191–192, 315, 318
Aguirre, Francisco de (IMS) 175, 197, 282, 293
Ah Toy (DF) 278, 312
Aka 20–21, 35–36, 45, 95, 114–117, 156, 165, 173, 179, 192, 198, 208, 210, 215, 226, 247, 253, 275, 291
Alcalufe (MIC) 200
Alcántara, Beatriz (OLS) 34, 43, 96, 97, 139, 187–188, 206, 211, 261, 318
alcohol 61, 65, 91, 103, 126–127, 200, 233, 259, 296, 307
allegory 14, 134, 135, 139, 154, 178, 205, 264, 266, 268, 299
Allende, Francisco 6, 10
Allende, Isabel 5–26, 30, **37–39**, 40, 58, 59, 64, 73, 79–80, 87, 94, 99, 103, 105, 112, 129, 133, 141, 186, 199–200, 217–218, 219–222, 232, 267–268, 271–273, 288, 295, 298; *see also* reading; writing
Allende, Juan 6
Allende, Salvador 8, 9, 10–11
Allende, Tomás 5, 9–10
Amalia (Z) 183
Amanda (HS) 63, 101, 106, 125, 183, 213, 218–219, 241, 250, 256, 278, 216
"The Amazon Queen" 4, 18, 48, 55, 205, 246
The Ambassador 10
ambition 32, **39–42**, 73, 94–95, 102, 185–186, 206, 210, 225, 230, 237, 249–250
Ampari (SEL) 205
"And of Clay Are We Created" (SEL) 15, 29, 38, 40, 60, 62, 88, 213, 219, 221, 224, 237, 240, 267–268, 276, 288, 295, 300, 316
Andieta, Elías "Chile Boy" (DF) 35, 69, 74, 83, 171, 194, 239
Andieta, Joaquin (PS) 30, 35, 47, 75, 83–84, 107, 147, 158, 170, 176, 179–180, 202, 207, 237, 251
Andieta, Widow (PS) 194, 218, 251
androcentrism 54, 98, 138, 217, 223; *see also machismo*; male persona
Angel, Uncle (SEL) 215
Antarctica (PS) 52
Antoine, Père (IBS) 82, 155, 158, 181, 189, 204, 246, 297, 311, 319
Aphrodite 11, 18, 24, **42–44**, 66, 99, 112, 130, 138, 159, 165, 184, 225, 269, 291
Araucan 5, 85, 154, 179, 184, 191, 285
La Araucana (PS) 154, 310
Aravena (EL) 250
Argentina 9, 11, 180, 217, 314
Ariosto, Captain (CB) 41, 48, 55–57, 71
Armadillo, Tex (KGD) 89, 92, 162–163, 205

arpilleras 94
art 7
Atahualpa (IMS) 286, 310
autodidacticism 152, 233; *see also* reading
awards 14, 15, 16, 17, 18, 19, 20, 21, 22, 23, 24
Aymara (MIC) 199–200, 228
Aztec (IMS) 121
Azucena (SEL) 60, 62, 157, 219, 267, 276, 288, 295

Babalú the Bad (DF) 35, 69, 176, 250
Bahadur, Dil (KGD) 33, 35, 41, 148, 61, 84, 113, 131, 163, 176, 196, 201, 205, 292, 297
Balcells, Carmen 15
Bal de Cordon Bleu (IBS) 34, 66, 161, 185, 262–263
The Ballad of a Nobody 10
Balmaceda, José Manuel (PS) 65, 145–146, 156, 282, 293, 313
Bantu (KGD) 21, 33, 35, 38, 45, 48, 93, 115, 117, 156, 164, 179, 215, 252–253, 275, 308
Barrabás (HS) 23, 77, 125, 138, 174, 192, 205, 276, 330
Barros, Rosa 118, 224
Barros Moreira, Isabel "Memé" 5, 6, 7, 12, 16, 119, 199
Basque 5, 6, 16, 179, 200, 206, 311
Battle of Las Salinas (IMS) 108, 244
beast fable (HS) 29, 124, 154, 164, 196, 214, 233, 268, 270, 291, 318
Beirut 7–8
Belalcázar, Daniel (IMS) 295
Belgium 9
belonging 14, 26, 30, **44–46**, 64, 318
Beltrán, Eusebio (OLS) 46, 139, 176, 187, 211, 317
Beltrán, Irene (OLS) 7, 12, 29–30, 34, 40, 43–44, 46, 53–54, 49, 64, 68, 88, 90, 96–97, 107, 120, 165–166, 187–188, 190, 202, 206, 212, 214, 216–217, 219, 234, 251, 278, 284–285, 299, 315, 317–319
Beltrán-Leal genealogy (OLS) **46**
El Benefactor (EL) 41, 313
Berastegui, Pedro (GL) 288, 315, 317
Bernal, Juan José (SEL) 116, 265–266
Bernardo (Z) 59, 72–73, 85, 123, 155, 167–168, 176, 196, 204, 209, 232, 235, 277, 302–303, 317
betrayal 6, 22, 35, 42, **47–49**, 65, 72, 75–76, 91, 152, 155, 157, 160, 165, 230, 263, 265–266, 287, 299, 316–317; *see also* "Letters of a Love Betrayed."
Beyé-Dokou (FP) 93, 115, 215, 267, 275
Bible 7, 52, 56, 73–74, 87, 107, 118, 126, 128, 138, 140–141, 145, 169–170, 205, 214, 215, 228, 230, 233, 235, 276, 286, 292, 302, 316
birth 5, 9, 11, 17, 30, 33, 45, 60–61, 63–65, 73–76, 78, 85, 87–88, 97, 98, 104, 110–111, 121, 128, 130, 138, 143, 155–156, 169–170, 178, 180, 187, 193, 195–197, 201, 203, 206, 209, 214, 217, 220–221, 223, 231, 245, 251, 253, 255, 257, 261–264, 275, 276, 279–280, 282, 285, 290, 295, 299, 318–320; *see also* mothering; stillbirth
Blancheland, Philippe (IBS) 207, 230
Blaum, Ana (SEL) 66–67, 181, 190, 319
Blaum, Roberto (SEL) 66–67, 79, 126, 181, 190
Blue Warriors (KGD) 201
Boisier, Violette (IBS) 34, 66, 71, 96–97, 101, 142, 160–161, 172–173, 178, 183, 185, 192, 195, 199, 219, 224, 226, 253, 258, 260, 262, 297
Bolivia 7, 112, 285, 293, 312, 314
Bonecrusher, Joe (DF) 41, 69, 74, 96–97, 101, 194, 227, 248, 250, 278, 319
Borobá (CB, FP, KGD) 142, 163, 210
Boukman, Dutty (IBS) 32, 123, 160, 203, 207, 270, 311
Boukman, Zambo (IBS) 110
Boulton, Filomena (SEL) 124, 190
Boulton, Gilberto (SEL) 190, 232
Boulton, Miguel (SEL) 190
Bretzner, Karl (DF) 68, 251
Bruce, Timothy (FP) 131–132
Buddhism (PS) 78, 113, 117, 141, 162, 186, 205, 242, 244–245, 287, 309–310, 319
Burgel, Aunt (SEL) 42, 106, 266
Burns, Cecilia (CB, FP, KGD) 62
Bush, George H.W. 18
Bush, George W. 20, 45, 314

Caleuche (MIC) 201
Cambray, Prosper (IBS) 41, 65, 81, 86, 155, 191, 207, 230, 272, 274, 287
cannibalism 100, 113, 122, 124, 154, 203, 229, 270, 274
Canuto, Sebastián (EL) 206
capitalism 56, 225, 249
El Capitán (SEL) 165–196
Cardinal (OLS) 54, 212, 243
Carías, Mauro (CB) 41, 48, 55–57, 89, 92, 112, 186, 210, 255
Carlé, Frau (OLS) 49, 60
Carlé, Katherina (EL) 49, 62, 240
Carlé, Lukas (EL) 60, 70, 87, 139, 147, 176, 178, 291
Carlé, Rolf (EL) 40, 60, 62, 87, 88, 106, 147, 167, 177, 213, 224, 240, 264, 267, 276, 300
Carlé-Luna genealogy **49–50**
Cartland, Barbara 8
Castro, Fidel 8, 9, 18, 260, 313
Catalina (IMS) 98, 121, 130–131, 175, 231, 244, 272, 317, 318
Catholicism 6–8, 15, 21, 43, 45, 53–54, 70, 72, 90, 94, 96, 98, 102, 126, 138–139, 141, 143, 145, 150, 155, 158, 160, 170, 175, 178, 182, 197, 200, 218, 234, 238, 242–245, 247, 261–262, 274, 280, 300, 320
Caupolicán (IMS) 184
Cecilia, Princess (IBS) 62, 71, 109, 130, 145, 179, 290
Célestine (IBS) 110
censorship 7, 10–11, 18, 37, 90, 146, 216, 234
Céspedes, Tadeo (SEL) 24, 90, 266, 283
Charles V (IMS) 148, 150, 184, 310
Chi'en, Ebanizer "Lucky" (PS) 51, 222, 263
Chi'en, Lin (DF, PS) 120, 252, 290
Chi'en, Tao (DF, PS) 30–33, 35, 38, 41, 56, 64, 69, 73–75, 78, 80, 84, 93, 101–102, 108, 121, 157, 169, 172, 177, 182, 188, 207, 216, 218, 223, 227, 229, 232, 237, 245, 249, 251, 252, 257–258, 263–264, 278–

279, 290, 295, 296, 315, 317, 318, 320
Chi'en del Valle–Sommers genealogy (DF, PS) **50–51**
Chile 5–13, 15–16, 18, 20–25, 29, 31, 35–37, 40–41, 45, 47, 50, **51–55**, 59, 68–69, 71, 74–76, 83, 85, 88, 90, 93–95, 98–99, 101, 103–105, 107–108, 110–112, 118, 121, 127, 130, 132–136, 141, 143–148, 150–151, 153–154, 156, 166, 168–171, 173–175, 179–180, 182, 188, 190–191, 194, 197, 199–200, 202, 208, 212, 214, 216–218, 220, 223, 227, 231–232, 236–239, 243–244, 248–249, 257, 263–264, 266–267, 272, 276–278, 281–286, 288, 290, 292–294, 299–301, 306–308, 310, 314, 318–319; *see also My Invented Country*; Santiago; War of the Pacific
Chilean Civil War of 1891 (PS) 94, 145, 286, 293, 313
Chiloé 23, 51, 319
Chinatown 19, 169, 212, 222–223, 227, 245, 263–264
Christianity 15, 20, 24, 30, 48, 52, 73, 99, 113, 116, 119, 132, 145, 149, 166, 174, 184, 190, 197, 220, 229, 231–233, 240, 242, 244, 246–247, 257, 266, 276, 284, 293, 308; *see also* Catholicism
CIA (HS) 10, 18, 54, 89–91, 302, 314
Cirilo, Father (OLS) 126
The City of the Beasts 5, 18–21, 32–33, 35, 38, 41, 45, 48, **55–57**, 60, 62, 70, 80–81, 83, 92–93, 96, 100, 112, 115, 117, 123, 130–131, 142, 156, 162, 164, 173, 175–178, 186, 196, 198, 201, 205, 207–208, 210, 214–215, 228, 233, 246, 248, 252, 269–270, 274–275, 279, 287, 289, 291, 294, 297, 317–319, 321
"Civilize Your Troglodyte" 11, 319
"Clarisa" (SEL) 39, 86, 89, 118, 124, 164, 173, 185, 222–223, 242, 250, 316–317
Clayton, Tom (IP) 194
Cobb, Harrison (IBS) 181, 189, 297, 316
Cold, Alexander "Jaguar" (CB, FP, KGD) 19, 35–36, 55–56, 60–62, 70, 80–81, 87, 92–93, 112–115, 123, 131–132, 142, 156, 162–165, 175–176, 178, 186, 198, 201, 203, 205, 205, 210, 233, 246–247, 252–253, 256, 267, 269, 270, 274–275, 279, 287, 292, 297–298, 315, 317
Cold, John (CB, FP, KGD) 57, 123, 297
Cold, Joseph (CB) 199
Cold, Kate (CB, FP, KGD) 21, 48, 55, 61, 87, 95, 96, 100, 132, 142, 162, 164, 165, 201, 205, 210, 215, 256, 257, 253, 295, 297, 316, 317, 320
Cold, Lisa (CB, FP, KGD) 56, 61, 80, 112, 123, 196, 198, 207, 275, 279, 287, 318
Cold genealogy **57–58**
the Collector (KGD) 93, 162, 186, 319
colonialism 11, 12, 20, 31, 37, 41, 42, 45, 47–48, 52, 53, 55, 56, 65–66, 72, 74, 71, 82, 85, 89, 92, 94, 96, 98, 101, 104, 107, 108, 109–110, 111, 116, 118, 120, 121, 122–123, 127, 128, 129, 130, 132, 133, 135–136, 137, 139, 142, 143, 145, 147, 148–151, 153–154, 157, 159–161, 164, 168, 167, 172–173, 175, 178, 180, 184, 187, 188, 190, 191–192, 196, 197, 200, 206, 207, 209, 213, 229–230, 231, 233, 236, 238, 239, 240, 242, 243, 244, 245, 255, 258, 261, 265, 266, 268–269, 270, 273, 275, 277, 278, 280–281, 282, 284, 286, 287, 290–291, 292, 293, 296, 300, 301, 306, 307, 308, 310, 311, 315, 318, 320
Columbus, Christopher 68, 231, 310
comic book 22, 232
coming of age 35–36, 56, **58–62**, 65, 75, 132, 209, 224, 236, 259, 303
concentration camp 64, 268, 295
confinement 30, 33, 52, 53, **62–66**, 68, 101, 102, 106, 115, 118–120, 123, 128, 134, 136, 144, 149, 164, 172, 174, 177, 180, 204, 216, 217, 225, 227, 243, 245, 246, 251, 260, 268, 276–278, 281, 283, 285, 290, 296, 297, 299, 306, 311, 313, 317
Conquistadors (IMS) 11, 31, 52, 56, 71, 96, 101, 104, 109, 139, 142, 147, 148, 154, 157, 168, 173, 184, 190, 197, 200, 231, 244, 258, 266, 282, 293, 300, 310, 315
conservatism 8, 53, 63, 68, 89, 101, 106, 118–119, 135, 146, 166, 200, 206, 216, 218–219, 240, 243, 261, 282, 292, 293
Consuelo (EL) 49, 86–87, 96, 100, 106, 120, 126, 167, 173, 207, 217, 235, 251, 270, 316–317
contraception 54, 59, 143
cooking 30, 32, 34, 41–44, 63–64, 74–75, 83, 88, 93, 96, 100, 102, 105–110, 111–114, 120, 121, 126–127, 181, 189, 193, 204, 217, 237, 239, 248, 251, 258, 270, 276, 296, 318; *see also* food
cordillera 51–52, 138, 149, 197, 306, 315
costume 12, 30, 32, 40, **66–73**, 74–75, 119, 154, 161, 181, 210, 248–249, 275, 279, 302–303, 318
creativity 7, 15, 18, 30, 52, 79, 94, 101, 103, 115, 119, 136, 170, 188, 196k 249, 251, 300, 320
Crepusculario, Belisa (SEL) 40, 44, 164, 205, 215, 265
Crías, Mauro (CB) 41, 48, 55–56, 89, 92, 112, 186, 210, 255
Cuban Revolution 8, 160, 290, 314
Cuevas, Dr. (HS) 11, 119, 174, 205–206, 239
Cyrus (IP) 91, 141, 152, 156, 176, 252, 295, 317

dance 24, 66, 68, 88, 115, 124, 142, 165, 196–198, 208, 210, 245, 259, 261, 291, 305–308, 313, 316, 319
Daughter of Fortune 15, 18, 30, 32, 33, 35, 38–41, 45, 47, 52, 55, 63, 68, **73–76**, 78, 83, 88, 93, 96–97, 99, 101, 105, 107, 116, 121, 126–127, 133, 137, 139, 140, 145, 147, 153, 154, 157, 158, 164, 166, 168, 170, 172, 176–177, 179–180, 182, 186, 188, 190–191, 194, 201–202, 207, 214–216, 218–219, 222, 224, 226, 228, 232, 235, 237, 239, 243, 248=251, 269, 277–278, 283, 285, 290, 294–296, 298, 300, 310, 317, 319, 320–321
de Alderete, Jerónimo (IBS) 130, 150

de Almagro, Diego (IMS) 42, 52, 244, 286, 310
death 7–8, 11–12, 16–17, 21, 31–33, 38, 41–44, 47, 56, 60–63, 67, 71, 74, **76–82**, 84, 87–88, 91–92, 106, 110–111, 117, 119, 121, 123–124, 128, 130, 132, 140, 145–147, 149, 155, 158, 171–174, 177, 186–189, 193–194, 196, 198, 202, 204–205, 208, 210, 212–214, 217, 219–221, 223–225, 228, 230–231, 233, 235–237, 243, 246, 251–252, 256, 258, 260, 262–264, 267–271, 273–277, 279–281, 283, 285, 288–290, 292, 295, 299, 301–303, 310, 315–318
de Callís, Eulalia (Z) 142, 183–184
Dédé, Sanité (IBS) 81, 123, 181, 246, 317
de Ercilla y Zúñiga, Alonso (PS) 85, 154, 310
de la Fuente, Fernando (FP) 20–21, 114
de la Gasca, Pedro (IMS) 184
de la Vega, Alejandro (Z) 155–156, 182–183, 231, 296, 302
de la Vega, Diego *SEE* Zorro
de León, Santiago (Z) 132, 197, 232–233, 296
Delphine, Madame (IBS) 142, 167
del Valle, Agustín (PS) 129, 145, 182, 218, 283
del Valle, Alba (HS) 10, 23, 33, 34, 39, 44, 47, 59, 63, 64, 67, 68, 78, 87, 93–94, 95, 100, 101, 106, 116, 117, 119, 120, 125, 133, 134, 135, 136, 137, 139, 144, 166–167, 168, 170, 174, 178, 180, 182, 193, 196, 206, 222, 225, 226, 233, 234, 235, 240, 256, 268–269, 276–277, 278, 280, 281, 284, 292, 295, 298–299, 300
del Valle, Aurora (PS) 11, 18, 30–31, 35, 40–42, 53, 56, 58, 65, 83, 96–98, 103, 111, 129, 169, 188, 193, 199, 207, 219, 222–226, 238–240, 244, 249, 257, 263–264, 268, 279, 286, 296, 299, 315
del Valle, Blanca (HS) 10, 30, 34, 44, 59, 64, 677, 82, 94, 96, 100–101, 103, 105–106, 119, 125, 133–134, 136, 139, 166, 170, 177, 181, 184, 187, 192, 196, 202, 206, 209, 213, 233–234, 236, 240, 256, 273, 276–277, 281, 289, 292, 299–300, 318–320
del Valle, Clara (HS) 5, 10–12, 22, 31, 33, 37, 40–41, 44, 47, 62–63, 67, 75, 77–778, 83, 94–96, 101, 105–106, 116–117, 119–120, 125, 133–139, 141, 146, 154, 157–158, 164, 166–170, 174, 177–178, 183, 187, 192–193, 206–207, 213, 216, 228, 236, 239–240, 255–256, 261, 268, 273, 276–278, 280–281, 283, 289, 295, 298–299, 311, 315, 317–318, 320
del Valle, Jaime (HS) 33–34, 39, 78, 89, 119, 125, 134, 136, 170, 174, 176, 213, 233–234, 235, 236, 240, 256, 278, 280, 292, 317
del Valle, Nicolás (HS) 33–34, 39, 73, 76, 78, 89, 119, 125, 134, 136, 146–147, 170, 174, 176, 213, 233–236, 240, 250, 256, 278, 280, 292, 317
del Valle, Nívea (HS, PS) 65, 78, 82, 94, 96, 98, 100, 103, 118, 119, 129–130, 133, 134–136, 138, 146, 166, 206, 213, 218–219, 223, 249, 255–256, 257, 261, 276, 286, 296
del Valle, Paulina (PS) 53, 63, 70, 71, 73, 78, 96, 97, 98, 103, 108, 110, 111, 130, 140, 145, 146, 169, 170, 183, 188, 192, 193, 216, 218, 219, 222, 223, 224, 238, 240, 241, 250, 263–264, 286, 296, 217, 320
del Valle, Rosa (HS) 11, 40, 77, 97, 105, 118–119, 125, 133, 138, 166, 169–170, 173–174, 196, 206, 276, 278
del Valle, Severo (HS, PS) 41–42, 78, 105, 129–130, 140, 177, 188, 218–219, 223–224, 243, 257, 263, 285–286, 296
del Valle–García–Trueba genealogy (HS) 34, **82–83**; *see also* Chi'en–del Valle–Sommers genealogy
de Málaga, Juan (IMS) 149
de Marmolejo, González (IMS) 142, 188
de Quiroga, Isabel (IMS) 193, 228
de Quiroga, Rodrigo (IMS) 31, 76, 109, 122, 145, 175, 184, 228, 258, 299
de Rameu, Tomás (Z) 118
de Romeu, Isabel (Z) 142, 167
de Romeu, Juliana (Z) 197, 303, 315, 317, 319
desaparecidos 11, 30, 44–45, 47, 54, 64, 68, 90, 120, 165, 170, 179, 190, 202, 278, 284, 315, 318
Dessalines, François (IBS) 32, 181, 204
diaspora 159, 190, 197; *see also* migration literature
Díaz, Ana (Z) 85, 196, 218, 266, 303
Díaz, Concha (SEL) 32, 265
Díaz, Ernesto 15–17, 129
dictator novel 13, 133, 318
"A Discreet Miracle" (SEL) 74, 124, 126, 190, 242, 264, 266–267, 300
disease 13, 15–16, 33, 43, 52, 56, 77, 79, 97, 108, 124–132, 134, 139, 157–158, 182, 194–195, 203–204, 217–218, 220, 225–227, 236, 248, 261, 291, 292, 294, 302, 312–313; *see also* health and healing; madness; venereal disease
disguise 67–68, 70, 72–74, 84, 90, 132, 138, 158, 194, 210
divorce 6, 14, 47, 54, 86, 139, 144, 271–272, 317
Domínguez, Diego (PS) 35, 47, 103, 257, 279, 315
Domínguez, Doña Elvira (PS) 58, 93, 96, 120, 193, 213, 224, 251, 316–318, 320
Domínguez, Sebastián (PS) 176
Domínguez, Susana (PS) 58, 257, 279, 318
Donaldina and Martha (PS) 188
Dorji (KGD) 33, 41, 48, 61, 79–80, 84, 117, 162, 163, 176, 205, 210, 214, 292, 298, 317
drama 6, 8, 10, 19, 21, 25, 31, 33, 40–42, 47–49, 59–60, 64 71, 73, 75–76, 84–85, 90, 92, 95, 97, 99–100, 102–103, 106, 108–109, 122, 125, 134–135, 139, 141, 147, 152, 154, 159–163, 165, 169, 182, 184, 195, 203, 206–207, 211, 216, 221 231, 233, 237–238, 244, 251, 255–256, 260, 263–264, 266, 272, 275, 279, 281–282, 287, 289, 299, 318
drugs 9, 19, 36, 55, 61, 65, 72, 91, 96, 127–128, 130, 143, 152, 226, 281, 294, 317
duality 31, 33–38, 43, 46, 56–57, 61, 63, 68, 70, 72–74, 77, **83–86**, 89–90, 94–95,

102, 107, 109, 115, 117, 120, 128, 130, 143, 153, 168, 183, 190, 195, 199–200, 202, 205, 209, 211, 223, 236, 239, 247, 252, 259, 269, 277, 283, 290, 298, 302, 318, 320
Duane, Timothy (IP) 252
Duchamp, Agnès (Z) 73, 233
Duchamp, Roland (Z) 73, 296

earthquake 22–23, 52, 77, 101, 105, 125, 134, 141, 157, 177, 180, 183, 187, 213, 277, 280, 313–314
ecofeminism 20, 315
education 7, 32, 50, 55, 57, 59–60, 74, 85, 96–98, 100–101, 125, 135–136, 142–143, 152, 208–210, 216, 229, 232, 234–235, 237, 244, 252, 255, 257, 261, 263, 274, 293, 297, 314, 318, 320; *see also* literacy
egalitarianism 54, 101, 115, 130, 156, 194, 206, 258, 289, 296
Eloísa (SEL) 107, 165, 196, 266
Elvira (EL) 96, 120, 251, 316, 320
Emancipation Proclamation (IBS) 66
Emilia (PS) 64
Erzulie (IBS) 98, 123, 197–198, 245–246, 306–307, 320
Escalante, Manuel (Z) 232, 287, 296, 303–304
Escapulario, Sor María (PS) 94, 98, 146, 219
Escobar (IMS) 274
"Ester Lucero" (SEL) 79, 112, 124, 138, 164, 205, 208, 266, 283, 285
ethnocentrism (FP) 93, 247
Etxebarría, Elena (GL) 137–138, 272, 288–289, 315
Eurocentrism 20–21
euthanasia (SEL) 79, 265, 319
Eva Luna 9, 14, 30, 32, 33, 38, 42, 47, 60, 64, 70, 84, **86–88**, 89, 95–96, 100, 103, 106–107, 115, 119, 120, 124, 126, 138, 139, 146, 147, 153, 154, 167, 170, 172, 173, 176–177, 178, 179, 182, 190, 197, 206, 207, 209, 212, 213, 217, 222, 224, 225, 226, 232, 233, 235, 236, 237, 239, 243, 250, 251, 255, 257, 265, 266, 268, 270, 271, 283, 285, 299, 300, 315, 316, 318, 319, 320
evil 7, 10, 19, 48, 56, 61–62, 77, 87, **89–93**, 113, 115, 116, 120, 122, 123, 125, 131, 132, 134, 148, 172, 188, 201, 216, 220, 243, 270, 274, 275, 276, 277, 284, 306
expatriation 15, 29, 53, 59–60, 75, 86, 179, 220, 278
Ezenji (FP) 198, 208

Fages, Pedro (Z) 183, 184
fantasy 5, 6, 8, 19, 20, 37, 40, 51, 52, 62, 68, 80, 84, 91, 94, 117, 119, 152, 157, 163, 175, 182, 191, 202, 216, 221, 233, 236, 237, 239, 257, 265, 266, 278, 279, 284, 290, 295, 318
fascism 10–11, 14, 19, 47, 53–54, 65, 89, 96, 97, 100, 101, 120, 133, 166, 211–210, 234, 237, 242, 261, 280, 289, 292
Felipe/Lautaro (IMS) 47, 48, 85, 109, 121, 122, 142, 150, 175, 176, 178, 184, 208, 282, 310, 317, 318
female persona 5, 6, 7, 8, 9, 11, 12, 13, 17, 19, 23, 24, 30, 31, 32, 34, 35, 40, 41, 42, 43, 45–46, 47, 48, 52, 54, 59, 61, 62–63, 66, 67, 68, 69, 70, 71, 75, 85, 88, 90, 91, **93–99**, 100, 101, 102, 103, 108, 112, 115, 117, 119, 123, 127, 128, 133, 134, 135, 138, 40, 141, 142, 143, 145, 149, 150, 152, 154, 155, 158, 165, 166, 167, 170, 174, 175, 178, 179, 180, 181, 182, 185, 192, 193, 194, 195, 196, 198, 200, 205, 206, 209, 210, 211, 212, 213, 215, 216, 217, 218, 225, 226, 227, 230, 237, 240, 241, 242, 245, 248, 250, 251, 252, 253, 255, 256, 257, 258, 259, 261, 262, 263, 265, 268, 269, 276, 278, 279, 280, 282, 283, 285, 288, 290, 291, 293, 295, 297, 298, 299, 300, 301, 314, 315, 316, 320
feminism 6–9, 10–11, 16, 18, 19, 20, 30, 34, 38, 42, 59, 74, 75, 86, 88, 94, 95, 96, 97, **99–104**, 117, 119, 133, 136, 140, 166, 170, 174, 182, 215, 217, 219, 234, 239, 240, 255, 257, 288, 289, 292, 293, 303, 315, 320
film 15, 16, 18, 20, 24, 36, 42, 60, 79, 86, 142, 163, 182, 183, 186, 200, 201, 217, 233, 234, 243, 279, 282, 303, 318
Flores, Antonio (OLS) 104
Flores, Evangelina (OLS) 44, 47, 104
Flores-Ranquileo genealogy (OLS) **104–105**
food 8, 11, 14, 18, 24, 33, 35, 42–44, 53–55, 74, **105–114**, 131, 141, 150, 153, 165–166, 170, 184, 188, 193, 200, 209, 225, 236, 240, 249–250, 261, 290–297, 306, 309, 316, 318–319; *see also* cooking
foot binding (DF) 74, 278
Forest of the Pygmies 20, 22, 25, 33, 35, 41, 45, 48, 55, 57, 62, 65–66, 85, 93, 95–97, 100, 113, **114–116**, 117, 124, 131, 142, 156, 164, 172–173, 176, 192, 198, 208, 210, 215, 226, 228, 247, 252, 267, 268, 285, 279, 283, 288, 291, 292, 298, 310, 316, 318, 319
forgiveness 24, **116–118**, 137, 155, 161, 188, 200, 209, 230, 241, 256, 295
Fortunato, Horacio (SEL) 205, 261, 265, 269
"Fox and Hens" (HS) 29, 130, 154, 196
Freemont, Jacob (DF) 202, 248
French Revolution (IBS) 32, 72, 145, 159, 231, 301, 311
Frías, Lori Barra 17, 18, 20, 23
Frías, Miguel (MIC, P) 8, 9, 12, 14, 16, 23, 315
Frías, Nicolás "Nico" 9, 12, 19, 20, 271
Frías, Paula (P) 9, 12, 14–16, 18, 19, 21, 22, 30, 32, 42, 43, 73, 126, 186, 193–194, 217–222, 273, 288, 315–319

Gabrieleno (Z) 302, 304
Galbaud, Général (IBS) 72, 311
Galupi, Leo (IP) 91, 252
Gambo La Liberté (IBS) 48, 72, 98–99, 109, 110, 128–129, 148, 160, 167, 176, 195, 203–204, 207, 258–259, 270, 274, 290, 301, 315
gangs (IP) 45, 60, 92–93, 102, 152, 252, 285, 320
García, Esteban (HS) 11, 43, 63, 67, 90, 101, 119, 135, 136, 167, 176, 180, 255, 268, 279–280, 281, 284
García, Pancha (HS) 135–136, 178, 180, 280
García, Pedro (HS)29, 77, 119, 130, 134, 136, 154, 177–178, 202, 208, 276–277, 295, 316, 320
García, Pedro Segundo (HS)

29, 67, 136, 157, 180, 187, 213, 277, 318
García, Pedro Tercero (HS) 29, 34, 44, 59, 63–64, 67, 82, 106, 120, 136–137, 139, 154, 158, 177, 180, 187, 196, 202, 209, 233, 240, 256, 276, 280, 283, 289, 317
García del Solar, Eugenia (IBS) 6, 65–66, 71, 80, 81, 97, 109, 122, 128, 167, 171, 195, 207, 219, 230, 244, 258, 261–262, 274
García del Solar, Sancho (IBS) 6, 91, 110, 145, 161, 262, 297
García Márquez, Gabriel 8, 12, 13, 26, 38, 134, 174, 211, 232, 236, 255, 316–317
"Gift for a Sweetheart" (SEL) 205, 261, 265, 266, 269, 298, 316–317
Godoy, Joaquín (PS) 64–65, 145–146
"The Gold of Tomás Vargas" (SEL) 32, 33, 38, 42, 95, 215, 240, 265, 295
gold rush (DF) 18, 30, 32, 75, 83, 98, 107, 145, 153, 154, 158, 168–169, 170, 194, 202–203, 227, 237, 239, 248–249, 312
Gómez, Pedro (IMS) 76, 130, 231, 290
González, Joel (CB) 131, 247
Gordon, Jennifer (SOD) 21, 271
Gordon, William "Willie" C. (MIC, P) 14–15, 18, 20–21, 44–45, 111, 140, 151–153, 165, 220, 252, 271, 294, 315
Gothic 6, 61, 63, 67, 80, 87, **118–124**, 128, 150, 159, 174, 176 201, 206, 217–218, 265, 276–277, 281, 299
Greer, Germaine 10
grief 7, 12, 16, 17, 23, 30, 42, 53, 63, 70, 73, 76, 77–78, 70, 80–81, 111, 117, 121, 132, 143, 168, 178, 194, 196, 197, 206, 218, 220, 221, 226, 235, 268, 271, 273, 292, 295, 299, 300, 315, 318
Grr-ympr (KGD) 57, 77, 164, 252
Guacolda (IMS) 85, 184, 208, 318
Guevara, Ernesto "Che" 160, 313, 314
"The Guggenheim Lovers" 29, 138, 172, 185, 201, 214, 255, 272, 276, 288, 291, 298, 216–217, 288–289
Guinea (IBS) 32, 34, 85–86, 148, 158, 171, 197, 203, 207, 226, 245–246, 258, 262, 270, 274, 283, 287, 290, 301, 318
Guizot, Hortense (IBS) 43, 110, 143, 145, 184, 259
Gypsies (Z) 22, 32, 67, 71–72, 98, 130, 183, 196, 199, 232, 272–273, 302, 304, 306, 308, 313

Habitation Saint Lazare (IBS) 159, 261, 319
hagiography (HS) 30, 77, 118, 139, 150, 201, 206, 245–246, 264, 270
Haiti (IBS) 22–23, 25–26, 32, 34, 40–41, 44, 48, 66, 71, 72–73, 81, 86, 91, 98–99, 102, 110, 122, 128–129, 145–146, 148, 155, 158–161, 171, 173, 180–181, 184–185, 189–191, 203–205, 207, 213, 226, 230, 235–236, 238, 245–246, 258, 261–262, 270, 274, 283, 287, 290–291, 293, 297, 301, 307–311, 319
Haitian Revolution (IBS) 23, 66, 81, 99, 109, 128, 148, 155, 158, 184, 191, 203, 245, 262, 293, 297, 311
Halabí, Riad (EL) 38, 86–87, 103, 107, 177, 190, 209, 217, 243, 251, 266, 281, 295, 315
Halabí, Zulema (EL) 64, 88, 96, 126, 167, 209, 255, 257, 281, 317
healing and health 17, 19, 25, 29, 31, 35, 37, 42, 38, 56, 64, 71, 74, 77–80, 82, 90, 96, 100, 105, 108, 110–111, 113–114, 117–118, **124–132**, 133, 136, 141, 156, 167–169, 171–172, 175, 177–178, 192, 194, 197–198, 202, 203 218, 221, 228–229, 236, 242, 247–249, 266, 272, 275, 279, 287, 289, 291, 296, 297, 306, 308, 309, 314, 315, 318, 319, 320
herbalism 30, 32, 34, 39, 64, 66, 69, 71, 73, 74, 78, 81, 84, 126, 128–130, 132, 141, 160, 170, 171, 182, 202–203, 218, 227, 248, 249, 252, 263, 296, 306, 308
Hermelinda (SEL) 208, 225, 255, 266
Hidalgo, Casilda (SEL) 266, 319
Hidalgo, Judge (SEL) 153, 205
Hinduism (KGD) 162
Hirondelle, Fleur (IBS) 181, 198
Hobbs, Ebanizer (DF) 74, 127, 251–252, 278, 296
homosexuality 35, 68, 154, 178, 179–180, 285, 307, 314; *see also* Mario; Mimí; Satigny, Jean de
Honoré (IBS) 13, 18, 24, 25, 95, 122, 160, 162, 192, 197, 268, 271
Hortensia (SEL) 118, 166, 266, 281, 288, 315
The House of the Spirits 5, 6, 10, 11, 13–16, 18, 20, 22–26, 29–31, 33, 37, 40, 43, 44, 47, 53, 55, 59, 62, 67–68, 71, 75, 77, 83, 87, 89–90, 93, 95–97, 100–101, 103–105, 116, 118, 120, 122, 124, 125, **132–137**, 138, 144, 146, 153–154, 157–158, 169, 173–174, 176–180, 182–183, 186, 190, 192, 196, 199, 202, 205–206, 208–209, 211, 213, 216, 218, 222, 224–225, 227–228, 233, 236–237, 239, 241, 243, 250–251, 255, 261, 267–268, 271, 273, 276, 279–280, 283, 289, 292, 294–295, 298, 310, 318, 319, 320
The House of the Spirits (film) 16
The House of the Spirits (play) 16, 22, 23, 24
Huidibro, Ramón 6–8, 9, 10
humor 10–11, 18, 35, 41–42, 45, 54, 60, 63, 70, 72, 87, 92, 95, 100, 103, 107, 114, 124, 125, 129, **137–143**, 146, 152, 157, 158, 164, 174, 184, 200, 205, 215, 323, 233, 243, 252, 271, 263, 273, 275, 280, 282, 288, 292, 294, 303, 317, 319
Hurtado, Général (HS) 134, 135
hypocrisy 73, 94, 139, 140, **143–146**, 155, 179, 182, 188, 219, 228, 243

idealism 8, 17, 29, 49, 55, 57, 69, 75, 87, 88, 91, 92, 96, 102, 118, 135–137, **146–148**, 149, 151, 155–157, 164, 176, 177, 180–183, 187–188, 194, 202, 209, 217, 223, 231, 233, 237, 250, 255, 270, 278–280, 283, 285, 292, 292, 293, 294, 296, 297, 302
illegitimacy 35, 59, 82, 89, 101, 135–136, 139, 144, 178, 180, 194, 216, 251, 255, 263, 280
Imagining Ourselves 94
"The Impertinents" 9, 11

Inca (IMS) 71, 119, 139, 208, 231, 310; *see also* Cecilia, Princess
incest (OLS) 44, 84, 104, 181, 253, 260
Inés (schoolteacher) (EL, SEL) 87, 126, 146, 250, 265, 266, 320
Inés of My Soul 14, 20, 21, 24, 31, 38, 40–43, 45, 47, 51, 52, 56, 71, 76, 85, 96, 99, 101, 103, 108, 121, 122, 130, 142, 145, 147, **148–151**, 154, 157, 161, 168, 173, 175–179, 182, 184, 188, 190, 192, 197, 199, 204, 208, 212, 225, 231, 235, 236, 238, 242, 244, 250, 257, 268, 272, 274, 281, 283, 286, 290, 293, 295, 298, 299, 300, 319
The Infinite Plan 11, 15, 16, 30, 32, 36, 39, 40, 43, 45, 47, 60, 65, 71, 75, 80, 82, 84, 90, 95, 96, 102, 111, 116, 140, 147, **151–153**, 156, 165, 167, 171, 173, 176, 179, 184, 188, 191, 193, 199, 226, 233, 236, 239, 248, 252, 260, 273, 283, 294, 296, 310, 317–319
injustice 12, 29, 37, 72, 87, 101, **153–157**, 173, 180, 188, 206, 228, 231, 281; *see also* racism
intergenerationalism 6, 9, 12, 13, 16, 21, 23, 29, 30–31, 38, 44, 48, 49, 55, 56, 57, 61, 63, 67, 68, 70, 78, 83, 87, 92, 94, 96, 97, 98, 99, 101, 103, 109, 114, 116, 117, 119, 130, 133, 135, 139, 162, 165, 174, 187, 188, 191, 196, 198, 199, 200, 201, 205, 219, 220, 222, 223, 224, 233, 240, 241, 249, 260, 264, 268, 270, 277, 280, 286, 295, 297, 299, 308, 317; *see also* Cold, Kate; del Valle, Clara; del Valle, Paulina; García, Pancha; Sommers, Eliza; Tété; Trueba, Esteban
"Interminable Life" (SEL) 12, 66–67, 78, 126, 146, 164, 181, 190, 267, 318
irony 18, 38, 45, 62, 64, 65, 69, 75, 78, 82, 84, 102, 103, 105, 109, 110, 129, 132, 139, 144, 147, 153, 156, **157–159**, 162, 166, 169, 180, 183, 187, 191, 200, 201, 207, 218, 220, 235, 238, 240, 242, 244, 247, 258, 263, 265, 274, 278, 286, 289
Isabel Allende Foundation 17, 22
Island Beneath the Sea 6, 23, 31, 32, 34, 38, 40, 41, 43, 44, 48, 58, 65, 66, 71, 72, 80, 81, 89, 91, 95–98, 101, 102, 109, 122, 123, 128, 142, 145, 146–148, 155, 158, **159–161**, 167, 171, 172, 176, 177–180, 182, 189–192, 195, 197, 201, 203, 205, 207, 213, 219, 224, 226, 229, 233, 235, 238, 239, 244, 245, 250, 258, 261, 269, 270, 272, 274, 282, 283, 287, 290, 291, 297, 301, 310, 316–320
Iyomi (CB) 5, 32, 57, 100, 113, 252, 317, 320

Jews 63, 120, 141, 180, 181, 191, 228, 232, 243, 277, 313
Jiménez, Juana (IMS) 150
Joan (IP) 43, 95, 102
Jones, Professor (EL) 87, 120, 177, 233, 235, 251
José Dulce María (HS) 77–78, 178, 234, 243
journalism 8–14, 29, 30, 34, 37, 53, 54, 59, 60, 64, 68, 77, 88, 116, 144, 147, 157, 166, 168, 177, 188, 202, 214, 220, 236, 237, 250, 264, 267, 276, 278, 284, 298, 300
Juana, Queen (IMS) 121
Juana la Triste (SEL) 153, 205
Juana of the Lilies (SEL) 267
Juanillo (Z) 273
Juarez, María Teresa (P) 273
"The Judge's Wife" (SEL) 153, 205, 240, 266, 269
La Justicia (Z) 232, 303

Kamal (EL) 88, 107, 126, 153, 167, 217, 255, 257, 281, 300, 317
"King of the Pressure Cookers" (HS) 63
Kingdom of the Golden Dragon 20, 33, 35, 38, 41, 48, 55, 57, 60, 61, 62, 66, 71, 77, 79, 80, 81, 84, 89, 92, 96, 100, 113, 115, 124, 131, 156, 160, **161–164**, 172, 176, 177, 186, 196, 201, 203, 205, 208, 210, 214, 228, 242, 246, 250, 252, 261, 275, 279, 283, 287, 288, 291, 292, 297, 310, 315, 318, 319, 320
Kinski, Judit (KGD) 48, 117, 214, 247
Kobi (FP) 57, 142, 210
Kunglung, Myar (KGD) 95, 163

Lacroix (IBS) 66, 81, 155, 191, 205, 230, 258, 262, 282, 283, 287, 301
Lafitte, Jean (Z) 20, 72, 97, 142, 180, 263, 303, 304, 312, 319
Lafitte, Pierre (Z) 20, 180, 312
language and silence 12, 14, 15, 16, 18, 21, 22, 24, 33, 35, 36, 45, 50, 53, 55, 59, 60, 73, 74, 78, 82, 92, 97, 112, 119, 120, 122, 125, 140, 142, 159, 160, **164–169**, 174, 176–178, 180, 183, 186, 190, 195, 196, 197, 198, 204, 208, 210, 212, 216, 217, 219, 221, 224, 229–230, 245, 248, 249, 253, 256, 265, 266, 268, 270, 271, 274, 276, 279, 283, 295, 300, 301, 303, 308, 318
Larramendi, Aitor (GL) 138, 289
Larraquibel, Padre (IP) 141
Laveau, Marie (Z) 20, 97
law 47, 91, 138, 140, 147, 149–150, 152, 155, 156, 159, 169, 184, 214, 262, 285, 310
Leal, Francisco (OLS) 30, 44, 46, 53, 88, 107, 165, 176, 178, 190, 212, 214, 224, 233, 234, 278, 281, 284–285, 299, 315, 319
Leal, Hilda (OLS) 44, 46, 96, 97, 107, 165–166, 181, 206, 294–295
Leal, Javier (OLS) 44, 46, 176, 181, 278, 281
Leal, José (OLS) 44, 46, 281
Leal, Professor (OLS) 44, 46, 147, 176, 181, 190, 212, 278, 284, 317, 320
Leblanc, Ludovic (CB) 57, 92, 176, 215, 270, 319
letter writing 8, 11, 13, 16, 18, 20, 22, 23, 30, 49, 59, 65, 137, 147, 165, 210, 220, 235, 265, 266, 273, 316, 317
Letters of a Love Betrayed (musical) 22, 49
"Letters of a Love Betrayed" (SEL) 22, 49, 265, 317
Letters to Paula 18, 273, 316
La Liberté *see* Gambo
Lieberman, Marcia (SEL) 33
Light-in-the-Night (Z) 96, 98, 197, 303, 317
Listen, Paula 17
Listen Up! 9
literacy 17, 30, 64, 88, 93, 136, 156, 233, 234, 235
"The Little Heidelberg" (SEL) 21, 42, 49, 107, 196, 266, 31

Llona Barros, Francisca "Panchita" 5, 8, 12, 17, 320
Llona Cuevas, Agustín "Tata" 6–9, 12, 16, 79
Los Riscos mine (OLS) 13, 54, 64, 68, 120, 202, 211, 237, 319
Louisiana Purchase (IBS) 66, 129, 155, 158, 167, 185, 189, 262, 311, 319
Loula (IBS) 34, 96, 181, 185, 192, 262, 272
"Love Mail" 9
Lowell, Amanda (PS) 53, 96, 106, 125, 183, 213, 218, 219, 241, 250, 256, 278, 317
Luna (play) 19

Má Bangesé (FP) 21, 93, 252, 253, 275, 298, 317
Macandal (IBS) 32, 85–86, 122, 178, 203, 270, 287, 290, 311, 319
machismo 6, 8, 54, 55, 90, 100, 103, 133, 138, 151–152, 157, 166, 177, 219, 222, 261, 280, 281, 290, 320; *see also* patriarchy
madness 80, 121, 128, **169–172**, 193, 195, 227
magical realism 6, 19, 25, 32, 37, 56, 61, 83, 95, 113, 134, 138, 157, **172–176**, 183, 193, 199, 203, 209, 220, 228, 233, 237, 267, 274, 275, 276, 277, 283, 286, 288
Málaga, Juan de (IMS) 149, 173, 182, 299
male persona 6, 9, 35, 40, 44, 54, 57, 59, 69, 82–83, 94, 95, 98, 100, 101–102, 114–115, 133, 138, 149, 151, 152–153, **176–179**, 181, 185, 200, 214, 217, 218, 223, 224, 250, 252, 255, 261–262, 265, 281, 291, 293; *see also machismo*; Mimí; patriarchy
Mama Fresia (DF) 69, 75, 96, 107, 126–127, 130, 168, 179–180, 184, 194, 201, 215, 228, 295
Mamita Encarnación (OLS) 125, 126, 130
Mampato 9
Manuel, Don (P) 79
Mapuche (IMS) 5, 31, 47, 50, 52, 73, 74, 75, 85, 99, 107, 121, 122, 126, 127, 142, 148, 149, 150, 153, 168, 175, 179, 184, 186, 190, 199–200, 204–205, 208, 225, 228, 231, 242, 243, 244, 249, 263, 264, 281, 282, 285, 286, 293, 307, 309, 310, 312, 318, 319
Marcos, Uncle (HS) 63, 77, 136, 138, 174, 234, 235, 250
marginalism 23, 34, 38, 46, 69, 75, 84, 87, 106, **179–181**, 216, 224, 237, 243, 269, 294, 316
marianismo 6–7, 102, 141, 142, 150, 152, 175, 219, 244, 245
Mario (OLS) 90, 178, 179, 299, 317, 318, 319
Mario, Doctor (SEL) 181
Maroons (IBS) 32, 40, 48, 66, 72, 98, 103, 110, 123, 155, 160, 189, 195, 201, 203, 204, 207, 259, 282, 301, 307, 311
marriage 6, 7, 12, 14, 15, 29, 30, 31, 41, 43, 44, 45, 46, 47, 49, 58, 62, 74, 77, 97, 98, 101, 102, 105, 106, 129, 134, 139, 140, 145, 147, 150, 152, 169, 172, 174, **181–185**, 187, 188, 190, 193, 197, 209, 215–216, 218, 219, 224, 252, 253, 256, 258, 259, 261, 262, 263, 264, 273, 281, 285, 308, 314, 316, 317, 319, 320; *see also* divorce; polygamy
Marxism 9, 10, 52–53, 89, 106, 135, 170, 176, 188, 225, 234, 240, 242–243, 283, 314
materialism 40, 162, **185–189**, 208, 210, 211, 239, 246, 248, 296
Mathilde, Tante (IBS) 109–110
Maya's Notebook 23, 165, 300, 315, 318
Mbembelé, Maurice (FP) 48, 62, 100, 114, 115–116, 117, 215, 275
McGovern, Abigail (SEL) 66–67, 185, 201
Mejías, Elena (SEL) 96, 205, 265
Melesio *see* Mimí
Mendoza, Padre (Z) 204
Mestizas/Mestizos 5, 20, 63, 74, 87, 89, 130, 183, 187, 197, 228, 231, 258, 302, 307, 315; *see also* Chi'en, Aurora; del Valle, Alba; Zorro
Michimalonko (IMS) 109, 175, 281–282, 310, 318
microfinancing (PS) 103
migration literature 11, 21, 24, 55, 60, 68, 73, 106, 121, 133, 169, **190–192**, 200, 226, 249, 269, 307, 313, 318
Miguel (lawyer) (HS) 83, 182, 256, 281
Miguel, Padre (SEL) 126, 190, 242, 264, 267
Mimí (EL) 30, 32, 49, 70, 84, 86, 103, 170, 178, 179, 251, 299, 316
miracles 113, 129, 175, 214, 243, 270, 272, 274, 275, 277, 288, 300, 318
missions 20–21, 42, 45, 73, 114, 116, 117, 126, 139, 140, 157, 164, 176, 188, 243, 292
Mokarita (CB) 80–81, 210
Moncada, Rafael (Z) 47, 72, 100, 116, 142, 175, 303, 317, 319
Montez, Lola (A) 269, 312
Mora sisters (HS) 44, 94, 96, 166, 213, 217, 234, 273, 276, 317
Morales, Carmen (IP) 30, 32, 36, 40, 60, 71, 75, 96, 97, 111, 260, 296–297, 315, 319
Morales, Dai (IP) 40, 71, 80, 194
Morales, Inmaculada (IP) 80, 96, 102, 111, 153, 193–194, 252, 318
Morales, Juan José (IP) 80, 116, 194, 265
Morales, Pedro (IP) 36, 80, 91, 111, 151, 153, 191, 252
Morales, Thui (IP) 80
Morante, Gustavo (OLS) 47, 176, 178, 216, 234, 251, 285, 317
Morton, Esther (DF) 102, 182, 194, 319
Morton, James (DF) 75, 102, 182, 282, 249, 319
mothering 5–9, 11–18, 20–21, 32, 35, 37, 40, 47, 48, 54, 55, 56, 57–64, 66–68, 70, 72, 74–76, 78–83, 85–87, 92, 94, 96–105, 109, 111–112, 114, 116, 119, 122–126, 129–133, 135, 137, 140, 141, 143, 148, 154, 157–158, 161–164, 166–169, 171, 174, 175, 182, 185, 186, 188, 189, **192–196**, 201, 205, 207, 216, 217, 219–224, 226, 229, 234, 236, 237, 240, 244, 245, 246, 247, 251, 252, 256, 257, 260, 262, 264, 266, 268, 270–273, 275, 277, 279, 280, 281, 286, 287, 290, 294, 295, 297, 299–302, 315, 317, 320
"Mouselets and Mice, Ratlets and Rats" 9
El Mulato (SEL) 215
mulattas/mulattos 34, 66, 71, 72, 86, 98, 110, 129, 147, 158,

160, 161, 181, 185, 192, 204, 219, 224, 226, 229, 230, 258, 261–263, 287, 305, 311, 318
Murieta, Joaquín (DF) 20, 32, 69, 83–84, 101, 102, 155, 169, 202, 203, 248, 249, 279, 285, 302, 312, 219, 320
Murphy, Leanna (IBS) 191–192
Murphy, Owen (IBS) 41, 155, 191–192, 250
Mushaha, Michael (FP) 100, 131–132
music 6, 20, 22, 24, 49, 54, 57, 61, 142, 148, 165, 168, **196–199**, 229, 234, 262, 267, 305, 307, 316; *see also* dance
My Invented Country 8, 20, 24, 30, 45, 53, 54, 94, 99, 112, 117, 118, 141, 143, 165, 169, 190, **199–200**, 201, 228, 232, 233, 239, 242, 268, 293, 299, 319
myth 6, 13, 16, 34, 51, 68, 69, 70, 84, 85, 101, 106, 120, 121–122, 123, 133, 155, 156, 158, 165, 168, 173, 178, 193, 194, **201–205**, 209, 212, 221, 223, 233, 248, 249, 258, 266, 268, 274, 277, 281, 283, 285, 287, 301, 302, 303, 306, 320

names 9, 11, 17, 19, 30, 32, 34, 37, 42, 66, 71, 72, 85, 91, 93, 100, 108, 110, 128, 152, 158, 160, 161–162, 164, 165, 168 174, 177, 180, 184, 187, 188, 190, 194, 195, **205–208**, 216, 228, 232, 245, 248, 250, 251, 256, 260, 263, 274, 280, 282, 287, 288, 296, 308, 313, 316, 319
Nana (HS) 42, 77, 97, 138, 187, 192, 239, 243, 255–256, 289, 318
Nana-Asante (FP) 5, 22, 48, 93, 96, 115–116, 117, 173, 205, 253, 317, 319
Napoleon (IBS) 23, 129, 183, 189, 191, 263, 269, 296, 301, 311, 312, 316, 319
Naranjo, Huberto (EL) 70, 84, 87, 88, 176, 182, 225, 251, 266, 285, 317
nativism 20, 52, 71, 73, 80–81, 85, 113, 116, 125, 129, 131, 150, **208–211**, 229, 246, 277, 284, 302, 303–304, 318; *see also* Aka; Araucan; Aymara; Aztec; Bantu; diaspora; Gabrieleno; Inca; Mapuche; Patagonians; Pehuenche; Quechua; Shoshone; Yanacona
Naziism (OLS, SEL) 60, 78, 313
El Negro (EL) 84, 106, 178
Neruda, Pablo 10, 11–12, 134, 141, 232, 234, 314
Ninderera, Angie (CB) 93, 96, 100, 113, 114, 115, 117, 142, 247, 253, 275, 292
9/11 19, 20, 45, 265
Nixon, Richard 9, 10
No-Tribe, Tom (DF) 74, 194
Nuñez, Lieutenant (IMS) 286
Nuria (Z) 132

O'Brien, Dr. Ming (IP) 36, 189
Odilia (Z) 97, 197, 317, 318
Of Love and Shadows 7, 10–11, 12, 13, 14, 16, 18, 29, 34, 37, 40, 42, 43, 44, 46, 47, 53, 59, 64, 68, 71, 88, 90, 96, 97, 100, 107, 118, 120, 122, 135, 138, 139, 147, 158, 165, 170, 172, 177, 178, 179, 181, 187, 190, 202, 206, 208, **211–212**, 214, 216, 219, 225, 233, 234, 236, 237, 243, 251, 255, 261, 266–267, 278, 284, 291, 315, 317, 318, 319
Of Love and Shadows (film) 16
Olga (IP) 71, 80, 96, 102, 111, 152, 193, 194, 273, 294
Oliver (IP) 152
opium (DF) 108, 127, 169, 171, 183, 224
Opium War of 1839 (DF) 229, 312, 319
optimism 34, 37, 38, 40, 41, 67, 77–78, 80, 86, 87, 91, 94, 100, 101, 108, 116, 121, 127, 129, 133, 136, 158, 159, 190, 191, 192, 193, 196, 206, 211, 220, 221, 248, 249, 270, 277, 288, 290–291, 294–295, 299
order 6, 19, 31, 36, 41, 48, 57, 68, 77–78, 88, 102, 103, 119, 120, 132, 136, 151, 153, 156–157, 165, 173, 177, 202, 211, **212–215**, 221, 262, 264, 271, 278, 297, 300
Orellano, Dulce Rosa (SEL) 29, 201, 266
Ortiz de Gaete, Marina (IMS) 184, 227, 244
"Our Secret" (SEL) 39, 165, 255, 266, 268, 269, 300, 317

Pablo, Tío 6, 232
Parmentier, Dr. (IBS) 81, 91, 128, 129, 148, 159, 171, 176, 181, 184, 185, 192, 230, 233, 238, 287, 297, 315
Patagonians (DF) 191, 229
patriarchy 6–7, 9, 16, 34, 36, 38, 39, 47, 54, 59, 63 97, 98–103, 123, 135, 136, 140, 143, 146, 166, 174, 176, 177, 178, 180, 181, 192, 206, **215–219**, 223, 225, 228, 236, 255, 261, 265, 281, 289, 301, 316, 320
patronage 30, 64, 67, 78, 88, 91, 139, 153, 177, 178, 180, 187, 206, 216, 217, 219, 233, 255, 274, 280, 283, 289, 308, 315, 318
Paula (biography) 7, 11, 17–18, 22, 32, 51, 52, 58, 59, 79, 94, 96, 99, 111, 118, 129, 143, 158, 179, 206, **219–222**, 239, 242, 268, 271, 272, 288, 295
Paula (magazine) 9, 10–11, 225
Paula Scholarship 17, 19
the Peaceable Kingdom 115, 117
pedophilia 7, 60, 139
Pehuenche (PS) 153–154
Pema, Queen (KGD) 33, 41, 48, 92, 95, 96, 100, 113, 163, 205, 292, 315, 317, 319
People of the Mist (CB) 33, 48, 56, 57, 81, 92, 113, 124, 142, 156, 201, 210, 214, 252, 269, 270, 289, 291
Peralta, Amadeo (SEL) 118, 166, 281, 315
Peru 5–8, 31, 42, 51, 52, 103, 108, 109, 121, 130, 149, 150, 154, 168, 169, 190, 197, 208, 217, 235, 238, 248, 268, 285, 286, 290, 293, 302, 306, 308, 310, 312, 313, 318, 319
"The Phantom Palace" (SEL) 33, 37, 41, 62, 107, 120, 172, 173, 196, 208, 212–213, 240, 266, 295, 317, 318
photography (EL, PS) 30, 35, 39–40, 58–96, 103, 107, 131, 157, 169, 176, 183, 210, 236, 247, 248, 264, 276, 279, 299, 319
Pierre (Z) 97
Pineda, Matilde (PS) 65, 94, 98, 146, 223
Pinochet Ugarte, Augusto (HS) 9–15, 18, 21, 29, 36, 37, 47, 53, 59, 62, 64, 89, 94, 116, 118, 134, 135, 141, 166, 177, 200, 206, 217, 242, 281, 300, 314
Pizarro, Francisco (IMS) 42, 47, 149, 231, 244, 258, 286, 319

Pizarro, Hernando (IMA) 42, 310
plaçage (IBS) 185, 308, 319
Placeres, Azucena (DF) 69, 73, 93, 139–140, 227
polygamy 142, 145, 185, 200, 242
The Porcelain Fat Lady 14, 321
pornography (DF) 17, 18, 42–43, 43, 73, 119, 147, 235, 249
Portrait in Sepia 11, 18, 19, 30, 31, 33, 35, 38, 39, 40, 41, 43, 47, 51, 53, 55, 58, 59, 63, 64, 70, 78, 80, 83, 94, 96, 97, 98, 99, 101, 103, 110, 129, 133, 140, 145, 146, 149, 153, 161, 168, 173, 176 183, 188, 192, 193, 199, 207, 21, 218, 219, **222–224**, 236, 238, 239, 240, 243, 244, 249–250, 257, 258, 263, 268, 279, 282 285, 286, 293, 296, 298, 299, 300, 316, 317, 319
post-traumatic stress disorder (IP) 91, 218, 260, 266, 294, 320
powerlessness *see* vulnerability
pregnancy 30, 59, 65, 68–69, 73–74, 82, 101, 120, 123, 127, 139, 144, 155, 180, 194, 195, 219, 224, 225, 240, 251, 256, 158, 259
prison 30, 33, 52, 53, 68, 101, 102, 106, 115, 118–120, 134, 136, 144, 149, 164, 172, 174, 177, 204, 216, 217, 225, 227, 243, 245, 246, 251, 260, 276–278, 281, 283, 285, 296, 297, 299, 306, 311, 313, 317
"The Proper Respect" (SEL) 66–67, 138, 164, 186, 190, 201, 205
prostitution 6, 17, 30, 34, 39, 40, 41, 47, 68, 69, 75, 83, 87, 93, 95, 96, 97, 101, 103, 121, 127, 135, 139, 140, 144, 145, 154, 170, 171, 179, 181, 182, 189, 194, 201–202, 204, 206, 214, 216, 223, **224–227**, 228, 229, 237, 239, 255, 258, 263, 266, 278, 285, 290, 312, 318; *see also* La Señora; singsong girls; Soto, Tránsito
pseudonym (OLS) 206
Pygmies *see* Aka

Quechua (IMS) 168, 180, 188, 200, 228, 244, 272, 308
Quiroga-Suarez-Valdivia genealogy (IMS) **227–228**

racism 41, 52, 54, 74, 133, 155, 156, 167, 179, 191, 180, 200, **228–232**, 232, 244, 247, 249, 285, 320; *see also* mestizas/mestizos; nativism
Radovic, Iván (PS) 31, 35, 130
Ramírez, Juan de Dios (OLS) 34, 43, 47, 54, 90, 121, 170, 176, 206, 216, 245, 251, 281, 291
Ramón (Z) 22, 183
Ranquileo, Digna (OLS) 44, 96–97, 100, 104, 125–126, 165, 166, 179, 181, 206, 212, 251, 281, 317
Ranquileo, Evangelina (OLS) 44, 47, 54, 68, 90, 96, 97, 104, 120, 125, 126, 166, 170, 206, 211, 212
Ranquileo, Hipólito (OLS) 68, 100, 126, 176, 179, 181, 251, 318
Ranquileo, Pradelio (OLS) 44, 68, 90, 104, 107, 211, 232–233, 243, 281
rape 90, 96, 97, 116–117, 118, 120–121, 125, 135, 136, 148, 154, 168, 170, 173, 178, 180, 185, 193, 195, 196, 216, 223, 228, 230, 231, 236, 238, 244, 245, 251, 255, 256, 258, 268, 274, 277, 283, 285, 286, 292, 293, 320
reading 6, 7–8, 10, 11–12, 20, 30, 63, 79, 85, 136, 149, 152, 165, 174, 194, 196, 211, 220, **232–236**, 238, 256, 273, 278, 291, 296; *see also* Neruda, Pablo
realism 6, 8, 19, 20, 24, 30, 37, 40, 54, 56, 59, 60, 68, 79, 86, 87, 103, 121, 123, 134, 150, 156, 163, 165, 171, 173, 174, 193, 199, 200, 211, 213–214, 221, 228, 231, **236–239**, 249, 251, 252, 262, 269, 271, 273, 278, 294, 300
rebellion 8, 9–10, 23, 29, 32, 47, 54, 65–66, 71–72, 86–87, 94, 96, 99, 97, 100, 101, 123, 129, 145, 146, 154–155, 158, 159, 160, 171, 176, 180, 189, 191, 195, 203, 207, 216, 229, 231, 239, 256, 261, 266, 270, 272, 274, 280, 282–283, 285, 286, 287, 291, 301, 311, 314, 318, 319, 320; *see also* Céspedes, Tadeo; Felipe/Lautaro; "Fox and Hens"; Gambo La Liberté; Macandal; Maroons
reclamation 30, 36, 54, 65, 79, 85, 101, 102, 106, 116, 137, 155, 161, 174, 178, 179, 180, 183, 191, 202, 203, 206, 215, **239–241**, 277, 278, 290
Reeves, Charles (IP) 36, 40, 60, 111, 140, 151, 170, 273, 283, 317
Reeves, David (IP) 36, 47, 60, 152, 153, 189, 193
Reeves, Gregory (IP) 11, 32, 33, 36, 38–39, 40, 45, 47, 60–61, 65, 71, 80, 84, 90–91, 111, 140, 141, 151–153, 156, 167, 171, 172, 173, 176, 179, 183–184, 188–189, 193, 194, 233, 239, 241, 248, 252, 260, 283, 294, 296–297, 315, 317
Reeves, Judy (IP) 60–61, 75, 116, 193, 252, 317
Reeves, Margaret (IP) 60, 91, 111, 152, 189, 226
Reeves, Nora (IP) 96, 111, 171, 172, 193, 252, 273, 320
Reeves, Samantha Ernst (IP) 47, 91, 111, 152, 183, 252
Reeves, Shannon (IP) 47, 152, 252
Reeves genealogy (IP) **241–242**
refugees 11, 12, 23, 34, 38, 44, 46, 53, 63, 96, 97, 129, 145, 147, 148, 165, 191, 192, 204, 277, 292, 313
rehabilitation 16, 38, 45, 65, 96, 152, 172, 273, 303
reincarnation (PS) 78, 140, 244
Relais, Etienne (IBS) 148, 158, 160–161, 172–173, 178, 183, 185, 226, 258, 291
Relais, Jean-Martin (IBS) 160–161, 195, 226, 238, 274
religion 11, 21, 34, 52, 73, 100, 114, 116, 130, 140, 144, 146, 167, 173, 179, 188, 190, 197, 200, 323, 214, 240, **242–247**, 249, 261, 269, 270, 274, 298, 307, 309, 316, 320
Restrepo (HS) 250
"Revenge" (SEL) 29, 37, 90, 201, 255, 265, 266, 269, 317
ritual 8, 13, 16, 20, 33–34, 45, 50, 70–71, 75, 77, 80–81, 88, 97, 98, 105, 106, 113, 119, 123, 128, 132, 129–140, 143, 146–147, 170, 184, 198, 204–205, 208, 210, 212, 221, **242–247**, 255, 265, 274, 303, 305–307, 309; *see also* animism; Catholicism; health and healing; voodoo
Rivera, Faustino (OLS) 54, 90, 120–121, 176, 251

"The Road North" (SEL) 9, 38, 118, 164, 186, 192, 205, 317
Rodríguez de Santa Cruz, Feliciano (PS) 41, 140, 173, 183, 218, 241, 263
Rodríguez de Santa Cruz, Matías (PS) 41–42, 47, 129, 188, 192, 223, 224, 241, 263, 268
Rogelio, Comandante (OLS) 84, 87, 326; *see also* Naranjo, Huberto
Romano, Giulio (A) 269
Romero, Sebastián (IMS) 238, 286
Rose, Tante (IBS) 86, 96, 98–99, 110, 122, 128, 129, 130, 160, 171, 181, 203, 238, 274, 317
Rosette (IBS) 34, 35, 58, 98, 122, 123, 155, 160, 161, 185, 189, 195, 197, 198, 207, 226, 229, 230, 259, 260, 261, 262, 297, 317
Rostipov (HS) 125
Rugieri, Maurizia (SEL) 266
Rupert, Uncle (EL) 70, 106, 213, 266

Sánchez, Angel (SEL) 164, 166, 283
Sánchez, Omaira 15, 221, 267
San Francisco (DP, PS) 14, 18, 21, 22, 31, 35, 36, 41, 51, 53, 63, 64, 69, 73, 74, 108, 111, 127, 145, 151, 154, 169, 172, 190, 212, 226, 229, 237, 240, 245, **247–250**, 248, 249, 250, 263, 285, 296, 311, 312, 314, 319
Santiago 6, 7–10, 13, 15, 17, 24, 53, 60, 65, 76, 85, 97, 98, 108, 109, 111, 139, 142, 145, 147, 148, 149, 150, 168, 169, 173, 175, 197, 199, 200, 208, 212, 247, 277, 282, 286, 293, 300, 310, 313, 314, 316, 319
Santiago Files 24
Santos, César (CB) 131, 246, 275, 318
Santos, Nadia "Eagle" (CB, FP, KGD) 19, 32, 33, 35, 56–57, 61, 62, 66, 70, 81, 93, 95, 96, 113, 114, 115, 117, 131, 142, 156, 163, 164, 175, 186, 198, 201, 208, 210, 252, 253, 255, 274, 275, 292, 315, 317, 318
Satigny, Jean de (HS) 10, 101, 105, 106, 119, 139, 144, 176, 177–178, 179, 181, 183, 184, 187, 190, 207, 224, 234 243, 250, 267, 277, 299
satire 9, 11, 39, 43, 65, 72, 81, 124, 128, 138, 140, 144, 158, 161, 164, 172, 182, 186, 187, 200, 233, 243, 262, 265, 270, 294, 318; *see also* humor; hypocrisy
Scheherazade 86, 87, 264, 269, 298
"The Schoolteacher's Guest" (SEL) 87, 118, 126, 146, 192, 250, 265, 266, 281, 298
Sebastián, Saint (HS) 77, 118, 206
secondary characters 38, **250–253**, 258, 266, 299, 317
Sedella, Zarité (IBS) *see* Tété
Sedella-Valmorain genealogy (IBS) **253–254**
La Señora (EL) 30, 64, 70, 86, 95, 144, 154, 179, 224, 225, 226, 251, 316
sensuality 12, 23, 86, 183–184, 214, 222, 226, 245, 259, 264, 318
Séraphine (IBS) 122, 238, 274
The Seven Mirrors 10
sex 6–7, 8, 17, 18–19, 23, 35, 36, 38, 40, 43, 54, 59, 62–63, 65, 66, 68, 70, 75, 77, 82, 84, 88, 89, 91, 94, 96, 97–98, 126, 128, 130, 138, 139, 143, 144, 147, 152, 159–160, 165, 179, 180, 182, 184, 199, 202, 203, 206, 208, 213, 216–217, 223, 224, 225, 226, 227, 228, 231, 242, 244, 245, 251, **255–260**, 261, 265, 266, 273, 284, 286, 299, 300, 303, 314, 319, 320; *see also* homosexuality; incest, rape; syphilis; venereal disease
Shakespeare, William 7, 233, 250, 282, 318
shapeshifting 48, 56, 57, 81, 84, 96, 115, 203, 204, 283, 303
Sheba (A) 66
Shoshone (Z) 85, 231, 302
Sierra, Antonia (SEL) 95, 265
Simón, Don (OLS) 125
"Simple María" (SEL) 42, 97, 124, 138, 172, 201, 226, 255, 266, 320
singsong girls (DF) 18, 38, 41, 75, 103, 145, 170, 188, 227, 237, 249, 278–279, 285, 312
slavery 12, 21, 22, 23, 31–32, 34, 39, 41, 48–49, 65–66, 71, 72, 81, 86, 91, 93, 95, 96, 98, 99, 102–103, 109–110, 114, 115, 117, 122, 123, 128, 145, 147, 148, 149, 153, 155, 156, 157, 158, 159–161, 167, 170, 171, 176, 177, 179, 180, 181, 185, 186, 188, 189, 191, 192, 193, 195, 197, 198, 203, 204, 207, 208, 215, 216, 226, 227, 229, 230, 231, 235, 236, 238, 245, 248, 249, 253, 258–259, 260, 261, 262, 263, 265, 270, 274, 287, 288, 289, 290, 291, 297, 301, 305, 306, 307, 311, 312, 316, 317, 319; *see also* singsong girls
social class 29, 45, 52–53, 59, 62, 71–72, 73, 74–75, 86, 90, 91, 142, 143, 138, 159, 162, 169, 180, 181, 190, 200, 211, 228, 229, 231, 250, 256, **261–264**, 267, 291, 302, 309, 316; *see also* racism
socialism 5, 9, 11, 52–53, 54, 59, 94, 135, 154, 157, 180, 190, 196, 206, 219, 234, 237, 283; *see also* Allende, Salvador
Solar, Justin (IBS) 260, 318
solidarity 11, 21, 22–23, 29, 44, 50, 75, 95, 107, 115, 135, 147, 174, 195, 208, 211, 212, 220, 255, 264, 280, 281, 284, 288, 316
Solomon (A) 66, 114, 286
Sommers, Dame Rose (PS) 50, 68–69, 70, 73, 75, 76, 96, 107, 140, 147, 166, 170, 194, 215–216, 229, 237, 251
Sommers, Eliza (DF, PS) 18, 30, 35, 38, 41, 50, 56, 59, 64, 68–69, 70, 74, 75, 83–34, 88, 96, 97, 101, 107, 127, 145, 158, 180, 182, 193, 202, 207, 214, 215, 222, 226, 235, 239, 240–241, 244, 249, 257, 258, 263, 300, 317, 319
Sommers, Jeremy (PS) 50, 52, 74, 105, 140, 147, 169, 176, 188, 191, 215
Sommers, John (PS) 50, 73, 89, 108, 127, 140, 170, 176, 218, 229, 235, 269
Sommers, Lin/Lynn (PS) 18, 31, 41–42, 78, 97, 169, 193, 222, 223, 244, 245, 257, 263
Soto, Tránsito (HS) 34, 40, 63, 68, 90, 95, 96, 118, 206, 224, 225, 226, 255, 257
Soupir, Adi (IBS) 263
Spain 9, 11, 14, 21, 23, 42, 46, 68, 85, 97, 107, 108, 114, 121, 132, 147, 149, 188, 190, 206, 231, 232, 242, 244, 257, 273,

284, 290, 292, 296, 299, 302, 305, 306, 310, 311, 312 313, 317; *see also* Conquistadors
stillbirth 30, 64, 75, 180, 251, 290, 318
The Stories of Eva Luna 15, 19, 21–22, 24, 37, 49, 96, 120, 157, 164, 196, 199, 201, 237, 240, **264–267**, 269
storytelling 6–8, 10, 12, 19, 24, 29, 40, 45, 70, 86, 87, 88, 96, 146, 154, 156, 165, 167, 182, 205, 211, 215, 233, 236, 255, 265, **267–271**, 276, 281, 300, 301, 302, 318
Suarez, Inés (IMS) 14, 20, 21, 24, 31–32, 38, 39–41, 45, 52, 71, 76, 85, 94, 96, 98, 101, 102, 103, 108, 109, 121, 130–131, 142, 145, 148–151, 154, 157, 173, 175, 184, 188, 192, 193, 197, 199, 227, 231, 235, 238, 244, 245, 257–258, 268, 286, 290, 295, 298, 299, 300–301, 319
Suffolk, Gerald (IBS) 111
suffrage (HS) 9, 94, 100–101, 135, 174, 213, 219, 316, 320
suicide 29, 44, 46, 53, 81, 36, 152, 238, 257, 281, 282, 314
Sultán (IMS) 85
The Sum of Our Days 6, 21, 22, 40, 52, 53, 76, 79, 165, 192, 171, **271–272**, 273, 295, 310, 316, 317, 318, 319, 320
superstition 21, 55, 93, 115, 131, 132, 138, 158, 175, 186, 214, 229, 240, 242, 247, **272–276**, 279, 304, 316; *see also* nativism; ritual
Susan (IP) 43, 95, 102
symbolism 13, 32, 33, 37, 54, 61, 62, 63, 66, 67, 70, 71, 75, 76, 77, 80, 84, 85, 89, 105, 106, 107, 109, 117, 118, 120, 133, 136, 162, 164, 172, 175, 184, 187, 188, 192, 196, 201, 202, 205, 206, 209, 211, 218, 219, 222, 233, 234, 243, 256, 259, 266, 267, 270, **276–279**, 281, 293, 302, 309; *see also* totemic animals

Tamar *see* Morales, Carmen
Tapestries of Hope 32, 40, 45, 319
teaching 18, 42, 91, 146, 175, 318; *see also* education; Inés (schoolteacher)
technology 35, 56, 61, 92, 93, 131, 132, 157, 163, 187, 209, 218, 268
telenovelas (EL) 6, 9, 86, 182, 235, 318
Tensing (KGD, FP) 41, 61, 84, 113, 115, 131, 162, 163, 164, 205, 208, 252, 287, 291, 292, 295, 297, 298, 317, 318, 319, 320
terrorism 10, 13, 18, 19, 20, 84, 88, 178, 290, 276, 314; *see also* García, Esteban; imprisonment; 9/11; torture
Tété (IBS) 23, 31, 34, 35, 48, 58, 64, 65–66, 71–72, 81, 85–86, 98, 102–103, 110, 122, 123, 128, 129, 142, 143, 155, 159–160, 167, 171, 179, 181, 185, 189, 195, 197–198, 204, 207, 226, 230, 245, 246, 253, 258, 259, 260, 270, 287, 290, 297, 301, 315, 317, 319
Tey, Don Pedro (PS) 65, 146, 286
Three-Finger Jack (DF) 69, 155, 202, 248, 285, 319
"Toad's Mouth" (SEL) 42, 44, 56, 120, 208, 225, 255, 265, 266, 269, 318
Todd, Jacob (PS) 50, 52, 69, 73, 107, 126, 140, 145, 147, 169, 191, 207, 229, 232, 248
Toledano, Romeiro (IBS) 181
tongs (PS) 154, 249
Tornado (Z) 168
Toro, Domingo (SEL) 66–67, 185, 205
Torres, Analía (SEL) 49, 165, 265, 266
Torres, Luis (SEL) 49, 165
Torres, Omayra (CB) 48, 55, 56, 57, 61, 131
torture 10, 11, 12, 13, 24, 37, 43, 47, 60, 63, 65, 72, 81, 88, 90, 93, 104, 118, 119, 126, 135, 136, 143, 144, 146, 154, 170, 180, 196, 203, 212, 251, 256, 266, 269, 277, 280, 284, 286, 292, 293, 295, 299, 310, 313
"Tosca" (SEL) 21, 181, 192, 265, 266
Tosca, Señora (SEL) 181
totemic animals 35, 56, 81, 115, 142, 165, 175, 210, 275, 303, 309, 319
Toussaint L'Ouverture (IBS) 32, 48, 86, 102, 110, 148, 160, 178, 181, 203, 204, 270, 290, 311
Toypurnia/Regina (Z) 69, 72, 96, 132, 167–168, 173, 175, 182, 183, 231, 302
translation 8, 13, 18, 22, 84, 163, 231, 235, 292, 298
transvestism (EL) 30, 32, 49, 70, 73, 84, 86, 103, 139, 143–144, 158, 170, 178, 179, 249, 251, 299, 316
Treaty of Guadalupe Hidalgo (DF) 20, 191, 312, 319
trial by ordeal 184, 201
Trueba, Esteban (HS) 29, 34, 37, 40, 47, 62, 77–78, 82, 89, 100, 105, 116, 119, 125, 133–139, 144, 153–155, 157, 169, 174, 176–178, 180, 183, 186, 192, 196, 206–207, 209, 213, 216–217, 225–226, 228, 233, 236, 243, 255–256, 261, 280, 283, 289, 292, 318
Trueba, Ester (HS) 77, 105, 119, 289, 318, 320
Trueba, Férula (HS) 11, 63, 67, 89, 96, 105, 119, 134, 250, 255, 256, 276, 278, 280, 289, 317
Two Words (play) 19
"Two Words" (SEL) 15, 40, 44, 97, 164, 205, 215, 265, 269, 276, 295, 317

underground 11, 128–129, 211
United Nations 8, 9, 11, 47, 105

Valdivia, Pedro de (IMS) 31, 41, 42, 47–48, 52, 71, 85, 98, 101–102, 108, 109, 121, 122, 130, 142, 147, 148, 150, 157, 168, 173, 177, 184, 188, 208, 227, 231, 235, 238, 244, 258, 282, 283, 286, 293, 294, 299, 310, 319
Valdomero, Padre (CB) 55, 131, 210
Valmorain, Maurice (IBS) 65, 110, 122, 123, 148, 159, 160, 161, 172, 181, 184, 195, 207, 229, 230, 245, 259, 260, 261, 274, 297, 317
Valmorain, Maurice, the elder (IBS) 147–148
Valmorain, Toulouse (IBS) 23, 32, 41, 43, 65, 71, 81, 85, 91, 109, 122, 128, 143, 145, 147–148, 155, 159, 160, 171, 172, 171, 181, 184, 189, 191, 219, 226, 229, 231, 235, 238, 245, 253, 254, 258, 259, 261, 262, 270, 274, 283, 287, 291, 320
venereal disease 42, 127, 130, 139, 147–148, 172, 192, 194, 202, 224, 226, 241
Venezuela (EL) 11–12, 14, 15,

35, 36, 37, 54, 55, 86, 131, 190, 236, 266, 272, 274, 281, 300, 307, 310, 312, 313
vengeance 20, 24, 34, 49, 63, 85, 86, 116, 117, 122, 123, 168, 192, 269, **280–283**, 284, 291, 293, 299, 302, 315, 319; *see also* Murieta, Joaquin; "Revenge"
Vergara, José Francisco (HS, PS) 218, 285
Vidal, Maya (MN) 165
Vidal, Nicolás (SEL) 266, 269, 317, 319
Vietnam (IP) 32, 36, 45, 65, 72, 80, 90–91, 111, 140, 152, 156, 167, 172, 179, 194, 199, 236, 252, 260, 294, 301, 314, 318, 319
Villars, Catherine (Z) 20, 97, 132, 173, 197, 262, 263
violence 12, 24, 29, 31, 33, 41, 44, 47, 53, 59, 88, 90, 91, 101, 105, 110, 115, 117, 118, 127, 128, 133, 134, 135, 136, 143, 148, 166, 177, 178, 185, 190, 206, 207, 211, 212, 215, 216, 223, 230, 236, 242, 251, 257, 265, 266, 276, 280, 282, **283–288**, 285, 286, 287, 288, 292, 293, 297, 302, 314, 320; *see also* rape; war
volcano 15, 150, 267, 314
voodoo (IBS) 20, 86, 87, 98, 123, 132, 170, 171, 181, 193, 198, 203, 207, 245, 246, 274, 305, 307, 308, 309, 311; *see also* Boukman Dutty; Laveau, Marie
vulnerability 15, 23, 45, 97, 120, 124, 181, 196, 267, 276, 284–285, **288–291**, 292, 318; *see also* marginalism; rape; torture; war

Walimai (CB, FP, KGD, SEL) 56–57, 92, 115–116, 131, 164, 177, 186, 201, 208, 246, 270, 274–275, 291, 292, 294–295, 317, 318, 320
"Walimai" (musical setting) 20
"Walimai" (SEL) 20, 39, 79, 81, 181, 186, 208, 240, 265, 266
war 10, 18, 24, 29, 31, 32, 36, 45, 52, 60, 64, 65, 72, 75, 76, 80, 84, 85, 88, 90, 91, 94, 98, 99, 102, 106, 108, 110, 111, 121, 122, 123, 129, 133, 140, 144, 145–146, 148, 149, 150, 152, 156, 160, 162, 163, 165, 167, 169, 171, 172, 173, 175, 176, 178, 179, 183–184, 188, 194, 199, 201, 205, 207, 218, 222, 225, 229, 232, 234, 236, 237, 239, 242, 244, 248, 249–250, 251, 252, 258, 260, 265, 266, 269, 275, 278, 282, 283, 285, 286, 288, **291–294**, 296, 297, 300–301, 302, 303, 306, 307, 311, 312, 313, 314, 316, 318, 319, 320
War of the Pacific (PS) 52, 78, 110–111, 239, 285, 319
War on the Underworld (EL) 144
White Owl (Z) 22, 59, 94, 96, 100, 132, 167–168, 174–175, 209–210, 268, 295, 317, 318, 320
"Wicked Girl" (SEL) 21, 59, 116, 205, 255, 265, 266, 319
widowhood 31, 70, 71, 76, 94, 96, 120, 123, 135, 140, 147, 148, 149, 171, 177, 190, 211, 216, 218, 22, 226, 243, 255, 264, 265, 315, 319
Williams, Frederick (PS) 53, 146, 169, 224, 264
wisdom 36, 40, 41, 43, 54, 59, 63, 75, 79, 98, 99, 100, 113, 127, 128, 134, 141, 151, 154, 163–164, 169, 203, 206, 223, 242, 246, 249, 252, 264, 270, 271, 272, **294–298**, 317, 319
women *see* female persona
World War I 135, 190
World War II 60, 106, 111, 160, 190
writing 12, 13, 15, 17, 18, 20, 29, 30–31, 33, 34, 38, 54, 58, 73, 76, 79, 85, 87, 116, 124, 128, 132, 133, 136, 141, 141, 143, 146, 147, 153, 164, 166–167, 173, 174, 176, 185, 190, 193, 196, 200, 201, 206, 215, 217, 219–222, 224, 225, 228, 229, 232, 235, 239, 240, 249, 255, 261, 269, 272, 278, 295, **298–301**, 316

Yanacona (IMS) 52, 149, 197, 231, 290
Yetis (KGD, FP) 33, 56, 57, 77, 93, 113, 115–116, 123, 124, 131, 156, 162, 162, 164, 196, 247, 252, 275, 291, 292

Zacharie (IBS) 72, 143, 161, 185, 189, 198, 260
Zimmerman, Patricia (SEL) 205, 261, 265, 269
Zorro 5, 20, 22, 23, 24, 32, 28, 47, 57, 59, 72, 73, 85, 86, 94, 96, 97, 98, 100, 116, 118, 130, 132, 141, 155, 156, 157, 158, 167, 168, 173, 175, 176, 178, 180, 182, 183, 190, 193, 196, 199, 204, 205, 206, 209, 210, 231, 233, 235, 236, 239, 262, 268, 269, 273, 277, 287, 296, 298, **302–303**, 304, 309, 310, 313, 315, 316, 317, 318, 320
Zorro (film) 24
Zorro (graphic novel) 22
Zorro (musical) 20, 22
Zorro genealogy **304**

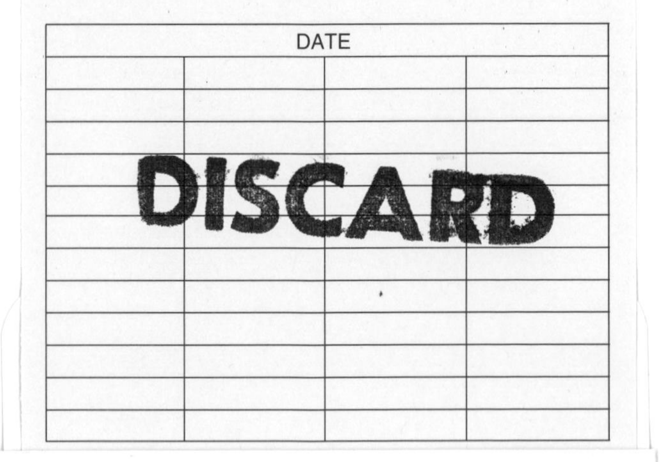